Learning Java

Joshua Crotts

Learning Java

A Test-Driven Approach

Springer

Joshua Crotts
Department of Computer Science
Indiana University Bloomington
Bloomington, IN, USA

ISBN 978-3-031-66637-7   ISBN 978-3-031-66638-4 (eBook)
https://doi.org/10.1007/978-3-031-66638-4

© The Editor(s) (if applicable) and The Author(s), under exclusive license to Springer Nature Switzerland AG 2024
This work is subject to copyright. All rights are solely and exclusively licensed by the Publisher, whether the whole or part of the material is concerned, specifically the rights of translation, reprinting, reuse of illustrations, recitation, broadcasting, reproduction on microfilms or in any other physical way, and transmission or information storage and retrieval, electronic adaptation, computer software, or by similar or dissimilar methodology now known or hereafter developed.
The use of general descriptive names, registered names, trademarks, service marks, etc. in this publication does not imply, even in the absence of a specific statement, that such names are exempt from the relevant protective laws and regulations and therefore free for general use.
The publisher, the authors and the editors are safe to assume that the advice and information in this book are believed to be true and accurate at the date of publication. Neither the publisher nor the authors or the editors give a warranty, expressed or implied, with respect to the material contained herein or for any errors or omissions that may have been made. The publisher remains neutral with regard to jurisdictional claims in published maps and institutional affiliations.

This Springer imprint is published by the registered company Springer Nature Switzerland AG
The registered company address is: Gewerbestrasse 11, 6330 Cham, Switzerland

If disposing of this product, please recycle the paper.

To my friends and family.

Preface

A course in Java programming is multifaceted. That is, it covers several core concepts, including basic datatypes, strings, simple-to-intermediate data structures, object-oriented programming, and beyond. What is commonly omitted from these courses is the notion of proper unit testing methodologies. Real-world companies often employ testing frameworks to bulletproof their codebases, and students who leave university without expose to such frameworks are behind their colleagues. Our textbook aims to rectify this delinquency by emphasizing testing from day one; we write tests before designing the implementation of our methods, a fundamental feature of test-driven development.

In our book, we *design* methods rather than write them, an idea stemming from Felleisen's *How to Design Programs*, wherein we determine the definition of our data, the method signature (i.e., parameter and return types), appropriate examples and test cases, and only then follow with the method implementation. Diving straight into a method implementation often results in endless hours of debugging that may have been saved by only a few minutes of preparation. Extending this idea into subsequent computer science courses is no doubt excellent.

At Indiana University, students take either a course in Python or the Beginner/Intermediate Student Languages (based on Scheme/Racket), the latter of which involves constant testing and remediation. Previous offerings of the successor course taught in Java lead students astray into a "plug and chug" mindset of re-running a program until it works. Our goal is to stop this once and for all (perhaps not truly "once and for all," but rather we aim to make it a less frequent habit) by teaching Java correctly and efficiently.

Object-oriented programming (and, more noteworthy, a second-semester computer science course) is tough for many students to grasp, but even more so if they lack the necessary prerequisite knowledge. Syntax is nothing short of a different way of spelling the same concept; we reinforce topics that students should already have exposure to: methods, variables, conditionals, recursion, loops, and simple data structures. We follow this with the Java Collections framework, generics, object-oriented programming, exceptions, I/O, searching and sorting algorithms, algorithm analysis, and modern Java features such as pattern matching and concurrency.

The ordering of topics presented in a Java course is hotly-debated and has been ever since its creation and use in higher education. Such questions include the location of object-oriented programming principles: do we start off with objects or hold off until later? Depending on the style of a text, either option can work. Even though we, personally, are more of a fan of the "early objects" approach, and is how we learned Java many moons ago, we choose to place objects later in the curriculum. We do this to place greater emphasis on testing, method design, recursion, and data structures through the Collections framework. Accordingly, after our midterm (roughly halfway through the semester), students should have a strong foundation of basic Java syntax sans objects and class design. The second half of the class is dedicated to just that: object-oriented programming and clearing up confusions that coincide and introduce themselves. Learning Java also includes two supplemental parts: one on searching, sorting, and algorithms, and another on modern Java features, the latter of which is not typically covered in its entirety within the span of a second-semester course.

We believe that this textbook can be used as any standard second-semester computer science course. At the high-school level, this book can be used as a substitute for the College Board's former AP Computer Science AB course. Certainly, this text may be well-suited for an AP Computer Science A course at the high-school level, but its material goes well beyond the scope of the AP exam and curriculum. Instructors are free to omit certain topics that may have been covered in a prerequisite (traditionally-styled) Java course. In those circumstances, it may be beneficial to dive further into the chapters on algorithm analysis and modern Java pragmatics (i.e., parts III and IV). For students without a Java background (or instructors of said students), which we assume, we take the time to quickly yet effectively build confidence in Java's quirky syntax. Additionally, we understand that our approach to teaching loops (through recursion and a translation pipeline) may appear odd to some long-time programmers. So, an instructor may reorder these sections however they choose, but we highly recommend retaining our chosen ordering for pedagogical purposes, particularly for those readers that are not taking an accompanying (college) class that uses this text.

At the end of Chapters 1–5, we present a slew of exercises to the readers, and we encourage them to do most, if not all, of the exercises. Some tasks in the exercises serve as simple reinforcement of topics, whereas others are long-haul marathons that take many hours to complete. Several exercises have also been used as (written) exam questions. We do not provide answers to the exercises because there are many "avenues to success." Readers should collaborate with others to solve the problems and discuss difficulties and points of confusion in aims of clarification.

The diction of our book is chosen very carefully, with hourly of scrutiny dedicated to the paragraphs, sentence structure, and their accompanying presentation. When we demonstrate an example, stop, and closely follow along. Do not rush through it. The words on the text remain in place, no matter the pace of the reader. A page, example, exercise, or chapter may require multiple passes to fully digest the content. Make notes in the margins, type out any examples and exercises, ask questions, and answer the questions posed by others. Perhaps they may answer one of yours.

In addition to the meticulously-selected diction, we have also made a conscious effort to place all code listings onto a single page, so as to prevent the reader from flipping back and forth between pages. The effort, while successful in most cases, is not perfect, and there are instances where a code listing spans multiple pages. Even so, we strongly encourage readers who cannot type out the code listings to read each line of code, ensuring that they understand its purpose in the context of the surrounding program.

Once again, by writing this book, we wish to ensure that students are better prepared for the more complex courses in a common computer science curriculum, e.g., data structures, operating systems, algorithms, programming languages, and whatever else lies ahead. A strong foundation keeps students motivated and pushes them to continue even when times are arduous, which we understand there to be plenty thereof. After all, not many moons ago were we in the shoes of our target audience!

Have a blast!
Joshua Crotts

Acknowledgements

I piloted *Learning Java* on the students in the Fall 2023 and Spring 2024 semesters of CSCI-C 212 (Introduction to Software Systems) at Indiana University. The inspiration came from those in the former, which drove me to continue writing and designing exercises. I sincerely appreciate all of the comments, suggestions, and corrections made. The following students and course staff members found mistakes: Ashley Won, Daniel Yang, Jack Liang, Shyam Makwana, and Muazzam Siddiqui.

Amr Sabry of Indiana University provided the suggestion to add streams to the Java curriculum, and as a consequence I now fully embrace and use them constantly.

I appreciate the help provided by my representative at Springer, Ralf Gerstner, and the fact that Springer took a bold chance to publish the work of a computer science PhD student.

Chandana Ariyawansa of UNC Greensboro and Nathaniel (Nat) Kell assigned brutal problem sets that shaped me into the skilled programmer and educator that I am today.

Steve Tate of UNC Greensboro put me through the ringer, figuratively, in his graduate algorithms, compilers, system programming, computer security, and software security classes. His mentorship through it all, and the fact that he was the chair of my master's thesis committee, is forever appreciated.

I attribute all of my love for Java (and computer science in general) to my former AP Computer Science A teacher: Tony Smith. Thanks for everything.

Contents

Preface vii

Part I Java Programming and Data Structures

1 Testing and Java Basics 3
   1.1   A First Glimpse at Java 3
   1.2   Strings 10
   1.3   Standard I/O 15
   1.4   Randomness 18
   1.5   Exercises 21

2 Conditionals, Recursion, and Loops 25
   2.1   Conditionals 25
   2.2   Recursion 30
   2.3   Loops 44
   2.4   Exercises 70

3 Arrays, Collections, and Generics 87
   3.1   Arrays 87
   3.2   Collections 110
   3.3   Iterators 146
   3.4   Streams 150
   3.5   Type Parameters 160
   3.6   Tree-Based Data Structures 165
   3.7   Exercises 172

Part II Objects, Classes, Exceptions, and I/O

4 Object-Oriented Programming 191
   4.1   Classes 191
   4.2   Object Mutation and Aliasing 222
   4.3   Interfaces 243
   4.4   Inheritance 261
   4.5   Abstract Classes 280
   4.6   Exercises 297

5 Exceptions and I/O ... 325
- 5.1 Exceptions ... 325
- 5.2 File I/O ... 330
- 5.3 Modern I/O Classes & Methods ... 342
- 5.4 Exercises ... 349

Part III Searching, Sorting, and Algorithms

6 Searching and Sorting ... 361
- 6.1 Searching ... 361
- 6.2 Sorting ... 368

7 Algorithm Analysis ... 387
- 7.1 Analyzing Algorithms ... 387

Part IV Modern Java

8 Modern Java and Advanced Topics ... 401
- 8.1 Verbosity ... 401
- 8.2 Pattern Matching ... 403
- 8.3 Reflection ... 413
- 8.4 Concurrent Programming ... 420
- 8.5 Design Patterns ... 442
- 8.6 API Connectivity ... 455

A JUnit Testing ... 461
- A.1 JUnit ... 461

B Binary Search Tree Library ... 465

References ... 469

Index ... 471

Part I
Java Programming and Data Structures

1 Testing and Java Basics

Abstract This chapter introduces readers to the basics of Java programming and testing. We will cover the fundamentals of Java syntax, including variables and data types. At the same time, we discuss the importance of test-driven development and how to write test cases in Java for methods. Our emphasis on testing makes work of the fact that testing is a critical part of writing correct and robust software. Test-driven development, in particular, is utilized as a "design recipe," of sorts, to guide programmers to solve a task.

1.1 A First Glimpse at Java

It makes little sense to avoid the topic at hand, so let's jump right in and write a program! We have seen *functions* before, as well as some mathematics operations, perhaps in a different (language) context.

Example 1.1. Our program will consist of a function that converts a given temperature in Fahrenheit to Celsius.

```
class TempConverter {

  /**
   * Converts a temperature from Fahrenheit to Celsius.
   * @param f temperature in degrees Fahrenheit.
   * @return temperature in degrees Celsius.
   */
  static double fToC(double f) {
    return 0.0;
  }
}
```

All code, in Java, belongs to a *class*. Classes have much more complex and concrete definitions that we will investigate in due time, but for now, we may think of them as the homes of our functions. By the way, functions in Java are called *methods*.[1] Again, this slight terminology differentiation is not without its reasons, but for all intents and purposes, functions are methods and vice versa. The class we have defined in the previous listing is called `TempConverter`, giving rise to believe that the class does something related to temperature conversion.

We wrote the `fToC` method *signature*, whose *return type* is a `double`, and has one *parameter*, which is also a `double`. A `double` is a floating-point value, meaning it potentially has

---
[1] The reasoning is simple: a method belongs to a class. Other programming languages, e.g., C++ or Python, do not restrict the programmer to writing code only within a class. Thus, there is a distinction between functions, which do not reside within a class, and methods.

decimals. For our method, this choice makes sense, because if we were to instead receive an integer int, we would not be able to convert temperatures such as 35.5 degrees Fahrenheit to Celsius.

The static keyword that we wrote also has significance, but for now, consider it a series of six mandatory key presses (plus one for the space thereafter).

Above this method *signature* is a Java documentation comment, providing a brief summary of the method's purpose, as well as the data it receives as parameters and its return value, should it be necessary.

Inside its *body* lies a single return, in which we return 0.0. The *return value* is what a *method call*, or *method invocation*, resolves to. For example, if we were to call fToC with any arbitrary double value, the call would be substituted with 0.0. Passing a value, or an *argument*, to a method is sometimes called *method application*.

```
fToC(5)     => 0.0
fToC(78)    => 0.0
fToC(-3123) => 0.0
```

The fToC method is meaningless without a complete implementation. Before we write the rest of the method body, however, we should design *test cases* to ensure it works as expected. Test cases verify the correctness (or incorrectness) of a method. We, as the readers, know how to convert a temperature from Fahrenheit to Celsius, but telling a computer to do such a conversion is not as obvious at first glance. To test our methods, we will use the *JUnit* testing framework. Creating tests for fToC is straightforward; we will make a second class called TempConverterTester to house a single method: testFToC.

```
class TempConverterTester {

  @Test
  void testfToC() {
    Assertions.assertAll(
      () -> Assertions.assertEquals(0, TempConverter.fToC(32)));
  }
}
```

We want JUnit to recognize that fToC contains testing code, so we prepend the @Test annotation to the method signature. In its body, we call Assertions.assertAll, which receives a series of methods that are ran in succession. In our case, we want to assert that our fToC method should return 0 degrees Celsius when given a temperature of 32 degrees Fahrenheit. The first parameter to assertEquals is the expected value of the test, i.e., what we want (and know) it to produce. The second parameter is the actual value of the test, i.e., what our code produces.

When writing tests, it is important to consider *edge cases* and all possible branches of a method implementation. Edge cases are inputs that are possibly missed by an implementation, e.g., -40, since it is the same in both Fahrenheit and Celsius, or 0. So, let us add a few more test cases.[2]

---

[2] To condense our code, we exclude the TempConverter class name out of conciseness. On the other hand, we can omit the Assertions class name by importing the two methods as shown in the listing.

1.1 A First Glimpse at Java

```java
import static Assertions.assertAll;
import static Assertions.assertEquals;

class TempConverterTester {

  @Test
  void testfToC() {
    assertAll(
      () -> assertEquals(0, fToC(32)),
      () -> assertEquals(100, fToC(212)),
      () -> assertEquals(-40, fToC(40)),
      () -> assertEquals(-17.778, fToC(0), .01),
      () -> assertEquals(-273.15, fToC(-459), .01));
  }
}
```

Computers are, unfortunately, not perfect; floating-point operations may result in precision/rounding errors. So, as an optional third argument to assertEquals, we can provide a *delta*, which allows for precision up to a certain amount to be accepted as a valid answer. For example, our tolerance for the fourth and fifth test cases is 0.01, meaning that if our actual value is less than ± 0.01 away from the expected value, the test case succeeds.

Now that we have copious amounts of tests, we can write our method definition. Of course, it is trivial and follows the well-known mathematical definition.

```java
class TempConverter {

  /**
   * Converts a temperature from Fahrenheit to Celsius.
   * @param temperature in F.
   * @return temperature in C.
   */
  static double fToC(double d) {
    return (d - 32) * (5.0 / 9.0)
  }
}
```

The definition of fToC brings up a few points about Java's type system. The primitive mathematics operations account for the types of its arguments. So, for instance, subtracting two integers will produce another integer. More noteworthy, perhaps, a division of two integers produces another integer, even if that result seems to be incorrect. Thus, 5 / 9 results in the integer 0. If, however, we treat at least one of the operands as a floating-point value, we receive a correct result of approximately 0.555555: 5.0 / 9. Java by default uses the standard order of operations when evaluating mathematics expressions, so we force certain operations to occur first via parentheses.[3]

Unlike some programming languages that are *dynamically-typed*, e.g., Scheme, Python, JavaScript, the Java programming language requires the programmer to specify the types of variables (Sebesta, 2012, Chapter 5).[4] Java has several default *primitive datatypes*, which are the simplest reducible form of a variable. Such types include int, char, double, boolean, and others. Integers, or int, are any positive or negative number without decimals. Doubles,

---

[3] By "standard," we mean the widely-accepted paradigm of parentheses first, then exponents, followed by left-to-right multiplication/division, and finally left-to-right addition/subtraction.

[4] In Java 10, the var keyword was introduced, which automatically infers the type of a given expression (Gosling et al., 2023, Chapter 14).

or double, are values with decimals.[5] Characters, or char, are a single character enclosed by single quotes, e.g., 'X'. Finally, booleans, or boolean, are either true or false. There are other Java data types that specify varying levels of precision for given values. Integers are 32-bit signed values, meaning they have a range of $[-2^{31}, 2^{31})$. The short data type, on the contrary, is 16-bit signed. Beyond this is the byte data type that, as its name suggests, stores 8-bit signed integers. Floating-point values are more tricky, but while double uses 64 bits of precision, the float data type uses 32 bits of precision.

Example 1.2. Let us design a method that receives two three-dimensional vectors and returns the distance between the two. We can, effectively, think of this as the distance between two points in a three-dimensional plane. Therefore, because each vector contains three components, we need six parameters, where each triplet represents the vectors v_1 and v_2.

```
class VectorDistance {

  /**
   * Computes the distance between two given vectors:
   * v_1=(x_1, y_1, z_1) and v_2=(x_2, y_2, z_2)
   */
  static double computeDistance(double x1, double y1, double z1,
                                double x2, double y2, double z2) {
    return 0.0;
  }
}
```

Again, we start by writing the appropriate method signature with its respective parameters and a Java documentation comment explaining its purpose. For tests, we know that the distance between two Cartesian points in a three-dimensional plane is

$$D(v_1, v_2) = \sqrt{(x_1 - x_2)^2 + (y_1 - y_2)^2 + (z_1 - z_2)^2}$$

So, let's now write a few test cases with some arbitrarily-chosen points that we can verify with a calculator or manual computation.

```
import static Assertions.assertAll;
import static Assertions.assertEquals;

class VectorDistanceTester {

  @Test
  void testComputeDistance() {
    assertAll(
      assertEquals(8.66, computeDistance(3, 2, 1, 8, 7, 6), .01),
      assertEquals(12.20, computeDistance(0, 0, 0, 8, 7, 6), .01),
      assertEquals(8.30, computeDistance(-8, -2, 1, 0, 0, 0), .01));
  }
}
```

Notice again our use of the optional delta parameter to allow us a bit of leeway with the rounding of our answer. Fortunately, the implementation of our method is just a retelling of the mathematical definition.

---

[5] The double data type cannot represent all real numbers. For example, the value π is an irrational (real) number, and thus cannot be represented exactly in a finite number of bits.

1.1 A First Glimpse at Java

```
class VectorDistance {

  /**
   * Computes the distance between two given vectors.
   * @param x1 x component of first vector.
   * @param y1 y component of first vector.
   * @param z1 z component of first vector.
   * @param x2 x component of second vector.
   * @param y2 y component of second vector.
   * @param z2 z component of second vector.
   * @return distance between v1 and v2.
   */
  static double computeDistance(double x1, double y1, double z1,
                                double x2, double y2, double z2) {
    return Math.sqrt(Math.pow(x1 - x2, 2) + Math.pow(y1 - y2, 2) + Math.pow(z1 - z2, 2));
  }
}
```

We make prolific use of Java's Math library in designing this method; we use the sqrt method for computing the square root of our result, as well as pow to square each intermediate difference.

Example 1.3. Slope-intercept is an incredibly common algebra and geometry problem, and even pokes its way into machine learning at times when computing best-fit lines. Let's design two methods, both of which receive two points (x_1, y_1), (x_2, y_2). The first method returns the slope m of the points, and the second returns the y-intercept b of the line. Their respective signatures are straightforward—each set of points is represented by two integer values and return doubles.

$$m = \frac{y_2 - y_1}{x_2 - x_1}$$
$$b = y_1 - mx_1$$

```
class SlopeIntercept {

  /**
   * Computes the slope of the line represented by the two points.
   * @param x1 x-coordinate of point 1.
   * @param y1 y-coordinate of point 1.
   * @param x2 x-coordinate of point 2.
   * @param y2 y-coordinate of point 2.
   * @return slope of points.
   */
  static double slope(int x1, int y1, int x2, int y2) { return 0.0; }

  /**
   * Computes the y-intercept of the line represented by the two points.
   * @param x1 x-coordinate of point 1.
   * @param y1 y-coordinate of point 1.
   * @param x2 x-coordinate of point 2.
   * @param y2 y-coordinate of point 2.
   * @return y-intercept of line represented by points.
   */
  static double yIntercept(x1, int y1, int x2, int y2) { return 0.0; }
}
```

The tests that we write are verifiable by a calculator or mental math. Our yIntercept method depends on a successful implementation of slope, as designated by the formula of the former. In the next chapter, we will consider cases that invalidate the formula, e.g., when two points share an x coordinate, in which the slope is undefined for those points.

```java
import static Assertions.assertAll;
import static Assertions.assertEquals;

class SlopeInterceptTester {

  @Test
  void testSlope() {
    assertAll(
      () -> assertEquals(1, slope(0, 0, 1, 1)),
      () -> assertEquals(0, slope(0, 0, 1, 0)),
      () -> assertEquals(2, slope(8, 4, 2, 4)),
      () -> assertEquals(0.5, slope(-1, 5, 3, 7)));
  }

  @Test
  void testYIntercept() {
    assertAll(
      () -> assertEquals(0, yIntercept(0, 0, 1, 1)),
      () -> assertEquals(0, yIntercept(0, 0, 1, 0)),
      () -> assertEquals(4, yIntercept(8, 4, 2, 4)),
      () -> assertEquals(5.5, yIntercept(-1, 5, 3, 7)));
  }
}
```

And the implementation of those two methods follows directly from the mathematical definitions. We replace our temporary 0.0 return values with the appropriate expressions, and all tests pass.

```java
class SlopeIntercept {

  /**
   * Computes the slope of the line represented by the two points.
   * @param x1 x-coordinate of point 1.
   * @param y1 y-coordinate of point 1.
   * @param x2 x-coordinate of point 2.
   * @param y2 y-coordinate of point 2.
   * @return slope of points.
   */
  static double slope(int x1, int y1, int x2, int y2) {
    return (y2 - y1) / (x2 - x1);
  }

  /**
   * Computes the y-intercept of the line represented by the two points.
   * @param x1 x-coordinate of point 1.
   * @param y1 y-coordinate of point 1.
   * @param x2 x-coordinate of point 2.
   * @param y2 y-coordinate of point 2.
   * @return y-intercept of points.
   */
  static double yIntercept(x1, int y1, int x2, int y2) {
    return y1 - slope(x1, y1, x2, y2) * x1;
  }
}
```

1.1 A First Glimpse at Java

Example 1.4. We are starting to get used to some of Java's verbosity! Let's now design a method that, when given a (numeric) value of x, evaluates the following quartic formula:

$$q(x) = 4x^4 + 7x^3 + 21x^2 - 65x + 3$$

Its signature is straightforward: we receive a value of x, namely a double, and return a double, since our operations work over double values. Again, we return zero as a temporary solution to ensure the program successfully compiles.

```java
class QuarticFormulaSolver {

  /**
   * Evaluates the equation 4x^4 + 7x^3 + 21x^2 - 65x + 3.
   * @param x the input variable.
   * @return the result of the expression after substituting x.
   */
  static double solveQuartic(double x) { return 0.0; }
}
```

Test cases are certainly warranted, but may be a bit tedious to compute by hand, so we recommend using a verified calculator to compute expected solutions![6]

```java
import static Assertions.assertAll;
import static Assertions.assertEquals;

class QuarticFormulaSolverTester {

  @Test
  void testSolveQuartic() {
    assertAll(
      () -> assertEquals(3, solveQuartic(0)),
      () -> assertEquals(313445.1875, solveQuartic(16.25)));
  }
}
```

We write tests *before* the method implementation because we know, intuitively, how to solve an equation for a variable, whereas a computer has to be told how to solve this task. Fortunately for us, a quartic equation solver is nothing more than returning the result of the expression. We have to use the exponential Math.pow method again (or conjoin several multiplicatives of x), but otherwise, nothing new is utilized.

```java
class QuarticFormulaSolver {

  /**
   * Evaluates the equation 4x^4 + 7x^3 + 21x^2 - 65x + 3.
   * @param x the input variable.
   * @return the result of the expression after substituting x.
   */
  static double solveQuartic(double x) {
    return 4 * Math.pow(x, 4) + 7 * Math.pow(x, 3) +
           21 * Math.pow(x, 2) - 65 * x + 3;
  }
}
```

---

[6] Remember that the coefficient is applied *after* applying the exponent to the variable. That is, if $x = 3$, then $4x^3$ is equal to $4 \cdot (3)^3$, which resolves to $4 \cdot 27$, which resolves to 108.

And, as expected, all tests pass. With only methods and math operations at our disposal, the capabilities of said methods are quite limited.

1.1.1 The Main Method

Java programming tutorials are quick to throw a lot of information at the reader/viewer, and our textbook is no exception to this practice. Unfortunately, Java is a verbose programming languages, and to begin designing a method, we must wrap its definition inside a class. After this step, we can design the static method implementation. Readers no doubt question the significance of static. For the first few chapters, we will intentionally omit its definition, as an explanation would almost certainly confuse the reader coming from another language. Therefore, for the time being, simply view it as six characters, plus a space, that must be typed in order to write a method that we can then test with JUnit.

Imagine, however, a situation where we want to output the result of an expression without using a test, as we will do in many examples. Java requires a main method in any executable Java class that does not use tests. For the sake of completeness, let's now write the traditional "Hello, world!" program in Java using the main method instead of tests.

```
class MainMethod {

  public static void main(String[] args) {
    System.out.println("Hello, world!");
  }
}
```

Yikes, that is a lot of required code to output some text to the console; what does public mean, and what are those [] brackets after the String word? Once again, we will not detail their importance, but view them as more mandatory characters to type when writing a main method. The only word we *will* explain is void, which means that the method does not return a value. If the readers are coming from a functional programming language, e.g., Scheme/Racket or OCaml, then it is almost certainly the case that they never worked with methods that did not return a value nor received no arguments.[7] The println method, for example, has no return value; its significance comes from the fact that it outputs text to the terminal/console, which is a *method side-effect*. We'll come back to what all of this means in subsequent chapters, but we could not avoid at least briefly mentioning it and its existence in the Java language.

1.2 Strings

Strings, as you might recall from another programming language, are sequences of characters. Characters are enclosed by single quotes, e.g., 'x'. A Java String is enclosed by double quotes. e.g., "Hello!". Strings may contain any number of characters and any kind of character, including no characters at all or only a single character. There is an apparent distinction between 'x' and "x": the former is a char and the latter is a String. Note the capitalization on the word String; the case sensitivity is important, because String is not one of the primitive datatypes that we described in the previous section. Rather, it is a sequence of char

---

[7] A method of no arguments is called a *thunk*, or a *nullary* method.

1.2 Strings

> **String Class**
>
> A *string* is an immutable sequence of characters. Strings are indexed from 0 to $|S|-1$, where $|S|$ is the number of characters of S.
>
> S_1 + S_2 adds the characters from S_2 onto the end of S_1, producing a new string.
> int S.length() returns the number of characters in S.
> char S.charAt(i) retrieves the $(i+1)^{\text{th}}$ character in S. We can also say that this retrieves the character at index i of S.
> String S.substring(i, j) returns a new string containing the characters from index i, inclusive, to index j, exclusive. The number of extracted characters is $j - i$. We will use the notation $S' \sqsubseteq S$ to denote that S' is a substring of S.
> String S.substring(i) returns a new string from index i to the end of S.
> int S.indexOf(S') returns the index of the first instance of S' in S, or -1 if $S' \not\sqsubseteq S$.
> boolean S.contains(S') returns true if $S' \sqsubseteq S$; false otherwise.
> String S.repeat(n) returns a new string containing n copies of S.
> String String.valueOf(v) returns a stringified version of v, where v is some primitive value.
> int Integer.parseInt(S) returns the integer representation of a string S if it can be parsed as such.

Fig. 1.1: Useful String Methods.

values coalesced into one value "under-the-hood," so to speak. We can declare a String as a variable using the keyword combined with a variable name, just as we do for primitives.

```
class NewStringTests {

  public static void main(String[] args) {
    String s1 = "Hello, world!";
    String s2 = "How are you doing?";
    String s3 = "This is another string!";
  }
}
```

We can conjoin, or *concatenate*, strings together with the + operator. Concatenating one string s_2 onto the end of another string s_1 creates a new string s_3 by copying the characters from s_1 and s_2, in that order.

Figure 1.1 states that strings are immutable, so how can we possibly combine them without altering one or the other? When concatenating two strings s_1 and s_2, Java creates a new string that is the result of the concatenation, leaving s_1 and s_2 unaltered.[8]

To retrieve the number of characters in a string, invoke .length on the string. The empty string has length zero, and spaces/whitespace characters count towards the length of a string, since spaces *are* characters. For instance, the length of " a " is five because there are two spaces, followed by a lowercase 'a', followed by two more spaces.

Comparing strings for equality seems straightforward: we can use == to compare one string versus another. Using == for determining string equality is a common Java beginner pitfall! Strings are *objects* and cannot be compared for value-equality using the == operator. Introducing this term "value-equality" insinuates that strings can, in fact, be compared using ==, which is theoretically correct. The problem is that the result of a comparison using == com-

---

[8] Hence, a series of repeated string concatenations is inefficient. The performance implications of this are addressed in a subsequent chapter.

pares the memory addresses of the strings. In other words, s_1 == s_2 returns whether the two strings reference, or point to, the same string in memory.

```java
class NewStringTests {

  public static void main(String[] args) {
    String s1 = "Hello";
    String s2 = s1;
    System.out.println(s1 == s2); // true
  }
}
```

In the above code snippet we declare s_1 as the *string literal* "Hello", then initialize s_2 to point to s_1. So there are, in effect, two references to the string literal "Hello". Let's try something a little more tricky: suppose we declare three strings, where s_1 is the same as before, s_2 is the string literal "Hello", and s_3 is the string literal "World". Comparing s_1 to s_2, strangely enough, also outputs true, but why? It seems that s_1 and s_2 reference different string literals, even though they contain the same characters. Indeed, the latter is obviously the case, but Java performs an optimization called *string pool caching*. That is, if two strings *are* the same string literal, it makes little sense for them to point to two distinct references, entirely because strings are immutable. Therefore, Java optimizes these references to point to a single allocated string literal. Comparing s_1 or s_2 with s_3 outputs false, which is the anticipated result.

```java
class NewStringTests {

  public static void main(String[] args) {
    String s1 = "Hello"; String s2 = "Hello";
    String s3 = "World";
    System.out.println(s1 == s2); // true (?)
    System.out.println(s2 == s3); // false
  }
}
```

If we want, for some reason, to circumvent Java's string caching capabilities, we need a way of *instantiating* a new string for our variables to reference. We use the power of new String to create a brand new, non-cached string reference. We treat this as a method, of sorts, called the *object constructor*. In Chapter 4, we will reintroduce constructors in our discussion on objects and classes, but for now, consider it (namely new String) as a method for creating distinct String instances. This method is *overloaded* to receive either zero or one parameter. The latter implementation receives a String, whose characters are copied into the new String instance. If we pass a string literal to the constructor, it copies the characters *from* the literal into the new string. At this point, the only possible object to be equal to s_1 is s_1 itself or another string that points to its value.

```java
class NewStringTests {

  public static void main(String[] args) {
    String s1 = new String("hello"); String s2 = new String("hello");
    String s3 = new String("world"); String s4 = s1;
    System.out.println(s1 == s1); // true
    System.out.println(s1 == s2); // false!
    System.out.println(s2 == s3); // false
    System.out.println(s1 == s4); // true
  }
}
```

1.2 Strings

Example 1.5. One final point to make about string equality is that string concatenation is not *always* subject to the same optimization as string literals. Consider the following code snippet, which creates two string literals s_1 and s_2. Then, we concatenate s_1 and s_2 into a string s_3, and separately concatenate the string literals themselves into the string s_4. What we observe is that s_3 and s_4 do not point to the same reference, even though they contain the same characters.

```
class NewStringTests {
  public static void main(String[] args) {
    String s1 = "Hello"; String s2 = "World";
    String s3 = s1 + s2; String s4 = "Hello" + "World";
    System.out.println(s3 == s4); // false
  }
}
```

On the other hand, consider the following code, where we create two strings s_1 and s_2 to both reference the concatenation of the string literals "x" and "y". Comparing s_1 and s_2 for object equality confusingly produces true. At compile-time, Java optimizes (and evaluates) the string literal concatenations, which leads to it being pooled to reference the same (string) object in memory.

```
class NewStringTests {
  public static void main(String[] args) {
    String s1 = "x" + "y";
    String s2 = "x" + "y";
    System.out.println(s1 == s2); // true
  }
}
```

Example 1.6. What if we want to compare strings based on their character content, rather than by memory reference? The String class provides a handy equals method that we invoke on instances of strings. Two strings s_1 and s_2 are equal if they are *lexicographically equal*. In essence, this is a long and scary word to represent the concept of "containing the same characters." Lexicographical comparisons are case-sensitive, meaning that uppercase and lowercase letters are report an unequal comparison.

```
class StringLexicographicallyEqual {
  public static void main(String[] args) {
    String s1 = new String("hello");
    String s2 = new String("hello");
    String s3 = new String("world");
    System.out.println(s1.equals(s2)); // true
    System.out.println(s2.equals(s3)); // false
  }
}
```

Let's veer into the discussion on the lexicographical ordering of strings. Like numbers, strings are comparable and can be, e.g., "less than" another. According to Java (as well as most other programming languages), one string is less than another if it is lexicographically less than another, and this idea extends to all (string) comparison operations; not just equality. Memorizing the string ordering rules is cumbersome, so we propose the S.N.U.L. acronym.

In general, special characters (S) are less than numbers (N), which are less than uppercase characters (U), which are less than lowercase characters (L).[9] For a full description with the modifications to our generalization, view an ASCII table, which provides the numerical equivalents of all standard American keyboard characters.

Example 1.7. Java returns the distance between the first non-equal characters in a string using compareTo. For instance, "hello".compareTo("hi") returns -4 because the distance from the first non-equal characters, those being 'e' and 'i', is minus four characters, since 'i' is greater than 'e'. If we compare "hello" against "Hello", we get 32, because according to the ASCII table, 'h' corresponds to the integer 104, and 'H' corresponds to the integer 72; their difference is 104 − 72. Comparing "hello" against "hello" produces zero, indicating that they contain the same characters.

Strings are *indexed from zero*, which means that the characters in the string are located at *indices* from zero to the length of the string minus one. So, for example, in the string "hello", the character 'h' is at index zero, 'e' is at index one, 'l' is at index two, 'l' is at index three, and 'o' is at index four. Knowing this fact is crucial to working with helper methods such as charAt, indexOf, and substring, which we will now discuss.

Example 1.8. To retrieve the character at a given index, we invoke charAt on the string: "hello".charAt(1) returns 'e'. Attempting to index out of bounds with either a negative number or a number that is equal to or exceeds the length of the string results in a StringIndexOutOfBoundsException exception.[10]

Example 1.9. We can use indexOf to find the index of the first occurrence of some value in a string. To demonstrate, "hello, how are you?".indexOf("are") returns 11 because the substring "are" occurs starting at index 11 of the provided string. If the supplied argument is not present in the string, indexOf returns −1.

Example 1.10. A *substring* of a string s is a sequence of subsequent characters inside s. We can extract a substring s' from some string s using the substring method: "abcde".substring(2, 4) returns "cd". Note that the last index is exclusive, meaning that, as a rule of thumb, the number of characters returned in the substring is equal to the second argument minus the first argument. There is also a handy second version of this method that receives only one argument: it returns the substring from the given index up to the end of the string. For example, "abcdefg".substring(1) returns everything but the first character, namely "bcdefg".

Example 1.11. We can convert between datatypes, such as an integer to a string and vice versa, using the String.valueOf and Integer.parseInt methods respectively. Passing any non-string primitive value as an argument to valueOf converts it into its string counterpart. Oppositely, if we pass a string that represents an integer to parseInt, we obtain the corresponding integer. The Double.parseDouble and Boolean.parseBoolean methods behave similarly. Passing an invalid string, i.e., one that does not represent the respective datatype, results in Java throwing a NumberFormatException exception.

```
String s1 = String.valueOf(1234);    // "1234"
```

---

[9] We say "in general" because certain characters that we might view as special, e.g., '@', have a larger numeric value than numbers, e.g., '2'.

[10] An *exception* in Java is a type of "error" that occurs while a program is running. We put "error" in quotes because "errors," at least in Java, are unpredictable and are usually a sign of a severe problem in the program such as running out of system memory.

```
String s2 = String.valueOf(Math.PI);  // "3.141592653589793"
int n1 = Integer.parseInt(s1);        // 1234
double n2 = Double.parseDouble(s2);   // 3.141593
```

1.3 Standard I/O

Early on in a Java programmer's career, they encounter the issue of reading from the "console," or standard input, as well as the dubiously useful act of debugging by printing data to standard output. Many programmers are aptly familiar with both of these topics when coming from other programming languages.

First, we need to discuss *standard data streams*. Java (and the operating system in general) utilizes three standard data streams: standard input, standard output, and standard error. We can think of these as sources for reading data from and writing data to. The *standard output stream* is often accessed using the System.out class and through its various methods, e.g., println, print, and printf. To output a line of data to standard output, we invoke System.out.println with some data, in this case, a string. For relaying messages to the user in a terminal-based application, or even when debugging, outputting information to standard output is a good idea. On the other hand, sometimes a program fails or the programmer wants to output an error message. It is possible to output error messages to standard output, since they are otherwise indistinguishable. Though, Java has a dedicated *standard error stream* for outputting error messages and logs via System.err. Now, let's discuss printf in more detail due to its inherent power.

The printf method originates from C, and is handy for printing multiple values at once without resorting to unnecessary string concatenation. In addition, it preserves the formatting of the data, which is useful when wanting to treat a double as a floating-point number in a string representation. It receives at least one argument: a *format string*, and is one of several *variadic methods* that we will discuss. A format string contains special *format characters* and possibly other characters.

Example 1.12. To output an int or long using printf, we use the %d format specifier.

```
int x = 42;
System.out.printf("The value of x is %d\n", x);
System.out.printf("We can inline ints 42 or as literals %d\n", 42);
```

Example 1.13. To output a double using printf, we use the %f format specifier. We can also specify the number of digits n to print after the decimal point by using the format specifier .%nf. Note that floating a decimal to *n* digits does not change the value of that variable; rather, it only changes its string/output representation.

```
double x = 42.0;
System.out.printf("The value of x is %f\n", x);
System.out.printf("PI to 2 decimals is %.2f\n", Math.PI);
System.out.printf("PI with all decimals is %f\n", Math.PI);
```

There are many ways to get creative with printf, including space padding, number formatting, left/right-alignment, and more. We will not discuss these in detail, but instead we provide Table 1.2 of the most common format specifiers.

Format Specifier	Description
%d	Integer (`int`/`long`)
%nf	Floating-point number to n decimals (`float`/`double`)
%s	String
%c	Character (`char`)
%b	Boolean (`boolean`)

Fig. 1.2: Common Format Specifiers

The *standard input stream* allows us to "read data from the console." We place this phrase in quotes because the standard input stream is not necessarily the console/terminal; it simply refers to reading characters from the keyboard that are then added into the data stream.

Example 1.14. Suppose we want to read an integer from the standard input stream. To do so, we first need to instantiate a `Scanner`, which declares a "pipe," so to speak, from which information is read. It is important to state that, while a `Scanner` may read from the standard input stream, it can also read from other input streams, e.g., files or network connections. We will explore this further in subsequent chapters, but for now, let's declare a `Scanner` object to read from standard input.

```
Scanner in = new Scanner(System.in);
```

The `Scanner` class has handy methods for retrieving data from the stream it is scanning (which we will dub the *scannee*). As we said in the example prompt, to read an integer from the scannee, we use `nextInt`, which retrieves and removes the next-available integer from the scannee data stream. Note that the `Scanner` class, by default, is line-buffered, meaning that the data will not be processed by the "retriever methods," e.g., `nextInt`, until there is a new-line character in the input stream. To force a new-line, we press the "Enter"/"Return" key.

```
Scanner in = new Scanner(System.in);
int x = in.nextInt();
System.out.println(x);
```

Running the program and typing in any 32-bit integer feeds it into the standard input stream, then echos it to standard output. Entering any non-integer value crashes the program with an `InputMismatchException` exception. So, what if we want to read in a `String` from the scannee; would we use `nextString`? Unfortunately, this is not correct. We need to instead use `nextLine`. The `nextLine` method reads a "line" of text, as a string, from the scannee. We define a "line" as all characters until the first occurrence of a line break. Invoking `nextLine` consumes these characters, including the newline, from the input stream, and stores them into a variable, if requested. It does not, however, store the new-line character in the returned string.

```
Scanner in = new Scanner(System.in);
String line = in.nextLine();
System.out.println(line);
```

Typing in some characters, which may or may not be numbers, followed by a new-line, stores them in the `line` variable, excluding said new-line. Though, what happens if we prompt for an integer, *then* a string? Our program behaves quite strangely. We type the integer, hit "Return," and the program terminates as if it did not prompt for a string. This is because of how both `nextInt` and `nextLine` work: `nextInt` consumes all data up to but excluding an integer

1.3 Standard I/O

from the input stream; ignoring any preceding whitespace characters. So, after consuming the integer, a new-line character remains in the input stream buffer. Then, nextLine intends to wait until a newline is in the buffer. Because the input stream buffer presently contains a new-line, it consumes everything before the new-line, which comprises the empty string, meaning that both the empty string and the new-line are removed the buffer. To circumvent this problem, we insert a call to nextLine in between the calls to nextInt and nextLine, thereby consuming the lone new-line character and, in effect, clearing the buffer. Notice that we do not put a return value on the left-hand side of this intermediate nextLine invocation; this is because such a variable would hold the empty string, which for the purposes of this program is a meaningless (variable) assignment.

```
Scanner in = new Scanner(System.in);
int x = in.nextInt();
in.nextLine();
String line = in.nextLine();
```

Example 1.15. Let's reimplement Python's input function, which receives a String serving as a prompt for the user to enter data. To make it a bit more user-friendly and elegant, we will add a colon and a space after the given prompt. Because we open a Scanner to read from the standard input stream, there is no need to worry about, say, calling nextInt prior to invoking input. If, on the other hand, we declared a static global Scanner that reads standard input, and we use that to read an integer *inside* input, we would be in trouble.

```
static String input(String prompt) {
  Scanner in = new Scanner(System.in);
  System.out.printf("%s: ", prompt);
  return in.nextLine();
}
```

Example 1.16. Suppose we want to design a method that reads three Cartesian points, as integers, from standard input, and computes the area of the triangle that comprises these points. We can type all integers on the same line, as separated by spaces, because nextInt only parses the *next* integer in the input stream, delimited by whitespace. And, as we said before, nextInt skips over existing trailing spaces in the input stream buffer, so those spaces are omitted. From there, we use the formula for computing the area of the triangle from those points.

$$\frac{x_1(y_2 - y_3) + x_2(y_3 - y_1) + x_3(y_1 - y_2)}{2}$$

```
import java.util.Scanner;

class ThreePointArea {

  /**
   * Computes the area of a triangle given three Cartesian points via standard input.
   * @return the area of the triangle.
   */
  static double computeThreePointArea() {
    Scanner in = new Scanner(System.in);
    int x1 = in.nextInt(); int y1 = in.nextInt(); int x2 = in.nextInt();
    int y2 = in.nextInt(); int x3 = in.nextInt(); int y3 = in.nextInt();
    return (x1 * (y2 - y3) + x2 * (y3 - y1) + x3 * (y1 - y2)) / 2.0;
  }
}
```

We make a note that reading data from a scanner inside a static method to compute some value is not a very good idea. A better alternative solution is to read the data inside a different, unrelated method, e.g., main, then call computeThreePointArea with the six arguments representing each point.

```java
import java.util.Scanner;

class ThreePointArea {

  /**
   * Computes the area of a triangle given three
   * Cartesian points as parameters.
   * @param x1 x coordinate of first point.
   * @param y1 y coordinate of first point.
   * @param x2 x coordinate of second point.
   * @param y2 y coordinate of second point.
   * @param x3 x coordinate of third point.
   * @param y3 y coordinate of third point.
   * @return the area of the triangle.
   */
  static double computeThreePointArea(double x1, double y1,
                                      double x2, double y2,
                                      double x3, double y3) {
    return (x1 * (y2 - y3) + x2 * (y3 - y1) + x3 * (y1 - y2)) / 2.0;
  }

  public static void main(String[] args) {
    Scanner in = new Scanner(System.in);
    int x1 = in.nextInt();
    int y1 = in.nextInt();
    ...
    System.out.println(computeThreePointArea(x1, y1, x2, y2, x3, y3));
  }
}
```

1.4 Randomness

So-called "true" randomness is difficult to implement from a computability standpoint. Thus, for most intents and purposes (i.e., all of those described in this textbook), it is sufficient to use *pseudorandomess* when generating random values. A *pseudorandom number generator* (PRNG) computes apparently random values using a deterministic algorithm, which means that the output values from the generator are predictable. Although it might be incredibly difficult to predict pseudorandomly-generated numbers, it is theoretically possible, which makes those numbers insufficient and insecure for cryptographic schemata and algorithms. For designing, perhaps, a word-guessing game that randomly chooses words from a list, it is perfectly reasonable to use a pseudorandom number generator.

Well, how do we generate pseudorandom numbers in Java? There are a few approaches, and many textbooks opt to use Math.random, which we will explain, but our examples will largely constitute the use of the Random class. Testing methods that rely on randomness is difficult, so our following code snippets do not come with testing suites.

Example 1.17. Using Random, let's generate an integer between 0 and 9, inclusive on both bounds. To do so, we first need to instantiate a Random object, which we will call random. Then, we should invoke nextInt on the random object with an argument of 10. Passing the argument n to nextInt returns an integer $x \in [0, n-1]$.[11]

```
Random random = new Random();
int x = random.nextInt(10); // x in [0, 9]
```

Example 1.18. Imagine we want to generate an integer between −50 and 50, inclusive on both bounds. The idea is to generate an integer between 0 and 100, inclusive, then subtract 50 from the result.

```
Random random = new Random();
int x = random.nextInt(101) - 50; // x in [-50, 50]
```

Example 1.19. When creating a Random object, we can pass a *seed* to the constructor, which is an integer that determines the sequence of pseudorandom numbers generated by our Random instance. Therefore, if we pass the same seed to two distinct Random objects, they will generate the same sequence of pseudorandom numbers. If we do not pass a seed to the constructor, then the Random object will use the current system time as the seed. In theory, we could select a predetermined seed to write JUnit tests for methods that rely on randomness.

```
import static Assertions.assertAll;
import static Assertions.assertEquals;

import java.util.Random;

class DualRandomTester {

  @Test
  void testDualRand() {
    Random r1 = new Random(212);
    Random r2 = new Random(212);
    for (int i = 0; i < 1_000_000_000; i++) {
      assertEquals(r1.nextInt(1_000_000_000), r2.nextInt(1_000_000_000));
    }
  }
}
```

Admittedly, the above test is somewhat useless since it only tests the efficacy of Java's Random class, rather than code that we wrote ourselves.[12] Regardless, it is interesting to observe the behavior of two random number generators to see that, in reality, pseudo-randomness is, as we stated, nothing more than slightly advanced math.

Example 1.20. Java's Math class provides a random method, which receives no arguments. To do anything significant, we must understand how this method works and what kinds of values it can return. The Math.random() method returns a random double between $[0, 1)$, where the upper-bound is exclusive. So, we could see Math.random() return floating-point

---

[11] Readers should be aware that this version of nextInt is different from the one provided by the Scanner class and cannot be used interchangeably.

[12] As a corollary point, the digits of integer literals can be separated via underscores to better visualize their size.

numbers such as 0.391283114421, 0, 0.999999999999, but never exactly one. We can use basic multiplicative offsets to convert this range into one that we might want. For example, to generate a random double value between [0, 10), we multiply the output by ten, e.g., Math.random() * 10.

Example 1.21. To generate a random integer between -5 and 15, inclusive, using the Math.random method, we need to create an offset similar to what we did in the Random example. First, we multiply the result of Math.random() by 21 to generate a floating-point value between [0, 21). *Casting* (i.e., explicitly treating the returned expression as another type) this expression to an integer produces an integer between [0, 20]. Finally, subtracting five therefrom gets us the desired range.

```
int x = ((int) (Math.random() * 21)) - 5;
```

1.5 Exercises

1.1 Design the `double celsiusToFahrenheit(double c)` method, which converts a given temperature from Celsius to Fahrenheit.

1.2 Design the `double fiToCm(double f, double in)` method, which receives two quantities in feet and inches respectively, and returns the combined amount in centimeters.

1.3 Design the `int combineDigits(int a, int b)` method, which receives two `int` values between 0 and 9, and combines them into a single two-digit number.

1.4 Design the `double gigameterToLightsecond(double gm)` method, which converts a distance in gigameters to light seconds (i.e., the distance that light travels in one second). There are $1,000,000,000$ meters in a gigameter, and light travels $299,792,458$ meters per second.

1.5 Design the `double billTotal(double t)` method, which computes the total for a bill. The total is the given subtotal t, plus 6.75% of t for the tax, and 20% of the taxed total for the tip.

1.6 Design the `double grocery(int a, int b, int o, int g, int p)` method, which receives five integers representing the number of apples, bananas, oranges, bunches of grapes, and pineapples purchased at a store. Use the following table to compute the total purchase cost in US dollars.

Item	Price Per Item
Apple	$0.59
Banana	$0.99
Orange	$0.45
Bunch of Grapes	$1.39
Pineapple	$2.24

1.7 Design the `double pointDistance(double px, double py, double qx, double qy)` method, which receives four double values representing two Cartesian coordinates. The method should return the distance between these points.

1.8 Design the `int sumOfSquares(int x, int y)` method, which computes and returns the sum of the squares of two integers x and y.

1.9 Design the `double octagonArea(double s)` method, which computes the area of an octagon with a given side length s. The formula is

$$A = 2(1+\sqrt{2})s^2$$

1.10 Design the `double pyramidSurfaceArea(double l, double w, double h)` method, which computes the surface area of a pyramid with a given base length l, base width w, and height h. The formula is

$$A = lw + l\sqrt{\left(\frac{w}{2}\right)^2 + h^2} + w\sqrt{\left(\frac{l}{2}\right)^2 + h^2}$$

1.11 Design the `double logBase(double n, double b)` that, when given a number n and a base b, returns $\log_b(n)$. You will need to make use of the change-of-base formula, which we provide below (n is the number to compute the logarithm of, b' is the old base, and b is the new base).

$$\log_b(n) = \frac{\log_{b'}(n)}{\log_{b'}(b)}$$

1.12 Design the `double crazyMath(double x)` method, which receives a value of x and computes the value of the following expression:

$$\sqrt{\left|\left(e^{-x} + \cos\frac{2}{x}\right) \cdot \left(\frac{\sin(\pi x - 2\pi) + 17x\pi}{\log_3 |x| \cdot \log_7 |x| \cdot \ln |x|}\right)\right|}$$

Below are some test cases. Hint: when testing this method, you may want to use the delta parameter of `assertEquals`!

```
crazyMath(0)       => NaN
crazyMath(1)       => Infinity
crazyMath(2)       => 21.52368973013284
crazyMath(3)       => 14.692493055407942
crazyMath(10)      => 9.574086130947974
crazyMath(100000)  => 86.49768321282015
```

1.13 The *z-score* is a measure of how far a given data point is away from the mean of a normally-distributed sample. In essence, roughly 68% of data falls between z-scores of $[-1, 1]$, roughly 95% falls between $[-2, 2]$, and 99.7% falls between $[-3, 3]$. This means that extreme outliers have z-scores of either less than -3 or greater than 3.

Design the `boolean isExtremeOutlier(double x, double avg, double stddev)` method that, when given a data point x, a mean μ, and a standard deviation σ, computes the corresponding z-score of x and returns whether it is an "extreme" outlier. Use the following formula:

$$Z = \frac{(x - \mu)}{\sigma}$$

1.14 Design the `double pdf(double mean, double stddev, double x)` that calculates the probability density of a given value x in a normal distribution with mean μ and standard deviation σ. The formula for the probability density function (PDF) of a normal distribution is as follows:

$$f(x) = \frac{1}{\sigma\sqrt{2\pi}} e^{-1/2(x-\mu/\sigma)^2}$$

1.15 Design the `double lawOfCosines(double a, double b, double th)` method that, when given two side lengths of a triangle a, b and the angle between those two sides θ in degrees, returns the length of the third side c. The formula is listed below. Hint: `Math.cos` receives a value in radians; we convert a value from degrees to radians with `Math.toRadians`.

$$c = \sqrt{a^2 + b^2 - 2ab\cos\theta}$$

1.5 Exercises

1.16 Design the `double angle(double a, double b, double c)` method that, when given three side lengths of a triangle a, b, and c, returns the angle θ opposite to that of c in degrees. The formula for this computation is listed below. Hint: arccosine in Java is `Math.acos`.

$$\theta = \cos^{-1}\left(\frac{a^2 + b^2 - c^2}{2ab}\right)$$

1.17 A physics formula for computing object distance displacement is

$$d = v_i t + 1/2at^2$$

where d is the final distance traveled in meters, v_i is the initial velocity, t is the time in seconds, and a is the acceleration in meters per second. Design the `double distanceTraveled(double vi, double a, double t)` method that, when given these variables as parameters, returns the distance that the object in question traveled.

1.18 Design the `String weekday(int d)` method that, when given an integer d from 1 to 7, returns the corresponding day of the week, with 1 corresponding to "Monday" and "Sunday" corresponding to 7. You **cannot** use any conditionals or data structures to solve this problem. Hint: declare a string containing each day of the week, with spaces to pad the days, and use `indexOf` and `substring`.

1.19 Design the `String flStrip(String s)` method that, when given a string, returns a new string with the first and last characters stripped. You may assume that the input string contains at least two characters.

1.20 Design the `double stats(double x, double y)` method that receives two `double` parameters, and returns a `String` containing the following information: the sum, product, difference, the average, the maximum, and the minimum. The string should be formatted as follows, where each category is separated by a newline '\n' character. Assume that XX is a placeholder for the calculated result.

```
"sum=XX
product=XX
difference=XX
average=XX
max=XX
min=XX"
```

1.21 Design the `String userId(String f, String l, int y)` method that computes a user ID based on three given values: a first name, a last name, and a birth year. A user ID is calculated by taking the the first five letters of their last name, the first letter of their first name, and the last two digits of their birth year, and combining the result. Your method should, therefore, receive two `String` parameters and an `int`. Do not convert the year to a `String`. Below are some test cases.

```
userId("Joshua", "Crotts", 1999)    => "CrottJ99"
userId("Katherine", "Johnson", 1918) => "JohnsK18"
userId("Fred", "Fu", 1957)           => "FuF57"
```

1.22 Design the `String cutUsername(String email)` method that receives an email address of the form X@Y.Z and returns the username. The username of an email address is X.

1.23 Design the `String cutDomain(String url)` method that returns the domain name of a website URL of the form `www.X.Z`, where `X` is the domain name and `Z` is the top-level domain.

1.24 Design the `int nextClosest(int m, int n)` method that, when given two positive (non-zero) integers m and n, finds the closest positive integer z to m such that z is a multiple of n and $z \leq m$. For example, if $m = 67$ and $n = 15$, then $z = 60$.

2   Conditionals, Recursion, and Loops

Abstract This chapter reintroduces three core concepts in programming to readers: conditionals, recursion, and loops. We explain the Java syntax and intracacies surrounding `if`, `else if`, and `else`, as well as the illustrious `switch`/`case` statement. Repetition joins the discussion with recursion as a means of breaking down a problem into easier-to-solve smaller problems. We conclude with an introduction to loops via a translation pipeline from tail recursion, and consequently demonstrate that loops can be used as a substitute for any recursive algorithm, and may in fact be simpler for certain problems.

2.1 Conditionals

Computer programs constantly make decisions through *conditionals*. We have seen conditionals before, but in this section we will reintroduce them as a concept and discuss the intricacies of Java's conditionals, including the different logical operators and behaviors thereof.

In Java, we use `if` to designate a branch in code. We supply to it a conditional expression, or a *predicate*, which resolves to either true or false. In essence, predicates resolve to boolean values. For example, if we want to return 5 when two integers a and b are the same value, we write the following:

```
static int foo() {
  int a = ...;
  int b = ...;
  if (a == b) { return 5; }
  return 0;
}
```

The `==` operator compares primitive values for equality, as we stated in our Java primer. If we want to use the result of a (boolean) method as the condition, we might want to inline the invocation.

```
static boolean bar() {
  ...
}

static int foo() {
  if (bar()) { return 5; }
  return 0;
}
```

We negate conditional expressions using the exclamation point operator, i.e., `!`. That is, if e is an expression that returns a boolean value, `!e` flips the output value from true to false and vice versa. We can chain conditional expressions together using the logical AND/OR operators, namely && and || respectively. All boolean subexpressions that comprise a larger expression, conjoined by &&, must be true for the overall expression to be true. On the other hand, when boolean expressions are conjoined by ||, only one must be true for the overall expression to be true.

Both logical AND and logical OR are *short-circuiting operators.* Regarding the former, if we have the expression $e = e_1$ && e_2, and e_1 resolves to false, then e_2 is not evaluated; recall that both operands of a logical AND must be true for the result to be true, so evaluating the second operand is unnecessary. Logical OR works similarly: if we have the expression $e = e_1$ || e_2, and e_1 resolves to true, then e_2 is not evaluated, because only one operand has to be true for the result of the OR to be true.

```
static int foo() {
  int a = 5;
  int b = 10;
  int c = 5;
  // We never check if c == 5.
  if (a == b && c == 5) { return 100; }
  // We never check if b != 10.
  if (a == c || b != 10) { return 200; }
  return 0;
}
```

In addition to if, Java also has else and else if for extending the possible outcomes of a condition. When the predicate of a preceding if is false and an else block is attached, its code is evaluated. Moreover, when the predicate of a preceding if is false and an else if block is attached, the condition to the else if is evaluated. The former pairing represents a binary outcome, whereas the latter corresponds to more than two possible outcomes. Multiple if statements "stacked above one another" results in their sequential evaluation, since Java assumes they are disjoint code segments. The else if block, on the contrary, executes exactly when its preceding if condition resolves to false. In the following code listing, we show an example of two sets of conditional statements; the former uses only if and the latter takes advantage of if, else if, and else. Accordingly, the left-hand listing returns 20 and the right-hand listing returns 10.

```
static int foo() {                  static int foo() {
  int x = 10;                         int x = 10;
  int y = 0;                          int y = 0;
  if (x == 10) { y = 5; }             if (x == 10) { y = 10; }
  if (y == 5) { y += 10; }            else if (y == 5) { y += 10; }
  if (x != 10 && y != 5) { y += 5; }  else { y += 5; }
  return y;                           return y;
}                                   }
```

Another piece of syntax that is worth an explanation is the use of operators such as +=, *=, and so forth. These operators introduce a form of variable reassignment, and while y = y + 5 is sufficient to express "assign to y the sum of y and 5," the augmented assignment operator shortens the statement to y += 5. Any simple binary operator, e.g., +, -, *, /, %, may take advantage of the augmented assignment operator, and our code will frequently use them in place of superfluous operations.

Example 2.1. Let's design the isPowerOfEight method, which determines whether a positive integer is a power of eight. For example, 64 is a power of eight because $8^2 = 64$, but 37 is not a power of 2 because there does not exist an integer x such that $2^x = 37$. We can use logarithms to our advantage to determine if a number is a power of eight. Java provides the

2.1 Conditionals

Math.log and Math.log10 methods to return the base e logarithm and base 10 logarithms respectively. It does not, however, provide a method for computing the base 8 logarithm, which we need. The change-of-base formula is necessary for such a calculation.[1] To change from a base c to a base b, we divide the logarithm base c of our number-of-interest n by the logarithm base c of our base b. So, to compute the base eight logarithm of an integer n, we can convert from base e to base 8 using a similar tactic. At the end of the chapter, we ask readers to apply the change-of-base method to any arbitrary base. So, to determine if an integer n is a power of eight, we check to see if it is an integer, which is possible via casting. That is, if x is a floating-point datatype, e..g, double, then x represents an integer number if the expression (int) x == x resolves to true.

```java
import static Assertions.assertAll;
import static Assertions.assertTrue;
import static Assertions.assertFalse;

class PowerOfEightTester {

  @Test
  void testIsPowerOfEight() {
    assertAll(
      () -> assertTrue(isPowerOfEight(8)),
      () -> assertTrue(isPowerOfEight(512)),
      () -> assertTrue(isPowerOfEight(262144)),
      () -> assertFalse(isPowerOfEight(0)),
      () -> assertFalse(isPowerOfEight(2)),
      () -> assertFalse(isPowerOfEight(47)),
      () -> assertFalse(isPowerOfEight(63)));
  }
}
```

```java
class PowerOfEight {

  /**
   * Determines whether a number is a power of eight.
   * @param n integer of interest.
   * @return true if 8^x = n for some x >= 0, false otherwise.
   */
  static boolean isPowerOfEight(int n) {
    if (n <= 0) {
      return false;
    } else {
      double cob = Math.log(n) / Math.log(8);
      return (int) cob == cob;
    }
  }
}
```

Example 2.2. Suppose we want to translate a String grade into its grade-point average equivalent, treating pluses and minuses as fractional grade increment or decrements. Our grading schema has no grade higher than a 4.0, and all failing grades (i.e., F+, F, F-) result in a 0.0 grade-point average. After writing the tests, we can use a series of if and else if statements as a case analysis on the letter grade. Once we have the base GPA according to the provided letter, we apply the plus or minus given the aforementioned criteria. When

---

[1] We presented this as an exercise in the previous chapter.

determining the initial GPA value, were we to use a series of if statements as opposed to if/else if/else, every predicate would need to be evaluated regardless of whether it is meaningful. By "meaningful," we mean to suggest that, for instance, once we know the GPA is a 4.0, it makes no sense to determine if the grade is a 'B', since we know from the previous branch that it is an 'A'. The else if statements are skipped over if a preceding condition resolves to true.

```
import static Assertions.assertAll;
import static Assertions.assertEquals;

class GpaCalculatorTesting {

  @Test
  void testGpa() {
    assertAll(
      () -> assertEquals(4.0, gpa("A+")),
      () -> assertEquals(3.7, gpa("A-")),
      () -> assertEquals(0.0, gpa("F-")));
  }
}
```

```
class GpaCalculator {

  /**
   * Computes the numeric GPA for a given letter grade.
   * @param letter - grade between A and F, with optional +.
   * @return numeric grade from 4.0 to 0.0.
   */
  static double gpa(String grade) {
    boolean plus = grade.contains("+");
    boolean minus = grade.contains("-");
    char letter = grade.charAt(0);
    double gpa = 0;

    // Compute the grade letter.
    if (letter == 'A') { gpa = 4.0; }
    else if (letter == 'B') { gpa = 3.0; }
    else if (letter == 'C') { gpa = 2.0; }
    else if (letter == 'D') { gpa = 1.0; }
    else { gpa = 0.0; }

    // Compute +/- if applicable.
    if (letter != 'A' && letter != 'F') { gpa = plus ? gpa + 0.3 : gpa; }
    if (letter != 'F') { gpa = minus ? gpa - 0.3 : gpa; }
    return gpa;
  }
}
```

The latter two if statements, as we said, apply increments or decrements based on whether the grade is a + or a -. We use the not-equal-to operator != to circumvent having to apply a negation on the outer condition, i.e., !(letter == 'A'). The bodies of these cases, however, are unfamiliar; here we introduce the *ternary operator*. Because if is a statement, there is no way to inline a conditional into an expression. Ternary operators are the remedy to this problem. We read $r = p \,?\, c \,:\, a$ as follows: "if p is true, assign c to r, otherwise assign a to r." Inlining conditional expressions in this fashion reduces code clutter, but should be used sparingly. We could write all if statements as ternary operations, but doing so possibly obfuscates the logic of our code.

2.1 Conditionals

Aside from the 'if'/'else if'/'else' trio and the ternary operator, Java has switch/case statements, which serve to help simplify repetitive case analysis problems. A switch statement receives an expression *e* that resolves to some value *v*. Inside the switch block exists case statements, corresponding to outcomes of *e*'s evaluation. For instance, if we wanted to design a method that determines the number of days there are in a given (non-leap year) month, we might be inclined to use several if statements. Instead, let's see the answer to this problem using switch and case statements.

```java
import static Assertions.assertAll;
import static Assertions.assertEquals;

class MonthToDaysTester {

  @Test
  void testMonthToDays() {
    assertAll(
      () -> assertEquals(31, monthToDays("January")),
      () -> assertEquals(28, monthToDays("February")),
      () -> assertEquals(31, monthToDays("May")),
      () -> assertEquals(31, monthToDays("July")),
      () -> assertEquals(31, monthToDays("August")),
      () -> assertEquals(30, monthToDays("September")),
      () -> assertEquals(31, monthToDays("December")));
  }
}
```

```java
class MonthToDays {

  /**
   * Determines how many days a given month has, not accounting for leap years.
   * @param m capitalized month, e.g., "July".
   * @return the number of days in the month
   */
  static int monthToDays(String m) {
    int days = 0;
    switch (m) {
      case "February":
        days = 28;
        break;
      case "April":
      case "June":
      case "September":
      case "November":
        days = 30;
        break;
      default:
        days = 31;
    }
    return days;
  }
}
```

We evaluate the argument *m* inside the switch statement, and it resolves to one of twelve possible strings, assuming the input is a valid and capitalized month. If, for instance, the string is "February", we assign *days* to 28 and perform a break. Cases that comprise a switch block can "fall through" to the next case, meaning that if we did not insert a break, the program would fall all the way to the default case and assign 31 to *days*. Default cases correspond to "anything other data," akin to else blocks. In our example, we place all months that have thirty-one days in the default case to reduce the number of lines in our code. When a month has thirty days, there are four possibilities, and so we stack these atop one another to state that these months should have 30 assigned to *days*. Should we wanted to omit break statements, we might instead inline return statements directly, since nothing else occurs outside the switch block aside from return *days* at the end of the method. Of course, this solution only works when the resulting target of a switch block *is* the desired value.

2.2 Recursion

In this section we reintroduce recursion as a means of problem decomposition and repetition. We present two forms: standard recursion and tail recursion, as well as the issues that come with both forms in Java. The discussion starts with a review of basic arithmetic and its relation to recursion.

2.2.1 Standard Recursion

You may or may not have seen recursion before, but in theory the concept is quite simple: a method f is *recursive* if, somewhere in the definition of f, it invokes itself. For example, in the following code segment, we define f to be a method of arbitrary arguments that calls itself from its body.

```
static int f(...) {
  ...
  f(...);
  ...
}
```

Some may question the need for recursive methods, as it appears to be circular; why would we ever want a method to call itself? There are two reasons, where the former is what we consider to be a less significant reason than the latter:

1. It allows the programmer to repeat a given segment of code.
2. We can compose the solution to a big problem by combining the solutions to smaller problems.

So, we may certainly use recursion to repeat a task, but we primarily design recursive methods to solve large problems by breaking them down into small, simple problems that we know how to solve.

Example 2.3. Let's consider the question of addition. Consider a context where we have access to only three methods: addOne, subOne, and isZero, all of which are trivially defined. We also have access to conditional statements and method calls. Finally, we have an identity that $m + 0 = m$ for any natural number m. Here's the problem that we want to solve: we want to add two natural numbers m and n, but how do we do that? Think about how humans calculate the sum of two natural numbers (perhaps some do it differently from others, but the general process is the same). Since we do not have a + operator in this context, we have to try a different approach. Recall the identity that we have at our disposal: $m + 0 = m$. Is

2.2 Recursion

there a way we can make use of the identity? Imagine that we want to solve $3 + 4$ in this context. Can we rewrite this expression that takes advantage of those methods that we have at our disposal? Indeed, we can rewrite $3 + 4$ as a series of calls to subOne and addOne, but we will first show this idea in math notation.

$$
\begin{aligned}
&= 3 + 4 \\
&= (3 + 3) + 1 \\
&= ((3 + 2) + 1) + 1 \\
&= (((3 + 1) + 1) + 1) + 1 \\
&= ((((3 + 0) + 1) + 1) + 1) + 1
\end{aligned}
$$

To solve $3 + 4$, we need to solve $3 + 3$, which means we need to solve $3 + 2$, which means we need to solve $3 + 1$, which means we need to solve $3 + 0$. Substituting 3 for m produces the identity, meaning this expression resolves to m, namely 3. Recursively breaking down a problem into smaller problems is called *invoking the recursion*. Namely, we invoke the method of interest, +, inside its own definition. As part of this, we decrement n by one in attempt to head towards the identity, or the problem that *we know* how to solve. Such a problem is called the *base case* to a recursive method. How do we know when and where to analyze m as a base case? We know that m is the base case when n is zero because of the known identity.

We still have work to do after reaching the base case, however. Even though we may substitute $3 + 0$ for 3, we have to add one to these resulting values. Let's examine this.

$$
\begin{aligned}
&= ((((3 + 0) + 1) + 1) + 1) + 1 \\
&= (((3 + 1) + 1) + 1) + 1 \\
&= ((4 + 1) + 1) + 1 \\
&= (5 + 1) + 1 \\
&= 6 + 1 \\
&= 7
\end{aligned}
$$

Upon reaching the base case, using the pieces generated by the recursion, we create the solution to our overall problem. In other words, to solve $3 + 1$, we had to solve $3 + 0$, whose base case resolves to 3. We subsequently walk back up through the series of recursive calls, filling in the gaps to previously-unknown solutions. Because $3 + 0 = 3$, we know the answer to $3 + 1$. The substitution continuously propagates back through the recursive calls, and we arrive at our desired solution of 7. Traversing through the recursive calls backwards, while building the solution to the overall problem, is called *unwinding the recursion*. Now that we understand the logic of our problem, let's design the method in Java. First, of course, we want to design our tests.

```
import static Assertions.assertAll;
import static Assertions.assertEquals;

class AddTester {

  @Test
  void testAdd() {
    assertAll(
      () -> assertEquals(7, add(3, 4)),
      () -> assertEquals(12, add(11, 1)),
      () -> assertEquals(6, add(0, 6)),
      () -> assertEquals(6, add(6, 0)));
  }
}
```

```
class Add {

  /**
   * Adds two natural numbers. Uses recursion and the addOne,
   * subOne, and isZero methods.
   * @param m the first number.
   * @param n the second number.
   * @return the sum.
   */
  static int add(int m, int n) {
    if (isZero(n)) {
      return m;
    } else {
      return addOne(add(m, subOne(n)));
    }
  }
}
```

Our recursive implementation is nothing more than a restatement of the mathematical definition, which is convenient. Let's trace through a sequence of recursive calls from invoking add(3, 4).

>Is 4 zero? No! return addOne(add(3, 3))
>Is 3 zero? No! return addOne(add(3, 2))
>Is 2 zero? No! return addOne(add(3, 1))
>Is 1 zero? No! return addOne(add(3, 0))
>Is 0 zero? Yes! return 3.

Once we reach the base case, we unwind the recursive calls, substituting our known values for their previously-unknown values.

>We now know add(3, 0) is 3. So, return addOne(add(3, 0)) is return 4
>We now know add(3, 1) is 4. So, return addOne(add(3, 1)) is return 5
>We now know add(3, 2) is 3. So, return addOne(add(3, 2)) is return 6
>We now know add(3, 3) is 3. So, return addOne(add(3, 3)) is return 7
>We now know add(3, 4) is 7. So, we are done.

2.2 Recursion

Recursion, as we stated before, composes the solution to a large problem by first solving smaller "easier" problems.

Example 2.4. Consider the factorial mathematical operation. The factorial of a natural number n obeys the following definition:

$$0! = 1$$
$$n! = n \cdot (n-1) \cdot (n-2) \cdot \ldots \cdot 1$$

Factorial is a naturally-recursive mathematical operation. To solve $n!$, we need to solve $(n-1)!$, which means we need to solve $(n-2)!$, all the way down to our base case of $0! = 1$. Rewriting the prior definition to use explicit recursion gets us the following:

$$0! = 1$$
$$n! = n \cdot (n-1)!$$

Let's trace through a factorial invocation.

$$5! = 5 \cdot 4!$$
$$4! = 4 \cdot 3!$$
$$3! = 3 \cdot 2!$$
$$2! = 2 \cdot 1!$$
$$1! = 1 \cdot 0!$$

So, after the recursive calls, we hit our base case. We still have work to do afterwards, much like how add unwinds its recursion. Rather than addOne, we extend our context to include multiplication for the sake of brevity, and use that as an operation. Therefore, when unwinding the recursive calls, we get the following trace:

$$0! = 1$$
$$1! = 1 \cdot 1$$
$$2! = 2 \cdot 1$$
$$3! = 3 \cdot 2$$
$$4! = 4 \cdot 6$$
$$5! = 5 \cdot 24$$
$$= 120$$

Now let's design the factorial method in Java, again with tests taking immediate precedence over the method definition.

```
import static Assertions.assertAll;
import static Assertions.assertEquals;

class FactorialTester {

  @Test
  void testFact() {
    assertEquals(1, fact(0));
    assertEquals(120, fact(5));
  }
}
```

```
class Factorial {

  /**
   * Computes the factorial of a number.
   * @param n the number to compute the factorial of.
   * @return factorial result.
   */
  static int fact(int n) {
    if (isZero(n)) {
      return 1;
    } else {
      return n * fact(subOne(n));
    }
  }
}
```

Once more will we derive a trace, but this time of the `fact` method when invoked with 5.

> Is 5 zero? No! return 5 * fact(4)
> Is 4 zero? No! return 4 * fact(3)
> Is 3 zero? No! return 3 * fact(2)
> Is 2 zero? No! return 2 * fact(1)
> Is 1 zero? No! return 1 * fact(0)
> Is 0 zero? Yes! return 1

Upon arriving at the base case, we begin to unwind the recursive calls.

> We now know `fact(0)` is 1. So, return 1 * 1 is return 1
> We now know `fact(1)` is 2. So, return 2 * 1 is return 2
> We now know `fact(2)` is 2. So, return 3 * 2 is return 6
> We now know `fact(3)` is 6. So, return 4 * 6 is return 24
> We now know `fact(4)` is 24. So, return 5 * 24 is return 120
> We now know `fact(5)` is 120. So, we are done.

Voilà, we get our desired solution.

2.2.2 Tail Recursion and Accumulators

In the previous section, we discussed recursion, or what we will refer to as *standard recursion*. This style of recursion is popular because of its ease-of-use and relative correlation to mathematical definitions. Unfortunately, there is a significant problem with standard recursion: it is a memory hog and potential recipe for disaster. The reason does not easily present itself to the programmer, and we have to dive deeper into how Java makes method calls to fully explain what goes awry.

Each time Java invokes a method, it pushes an *activation record* to its *method call stack*. The call stack is a location in memory where all method invocations reside. Activation records contain information about the method that was called, such as its arguments, the locally-

2.2 Recursion

defined variables, and other miscellaneous data. More importantly, activation records designate the "return location" of a method. When a method call returns, it is popped off the top of the call stack. The call stack's memory, or lack thereof, is the root cause of problems with standard recursion. Let us demonstrate this predicament with an example trace of add whose second argument is incredibly large; over two million.

As we stated, calling a method pushes its activation record to the method call stack, so invoking add(3, 2000000) pushes one record. Then, because two million is certainly not zero, we then recursively call add(3, 1999999) and push that record to the call stack. This idea continues until we reach a point where there is not enough memory to push another activation record onto the (call) stack, in which a StackOverflowError is thrown by the Java Virtual Machine. We need a way of writing recursive algorithms without having to waste so much memory and risk a stack overflow of the call stack. A potential solution to our problem is via *tail recursion* through *accumulator-passing style*.

...
...
...
...
add(3, 19996)
add(3, 19997)
add(3, 19998)
add(3, 19999)
add(3, 20000)

Fig. 2.1: Pushing of add Activation Records to the Call Stack

A method f is *tail recursive* if all recursive calls are in *tail position*. At first glance, this definition appears circular due to the similar terms used. But, consider this piece: an expression is in tail position if it is in the last-to-perform operation before a method returns. Both add and fact are non-tail recursive methods, because each have extra work to do; that work being an unwinding of the recursive calls. Tail recursive functions do not need to unwind anything because they (for the most part) accumulate the result to an overall problem in an argument to the tail recursive method.

Example 2.5. We want to compute the factorial of some number using tail recursion. Let's design a template for such a method. We know that the method must be called where the call is in tail position, so we can add it as a preliminary step. Up next, we can copy the logic of the previous standard recursive algorithm with the added exception that we do not return one from the base case, but instead return an accumulated result. The goal is to construct, or generate, the factorial of some n as an argument to the method.

```
class Factorial {

  /**
   * Tail recursive method for computing the factorial of a number.
   * @param n the number to compute the factorial of.
   * @param acc the accumulator for the result.
   * @return the factorial of the number.
   */
```

```
  static int factTR(int n, int acc) {
    if (isZero(n)) { return acc; }
    else { return factTR(n - 1, acc * n); }
  }
}
```

Observe that the only change to the base case occurs in the body of the condition. So, the first argument to factTR, i.e., n, still trends towards the base case and, hence, should be the decrement of n. Oppositely, acc stores an accumulated factorial result. We multiply the accumulator variable by n with every (tail) recursive call, meaning that the accumulator approaches the solution.

Let's perform a trace of factTR to see how we build the result in the acc parameter. One extra factor to consider is the initial/starting value of our accumulator argument. The starting value of a tail recursive method depends on the context of the problem, and for factorial, the only reasonable value is one. For example, if we initialize acc to zero, then we would continuously multiply and store zero as the argument to the recursive call and always return zero as the factorial of any number.

> Is 5 zero? No! return factTR(4, 5)
>
> Is 4 zero? No! return factTR(3, 20)
>
> Is 3 zero? No! return factTR(2, 60)
>
> Is 2 zero? No! return factTR(1, 120)
>
> Is 1 zero? No! return factTR(0, 120)
>
> Is 0 zero? Yes! return 120

The base case simply returns the accumulated value from the method. We do not need to unwind the recursive calls, since there is no extra work to be done after making the recursive calls in the first place. Even still, some may question how this avoids a stack overflow error, because we still push an activation record to the call stack each time we invoke factTR, right? Indeed, this solution does not solve the stack overflow problem, because Java does not employ the necessary optimizations to do so. What might one of those solutions be, in fact? As a hypothesis, because the method is tail recursive, the Java compiler could detect this and, instead of pushing a new activation record to the call stack, overwrite the preexisting record, hence using constant space and only one record. Overriding the existing activation record is permissible, since we do not unwind the stack. Recall with standard recursion that we push an activation record to the call stack to remember the context of "how deep we are" into the recursion, in addition to what values we must substitute back into the unknowns during the unwinding phase. Conversely, when examining the tail recursive approach, we build the result alongside heading towards the base case, meaning previous recursive calls are irrelevant. Let's see what this looks like in the model of a stack.

The transitions between each "stack" represent the same stack wherein they represent a point in time. Following the invocation of factTR(5, 1), we recursively call factTR(4, 5), and replace the previous activation record. This follows suit until we hit the base case and return the accumulator.

Tail recursion often exposes its use of an accumulator to the caller of the method. The user of such a factorial function should not need to worry about what value to pass as the initial accumulator; they only want a method that computes the factorial of some natural number. The solution is to write a *driver method* and introduce *method access modifiers*. Driver methods, in short, serve to "jump start" the logic for some other, perhaps more complex,

2.2 Recursion

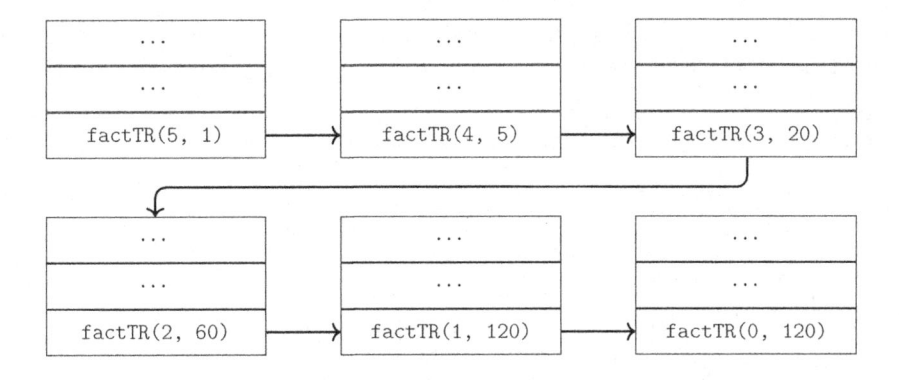

Fig. 2.2: Simulated Tail Recursion with "Multiple Stacks"

method. We should refactor the logic from factTR into a helper method that is inaccessible from outside the class. To do so, we affix the private keyword in front of static. Private methods are unreachable/not callable from outside the class in which it is declared.

```
class Factorial {

  /**
   * Tail recursive (driver) method for computing the factorial of a number.
   * @param n the number to compute the factorial of.
   * @return the factorial.
   */
  static int factTR(int n) {
    return factHelper(n, 1);
  }

  /**
   * Helper method to compute the factorial of a number using tail recursion.
   * @param n the number to compute the factorial of.
   * @param acc the accumulator for the result.
   * @return the factorial of the number.
   */
  private static int factHelper(int n, int acc) {
    if (isZero(n)) { return acc; }
    else { return factHelper(subOne(n), acc * n); }
  }
}
```

Notice that we localized the tail recursive method to this class and updated the signature of factTR to only have one parameter. We designate factTR as the driver method for jump-starting the tail recursion that occurs in factHelper. Driver methods should share the same signature with their standard recursion method counterparts so as to not expose the innard implementation of a method to the caller. Hiding method implementation in this fashion is called *encapsulation*.

Example 2.6. Let us get a bit more practice with recursion by integrating strings into the mixture. Suppose that we want to design a method that removes all characters whose position is a multiple of three. For example, given the string "ABCDEFGHI", we want to return

"ABDEGH", since "C", "F", and "I" are located at positions (note the use of position and not index) are divisible by three. Tests are, of course, warranted and necessary.

```java
import static Assertions.assertAll;
import static Assertions.assertEquals;

class RemoveDivThreeCharsTester {

  @Test
  void testRemoveDivThreeChars() {
    assertAll(
      () -> assertEquals("ABDEGH", removeDivThreeChars("ABCDEFGHI")),
      () -> assertEquals("CCC", removeDivThreeChars("CC")),
      () -> assertEquals("AB", removeDivThreeChars("AB")),
      () -> assertEquals("A", removeDivThreeChars("A")),
      () -> assertEquals("", removeDivThreeChars("")),
      () -> assertEquals("ABCD", removeDivThreeChars("ABD")));
  }
}
```

We break our input down into two cases: when the string does not have at least three characters, and otherwise. If the string has less than three characters, we return the string itself. If the string has at least three characters, we compose a new string containing the first two characters, skipping the third, and recursing on the rest. In the `else` case, we are guaranteed that the input string has at least three characters, implying that `substring(3)` can never fail. Because the `substring` method of one argument is exclusive, if the provided index is the end of the string, the empty string is returned.

```java
class RemoveDivThreeChars {

  /**
   * Removes characters at positions divisible by three.
   * @param s the given string.
   * @return the resulting string.
   */
  static String removeDivThreeChars(String s) {
    if (s.length() < 3) {
      return s;
    } else {
      return s.substring(0, 2) + removeDivThreeChars(s.substring(3));
    }
  }
}
```

Thinking recursively takes time, and there is no better way to get better than extensive practice. Let's now convert the method into its tail recursive counterpart. Due to the trivial nature of writing tests, we omit them for our tail recursive version. The algorithm remains largely the same, except for the added accumulator, which builds the resulting string rather than relying on the recursive unwinding to compose the solution. Our base case concatenates *s* onto the end of the accumulator.

2.2 Recursion

```
class RemoveDivThreeChars {

  /**
   * Tail recursive (driver) method to remove characters at
   * positions divisible by three.
   * @param s the given string.
   * @return the resulting string.
   */
  static String removeDivThreeCharsTR(String s) {
    return removeDivThreeCharsTRHelper(s, "");
  }

  /**
   * Helper method to remove characters at positions
   * divisible by three using tail recursion.
   * @param s the given string.
   * @param acc the accumulator for the result.
   * @return the resulting string.
   */
  private static String removeDivThreeCharsTRHelper(String s, String acc) {
    if (s.length() < 3) {
      return acc + s;
    } else {
      return removeDivThreeCharsTRHelper(s.substring(3), acc+s.substring(0, 2));
    }
  }
}
```

Example 2.7. Let's design a recursive method to remove sequences of duplicate characters. For example, consider "aaabbcdddc". Removing sequential characters from this string produces "abcdc".

Let's think about the base case and recursive step for the algorithm. One base case we can derive is when the string contains at most one character, meaning we return that string. On the other hand, the string must contain at least two characters that may be identical. At first, we may think to check whether the first and second characters and, if so, recurse without the second character and prepend the first. Sadly, this only removes every other duplicate character. We need to keep track of what character we are removing from the string in a sequence. If we are removing 'a' from the above example, we want to concatenate 'a' onto the front of the recursive call, then recurse on the rest of the string, but pass 'a' as a parameter. Until we reach a non-'a' character, we simply recurse on the rest of the string without concatenating a character. Notice that the initial call to the helper method, namely remSeqCharsHelper, contains the null character literal, i.e., '\0'.

```
class RemoveSequentialCharsTester {

  @Test
  void testRemoveSequentialChars() {
    assertAll(
      () -> assertEquals("abcdc", remSeqChars("aaabbcdddc")),
      () -> assertEquals("abcde", remSeqChars("abcde")),
      () -> assertEquals("aaaaa", remSeqChars("")),
      () -> assertEquals("a", remSeqChars("a")),
      () -> assertEquals("", remSeqChars("")));
  }
}
```

```
class RemoveSequentialChars {

  /**
   * Removes sequential characters from a string.
   * @param s the given string.
   * @return the resulting string.
   */
  static String remSeqChars(String s) {
    return remSeqCharsHelper(s, '\0');
  }

  /**
   * Helper method to remove sequential characters from a string.
   * @param s the given string.
   * @param c the character to remove from the string.
   * @return the resulting string.
   */
  private static String remSeqCharsHelper(String s, char c) {
    if (s.isEmpty()) {
      return "";
    } else if (s.charAt(0) != c) {
      return s.charAt(0) + remSeqCharsHelper(s.substring(1), s.charAt(0));
    } else {
      return remSeqCharsHelper(s.substring(1), c);
    }
  }
}
```

```
class RemoveSequentialChars {

  /**
   * Tail recursive (driver) method to remove sequential characters from a string.
   * @param s the given string.
   * @return the resulting string.
   */
  static String remSeqCharsTR(String s) {
    return remSeqCharsTRHelper(s, '\0', "");
  }

  /**
   * Tail recursive helper method for remSeqCharsTR.
   * @param s the given string.
   * @param c the character to remove from the string.
   * @param acc the accumulator for the result.
   * @return the resulting string.
   */
  private static String remSeqCharsHelper(String s, char c, String acc) {
    if (s.isEmpty()) {
      return acc;
    } else if (s.charAt(0) != c) {
      return remSeqCharsHelper(s.substring(1), s.charAt(0), acc + s.charAt(0));
    } else {
      return remSeqCharsHelper(s.substring(1), c, acc);
    }
  }
}
```

2.2 Recursion

Example 2.8. Exponentiation is an incredibly common mathematical operation that, like factorial, may be represented as a recurrence relation. That is, n^b where $n > 0$ and $b \geq 0$ is defined as $n \cdot n^{b-1}$ for $b > 0$, and 1 when $b = 0$. The simple algorithm is to naturally recurse on b until it is zero. Because we know that b is a natural number, we can design a substantially faster algorithm. Recall the rules of exponents, namely that $n^{2b} = (n^b)^2$. Using this equivalence, when the exponent is even, we square the result and divide the given exponent in half. If it is odd, we recurse with one less than the exponent.

The standard recursive pow method receives two arguments: n and b, and recurses over b until it is zero. On the other hand, the tail recursive counterpart accumulates the result as a parameter. In either method, we must handle a case analysis on the parity of b, i.e., determine whether b is even or odd. Both method implementations utilize the same test cases, and we will show both testing suites.

```java
import static Assertions.assertAll;
import static Assertions.assertEquals;

class PowTester {

  @Test
  void testPow() {
    assertAll(
      () -> assertEquals(1, pow(42, 0)),
      () -> assertEquals(81, pow(9, 2)),
      () -> assertEquals(16777216, pow(4, 12)));
  }

  @Test
  void testPowTR() {
    assertAll(
      () -> assertEquals(1, powTR(42, 0)),
      () -> assertEquals(81, powTR(9, 2)),
      () -> assertEquals(16777216, powTR(4, 12)));
  }
}
```

```java
class Pow {

  /**
   * Calculates the result of raising a base number to an exponent.
   * The method uses standard recursion over ints, so make sure that
   * neither parameter are very large!
   * @param n the base number.
   * @param b the exponent.
   * @return the result of n raised to the power of b.
   */
  static int pow(int n, int b) {
    if (b == 0) {
      return 1;
    } else if (b % 2 == 0) {
      return n * n * pow(n, b / 2);
    } else {
      return n * pow(n, b - 1);
    }
  }
}
```

```java
class Pow {

  /**
   * Calculates the result of raising a base number to an exponent.
   * The helper method uses tail recursion over ints, so make sure that
   * neither parameter are very large!
   * @param n the base number.
   * @param b the exponent.
   * @return the result of n raised to the power of b.
   */
  static int powTR(int n, int b) {
    return powTR(n, b, 1);
  }

  /**
   * Tail recursive helper method for powTR.
   * @param n the base number.
   * @param b the exponent.
   * @param acc the intermediary result of n^b.
   * @return acc.
   */
  private static int powTRHelper(int n, int b, int acc) {
    if (b == 0) {
      return acc;
    } else if (b % 2 == 0) {
      return powTRHelper(n, b / 2, n * n * acc);
    } else {
      return powTRHelper(n, b - 1, n * acc);
    }
  }
}
```

Example 2.9. Let's design a method to count the number of digits in a positive integer. It's important to realize that we can write an algorithm to compute such a value using only mathematical operations, i.e., exponents and logarithms. Let's first design the standard recursive algorithm and then write the tail recursive variant. The standard recursive algorithm has a base case, namely when its input is less than 10. If so, we know the number has only one digit and can return accordingly. We recurse on the number after removing a digit. Digits are removed by dividing the input by ten. The tail recursive algorithm delegates the return value to an accumulator. By designing the tests for one of the algorithms, we inadvertently write tests for the other!

```java
import static Assertions.assertAll;
import static Assertions.assertEquals;

class CountDigitTester {

  @Test
  void testCountDigit() {
    assertAll(
      () -> assertEquals(1, countDigits(0)),
      () -> assertEquals(3, countDigits(123)),
      () -> assertEquals(4, countDigits(5192)));
  }
```

2.2 Recursion

```java
@Test
void testCountDigitTR() {
  assertAll(
      () -> assertEquals(1, countDigitsTR(0)),
      () -> assertEquals(3, countDigitsTR(123)),
      () -> assertEquals(4, countDigitsTR(5192)));
}
}
```

```java
class CountDigit {

  /**
   * Counts the number of digits in a positive integer.
   * @param n positive integer.
   * @return number of digits.
   */
  static int countDigits(int n) {
    if (n < 10) {
      return 1;
    } else {
      return 1 + countDigits(n / 10);
    }
  }
}
```

```java
class CountDigit {

  /**
   * Counts the number of digits in a positive integer
   * using tail recursion.
   * @param n positive integer.
   * @return number of digits.
   */
  static int countDigitsTR(int n) {
    return countDigitsTRHelper(n, 1);
  }

  /**
   * Helper method for computing the number of digits.
   * @param n positive integer.
   * @param acc accumulator for # of digits.
   * @return number of digits.
   */
  private static int countDigitsTRHelper(int n, int acc) {
    if (n < 10) {
      return acc;
    } else {
      return countDigitsTRHelper(n / 10, acc + 1);
    }
  }
}
```

So, we have explored both standard and tail recursive methods, and how a programming language might optimize tail recursive calls. The thing is, tail recursion has a direct correspondence to loops, i.e., while. In fact, some programming languages convert all tail recursive functions into their iterative counterparts, alleviating the need for a stack whatsoever. Replacing tail recursion, or tail recursive calls, with iteration is known as *tail call optimization*. As we stated, Java is not a language that supports tail call optimization out of respect for maintaining the call stack when debugging. Moreover, Java allows the programmer to investigate the call stack explicitly in their program. Employing tail call optimization would break existing programs that rely on the ability to walk through stack frames. The fact that Java does not perform tail call optimization means that tail calls continue to blow up the call stack. In the next section, we will discuss a translation pipeline from tail recursion to loops in greater detail, as well as describe the syntax and semantics of Java iteration structures.

2.3 Loops

Looping is a fundamental concept in computer programming. Loops allow for repetition of actions or tasks. As we stated in the previous section on recursion, any tail recursive algorithm may be translated into an algorithm that uses loops. In this section, we will describe this translation as a sequential pipeline of steps, then begin to distance ourselves from recursion when it is suboptimal.

2.3.1 Translation Pipeline for Tail Recursive Methods

A Coarse-Grained Approach

What follows is a high-level introduction to converting from tail recursive methods to iteration. While you may not understand everything at first, we supplement this with a comprehensive translation schema.

Writing recursive methods is certainly fun.[2] Though, recursion is not always the best approach to solve a problem according to some programmers/students. Many programming languages offer *iteration* statements, which allow us to perform a task that we might otherwise use recursion to complete. Suppose we have a standard recursive *fact* method.

```
static int fact(int n) {
  if (isZero(n)) {
    return 1;
  } else {
    return n * fact(n - 1);
  }
}
```

```
static int factTR(int n,
                  int acc) {
  if (isZero(n)) {
    return acc;
  } else {
    return factTR(subOne(n),
                  n * acc);
  }
}
```

The first step in converting a recursive method into its iterative counterpart is to rewrite it using tail recursion. Notice that, in order to "tail-recursify" fact, we had to add an extra parameter that keeps track of the "current result."[3] We convert recursive methods into tail

---

[2] The definition of "fun" is, of course, relative.

[3] Some tail recursive methods need more than one extra parameter—it is a case-by-case basis.

2.3 Loops

recursion because of their direct relation to iteration.[4] Let us look a little deeper into this idea and discover why the relation is true.

Our iterative version of `fact` moves all "accumulator" variables into the method body. For instance, `acc` is now declared locally within the `fact` method. In addition to this modification, all accumulator-to-local variables should have an "iterative purpose statement," which mimics the documentation comment for the accumulator parameter.

```
static int fact(int n) {
  // acc stores the current factorial value as n goes to zero.
  int acc = 1;
  // TODO.
}
```

Second, we must describe the syntax of a loop. A `while` loop is the construct of choice, and it has two components: a condition denoted as a predicate, and a body. The loop checks to see if the given predicate is true and, if so, executes the body of the loop. On the other hand, if the predicate is false, program control jumps down to immediately below the loop body. Each pass through the loop, it re-verifies that the predicate has not been falsified. Unlike expressions, however, a `while` loop itself does not resolve to a value and is therefore a statement. Let's continue by defining the predicate of our loop. To do so, we ask, then answer, the question of the base case(s) for our tail recursive method. As shown, the base case is true when n is zero. Therefore, our loop continues to execute its body as long as n is not zero. One tail recursive method call correlates directly with one loop iteration. So, let's remove the `if/else` statement chain, and substitute them with a loop, whose predicate is nothing more than the negated base case(s).

```
static int fact(n) {
  // acc stores the current factorial value as n goes to zero.
  int acc = 1;
  while (!(n == 0)) {
    // TODO.
  }
}
```

Finally, we come to the heart of the loop: its body. Within, we update variables according to how they are updated in the tail recursive call. Namely, n is decremented by 1, and acc is multiplied by n. We must be cautious, however, because the order of these statements is significant! In the tail recursive method call to `fact`, the n that is decremented is passed to the method, whereas the original value of n is used when multiplying by acc. As a result, the accumulator update should come first.

```
static int fact(int n) {
  // acc stores the current factorial value as n goes to zero.
  int acc = 1;
  while (!(n == 0)) {
    acc = acc * n;
    n = n - 1;
  }
}
```

We are almost done; the loop body is now complete, with each modification corresponding precisely with a piece of the tail recursive version. All that remains is the base case return statement. In our tail recursive method, once we hit the base case, we return `acc`. We model returning (a value) from the base case with a return statement beneath the loop.

---

[4] A method definition may already be tail recursive depending on the circumstance.

```
static int fact(int n) {
  // acc stores the current factorial value as n goes to zero.
  int acc = 1;
  while (!(n == 0)) {
    acc = acc * n;
    n = n - 1;
  }
  return acc;
}
```

Excellent, we now have an iterative version of the factorial method! Let's compare these two implementations side-by-side, color-coding their similarities. Base cases are red, accumulated variables/steps are yellow, and return values are green.

```
static int fact(int n, int acc) {          static int fact(int n) {
  if (n == 0) {                              // acc stores the current
    return acc;                              // factorial value as n
  } else {                                   // goes to zero.
    return fact(n - 1, acc * n);             int acc = 1;
  }                                          while (!(n == 0)) {
}                                              acc = acc * n;
                                               n = n - 1;
                                             }
                                             return acc;
                                           }
```

A Fine-Grained Approach

What we just saw was a fast-paced, high-level overview of the conversion process from tail recursive methods into methods that use while loops. Let's take a step back and slow our approach to better understand each part. We first want to describe a general outline of the steps-to-success in the translation pipeline.

The goal, in due time, is to work our way from TR to I, but there are a few highly important intermediary components to this process. Note that the lines from P to R, and R to TR are not as important for this section of the transformation.

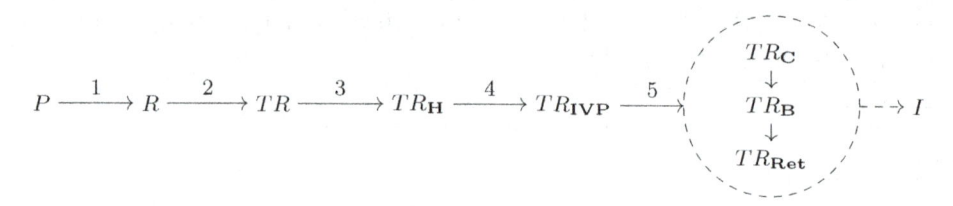

$$P \xrightarrow{1} R \xrightarrow{2} TR \xrightarrow{3} TR_{\mathbf{H}} \xrightarrow{4} TR_{\mathbf{IVP}} \xrightarrow{5} \begin{pmatrix} TR_{\mathbf{C}} \\ \downarrow \\ TR_{\mathbf{B}} \\ \downarrow \\ TR_{\mathbf{Ret}} \end{pmatrix} \dashrightarrow I$$

Fig. 2.3: Fine-Grained Translation Pipeline

TR is the tail recursive method derived either from the problem statement P or the standard recursive step R. From here, we make our way to $TR_{\mathbf{H}}$, denoting the "color-coding" phase, wherein we mark the three sub components of a tail recursive method, those being the base case(s), updated variables in the tail recursive call, and returned values from the base case.

2.3 Loops

$TR_{\mathbf{IVP}}$, or "Iterative Variable Purpose," is a step following the method signature, but preceding the loop definition. In $TR_{\mathbf{IVP}}$, we examine the updated variables/accumulators marked in $TR_{\mathbf{H}}$ and localize them into variables that are not passed as arguments to a method, but rather as a sequence of value updates. Moreover, we add comments to these variable declarations explaining their purpose.

$TR_{\mathbf{C}}$ is the step wherein we write the while keyword, followed by the negated base case condition(s) as a series of conjunctions (i.e., logical AND).

$TR_{\mathbf{B}}$ is where we design the body of our loop, which contains update statements to our localized iterative variables, rather than arguments to a recursive call.

Finally, in $TR_{\mathbf{Ret}}$, we add the line to return the accumulated local variable(s). I is the output translation.

$TR_{\mathbf{H}}$:

When designing a tail recursive method, there are several values to keep in mind: base cases (i.e., terminating conditions), returned values that are not method calls, and accumulators. Each of these play a crucial role in the transition to I, and quickly yet correctly identifying these as they fit in tail recursive methods, is paramount. Let us re-look at our old factorial friend to see what this entails.

```
static int fact(int n, int acc) {
  if (n == 0) {
    return acc;
  } else {
    return fact(n - 1, acc * n);
  }
}
```

Marking the base case(s) is usually rather simple, as they are most often the selection statements that return a value rather than a recursive method invocation. So, the only instance of this in the above definition is $n == 0$, meaning we highlight it in red.

```
static int fact(int n, int acc) {
  if (n == 0) {
    return acc;
  } else {
    return fact(n - 1, acc * n);
  }
}
```

To coincide with the base case(s), we also want to highlight the returned values that are not recursive calls. Only one exists, namely *acc*. Let's highlight *acc* in green.

```
static int fact(int n, int acc) {
  if (n == 0) {
    return acc;
  } else {
    return fact(n - 1, acc * n);
  }
}
```

Now, we want to highlight updated variables that are passed to the (tail) recursive call(s). When we say updated, we mean "modified" insofar as they are not copied verbatim, e.g., $f(n) = f(n)$, in which we see n remains unaltered across method calls. Conveniently, both n

and *acc* are updated (*n* is decremented by one; *acc* is multiplied by *n*). Let's highlight these changes in yellow.

```
static int fact(int n, int acc) {
  if (n == 0) {
    return acc;
  } else {
    return fact(n - 1, acc * n);
  }
}
```

$TR_{\mathbf{IVP}}$:

All accumulator variables in tail recursive methods serve some purpose, one way or another, hence their necessity. The necessity also holds true for local variables defined as accumulator substitutions. Conveniently enough, every variable designated as an accumulator morphs nicely into a local variable when writing the iterative counterpart. Consider, once more, the tail recursive factorial definition. We use *acc* to accumulate the result as a parameter, indicating the need for an accumulator statement. We can simply insert this as an addendum to our Java documentation comment.

```
/**
 * @accumulator acc stores the current factorial product.
 */
static int fact(int n, int acc) {
  if (n == 0) {
    return acc;
  } else {
    return fact(n - 1, acc * n);
  }
}
```

In the translation to a loop, we move *acc* to the body of the method, and write a similar iterative variable purpose.[5] The value that we initialize a local accumulator variable to depends on the problem/context, but it always matches whatever value is passed to a tail recursive helper method.

```
static int fact(int n) {
  // acc stores the current factorial product.
  int acc = 1;
}
```

Writing these imperative variable purposes, akin to accumulator statements, help us organize what variables change and, more importantly, how they change.

$TR_{\mathbf{C}}$:

Up next is where we take our base case condition, highlighted in red, and insert it as the negated condition for our loop. First, we add the `while` keyword to our method, then follow this with a set of parentheses, and an exclamation point immediately after the opening parenthesis but before the closing parenthesis. Inside these parentheses, we place the base case

---

[5] By "move," we mean "remove" but not "delete."

2.3 Loops

condition. To be safe, one should also insert parentheses for the base case, which ensures that the correct expression is negated by the logical 'not' operator. Follow this with an opening and closing brace set.

```
static int fact(int n) {
  // acc stores the current factorial product.
  int acc = 1;
  while (!(n == 0)) {
    // TODO.
  }
}
```

TR_B:

Finally, we get to the fun part of this translation process: the body of our loop. We need to make a design choice of what variables to update and how they should be updated. We take the yellow highlighted tail recursive arguments, create assignment statements out of them, and insert them into the body of our loop. To this end, we need to follow two principles:

Rule of Reassignment: In any tail recursive call, if we pass an expression e which updates parameter p, then in the loop body, we directly reassign p to e.

Rule of Update: If we have two parameters p and q that are updated as part of the tail recursive call, and p's value is used as part of updating q, then q must be modified before p.

The rule of reassignment is straightforward: we have an expression that resolves to some value, which corresponds precisely to those highlighted arguments. This expression is converted into an assignment statement to the locally-declared variable.

The rule of update, on the other hand, is not as straightforward. Essentially, we use this rule to ensure that variables whose value depends on another are not prematurely updated. Consider the following incorrect update of n before updating acc:

```
n = n - 1
acc = acc * n
```

Iteration #	n	acc
0	5	1
1	4	4
2	3	12
3	2	24
4	1	24
5	0	0

We see that this variable update ordering produces 0, which does not match our recursive trace! We receive zero thanks in part due to the final multiplication before our loop condition is falsified. Let's now try the other possible ordering, in which acc is updated before n. Hence, we are now in the second attempt of completing TR_B:

```
acc = acc * n
n = n - 1
```

Iteration #	n	acc
0	5	1
1	4	5
2	3	20
3	2	60
4	1	120
5	0	120

This ordering correctly results in 120, which matches our recursive trace. Therefore, without loss of generality, we can conclude that we should update the accumulator variable before updating n in this circumstance.

Determining the correct order of update, according to the rules we specify, may take a few tries to get right. The idea is to match the result of previously-verified tail recursive traces.

$TR_{\textbf{Ret}}$:

In our final translation stage, we add the necessary return statement(s) that serve to return the accumulated result from our loop. We highlighted these return values in green during the highlighting/color-coding stage.

```
static int fact(int n) {
  // acc stores the current factorial product.
  int acc = 1;
  while (!(n == 0)) {
    acc = acc * n;
    n = n - 1;
  }
  return acc;
}
```

The translation pipeline is complete, and we now know how to mechanically translate a tail recursive method into one that uses a loop.

The astute reader might question the need for a tail recursion-to-iteration translation schema. We mentioned the term tail call optimization in the previous section on recursion, and will now explain the relation to loops.

Recall the benefit of tail recursion over standard recursion: it uses only one (replaceable) activation record. Though, because we can translate any tail recursive method into an iterative algorithm, we forgo the stack in its entirety.

From here we might ask a similar question: can we translate any standard recursive method into one that uses tail recursion (and by transitivity, iteration)? In general, the answer is yes, through a concept called *continuation-passing style*. Because of how difficult it is to implement continuations in Java, we will omit any further discussion, but interested readers should delve into functional programming if this equivalence is intriguing (Friedman and Wand, 2008; Friedman and Felleisen, 1996; Sussman and Steele, 1975).

Example 2.10. Let's design the isDisarium method, which returns whether a given positive integer is a *Disarium number* (Code, 2024). A Disarium number is a positive integer such that the sum of its digits, where each digit is raised to the power of its position, is equal to the number itself. For example, 135 is a Disarium number because $1^1 + 3^2 + 5^3 = 1 + 9 + 125 = 135$.

We will design the standard recursive, tail recursive, and loop variants of the algorithm using the translation pipeline. As usual, we should write tests for all three variants of the method, which trivially carry over to one another. Because all three sets of tests are identical, we will only show those of the standard recursive variant.

```
import static Assertions.assertAll;
import static Assertions.assertTrue;
import static Assertions.assertFalse;

class DisariumTester {
```

2.3 Loops

```
@Test
void testDisariumSr() {
  assertAll(
    () -> assertTrue(isDisarium(135)),
    () -> assertTrue(isDisarium(89)),
    () -> assertFalse(isDisarium(101)),
    () -> assertFalse(isDisarium(202)),
    () -> assertFalse(isDisarium(0)),
    () -> assertFalse(isDisarium(1)));
  }
}
```

The standard recursive helper method has two parameters. The first parameter, n, is the number we are checking for "Disarium-ness." The third accumulator, p, is the position of the digit we are currently checking. The helper method is also an example of the fact that the return type may differ from the driver method signature. That is, isDisariumSr returns a boolean, whereas its helper method returns the sum of the digits raised to their respective positions.

```
class Disarium {

  /**
   * Determines if a given integer is a Disarium number.
   * @param n positive integer.
   * @return true if Disarium, false otherwise.
   */
  static boolean isDisariumSr(int n) {
    return isDisariumSrHelper(n, 1) == n;
  }

  /**
   * Recursively computes the sum of the digits of n raised
   * to their respective positions.
   * @param n positive integer.
   * @param p position of the digit that is currently being checked.
   * @return sum of digits raised to their respective positions.
   */
  private static int isDisariumSrHelper(int n, int p) {
    if (n == 0) { return 0; }
    else { return Math.pow(n % 10, p) + isDisariumSrHelper(n / 10, p + 1); }
  }
}
```

The tail recursive variant is similar to the standard recursive variant, but with an additional parameter, s, which accumulates the result as a parameter.

```
class Disarium {

  /**
   * Determines if a given integer is a Disarium number.
   * @param n positive integer.
   * @return true if Disarium, false otherwise.
   */
  static boolean isDisariumTr(int n) {
    return isDisariumTrHelper(n, 1, 0) == n;
  }
```

```java
/**
 * Tail-recursively computes the sum of the digits of n raised to
 * their respective positions.
 * @param n positive integer.
 * @param p position of the digit that is currently being checked.
 * @param s sum of digits raised to their respective positions.
 * @return sum of digits raised to their respective positions.
 */
private static int isDisariumTrHelper(int n, int p, int s) {
  if (n == 0) {
    return s;
  } else {
    return isDisariumTrHelper(n / 10,
                              p + 1,
                              s + (int) Math.pow(n % 10, p));
  }
}
}
```

The iterative variant is the most verbose of the three, but it is also the most efficient due to the lack of overhead from method calls. The method uses a counter c to keep track of the position of the digit we are currently checking.

```java
class Disarium {

  /**
   * Determines if a given integer is a Disarium number.
   * @param n positive integer.
   * @return true if Disarium, false otherwise.
   */
  static boolean isDisarium(int n) {
    int c = 1;
    // s stores the sum of the digits raised to their respective positions.
    int s = 0;
    while (n != 0) {
      s += (int) Math.pow(n % 10, c);
      n /= 10;
      c++;
    }
    return s == n;
  }
}
```

2.3.2 Iteration Constructs

Perhaps the related equivalence to tail recursion is too abstract for some to digest. Indeed, we believe the relationship is somewhat far-fetched at first glance, but after enough practice, it becomes clearer. We will now discuss loops from a non-translation perspective. That is, if we assume the translation diagram from before, we are going straight from the problem statement P to the iterative solution I, or at least, we will not design I from translating a recursive solution R or a tail recursive solution.

2.3 Loops

As we stated before, loops are statements in Java, meaning they do not, themselves, resolve to a value. Therefore, any and all lines of code executed inside the body of a loop must be statements rather than expressions.

Example 2.11. Suppose we want to print the first one hundred prime integers. Recall the definition of primality: a positive integer n is prime if it is divisible by only one and itself. Without loops, we would otherwise solve this task using recursion. Although summing prime values is not a too terribly complicated task, it requires a verbose set of methods, should we choose to do it tail recursively. Instead, let's try and use loops to solve the problem. We want to continue looping until we have summed one hundred prime values. Fortunately, there is exactly one correct test case for this method, so writing an elaborate test suite is superfluous.

Declaring an integer counter c is mandatory. Our loop condition, therefore, executes so long as we have not encountered one hundred prime values. When designing loop conditions, we ask ourselves the question, "What should be true after the loop?," and design the condition around the answer. Our counter c will be exactly one hundred upon loop completion, so the condition is the negated version of this expression.[6]

Up next, we need to write a method that determines the primality of an integer. We presented the definition of primality before, and it is also known mathematically that we only need to check up to $\sqrt{n}$ for primality (Riesel, 1994). Let's design such a method, writing the appropriate tests. The loop condition is to continue so long as a variable, i, is less than or equal to the square root of our input number. The variable i serves as a counter towards our number; if we find that n is not divisible by any numbers from two up to $\sqrt{n}$, then it must be prime.[7] Note the edge cases of zero and one, both of which are non-prime.

```java
class SumPrimes {

  /**
   * Computes the sum of the first 100 prime integers.
   * @return sum of first 100 primes.
   */
  static int sum100Primes() {
    int c = 0;
    while (c != 100) {
      /* TODO. */
    }
    return 0;
  }
}
```

```java
import static Assertions.assertAll;
import static Assertions.assertTrue;
import static Assertions.assertFalse;

class PrimeTester {

  @Test
  void testPrime() {
    assertAll(
```

---

[6] Rather than (!(c == 100)), we can write (c != 100) to achieve the same effect.

[7] We cast the result of `Math.sqrt` to an integer because it returns a `double` rather than an `int` datatype.

```
            () -> assertTrue(isPrime(101)),
            () -> assertTrue(isPrime(3)),
            () -> assertFalse(isPrime(0)),
            () -> assertFalse(isPrime(1)),
            () -> assertFalse(isPrime(2)),
            () -> assertFalse(isPrime(202)));
    }
}
```

```
class Prime {

    /**
     * Determines if a given integer is prime.
     * @param n positive integer.
     * @return true if prime, false otherwise.
     */
    static boolean isPrime(int n) {
        if (n < 2) {
            return false;
        } else {
            int bound = (int) Math.sqrt(n);
            int i = 2;
            while (i <= bound) {
                if (n % i == 0) {
                    return false;
                } else {
                    i++;
                }
            }
            return true;
        }
    }
}
```

The primality tests pass, which means we can put isPrime to work inside of sum100Primes. The method logic is straightforward: initialize our counter c to one. We also need a variable to track the last-found prime integer, so we know from where to start the search. We will call this variable l and initialize it to zero. Finally, a *sum* variable accumulates the sum of each prime. Inside the loop, we declare another variable v, which serves as the value to check for primality, taking on the value of $l+1$ (if it were just l, it would forever check the same value for primality!). Run v through the isPrime method and, if it is prime, assign to l the value of v, add v to the sum, and increment c. Otherwise, increment l by one.[8] Running the code produces 24133: the desired answer.

```
class SumPrimes {

    /**
     * Computes the sum of the first 100 prime integers.
     * @return sum of first 100 primes.
     */
    static int sum100Primes() {
        int c = 0; // Counter for no. of primes.
        int l = 0; // Current "prime value".
        int sum = 0; // Running sum.
        while (c != 100) {
            int v = l + 1;
```

---

[8] We will note that this code is overly verbose for pedagogical purposes.

2.3 Loops

```
      if (isPrime(v)) {
        l = v;
        sum += v;
        c++;
      } else {
        l++;
      }
    }
    return sum;
  }
}
```

Example 2.12. Continuing with the theme of number theory, let's design the isDePolignac method, which returns whether a given positive integer is a *De Polignac number* (Polignac, 2013).

A de Polignac number is an odd positive integer n that cannot be expressed as the sum of 2^k and p, where k is a non-negative integer and p is a prime number. We just recently designed a method to check for primality, so we can use it when determining if a number is a de Polignac number.

This algorithm cannot be easily expressed as a standard recursive problem, because while we can decompose the problem, there is no result to accumulate; we are only checking for a condition. So, the tail recursive method receives the value n and a value i that starts at the nearest power of two less than n. We check whether $n - i$ is prime, and if so, we return false. If i is equal to one, we return true, because we have exhausted all possible powers of two. Each recursive call divides the power of two in half. Once again, we write tests for the tail recursive variant, but omit those of the iterative algorithm. We emphasized the tail recursive method for de Polignac numbers primarily as a means of continued practice with recursion.

```
import static Assertions.assertAll;
import static Assertions.assertTrue;
import static Assertions.assertFalse;

class DePolignacTester {

  @Test
  void testDePolignacTr() {
    assertAll(
      () -> assertTrue(isDePolignacTr(1)),
      () -> assertTrue(isDePolignacTr(959)),
      () -> assertFalse(DePolignac.isDePolignacTr(7)),
      () -> assertFalse(DePolignac.isDePolignacTr(1001)));
  }
}

class DePolignac {

  /**
   * Determines if a given integer is a De Polignac number.
   * @param n positive integer.
   * @return true if De Polignac, false otherwise.
   */
  static boolean isDePolignacTr(int n) {
    int nextPower = (int) Math.pow(2, (int) (Math.log(n) / Math.log(2)));
    return isDePolignacTrHelper(n, 1);
  }
```

```java
/**
 * Tail recursive helper method for De Polignac number.
 * @param n positive integer.
 * @param i power of two to check, starts at nearest power of 2 < n.
 * @return true if De Polignac, false otherwise.
 */
private static boolean isDePolignacTrHelper(int n, int i) {
  if (n % 2 == 0) { return false; }
  else if (i <= 1) { return true; }
  else if (isPrime(n - i)) { return false; }
  else { return isDePolignacTrHelper(n, i / 2); }
}
```

The loop counterpart localizes the accumulator into a variable i that starts at the nearest power of two less than n.

```java
class DePolignac {

  /**
   * Determines if a given integer is a De Polignac number.
   * @param n positive integer.
   * @return true if De Polignac, false otherwise.
   */
  static boolean isDePolignac(int n) {
    if (n % 2 == 0) {
      return false;
    } else {
      int i = (int) Math.pow(2, (int) (Math.log(n) / Math.log(2)));
      while (i > 1) {
        if (isPrime(n - i)) {
          return false;
        } else {
          i /= 2;
        }
      }
      return true;
    }
  }
}
```

Example 2.13. Suppose that we want to compute the sum of the first n odd reciprocals. That is, $1/1 + 1/3 + 1/5 + \cdots + 1/(2n-1)$. Again, we might choose to this recursively, but let's try and design an iterative algorithm from the start. Its signature is straightforward: the method receives some integer n, and compute the sum of n odd reciprocals. Our tests are trivial to write with the employment of a calculator.

```java
import static Assertions.assertAll;
import static Assertions.assertEquals;

class OddReciprocalSumTester {

  static final double DELTA = 0.001;

  @Test
  void testOddRecipSum() {
```

```
        assertAll(
          () -> assertEquals(1.67619, oddRecipSum(4), DELTA),
          () -> assertEquals(0, oddRecipSum(0), DELTA),
          () -> assertEquals(1, oddRecipSum(1), DELTA),
          () -> assertEquals(2.26435, oddRecipSum(13), DELTA));
    }
}
```

The implementation is similarly simple: we create a counter c that increments so long as c is not equal to n, accumulating the *sum* of 1 divided by $2c - 1$.

```
class OddReciprocalSum {

  /**
   * Computes the sum of the first n odd reciprocals.
   * @param n number of reciprocals to compute.
   * @return sum of first n odd reciprocals.
   */
  static double oddRecipSum(int n) {
    int c = 0;
    double sum = 0;
    while (c != n) {
      sum += c / (double) (2 * c - 1);
      c++;
    }
    return sum;
  }
}
```

Note the cast of the denominator from an int to a double; what happens if we omit the cast? Our tests would fail, because dividing two integers produces another integer, which is not desired when all of our numbers are less than or equal to one.[9]

While loops are reserved for when we do not know the point of termination. Thus far, all methods that we have written use predictable termination cases; we increment a counter until hitting an upper-bound. The while loop is unnecessary in these circumstances due to the equivalent for construct.

With a for loop, we supply to it three constructs: an *initializer statement*, a conditional expression, and a *step statement*. We have previously seen conditional expressions being that they are the basis for our while loop condition. An initializer statement, as its name suggests, declares a variable and initializes it to a value. Stepping statements determine how to change a value between iterations of the loop. In our while loops, notice how we always increment the counter by one at the end of the loop body. Stepping statements take care of this action for us, reducing the need for such simple statements in the loop body.

Example 2.14. Suppose we want to design a method that returns the sum of the integers between two integers a and b, inclusive. We know a priori how many integers there are between a and b, assuming $a \leq b$, so we should use a for loop to solve this problem. Namely, we want to iterate from $i = a$ so long as $i \leq b$. We use the variable i out of convention; one could easily use any other unused identifier.

---

[9] Equivalently, we might multiply c by 2.0, or subtract 1.0; all of these *coerce* the int into a double, thereby allowing correct division.

```
import static Assertions.assertAll;
import static Assertions.assertEquals;

class SumIntervalTester {

  @Test
  void testSumInterval() {
    assertAll(
        () -> assertEquals(0, sum(5, 0)),
        () -> assertEquals(0, sum(0, 0)),
        () -> assertEquals(55, sum(0, 10)),
        () -> assertEquals(55, sum(1, 10)),
        () -> assertEquals(110, sum(5, 15)));
  }
}
```

```
class SumInterval {

  /**
   * Computes the sum of the integers between a and b inclusive.
   * @param a lower-bound inclusive.
   * @param b upper-bound inclusive.
   * @return sum of values.
   */
  static int sum(int a, int b) {
    if (a > b) {
      return 0;
    } else {
      int sum = 0;
      for (int i = a; i <= b; i++) {
        sum += i;
      }
      return sum;
    }
  }
}
```

Example 2.15. Let's write an example of an unpredictable loop; one that best suits the use of while. Suppose we want to manually compute the square root of some positive value, i.e., without Java's implementation. A simple algorithm to use is *Newton's Approximation*:

$$g_{x+1} = \frac{\left(g_x + \dfrac{n}{g_x}\right)}{2}$$

Where g_x is called a "guess." The idea is to continuously apply the Newton's Approximation formula until we are "close enough" to the square root. "Close-enough" is a heuristic whose value, when very small, increases the running time of our loop. Small values of g_x indicate a closer approximation to the true square root of n. For instance, suppose $n = 64$ and $\Delta = 0.1$. Applying the formula (initializing g_0 to n) gets us the following trace:

2.3 Loops

$$g_1 = \frac{\left(64 + \frac{64}{64}\right)}{2} = 32.500$$

$$g_2 = \frac{\left(32.5 + \frac{64}{32.5}\right)}{2} = 17.234$$

$$g_3 = \frac{\left(17.234 + \frac{64}{17.234}\right)}{2} = 10.474$$

$$g_4 = \frac{\left(10.474 + \frac{64}{10.474}\right)}{2} = 8.2921$$

$$g_5 = \frac{\left(8.2921 + \frac{64}{8.2921}\right)}{2} = 8.0051$$

At each iteration, we square the current guess and determine if the absolute difference between it and n is less than the guess. When so, that iteration of g_x is the square root approximation. Otherwise, we continue to approach the square root value. We cannot reasonably predict when this will occur (that is, how many iterations are necessary), so we use a while loop. Because there are multiple potential points of failure in this algorithm, we make sure to write an extensive test suite. The method itself is a re-telling of the mathematical definition with bits of Java syntax sprinkled about.

```
import static Assertions.assertAll;
import static Assertions.assertEquals;

class NewtonApproximationTester {

  final double DELTA = 0.1;

  @Test
  void testNewtonApproximation() {
    assertAll(
      () -> assertEquals(Math.sqrt(0), sqrtApprox(0, DELTA)),
      () -> assertEquals(Math.sqrt(1), sqrtApprox(1, DELTA)),
      () -> assertEquals(Math.sqrt(3), sqrtApprox(3, DELTA)),
      () -> assertEquals(Math.sqrt(16), sqrtApprox(16, DELTA)),
      () -> assertEquals(Math.sqrt(64), sqrtApprox(64, DELTA)),
      () -> assertEquals(Math.sqrt(256), sqrtApprox(256, DELTA)),
      () -> assertEquals(Math.sqrt(4000), sqrtApprox(4000, DELTA)),
      () -> assertEquals(Math.sqrt(129500), sqrtApprox(1295000, DELTA)));
  }
}
```

```
class NewtonApproximation {

  /**
   * Computes an approximation of the square root of a # via Newton's Approximation.
   * @param n number to square root.
   * @param delta approximation range.
   * @return approximation of sqrt of n.
   */
```

```
  static double sqrtApprox(double n, double delta) {
    double g = n;
    // As long as the guess is too far from the real value...
    while (Math.abs(g * g - n) > delta) {
      g = (g + (n / g)) / 2;
    }
    return g;
  }
}
```

To decrease the level of accuracy, we should pass a different value for the *delta* argument. Conversely, to see a higher level of precision, a *delta* that is closer (but not equal to) to zero is necessary. Our implementation of the square root algorithm is far from optimal, but it exists to demonstrate the unapparent necessity of while loops. Though, it is important to note that, the power of both for and while is largely irrelevant when we concern ourselves only with their semantics; they are equal in their expressibility. This means that any for loop is representable with a while and vice-versa. Depending on the circumstance, however, one might be preferable over the other. We reiterate that for loops should be used when we know how many iterations there are for a certain task, whereas while loops are for indeterminate termination conditions.

Example 2.16. Let's design the generateAcronym method, which returns the acronym of a given string. For our purposes, an acronym is the first letter of each word in a string, where words are strings separated by a single space. No other kinds of strings will be present in the input, e.g., strings with multiple spaces between words, nor leading/trailing spaces.

The idea behind the recursive algorithm is to keep track of when we are at the beginning of a word. We can do this by checking if the current character is a space, and if so, we know that the next character is the beginning of a word, meaning we should add it to the acronym. The base case is when we reach the end of the string, at which point we return the empty string. Our standard recursive method needs a helper method to keep track of whether we are at the beginning of a word. The acronym itself is constructed via a series of concatenating recursive calls.

```
import static Assertions.assertAll;
import static Assertions.assertEquals;

class GenerateAcronymTester {

  @Test
  void testGenerateAcronym() {
    assertAll(
      () -> assertEquals("gafia, generateAcronym("get away from it all")),
      () -> assertEquals("NESW", generateAcronym("Never Eat Soggy Waffles")),
      () -> assertEquals("abc", generateAcronym("a b c")),
      () -> assertEquals("abc", generateAcronym("a b c")),
      () -> assertEquals("FBI", generateAcronym("Federal Bureau of Investigation")),
      () -> assertEquals("CIA", generateAcronym("Central Intelligence Agency")),
      () -> assertEquals("HVAC", generateAcronym("Heating Ventilation Air Conditioning")),
      () -> assertEquals("W", generateAcronym("Word")));
  }
}
```

2.3 Loops

```
class GenerateAcronym {

  /**
   * Generates the acronym of a given string.
   * @param s string to generate acronym from.
   * @return acronym of s.
   */
  static String generateAcronym(String s) {
    return genAcronymHelper(s, true);
  }

  /**
   * Recursively generates the acronym of a given string.
   * @param s string to generate acronym from.
   * @param isStart true if at the beginning of a word.
   * @return acronym of s.
   */
  private static String genAcronymHelper(String s, boolean isStart) {
    if (s.isEmpty()) { return ""; }
    else if (isStart) { return s.charAt(0) + genAcronymHelper(s.substring(1), false); }
    else if (s.charAt(0) == ' ') { return genAcronymHelper(s.substring(1), true); }
    else { return genAcronymHelper(s.substring(1), false); }
  }
}
```

As is usual with tail recursive methods, we need to keep track of the state of the algorithm via an accumulator. So, the tail recursive method has an additional parameter, *acc*, which is the acronym we are building.

```
class GenerateAcronym {

  /**
   * Generates the acronym of a given string.
   * @param s string to generate acronym from.
   * @return acronym of s.
   */
  static String generateAcronymTr(String s) {
    return genAcronymTrHelper(s, true, "");
  }

  /**
   * Tail-recursively generates the acronym of a given string.
   * @param s string to generate acronym from.
   * @param isStart true if at the beginning of a word.
   * @param acc accumulator for acronym.
   * @return acronym of s.
   */
  private static String genAcronymTrHelper(String s, boolean isStart, String acc) {
    if (s.isEmpty()) {
      return acc;
    } else if (isStart) {
      return genAcronymTrHelper(s.substring(1), false, acc + s.charAt(0));
    } else if (s.charAt(0) == ' ') {
      return genAcronymTrHelper(s.substring(1), true, acc);
    } else {
      return genAcronymTrHelper(s.substring(1), false, acc);
    }
  }
}
```

If we follow the translation pipeline, we observe that, yet again, the iterative algorithm is a straightforward conversion of the tail recursive method. We can make the iterative method more efficient by using a `StringBuilder` to accumulate the acronym, rather than concatenating strings. We could similarly reduce the number of lines in the method by using a `for` loop and not invoke `substring` in every branch of the conditional, but we will keep the code as is for relation to the tail recursive method and the translation pipeline.

As a word of caution, however, if we choose to update the string *s* *before* updating the accumulator, we run into a problem imposed by the rule of update: we lose the first character of the string, which is the character we want to add to the acronym. Thus, we must update the accumulator *before* updating the string.

```
class GenerateAcronym {

  /**
   * Generates the acronym of a given string.
   * @param s string to generate acronym from.
   * @return acronym of s.
   */
  static String generateAcronym(String s) {
    String acc = "";
    boolean isStart = true;
    while (!(s.isEmpty())) {
      if (isStart) {
        acc = acc + s.charAt(0);
        isStart = false;
        s = s.substring(1);
      } else if (s.charAt(0) == ' ') {
        isStart = true;
        s = s.substring(1);
      } else {
        isStart = false;
        s = s.substring(1);
      }
    }
    return acc;
  }
}
```

Example 2.17. We will write one more example of first writing a recursive algorithm, then its tail recursive version, then its iterative counterpart to describe a problem that occurs when translating specific tail recursive algorithms. Suppose we want to write a method to determine the nth Fibonacci number. The *Fibonacci sequence* is defined recursively as follows:

$$Fib(0) = 0$$
$$Fib(1) = 1$$
$$Fib(n) = Fib(n-1) + Fib(n-2)$$

Writing tests for a Fibonacci algorithm is trivial to do and propagates through to the other variants. So, writing tests for the standard recursive algorithm, assuming they are correct, allows us to easily propagate tests for the tail recursive and iterative algorithms.

2.3 Loops

```
import static Assertions.assertAll;
import static Assertions.assertEquals;

class FibonacciTester {

  @Test
  void testFib() {
    assertAll(
      () -> assertEquals(0, fib(0)),
      () -> assertEquals(1, fib(1)),
      () -> assertEquals(1, fib(2)),
      () -> assertEquals(8, fib(5)),
      () -> assertEquals(55, fib(10)));
  }
}
```

The standard recursive algorithm is trivial to write, but is also horribly inefficient. Because we make two recursive calls to *Fib*, we end up computing the same data multiple times, resulting in an *exponential time algorithm*. In other words, small inputs, e.g., *Fib*(40), will take an absurdly long time to finish.

```
class Fibonacci {

  static int fib(int n) {
    if (n <= 1) { return n; }
    else { return fib(n - 1) + fib(n - 2); }
  }
}
```

Our method works and all tests pass, which is great, but we can do better by using tail recursion. The tail recursive variant, however, is slightly more complicated than prior tail recursive definitions, due to the need to use two accumulators. We use two variables to compute the "next" Fibonacci number: the previous, and the previous' previous. So, storing these values as variables, say, a and b, is sensible, where a is the "previous' previous," and b is the previous. Thus, when making a tail recursive call, we assign b as $a + b$, and a as b. We cannot forget the driver method!

```
class Fibonacci {

  static int fibTR(int n) {
    return fibHelp(n, 0, 1);
  }

  /**
   * Computes the nth Fibonacci number using tail recursion.
   * @param n nth Fibonacci number.
   * @accumulator a - "previous' previous" fib.
   * @accumulator b - "previous" fib.
   * @return result.
   */
  static int fibHelp(int n, int a, int b) {
    if (n == 0) { return a; }
    else if (n == 1) { return b; }
    else { return fibHelp(n - 1, b, a + b); }
  }
}
```

Our tail recursive implementation has two base cases instead of one due to the two base cases of the mathematical recursive definition. It may be difficult to visualize the initial accumulator values (i.e., the starting values of a and b), but just consider the base case(s) of the standard recursive algorithm, and let this/these guide your decision.

Finally we arrive at the iterative algorithm. To avoid any confusion in the conversion process, we will use our translation pipeline. Skipping a few steps up to $TR_\mathbf{C}$:

```
static int fibHelp(int n, int a, int b) {      static int fib(int n) {
  if (n == 0) {                                  // Holds the previous' prev.
    return a;                                    int a = 0;
  } else if (n == 1) {                           // Holds the prev.
    return b;                                    int b = 1;
  } else {                                       while (???) {
    return fibHelp(n - 1, b, a + b);               // TODO.
  }                                              }
}                                              }
```

The question now is, what do we use as the `while` loop condition? We are obviously decreasing n by one with each (tail) recursive call, but since we have two base cases, what do we do? Realistically, we only need to use the loop for one base case: namely $n == 1$, since the only other possibility for n is if it is zero (meaning that we return zero). Therefore, our loop conditional is the negated condition of $n == 1$, namely (!($n == 1$)). At this point, we run into another problem: according to the rule of update, because b's value depends on a, we need to update b before a, but because a's value depends on b, we are at a bit of an impasse. Fear not, because we have an amendment to TR_B, which introduces the *rule of temporary*.

Rule of Temporary: If two parameters p and q depend on each other, introduce a temporary variable t_p, assign p to t_p, update p, then update q using t_p in place of p.

In essence, we generate a local temporary variable to hold onto the old value of one of our accumulators. Following this logic, we create the variable t_a, assign to it a, update a, then update b using t_a in place of a. Since n does not a dependent variable, its ordering in the mix is irrelevant.

The last stage is simple; we return the result of the other base case, namely b when n is one.

```
static int fib(int n) {
  // Holds the previous' prev.
  int a = 0;
  // Holds the prev.
  int b = 1;
  // Initial base case.
  if (n == 0) {
    return a;
  } else {
    while (!(n == 1)) {
      int ta = a;
      a = b;
      b = ta + b;
      n = n - 1;
    }
    return b;
  }
}
```

The Fibonacci sequence is predictable, in that we know how many iterations are necessary to compute a result. Therefore, a `for` loop seems like a reasonable substitute to `while` in this circumstance.

2.3 Loops

We still must declare variables a and b, but instead of decrementing n, we instead localize an accumulator i (initialized as n) to, counter-intuitively, decrement towards the base case.

No significant changes to the implementation are made, aside from a new local variable to count down from n until it hits one.

```
static int fib(int n) {
  int a = 0;
  int b = 1;
  if (a == 0) {
    return a;
  } else {
    for (int i = n; !(n == 1); i--) {
      int ta = a;
      a = b;
      b = ta + b;
    }
  }
  return b;
}
```

Example 2.18. We can use two keywords to alter the control flow of a loop: break and continue. We saw break when working with the switch keyword and statement, but in the context of loops, its meaning is more significant.

Suppose that we're designing the int findFirstVowel(String s) method, which returns the first occurrence of a vowel in a string s, and -1 if it has no vowels. The break statement allows us to exit the loop body early upon finding a vowel. We will traverse over the string characters using a for loop and terminate if we reach the end of the string, hence the inclusion of the i < s.length() condition. Our implementation must also include a method to determine whether a character is a vowel. We *could* write ten separate clauses for checking if a character is the uppercase or lowercase version of the vowel, but we can eliminate half of those checks by converting the character to either case, and check only those.

```
import static Assertions.assertAll;
import static Assertions.assertEquals;

class FindFirstVowelTester {

  @Test
  void testFindFirstVowel() {
    assertAll(
      () -> assertEquals(-1, findFirstVowel("")),
      () -> assertEquals(-1, findFirstVowel("BDFG")),
      () -> assertEquals(-1, findFirstVowel("111122223333")),
      () -> assertEquals(0, findFirstVowel("ABCD")),
      () -> assertEquals(0, findFirstVowel("aBCd")),
      () -> assertEquals(1, findFirstVowel("bEdFGhiOnP")),
      () -> assertEquals(7, findFirstVowel("BDFGHJKO")),
    )
  }
}
```

```
class FindFirstVowel {

  /**
   * Finds the index of the first vowel in a given string.
   * If there are no vowels in the string, we return -1.
   * @param s input string.
   * @return index of first vowel occurrence, or -1 if it has no vowels.
   */
  static int findFirstVowel(String s) {
    int idx = -1;
    for (int i = 0; i < s.length(); i++) {
      if (isVowel(s.charAt(i))) {
        idx = i;
        break;
      }
    }
    return idx;
  }

  /**
   * Determines whether or not the character is a vowel.
   * We convert it to lowercase, then check it against
   * those five vowels.
   * @param ch character to check.
   * @return true if ch is a vowel, false otherwise.
   */
  static boolean isVowel(char ch) {
    char lch = Character.toLowercase(ch);
    return ch == 'a' || ch == 'e' || ch == 'i' || ch == 'o' || ch == 'u';
  }
}
```

Example 2.19. To better illustrate how break and continue work, let's write a method that has no real purpose, but serves to demonstrate the utility of these keywords. Our method, namely countOdds, counts the number of odd integers generated by a random number generator from 1 to 100.

To spice it up, we will not count odd integers less than 50, and if we ever generate a number greater than 95, we stop looping and return the count. The idea is to use break when we generate a integer between 96 and 100, and to use continue to skip over incrementing the counter if we find a number less than 50. The continue keyword shifts program control to the top of the loop, skipping over any remaining statements in the body.

Because the countOdds method relies solely on random chance, writing unit tests is not helpful in determining whether the method in question works as intended.[10]

In the following code snippet, an else statement is preferred over the superfluous use of continue, but we demo it to, at a minimum, portray its existence. The only way to exit the infinite while loop is to either break out, return from the method, or halt the program via another means (e.g., through a program crash or forced termination).

---

[10] Some testing frameworks provide methods that allow the programmer to verify the correctness of functions/methods that utilize randomness (Felleisen et al., 2018). We *could* prove/assert that the method, without the randomness component, is correct, then later on inject a means of generating random numbers.

2.3 Loops

```java
import java.util.Random;

class RandomNumbers {

  /**
   * Counts the number of odd values generated by a random # generator.
   * @return the number of odd values counted.
   */
  static int countOdds() {
    int cnt = 0;
    Random rng = new Random();
    while (true) {
      int r = 1 + rng.nextInt(100);
      if (r > 95) { break; }
      else if (r < 50 || r % 2 == 0) { continue; }
      cnt++;
    }
    return cnt;
  }
}
```

Example 2.20. Let's write one more example of a loop where we go directly from the problem statement to the code in question. Suppose we're designing a method that receives some string s, a "search string" f, and a replacement string r, with a goal of replacing all occurrences of f with r without helper methods in the String class, e.g., indexOf, contains, and certainly not replace. We start by writing the signature, documentation comments, and a handful of tests. We emphasize writing more tests than what may be considered normal for this specific problem due to its complexity and number of "edge cases," i.e., cases in which a method might not account for because of their obscurity.

```java
import static Assertions.assertAll;
import static Assertions.assertEquals;

class FindReplaceTester {

  @Test
  void testFindReplace() {
    assertAll(
      () -> assertEquals("hiya there!",
                         replace("hiya there!", "", "replace!")),
      () -> assertEquals("hiya there!",
                         replace("hiya there!" "ya T", "replace!")),
      () -> assertEquals("Spaces_With_Underscores",
                         replace("Spaces With Underscores", " ", "_")),
      () -> assertEquals("heyyyyyay",
                         replace("heyaaaaay", "aa", "yy")),
      () -> assertEquals("hello",
                         replace("hillo", "i", "e")),
      () -> assertEquals("heyheyhey",
                         replace("hiyhiyhiy", "i", "e")),
      () -> assertEquals("We replaced the entire string!",
                         replace("Hello world, how are you?",
                                 "Hello world, how are you?"
                                 "We replaced the entire string!")));
  }
}
```

Subsequently, we complete the implementation of replace, which reduces into a few cases: while traversing, did we find the start of the search string f, did we find the end of f, and did we encounter a break in f? Let's go from the start to the end in our analysis.

When traversing over the input string s, if we find the character that starts f in s, we increment a counter c, and continue counting as long as the characters in the particular substring of s match the characters in f.

As an example, in the string $s =$ "hello", if $f =$ "ell", once our traversal finds "e", we increment c by one to designate that we matched one character of f. We continue this process until we either reach the end of f, the end of s, or we find a non-matching character.

In the former instance, we append the replacement string r onto our newly-constructed string s', because it indicates that we encountered a full match of f inside s, meaning it is to be replaced by r.

In the second instance, we reach the end of s, meaning that we are out of characters to match. Therefore, we either copy over the last c characters from s into s' if we have not also reached the end of f, or r otherwise. For example, if $s =$ "hello", and $f =$ "low", we reach the end of s prior to finishing the substring f, meaning that we only copy over those final characters of s and do not append r. Conversely, if $f =$ "lo" in that instance, we instead substitute the suffix "lo" with r.

Finally, when we encounter a non-matching character, we terminate the current replacement strategy and simply append the last c characters of s onto s' and move the index forward.

A small intricacy that we have not discussed is StringBuilder. As previously mentioned, strings are immutable, and concatenating two strings produces another integer. Combining repeated concatenation operations together with a loop or recursion is highly inefficient. To remedy the problem, Java provides the StringBuilder class to make repeated string append operations much faster and less of a memory hog.[11]

To summarize, the StringBuilder class allocates a buffer that stores the characters of a string, and any "append" operations manipulate the buffer, rather than having to reallocate an entirely new string of the previous size, plus the number of characters in the string-to-conjoin.

---

[11] Java's library also has the StringBuffer class to achieve the same effect, but it is suboptimal when writing single-threaded programs (i.e., programs that are concurrent).

2.3 Loops

```java
import java.lang.StringBuilder;

class FindReplace {

  /**
   * Searches through a string s for occurrences of "find",
   * and replaces them with "repl".
   * @param s string to search through.
   * @param find string to find.
   * @param repl string to replace "find" with.
   * @return new replaced string.
   */
  static String replace(String s, String find, String repl) {
    StringBuilder sb = new StringBuilder(s.length());
    for (int i = 0; i < s.length(); i++) {
      int pos = 0;
      int j;
      for (j = i; j < s.length(); j++) {
        // If we find the entire "find" string, append the replacement.
        if (pos >= find.length()) {
          sb.append(repl);
          i = j - 1;
          break;
        }
        // If we are in the middle of searching and we find a non-matching
        // character, append everything up until this point and break.
        else if (s.charAt(j) != find.charAt(pos)) {
          sb.append(s, i, i + pos + 1);
          i = j;
          break;
        }
        // If we are matching, continue to search.
        else if (s.charAt(j) == find.charAt(pos)) {
          pos++;
        }
      }
      // If we reach the end of the string and are in the middle of searching, we append.
      if (pos > 0 && j >= s.length()) {
        sb.append(repl);
        break;
      }
    }
    return sb.toString();
  }
}
```

2.4 Exercises

2.1 Design the `boolean isStrictlyIncreasing(int x, int y, int z)` that determines if three integers x, y, and z are strictly increasing. By this, we mean that $x < y < z$.

2.2 Design the `String numStuff(int n)` that determines if an integer n is greater than 100. If so, return the string of n divided by two. If the number is less than 50, return the string of n divided by five. In any other case, return the string `"N/A"`.

2.3 Design the `boolean canVote(int age)` that, when given an integer variable *age* in years, returns whether or not someone who is that age is able to legally vote in the United States. For reference, someone may legally vote once they turn eighteen years old.

2.4 Design the `int max(int x, int y, int z)` that returns the maximum of three integers x, y, and z. Do not use any built-in (Math library) methods.

2.5 Design the `int computeRoundSum(int x, int y, int z)` method that computes the sum of the rounded values of three integers x, y, and z. By "rounded values," we mean that we round their least significant digit, i.e., the rightmost digit either up or down depending on its value. For instance, 12 rounds down to 10, 59 rounds up to 60, and 1009 rounds up to 1010. If the number is negative, round towards zero when necessary, e.g., -7 rounds down to -10, -2 rounds up to zero.

2.6 Design the `boolean lessThan20(int x, int y, int z)` method that, when given three integers x, y, and z, returns whether or not one of them is less than twenty away from another. For example, `lessThan20(19, 2, 412)` returns true because 2 is less than 20 away from 19. Another example is `lessThan20(999, 888, 777)`, which returns false because none of the numbers have a difference less than twenty.

2.7 Design the `boolean canSleepIn(String d, boolean onVacation)` method, which determines whether or not someone can sleep in. Someone is able to sleep in if it is a weekend or they are on vacation. The input d is passed as a day of the week, e.g., `"Monday"`, ..., `"Sunday"`.

2.8 Design the `boolean isEvenlySpaced(int x, int y, int z)` method, which receives three integers x, y, and z, and returns whether they are evenly spaced. Evenly spaced means that the difference between the smallest and medium number is the same as the difference between the medium and largest number.

2.9 Design the `String cutTry(String s)` method, which receives a string s and, if s ends with `"try"`, it is removed. Otherwise, the original string is returned.

2.10 Design the `String popChars(String s, char c, char d)` method, which receives a string s and two characters c, d. The method removes c if s starts with c, and removes d if the second character of s is d. The remainder of the string is the same.

2.11 Design the `String middleString(String a, String b, String c)` method, which receives three strings a, b, and c, and returns the string that is "in between" the others in terms of their lexicographical content. You cannot sort the strings or use an array.

2.4 Exercises

2.12 In propositional logic, there are several *connectives* that act on boolean truth values. These include logical conjunction ∧, disjunction ∨, conditional →, biconditional ↔, and negation ¬. We can represent *schemata* as a series of composed method calls. For example, an evaluation of

$$`P \to \neg(Q \leftrightarrow \neg R)`$$

where 'P' and 'R' are assigned to false and 'Q' is assigned to true, is equivalent to

```
static final boolean P = false;
static final boolean Q = true;
static final boolean R = false;
cond(P, not(bicond(Q, not(R))))
```

The presented schema resolves to true.

Design methods for the five connectives according to the following truth tables. These methods should be called cond, bicond, and, or, and not. Assume that T is true and F is false.

P	$\neg P$
T	F
F	T

Truth Table of '$\neg P$'

P	Q	$P \wedge Q$
T	T	T
T	F	F
F	T	F
F	F	F

Truth Table of '$P \wedge Q$'.

P	Q	$P \vee Q$
T	T	T
T	F	T
F	T	T
F	F	F

Truth Table of '$P \vee Q$'.

P	Q	$P \to Q$
T	T	T
T	F	F
F	T	T
F	F	T

Truth Table of '$P \to Q$'.

P	Q	$P \leftrightarrow Q$
T	T	T
T	F	F
F	T	F
F	F	T

Truth Table of '$P \leftrightarrow Q$'.

2.13 Design the boolean isInsideCircle(double cx, double cy, double r, double px, double py) method that, when given a circle centered at (c_x, c_y) and radius r as well as a point at (p_x, p_y), returns whether the point is located strictly inside the circle.

2.14 Design the boolean isInsideRectangle(double rx, double ry, double w, double h, double px, double py) method that, when given a rectangle centered at (r_x, r_y), width w and height h as well as a point (p_x, p_y), returns whether the point is located strictly inside the rectangle.

2.15 (⋆) Carlo is shipping out orders of candy to local grocery stores. Boxes have a maximum weight defined by a value w, and we can (potentially) fit both small and large bars of candy in a box. Design the int fitCandy(int s, int l, int w) method that, when given a number of small bars s, large bars l, and maximum weight w, determines the number of small candy bars he can fit in the box. Large bars weigh five kilograms, and small bars weigh one kilogram. Note that Carlo always tries to fit large candies first before small. Return -1 if it is impossible to fill the box with the given criteria. Below are some test examples. Hint: consider this as an analysis of three cases.

```
fitCandy(4, 1, 9)       => 4
fitCandy(4, 1, 4)       => 4
fitCandy(1, 2, 6)       => 1
fitCandy(6, 1, 13)      => -1
fitCandy(60, 100, 550)  => 50
fitCandy(7, 1, 12)      => 7
fitCandy(7, 1, 13)      => -1
```

2.16 (⋆) An IPv4 address contains four integer values stored in four octets, separated by dots. For instance, 192.168.1.244 is a valid IPv4 address. Another example is 149.165.192.52. Design the boolean isValidIpv4(String ip) method that, when given a string, determines whether or not it represents a valid IPv4 address. Each octet must be an integer between zero and 255 inclusive. Note that some IPv4 addresses are, in reality, nonsensical, e.g., 0.0.0.0, but we will not consider these as invalid. Below the examples is a helper method, isNumeric, to determine whether or not a string is "numeric." Understanding *how* this helper method works is unimportant for the time being. You **cannot** use arrays, loops, or regular expressions to solve this problem. Finally, you will need to use Integer.parseInt, substring, and indexOf.

```
isValidIpv4("192.168.1.244")     => true
isValidIpv4("149.165.192.52")    => true
isValidIpv4("192.168.1.256")     => false
isValidIpv4("192.168.1201.23")   => false
isValidIpv4("192.168.1201.ABC")  => false
isValidIpv4("ABC.DEF.GHI")       => false
isValidIpv4("192.168.1A6.201")   => false
```

```
/**
 * Determines whether or not we can convert a given string into
 * an integer datatype.
 * @param n input string.
 * @return true if we can convert n to an int, false otherwise.
 */
static boolean isNumeric(String n) {
  try {
    Integer.parseInt(n);
    return true;
  } catch (NumberFormatException ex) {
    return false;
  }
}
```

2.17 Design the String stateOfMatter(double t, char u) method that receives a water temperature as a double and a unit as a char, i.e., either 'C' or 'F' for Celsius and Fahrenheit

2.4 Exercises

respectively. Return a string representing whether the water is a liquid, solid, or gas at sea level.

2.18 Design the `String sortStrings(String a, String b, String c)` method that receives three strings and sorts them lexicographically. Return the sorted set of strings as a string itself, separated by commas. For example, if the input is `Charlie, Able, Baker`, you should return `Able,Baker,Charlie`.

2.19 Design the `int trickSum(int x, int y, int z)` method that sums the three integer inputs. If one of those values is 17, however, it and any numbers to its right should not be included in the sum. For example, `trickSum(13, 17, 3)` resolves to 13 because, when $y = 17$, we add neither y nor z to the resulting sum.

2.20 A year with 366 days is called a leap year. Leap years are necessary to keep the calendar synchronized with the sun because the earth revolves around the sun once every 365.25 days. Actually, that figure is not entirely precise, and for all dates after 1582 the Gregorian correction applies. Usually years that are divisible by 4 are leap years, for example 1996. However, years that are divisible by 100 (for example, 1900) are not leap years, but years that are divisible by 400 are leap years (for example, 2000). Design the `boolean isLeapYear(int y)` method that receives a year (as an integer) y and computes whether y is a leap year. Use a single `if` statement and Boolean operators.

2.21 Design the `double getDiscount(double c, int age, boolean isStudent)` method that computes a discount for some item cost c based on their age age and student status. Your method should return the total cost of the item after applying the discount. Use the following criteria for computing the discount:

- If $age < 18$, apply a 20% discount.
- If $18 \leq age \leq 25$ and they are a student, apply a 25% discount. If they are not a student, do not apply a discount.
- If $age \geq 65$ and they are a student, apply a 30% discount. If they are not a student, apply a 15% discount.
- All other cases should not have a discount applied.

2.22 Design the `double getTaxCost(double itemCost, String state)` method that computes the tax for some item based on the state in which it is purchased. The method should return the total cost of the item, which includes the taxed amount. The tax rates are as follows:

- "CA": 9.25%
- "NY": 4.0%
- "NC": 6.625%
- "SC": 6.0%
- "VA": 6.25%
- "WA": 6.5%
- "IN": 8.0%

2.23 Design the `double computeOvertimePay(double hrRate, double noHrs, boolean onVacation, double taxRate)` method that computes the amount of overtime pay (note: **only** the overtime pay) given to an employee. Overtime pay is defined as the pay an employee receives after working more than 40 hours. The method should consider the following:

- An employee's base overtime pay rate is 1.5 times their hourly rate.
- If the employee is on vacation, their pay rate is double their hourly rate rather than a factor of 1.5.
- If the number of hours is less than or equal to 40, then no overtime pay is given.
- If the number of hours is greater than 70, then the resulting gross pay (before taxes) is increased by 15%.
- The gross pay is subject to the tax *percentage* passed to the method.

Overtime pay is defined as the pay an employee receives after working 40 hours.

2.24 Design the `double computeBonusPay(double baseSalary, int yearsOfService, boolean achievedTarget, double salesAmount, double targetSales)` method that calculates the amount of bonus pay (note: **only** the bonus pay) given to an employee under the following conditions:

- A base bonus rate of 10% of the base salary is given to employees who have achieved their sales target.
- Employees with more than 5 years of service receive an additional 5% bonus of their base salary.
- If the sales amount exceeds the target sales by more than 50%, the employee receives an additional bonus of 25% of the base salary.
- If the employee has not achieved their sales target, they receive a flat bonus of 2% of their base salary, regardless of sales amount or years of service.
- The total bonus amount is reduced by a flat tax rate of 25%.

2.25 Design the `double cookingScore(String type, double oz, int costDollars, int costCents, boolean isAppealing)` method, which scores a culinary piece in a cooking contest. **The returned score is a value in the interval $[0, 10]$.**

A type is one of:
- "Cake"
- "Pasta"
- "Pie"
- "Burger"

Below are the criteria for scoring the piece:

- If the `type` is "Cake" or "Pasta", the base score is 1. If the `type` is "Burger", the base score is 0.5. If the `type` is "Pie", the base score is 0.75. Any other `type` is an automatic zero.
- If the weight `oz` is less than 4, their (current) score is multiplied by 0.9. If $4 \leq oz \leq 20$, their (current) score is multiplied by y such that $y = 1/16oz + 0.25$. Otherwise, their (current) score is multiplied by 0.2.
- The *combined* price of the piece adds a fixed amount to the score up to a total of $5.00. Anything beyond this subtracts that amount from the score. For example, if the combined cost of a piece is $1.25, then its score is increased by 1.25. On the other hand, if the combined cost of a piece is $6.75, then its score is decreased by $1.75.
- If the piece is appealing, add a constant factor of 1.5 to the piece.

2.26 Design the `String createPalindrome(String s, boolean mirror)` method that receives a string s and a boolean. If the boolean is true, then return a string ss', where s'

2.4 Exercises

is the mirror of *s*. If the boolean is false, then return a string *st*, where *t* contains all but the last character of *s*, and is reversed. You cannot use any helper classes, e.g., String-Builder/StringBuffer to solve this problem.

2.27 This exercise has two parts.

(a) Design the recursive `int countStr(String s)` that counts the number of times the substring "str" appears in a given string *s*.
(b) Design the `countStrTR` method that solves the same problem, but instead uses tail recursion. Hint: you will need to design a `private static` helper method. The `countStrTR` method should only have one parameter.

If you write tests for one of these methods, you should be able to propagate it through the other, so write plenty!

2.28 This exercise has two parts.

(a) Design the recursive `String replaceAB(String s)` method that replaces any occurrence of the character 'A' with the character 'B' in a given string *s*.
(b) Design the `replaceABTR` method that solves the same problem, but instead uses tail recursion. Hint: you will need to design a `private static` helper method. The `replaceABTR` method should only have one parameter.

If you write tests for one of these methods, you should be able to propagate it through the other, so write plenty!

2.29 This exercise has two parts.

(a) Elephants have two ears, right? Design the recursive `int countElephantEars(int n)` that returns the total number of elephant ears that are in a group of *n* elephants. You must solve this recursively!
(b) Design the `countElephantEarsTR` method that solves the same problem, but instead uses tail recursion. Hint: you will need to design a `private static` helper method. The `countElephantEarsTR` method should only have one parameter.

If you write tests for one of these methods, you should be able to propagate it through the other, so write plenty!

2.30 This question has two parts.

(a) Design the `raiseLowerToUpperTR` tail recursive method, which receives a string and returns the number of lowercase characters raised to the number of uppercase characters, ignoring any other character. If there are no lowercase or uppercase characters, return zero. Hint: you will need to design a `private static` helper method to solve this problem.
(b) Design the `raiseLowerToUpperLoop` method that solves this problem using a loop.

If you write tests for one of these methods, you should be able to propagate it through the other, so write plenty!

2.31 This question has two parts.

(a) Design the `isPalindromeTR` tail recursive method, which receives a string and determines if it is a palindrome. Recall that a palindrome is a string that is the same backwards as it is forwards. E.g., "racecar." **Do not** use a (character) array, StringBuilder, StringBuffer, or similar, to solve this problem. It *must* be naturally recursive.

(b) Design the `isPalindromeLoop` method that solves the problem using a loop. The same restrictions from the previous problem hold true for this one.

If you write tests for one of these methods, you should be able to propagate it through the other, so write plenty!

2.32 This question has two parts.

(a) Design the `gcdTR` tail recursive method, which receives two integers and returns the greatest common divisor between the two. Euclid's algorithm is the basis for this approach and is a tail recursive algorithm by design.
(b) Design the `gcdLoop` method that solves the problem using a loop.

If you write tests for one of these methods, you should be able to propagate it through the other, so write plenty!

2.33 This question has two parts.

(a) Design the `isNestedParenthesesTR` tail recursive method, which receives a string and determines if its parentheses pairs are "balanced." A pair of parentheses is balanced if it is a nesting of zero or more pairs of parenthesis, like "(())" or "((()))." Note that pairs like "(()())" will not be tested.
(b) Design the `isNestedParenthesesLoop` method that solves the problem using a loop.

If you write tests for one of these methods, you should be able to propagate it through the other, so write plenty!

2.34 This question has three parts.

(a) A *factorion* is a number that is equal to the sum of the factorials of its digits (Gardner, 1990). For example, 145 is a factorion because $1! + 4! + 5! = 1 + 24 + 120 = 145$. Design the standard recursive `isFactorion` method, which receives an integer n and returns whether or not it is a factorion.
(b) Design the `isFactorionTR` tail recursive method, which receives two integers and returns the greatest common divisor between the two. Euclid's algorithm is the basis for this approach and is a tail recursive algorithm by design.
(c) Design the `isFactorionLoop` method that solves the problem using a loop.

If you write tests for one of these methods, you should be able to propagate it through the rest, so write plenty!

2.35 This question has three parts.

(a) The *hyperfactorial* of a number, namely $H(n)$, is the value of $1^1 \cdot 2^2 \cdot \ldots \cdot n^n$. As you might imagine, the resulting numbers from a hyperfactorial are outrageously large. Therefore we will make use of the `long` datatype rather than `int` for this problem. Design the standard recursive `hyperfactorial` method, which receives a long integer n and returns its hyperfactorial.
(b) Then, design the `hyperfactorialTR` method that uses tail recursion and accumulators to solve the problem. Hint: you will need to design a `private static` helper method to solve this problem.
(c) Finally, design the `hyperfactorialLoop` method that solves the problem using a loop.

If you write tests for one of these methods, you should be able to propagate it through the rest, so write plenty!

2.4 Exercises

2.36 This question has three parts.

(a) The *subfactorial* of a number, namely !n, is the number of permutations of n objects such that no object appears in its natural spot. For example, take the collection of objects $\{a, b, c\}$. There are 6 possible permutations (because we choose arrangements for three items, and $3! = 6$): $\{a, b, c\}, \{a, c, b\}, \{b, c, a\}, \{c, b, a\}, \{c, a, b\}, \{b, a, c\}$, but only two of these are *derangements*: $\{b, c, a\}$ and $\{c, a, b\}$, because no element is in the same spot as the original collection. Therefore, we say that $!3 = 2$. We can describe subfactorial as a recursive formula:

$$!0 = 1$$
$$!1 = 0$$
$$!n = (n-1) \cdot (!(n-1) + !(n-2))$$

Design the standard recursive subfactorial method, which receives an long integer n and returns its subfactorial. Because the resulting subfactorial values can grow insanely large, we will use the long datatype instead of int.

(b) Then, design the subfactorialTR method that uses tail recursion and accumulators to solve the problem. Hint: you will need to design a private static helper method to solve this problem.

(c) Finally, design the subfactorialLoop method that solves the problem using a loop.

If you write tests for one of these methods, you should be able to propagate it through the rest, so write plenty!

2.37 This question has three parts.

(a) Design the standard recursive collatz method, which receives a positive integer and returns the Collatz sequence for said integer. This sequence is defined by the following recursive process:

```
collatz(1) = 1
collatz(n) = collatz(3 * n + 1) if n is odd.
collatz(n) = collatz(n / 2) if n is even.
```

The sequence generated is the numbers received by the method until the sequence reaches one (note that it is an open research question as to whether this sequence converges to one for every positive integer). So, collatz(5) returns the following String of comma-separated integers: "5,16,8,4,2,1". **The last number cannot have a comma afterwards**.

(b) Then, design the collatzTR method that uses tail recursion and accumulators to solve the problem. Hint: you will need to design a private static helper method to solve this problem.

(c) Finally, design the collatzLoop method that solves the problem using a loop.

If you write tests for one of these methods, you should be able to propagate it through the rest, so write plenty!

2.38 This question has three parts.

(a) Design the standard recursive parenthesesDepth method, which receives a string of parentheses and returns an integer representing the "depth" at the end of the string.

Each instance of (increments the depth counter, and each instance of) decrements the depth counter. So, e.g., "((())()))))(()" is $1+1+1-1-1+1+1-1-1-1-1-1+1+1 = -2$.

(b) Then, design the parenthesesDepthTR method that uses tail recursion and accumulators to solve the problem. Hint: you will need to design a `private static` helper method to solve this problem.

(c) Finally, design the parenthesesDepthLoop method that solves the problem using a loop.

If you write tests for one of these methods, you should be able to propagate it through the rest, so write plenty!

2.39 This question has three parts.

A *parenthesized string* is a string enclosed by parentheses. For example, the string "(abc)pqr(de)" contains two parenthesized strings: "abc", and "de".

For the following problems, you may assume that there are no nested parentheses, all parentheses are balanced, and if there is a parenthesized string, it contains at least one character.

(a) *(9 points)* Design the standard recursive collectParenthesizedStrings method, which receives a String S and returns a List of all the parenthesized strings of S.

(b) Design the collectParenthesizedStringsTR method and its accompanying helper method collectParenthesizedStringsTRHelper. The former acts as the driver to the latter; the latter solves the same problem as collectParenthesizedStrings does, but it instead uses tail recursion. Remember to include the relevant access modifiers!

(c) Design the collectParenthesizedStringsLoop method, which solves the problem using either a `while` or `for` loop.

2.40 This question has three parts.

(a) Design the standard recursive countdown method, which receives an `int` $n \geq 0$ and returns a String containing a sequence of the even numbers from n down to 0 inclusive, separated by commas.

(b) Then, design the countdownTR method that uses tail recursion and accumulators to solve the problem. Hint: you will need to design a `private static` helper method to solve this problem.

(c) Finally, design the countdownLoop method that solves the problem using a loop.

If you write tests for one of these methods, you should be able to propagate it through the rest, so write plenty!

2.41 This question has three parts.

(a) Design the standard recursive chickenCounter method, which receives a string s and returns the number of times the substring "chicken" appears in s. You must account for overlapping instances of "chicken". For example, calling the method with "abc-chickechickenn" returns 2 because, after removing the substring "chicken" from the original string, we are left with "abcchicken", which itself contains another instance of "chicken".

(b) Then, design the chickenCounterTR method that uses tail recursion and accumulators to solve the problem. Hint: you will need to design a `private static` helper method to solve this problem.

(c) Finally, design the chickenCounterLoop method that solves the problem using a loop.

2.4 Exercises

If you write tests for one of these methods, you should be able to propagate it through the rest, so write plenty!

2.42 This question has five parts. We need to provide some background for the question first. An *encoded string* S is one of the form:

$$S = G^*$$
$$G = N \text{ "[" } L \text{ "]"}$$
$$N = [0\text{---}9]^+$$
$$L = [a\text{---}z]^+$$

We imagine this didn't clear up what the definition means. Take the encoded string "3[a]2[b]" as an example. The resulting decoded string is "aaabb", because we create three copies of "a", followed by two copies of "b". Another example is "4[abcd]", which returns the string containing "abcdabcdabcdabcd".

(a) First, design the `int retrieveN(String s)` that returns the integer at the start of an encoded string. Take the following examples as motivation.

```
retrieveN("3[a]2[b]")      => 3
retrieveN("47[abcd]")      => 47
retrieveN("1[bbbbb]3[a]")  => 1
```

(b) Next, design the `String cutN(String s)` method that returns a string without the integer at the start of an encoded string. Hint: use `indexOf` and `substring`.

```
cutN("3[a]2[b]")      => "[a]2[b]"
cutN("47[abcd]")      => "[abcd]"
cutN("1[bbbbb]3[a]")  => "[bbbbb]3[a]"
```

(c) Design the *standard recursive* decode method, which receives an encoded string and performs a decoding operation.
(d) Design the `decodeTR` and `decodeTRHelper` methods. The former acts as the driver to the latter; the latter solves the same problem that decode does, but it instead uses tail recursion. Remember to include the relevant access modifiers!
(e) Design the `decodeLoop` method, which solves the problem using either a `while` or `for` loop.

2.43 Design the `boolean isNumberPalindrome(int n)` method that, when given an integer n, returns whether or not that number is a palindrome. You cannot convert the number to a string.

2.44 (⋆) The C programming language contains the atoi "ascii-to-integer" function, which receives a string and, if the string represents some integer, returns the number converted to an integer. Design the `int atoi(String s)` method that, when given a string s, returns its value as an integer if it can be parsed as an integer. When parsing the integer, ignore all leading zeroes and leading non-digits. Upon finding the first non-zero digit, if it exists, begin interpreting the string as a number. At any point thereafter, if a non-digit is encountered, return the number parsed up to that point. The given integer can also contain a sign, e.g., + or −. If the value exceeds the bounds of an integer (i.e., `Integer.MAX_VALUE` or `Integer.MIN_VALUE`), return zero. Writing enough tests is *crucial* to getting this correct! We provide some examples below.

```
atoi("ABCD")              => 0
atoi("42")                => 42
atoi("000042")            => 42
atoi("004200")            => 4200
atoi("ABCD42ABCD)         => 42
atoi("ABCD-+42ABCD)       => 42
atoi("ABCD+-42ABCD)       => -42
atoi("9999999999999")     => 0
atoi("-9999999999999")    => 0
atoi("000-42000")         => -42000
atoi("000-ABCD)           => 0
atoi("000+42ABCD)         => 42
atoi("8080*8080")         => 8080
```

2.45 (⋆) Similar to atoi, the C programming language also has a way of converting floating-point values represented as strings to double values via atof. Design the double atof(String s) method, which receives a string and converts it into a double if the input can be interpreted as such. To make this a bit easier, assume that only valid floating-point values can be passed to the method. Below are some examples. Due to potential inaccuracies with floating-point precision, as long as you are close to the given number, that is fine.

```
atof("3.1415")      => 3.1415
atof("+3.1415")     => -3.1415
atof("-3.1415")     => -3.1415
atof("100.0005")    => 100.0005
atof("6.28")        => 6.28
atof("3")           => 3.0
atof("0")           => 0.0
atof("-0.000000")   => -0.000000
```

2.46 Wordle is a game created by Josh Wardle, where the objective is to guess a word with a given number of turns, inspired by Mastermind (Katherine Ritchey and Ritchey, 2023). In this exercise, you will implement a stage of the Wordle game.

Design the String guessWord(String W, String G) method that, when given a string W and a "guess" string G, returns a new string with the following properties:

- If $|W| \neq |G|$, return null.
- For every index i, if $W_i = G_i$, append W_i to the output string. If $W_i \neq G_i$ but $G_i \in W$, append an asterisk to the output string. Otherwise, output a dash.

Below are some example inputs and outputs.

```
guessWord("PLANS", "TRAP")   => null
guessWord("PLANS", "TRAIN")  => "--A-*"
guessWord("PLANS", "PLANE")  => "PLAN-"
guessWord("PLANS", "PLANS")  => "PLANS"
guessWord("PLANS", "SNLPA")  => "*****";
```

2.47 Design the int indexOf(String s, String k) method, which receives two strings s, k, and returns the first index of k in s. Note that k may be any arbitrary string and not just a a single character. If k is not in s, return -1. You **cannot** use the indexOf method provided by the String class.

2.48 Design the String substring(String s, int a, int b) method, which receives a string and two integers a, b, and returns the substring between these indices. If either are out of bounds of the string, return null. You **cannot** use the substring method(s) provided by the String class.

2.49 Design the boolean isEqualTo(String s1, String s2) method, which receives two strings s_1 and s_2, and determines whether they are lexicographically equal. You cannot use the built-in equals or compareTo methods.

2.50 Design the int compareTo(String s1, String s2) method that receives two strings s_1 and s_2, and compares their contents lexicographically. If s1 is less than s2, return -1. If s1 is greater than s2, return 1. Otherwise, return 0. Note that our implementation of compareTo will differ from Java's in that, if s1 has less characters than s2, we return -1; if s2 has less characters than s1, we return 1. Otherwise, we do the character-by-character comparison.

2.51 File names are often compared lexicographically. For example, a file with name "File12.txt" is greater than "File1.txt" because '.' is less than '2'. Design the int compareFiles(String f1, String f2) method that would fix this ordering to return the more sensible ordering. That is, if a file has a prefix and a suffix, where the only differing piece is the number, then make the file with the lower number return a negative number. Take the following examples as motivation.

```
compareFiles("File12.txt", "File1.txt")  => 1
compareFiles("File10.txt", "File11.txt") => -1
compareFiles("File1.txt", "File12.txt")  => -1
compareFiles("File1.txt", "File1.txt")   => 0
```

2.52 Design the String trim(String s) method, which receives a string s and a character ch, and returns a string with all leading and trailing occurrences of ch removed. For instance, trim("aaHelloa", 'a') returns "Hello". Hint: while you cannot use Java's substring method, you can certainly use the one you wrote previously to solve this problem!

2.53 Design the String trimSpace(String s) method, which receives a string s and returns a new string with all leading and trailing spaces removed. You cannot use the trim method provided by the String class.

2.54 Design the boolean containsMiddleABC(String s) method, which receives a string s and returns whether s contains the substring "ABC" in the "middle." We define the "middle" as the point where number of characters on the left and right differ by at most one. You **cannot** use any String methods to solve this problem except .length and .charAt.

```
assertTrue(middleABC("helloABChiya!"));
assertTrue(middleABC("ABC"));
assertTrue(middleABC("aABCc!"));
assertFalse(middleABC("notInTheMiddleABCmid!"));
```

2.55 (⋆) Design the String censor(String s, String c) method, which receives a string s and another string c. It should return a "censored" version of s, wherein each instance of c in s is replaced by asterisks. You **cannot** use any String methods to solve this problem except .length and .charAt. This problem is harder than it looks due to these limitations.

2.56 Design the boolean isSelfDividing(int n) method, which receives an integer n and returns whether the sum of its digits evenly divide n. You must perform the arithmetic manually; you **cannot** convert the value to a String or use an array.

2.57 Design the `boolean allSelfDividing(int n)` method, which receives an integer n and returns whether each digit evenly divides n. If any digit is zero, then return `false`. You must perform the arithmetic manually; you **cannot** convert the value to a `String` or use an array.

2.58 Design the `int strSumNums(String s)` that computes the sum of each *positive integer* (≥ 0) in a string s. See the below test cases for examples. You may assume that each integer in s, should there be any, is in the bounds of a positive int, i.e., 0 and $2^{31} - 1$. Hint: use `Character.isDigit` to test whether a character c is a digit, and `Integer.parseInt` to convert a `String` to an `int`.

```
assertEquals(100, strSumNums("hello50how20are30you?"));
assertEquals(10, strSumNums("t1h1i1s1i1s1e1a1s1y1!"));
assertEquals(0, strSumNums("there are no numbers :("));
assertEquals(0, strSumNums("still 0 just 0 zero0!"));
assertEquals(500000, strSumNums("500000"));
```

2.59 (⋆) Design the `String stripComments(String s)` method that, when given a string s representing a (valid) Java program, returns a string where all comments (single-line, multi-line, and Java documentation) have been removed. You **cannot** use any `String` helper methods (e.g., `strip`, `split`) to solve this problem nor can you use regular expressions.

2.60 Design the `double approxPi(int n)` that approximates π using the following formula:

$$\pi = 4 \cdot \left(1 - \frac{1}{3} + \frac{1}{5} - \frac{1}{7} + \frac{1}{9} - \frac{1}{11} + \frac{1}{13} - \frac{1}{15} + \frac{1}{17} - \cdots\right)$$

That is, given an input number n, compute that many terms of the above sequence. Return the difference between this approximation and Java's built-in `Math.PI` using `Math.abs`.

2.61 Design the `String toBinary(int n)` that converts a positive integer n into a `String` that represents its binary counterpart. We present some examples below.

```
toBinary(13)   => "1101"
toBinary(144)  => "10010000"
toBinary(25)   => "11001"
```

2.62 Design the `String toBase(int n, int u, int v)` method that converts a positive integer n_u in base u to base v, as a `String`. You may assume that $2 \leq u, v \leq 16$. Any base above ten uses $A, B, \ldots, F$ for $11, 12, \ldots, 15$ respectively. Hint: multiply when going down in bases ($v < u$), divide when going up ($v > u$).

2.63 Design the `int countPairs(int n)` method that computes the number of pairs (a, b) that satisfy the equation $(a^2 + b^2 + 1)/(ab)$ such that $1 \leq a \leq b < n$. To "satisfy the equation," in this context, means that the quotient is an integer.

2.64 Design the `String mirrorEnds(String s)` method that, when given a string s, looks for a mirror image (backwards) string at both the beginning and end of the given string. In other words, zero or more characters at the very beginning of the given string, and at the very end of the string in reverse order (possibly overlapping). For example, the string `"abXYZba"` has the mirror end `"ab"`. If there is no such string, return `null`.

```
mirrorEnds("abXYZba") => "ab"
```

2.4 Exercises

```
mirrorEnds("abca")    => "a"
mirrorEnds("aba")     => "aba"
mirrorEnds("abc")     => null
```

2.65 Design the `String multTable(int a, int b)` method that, when given two integers a and b such that $a \leq b$, computes the "multiplication table" from a to b. We provide some test cases below. Note that the newline is just for formatting purposes.

```
multTable(3, 3) => "1*1=1,1*2=2,1*3=3,2*1=2,2*2=4,
                    2*3=6,3*1=3,3*2=6,3*3=9"
multTable(2, 6) => "1*1=1,1*2=2,1*3=3,1*4=4,1*5=5,
                    1*6=6,2*1=2,2*2=4,2*3=6,2*4=8,
                    2*5=10,2*6=12"
```

2.66 (⋆) This exercise has two parts.

(a) Design the `int nCk(int n, int k)` method that returns the number of ways that one can choose k elements from a set of n values without care for the order. The formula, also called the binomial coefficient (represented as $\binom{n}{k}$), is listed below.

$$\binom{n}{k} = \frac{n!}{k!(n-k)!}$$

(b) Use the nCk method that you designed to design another method: `String binomial(int x, int y, int n)`, which returns a string representation of the expansion of powers of a binomial, namely $(x+y)^n$. The formula is as follows, where $\binom{n}{k}$ stands in place for nCk:

$$(x+y)^n = \binom{n}{0}x^n y^0 + \binom{n}{1}x^{n-1}y^1 + \cdots + \binom{n}{n-1}x^1 y^{n-1} + \binom{n}{n}x^0 y^n$$

2.67 (⋆) We can "speak" a sequence of numbers by saying each number as its quantity and the number itself. For example, the number 11 is spoken as `"two 1s"`, or `"21"`. Similarly, `"21"` is spoken as `"one 2, one 1"`, or `"1211"`. Finally, `"1211"` is spoken as `"one 1, one 2, two 1s"`, or `"111221"`. We can derive a recursive sequence to express the algorithm.

$$a_1 = \texttt{"1"}$$
$$a_2 = \texttt{"11"}$$
$$a_3 = \texttt{"21"}$$
$$a_4 = \texttt{"1211"}$$
$$a_n = \text{the String representation of } a_{n-1}, \text{ but spoken.}$$

Design the `String speakSequence(int n)` method that returns the nth number in this sequence. Hint: design a helper method that, when given the $(n-1)^{\text{th}}$ "spoken number," returns the nth spoken number. To this end, you should also design a helper method, namely `countPrefix`, that counts the number of times a character appears consecutively in the prefix of a string. For example, `countPrefix("111221")` returns 3 because the character 1 appears three times consecutively in the prefix of the given string.

2.68 (⋆) The *definite integral* of a function f, defined as $\int_a^b f(x)\,dx$, produces the area under the curve of f on the interval $[a,b]$. The thing is, though, integrals are defined in terms of *Riemann summations*, which provide estimations on the area under a curve. Riemann sums approximate the area by creating rectangles of a fixed width Δ, as shown in 2.4 for an arbitrary function f. Left-Riemann, right-Riemann, and midpoint-Riemann approximations define the focal point, i.e., the height, of the rectangle. Notice that, in Figure 2.4, we use a midpoint-Riemann sum with $\Delta = 0.2$, in which the collective sum of all the rectangle areas is the Riemann approximation. Your job is to use this idea to approximate the area of a circle.

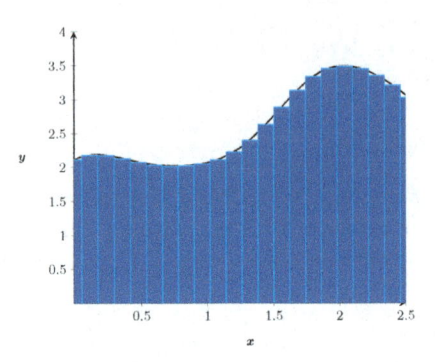

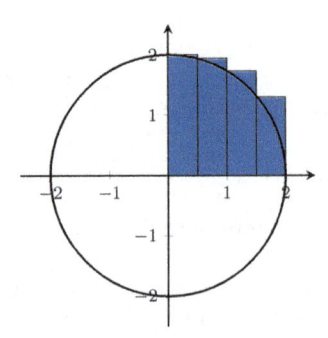

Fig. 2.4: Midpoint-Riemann Approximation of a Function

Design the `double circleArea(double r, double delta)` method, which receives a radius r and a delta Δ. It computes (and returns) a left/right-Riemann approximation of the area of a circle. Hint: if you compute the left/right-Riemann approximation of one quadrant, you can very easily obtain an approximation of the total circle area. We illustrate this hint in Figure 2.5 where $\Delta = 0.5$ and its radius $r = 2$. Note that the approximated area will vary based on the chosen Riemann approximation.[12] Further note that no calculus knowledge is necessary to solve this exercise.[13]

Fig. 2.5: Left-Riemann Approximation of a Function

---

[12] A left-Riemann sum over-approximates the area, whereas a right-Riemann sum provides an under-approximation. A midpoint approximation uses the average between the left and right approximations.
[13] This exercise comes directly from (Crotts, 2023). Thanks, past me! Further thanks to Chandana Ariyawansa for the problem.

2.4 Exercises

2.69 In 1964, Willans (1964) derived the following formula for computing the nth prime number:

$$p_n = 1 + \sum_{i=1}^{2^n} \left\lfloor \left(\frac{n}{\sum_{j=1}^{i} \left\lfloor (\cos(j-1)! + 1/j\pi)^2 \right\rfloor} \right)^{1/n} \right\rfloor$$

While this looks frightening, it is actually straightforward and requires no conditionals. We know that '$n!$' is the factorial of some integer n. The summation, $\sum_{j=1}^{n} f(i)$ is, effectively, a loop from $j = 1$ to n, inclusive, which sums the value returned from $f(i)$. Finally, $\lfloor n \rfloor$ computes the floor of a number n, which is the next-closest integer to n. E.g., the floor of 3.7 is 3. Use this formula to design the `int nthPrime(int n)` method, which returns the nth prime number. You *must* use this formula exactly as specified.

2.70 (⋆) Speech-to-text software plays a significant role in accessibility for those who may not be able to type quickly or at all. Design the `String speechToText(String s)` method that, when given a "speech string", returns the corresponding text. A speech string, in this context, is a string spoken, in English, by a person, which may or may not contain punctuation. If a speech string contains a word that represents punctuation, e.g., "period", "question mark", encode this punctuation in the returned text. For example, speechToText("hello period how are you question mark") returns the string "Hello. How are you?". You should also account for quotations, e.g., speechToText("hello quote how are you question mark unquote") returns the string Hello. "how are you?".

3 Arrays, Collections, and Generics

Abstract Data structures are fundamental to programming languages, and fortunately, Java provides a plethora of options to choose for differing situations. In this chapter, we will analyze and exemplify the popular data structures that Java has to offer. We begin the discussion with primitive (and statically-sized) arrays, then move into dynamically-resizable lists, stacks, queues, sets, and maps. We also explain the Java Stream API and its advantages over standard data structure manipulation.

We follow the data structure section with type parameterization, or generics, over static methods. While generics are not very powerful when paired only with static methods, we need to understand their role within Java's Collections framework.

The last section is a basic overview of the tree data structure, which will be covered in greater detail in a subsequent computer science text. Java does not provide a tree data structure in the collections framework, so we wrote one for readers to work with.

3.1 Arrays

Thus far, all data that we work with has been passed as method parameters. When we invoke a method, we have access to the arguments at that point in time. *Arrays* allow us to store values, similar to how we use variables, but with the added benefit of storing multiple values in one location.

Arrays store *elements* and *indices* of some type. An element is just a value in an array. The *index* of an element is its location in the array. Indices of an array are indexed from zero, much like strings. Thus, the first element of an array is at index zero, whereas the last element is located at the index $|A| - 1$, where $|A|$ denotes the number of elements, or *cardinality*, of some array A.

We store elements contiguously in arrays, where all are of the same type. This means that, if we declare an array of type `int`, we cannot store, for example, a `String` in that array. We can declare an array variable with preset values using *initializer lists*:

```
int[] array = {5, 10, 15, 20, 100, 50};
```

To retrieve the size of an array, the number of elements it can store, we access the *.length* field of the array, e.g., `array.length`. For our example array, we see that its size is six. Moreover, `array[0]` stores 5 and `array[5]` stores 50. Accessing a negative index or an index beyond the bounds of the length results in an `ArrayIndexOutOfBoundsException`. So, accessing `array[-1]` or `array[6]`, for instance, crashes the program. A common mistake is to access the index at the length of the array to retrieve the last element, which represents a misunderstanding of array indexing.

> **Java Arrays**
>
> An *array* stores a fixed-size collection of elements of some type.
>
> $T[]\ A =$ new $T[n]$ creates an array of type T, named A, that stores n elements.
> $A[i]$ retrieves the element at index i^{th} of A. We refer to this as position $i + 1$.
> $A[i] = v$ assigns v to index i of A.
> A.length returns the number of elements that the array can store.
> Arrays.equals(A_1, A_2) returns whether or not the elements of A_1 are equal to the elements of A_2.
> Arrays.toString(A) returns a string representation of the elements in A, separated by commas and enclosed by brackets.
> Arrays.fill(A, v) populates A with v in every index.
> Arrays.copyOf(A, n) returns a new array A' of the same type with the new size, padding with the necessary default elements or truncating.
> Arrays.sort(A) performs an in-place sort of A, meaning the contents of A are modified.

Fig. 3.1: Useful Array Methods.

To declare an array of type T, called A, that stores N elements, we write the following:

```
T[] A = new T[N];
```

We can store a value e at an arbitrary index i of array A, in addition to accessing the value at some index.

```
// Store "e" at index i of A.
A[i] = e;
// Print out the value at A[i].
System.out.println(A[i]);
```

Example 3.1. Let's declare an integer array A to store the integers from zero to one hundred in increments of ten.

```
int[] A = {0, 10, 20, 30, 40, 50, 60, 70, 80, 90, 100};
```

Initializer lists are verbose and require us to explicitly specify each constant. A better solution is to initialize the array to a size, and populate its elements using a loop.

```
final int SIZE = 11;
int[] A = new int[SIZE];
for (int i = 0; i < A.length; i++) { A[i] = i * 10; }
```

We use i to iterate over the possible indices of our array. Before we explained that i is used out of standard loop convention, but we now say that i, in general, stands for either "iteration" or "index." We assign, to A at index i, the value of i multiplied by ten. We can convert the array to a String using a utility method from the Arrays class (note the plural!); a "string-ified" array separates each element by commas and surrounds them with braces.

```
String s1 = Arrays.toString(A);
s1 => [0, 10, 20, 30, 40, 50, 60, 70, 80, 90, 100]
```

3.1 Arrays

Example 3.2. Let's design a method that receives an array of `double` values and returns the sum of those elements.

```java
import static Assertions.assertAll;
import static Assertions.assertEquals;

class SumOfDoubleArrayTester {

  @Test
  void testSumOfDoubleArray() {
    assertAll(
      () -> assertEquals(0.0, sumOfDoubles(new double[]{})),
      () -> assertEquals(100.0, sumOfDoubles(new double[]{25.0, 50.0, 25.0})));
  }
}
```

Our method uses a local variable to accumulate the "running sum," so to speak, of the values seen so far in the passed array.

```java
class SumOfDoubleArray {

  /**
   * Computes the sum of the values in a double array.
   * @param arr double [] array of double values.
   * @return sum of those values.
   */
  static double sumOfDoubles(double[] arr) {
    double sum = 0;
    for (int i = 0; i < arr.length; i++) {
      sum += arr[i];
    }
    return sum;
  }
}
```

Even though our code works and the tests that we wrote pass without question, there is a bit of verbosity with our loop: *i*'s purpose is solely for accessing an index into the array. In such circumstances, we may prefer using the enhanced `for` loop, which abstracts away the index and provides an iteration construct for accessing elements sequentially. Why might someone want to use the enhanced `for` loop over a standard `for`? When we only want to access the elements themselves and not care about their position, the enhanced counterpart is favored; not having to concern ourselves with indices completely removes the possibility of accessing an out-of-bounds index.

```java
class SumOfDoubleArray {

  static double sumOfDoubles(double arr) {
    double sum = 0;
    for (double e : arr) {
      sum += e;
    }
    return sum;
  }
}
```

Example 3.3. Let's design the `int countOccurs(int[] A, int n)` method, which receives an integer n and returns the number of times it appears in an array of integers. Fortunately this requires exactly one traversal over A to count the occurrences of n, with no complex cases to consider.

```java
import static Assertions.assertAll;
import static Assertions.assertEquals;

class CountOccursTester {

  @Test
  void testCountOccurs() {
    assertAll(
      () -> assertEquals(0, countOccurs(new int[]{}, 5)),
      () -> assertEquals(3, countOccurs(new int[]{5, 3, 5, 5}, 5)),
      () -> assertEquals(1, countOccurs(new int[]{1, 2, 3, 4, 5}, 5)),
      () -> assertEquals(0, countOccurs(new int[]{1, 2, 3, 4, 5}, 6)));
  }
}
```

```java
class CountOccurs {

  /**
   * Counts the number of occurrences of a value in an int array.
   * @param A array of integers.
   * @param n value to count.
   * @return number of occurrences of n in A.
   */
  static int countOccurs(int[] A, int n) {
    int count = 0;
    for (int e : A) {
      if (e == n) { count++; }
    }
    return count;
  }
}
```

Example 3.4. Consider the `int[] wordLengths(String[] S)` method. Its purpose is, for every index i of the array S, to store the length of the string at that index in the corresponding index of the returned array. For example, if S contains the strings `"hello"`, `"world"`, and `"!"`, the returned array should contain the values 5, 5, and 1, respectively.

```java
import static Assertions.assertAll;
import static Assertions.assertEquals;

class WordLengthsTester {

  @Test
  void testWordLengths() {
    assertAll(
      () -> assertEquals(new int[]{5, 1}, wordLengths(new String[]{"hello", "!"})),
      () -> assertEquals(new int[]{0, 0, 0}, wordLengths(new String[]{"", "", ""})),
      () -> assertEquals(new int[]{3}, wordLengths(new String[]{"abc"})));
  }
}
```

3.1 Arrays

```java
class WordLengths {

  /**
   * Computes the lengths of the strings in an array.
   * @param S array of strings.
   * @return array of lengths of the strings in S.
   */
  static int[] wordLengths(String[] S) {
    int[] lengths = new int[S.length];
    for (int i = 0; i < S.length; i++) {
      lengths[i] = S[i].length();
    }
    return lengths;
  }
}
```

Example 3.5. Let's design a method that returns the largest integer in an array of integers. Its algorithm appears straightforward, but can be a little tricky to correctly design because of how we determine the "largest integer." Some programmers may choose to declare a value `largest` and assign it, say, -1, and then if we find a larger value, overwrite the existing value. Such an algorithm works well when the provided array contains only positive integers, but what if our array contains only negative numbers less than -1? In that scenario, our algorithm would return -1, which is not the largest integer in the array. To avoid this issue, we can initialize `largest` to the first element of the array, and then iterate over the remaining elements, updating `largest` when we find a larger value. To simplify the implementation, we assume a precondition that the given array is non-empty.

```java
import static Assertions.assertAll;
import static Assertions.assertEquals;

class LargestIntTester {

  @Test
  void largestIntTester() {
    assertAll(
      assertEquals(4, largestInt(new int[]{4})),
      assertEquals(13, largestInt(new int[]{12, 13, 10, 9})),
      assertEquals(-5, largestInt(new int[]{-5, -7, -1932, -6, -6})),
      assertEquals(9, largestInt(new int[]{9, 9, 9, 9, 9, 9, 9, 9})),
      assertEquals(0, largestInt(new int[]{-321, -43, 0, -43, -321})),
      assertEquals(0, largestInt(new int[]{-9, 0, -8, -7, -1234})));
  }
}
```

```java
class LargestInt {

  static int largestInt(int[] arr) {
    int max = arr[0];
    for (int i = 1; i < arr.length; i++) {
      if (arr[i] > max) { max = arr[i]; }
    }
    return max;
  }
}
```

A slightly more compact solution is to wrap the conditional inside a call to Math.max, since the logic is effectively identical: max = Math.max(arr[i], max).

Java arrays are rather primitive compared to other more-complex data structures.[1] The Arrays class provides a few convenient methods for working with arrays, but for the most part, arrays serve as the backbone of other data structures. Arrays guarantee *constant access* times for elements. That is, if we know the index of an element e, we retrieve or modify it using the aforementioned array bracket syntax.

Example 3.6. Suppose we want to design a method that returns the index of an element e of an array of String values. Doing so is not a challenge: check each element, one-by-one, until we find the desired element, or return -1. Note the parallelism to the String class' indexOf method. To get practice using both recursion and iteration, we will design two versions of this method: one that uses tail recursion and the other that uses a loop.[2] The tail recursive method recurses over the accumulator, which serves as the current index to check.[3] If this value exceeds the bounds of the array, we return -1. If $S[i]$ is equal to k, we return i. Otherwise, we recurse and increment i by one. The tests for these two are both trivial to design.

```java
import static Assertions.assertAll;
import static Assertions.assertEquals;

class ArrayFinderTailRecursiveTester {

  @Test
  void testArrayFinderTailRecursive() {
    String[] arrS = new String[]{"Hello", "hi", "hiya", "howdy", "hello"};
    assertAll(
      () -> assertEquals(2, indexOfTR(arrS, "hiya")),
      () -> assertEquals(0, indexOfTR(arrS, "Hello")),
      () -> assertEquals(4, indexOfTR(arrS, "hello")),
      () -> assertEquals(-1, indexOfTR(arrS, "ahoy")));
  }
}
```

```java
class ArrayFinder {

  static int indexOfTR(String[] arrS, String k) {
    return indexOf(arrS, k, 0);
  }

  private static int indexOfTRHelper(String[] arrS, String k, int i) {
    if (i >= arrS.length) { return -1; }
    else if (arrS[i].equals(k)) { return i; }
    else { return indexOfHelper(arrS, k, i + 1); }
  }
}
```

In converting the tail recursive solution to use iteration, we will use the translation pipeline. Our base case is when i equals or exceeds the length of the array, so the negated expression

---

[1] Do not conflate this use of the "primitive" term with its use in describing "primitive datatypes."

[2] When recursing over an array, it is common to always have a parameter to represent the ith index, which corresponds to the current element. Note that this can be accomplished through both standard and tail recursion.

[3] We do *not* use standard recursion for this particular problem because returning -1 would result in an incorrect final value when unwinding the recursive calls.

3.1 Arrays

is our loop condition. Moreover, we place a conditional statement inside the loop, which returns whether $S[i]$ equals k for that value of i and, if so, we return i. We might also form a conjunction between the two conditions whose exit condition is when one of those conditions is falsified. Because we have two different atomic return values, though, we will use the former approach. The test cases for this method are identical to the tail recursive version.

```
class ArrayFinder {

  static int indexOfLoop(String[] arrS, String k) {
    int i = 0;
    while (!(i >= arrS.length)) {
      if (arrS[i].equals(k)) {
        return i;
      }
    }
    return -1;
  }
}
```

The conventional solution to this problem, especially since we know the upper bound on the number of iterations, involves a `for` loop. A `for` loop, as we now know, localizes the accumulator variable. Moreover, we *could* use the translation pipeline conditional expression, but it is idiomatic to loop while the index is less than the length of the array, and use an expression that describes this relationship.

```
class ArrayFinder {

  static int indexOfLoop(String[] arrS, String k) {
    for (int i = 0; i < arrS.length; i++) {
      if (arrS[i].equals(k)) {
        return i;
      }
    }
    return -1;
  }
}
```

Example 3.7. Imagine that we are writing a multiple choice question exam score calculator. Correct answers award three points, incorrect answers remove one point, and a "?" represents a guess, which neither awards nor removes points. Let's design a method that receives two String arrays representing the expected answers E and the actual answers A, and returns the score as a percentage. We will assume that $|E| = |A|$. Again, to gain practice with recursion and iteration, we'll design three versions of the score method.

First, we need to once again recognize that, because the method receives an array to recurse over, the method must receive a parameter representing the index-to-check. Though, we do not wish to expose to the caller how score works, so we can design a private helper method. Our base case occurs when $i \geq |E|$, in which we return zero. Otherwise, we have a case analysis on the ith actual answer: if it equals the ith expected answer, we award three points. If it is equal to a question mark string, i.e., "?" then we award no points. Otherwise, the answer is incorrect, meaning we deduct one point. Because a negative score is nonsensical, our driver method returns the maximum of zero and the score to filter out negative values.

```java
import static Assertions.assertAll;
import static Assertions.assertEquals;

class McqScoreCalculatorTester {

  @Test
  void testScore() {
    String[] E  = new String[]{"A","C","D","A","B","B","D","C","C"};
    String[] A1 = new String[]{"A","C","D","C","B","B","C","C","C"};
    String[] A2 = new String[]{"A","C","D","A","B","B","D","C","C"};
    String[] A3 = new String[]{"A","C","?","C","?","B","?","C","C"};
    assertAll(
        () -> assertEquals(70.3, score(E, A1)),
        () -> assertEquals(100.0, score(E, A2)),
        () -> assertEquals(51.8, score(E, A3)));
  }
}
```

```java
class McqScoreCalculator {

  /**
   * Computes the score of a test.
   * @param E expected test answers.
   * @param A answers provided.
   * @return score of test, >= 0.
   */
  static double score(String[] E, String[] A) {
    int maxScore = E.length * 3;
    return Math.max(0, scoreHelper(E, A, 0)) / maxScore * 100;
  }

  /**
   * Recursively computes the score of an exam.
   * @param E expected answers.
   * @param A answers provided.
   * @param i index-to-check.
   * @return score of test.
   */
  private static double scoreHelper(String[] E, String[] A, int i) {
    if (i >= A.length) { return 0; }
    else if (A[i].equals(E[i])) { return 3 + scoreHelper(E, A, i + 1); }
    else if (A[i].equals("?")) { return scoreHelper(E, A, i + 1); }
    else { return -1 + scoreHelper(E, A, i + 1); }
  }
}
```

The tail recursive solution is almost identical to the standard recursive variant. The essential difference is that we accumulate the score as a parameter in between recursive calls instead of summing the points when unwinding the calls. Aside from that, everything else remains the same. Our tests from score are likewise suitable for both the tail recursive and loop methods.

3.1 Arrays

```
class McqScoreCalculator {

  /**
   * Computes the score of a test.
   * @param E expected test answers.
   * @param A answers provided.
   * @return score of test, >= 0.
   */
  static double scoreTR(String[] E, String[] A) {
    return Math.max(0, scoreTRHelper(E, A, 0, 0)) / (E.length * 3) * 100;
  }

  /**
   * Recursively computes the score of an exam.
   * @param E expected answers.
   * @param A answers provided.
   * @param i index-to-check.
   * @param s currently-accumulated score.
   * @return score of test.
   */
  private static double scoreTRHelper(String[] E, String[] A,
                                      int i, int s) {
    if (i >= E.length) { return s; }
    else if (A[i].equals(E[i])) { return scoreTRHelper(E, A, i+1, s+3); }
    else if (A[i].equals("?")) { return scoreTRHelper(E, A, i+1, s); }
    else { return scoreTRHelper(E, A, i + 1, s + -1); }
  }
}
```

Lastly, the loop variant is just a translation pipeline away. When traversing over arrays, though, it is much more colloquial to use a `for` loop, since the bounds are known a priori.

```
class McqScoreCalculator {

  /**
   * Computes the score of a test.
   * @param E expected test answers.
   * @param A answers provided.
   * @return score of test, >= 0.
   */
  static double scoreLoop(String[] E, String[] A) {
    int score = 0;
    int i = 0;
    while (!(i >= A.length)) {
      if (A[i].equals(E[i])) { score += 3; }
      else if (A[i].equals("?")) { score += 0; }
      else { score += -1; }
      i++;
    }
    int maxScore = E.length * 3;
    return Math.max(0, score) / maxScore * 100;
  }
}
```

The key ideas with this example are twofold: first, a helper method does not always have to be tail recursive. Second, a standard recursive method can leverage a helper method when necessary.

We are on our way to understanding the full signature of the main method. Now that we have covered arrays, we know what the String[] args parameter represents, but *why* it receives that array of strings remains a mystery. We can compile Java files using the terminal and the javac command. Moreover, when executing a Java file, we may pass to it *terminal arguments*, which are values that the program might use to configure settings or process at runtime.

Example 3.8. Suppose we want to write a program, using the main method and terminal arguments, that evaluates an arithmetic operation on a collection of integers values, e.g., $5 + 3 + 17$. Additionally, we might want to let the user pass *flags* to denote these different operations, such as --add for addition, --sub for subtraction, and so on. So the user is not confused, we might also provide a "help" option that is displayed either upon request or when incorrect arguments are supplied.

First, we must explain how terminal arguments work. Terminal arguments are specified after the executable (name) and are separated by spaces. For instance, if our program name is calculator, we might use ./calculator --add 5 4 17. Thus, args[0] is --add, args[1] is "5", args[2] is "4", and args[3] is "17". For simplification purposes, we will assume that the first argument is always the operation/help flag, and the remaining values are operands. This means that the program should output 26. Let's design a method that parses the operation/help flag. Upon success, it returns true and upon failure, it returns false. This prevents the program from further interpreting bad terminal arguments, e.g., ./calculator --wrong 5 12. We will also use false as an indication that the help menu was requested or prompted. Thus, to not duplicate code, we should design another method that displays the relevant program usage information.

```
class Calculator {

  public static void main(String[] args) {
    if (parseCommand(argv[0])) {
      // Continue.
    }
    // Otherwise, stop.
  }

  static boolean parseCommand(String cmd) {
    if (cmd.equals("--add") || cmd.equals("--sub")) {
      return true;
    } else {
      displayHelp();
      return false;
    }
  }

  static void displayHelp() {
    System.out.println("usage: ./calculator --(help | add | sub) <n1>
                        [n...]");
  }
}
```

Up next is the process of interpreting each valid operation, i.e., --add and --sub. The former will add each successive argument one-by-one while the latter subtracts them from left-to-right. Because we receive the terminal arguments as strings, we will need to convert their values from strings to double values using Double.parseDouble. For the time being, we will assume that these *are*, in fact, double values, rather than working through the painstaking

3.1 Arrays

process of parsing a string for the existence of a proper `double` datatype value. We encourage the readers to implement this method themselves, along with the appropriate tests.

Note that in the code below, we utilize an `if`/`else if` combination without an accompanying `else`, which we would normally discourage. Because we exhaust the possibilities with `parseCommand`, however, we will allow its usage. The `parseAdd` and `parseSub` methods are trivial and we have shown an example of their implementation previously, so we will also omit these to preserve space and avoid unnecessary repetition.

```
class Calculator {

  public static void main(String[] args) {
    if (parseCommand(args[0])) {
      String cmd = args[0];
      double[] operands = convertToDoubleArray(args);
      if (cmd.equals("--add")) {
        System.out.println(parseAdd(operands));
      } else if (cmd.equals("--sub")) {
        System.out.println(parseSub(operands));
      }
    }
  }
}
```

Example 3.9. Let's write a program that receives a list of integers through the terminal, as an "argument array" of sorts, and allow the user to pass flags to denote the operation to perform on the list. Our program will support the following operations: `--sum`, `--product`, `--min`, and `--max` command. We will also provide a `--help` flag that displays the program usage information. This is a substantial project, but doing so allows us to practice using arrays and integrating more complex terminal arguments. As a measure of simplification, we will assume that the first n arguments are the numeric values, and the remaining arguments are the operation flags. Let's further assume that the user will not pass an invalid command. Lastly, we shall not consider invalid inputs for a given context, e.g., the minimum/maximum when no input values are provided. The first terminal argument denotes the number of values to expect, so we will use it to initialize our array.

To start, let's see a few example runs of our program, containing a mixture of flags.

```
./ArrayArguments 5 1 2 3 4 5 --sum --max
sum: 15.000000
max: 5.000000

./ArrayArguments 3 100 200 -100 --product --sum --min
sum: 200.000000
product: -2000000.000000
min: -100.000000

./ArrayArguments --help
usage: ./ArrayArguments <n> <n1> [n...] [--(sum | product | min | max)]
```

The ordering of the output is irrelevant, and depends on how we parse the input flags in the main method. To scan for a given flag, let's design a static method to return whether or not the flag exists in the arguments array.

```
import static Assertions.assertAll;
import static Assertions.assertEquals;

class ArrayArgumentsTester {

  @Test
  void testScanForFlag() {
    String[] args = new String[]{"--sum", "--max", "--min"};
    assertAll(
      () -> assertEquals(true, isFlagPresent(args, "--sum")),
      () -> assertEquals(true, isFlagPresent(args, "--max")),
      () -> assertEquals(true, isFlagPresent(args, "--min")),
      () -> assertEquals(false, isFlagPresent(args, "--product")));
  }
}
```

```
class ArrayArguments {

  /**
   * Returns whether or not a given flag exists in the arguments array.
   * @param args array of arguments.
   * @param flag flag to search for.
   * @return whether or not the flag exists.
   */
  static boolean isFlagPresent(String[] args, String flag) {
    for (String arg : args) {
      if (arg.equals(flag)) {
        return true;
      }
    }
    return false;
  }
}
```

The other "operations" methods, as well as their tests, are simple to create, and we will omit their implementation.

Our main method first checks to see if the user entered the "help" command and, if so, presents the necessary information for running the program. Otherwise, we perform a case analysis on the terminal arguments, looking for the presence of the operation flags. For arbitrary reasons, we output the sum, then the product, then the minimum, and finally the maximum, in that order, despite the ordering of the flags. As an exercise, we encourage the readers to modify the program to instead output the values in the order of the presented flags.

An important detail that some may miss is that we use a sequence of if statements, instead than if/else if statements. This is because we want to allow the user to pass multiple flags; we would unintentionally restrict them to exactly one flag with if/else if statements. Each flag is checked independently from one another, and whether a flag is entered does not affect the state of another.

3.1 Arrays

```
class ArrayArguments {

  public static void main(String[] args) {
    if (isFlagPresent(args, "--help")) {
      displayHelp();
    } else {
      int n = Integer.parseInt(args[0]);
      double[] values = new double[n];
      for (int i = 0; i < n; i++) {
        values[i] = Double.parseDouble(args[i + 1]);
      }
      if (isFlagPresent(args, "--sum")) {
        System.out.printf("sum: %f\n", sum(values));
      }
      if (isFlagPresent(args, "--product")) {
        System.out.printf("product: %f\n", product(values));
      }
      if (isFlagPresent(args, "--min")) {
        System.out.printf("min: %f\n", min(values));
      }
      if (isFlagPresent(args, "--max")) {
        System.out.printf("max: %f\n", max(values));
      }
    }
  }
}
```

Example 3.10. Arrays are not restricted to being only one dimensional. In this problem, we will make use of a two-dimensional array, which might be thought of as a matrix or a grid. Namely, we'll design a method that returns the sum of the elements of a two-dimensional array of integers. Traversing over an n-dimensional array generally involves nested loops. The order in which we traverse over the array can be significant. For example, the following code uses *row-major* ordering, since we iterate over the rows first, and then the columns, meaning that we visit the elements (of a 3 × 3 array) in the order

$$A_{0,0}, A_{0,1}, A_{0,2}, A_{1,0}, A_{1,1}, A_{1,2}, A_{2,0}, A_{2,1}, A_{2,2}$$

Conversely, *column-major* ordering would visit the elements in the order

$$A_{0,0}, A_{1,0}, A_{2,0}, A_{0,1}, A_{1,1}, A_{2,1}, A_{0,2}, A_{1,2}, A_{2,2}$$

Multi-dimensional arrays are nothing more than arrays of arrays. As an example, we can declare a 3 × 4 two-dimensional array of integers (with three rows and four columns) as follows:[4]

```
int[][] A = {{1, 2, 3, 4},
             {5, 6, 7, 8},
             {9, 10, 11, 12}};
```

---

[4] The spacing/positioning of the rows/elements is irrelevant; we could type the rows side-by-side and we would have the same resulting array.

```
import static Assertions.assertAll;
import static Assertions.assertEquals;

class SumOf2DArrayTester {

  @Test
  void testSumOf2DArray() {
    int[][] A = {{1, 2, 3, 4}, {5, 6, 7, 8}, {9, 10, 11, 12}};
    assertAll(
      () -> assertEquals(78, sumOf2DArray(A)),
      () -> assertEquals(0, sumOf2DArray(new int[][]{})),
      () -> assertEquals(1, sumOf2DArray(new int[][]{{1}})));
  }
}
```

We need to know both the number of rows and the number of columns to traverse over a two-dimensional array. To retrieve the number of rows, we refer to the array's length via A.length. To get the number of columns, again, because we know that A is an array of one-dimensional arrays, we use $A[0]$.length, or in general, $A[i]$.length for any i such that $0 \leq i < A$.length.[5] To access the element at row i and column j, we use $A[i][j]$.

```
class SumOf2DArray {

  /**
   * Computes the sum of the values in a two-dimensional array.
   * @param arr two-dimensional array of integers.
   * @return sum of those values.
   */
  static int sumOf2DArray(int[][] arr) {
    int sum = 0;
    for (int i = 0; i < arr.length; i++) {
      for (int j = 0; j < arr[i].length; j++) {
        sum += arr[i][j];
      }
    }
    return sum;
  }
}
```

Example 3.11. Let's design the int[][] removeAllZeroRows(int[][] A) method that removes all rows from a two-dimensional array of integers that contain a 0. Remember that arrays are immutable, so we instead return a new array with the appropriate alterations. For example, suppose our array A contains the following values:

$$\begin{bmatrix} 3 & 4 & 5 & 6 \\ 7 & 0 & 8 & 9 \\ 10 & 11 & 21 & 13 \\ 2 & 2 & 2 & 0 \\ 0 & 2 & 2 & 2 \end{bmatrix}$$

---

[5] This generalization applies because arrays in Java cannot be *ragged*: where different rows/columns have differing sizes.

3.1 Arrays

Invoking removeAllZeroRows returns a new array A':

$$\begin{bmatrix} 3 & 4 & 5 & 6 \\ 10 & 11 & 21 & 13 \end{bmatrix}$$

A problem that we immediately stumble upon is not knowing the resulting array size. Before a traversal over the input array A, we cannot predict how many rows will need to be removed. Thus, to design the removeAllZeroRows method, we need two helper methods, namely boolean containsZero(int[] A) and int countZeroRows(int[][] A), which returns whether a row contains a zero and the number of rows that contain at least one 0 respectively. Both implementations are nothing more than a single traversal over all elements in the array, so we will not design a test suite. Moreover, because they are private, a global test suite for either is not appropriate. After its implementation is complete, we can work on removeAllZeroRows. The number of columns in the resulting array is fixed. The number of rows, however, is not, so we invoke countZeroRows and instantiate the resulting array to the correct size. Thereafter we traverse over the array twice: one to determine if it contains a zero and, if not, add every element to the new array. We must be careful to correctly access the resulting array; recall that its number of rows is at most equal to A's row count, so we need a separate variable to index into its rows.

```java
import static Assertions.assertAll;
import static Assertions.assertArrayEquals;

class RemoveAllZeroRowsTester {

  @Test
  void testRemoveAllZeroRowsTester() {
    int[][] A1 = {{3, 4, 5, 6},
                  {7, 0, 8, 9},
                  {10, 11, 21, 13},
                  {2, 2, 2, 0},
                  {0, 2, 2, 2}};
    int[][] R1 = {{3, 4, 5, 6},
                  {10, 11, 21, 13}};
    int[][] A2 = {{2, 4},
                  {5, 6}};
    int[][] R2 = {{2, 4},
                  {5, 6}};
    int[][] A3 = {{0, 10, 30},
                  {90, 100, 0}};
    int[][] R3 = {{}};
    assertAll(
      () -> assertArrayEquals(R1, removeAllZeroRows(A1)),
      () -> assertArrayEquals(R2, removeAllZeroRows(A2)),
      () -> assertArrayEquals(R3, removeAllZeroRows(A3)));
  }
}
```

```java
class RemoveAllZeroRows {

  /**
   * Removes all rows from a 2D array that contain at least one zero.
   * @param A a 2D array of integers.
   * @return a new 2D array with all zero rows removed.
   */
  static int[][] removeAllZeroRows(int[][] A) {
    int numRows = A.length - countZeroRows(A);
    int numCols = A[0].length;
    int[][] res = new int[numRows][numCols];
    for (int i = 0, rIdx = 0; i < A.length; i++) {
      if (!containsZero(A[i])) {
        for (int j = 0; j < A[i].length; j++) {
          res[rIdx][j] = A[i][j];
        }
        rIdx++;
      }
    }
    return res;
  }

  /**
   * Checks if an array contains a zero.
   * @param A an array of integers.
   * @return true if the array contains a zero, false otherwise.
   */
  private static boolean containsZero(int[] A) {
    for (int x : A) {
      if (x == 0) {
        return true;
      }
    }
    return false;
  }

  /**
   * Counts the number of rows in a 2D array that contain at least one zero.
   * @param A a 2D array of integers.
   * @return number of rows that have at least one zero.
   */
  private static int countZeroRows(int[][] A) {
    int count = 0;
    for (int[] r : A) {
      if (containsZero(r)) {
        count++;
      }
    }
    return count;
  }
}
```

Example 3.12. Let's solve a slightly harder problem using two-dimensional arrays. Suppose that we want to design a method that returns the number of possible moves that a rook can take to go from the top-left of a (not-necessarily rectangular) board to the bottom-right, assuming that it cannot move left or up. The naive solution to this problem is to use a recursive method that changes its position by one in either direction, stopping once we hit

3.1 Arrays

the bottom-right of the board. Assuming the rook starts at (x,y) and the board is $n \times m$, we can design the following method:

```
import static Assertions.assertAll;
import static Assertions.assertEquals;

class RookPathTester {

  @Test
  void testRookPath() {
    assertAll(
      () -> assertEquals(2, rook(0, 0, 1, 1)),
      () -> assertEquals(6, rook(0, 0, 2, 2)),
      () -> assertEquals(10, rook(0, 0, 2, 3)),
      () -> assertEquals(70, rook(0, 0, 4, 4)));
  }
}
```

```
class RookPath {

  /**
   * Computes the number of possible paths that a rook
   * can take to go from the top-left of a board to the
   * bottom-right, assuming that it cannot move left or up.
   * @param x x-coordinate of the rook's starting position.
   * @param y y-coordinate of the rook's starting position.
   * @param n number of rows of the board.
   * @param m number of columns of the board.
   * @return number of possible paths.
   */
  static int rook(int x, int y, int n, int m) {
    if (x == n || y == m) {
      return 1;
    } else {
      return rook(x + 1, y, n, m) + rook(x, y + 1, n, m);
    }
  }
}
```

Much like how the recursive definition of Fibonacci is horrendously slow, so is this implementation of the rook path problem. We need a faster algorithm, and indeed, we can take advantage of a two-dimensional array because of an emerging pattern. Notice that, in the bottom-right corner, there is only one possible solution. We can generalize this to say that there is only one solution for any position in the bottom row or the far-right column. From here, we can work our way up and to the left, filling in the number of possible solutions for each position.

For example, the position $(n-1, m-1)$ has a value of two, since it can move either right or down. The position $(n-2, m-1)$ has a value of three, since it can move right, down, or down and then right. We continue this process until we reach the top-left corner, which contains the value of the number of possible paths from $(0,0)$ to (n,m).[6] We can design a method that computes this value using a two-dimensional array. Composing the solution using this style is called *dynamic programming*, which comes up often when attempting to optimize problems that have naive and outrageously recursive solutions.

---

[6] Should we want to choose an arbitrary starting point, we can retrieve that index rather than $(0,0)$ in the resulting two-dimensional array.

To prevent our code from going out of bounds, we need to add one to the bounds of our input array. That is, if we want to compute the number of possible paths from $(0,0)$ to (n,m), we need to create an array of size $(n+1) \times (m+1)$, because the current value of the array at (n,m) depends on the values of the array at $(n+1,m)$ and $(n,m+1)$.[7]

Dynamic programming problems are often solved using two-dimensional arrays using the following three-step process:

1. For a problem size of n and m, we first initialize a two-dimensional array of size $(n+1) \times (m+1)$.
2. Populate the array with the necessary base cases.
3. Iterate over the array, filling in the values using a recurrence relation.

```
import static Assertions.assertAll;
import static Assertions.assertEquals;

class RookPathTester {

  @Test
  void testRookPathDp() {
    assertAll(
      () -> assertEquals(2, rookDp(0, 0, 1, 1)),
      () -> assertEquals(10, rookDp(0, 0, 2, 3)),
      () -> assertEquals(70, rookDp(0, 0, 4, 4)));
  }
}
```

```
class RookPath {

  /**
   * Computes the number of possible paths that a rook
   * can take to go from the (x, y) position of a board
   * to the bottom-right, assuming that it cannot move left or up.
   * @param x x-coordinate of the rook's starting position.
   * @param y y-coordinate of the rook's starting position.
   * @param n number of rows of the board.
   * @param m number of columns of the board.
   * @return number of possible paths.
   */
  static int rookDp(int x, int y, int n, int m) {
    int[][] dp = new int[n + 1][m + 1];
    // Compose the initial bottom-row solutions.
    for (int i = 0; i < n + 1; i++) { dp[i][m] = 1; }
    // Compose the initial far-right solutions.
    for (int i = 0; i < m + 1; i++) { dp[n][i] = 1; }
    // Now do the dynamic programming algorithm.
    for (int i = n - 1; i >= 0; i--) {
      for (int j = m - 1; j >= 0; j--) {
        dp[i][j] = dp[i + 1][j] + dp[i][j + 1];
      }
    }
    return dp[x][y];
  }
}
```

---

[7] When writing dynamic programming algorithms, it is commonplace to call the auxiliary data structure dp out of convention.

3.1 Arrays

Example 3.13. Let's solve another foundational dynamic programming problem, only this time we utilize only a one-dimensional array. Imagine that we're working at a lumber store that saws wood logs for manufacturing purposes. We sell and saw wood logs by the meter. Different lengths of a log cost different amounts, and we want to maximize the profits made when sawing the logs. For example, consider the following table:

Length (meters)	0	1	2	3	4	5	6	7	8
Cost (USD)	0	1	4	6	7	12	18	25	30

Suppose our wood log is 4 meters long. There are, therefore, $2^{(4-1)} = 2^3 = 8$ ways to saw the log: '1|1|1|1', '1|1|2', '1|2|1', '1|3', '2|1|1', '2|2', '3|1', and '4|0.' If we compute the prices of these sawings, we get $1+1+1+1 = 4$, $1+4+1 = 6$, $1+1+4 = 6$, $1+6 = 7$, $4+1+1 = 6$, $4+4 = 8$, $6+1 = 7$, and $7 = 7$. So, to maximize our profit, we want to saw the log into two pieces, each of which are 2 meters long.

The question is, how do we determine the maximum profit algorithmically? Decomposing the problem shows us that we first saw the log into size i meters, then try to maximize the profit made from sawing the rest of the log, which has size $n - i$ meters. The relationship is recursive, and we can design a method to simulate it. Namely, we try all possible sawings of size i using a loop, then recursively decompose the problem.

```
import static Assertions.assertAll;
import static Assertions.assertEquals;

class LogSawTester {

  @Test
  void testLogSaw() {
    assertAll(
      () -> assertEquals(0, logSaw(new int[]{0})),
      () -> assertEquals(8, logSaw(new int[]{0,1,4,6,7,12,18,25,30})));
  }
}
```

```
class LogSaw {

  /**
   * Performs a traditional recursive sawing of the given log.
   * Warning: this algorithm is outrageously slow!
   * @param P array of saw prices from 0 to n.
   * @param n length of log to saw in meters.
   * @return maximum profit of sawing log of length n.
   */
  static int logSaw(int[] P, int n) {
    if (n == 0) {
      return 0;
    } else {
      int r = 0;
      for (int i = 1; i <= n; i++) {
        r = Math.max(r, P[i] + logSaw(P, n - i));
      }
      return r;
    }
  }
}
```

While the recursive algorithm works, it is horribly inefficient; we saw the log at *all* possible intervals, meaning there are several repeated computations. Similar to Fibonacci, `logSaw` is an exponential-time algorithm! We can do better.

Like we said, we're repeatedly sawing at places whose maximal price has already been determined. So, let's design another recursive method that passes along an array L of stored (maximal) sawings. After trying all sawings from 1 to n, we store the maximum saw price for length n in L at index n. When recursing, if there is a non-zero element at index n, we know that its value was computed earlier and can return it accordingly.

This variant is leaps and bounds better than the original algorithm, taking its runtime from exponential down to quadratic in the length of the given log. We consider the algorithm to be "top-down memoized," because the solution recurses from n down to 1, and it stores partial solutions in an array (i.e., memoizing).

```java
class LogSaw {

  /**
   * Performs a top-down sawing of the given log.
   * @param P array of saw prices from 0 to n.
   * @param n length of log to saw in meters.
   * @return maximum profit of sawing log of length n.
   */
  static int logSawTopDown(int[] P, int n) {
    int[] R = new int[P.length];
    return logSawTopDownHelper(P, R, n);
  }

  /**
   * Helper method for top-down log saw algorithm.
   * @param P array of saw prices from 0 to n.
   * @param R intermittient saw prices; memoized.
   * @param n length of log in meters.
   * @return maximum profit for log of size n.
   */
  private static int logSawHelper(int[] P, int[] R, int n) {
    if (R[n] > 0) {
      return R[n];
    } else if (n == 0) {
      return n;
    } else {
      int pr = 0;
      for (int i = 1; i <= n; i++) {
        pr = Math.max(pr, P[i] + logSawHelper(P, R, n - i));
      }
      R[n] = pr;
      return pr;
    }
  }
}
```

Though, we still have to worry about recursive depth for sufficiently large values of n. Let's take the algorithm one step further and convert it into a "bottom-up" iterative algorithm. In essence, rather than making recursive calls, we use two loops and compose the solution to larger problems (i.e., larger values of n) by saving (intermittent) solutions to smaller problems (i.e., smaller values of n). The tests for the top-down and bottom-up methods are the same as the standard recursive version.

3.1 Arrays

```
class LogSaw {

  /**
   * Performs a bottom-up sawing of the given log.
   * @param P array of saw prices from 0 to n.
   * @param n length of log to saw in meters.
   * @return maximum profit of sawing log of length n.
   */
  static int logSawBottomUp(int[] P, int n) {
    int[] r = new int[p.length];
    for (int i = 1; i <= n; i++) {
      int pr = 0;
      for (int j = 1; j <= i; j++) {
        pr = Math.max(pr, P[j] + R[i - j]);
      }
      R[i] = pr;
    }
    return R[n];
  }
}
```

Example 3.14. A bank robber is heisting a local jewelry store, and a priori knows the weight and value of each item in the showcases.[8] The robber can only carry up to a maximum of m ounces of jewelry and wants to develop an algorithm that calculates the highest attainable profit.

Given an array of jewelry values V and weights in ounces W, we can find the maximum possible profit by brute forcing every combination of items. That is, at each choice of jewelry, the robber either does or does not steal the item in the showcase. Making two recursive calls that represent these decisions is easily conceivable; the base case is whether or not we are out of items to check, in which case we return zero as the profit. If the item-in-question exceeds the weight of the items currently in the robber's bag, then we must skip over it. For example, if a piece of jewelry j weighs 3 ounces and the robber has a 16oz bag that contains 14oz of jewelry, the robber cannot add j to their bag.

```
import static Assertions.assertAll;
import static Assertions.assertEquals;

class MaxJewelProfitTester {

  @Test
  void testMaxJewelProfit() {
    int[] V1 = new int[]{1, 2, 4, 2, 5};
    int[] W1 = new int[]{5, 3, 5, 3, 2};
    int[] V2 = new int[]{7, 5, 5};
    int[] W2 = new int[]{4, 2, 2};
    assertAll(
      () -> assertEquals(9, maxJewelProfit(V1, W1, 8)),
      () -> assertEquals(10, maxJewelProfit(V2, W2, 4)));
  }
}
```

---

[8] We, the authors, do not condone robbing your local jewelry store.

```
class MaxJewelProfit {

  /**
   * Given a list of jewels with values V and weights W, and a
   * bag with a maximum weight m, returns the maximum value of
   * jewels that can be picked.
   * @param V values of the jewels.
   * @param W weights of the jewels.
   * @param m maximum weight that the bag can hold.
   * @return the maximum value of jewels that can be picked.
   */
  static int maxJewelProfit(int[] V, int[] W, int m) {
    return maxJewelProfitHelper(V, W, m, 0);
  }

  /**
   * Helper method for maxJewelProfit. Uses the brute-force approach
   * of trying all possible combinations of picking and not picking each jewel.
   * @param V values of the jewels.
   * @param W weights of the jewels.
   * @param m current weight remaining in the bag.
   * @param i current index of the jewel we are considering.
   * @return the maximum value of jewels that can be picked.
   */
  private static int maxJewelProfitHelper(int[] V, int[] W, int m, int i) {
    if (i >= V.length || m == 0) {
      return 0;
    } else {
      int noPick = maxJewelProfitHelper(V, W, m, i + 1);
      // If we can fit it, then do so.
      if (m - W[i] >= 0) {
        int pick = V[i] + maxJewelProfitHelper(V, W, m - W[i], i + 1);
        return Math.max(pick, noPick);
      } else {
        // If we can't, then just use the result from "no pick."
        return noPick;
      }
    }
  }
}
```

Like many algorithm that makes two subsequent recursive calls, this is horribly inefficient, being yet again an exponential time algorithm. Dynamic programmingg rescues us once more by caching the results to intermediate "robberies." By intermediate "robberies," we mean that, for every item in the store, the robber either chooses to or not to steal it. When making this decision, the robber determines whether adding the item is advantageous to maximizing the profit by looking at past calculations. We will store these intermediate robberies in a two-dimensional array whose rows correspond to items in the store and whose columns correspond to weights of the bag. The idea is to iteratively build a table of maximum profits, and at intermediate steps, figure out if including the item maximizes the profit.

Let's consider an example. Suppose that we have a bag that weighs 7oz, and we know that a bag of 4oz has a maximum profit of $80. If we are currently eyeing an item that weighs 3oz at a value of $10, then we conclude that $90 is the maximum possible profit by stealing the 3oz item. This is because, if we steal the item, our bag now has 4oz of remaining capacity. We know the maximum possible profit of a 4oz bag, which is $80. So, the sum of these two values is $90. On the other hand, choosing not to take the item means that we copy over whatever

3.1 Arrays

value is stored for a 6oz bag. The decision to include or not include is made, similar to the model in the recursive approach, by taking the maximum of the two profits.

Let's initialize the dynamic programming array dp to be of sizes $|V|+1$, $m+1$. The base cases are trivial: if the total bag weight is 0, then no profits can be made. Similarly, on the 0th item, no profits are possible. In all other cases, for every item and for every bag weight from 0 to m (corresponding to an entry in the dp table), if an item i *can* fit in the bag, then we take the maximum of either the profit *without* i and the profit obtained after adding i. The latter amount is calculated by adding the value of i to the maximum profit achievable with the remaining capacity of the bag, which is determined after subtracting the weight of i from the bag's current capacity. We will note that our code is a bit more verbose than it could be as a consequence of wanting to label and clarify each variable. This is already a complex problem, and shoving multiple expressions into one does not make it easier for beginning (or even more advanced readers) readers to understand.

```java
class MaxJewelProfit {

  /**
   * Computes the maximum jewel profit using dynamic programming.
   * @param V values of the jewels.
   * @param W weights of the jewels.
   * @param m maximum weight that the bag can hold.
   * @return the maximum value of jewels that can be picked.
   */
  static int maxJewelProfitDp(int[] V, int[] W, int m) {
    int[][] dp = new int[V.length + 1][m + 1];
    // A jewel with 0 value should not be picked.
    for (int i = 0; i <= V.length; i++) {
      dp[i][0] = 0;
    }

    // A bag with 0 weight can't hold any jewels.
    for (int i = 0; i <= m; i++) {
      dp[0][i] = 0;
    }

    for (int i = 1; i < dp.length; i++) {
      for (int j = 1; j < dp[i].length; j++) {
        // If we can fit it, then do so. Remember that j
        // represents the remaining weight in the bag.
        if (j - W[i - 1] >= 0) {
          int currValue = V[i - 1];
          int prevMaxProfit = dp[i - 1][j];
          int remainingWeight = j - W[i - 1];
          int remainingWeightMaxProfit = dp[i - 1][remainingWeight];
          dp[i][j] = Math.max(prevMaxProfit, currValue + remainingWeightMaxProfit);
        } else {
          dp[i][j] = dp[i - 1][j];
        }
      }
    }
    return dp[V.length][m];
  }
}
```

3.2 Collections

In this section we will introduce the *Java Collections framework*. In doing so we will discuss three broad classifications of data structures provided by the API:

1. Sequential-based
2. Dictionary-based
3. Set-based

Our discussion will not be all-inclusive of every data structure in the API, but we present those that we feel are most valuable to readers.

3.2.1 Sequential-Based Data Structures

We categorize data structures that have an ordering over the natural numbers as *sequential-based*. That is, each element has an index where it "lives" for its lifetime. Each index is, similar to standard arrays, numbered from zero to the size of the collection minus one. Let's now dive into these different sequential collections.

ArrayList Class

Arrays are fixed-size data structures; once they are initialized, they cannot, themselves, be resized. A solution to this problem (i.e., the problem of non-resizable arrays) is to create a new array A' of the same type with a new size, and copy the elements from the old array into A'. Doing so is not difficult, but cumbersome to repeatedly implement. Consider a situation in which the number of elements to store is unknown at compile-time. We, therefore, cannot use an array without repeated resizing. The correct and colloquial solution involves the ArrayList class.

First, however, let's see how we might go about implementing a *dynamic array*, called a *list*, using only methods. Suppose we want to store positive integers in this list. We also want to be able to add, set, and retrieve elements at a specified index. We will continue to work with arrays for the time being to demonstrate what roadblocks we encounter with this approach, and then to understand the power of the ArrayList.

We need to design a few methods: makeList, addToList, getFromList, and setInList. At the end of the day, we want the programmer who uses these methods to not worry about resizing the array themselves; the logic within handles the "dirty work."

To better relate the problem to the ArrayList class implementation, we will design two versions of the makeList method: one that receives an initial size and one that does not. Designing two methods of the same name that receive different parameter types/quantities is known as *method overloading*, and we will see this further in our discussion on *classes* in Chapter 4. The makeList method returns an array of integers instantiated to the given size, or a base size of ten elements in the method that does not receive a parameter. Inside of the makeList method that does not receive a parameter, we invoke makeList(10) so as to not repeat code logic.

3.2 Collections

```java
class DIntArray {

  /**
   * Creates a "dynamic array" of the given size. Each free slot
   * is simulated with a value of -1.
   * @param size initial size of the list.
   * @return integer array with size slots.
   */
  static int[] makeList(int size) {
    int[] array = new int[size];
    for (int i = 0; i < array.length; i++) {
      array[i] = -1;
    }
    return array;
  }

  /**
   * Creates a "dynamic array" with ten spaces.
   * @return integer array with ten slots.
   */
  static int[] makeList() {
    return makeList(10);
  }
}
```

We now want a method that adds a value to a given "dynamic list," in this fashion. In particular, we know that indices whose elements are −1 correspond to "free/available" slots for the next value to-be added. The thing is, there is more to consider than just replacing the first-found instance of −1 with the desired value. We need to ensure that room exists for this new value, i.e., whether there is a −1 (free slot) to begin with. As such, we should design a local helper method that returns a resized list with the values copied over from the old list; the only difference being a doubling in element capacity. Then, inside addToList, we check to see if we were able to properly insert v into the list and, if not, resize and make a recursive call to addToList.[9] Regarding performance and memory usage, this is a suboptimal solution, since we could simply add v to index $|A|$ of the new array A', knowing that $|A'| = |A|$.

```java
import static Assertions.assertAll;
import static Assertions.assertArrayEquals;

class DIntArrayTester {

  @Test
  void testAdd() {
    int[] arr1 = makeList(5);
    int[] arr2 = addToList(arr1, 20);
    int[] arr3 = addToList(arr2, 350);
    assertAll(
      () -> assertArrayEquals(new int[]{20, -1, -1, -1, -1}, arr2),
      () -> assertArrayEquals(new int[]{20, 350, -1, -1, -1}, arr3));
  }
}
```

---

[9] We could use Arrays.copyOf, but it is important to understand *how* the copying occurs.

```
class DIntArray {

  /**
   * Doubles the capacity of a list, returning a
   * new list with the old elements copied over.
   * @param list old dynamic list to resize.
   * @return a new resized dynamic list.
   */
  private static int[] resize(int[] list) {
    int[] newList = new int[list.length * 2];
    for (int i = 0; i < list.length; i++) {
      newList[i] = list[i];
    }
    return newList;
  }
}
```

```
class DIntArray {

  /**
   * Adds a value to the next-available spot in the list.
   * We define next-available as the first -1 we find from the left.
   * @param list list to add v into.
   * @param v integer to insert.
   * @return new list with v added.
   */
  static int[] addToList(int[] list, int v) {
    boolean added = false;
    int[] newList = makeList(list.length);
    for (int i = 0; i < list.length; i++) {
      // If we haven't inserted the value yet and we found
      // a free slot, insert it and mark added as true.
      if (list[i] == -1 && !added) {
        newList[i] = v;
        added = true;
      } else {
        // Otherwise, just copy over the old value.
        newList[i] = list[i];
      }
    }
    if (!added) { return addToList(resize(newList), v); }
    else { return newList; }
  }
}
```

We have two remaining methods to design: getFromList and setInList. The former retrieves an element at a given index and the latter replaces the element at a given index. Both methods receive an index i that must be in-bounds, where in-bounds refers to not only the bounds of the array, i.e., neither negative nor exceeding the length of the list, but also the logical indices. The *logical indices* of a list are the indices in which (real) elements exist. For our purposes, these indices are from zero up until and excluding the first instance of -1. We will also design a helper method to retrieve the index of the first "free" slot of a list, i.e., the (index of the) first occurrence of -1.

3.2 Collections

```java
class DIntArray {

  /**
   * Retrieves a value at a given index from the specified
   * dynamic list.
   * @param list dynamic list.
   * @param idx index to retrieve.
   * @return value at the given index.
   */
  static int getFromList(int[] list, int idx) {
    int upperBound = getFirstFreeSlot(list);
    return (idx < 0 || >= upperBound) ? -1 : list[idx];
  }

  /**
   * Finds the first "free slot" in a given dynamic list.
   * @param list dynamic list.
   * @return index of first occurrence of -1, or -1 if it doesn't exist.
   */
  private static int getFirstFreeSlot(int[] list) {
    for (int i = 0; i < list.length; i++) {
      if (list[i] == -1) { return i; }
    }
    return -1;
  }
}
```

```java
class DIntArray {

  /**
   * Sets a value in a dynamic list.
   * @param list dynamic list.
   * @param idx index to replace.
   * @param v value to replace at the index.
   * @return new dynamic list with the replaced value,
   * or null if the index is incorrect.
   */
  static int[] setInList(int[] list, int idx, int v) {
    int upperBound = getFirstFreeSlot(list);
    if (idx < 0 || idx >= upperBound) {
      return null;
    } else {
      // Copy over old elements.
      int[] newList = makeList(list.length);
      for (int i = 0; i < list.length; i++) {
        newList[i] = i == idx ? v : list[i];
      }
      return newList;
    }
  }
}
```

It should be noted that our implementation is a *persistent list*, which means that the (old) passed list, in and of itself, is not altered. Rather, we create a new list with each successive modification.

So, the problems of relying only on methods become clear: we have no way of keeping track of when/where the last *logical element* is located. By assuming an input of only positive integers, we can say that the first occurrence of a -1 marks the next-available spot to add

> **Java Array Lists**
>
> An *ArrayList* is a dynamically-sized data structure for storing elements.
>
> `List<T> A = new ArrayList<>()` creates an `ArrayList` of type T named A.
> T `A.get(`i`)` retrieves the element at index i^{th} of A. We refer to this as position $i+1$.
> `void A.set(`i, v`)` assigns v to index i of A.
> `int A.size()` returns the number of logical elements in the list, i.e., the logical size.
> `boolean` A_1`.equals(`A_2`)` returns whether or not the elements of A_1 are equal to the elements of A_2, using the equals method implementation of A_1.
> `String A.toString()` returns a string representation of the elements in A, separated by commas and enclosed by brackets.
> `void Collections.sort(`A`)` performs an in-place sort of A, meaning the contents of A are modified.

Fig. 3.2: Useful `ArrayList`-based Methods.

a value. *Sentinel indicators* like these fall apart once we allow different kinds of inputs, e.g., negative numbers.

The Java `ArrayList` class is a dynamic list data structure, is our first look at a "powerful" data structure insofar as its capabilities are concerned. Additionally, it is the first class that we have seen to incorporate *parameterized types*. With arrays, we specify the type upon declaration; the `ArrayList` class is *generic* in the sense that it operates over any type, whether that is `Integer`, `String`, or anything else, making it an incredibly flexible data structure.

What makes an `ArrayList` so convenient is the abstraction and encapsulation of the underlying data structure. Underneath lies a primitive array that is resized whenever necessary, similar to our resizing method. Thankfully, us as the programmers need not to worry about its implementation, but understanding it is key to grasping just what makes an improvement over our previous design of creating static methods that receive and return lists. First, like we said, our methods-based implementation of dynamic lists is restricted to one datatype, namely `int`, and also uses -1 as a "sentinel." Conversely, `ArrayList` stores a number that references the next-available spot, meaning we do not need to waste time traversing the list for every instance of adding or modifying elements. The `ArrayList` class also does not use an arbitrary sentinel value that cannot be used as an element.

To declare an `ArrayList` called A, we write the following, where T is a class representing the type of A's elements:

```
List<T> A = new ArrayList<>();
```

This line of code initializes a `List` A, but instantiates it as a new `ArrayList`.[10] Notice that we do not specify the capacity, like we would an array. Indeed, because lists are dynamic, there is no need to specify a default. Java defaults the starting size of a newly-declared `ArrayList` to ten elements, although this *can* be changed by passing a size argument between the parentheses.

```
List<T> A = new ArrayList<>(100);
```

You might be tempted to ask, "Why might it be a good idea to provide a capacity of my own?", which is a great question. Remember that resizing an array depends on the number

---

[10] The reason behind this *polymorphic* choice will become apparent in subsequent chapters. Moreover, all examples until our section on `LinkedList` will initialize lists as `List`, but instantiate them as `ArrayList`.

of pre-existing elements. Thus, the fewer (number of) resizes there are, the better, hence why we double the array capacity in our functional list implementation. If we know that we might have a lot of elements to add to the list from the start, it is helpful to provide this as an argument to the `ArrayList`. On average, adding a value to the end of an `ArrayList` is a *constant cost*, or occurs instantaneously, because we know exactly where the next free spot is located. We cannot forget the time needed to resize, however, so we declare that the `.add` method takes constant time with respect to *amortized analysis*. In essence, sometimes we perform a resize-and-copy operation, but on average, we do not, meaning the considered cost is negligible.

Like arrays, modifying elements in-place and retrieval also has a constant cost; the underlying data structure is an array after all. We retrieve a value at a given index using `.get`, and we replace an existing value at a given index using `.set`.

Example 3.15. If we instantiate an `ArrayList` of integers ls1, we can perform several operations to demonstrate our understanding.

```
List<Integer> ls1 = new ArrayList<>();
ls1.add(439);
ls1.add(311);
ls1.add(654);
ls1.add(523);
ls1.toString();    => {439, 311, 654, 523}
ls1.get(0);        => 439
ls1.set(1, 212);
ls1.add(677);
ls1.toString()     => {439, 212, 654, 523, 677}
```

Finally, we can remove an element, when given its index, using `.remove`. Be aware that removing elements is not as simple as adding one. Suppose that, from the previous example, we invoke ls1.remove(2), which removes the value 654. The slot where 654 previously existed cannot be vacant, so the `ArrayList` class compensates by shifting all elements to the right of the removed element one index to the left.

Example 3.16. Consider a situation in which we have an `ArrayList` that contains $1,000,000$ arbitrary integers. If we continuously remove elements from its front, each value is shifted down by one index. Propagating the act of shifting through all one million elements results in a hefty operational cost of $999,999 + 999,998 + \cdots + 3 + 2 + 1$ shifts. So, removing n elements from the front of an `ArrayList` is representable as an equation of time T:

$$T(n) = (n-1) + (n-2) + (n-3) + \cdots + 3 + 2 + 1$$

We can collapse this into an arithmetic series from 1 to $n-1$:

$$T(n) = \sum_{i=1}^{n-1} i$$
$$= n \cdot \left(\frac{1+n-1}{2}\right)$$
$$= n \cdot \left(\frac{n}{2}\right)$$
$$= \frac{n^2}{2}$$

Therefore, to remove 1,000,000 elements from the front of an `ArrayList`, we need to perform roughly $1,000,000^2/2$ operations, which is an astronomical number, even for computers of today. Removing elements from other indices, excluding the rear, will incur a (smaller) similar penalty due to shifts. As we will examine later in this chapter, there are better data structure choices when we need to consistently remove elements from the front of a list.

Example 3.17. We made a big deal about growing the underlying array when we run out of room to add new elements. We could ask a similar question about what to do when we remove lots of elements from a substantially large list. For instance, if our list contains one million elements, and we then clear the list, it makes little sense (at first glance) to have allocated space for one million non-existent values. Though, Java's implementation of `ArrayList` does *not* decrease the size of the backing array, preferring performance over memory usage. The reasoning behind this design choice is as follows: suppose we have an `ArrayList` of 500 elements and we remove 250 elements. Is it a good idea to decrease the size of the list by a factor of two? If so, what happens when we add one more element, totaling to 251? We then have to grow the underlying array, again, wasting valuable time.

Example 3.18. Consider the following code. What does s contain after execution?

```
List<Integer> ls1 = new ArrayList<>();
ls1.add(10);
List<Integer> ls2 = ls1;
ls2.add(20);
ls1.add(30);
String s = ls1.toString() + " " + ls2.toString();
```

Should you be unaware of aliasing, you might say it resolves to `"[10, 30] [20]"`. *Aliasing* is a form of object-sharing. When allocating any type of *object*, whether that object is an array, an `ArrayList`, a `String`, or something else, we assign a reference *to* that object in memory via the variable declaration. That is, in the preceding code, ls1 references the location, in memory, of an `ArrayList`. Correspondingly, when we declare ls2 and assign to it ls1, we are not copying over the values from ls1 into ls2. Rather, we are expressing that ls2 references the same list as referenced by ls1. Therefore, by asserting that ls2 as an alias of ls1, any modifications made to either is reflected when referencing the other. In this instance, s resolves to `"[10, 20, 30] [10, 20, 30]"`

Example 3.19. Consider two methods `void increment(int x)`, which increments an integer variable, and `void increment(ArrayList<Integer> ls, int idx)`, which increments the value at a given index in a list of integers.

```
static void incrementInt(int x) {
  x = x + 1;
}
static void incrementList(ArrayList<Integer> ls, int idx) {
  ls.set(idx, ls.get(idx) + 1);
}
```

If we pass a variable to the `incrementInt` method, we might expect the resulting value, outside of the method, to also be incremented. This is a misconception—in the following code segment, we observe that the primitive variable y remains unchanged outside of the method invocation. This happens because primitive values are *passed by value*. Methods receive a copy of the variable value, which means that the original variable is not modified, and the change(s) made inside the scope of `incrementInt` are non-existent outside its scope. Compare this to what happens if we pass an `ArrayList<Integer>` to `incrementList`: we see that the

3.2 Collections

change occurs both inside and outside the scope of the method body. Objects, e.g., String, ArrayList, arrays, and so forth, when supplied as arguments to methods, are passed by what we call *pseudo-reference*.[11] Passing by pseudo-reference means to suggest that we are not truly passing the argument by reference, and this is correct. Objects in Java are still passed by value, but instead of creating a copy of the object, the method receives an object reference value, which points to the location in memory where the object is allocated. Therefore, any changes made to the value inside the method are reflected outside the method.

```
int y = 5;
assertEquals(5, y);        // Assertion before increment.
incrementInt(y);
assertEquals(5, y);        // Assertion after increment.

List<Integer> ls = new ArrayList<>();
ls.add(5);
assertEquals(5, ls.get(0)); // Assertion before increment.
incrementList(ls, 0);
assertEquals(6, ls.get(0)); // Assertion after increment.
```

Example 3.20. We have seen the repeated use of the Integer and Double classes when parameterizing the types for ArrayList, but what is the point? Could we not instead opt for int and double, as we have traditionally? The answer is a resounding no; we must take advantage of the luxury that is Java *autoboxing* and *autounboxing* through the *wrapper classes*. The classes Integer, Double, as well as Short, Byte, Long, Character, and Boolean are classes that encapsulate, or box, a corresponding primitive value. Parameterized types only work with class types; not primitives. So, for instance, if we want to work with an ArrayList of int elements, we are required to use the Integer wrapper class in our type declaration. We can declare an Integer using the following overly-verbose syntax:

```
Integer x = new Integer(42);
int y = x.getValue(); // y = 42.
```

We explicitly wrap the integer literal 42 in x, which is of Integer type, then unwrap its value to be stored in y. Manually wrapping and unwrapping primitives is tiresome and results in redundant code, hence why Java autoboxes and autounboxes values as necessary. For example, if we declare an ArrayList of Integer values, then add the primitive integer literal 42 to the list, Java autoboxes the literal into its Integer wrapper class. Going the other direction, if we want to iterate over the values in the list, we might use the enhanced-for loop. If Java did not natively support autounboxing, we instead have to use Integer in the loop variable declaration.

```
ArrayList<Integer> al = new ArrayList<>();
al.add(42);
for (int e : al) {
  ...
}
```

Example 3.21. Testing is always important when writing programs, as this text has emphasized from the first page. Naively writing test cases for lists is cumbersome due to the repetition of .add method calls. As an alternative, Java has the convenient List.of method,

---

[11] The emphasis on calling this "pseudo-reference" is to provide an intuition for those readers who may know about true pass-by-reference, while satisfying those who want to angrily shout that Java is strictly pass-by-value.

which receives any number of arguments and stores them in an *immutable list*. Because the resulting list is immutable, its contents cannot be updated/added/removed. If we want the list to be mutable, we can pass it to a new `ArrayList<>(...)`, which is exemplified at the bottom of the following listing:

```
// Old way:
List<Integer> ls1 = new ArrayList<>();
ls1.add(5);
ls1.add(40);
ls1.add(4);
ls1.add(42);
// New way:
List<Integer> ls2 = new ArrayList<>(List.of(5, 40, 4, 42));
```

Using `List.of` raises a question: does `List.of` only receive four integer arguments? What if I want to specify more than four arguments, or less than four? The answer to this excellent question is that `List.of` is a *variadic-argument method*. Variadic methods receive any number of arguments, which collapse into an iterable data structure.

Example 3.22. Suppose we want to design a variadic method that computes the average of some `double` values. Without variadic-argument methods, we would need to explicitly wrap these values into a list or an array, then pass it to the method. With them, we invoke the method with however many values we wish.

```
import static Assertions.assertAll;
import static Assertions.assertEquals;

class NumAverageTester {

  @Test
  void testNumAverage() {
    assertAll(
      () -> assertEquals(0, numAverage()),
      () -> assertEquals(5.66, numAverage(5, 2, 10)),
      () -> assertEquals(55.2, numAverage(10, 65, 77, 81, 43)));
  }
}
```

```
class NumAverage {

  /**
   * Computes the average of a sequence of provided integers.
   * @param nums variadic integers.
   * @return average if there is at least one number or zero otherwise.
   */
  static int numAverage(int ... nums) {
    double sum = 0;
    for (int e : nums) { sum += e; }
    return nums.length == 0 ? 0 : sum / nums.length;
  }
}
```

Example 3.23. If we want to, say, specify that a method receives at least two parameters, those being a `String` and an `int`, followed by zero or more `String` values, we may declare the first two parameters, then incorporate the variadic notation for the those remaining parameters. Doing so ensures that we pass the required parameters, but any thereafter are optional but variadic nonetheless.

3.2 Collections

```java
class RequiredVariadicParameters {

  static int doSomething(String s, int v, String ... vals) { ... }
}
```

Example 3.24. Let's design the `List<Character> explode(String s)` method, which receives a `String` and returns a list of its characters. We can solve the problem using recursion and iteration, so we shall develop all three versions. The recursive versions are, in this instance, more verbose than the iterative counterpart: the base case is when the string is empty, and in the recursive step, we add the first character of the string to a list and call the method with the remaining characters. The iterative version uses a loop over the characters and adds each to the list. This example proves yet again that, while recursion is beneficial for tasks that inhibit a recursive structure, iteration may express the solution more succinctly.

```java
import static Assertions.assertAll;
import static Assertions.assertEquals;

import java.util.List;

class ExplodeTester {

  @Test
  void testExplode() {
    assertAll(
      () -> assertEquals(List.of(), explode("")),
      () -> assertEquals(List.of('H', 'e', 'l', 'l', 'o'), explode("Hello")));
  }
}
```

```java
import java.util.List;

class Explode {

  /**
   * Explodes a string into a list of its characters.
   * @param s string to explode.
   * @return list of characters in the string.
   */
  static List<Character> explode(String s) {
    if (s.isEmpty()) {
      return new ArrayList<>();
    } else {
      List<Character> ls = new ArrayList<>();
      ls.add(s.charAt(0));
      ls.addAll(explode(s.substring(1)));
      return ls;
    }
  }
}
```

```java
class Explode {

  /**
   * Explodes a string into a list of its characters using tail recursion.
   * @param s string to explode.
   * @return list of chars in string.
   */
  static List<Character> explodeTR(String s) {
    List<Character> ls = new ArrayList<>();
    return explodeTR(s, ls);
  }

  /**
   * Tail recursive helper method for explodeTr.
   * @param s string to explode.
   * @param ls list to store characters.
   * @return list of chars in the string.
   */
  private static List<Character> explodeTRHelper(String s, List<Character> ls) {
    if (s.isEmpty()) {
      return ls;
    } else {
      ls.add(s.charAt(0));
      return explodeTRHelper(s.substring(1), ls);
    }
  }
}
```

```java
import java.util.List;

class Explode {

  /**
   * Explodes a string into a list of its characters.
   * @param s string to explode.
   * @return list of characters in the string.
   */
  static List<Character> explode(String s) {
    List<Character> ls = new ArrayList<>();
    for (int i = 0; i < s.length(); i++) {
      ls.add(s.charAt(i));
    }
    return ls;
  }
}
```

Example 3.25. Let's design the List<Integer> takeEvens(List<Integer> ls, int n) method that retrieves the first n even integers from a list of integers ls. If there are less than n even integers, then all of those are retrieved. Note that the given list is *not* modified; we instead return a new list with the desired contents. All we must do is keep track of a counter as to how many even numbers we have seen thus far and ensure that we have not gone out of bounds of the list. Now, we *could* declare a local variable, say countEvens, to keep track of the number of even values seen. Though, a for loop is not restricted to only one variable declaration, so why not include it in the mix? In addition to our index variable i, let's also declare countEvens as zero, and have the loop condition terminate when either i is at the end of the list or countEvens is equal to n. We only increment countEvens when we encounter an even integer. Furthermore, note that we need enough tests to account for all possible inputs, those being when n is less than the number of evens and when it exceeds or is greater than that count.

```java
import static Assertions.assertAll;
import static Assertions.assertEquals;

import java.util.List;

class TakeEvensTester {

  @Test
  void testTakeEvens() {
    List<Integer> l1 = List.of(41, 42, 90, 50, 80, 75, 73);
    List<Integer> l2 = List.of();
    assertAll(
       () -> assertEquals(List.of(42, 90, 50), takeEvens(l1, 3)),
       () -> assertEquals(List.of(42), takeEvens(l1, 1)),
       () -> assertEquals(List.of(), takeEvens(l2, 5)),
       () -> assertEquals(List.of(), takeEvens(l2, 0)));
  }
}
```

```java
import java.util.List;

class TakeEvens {

  /**
   * Returns a list of a given number of even integers from the list.
   * If there are less than n even integers, all of them are returned,
   * and if there are at least n even integers, those n are returned.
   * @param ls list of integers.
   * @param n number of even integers to potentially retrieve.
   * @return a list of even integers.
   */
  static List<Integer> takeEvens(List<Integer> ls, int n) {
    List<Integer> res = new ArrayList<>();
    for (int i = 0, countEvens = 0; i < ls.size() && countEvens < n; i++) {
      if (ls.get(i) % 2 == 0) {
        res.add(ls.get(i));
        countEvens++;
      }
    }
    return res;
  }
}
```

Example 3.26. Let's design the `void filterQuarters(List<String> times)` method that, when given a list of strings representing times in the 24-hour format, e.g., "12:30" or "17:55", removes all times that are in fifteen-minute intervals. First, we should design a helper method that returns whether a time *is* a fifteen-minute interval. That is, its number of minutes is either "0", "15", "30", or "45". Aside from the helper, the method definition itself is nothing special–requiring exactly one traversal over the data. Importantly, though, notice that `filterQuarters` returns `void` rather than, say, a list of strings. The method updates the `times` list itself, which means that any list we pass is updated/changed inside the method. In Chapter 4, we will explore methods like these that cause *side-effects* in relation

to user-defined classes. For now, testing a void method means that we must instantiate a
List<String> above the test, pass it to filterQuarters, and then check to see if the change
occurred. Normally, we pass the filterQuarters invocation as the second argument to assertEquals, since it traditionally returns the value-to-check. In this circumstance, however,
we must separately call filterQuarters, then assert whether the list that we pass, after
being affected on by filterQuarters, now contains the desired result.

```java
import static Assertions.assertAll;
import static Assertions.assertEquals;

import java.util.List;

class FilterQuartersTester {

  @Test
  void testFilterQuarters() {
    List<String> t1 = List.of("11:37", "12:00", "18:15", "19:25", "10:30" "9:45");
    List<String> t2 = List.of();
    assertAll(
      () -> filterQuarters(t1),
      () -> assertEquals(List.of("11:37", "19:25"), t1),
      () -> filterQuarters(t2),
      () -> assertEquals(List.of(), t2));
  }
}
```

```java
import java.util.List;

class FilterQuarters {

  /**
   * Removes all times from a list of "times." A time is a string "XX:YY"
   * such that 0 <=XX<= 23, and 00<=YY<= 59;
   * This method modifies the list in-place.
   * @param times list of times.
   */
  static void filterQuarters(List<String> times) {
    for (int i = 0; i < times.length(); i++) {
      if (isQuarterHour(times.get(i))) {
        times.remove(i);
        i--; // We need to subtract one so we don't go out of bounds!
      }
    }
  }

  /**
   * Returns whether a time is a "quarter." A quarter is either 0, 15, 30, or 45.
   * @param t string representing time as XX:YY, where 00<=XX<=23, and 00<=YY<= 59.
   * @return true if quarter; false otherwise.
   */
  private static boolean isQuarterHour(String t) {
    int mins = Integer.parseInt(t.substring(t.length() - 2));
    return mins == 0 || mins == 15 || mins == 30 || mins == 45;
  }
}
```

Example 3.27. Let's design another method that processes units of time, only instead, we
will parse the strings as "airplane travel information." A string containing airplane travel

3.2 Collections

information is a four-segment string, separated by semicolons:

"FLIGHT-ID;NUM-PASSENGERS;START-TIME;END-TIME"

where FLIGHT-ID is a two-character identifier for the flight, NUM-PASSENGERS is an integer denoting how many passengers are on the flight, START-TIME and END-TIME are units of time denoting the flight's start time and ending-time respectively. The difference between these units and those of the previous question is that START-TIME and END-TIME do not have a colon between the hour and minute components. An example of airplane travel information is U2;265;0900;1215.

We will design the String getShortestFlight(List<String> L) method that, when given a list of airplane travel information, returns the flight identifier of the flight whose trip duration is the shortest. Trip duration is the difference in a flight's end-time and start-time. There are two possible kinds of differences to consider:

- When both times are before midnight.
- When the start time is before midnight and the ending time is after midnight.

In the first case, suppose we have the airplane travel information "L4;65;1825;2100". Its flight is 2 hours and 35 minutes, or 155 minutes. To figure this out, we multiply the number of hours of both times by 60, add the minutes, then take the difference. Using the example, we get

$$\begin{aligned} &= (21 \cdot 60 + 0) - (18 \cdot 60 + 25) \\ &= 1260 - 1105 \\ &= 155 \end{aligned}$$

On the other hand, consider a flight that meets the second case criteria: "K16;280;2230;0128". If we naively apply the same approach to these times, we get a negative time result rather than the actual time duration of 178 minutes. A negative time duration is nonsensical. The solution, only in these circumstances, is to add 24 hours to the ending time, which amounts to 1440 minutes. After this modification, everything remains the same.

$$\begin{aligned} &= (24 \cdot 60 + 1 \cdot 60 + 28) - (22 \cdot 60 + 30) \\ &= (1440 + 88) - (1320 + 30) \\ &= 1528 - 1350 \\ &= 178 \end{aligned}$$

We'll design a helper method that computes the time difference, in minutes, when supplied with starting and ending (flight) times. Because it is easy to make arithmetic mistakes, we won't privatize the method, so we can handle test cases.[12]

To retrieve the start and end times of a flight, we can partition the data into four substrings using split on a string, passing to it the semicolon character. The split method returns an array of the substrings between the provided delimiter. For example, "123.456.789.012".split(".") returns an array ["123", "456", "789", "012"]. The start time, therefore, is the third substring, and the end time is the fourth substring.

---

[12] In our code, we have "magic numbers" such as 60, 24, and 1440. In larger projects, such numbers should be refactored into named constants, but due to the limited scope of the method, we will not do so.

```java
import static Assertions.assertAll;
import static Assertions.assertEquals;

import java.util.List;

class AirplaneTravelInformationTester {

  @Test
  void testAirplaneTravelInformation() {
    List<String> l1 = List.of("Z4;215;1700;1645");
    List<String> l2 = List.of("P3;240;0930;1130",
                              "L9;500;2245;0223",
                              "K2;330;1230;1800",
                              "L1;400;1955;2050",
                              "C1;110;0000;1330");
    assertAll(
        () -> assertEquals("Z4", shortestDurationFlight(l1)),
        () -> assertEquals("L1", shortestDurationFlight(l2)));
  }

  @Test
  void testTimeDurationDifference() {
    assertAll(
        () -> assertEquals(330, timeDifference("1230", "1800")),
        () -> assertEquals(257, timeDifference("2130", "0147")),
        () -> assertEquals(810, timeDifference("0000", "1330")),
        () -> assertEquals(245, timeDifference("1955", "0000")));
  }
}
```

```java
import java.util.List;

class AirplaneTravelInformation {

  /**
   * Given two times in the format "HHMM", return the difference in minutes.
   * @param t1 first time.
   * @param t2 second time.
   * @return the difference in minutes between t1 and t2.
   */
  static int timeDifference(String t1, String t2) {
    int hrT1 = Integer.parseInt(t1.substring(0, 2));
    int minT1 = Integer.parseInt(t1.substring(2));
    int hrT2 = Integer.parseInt(t2.substring(0, 2));
    int minT2 = Integer.parseInt(t2.substring(2));

    // Case 1: when t1 <= t2.
    if (hrT1 < hrT2 || (hrT1 <= hrT2 && minT1 <= minT2)) {
      return (hrT2 * 60 + minT2) - (hrT1 * 60 + minT1);
    } else {
      // Case 2: when t1 > t2.
      return (1440 + hrT2 * 60 + minT2) - (hrT1 * 60 + minT1);
    }
  }

  /**
   * Given a non-empty list of flights, return the flight id of
   * the flight with the shortest duration.
   * A flight is represented by a string with the following format:
```

```
 * "FLIGHT-ID;NUM-PASSENGERS;START-TIME;END-TIME"
 * @param flights non-empty list of flights.
 * @return the flight id of the flight with the shortest duration.
 */
static String shortestDurationFlight(List<String> flights) {
  int shortestFlight = Integer.MAX_VALUE;
  String shortestFlightId = null;
  for (String flightInfo : flights) {
    String[] flightDetails = flightInfo.split(";");
    int duration = timeDifference(flightDetails[2], flightDetails[3]);
    if (duration < shortestFlight) {
      shortestFlight = duration;
      shortestFlightId = flightDetails[0];
    }
  }
  return shortestFlightId;
}
```

Example 3.28. Let's complete one final problem using array lists. Given a list of lists of integers that forms a triangle, we want to return the maximum sum of any path from the top to the bottom.[13]

While faster solutions exist (as demonstrated later), we will use a brute-force approach that recursively computes the sum of all possible paths from the top to the bottom. We need to keep track of what row we are on, as well as the index of the element in that row. Each element can visit two other elements in the row: the element at its index and the element at its index plus one. Let's break the problem down by first designing a method that returns the two indices that a given index can visit. Given an index and a level, the getAdjacentPaths method returns a two-element array containing the indices of the two elements that the given index can visit. For example, if the index is 1 and the level is 2, it can visit the elements in level 3 at indices 1 and 2.

Without a visualization, this problem can be difficult to understand, so let's provide an example. The below triangle has four rows of 1, 2, 3, and 4 elements respectively. For any triangle of n rows, there are 2^{n-1} possible paths from the top to the bottom, given the aforesaid constraints. The goal is to find the sum of the path that has the maximum sum of all paths in the triangle. The possible paths are also calculated, in which we observe that path $9 + 2 + 8 + 5$, marked in red with a sum of 24, is the max.

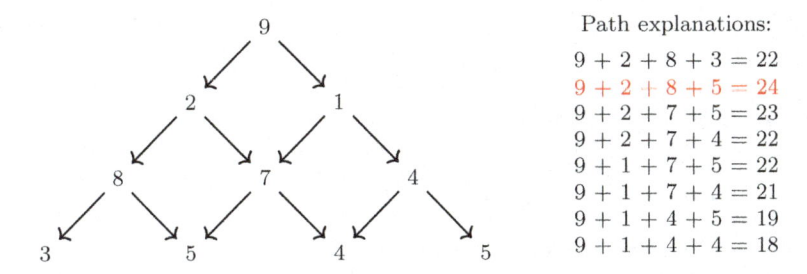

Path explanations:

$9 + 2 + 8 + 3 = 22$
$9 + 2 + 8 + 5 = 24$
$9 + 2 + 7 + 5 = 23$
$9 + 2 + 7 + 4 = 22$
$9 + 1 + 7 + 5 = 22$
$9 + 1 + 7 + 4 = 21$
$9 + 1 + 4 + 5 = 19$
$9 + 1 + 4 + 4 = 18$

Now, we will design the method itself. When designing recursive algorithms, we must consider all valid base cases. In this case, we have one: if we are at the bottom of the triangle,

---

[13] This problem comes courtesy of Project Euler. Thanks!

we return the value at the given index. Otherwise, we recursively call the method on the two adjacent paths, sum the value at the current index, and return the maximum of the two recursive calls. We store the result of the left and right recursive calls, and add the maximum of the two to the current value. Disappointingly, the solution is nowhere near efficient, requiring exponential time, but it serves as a good exercise in recursion.

```java
import static Assertions.assertAll;
import static Assertions.assertEquals;

class MaxPathSumTester {

  @Test
  void testGetAdjacentPaths() {
    assertAll(
      () -> assertArrayEquals(new int[]{2, 3}, getAdjacentPaths(1, 1)),
      () -> assertArrayEquals(new int[]{4, 5}, getAdjacentPaths(2, 2)),
      () -> assertArrayEquals(new int[]{6, 7}, getAdjacentPaths(3, 3)));
  }

  @Test
  void testMaxSum() {
    List<List<Integer>> t0 = List.of();
    List<List<Integer>> t1 = List.of(
      List.of(3),
      List.of(7, 4),
      List.of(2, 4, 6),
      List.of(8, 5, 9, 3));
    assertAll(
      () -> assertEquals(0, maxSum(t0)),
      () -> assertEquals(23, maxSum(t1)));
  }
}
```

```java
class MaxPathSum {

  /**
   * Computes the maximum sum of any path from the top to the bottom
   * of a triangle.
   * @param ls list of lists of integers.
   * @return max sum.
   */
  static int maxPathSum(List<List<Integer>> ls) {
    return ls.isEmpty() ? 0 : maxPathSumHelper(ls, 0, 0);
  }

  /**
   * Returns the two indices that a given index can visit.
   * @param idx index of element.
   * @param level level of element.
   * @return two indices that the given index can visit.
   */
  static int[] getAdjacentPaths(int idx, int level) {
    return new int[]{idx, idx + 1};
  }
```

```
/**
 * Computes the maximum sum of any path from the top to the bottom.
 * @param triangle list of lists of integers.
 * @param i index of element.
 * @param l level of element.
 * @return maximum sum of any path from the top to the bottom.
 */
private static int maxPathSizeHelper(List<List<Integer>> triangle, int i, int l) {
  if (l == triangle.size() - 1) {
    return triangle.get(l).get(i);
  } else {
    int[] adjacentPaths = getAdjacentPaths(idx, level);
    int left = maxSum(ls, level + 1, adjacentPaths[0]);
    int right = maxSum(ls, level + 1, adjacentPaths[1]);
    return ls.get(level).get(idx) + Math.max(left, right);
  }
}
```

We can substantially improve (the performance of) our solution by once again using dynamic programming. Rather than computing paths recursively from the top to the bottom, we can start from the bottom and work our way up, storing the maximum sum of any path from the bottom to the current element. Though, because the structure-of-interest is not rectangular, a two-dimensional array is not an optimal dynamic programming data structure choice. Our input L is a list of lists, so let's utilize another list of lists L' to hold precomputed values. We need to instantiate each element to a new array list, then add the last row of values from the input list into the dynamic programming list. From here, we traverse up through the triangle, for every row $r \in L$, and for every element r_i of r, if r is the nth row in L, compute the adjacent cells in the $(i+1)^{\text{th}}$ row of L', then assign to r_i in L' the maximum of the sum of r_i and the adjacent cells. That was a lot of notation, so let's walk through an example. To follow along, recall that the inputs to max are the adjacent cells in the row immediately below the row-of-interest.

Assume $L = [[2], [9, 4], [3, 5, 4], [7, 8, 6, 10]]$. Then, L' is initialized to $[[], [], [], [7, 8, 6, 10]]$. Row 3 of L', therefore, becomes

$$[3 + \max\{7, 8\}, 5 + \max\{8, 6\}, 4 + \max\{6, 10\}]$$
$$[11, 13, 14]$$

Row 2 of L', therefore, becomes

$$[9 + \max\{11, 13\}, 4 + \max\{13, 14\}]$$
$$[22, 18]$$

Finally, row 1 of L', therefore, becomes

$$[2 + \max\{22, 18\}]$$
$$[24]$$

```java
import java.util.ArrayList;
import java.util.List;

class MaxPathSum {

  /**
   * Dynamic programming solution to the maximum path sum problem.
   * @param ls given triangle.
   * @return the maximum path sum.
   */
  static int maxSumDp(List<List<Integer>> ls) {
    List<Integer> lastRow = ls.getLast();
    List<List<Integer>> dp = new ArrayList<>();

    // Initialize each row with an empty list.
    for (int i = 0; i < ls.size(); i++) {
      dp.add(new ArrayList<>());
    }

    // Initialize the last row with the values from the last row of the triangle.
    for (int i = 0; i < lastRow.size(); i++) {
      dp.get(ls.size() - 1).add(lastRow.get(i));
    }

    // Get the ith row in the triangle and the (i+1)th row in the dp table.
    for (int i = ls.size() - 2; i >= 0; i--) {
      List<Integer> row = ls.get(i); // The current row.
      List<Integer> dpRow = dp.get(i + 1); // The prev. row with already computed vals.
      for (int j = 0; j < row.size(); j++) {
        // Add the current val to the max of the two adjacent values in the next row.
        int[] adjPaths = getAdjacentPaths(j, i);
        int left = dpRow.get(adjPaths[0]);
        int right = dpRow.get(adjPaths[1]);
        int curr = row.get(j);
        dp.get(i).add(curr + Math.max(left, right));
      }
    }
    return dp.getFirst().getFirst();
  }
}
```

LinkedList Class

Linked lists remove us from the shackles of array-based data structures in that, as their name implies, they are a series of *nodes*, or elements, linked together in a chain of sorts. These nodes need not be adjacent in memory (like the elements of arrays), but rather reference each other to find what comes next in the chain/list. For instance, if we create a linked list, it has a *front/head* element that always references, or points, to the first element in the list (upon initialization, the head refers to nothing). If we add a new element, the head now points to this first element. Subsequent additions to the list continue growing the chain and links. Namely, element 1 points to element 2, element 2 to 3, and so on.

Elements have an associated index and value, but linked lists are not constrained to a static size, even in the underlying implementation. So, we can add and remove links from the chain whenever we please with no shuffling of values around aside from links within the chain.

3.2 Collections

> **Java Linked Lists**
>
> A *LinkedList* is a node-based data structure where each element contains a link to its successor (and potentially predecessor).
>
> List<T> A = new LinkedList<>() creates a LinkedList of type T named A.
> T A.get(i) retrieves the element at index i^{th} of A. We refer to this as position $i + 1$.
> void A.set(i, v) assigns v to index i of A.
> int A.size() returns the number of logical elements in the list, i.e., the logical size.

Fig. 3.3: Useful LinkedList-based Methods.

> **Java Stacks**
>
> A *Stack* is a last-in-first-out (LIFO) data structure where each element is linked to the element immediately below.
>
> Stack<T> S = new Stack<>() creates a Stack of type T, named S.
> T S.peek() returns, but does not remove, the top element of S.
> T S.pop() returns and removes the top element of S.
> void S.push(e) pushes e to the top of S, making e the element on the top of the stack.
> int S.size() returns the number of logical elements in the stack.

Fig. 3.4: Useful Stack-based Methods.

Removing elements from the front of a linked list takes constant time, and scales linearly with the number of elements in the list rather than as a quadratic growth.

Of course, these advantages are not without their disadvantages. Reading and modifying elements are slower operations than their array counterparts since the elements are not contiguous blocks in memory. Recall that, with an ArrayList, because elements sequentially located in memory, we know the location of any arbitrary index in the array list as a multiplicative offset of the starting index and the "byte-size" of each element. Accordingly, each node is located at an unpredictable place in memory, meaning we lose the constant access time granted by array lists. Adding and removing elements are "faster" in the sense that, as we stated, linked lists do not copy and resize buffers. Because of this, we need to iterate/-traverse through the linked list every time we want to reference a provided index. The same goes for inserting elements into the list. Adding or removing elements from the front or rear of the list, on the other hand, are instant (constant time) operations, since we keep track of the first element of the list (and we can, similarly, keep track of the last!). Linked lists are also the backbone of many other data structures, as we will soon see.

Stack Class

Imagine you are washing dishes, by hand, at the kitchen sink. The dishes are assorted in a single stack to your left. A dish cannot be removed from anywhere but the top of the stack, because displacement anywhere else will destroy the stack. Additionally, further imagine that people are, to your dismay, adding more dishes to the stack. Again, dishes cannot be added anywhere else but the top of the stack, otherwise it disrupts the stack.

The *stack* data structure is as simple as it sounds—a collection of elements that operate on the principle of last-in-first-out, or LIFO. In other words, the last thing that we enter is the first thing removed. Stack implementations contain at least the following operations: POP and PUSH, where the former removes the top-most element from the stack (if one exists), and the latter adds a new element to the top of the stack. There may also exist an operation to view, but not remove, the top-most element via PEEK.

Stacks have the advantages of instant insertion and removal times, but are obviously not as flexible as an array or linked list. A practical example of a stack data structure would be to implement an "undo" function in a document-editing program—whenever an action is made, it is pushed to an event stack. An "undo" event resembles popping an action off this stack. We illustrate this concept in Figure 3.5.

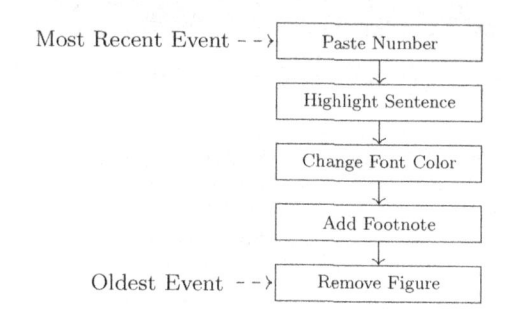

```
Most Recent Event --> | Paste Number |
                              ↓
                      | Highlight Sentence |
                              ↓
                      | Change Font Color |
                              ↓
                      | Add Footnote |
                              ↓
   Oldest Event   --> | Remove Figure |
```

Fig. 3.5: Example of "Undo" Event Stack in Text-Editing Program

Example 3.29. As a very basic example of working with the Stack data structure, let's design the int sumOdds(Stack<Integer> S) method that, when given a stack of integers S, returns the sum of all odd integer elements. Remember that we cannot access arbitrary elements of the stack. So, for now, all we can do is traverse over the stack using a while loop until it has no elements remaining. That is, while the stack is non-empty, pop the top-most element, examine if it is odd and, if so, add it to our running total. We present the following example to demonstrate some of the methods that Java's Stack class provides.[14]

```java
import static Assertions.assertAll;
import static Assertions.assertEquals;
import java.util.Stack;

class StackSumOddsTester {

  @Test
  void testSumOdds() {
    Stack<Integer> S1 = new Stack<>();
    Stack<Integer> S2 = new Stack<>(List.of(5, 12, 13, 24, 91, 108));
    assertAll(
      () -> assertEquals(0, sumOdds(S1)),
      () -> assertEquals(109, sumOdds(S2)));
  }
}
```

---

[14] By providing a List to the Stack constructor, i.e., new Stack<>(List.of(...)), we do not need to write repeated calls to push on the stack object.

```java
import java.util.Stack;

class StackSumOdds {

  /**
   * Sums the odd numbers in a given stack of integers.
   * @param S stack of integers.
   * @return sum of odd integers.
   */
  static int sumOdds(Stack<Integer> S) {
    int sum = 0;
    while (!S.isEmpty()) {
      int top = S.pop();
      sum += top % 2 != 0 ? top : 0;
    }
    return sum;
  }
}
```

Queue Interface

Imagine you are in line at an amusement park for the most intense roller coaster in the world. Another, perhaps more generic term for a "line" is a *queue*. In this metaphor, riders enqueue the line at the back and board the roller coaster (and hence dequeue from the line) at the front.

What we have described is a practical example of the queue data structure. In a queue, elements are enqueued, or inserted, onto the back of the queue, and are dequeued, or removed, from the front. Queues operate on the principle of first-in-first-out, or FIFO. The implementation of a queue data structure may contain different names for their operations, but at their core should contain operations for inserting an element to the back of the queue (e.g., ENQUEUE) and removing an element from the front of the queue (e.g., DEQUEUE).

Like the operations of a stack, ENQUEUE and DEQUEUE are also constant-time, since we store references to the front and rear elements of a queue. Queues, consequently, share similar drawbacks to stacks in that elements are not randomly accessible, i.e., we only know what exists at the front and rear of a queue instantaneously. Figure 3.6 demonstrates the task queue of a printer, which has a sequence of files to print, one after another.

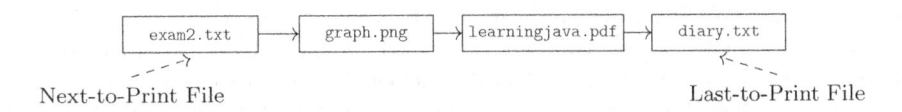

| exam2.txt | → | graph.png | → | learningjava.pdf | → | diary.txt |

Next-to-Print File   Last-to-Print File

Fig. 3.6: Example of Printer Task Queue

Unfortunately and inconveniently, there is no Queue class in Java. Instead, Queue is an *interface* that other classes implement whose structure models the behavior of a queue. To create a first-in-first-out queue data structure, we initialize a variable to be a Queue, then instantiate it as a LinkedList. Thankfully, the LinkedList class contains all the relevant methods for operating a FIFO-based queue.

```java
Queue<Integer> q = new LinkedList<>();
```

> **Java Queue**
>
> A *Queue* is a first-in-first-out (FIFO) sequential data structure where each element is linked to the element immediately after.
>
> Queue<*T*> *Q* = new LinkedList<>() creates a Queue of type *T*, named *Q*.
> void *Q*.addLast(*e*) adds *e* to the end of *Q*, placing it at the end of the queue structure.
> *T Q*.poll() returns and removes the element from the front of the queue.
> *T Q*.peek() returns the front-most element in the queue.
> int *Q*.size() returns the number of logical elements in the queue.

Fig. 3.7: Useful Queue-based Methods.

> **Java PriorityQueue**
>
> A *Priority queue* is a rank/score-based data structure wherein the ordering of elements is determined by either their natural ordering or a Comparator.
>
> PriorityQueue<*T*> *PQ* = new PriorityQueue<>(*c*) creates a PriorityQueue of type *T*, named *PQ*, with a Comparator *c* that is used to compare objects of type *T* within the priority queue.
> void *PQ*.add(*e*) inserts *e* into *PQ*, whose position in the priority queue depends on the currently-existing elements.
> *T PQ*.poll() returns and removes the element with the highest priority.
> *T PQ*.peek() returns the element with the highest priority.
> int *PQ*.size() returns the number of logical elements in the priority queue.

Fig. 3.8: Useful PriorityQueue-based Methods.

Treating q as a queue rather than a linked list is easy thanks to the methods supplied by the LinkedList implementation. Figure 3.7 shows some of these handy methods.

PriorityQueue Class

Priority queues are the final sequential data structure that we will discuss from the Collections framework. Though, placing priority queues in this section feels a bit disingenuous because, while priority queues have an ordering in their underlying data structure, saying that elements correspond to an index is a misnomer. Priority queues, as the name suggests, rank items in the queue by a score called the *priority*. Elements with the highest priority are at the "front" of the priority queue. Inserting elements into a priority queue potentially alters the positioning of preexisting elements.

Priority queues base priority on one of two contributing factors: either the *natural ordering* of elements, or a *comparator object*. The natural ordering of elements is straightforward: natural ordering for numbers is their standard numeric ordering from least to greatest. For strings, the natural ordering is their lexicographical ordering. Natural ordering, however, are not as interesting as comparators, which we will now discuss.

3.2 Collections

A *comparator* is a way of comparing two arbitrary "things." Whether these "things" are numbers (i.e., the wrapper classes), strings, or another kind of object, we can define custom ways of comparing *any* non-primitive datatype.

Example 3.30. Let's design a Comparator for prioritizing strings that start with the lowercase letter 'p' . Comparators are constructed like all other objects via new, but something interesting about their implementation is that we must specify *how* to compare two objects. Therefore, when we create a new instance of Comparator, we must also override its compare method. The compare method's signature varies based on the parameterized type provided to the comparator, but since we want to compare strings, we should declare it as follows:

```java
import java.util.Comparator;
import java.util.PriorityQueue;

class PriorityQueueByP {

  /**
   * Returns a priority queue that prioritizes strings
   * that start with `p'.
   * @return priority queue instance.
   */
  static PriorityQueue<String> priorityByP() {
    Comparator<String> c = new Comparator<>(
      @Override
      public int compare(String s1, String s2) { /* TODO. */ }
    );
  }
}
```

We now must describe how we want to compare s1 and s2 to achieve our goal. Strangely enough, if we want to say that s1 has a higher priority than s2, we must return a negative value, similar to the natural ordering of strings (this idea extends to any type we wish to compare, however). Fortunately, this is not as strange once we understand *why* the negative value is required. A value of −1 comes before 1 when placing numbers in ascending order. Consequently, when comparing an arbitrary value t_1 against t_2, to say that t_1 comes before t_2, we return a negative integer. Conversely, to say that t_1 comes after t_2, we return a positive number.

Let's perform a case analysis on the input strings. If both provided strings are non-empty, we retrieve their first character. If both start with 'p', then their ordering depends on a standard lexicographical comparison of the rest of the strings. If the first character of s_1 is 'p', however, we return −1 to designate that s_1 has a higher priority than s_2. Conversely, if s_2 starts with 'p', then we return 1 to designate the opposite. If neither start with p, then again we perform a lexicographical comparison on the entire strings. Algorithm 1 displays the pseudocode for the comparator, but as we will see, we can translate this, verbatim, into Java syntax. The last line of priorityByP instantiates a new PriorityQueue whose constructor receives the Comparator that we just designed.

Algorithm 1 Pseudocode for Comparing Two Strings For 'p' Priority

procedure COMPARE(s_1, s_2)
    if s_1 and s_2 are non-empty **then**
        $c_1 \leftarrow$ **First**(s_1)
        $c_2 \leftarrow$ **First**(s_2)
        if c_1 is 'p' **and** c_2 is 'p' **then**
            $xs_1 \leftarrow s_1.substring(1)$
            $xs_2 \leftarrow s_2.substring(1)$
            return $xs_1.compareTo(xs_2)$
        else if c_1 is 'p' **then**
            return -1
        else if c_2 is 'p' **then**
            return 1
        else
            return $s_1.compareTo(s_2)$
        end if
    else
        return $s_1.compareTo(s_2)$
    end if
end procedure

```java
import java.util.Comparator;
import java.util.PriorityQueue;

class PriorityQueueByP {

  static PriorityQueue<String> priorityByP() {
    Comparator<String> c = new Comparator<>() {
      @Override
      public int compare(String s1, String s2) {
        if (!s1.isEmpty() && !s2.isEmpty()) {
          char c1 = s1.charAt(0);
          char c2 = s2.charAt(0);
          if (c1 == 'p' && c2 == 'p') {
            return s1.substring(1).compareTo(s2.substring(1));
          } else if (c1 == 'p') {
            return -1;
          } else if (c2 == 'p') {
            return 1;
          } else {
            return s1.compareTo(s2);
          }
        } else {
          return s1.compareTo(s2);
        }
      }
    };
    return new PriorityQueue<String>(c);
  }
}
```

Let us add a few elements to a priority queue with our custom comparator to exemplify the idea. To add elements, we use .add, and to remove the element with the highest priority, we invoke .poll.

```
import java.util.Comparator;
import java.util.PriorityQueue;

class PriorityQueueByP {

  static PriorityQueue<String> priorityByP() { /* Code hidden. */ }

  public static void main(String[] args) {
    PriorityQueue<String> pq1 = priorityByP();
    // Add a few values.
    pq1.add("pool"); pq1.add("peek"); pq1.add("hello"); pq1.add("barks");
    pq1.add("park"); pq1.add("pecking"); pq1.add("shrub");

    // Poll each from the queue and print them out.
    while (!pq1.isEmpty()) { System.out.println(pq1.poll()); }
  }
}
```

The output is as follows:

```
park
pecking
peek
pool
barks
hello
shrub
```

With the provided comparator, `park` has the highest priority because it starts with `'p'` and has a substring that comes before the rest of those strings starting with `'p'`. The strings `pecking`, `peek`, and `pool` come next for similar reasons. Finally, none of the strings `barks`, `hello`, and `shrub` start with `'p'`, so we compare based on the strings themselves. The underlying implementation of *how* the priority queue works and enforces ordering is beyond the scope of this textbook. Such details are reserved for a textbook or course on advanced data structures, which follows the course designed for the audience of this text.

3.2.2 Set-Based Data Structures

Sets are unordered collections of non-duplicate elements. Does this definition sound familiar? It should; it perfectly mirrors the mathematical definition of a set. Java has a few nuances to its definition of sets that we will now see. We consider these data structures *set-based* since they all rely on the "no-duplicate" philosophy.

Set Interface

A *Set* in Java is an interface rather than a class. This is because Java has a hierarchy for differing implementations of sets. We will discuss three such implementations: *HashSet*, *TreeSet*, and *LinkedHashSet*. While all three disallow duplicate elements, the latter two impose an ordering on their elements, which goes against the standard mathematical definition, but for practical reasons.

> **Java Sets**
>
> A *Set* is a data structure of non-duplicate elements, with HashSet being the most common implementation/usage of sets.
>
> Set<T> $S =$ new HashSet<>() creates a HashSet of type T, named S.
> boolean S.contains(e) returns whether or not e is in the set S.
> boolean S.add(e) adds e to the set S only if it is not present. If e is not in S, it returns false; otherwise, it returns true.
> boolean S.remove(e) removes e from the set S only if it is present. If e is not in S, it returns false; otherwise, it returns true.
> int S.size() returns the number of logical elements in the set.

Fig. 3.9: Useful Sets-based Methods.

HashSet Class

In the implementation of a HashSet, the existence of objects in the set is determined by the hashCode() method of the objects, which computes their hash codes. These hash codes are used to decide in which 'bucket' within the hash table an object should be placed. It's important, though, to note that hash codes are not used for comparing the equality of the content of objects. Unlike the == operator, which checks if two references point to the same object in memory, the respective equals() method is used to compare the actual content of the objects. When adding an object to a HashSet, if the hash code of the object matches the hash code of any existing object in the corresponding bucket, the equals() method is then used to check for actual content equality to ensure that no duplicate objects (in terms of content) are added to the set. In other words, two objects that are equal in terms of equals() must have the same hash code, but the converse is not necessarily true. Anything more than these details goes beyond the scope of this textbook, but we will provide a small synopsis of hashable data structures.

A hashable data structure is most often designed as a hash table, which is similar to an array, where elements are stored. Hashable data structures are known for their fast lookup times, thanks to a *hash function*: a mathematical function used to compute the location to store a value in a hash table. Consider a hash function $H(v)$, whose range is the set of integers $[0, n)$, where n is the number of elements of the hash table. Running v (which is an arbitrary argument) through the hash function H returns an index of the hash table. Evaluating H is, in optimal conditions, a constant-time algorithm, hence determining value existence in a hash table also runs in constant-time. This begs the question of what happens if there exists an output of H such that $H(v') = H(v)$, but $v' \neq v$. In subsequent computer science courses, students learn how to resolve *hash collisions* through techniques such as linear and quadratic probing, as well as chaining.[15]

Use hash sets when you do not care about element ordering or "position" in the set, and want to ensure no duplicates exist.

---

[15] In Chapter 4, we will implement a simple hash table that uses chaining to resolve hash collisions.

TreeSet Class

A *TreeSet* is a set with determined order, either by the natural ordering of the elements or one defined by a Comparator, similar to a priority queue. All methods in a Set are, definitionally, implemented by a TreeSet.

LinkedHashSet Class

A *LinkedHashSet* is a set with an ordering based on the insertion order of the elements. All methods in a Set are, definitionally, implemented by a LinkedHashSet.

Example 3.31. The canonical usage of a set is to remove duplicates from a list. Indeed, let's design the removeDuplicatesList method that receives a list of integers and returns a new list without any duplicates. We will add a post-condition requirement that the output order of the integers must match the input order. To solve this problem, we will create an auxiliary linked hash set data structure, add all elements from the list into the set, then add those values from the set to a new list. When adding a value into a set, if it already exists, it is not re-added.

```
import static Assertions.assertAll;
import static Assertions.assertEquals;

import java.util.List;

class RemoveDuplicatesListTester {

  @Test
  void testRemoveDuplicatesList() {
    assertAll(
        () -> assertEquals(List.of(), removeDuplicatesList(List.of())),
        () -> assertEquals(List.of(3, 4), removeDuplicatesList(List.of(3, 3, 4, 4, 3, 4))));
  }
}
```

```
import java.util.List;
import java.util.ArrayList;
import java.util.Set;
import java.util.LinkedHashSet;

class RemoveDuplicatesList {

  /**
   * Removes duplicates from a list of integers.
   * @param ls list of integers.
   * @return new list without duplicates.
   */
  static List<Integer> removeDuplicatesList(List<Integer> ls) {
    List<Integer> newLs = new ArrayList<>();
    Set<Integer> set = new LinkedHashSet<>();
    for (int x : ls) { set.add(x); }
    for (int x : s) { newLs.add(x); }
    return newLs;
  }
}
```

Example 3.32. Suppose we want to find all common elements shared between two linked lists of elements, which are unordered. Let's design the `commonValues` method that, when given two linked lists of integers, returns a sorted-ordered list of the values that occur in both lists. We should not count values twice, e.g., if 2 occurs twice in the first list, then the resulting output list should only contain one occurrence of 2. Let's take advantage of a tree set to store the common values in order, and then add those values to a new linked list.

```
import static Assertions.assertAll;
import static Assertions.assertEquals;

import java.util.List;
import java.util.LinkedList;
import java.util.Set;
import java.util.TreeSet;

class CommonValuesTester {

  @Test
  void testCommonValues() {
    assertAll(
      () -> assertEquals(List.of(), commonValues(List.of(),
                                      List.of(5, 4, 3, 2, 1))),
      () -> assertEquals(List.of(), commonValues(List.of(10, 20, 30, 40, 50),
                                      List.of(5, 4, 3, 2, 1))),
      () -> assertEquals(List.of(1, 3, 4), commonValues(List.of(2, 4, 1, 3, 5, 6),
                                      List.of(1, 4, 3, 10, 20))),
      () -> assertEquals(List.of(-2, 0, 2), commonValues(List.of(2, -2, 0, 0, -2, 2),
                                      List.of(-2, 2, 0))));
  }
}
```

```
import java.util.List;
import java.util.LinkedList;
import java.util.Set;
import java.util.TreeSet;

class CommonValuesTester {

  /**
   * Finds all common values between two linked lists of integers.
   * @param ls1 first linked list.
   * @param ls2 second linked list.
   * @return list of (distinct) common values.
   */
  static List<Integer> commonValues(LinkedList<Integer> ls1, LinkedList<Integer> ls2) {
    Set<Integer> set = new TreeSet<>();
    for (int x : ls1) {
      if (ls2.contains(x)) { set.add(x); }
    }
    List<Integer> newLs = new LinkedList<>();
    newLs.addAll(set);
    return newLs;
  }
}
```

3.2 Collections

Example 3.33. We are given an array of numbers from 1 to n, where one number is missing and one is duplicated. Let's design the `findDupMissing` method that returns an array of two elements: the first of which is the missing number and the second of which is the duplicate value. It makes sense to use a `TreeSet` since, that way, we can store the numbers in order and find out which one is omitted through one traversal, and find the only duplicate.

```java
import static Assertions.assertAll;
import static Assertions.assertArrayEquals;

class FindDupMissingTester {

  @Test
  void testFindDupMissing() {
    assertAll(
      () -> assertArrayEquals(new int[]{2, 3},
                              findDupMissing(new int[]{1, 3, 3, 4})),
      () -> assertArrayEquals(new int[]{5, 1},
                              findDupMissing(new int[]{8, 1, 4, 1, 3, 2, 6, 7})),
      () -> assertArrayEquals(new int[]{6, 7},
                              findDupMissing(new int[]{3, 2, 7, 7, 4, 5, 1})));
  }
}
```

```java
import java.util.Set;
import java.util.TreeSet;

class FindDupMissing {

  /**
   * Finds a duplicate number and a missing number from
   * an array of numbers within a specific interval.
   * @param A array of integers where each number is in [1, n],
   * with one missing and one duplicate.
   * @return two-element array where [0] is the missing number
   * and [1] is the duplicate number.
   */
  static int[] findDupMissing(int[] A) {
    Set<Integer> set = new TreeSet<>();
    int[] res = new int[2];
    // Add the values to the set and find the duplicate one.
    for (int x : A) {
      if (set.contains(x)) { res[1] = x; }
      else { set.add(x); }
    }
    // Now find the missing number.
    int prev = 0;
    for (int x : set) {
      if (x != prev + 1) {
        res[0] = prev + 1;
        break;
      } else {
        prev = x;
      }
    }
    return res;
  }
}
```

> **Java Maps**
>
> A *Map* is a dictionary-based data structure wherein we map *keys* to *values*, with HashMap being the most common implementation/usage of maps.
>
> Map<K,V> M = new HashMap<>() creates a HashMap named M whose keys are of type K and whose values are of type V. Namely, the keys map to the values.
> M.containsKey(k) returns whether or not k is a key in the map M.
> void M.put(k,v) maps the key k to the value v in M.
> V M.get(k) returns the value associated with k in M, or null if k has no association.
> V M.getOrDefault(k, x) returns the value associated with k in M, or x if k does not have an association.
> int M.size() returns the number of logical elements in the set.
> Set<K> keySet() returns a set of the keys in the map.

Fig. 3.10: Useful Map-based Methods.

3.2.3 Dictionary-Based Data Structures

Dictionaries map elements from one type K to elements of another type V. The types K and V do not necessarily need to be distinct.

Map Interface

Java has an interface called Map rather than a class because, like sets, there is a hierarchy for differing implementations of maps. We will discuss three: *HashMap*, *TreeMap*, and *LinkedHashMap*. Maps contain keys and values; the keys are mapped to values in the map. A key/value pairing is called an *entry*, or an *association*. Maps cannot contain duplicate keys, because it would be ambiguous to have two identical keys mapping to different values.

HashMap Class

HashMaps base existence of keys in the map by their hashcode and a hash table, identical to a hash set. For a greater detail of how hashable data structures work, please refer to the previous subsection.

TreeMap Class

A *TreeMap* is a map with a determined order, either by a natural ordering of the keys or that defined by a comparator. All methods in Map are, definitionally, implemented by a TreeMap.

LinkedHashMap Class

A *LinkedHashMap* is a map with an ordering based on the insertion order of the key/value pairs. All methods in a `Map` are, definitionally, implemented by a `LinkedHashMap`.

Example 3.34. Perhaps one of the most common use cases for a dictionary-based data structure is to compute the frequency, or count, of some values. Suppose we want to design the `mode` method that, when given a list of integers, returns the mode(s), i.e., the most-frequent value(s). We can use a map to keep track of the numbers seen so far, which are the keys, and their respective frequencies being the values. Because a list of numbers may have multiple modes, we will need to use a three-step algorithm:

1. Compute the frequencies of each number.
2. Find the highest frequency.
3. Find all numbers that match this frequency.

Traversing over a map is straightforward: we obtain a *key set*, which is a set of the keys in a map, and each corresponding value is retrieved via one call to the `.get` method.

```java
import static Assertions.assertAll;
import static Assertions.assertEquals;

import java.util.List;
import java.util.Set;

class ComputeModeTester {

  @Test
  void testMode() {
    assertAll(
        () -> assertEquals(Set.of(), mode(List.of())),
        () -> assertEquals(Set.of(3), mode(List.of(4, 5, 2, 3, 3, 4, 3))),
        () -> assertEquals(Set.of(2, 3), mode(List.of(2, 3, 2, 3, 3, 2))),
        () -> assertEquals(Set.of(2), mode(List.of(2, 2, 2, 2, 2, 2, 2))));
  }
}
```

```java
import java.util.HashMap;
import java.util.HashSet;
import java.util.List;
import java.util.Map;
import java.util.Set;

class ComputeMode {

  /**
   * Computes the mode of a list of numbers, which is the most-frequent value(s).
   * @param ls list of numbers.
   * @return set of mode values, if they exist.
   */
  static Set<Integer> mode(List<Integer> ls) {
    if (ls.isEmpty()) { return new HashSet<>(); }
    else {
      // First, compute the frequencies.
      Map<Integer, Integer> frequencies = new HashMap<>();
      for (int v : ls) {
        if (!frequencies.containsKey(v)) {
```

```java
          frequencies.put(v, 1);
        } else {
          frequencies.put(v, frequencies.get(v) + 1);
        }
      }

      // Find the highest frequency.
      int highestFreq = -1;
      for (int k : frequencies.keySet()) {
        highestFreq = Math.max(highestFreq, frequencies.get(k));
      }

      // Now, find the values that match that frequency.
      return frequencies.keySet()
                        .stream()
                        .filter(k -> frequencies.get(k) == highestFreq)
                        .collect(Collectors.toSet());
    }
  }
}
```

Example 3.35. Let's design the `sharesFirstChar` method that, when given an array of strings, returns a Map<Character, Set<String>> such that each alphabetized character maps to a set of alphabetized strings that start with that character. We will further assume a case-insensitive mapping. Consider the following input and output example:

```
sharesFirstChar(["she", "sells", "sea", "shells", "by", "the", "sea"])
 => [<'b' : {"by"}>,
     <'s' : {"sea", "sells", "she", "shells"}>
     <'t' : {"the"}>]
```

Because we want both the sets and maps to be alphabetized, the use of a `TreeSet` and `TreeMap` is appropriate. So, we will first traverse over the input list and instantiate a map whose keys are the first letters of each word, and whose value is a new instance of a `TreeSet`. We then populate the sets via a second traversal over the list.

```java
import static Assertions.assertAll;
import static Assertions.assertEquals;

import java.util.List;
import java.util.Map;
import java.util.Set;
import java.util.TreeMap;

class ShareFirstCharacterTester {

  @Test
  void testShareFirstChar() {
    Map<Character, Set<String>> exp1 = new TreeMap<>();
    assertEquals(exp1, shareFirstChar(List.of()));

    Map<Character, Set<String>> exp2 = new TreeMap<>();
    exp2.put('b', new TreeSet<>());
    exp2.put('s', new TreeSet<>());
    exp2.put('t', new TreeSet<>());
    exp2.get('s').addAll(Set.of("she", "sells", "sea", "shells"));
    exp2.get('t').addAll(Set.of("the"));
    exp2.get('b').addAll(Set.of("by"));
```

```
    assertEquals(exp2,
                 shareFirstChar(List.of("she", "sells", "sea", "shells",
                                        "by", "the", "sea")));
  }
}
```

```
import java.util.HashMap;
import java.util.List;
import java.util.Map;
import java.util.Set;
import java.util.TreeSet;

class ShareFirstCharacter {

  /**
   * Returns a map whose keys are the first characters of the strings
   * and whose values are sets of strings that start with that character.
   * @param ls list of strings.
   * @return map of sets of strings.
   */
  static Map<Character, Set<String>> shareFirstChar(List<String> ls) {
    Map<Character, Set<String>> M = new HashMap<>();
    // Populate the map with the initial TreeSets.
    for (String s : ls) {
      char lc = Character.toLowerCase(s.charAt(0));
      if (!M.containsKey(lc)) {
        M.put(lc, new TreeSet<>());
      }
    }

    // Add the strings to each set.
    for (String s : ls) {
      M.get(Character.toLowerCase(s.charAt(0))).add(s);
    }
    return M;
  }
}
```

Example 3.36. Let's design the firstUniqueDigit method that, when given a string, returns the first non-repeated digit. If there is no non-repeated digit, then return the empty string. Because we care about the insertion order, we should use a LinkedHashMap whose keys are characters in the string and whose values are frequency counts. The idea is to count the frequency of each (digit) character, then traverse over the linked map and find the first key whose (value) frequency is one. Because we now understand how to combine get and put to insert and increment frequency counts, we will instead opt to use getOrDefault, which removes the need for the conditional.[16]

```
import static Assertions.assertAll;
import static Assertions.assertEquals;

class FirstUniqueDigitTester {

  @Test
```

---

[16] This problem is similar to one created by frew@mclean.com on codingbat.com. Thanks!

```java
  void testFirstUniqueDigit() {
    assertAll(
      () -> assertEquals("3", firstUniqueDigit("1211312121")),
      () -> assertEquals("2", firstUniqueDigit("0099828776")),
      () -> assertEquals("", firstUniqueDigit("11223344")));
  }
}
```

```java
import java.util.HashMap;
import java.util.Map;

class FirstUniqueDigit {

  /**
   * Returns the first unique digit in a string, as a string.
   * If there is no unique digit, then the empty string is returned.
   * @param s string.
   * @return first unique digit as a string.
   */
  static String firstUniqueDigit(String s) {
    Map<Character, Integer> M = new LinkedHashMap<>();
    // Count the frequency of each digit
    for (int i = 0; i < s.length(); i++) {
      String c = s.substring(i, i + 1);
      if (Character.isDigit(c.charAt(0))) {
        M.put(c.charAt(0), M.getOrDefault(c.charAt(0), 0) + 1);
      }
    }

    // Find the first unique letter.
    for (char c : M.keySet()) {
      if (M.get(c) == 1) {
        return String.valueOf(c);
      }
    }
    return "";
  }
}
```

Example 3.37. One final example that we will consider is the nthMostFrequentChar method that, when given a string s and an integer n, returns the nth most frequent character in the string, or null if there is no such character. If there are multiple characters that share the same position, we return the first one in terms of lexicographical ordering.

For example, consider the string "abbabdcaadaababcdcc" and $n = 3$. The most frequent characters are 'a', 'b', 'c', in that order. So, the third most frequent character is 'c'.

Another example is the string "aabbcc" and $n = 2$. The most frequent characters are 'a', 'b', 'c', in that order, but all three characters share a frequency of two, meaning they are all equally frequent. In this case, we return the empty string.

A third example is the string "aaaabccccc" and $n = 2$. The most frequent characters are 'c', 'a', 'b', in that order. So, the second most frequent character is 'a'.

First, we will count the frequency of each character, then use a PriorityQueue to store the characters in order of their frequency from greatest to least. We will then remove the first $n - 1$ characters from the priority queue, and return the first character of the remaining queue. This approach may raise some eyebrows, because if the frequency is the value in a map, how can we construct a comparator? In other circumstances, one needs access to a particular key to obtain its corresponding value. In this instance, though, we can generate the *entry set* for the map of characters to frequencies, which is a set of Map.Entry<K, V> objects, where K is the key type and V is the value type. Our priority queue comparator receives two such entries e and f, and performs the following comparison:

- If $e_k \neq f_k$, return $f_v - e_v$.
- Else, return the lesser of e_k and f_k.

We know that K is Character and V is Integer representing the characters mapped to their frequencies. To retrieve the key and value from an Map.Entry object, we use the getKey() and getValue() methods respectively. In an effort to keep our code a bit more concise, we will design a private and static helper method to create a Comparator object using the aforementioned criteria.

```java
import static Assertions.assertAll;
import static Assertions.assertEquals;

class NthMostFrequentCharTester {

  @Test
  void testNthMostFrequentChar() {
    assertAll(
      () -> assertEquals("a", nthMostFrequentChar("abacab", 1)),
      () -> assertEquals("d", nthMostFrequentChar("aaaadddccccbbee", 3)),
      () -> assertEquals("q", nthMostFrequentChar("ppqrrss", 2)),
      () -> assertEquals(null, nthMostFrequentChar("aabbccdd", 2)));
  }
}
```

```java
import java.util.Comparator;
import java.util.HashMap;
import java.util.Map;
import java.util.PriorityQueue;

class NthMostFrequentChar {

  /**
   * Given a string, returns the nth most
   * frequent character in that string.
   * @param s string to examine.
   * @param n int n >= 0.
   * @return the nth most frequent character as a String or null if nonexistent.
   */
  static String nthMostFrequentChar(String s, int n) {
    // Step 1: compute the frequencies.
    Map<Character, Integer> M = new HashMap<>();
    s.chars().forEach(c -> M.put(c, M.getOrDefault(c, 0)));

    // Step 2: populate the priority queue with entry objects. Use the comparator.
    PriorityQueue<Map.Entry<Character, Integer>> Q = new PriorityQueue<>(getCmp());
    M.entrySet().forEach(e -> Q.add(e));

    // Step 4: poll n - 1 items from the queue.
    while (!Q.isEmpty()) {
      n--;
      if (n == 0) { return String.valueOf(Q.peek().getKey()); }
      else { Q.poll(); }
    }
```

```
      return null;
    }

    private static Comparator<Entry<Character, Integer>> getCmp() {
      return new Comparator<>() {
        @Override
        public int compare(Map.Entry<Character, Integer> e,
                           Map.Entry<Character, Integer> f) {
          if (e.getKey() != f.getKey()) {
            return Character.compare(e.getKey(), f.getKey());
          } else {
            return f.getValue() - e.getValue();
          }
        }
      };
    }
}
```

3.3 Iterators

We know how to iterate, or traverse, over a simple data structure such as an array. The idea is to use a variable for the index and continuously increment it until we reach the upper bound of the array. Below is a simple example where we sum the elements of an array.

```
static int sum(int[] arr) {
  int sum = 0;
  for (int i = 0; i < arr.size; i++) { sum += arr[i]; }
  return sum;
}
```

    The problem is that not all data structures, as we have undoubtedly seen, are sequential; sets and maps are two examples of non-sequential data structures, so how do we traverse over those? One option is the enhanced-for loop, but as we will show later, this approach has its drawbacks, even though its syntax is straightforward. Stacks and queues are another example of data structures that are not necessarily sequential. *Iterator* objects are one answer to the issue of traversability. Iterators provide a mechanism for traversing over a data structure. Any data structure whose class definition implements `Iterator` must define at least two methods: `boolean hasNext` and `T next`, which determines whether we are at the end of the traversal, and retrieves the next element, respectively. Note that T, for the time being, simply means "any type," and is related to type parameterization. All of the Java collections implement `Iterator`, and we can retrieve the corresponding `Iterator` object via the `.iterator` method.

    Upon retrieving an iterator, we can use a `while` loop to continuously retrieve elements in the data structure until no more elements remain to be visited. The elements of the iterator are generated on-the-fly; only upon calling `next` is the value truly read from the data structure itself. Much like the rest of the Collections framework, we must pass the parameterized type to the `Iterator` initialization, so that it knows what type to substitute for T.

Example 3.38. Let's use an iterator to traverse over a `LinkedHashSet`, whose element ordering is determined by their insertion order, meaning that the iterator should produce them in the order that they were inserted.

3.3 Iterators

```java
import static Assertions.assertAll;
import static Assertions.assertEquals;

import java.util.Set;
import java.util.LinkedHashSet;
import java.util.Iterator;

class IteratorTester {

  @Test
  void testIterator() {
    Set<Integer> lhs = new LinkedHashSet<>(Set.of(8, 90));
    Iterator<Integer> it = lhs.iterator();
    assertAll(
      () -> assertTrue(it.hasNext());
      () -> assertEquals(8, it.next()),
      () -> assertEquals(90, it.next()),
      () -> assertFalse(it.hasNext()));
  }
}
```

Should we want to traverse over the data again, we need to instantiate another instance of the iterator, because there is no way to reset the "position" of an iterator; they are a kind of "one-time use" objects.

It should be stated that the enhanced `for` loop is nearly identical to the job of an `Iterator`, so a programmer may wonder why not use the former over the latter. Inside an enhanced `for` loop, the data structure in question is immutable, meaning that we cannot add, insert, remove, or change elements. On the other hand, iterators allow structural modification. We would recommend not altering the data structure while traversing, even if it is permissible by Java, because doing so can produce irksome bugs.

Example 3.39. Let's now iterate over the `LinkedHashSet` using an enhanced `for` loop. We can do so by placing the type on the left-hand side of the element declaration. Our test subtracts the elements from left-to-right.

```java
import static Assertions.assertEquals;

import java.util.Set;
import java.util.LinkedHashSet;

class EnhancedForLoopTester {

  @Test
  void testEnhancedForLoop() {
    Set<Integer> lhs = new LinkedHashSet<>();
    lhs.add(1); lhs.add(2); lhs.add(3); lhs.add(4);
    int diff = 0;
    for (Integer e : lhs) { diff -= e; }
    assertEquals(-10, diff);
  }
}
```

Example 3.40. Not only does the use of an enhanced `for` loop disallow structural modification, it also does not preserve the order of specific data structures. For example, suppose we have a stack $S = [10, 20, 30, 40, 50]$, where 50 is the top of the stack. If we want to print each element of S without iterators or modifying the stack itself, the obvious option is to use an enhanced `for` loop. Unfortunately, this does not go as expected: it prints the elements in the order they are inserted, i.e., first-in-first-out. Intuitively, we may expect the program to output the values via last-in-first-out, i.e., 50, 40, 30, 20, 10. What's worse is that its `Iterator` implementation also makes the glaring mistake. The solution proposed by Oracle is to instead use the `ArrayDeque` class, which is a type of `Deque` object.[17][18]

```java
import java.util.ArrayDeque;
import java.util.Deque;
import java.util.Iterator;
import java.util.List;
import java.util.Stack;

class StackPrinter {

  public static void main(String[] args) {
    Stack<Integer> S = new Stack<>(List.of(10, 20, 30, 40, 50));

    // Enhanced for loop prints them "incorrectly!"
    // An Iterator also has this issue.
    // We get "10, 20, 30, 40, 50" separated by newlines.
    S.forEach(x -> System.out.println(x));

    Deque<Integer> D = new ArrayDeque<>(List.of(10, 20, 30, 40, 50));

    // An ArrayDeque corrects this problem.
    // We correctly get "50, 40, 30, 20, 10" separated by newlines.
    D.forEach(x -> System.out.println(x));
  }
}
```

Example 3.41. The unintuitive nature of the enhanced `for` loop and certain iterator behavior does not stop with stacks, unfortunately. Priority queues are also afflicted as a consequence of their implementation. Let's see what happens when we create a priority queue whose comparator prioritizes the string `"Joshua"` over all strings and makes the string `"Jack"` have the lowest priority. In other words, any occurrence of `"Joshua"` should come before all other strings in the priority queue, whereas any occurrence of `"Jack"` should come after all other strings in the priority queue. Any strings in between are ordered naturally, i.e., via lexicographical ordering.

```java
import java.util.List;
import java.util.PriorityQueue;
import java.util.Comparator;

class PriorityQueuePrinting {

  private static PriorityQueue<String> initPriorityQueue() {
    Comparator<String> S = new Comparator<>() {
      @Override
      public int compare(String s1, String s2) {
        // If Joshua comes first or Jack comes last,
        // then s1 is prioritized.
        if (s1.equals("Joshua") || s2.equals("Jack")) { return -1; }
```

---

[17] A *deque*, pronounced as 'deck,' is a double-ended queue, meaning we can insert and remove elements from either the front or the rear.

[18] See the note listed on Oracle's Stack documentation: https://docs.oracle.com/javase/8/docs/api/java/util/Stack.html

```
      // If Jack comes first or Joshua comes last,
      // then s2 is prioritized.
      else if (s1.equals("Jack") || s2.equals("Joshua")) { return 1; }
      // All other strings take standard priority (natural ordering).
      else { return s1.compareTo(s2); }
    }
  };
  return new PriorityQueue(S);
}

public static void main(String[] args) {
  PriorityQueue<String> pq = initPriorityQueue();
  pq.add("Peter"); pq.add("Joshua"); pq.add("Gautam"); pq.add("Jane");
  pq.add("Jack"); pq.add("Ratan"); pq.add("Dharmik"); pq.add("Sakshi");

  // Prints a seemingly random order!
  for (String s : pq) { System.out.println(s); }

  // Uses Arrays to sort the elements according to the PQ's comparator.
  String[] elements = pq.toArray(new String[0]);
  Arrays.sort(elements, pq.comparator());
  System.out.println(Arrays.toString(elements));
}
}
```

By traversing over the elements with an enhanced for loop, we notice that the elements are printed in a seemingly random order that does not obey our comparator. One solution here is to convert the priority queue to an array, sort the array using Arrays.sort, then print the contents of the array using Arrays.toString. Remember that, if we only pass the array itself to println, we see the hash code of the array is printed instead of its elements.

One complication to concern ourselves with is how we convert the priority queue (or any collection) to an array using .toArray(...). It receives an array of some type T and, if it is large enough to store all the elements of the collection, it is populated. Otherwise, an array of the same type T is returned. To summarize, if we want to convert the priority queue of strings into an array, we must pass new String[0] to the .toArray method. The returned array is then sorted and printed.[19]

A final intricacy of conversion process is that we need to pass the comparator of the priority queue to Arrays.sort, otherwise it sorts the elements based on their natural ordering, which is certainly undesired. We do not have direct access to the comparator that we created in the initPriorityQueue method, but we can retrieve the comparator used by the priority queue via the priority queue .comparator method.

Example 3.42. Gilmore and Kushagra are playing a game of "pick the maximum." The rules are that Gilmore removes the maximum value from a given list of numbers, then Kushagra does the same. Kushagra then puts their number into another list, followed by Gilmore's number (okay, this isn't exactly a competitive game). We want to see what the resulting list would be for a given input. Let's design the List<Integer> maximalMoves(List<Integer> ls) method that, when given a list of numbers, and playing the game as aforementioned, returns the moves made by the players. The naive approach is to traverse the list and remove the maximum element for every value. Unfortunately, this algorithm is terribly slow, being quadratic in the number of required iterations. A more performant method is to add each item to a maximal priority queue (i.e., a priority queue whose comparator sorts items from

---

[19] In the next section, we will discuss a much easier way to replicate toArray using a new collection type called *streams*.

greatest to least), withdraw two items at a time, and add them to the resulting list in the opposite order. To create a comparator that uses "greatest" as the "highest" priority metric, we can use the `Collections.reverseOrder` method, which returns a comparator that sorts items in reverse order.

```java
import static Assertions.assertAll;
import static Assertions.assertEquals;

import java.util.List;

class MaximalMovesTester {

  @Test
  void testMaximalMoves() {
    assertAll(
      () -> assertEquals(List.of(),
                         maximalMoves(List.of())),
      () -> assertEquals(List.of(4, 5, 3, 2, 0, 1),
                         maximalMoves(List.of(0, 1, 2, 3, 4, 5))),
      () -> assertEquals(List.of(45, 60, 35, 25, 45, 25, 15, 5),
                         maximalMoves(List.of(20, 40, 30, 25, 45, 25, 15, 5, 60, 35))));
  }
}
```

```java
import java.util.Collections;
import java.util.List;
import java.util.PriorityQueue;

class MaximalMoves {

  /**
   * Given a list of numbers, returns the moves made by the players
   * @param ls list of numbers with even length.
   * @return list of moves.
   */
  static List<Integer> maximalMoves(List<Integer> ls) {
    PriorityQueue<Integer> pq = new PriorityQueue<>(Collections.reverseOrder());
    pq.addAll(ls);
    List<Integer> moves = new ArrayList<>();
    for (int i = 0; i < ls.size() - 1; i += 2) {
      moves.add(pq.poll());
      moves.add(pq.poll());
    }
    return moves;
  }
}
```

3.4 Streams

Streams are, in effect, a *lazy* collection of "things." By "lazy," we mean to say that, if a result is not necessary nor requested, then it is not computed.

Example 3.43. Consider a situation where we invoke the `omega()` method, which is defined as an infinite loop, as the argument to the `foo` method, giving us `foo(omega())`. In Java, all arguments are evaluated *eagerly*, meaning that the arguments are evaluated before the method is applied. Unfortunately for the caller of foo, the body thereof does not make use of x, meaning we evaluate omega() for no reason whatsoever. This means that, because omega never terminates, foo similarly never returns a result.

```
static int omega() {
  while (true) {}
  return 10;
}
static int foo(int x) {
  return 5;
}
```

If Java supported *lazy evaluation* for method calls, we would not have this problem. Our discussion is not entirely driven by a desire for lazy evaluation, but rather the desire for easily-composable operations; lazy evaluation is a perk in that it allows us to design infinite data structures! An "infinite" data structure raises some important questions about how to store "infinite" data. Imagine that we want to compute a list that contains every positive even integer. We can represent this as the following inductive set:

$$0 \in S$$
$$\text{If } x \in S, \text{ then } x + 2 \in S$$

Therefore, S is a set containing countably-infinite values. Implementing S in Java, as an ArrayList, might contain a for loop with a condition that we do not know how to solve! Because we do not know how many values to add, we may be tempted to design an infinite loop via while (true), but then the loop never ends, and eventually the program runs out of memory due to adding values to the never-ending list. The solution, as we have suggested, is to use streams.[20]

To create a stream of infinite data is to recreate our inductive set definition inside a IntStream instance and invoke the iterate static method.

```
IntStream is = IntStream.iterate(0, x -> x + 2);
```

Let's explain this method, but to do so we must simultaneously introduce *lambda expressions*. A lambda expression is an anonymous function, i.e., a function definition without a name. In the above code snippet, we define a function that receives a value x and returns x plus two. It would be identical to defining a private static method to add 2 to some given integer, but we like lambda expressions due to their locality; it might come across as superfluous to design a method that is used in only one context. It is also possible to pass a *method reference* instead of a lambda expression.

```
import java.util.IntStream;

class PositiveEvens {

  private static int addTwo(int x) { return x + 2; }

  public static void main(String[] args) {
    IntStream is = IntStream.iterate(0, PositiveEvens::addTwo);
  }
}
```

---

[20] For those coming from another language such as Python, a stream is equivalent to a *generator*.

The `IntStream` instance declares a stream that, when requested/prompted, invokes and populates the stream. Because it is impossible to represent a truly infinite data structure in Java with modern computers, we need to limit how many values we want from this stream. Indeed, the `.limit` method computes exactly n elements from the stream. So, to compute the first ten elements of our *is* `IntStream`, we invoke `.limit(10)` on our *is* stream.

```java
import java.util.IntStream;

class PositiveEvens {

  public static void main(String[] args) {
    IntStream is = IntStream.iterate(0, x -> x + 2).limit(10);
  }
}
```

Now, suppose we want to view these ten elements. Right now, they are consolidated to an `IntStream`, but we need to convert them to a list of sorts. The solution is to convert the values into a `Stream<Integer>` via `.boxed()`, and then to a list using the convenient `.toList()` method.

```java
import java.util.IntStream;
import java.util.List;

class PositiveEvens {

  public static void main(String[] args) {
    IntStream is = IntStream.iterate(0, x -> x + 2).limit(10);
    List<Integer> ls = is.boxed().toList();
    System.out.println(ls); // [0, 2, 4, 6, 8, 10, 12, 14, 16, 18]
  }
}
```

Example 3.44. Suppose we want a stream of infinitely repeating "a" strings. We can easily create one via the generate method, which acts as the stream constructor, receiving a lambda expression to continuously generate new elements.

```java
import java.util.Stream;

class AGenerator {

  public static void main(String[] args) {
    Stream<String> as = Stream.generate(() -> "a");
    // ["a", "a", "a", "a", "a", "a", "a", "a", "a", "a"]
    System.out.println(as.limit(10).boxed().toList());
  }
}
```

Again, it is important to understand what happens under the hood of a stream. Elements thereof only generate when we request them through some accessory means, e.g., `limit`. As we previously suggested, attempting to access an infinite stream (without a limit) causes the program to hang and eventually crash with an `OutOfMemoryError` error.

Example 3.45. Imagine we want to create a stream of all of the Fibonacci numbers. The thing is, we eventually reach the 32-bit limit of the `int` datatype, so we should take advantage

3.4 Streams

of the `BigInteger` class, allowing us to represent arbitrarily-large integers.[21] Also, this time, we will design a method that returns the stream instance rather than creating one in the `main` method.

Here's what we need to do: let's use `iterate` to generate new values in the sequence. There is a slight problem in that the Fibonacci sequence has two starting (accumulator) values: 0 and 1. The issue is that `iterate` receives only one "initializer" value. To circumvent this predicament, we can pass an array that contains the current and "next" Fibonacci values. Inside the lambda expression, we receive an array of values, from which we compute the next Fibonacci number. Instead of using `IntStream`, however, we generalize to the `Stream` class, since our initial value(s) is not an integer.

```java
import static Assertions.assertEquals;
import static Assertions.assertArrayEquals;

import java.util.Stream;
import java.util.List;
import java.util.ArrayList;
import java.util.BigInteger;

class BigIntFibStreamTester {

  @Test
  void testBigIntFibStream() {
    // Get the stream, test ten values, make sure the lists are the same.
    Stream<BigInteger[]> s = StreamExample.fibonacciStream();
    List<BigInteger[]> actualLs = s.limit(10).toList();
    List<BigInteger[]> expectedLs =
        List.of(new BigInteger[]{new BigInteger("0"), new BigInteger("1")},
                new BigInteger[]{new BigInteger("1"), new BigInteger("1")},
                ...);

    // Check each array of BigIntegers of the expected and actual.
    assertTrue(expectedLs.size() == actualLs.size());
    for (int i = 0; i < expectedLs.size(); i++) {
      assertArrayEquals(expectedLs.get(i), actualLs.get(i));
    }
  }
}
```

```java
import java.util.Stream;
import java.util.BigInteger;

class BigIntFibStream {

  /**
   * Computes a stream of BigInteger values of the nth Fibonacci value.
   * @return stream containing arrays of the next sequential BigIntegers.
   */
  static Stream<BigInteger[]> fibonacciStream() {
    BigInteger[] vals = new BigInteger[]{new BigInteger("0"), new BigInteger("1")};
    return Stream.iterate(vals, v -> new BigInteger[]{v[1], v[0].add(v[1])});
  }
}
```

---

[21] Worrying about *how* the `BigInteger` class works for now is unnecessary as our current plan is to demonstrate stream properties.

> **Java Streams**
>
> A *stream* is a lazy collection of elements that are computed only when requested.
>
> int S.count() returns the number of elements in the stream.
> Stream<T> S.map(f) returns a new stream whose elements are the result of applying f to each element of S.
> Stream<T> S.filter(p) returns a new stream of values in S that satisfy the predicate p.
> T S.reduce(a, f) returns the result of applying the binary function f to each element of S, starting from a, which serves as the accumulator's initial value. The type of a is T, which matches the elements of the stream.
> Stream<T> S.limit(n) returns a new stream containing the first n elements of S.
> Stream<T> S.skip(n) returns a new stream containing the elements of S after the first n.
> Optional<T> S.min/max(c) returns the minimum/maximum element of S according to the comparator c. If S is empty, returns Optional.empty().

Fig. 3.11: Useful Stream-based Methods.

> **Java Stream–Searching Methods**
>
> We can search for the existence of types of elements in a stream.
>
> boolean S.anyMatch(p) returns true if **at least one** element of S satisfies the predicate p; otherwise, returns false.
> boolean S.allMatch(p) returns true if **all** elements of S satisfy the predicate p; otherwise, returns false.
> boolean S.noneMatch(p) returns true if **no** elements of S satisfy the predicate p; otherwise, returns false.

Fig. 3.12: Useful Stream-Searching Methods.

Our code now produces a list of BigInteger arrays containing the current Fibonacci value and its successor. Though, is this really what we want? A better solution would be to return the *first* element of the tuple/two-element array, which is attainable via the map method. map receives a lambda expression as an argument and applies it to every element of the acting stream. Let's modify the code to see an improved output. Conveniently, the change means we need not loop over our expected/actual lists in the unit testing method, as assertEquals works operates correctly over List objects.

```
import static Assertions.assertEquals;

import java.util.Stream;
import java.util.List;
import java.util.ArrayList;
import java.util.BigInteger;

class BigIntFibStreamTester {

  @Test
  void testBigIntFibStream() {
    Stream<BigInteger> s = StreamExample.fibonacciStream();
    List<BigInteger> actualLs = s.limit(10).toList();
    List<BigInteger[]> expectedLs =
```

3.4 Streams

```
            List.of(new BigInteger[]{new BigInteger("0"), new BigInteger("1")},
                    new BigInteger[]{new BigInteger("1"), new BigInteger("1")},
                    ...);
        assertEquals(expectedLs, actualLs);
    }
}
```

```
import java.util.Stream;
import java.util.BigInteger;

class BigIntFibStream {

  /**
   * Computes a stream of BigInteger values of the nth Fibonacci value.
   * @return stream containing arrays of the next
   * sequential Fibonacci BigIntegers.
   */
  static Stream<BigInteger> fibonacciStream() {
    BigInteger[] vals = new BigInteger[]{new BigInteger("0"), new BigInteger("1")};
    return Stream.iterate(vals, v -> new BigInteger[]{v[1], v[0].add(v[1])})
                 .map(v -> v[0]);
  }
}
```

Let's now look a bit more at map, as well as other useful *higher-order functions* such as filter and reduce.

A *higher-order function* is a function that receives functions as parameters. We saw that map receives a lambda expression and applies it to every element of a stream.

Example 3.46. Let's design the sqList method that receives a List<Integer> and squares each element using the Stream API. The method should return a new list. A motif presented throughout stream methods is that they do not modify the original data. We should use map to apply a lambda expression that receives an integer and returns its square. Fortunately for us, we can convert any collection into a stream using the .stream() method. From there, we use a map invocation to arrive at our desired outcome.

```
import static Assertions.assertAll;
import static Assertions.assertEquals;

import java.util.List;
import java.util.ArrayList;

class SqListTester {

  @Test
  void testSqList() {
    List<Integer> ls1 = new ArrayList<>(List.of(0, 100, 49));
    List<Integer> ls2 = new ArrayList<>();
    assertAll(
        () -> assertEquals(ls1, sqList(new ArrayList<>(List.of(0, 10, 7)))),
        () -> assertEquals(ls2, sqList(new ArrayList<>())));
  }
}
```

```
import java.util.List;

class SqList {

  /**
   * Returns a list of squared integers from a list of integers.
   * @param ls list of integers.
   * @return list of squared integers.
   */
  static List<Integer> sqList(List<Integer> ls) {
    return ls.stream()
            .map(x -> x * x)
            .toList();
  }
}
```

Example 3.47. Now, let's design the removeVowels method, which receives a string and removes all vowels, returning a new string in the process. This requires a few techniques that we have learned, but also means we need to use filter and reduce. Here's the idea:

1. Convert the given String into a stream of integers representing the numeric ASCII values of characters.
2. Convert each integer to a "one-string," i.e., a String of one character. The reasoning behind this decision will become clear later.
3. Filter out vowels from the stream.
4. Accumulate the characters in a new string.

We always begin by writing a few tests. Although the tests are simple, the method implementation is the most complex seen thus far.

```
import static Assertions.assertAll;
import static Assertions.assertEquals;

class RemoveVowelsStreamTester {

  @Test
  void testRemoveVowels() {
    assertAll(
      () -> assertEquals("hll", removeVowels("hello")),
      () -> assertEquals("hw r y?", removeVowels("how are you?")),
      () -> assertEquals("", removeVowels("aaaaaaaaaaaa")),
      () -> assertEquals("bbbbbbbbbb", removeVowels("bbbbbbbbbb")),
      () -> assertEquals("bbbbb", removeVowels("ababababab")),
      () -> assertEquals("hll", removeVowels("aeiouAEIOU")));
  }
}
```

Onto the definition: we start by writing the method signature and purpose. Then, we need to complete step one of the algorithm: convert the given string into a stream of ASCII integers, which is achievable via the .chars method. It returns an IntStream of integer ASCII values.

Step two of the algorithm is to convert each integer into a "one-string," which we can do via the constructor for a String object. Step three requires filter, which is another higher-order function; it receives a lambda expression and returns those objects from the stream that satisfy the filter. Since we want to filter *out* the vowels, we should design a method that determines if a character is vowel, then negate the expression as part of the lambda definition.

3.4 Streams

Lastly, we arrive at accumulating the characters into a new string, requiring us to use reduce: yet another higher-order function. The reduce method receives an initial value, i.e., an accumulator a and a binary function/method f. It then applies the binary function to each value in the stream and the running accumulator. If this reminds you of tail recursion, then indeed, that is exactly how reduce works it folds over the list/stream of values, building the result in the accumulator variable.[22] Due to the simplicity of the isVowel predicate and its inclusion in Chapter 2, we omit its definition.

```
class RemoveVowelsStream {

  /**
   * Removes all vowels from a given string using streams.
   * @param s string to remove vowels from.
   * @return new string.
   */
  static String removeVowels(String s) {
    return s.chars()
            .mapToObj(c -> String.valueOf(c))
            .filter(c -> !isVowel(c))
            .reduce("", (acc, c) -> acc + c);
  }
}
```

Example 3.48. While the stream API is convenient and helps us to write complicated code quickly, it is not always a performant solution. Consider the following problem: we are given a Set<Integer>, and we want to return a Map<Integer, Integer> where each integer in the given set is mapped to its "rank." A value's "rank" is denoted by how many elements are larger than (or equal to) it in the list. For example, the rank map of $\{44, 41, 23, 94, 10, 0\}$ is

$$\{<0:6>, <10:5>, <23:4>, <41:3>, <44:2>, <94:1>\}$$

Because there are 6 elements greater than or equal to 0, and so forth. The naïve algorithm is to traverse over the elements of the set, and create a map where the key is the element and its value is the result of a filter. While concise, the code traverses over each element for every element, making this a quadratic-time algorithm.

```
import static Assertions.assertAll;
import static Assertions.assertEquals;

import java.util.Map;
import java.util.Set;
import java.util.TreeMap;

class RankMapTester {

  @Test
  void testRankMap() {
    Map<Integer, Integer> M1 = new TreeMap<>();
    M1.put(0, 6);
    M1.put(10, 5);
    M1.put(23, 4);
    M1.put(41, 3);
    M1.put(44, 2);
```

---

[22] In other functional programming languages, reduce is commonly called foldr.

```
        M1.put(94, 1);
        assertAll(
            () -> assertEquals(Map.of(), rankMap(Set.of())),
            () -> assertEquals(M2, rankMap(Set.of(44, 41, 23, 94, 10, 0))));
    }
}
```

```
import java.util.Set;
import java.util.Map;
import java.util.TreeMap;

class RankMap {

    /**
     * Creates a rank map for a given set of numbers. A rank map
     * is an association of a number to how many numbers are >=
     * the number. This method uses the stream approach.
     * @param S set of integers.
     * @return rank map.
     */
    static Map<Integer, Integer> rankMap(Set<Integer> S) {
        Map<Integer, Integer> M = new TreeMap<>();
        S.forEach(n -> M.put(n, (int) S.stream().filter(m -> m >= n).count()));
        return M;
    }
}
```

Let's design an improved version of `rankMap`, where we sort the elements of the set, then insert them into a map based on position. There is a fixed cost associated with sorting, but it is ultimately faster than the stream and filter approach. The lesson here is not to discourage readers from the stream API; in fact, we claim the opposite. Streams are an amazing addition to Java, but programmers should always consider the performance implications of stream methods, as they would any other method.

```
import java.util.ArrayList;
import java.util.Collections;
import java.util.LinkedHashMap;
import java.util.List;
import java.util.Map;
import java.util.Set;
import java.util.TreeMap;

class RankMap {

    /**
     * Creates a rank map for a given set of numbers. A rank map
     * is an association of a number to how many numbers are >=
     * the number. This method is faster than the stream approach.
     * @param S set of integers.
     * @return rank map.
     */
    static Map<Integer, Integer> fasterRankMap(Set<Integer> S) {
        // Step 1: create a list and sort the elements.
        List<Integer> ls = new ArrayList<>();
        S.forEach(x -> ls.add(x));
        Collections.sort(ls);

        // Step 2: traverse over the list and add the elements to a map.
        Map<Integer, Integer> M = new LinkedHashMap<>();
```

3.4 Streams

```
    for (int i = 0; i < ls.size(); i++) {
      M.put(ls.get(i), ls.size() - i);
    }
    return M;
  }
}
```

Optional Type

The primary benefit of streams is their compositionality; we can chain together multiple operations, sequentially, to compute a result. Though, there are instances in which a value may not exist, and the stream has to account for these cases somehow.

Example 3.49. Consider a series of stream operations to find the maximum integer of a list. For the general case, this is straightforward, but what about when the list is empty? It does not make sense to return 0, since the maximum integer in a list may very well be 0, which leads to a false conclusion. The solution, in this case, is the Optional class. An Optional is a container that may or may not contain a value. If an Optional does contain a value, we access the value directly via .get. If we do not know whether or not it contains a value, we can use .orElse(t), which returns the encapsulated value if it exists, or t otherwise. We can also check, prior to a retrieval, if the Optional contains a value via the .isPresent method. Optional is generic and works over any class type, like almost all other classes from the collections framework. To test the return value of a stream operation that returns an Optional, e.g., max, we instantiate an Optional that wraps the resulting value if it exists, or Optional.empty() otherwise.

```
import static Assertions.assertAll;
import static Assertions.assertEquals;
import static Assertions.assertNull;

import java.util.Optional;
import java.util.List;

class OptionalTester {

  private static final List<Integer> LS1 = List.of(10, 20, 42, 12, 5);
  private static final List<Integer> LS2 = List.of();

  @Test
  void testMaxValue() {
    Optional<Integer> op1 = Optional.of(42);
    Optional<Integer> op2 = Optional.empty();
    assertAll(
        () -> assertEquals(op1, LS1.stream().max((a, b) -> a - b)),
        () -> assertEquals(op2, LS2.stream().max((a, b) -> a - b)),
        () -> assertEquals(42, LS1.stream().max((a, b) -> a - b).orElse(null)),
        () -> assertNull(LS2.stream().max((a, b) -> a - b).orElse(null)));
  }
}
```

Optional values, like we stated, work wonders with the compositionality of streams; if a value does not exist, the stream API will propagate an empty instance of Optional up the chain rather than displaying an error or crashing the program. As part of the design philosophy of the text, those decisions, i.e., whether to crash the program or not, remain as a choice to the implementing programmer.

3.5 Type Parameters

Generics as a concept go far back in programming history, generally renown as type parameterization or *parametric polymorphism*, which we briefly touched on during our discussion of how to instantiate instances of `ArrayList` from the Collections framework. Imagine, for a moment, if Java programmers had to, by hand, design different implementation of `ArrayList` for Integer, String, Double, and so on for every object type. Not only is this impossible (because there are a countably-infinite number of types), it is also extremely cumbersome and redundant, since the only altering parameter is the underlying element type in the data structure. Before Java 5, we could only use "generics" via collections of type `Object`, since it is the root class object type, meaning any element could be stored in any type of collection.

```java
import java.util.ArrayList;

class WeakGenerics {
  public static void main(String[] args) {
    ArrayList al1 = new ArrayList();
    al1.add(new Integer(42));
    al1.add(new Integer(43));
    Integer x = (Integer) al1.get(0);
  }
}
```

Performing runtime casts in the Java 5 sense is prone to errors, not to mention the possibility of adding disjoint types into a collection. For example, nothing prevents us from adding objects of type `String` or `Integer` into an `ArrayList`. Generics were introduced to convert the problem from one encountered at runtime to one encountered more so at compile-time.

Since we have yet to discuss objects in detail, we will hold off on a significant discussion of generic class implementations. To keep everything to the point, we can write any class to be generic and store objects of an arbitrary type. Fortunately, we can also design generic static methods.

To declare a static method as generic, we must specify the type variable(s) necessary to use the method. These *quantifier* come after the `static` keyword but before the return type. For instance, if we want to say that an object of type T is used in the static method `foo`, we declare it as `static <T> void foo(...){...}`. Then, if we want to say that the method returns or receives an object of type T, we substitute the return/parameter type with T, e.g., `static <T> T foo(T arg){...}`. At compile-time, Java looks for method invocations of `foo` and substitutes the T for the type `foo` is invoked with.

Example 3.50. Let's design the search method, which receives a list t and an object k, where the elements of t are of type T and k is also of type T. Its purpose is to return the index of the first occurrence of k in t, and -1 if it does not exist. Because all objects have a `equals` method for object equality, we can take advantage of that when comparing objects in the list against the search parameter. When testing, we will instantiate the type parameter to several different object types to demonstrate.

3.5 Type Parameters

```
import static Assertions.assertAll;
import static Assertions.assertEquals;

import java.util.List;
import java.util.ArrayList;

class GenericSearchTester {

  @Test
  void testGenericSearch() {
    List<Integer> l1 = new ArrayList<>(List.of(1, 2, 3, 4, 5));
    List<String> l2 = new ArrayList<>(List.of("a", "b", "c", "d", "e"));
    List<Double> l3 = new ArrayList<>(List.of(1.0, 2.0, 3.0, 4.0, 5.0));
    List<Character> l4 = new ArrayList<>(List.of('a', 'b', 'c', 'd', 'e'));
    List<List<Integer>> l5 = new ArrayList<>();
    assertAll (
      () -> assertEquals(1, genericSearch(l1, 2)),
      () -> assertEquals(-1, genericSearch(l1, 6)),
      () -> assertEquals(1, genericSearch(l2, "b")),
      () -> assertEquals(-1, genericSearch(l2, "f")),
      () -> assertEquals(1, genericSearch(l3, 2.0)),
      () -> assertEquals(-1, genericSearch(l3, 6.0)),
      () -> assertEquals(1, genericSearch(l4, 'b')),
      () -> assertEquals(-1, genericSearch(l4, 'f')),
      () -> assertEquals(-1, genericSearch(l5, List.of(1, 2, 3))));
  }
}
```

```
import java.util.List;

class GenericSearch {

  /**
   * Returns the index of the first occurrence of k in t or -1 if it does not exist.
   * @param t the list of type T.
   * @param k the object of type T to search for.
   * @return the index of k or -1.
   */
  static <T> int genericSearch(List<T> t, T k) {
    for (int i = 0; i < t.size(); i++) {
      if (t.get(i).equals(k)) {
        return i;
      }
    }
    return -1;
  }
}
```

3.5.1 Bounded Type Parameters

To restrict the type parameter to a certain subset of types, we can use *bounded type parameters*. As an example, we might wish to restrict a type parameter for a method to only types that implement the Comparable interface.[23] Doing so means that the type parameter has access to any methods defined by the interface, in this case, compareTo being the only available method. To specify a bounded type parameter, we use the extends keyword, e.g., <T extends Comparable>, which serves as an upper-bound on the type parameter, since we are restricting the type parameter to a subset of types that are "above" the specified type. We might also wish to use a lower-bound, which restricts the type parameter to a subset of types that are "below" the specified type. For example, if we want to restrict the type parameter to only types that are superclasses of Integer, we can use <T super Integer>.

Example 3.51. Let's design the T max(List<T> ls) method, which receives a list *t* whose elements are of type T, and returns the maximum element in the list. Because determining the max element of a list involves comparison-based checking, we restrict the type parameter to only types that implement Comparable. In the previous section, we discussed that Optional is a container class that either holds a value or is empty. An exercise at the end of this section asks you to use Optional in designing a similar method, rather than returning null, as we do here.

```java
import static Assertions.assertAll;
import static Assertions.assertEquals;

import java.util.List;
import java.util.ArrayList;

class GenericMaxTester {

  @Test
  void testGenericMax() {
    List<Integer> l1 = new ArrayList<>(List.of(5, 10, 20, 7, 2));
    List<String> l2 = new ArrayList<>(List.of("A", "e", "x", "3", "N"));
    List<Double> l3 = new ArrayList<>(List.of(500.0, 3.0, Math.PI));
    List<Character> l4 = new ArrayList<>(List.of('?','@','A','a','Z'));
    List<List<Integer>> l5 = new ArrayList<>();
    assertAll (
      () -> assertEquals(20, genericMax(l1)),
      () -> assertEquals("x", genericMax(l2)),
      () -> assertEquals(500.0, genericMax(l3)),
      () -> assertEquals('a', genericMax(l4)),
      () -> assertEquals(null, genericMax(l5)));
  }
}
```

```java
import java.util.Comparable;
import java.util.List;

class GenericMax {

  /**
   * Returns the maximum element in the list according compareTo of type T.
   * @param t the list of type T, where T is a type that implements Comparable.
   * @return the maximum element in the list.
   */
  static <T extends Comparable<T>> T genericMax(List<T> t) {
    if (t.isEmpty()) { return null; }
    else {
```

---

[23] For now, "implementing" an "interface" means that a type "behaves like" another type. So, a type that implements Comparable means that it behaves like a "comparable" object.

```
    T max = t.get(0);
    for (int i = 1; i < t.size(); i++) {
      if (t.get(i).compareTo(max) > 0) {
        max = t.get(i);
      }
    }
    return max;
  }
}
```

Wildcards and Unspecific Bounds

Sometimes we want to specify that a collection contains different, but related, types. If we declare a List<Integer>, then Java throws a compile-time error if we attempt to pass, say, an unboxed double, since a Double is not of type Integer. As a solution, Java allows the programmer to enforce *wildcard* bounds on the type of a generic.

Example 3.52. Reusing the example that we just talked about, if we want to store both Integer and Double objects in the same collection, we need to examine how they are related. Both of these classes extend the Number superclass, so we can place an upper-bound on the type parameter to say that anything that extends Number, whatever it may be, can be stored in the collection. Wildcards are denoted via the question mark: '?', to represent that it can be substituted with any other type that satisfies the bound criteria. Our example method, which computes the sum of a list of numbers, requires the substitutable type to be a subclass of Number.

```
import static Assertions.assertAll;
import static Assertions.assertEquals;

import java.util.List;

class NumberListTester {

  private static final double DELTA = 0.0000001;

  @Test
  void testSum() {
    assertAll(
      () -> assertEquals(0, sum(List.of())),
      () -> assertEquals(42, sum(List.of(-1, (short) 138.2,
                                         2.6d, -95L, -2.8f)), DELTA));
  }
}
```

```
import java.util.List;

class NumberList {

  /**
   * Computes the sum of a list of Number subclasses.
   * @param ls list of Number instances.
   * @return sum as a double.
   */
```

```java
  static double sum(List<? extends Number> ls) {
    return ls.stream()
            .mapToDouble(Number::doubleValue)
            .sum();
  }
}
```

Example 3.53. Lower-bounded type parameters are the dual to upper-bounded type parameters. If we want to restrict our possible types in a generic implementation to be only superclasses of a type, we can easily do so. For instance, the following code specifies that the input list must only contain objects that are superclasses of Integer, or are Integer itself. Unfortunately, the only classes that are ancestors/superclasses of Integer are Number and Object, which severely limits the capabilities of our list. For the sake of an example, we might return a string containing the "stringified" elements, separated by commas, enclosed by brackets.

```java
import static Assertions.assertAll;
import static Assertions.assertEquals;

import java.util.List;

class NumberListTester {

  @Test
  void testStringify() {
    assertAll(
      () -> assertEquals("[]", stringify(List.of())),
      () -> assertEquals("[42, 32, Hi]", stringify(List.of(42, 32, (Object) "Hi"))));
  }
}
```

```java
import java.util.List;
import java.util.stream.Collectors;

class NumberList {

  /**
   * Receives a list of objects that are superclasses of Integer
   * and converts them to their string counterparts and puts them
   * in a list representation.
   * @param ls list of instances that are superclasses of Integer.
   * @return stringified list.
   */
  static String stringify(List<? super Integer> ls) {
    return ls.stream()
            .map(Object::toString)
            .collect(Collectors.joining(", ", "[", "]"));
  }
}
```

Without our own classes to work with, the potential benefits for wildcards and type parameter bounds are not easy to see. We present them in this chapter, though, to minimally demo their existence.

3.6 Tree-Based Data Structures

At the start of section 3.2, we distinguished between three types of data structures: array-based, dictionary-based, and set-based. To close off this part of the chapter, we will dive into a more advanced data structure category: tree-based structures.

A *tree* is a recursive data structure by nature. Trees comprise *nodes* and *edges* between nodes. Let's draw a simple tree that stores some arbitrary numbers.

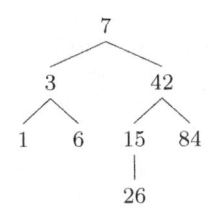

```
          7
         / \
        3   42
       / \  / \
      1  6 15  84
           |
           26
```

Fig. 3.13: Example of a Binary Tree

The example in Figure 3.13 is called a *binary tree* because all nodes have at most two children. The top-most node in the tree, 7 is called the *root*, which has two children that are trees themselves 3 and 41. The root has a *depth* of zero, whereas 3 and 41 have depth of one. A node m is a child of node a if there is a direct edge between a and m, where the depth level of a is exactly one fewer than m's depth level. We consider a node m to be a *descendant* of node a if there is a sequence of edges from a to m, where the depth level of a is at least one fewer than m's depth level. The *height* of a tree T is the maximum of the depth of T's root and its children. In the example, the tree's height is three due to the path from 7 to 26.

At this point the reader may await us to show them a collections framework implementation of a tree. Unfortunately, Java provides no implementation of trees in its collections framework. To compensate, we provide a library that mimics what Java might provide (see Appendix B for the code implementation). In this library we include the BinarySearchTree class, alongside a few other tree implementations that are more complex. The difference between a binary search tree and a standard binary tree is that the elements are ordered. All nodes to the left of a node T are "less than" T, whereas all nodes to the right of T are greater than T. The tree example from Figure 3.13 is, coincidentally, a binary search tree.

To create a binary search tree, we initialize and instantiate an object of type Binary-SearchTree.[24] Similar to how ArrayList and LinkedList are "kinds of" List objects, a BinarySearchTree is a "kind of" Tree object. To add an element to the binary search tree, we invoke its add method. Nodes are inserted according to their natural ordering if a Comparator is not specified when instantiating the binary search tree, identical to priority queues. Be aware that the elements of the tree must be Comparable.

Example 3.54. To visit the elements of a binary tree, we can write one of three methods: preorderTraversal, inorderTraversal, or postorderTraversal. All three traversal types are recursive by design.

- A *preorder traversal* visits the current node, then recurses on its left child, then recurses on its right child.

---

[24] We do *not* initialize the type to Tree because a Tree does not contain methods for accessing the children of the tree.

> **Teaching Java Binary Search Trees**
>
> A *binary search tree* is a data structure that stores elements in sorted order.
>
> BinarySearchTree<T> t = new BinarySearchTree<>(v) creates a binary search tree t whose root has the value v.
> BinarySearchTree<T> t = new BinarySearchTree<>(v, cmp) creates a binary search tree t whose root has the value v and uses cmp as a comparator when inserting values.
> void insert(v) inserts v into the existing tree using either the stored comparator or the natural ordering of the T type.
> BinarySearchTree<T> contains(v) determines whether or not v is in the tree. If so, the subtree where v is the root is returned; null otherwise.
> int size() returns the number of elements in the tree.
> BinarySearchTree<T> getLeft() returns the left child of the tree, or null if non-existent.
> BinarySearchTree<T> getRight() returns the right child of the tree, or null if non-existent.
> BinarySearchTree<T> getParent() returns the parent of the tree, or null if non-existent.
> boolean isLeaf() returns true if this tree has no children, and false otherwise.
> boolean isRoot() returns true if this tree has no parent, and false otherwise.

Fig. 3.14: Useful Binary Search Tree Methods.

- An *inorder traversal* recurses on its left child, then visits the current node, then recurses on its right child.
- A *postorder traversal* recurses on its left child, then recurses on its right child, then visits the current node.

Let's design the List<T> inorderTraversal(Tree<T> t) method, which returns a list of the elements in the tree after an inorder traversal. An interesting (and mathematically-provable) property of this traversal is that it always visits the elements in sorted order (according to the natural ordering or the comparator). To make testing this method easier, we will take advantage of the fact that we can pass a list of values to the BinarySearchTree constructor, which "bulk adds" them to the tree.

```java
import static Assertions.assertAll;
import static Assertions.assertEquals;

import java.util.List;
import learningjava.trees.BinarySearchTree;

class InorderTraversalTester {

  @Test
  void testInorderTraversal() {
    BinarySearchTree<Integer> t1 = new BinarySearchTree<>();
    BinarySearchTree<Integer> t2 = new BinarySearchTree<>(List.of(7,42,1,6,15,84,26));
    assertAll(
      () -> assertEquals(List.of(), inorderTraversal(t1)),
      () -> assertEquals(List.of(1, 6, 7, 15, 26, 42, 84), inorderTraversal(t2)));
  }
}
```

3.6 Tree-Based Data Structures

```java
import java.util.Comparable;
import java.util.List;
import java.util.ArrayList;
import learningjava.trees.Tree;
import learningjava.trees.BinarySearchTree;

class InorderTraversal {

  /**
   * Returns a list of the elements in the tree after an inorder traversal.
   * @param t the tree to traverse.
   * @return a list of elements.
   */
  static <T extends Comparable<T>> List<T> inorder(BinarySearchTree<T> t) {
    if (t == null) { return new ArrayList<>(); }
    else {
      List<T> left = inorder(t.getLeft());
      List<T> right = inorder(t.getRight());
      List<T> res = new ArrayList<>();
      res.addAll(left);
      res.add(t.getValue());
      res.addAll(right);
      return res;
    }
  }
}
```

A tree is said to be *balanced* if the heights of its left and right children differ by at most one. This property allows for very fast object lookup times, insertions, and removals. Maintaining the balance factor of a tree is a non-trivial task, though, and the `BinarySearchTree` class does not balance the tree, meaning the fast operation times are not guaranteed. In fact, these operations are, in their worst case, the same as a linked list, because the shape of a *totally unbalanced* binary search tree resembles a list. By "totally unbalanced," we mean that all elements are to the left or right of the root, a property that applies recursively to its children.

Example 3.55. Let's design the `T findMax(BinarySearchTree t)` method that finds the largest element of a binary search tree. All this involves is following the right-most child until we reach a dead-end. Because all elements to the right of another are larger than the node, this task is trivial.

```java
import static Assertions.assertEquals;
import static Assertions.assertAll;

import java.util.List;
import learningjava.trees.BinarySearchTree;

class FindMaxTester {

  @Test
  void testFindMax() {
    BinarySearchTree<Integer> t1 = new BinarySearchTree<>();
    BinarySearchTree<Integer> t2 = new BinarySearchTree<>(List.of(7, 42, 1, 6, 84, 26));
    assertAll(
      () -> assertEquals(null, findMax(t1)),
      () -> assertEquals(84, findMax(t2)));
  }
}
```

```
import java.util.Comparable;
import learningjava.trees.BinarySearchTree;

class FindMax {

  /**
   * Finds the maximum value in a tree.
   * @param t the tree to search.
   * @return the maximum value in the tree, or null if the tree is empty.
   */
  static <T extends Comparable<T>> T findMax(BinarySearchTree<T> t) {
    if (t.isEmpty()) { return null; }
    else if (t.getRight().isEmpty()) { return t.getValue(); }
    else { return findMax(t.getRight()); }
  }
}
```

Example 3.56. Let's design the `boolean isBalanced(Tree t)` method to determine whether or not a tree is balanced. As we stated, a tree is balanced if the difference between the heights of its left and right subtrees differ by at most one. The idea is to recursively traverse each subtree until we reach a leaf, at which we know that the tree is balanced. We then compare the heights of the left and right subtrees, and if they differ by more than one, we return `false`. Because we use a logical `AND` operator, if any subtree is unbalanced, the entire tree is unbalanced, because the `false` return value propagates upward.

```
import static Assertions.assertTrue;
import static Assertions.assertFalse;
import static Assertions.assertAll;

import java.util.List;
import learningjava.trees.BinarySearchTree;

class IsBalancedTester {

  @Test
  void testIsBalanced() {
    BinarySearchTree<Integer> t1 = new BinarySearchTree<>();
    BinarySearchTree<Integer> t2 = new BinarySearchTree<>(List.of(7,42,1,6,15,84,26));
    BinarySearchTree<Integer> t3 = new BinarySearchTree<>(List.of(10, 5, 20));
    assertAll(
        () -> assertTrue(isBalanced(t1)),
        () -> assertFalse(isBalanced(t2)),
        () -> assertTrue(isBalanced(t3)));
  }
}
```

```
import java.util.Comparable;
import learningjava.trees.BinarySearchTree;

class IsBalanced {

  /**
   * Determines whether a tree is balanced. A tree is balanced if the difference
   * between the heights of its left and right subtrees differ by at most one.
   * @param t the tree to check.
   * @return true if the tree is balanced, false otherwise.
   */
```

3.6 Tree-Based Data Structures

```
static <T extends Comparable<T>> boolean isBalanced(BinarySearchTree<T> t) {
  if (t.isEmpty()) {
    return true;
  } else {
    boolean left = isBalanced(t.getLeft());
    boolean right = isBalanced(t.getRight());
    int leftHeight = t.getLeft().height();
    int rightHeight = t.getRight().height();
    return left && right && Math.abs(leftHeight - rightHeight) <= 1;
  }
}
```

Example 3.57. Let's design the `BinarySearchTree<T> inorderSucc(BinarySearchTree<T> t)` method, which returns the inorder successor of a node in a given binary search tree. The inorder successor of a node n is the node with the smallest value that is greater than n's value. Another way to phrase it is the next-greatest element in the tree. The algorithm to find the inorder successor of a node n is as follows:

- If n has a right child, then the inorder successor is the left-most child of n's right subtree.
- If n has no right child, then the inorder successor is the first ancestor of n that is a left child.

Following the first case is trivial, because we only need to traverse the left subtree of n's right child. The second case is more difficult, because we need to traverse the tree *upwards* until we find the first ancestor that is a left child. We can do this by keeping track of the parent of n, and if n is its parent's left child, we return the parent.

```
import static Assertions.assertAll;
import static Assertions.assertEquals;
import java.util.List;
import learningjava.trees.BinarySearchTree;

class InorderSuccTester {

  @Test
  void testInorderSucc() {
    BinarySearchTree<Integer> t1 = new BinarySearchTree<>();
    BinarySearchTree<Integer> t2 = new BinarySearchTree<>(List.of(7, 42, 1, 6, 84, 26));
    assertAll(
      () -> assertEquals(null, inorderSucc(t1)),
      () -> assertEquals(null, inorderSucc(t2.contains(42))),
      () -> assertEquals(15, inorderSucc(t2.contains(7))),
      () -> assertEquals(42, inorderSucc(t2.contains(26))));
  }
}
```

```
import java.util.Comparable;
import learningjava.trees.BinarySearchTree;

class InorderSuccessor {

  /**
   * Returns the inorder successor of a node in a binary search tree.
   * @param t the node to find the successor of.
   * @return the inorder successor of the node, or null if the node has no successor.
   */
```

```
  static <T extends Comparable<T>> T inorderSuccessor(BinarySearchTree<T> t) {
    if (t.isEmpty()) { return null; }
    else if (t.getRight() != null) {
      BinarySearchTree<T> temp = t.getRight();
      while (temp != null) {
        temp = temp.getLeft();
      }
      return temp;
    } else {
      BinarySearchTree<T> parent = t.getParent();
      while (parent != null && t == parent.getRight()) {
        t = parent;
        parent = parent.getParent();
      }
      return parent;
    }
  }
}
```

Example 3.58. Let's see an example of why we might care about finding the inorder successor of a node. We will design the Set<T> findBetween(BinarySearchTree<T> t, T min, T max) method, which returns a set of all elements in the tree that are between min and max. There are two ways we can solve this problem: (1) traverse the tree and add elements to the set if they are between min and max, or (2) find the inorder successor of min, and then traverse the tree until we reach max. The former approach is more straightforward, but the latter is more efficient, because it takes advantage of the fact that the tree is ordered. The latter algorithm is as follows:

- Find the inorder predecessor to min, or min itself if it is in the tree.
- Traverse the tree until we reach max, adding elements to the set as we go, computing the inorder successor of each node.

First, we need an algorithm to find the inorder predecessor of a node. This encompasses searching for the location of the node in the tree and returning it, if it exists. Otherwise we return the parent of the last node we visited. We will explicitly show the findPredecessor method, but it will be used in the implementation of our findBetween method.

```
import static Assertions.assertEquals;
import static Assertions.assertAll;

import learningjava.trees.BinarySearchTree;

class FindBetweenTester {

  @Test
  void testFindBetween() {
    BinarySearchTree<Integer> t1 = new BinarySearchTree<>();
    BinarySearchTree<Integer> t2 = new BinarySearchTree<>(List.of(7, 42, 1, 6, 84, 26));
    assertAll(
      () -> assertEquals(Set.of(), findBetween(t1, 0, 100)),
      () -> assertEquals(Set.of(1, 6, 7, 26, 42), findBetween(t2, 0, 100)),
      () -> assertEquals(Set.of(6, 7, 26), findBetween(t2, 3, 26)),
      () -> assertEquals(Set.of(6, 7), findBetween(t2, 3, 25)));
  }
}
```

3.6 Tree-Based Data Structures

```java
import java.util.Comparable;
import java.util.HashSet;
import java.util.Set;
import learningjava.trees.BinarySearchTree;

class FindBetween {

  /**
   * Returns a set of all elements in the tree that are between min and max.
   * @param t the tree to search.
   * @param u the minimum value.
   * @param v the maximum value.
   * @return a set of elements between u and v.
   */
  static <T extends Comparable<T>> Set<T> findBetween(BinarySearchTree<T> t, T u, T v) {
    Set<T> res = new HashSet<>();
    BinarySearchTree<T> temp = findPredecessor(t, u);
    while (temp != null && temp.getValue().compareTo(v) <= 0) {
      // Add the element to the set if it is between u and v.
      if (temp.getValue().compareTo(u) >= 0) {
        res.add(temp.getValue());
      }
      temp = inorderSuccessor(temp);
    }
    return res;
  }
}
```

Maintaining a balanced binary tree, as we suggested earlier, guarantees fast operations. This invariant is non-trivial to maintain, and there are several *height-balancing* tree data structures that do so. For example, there are *AVL* trees, *red-black* trees, and *splay* trees (the list is by no means exhaustive) (Cormen et al., 2009; Weiss, 1998). Trees are a natural fit for programming language interpreters and design. Moreover, height-balancing trees are the basis for the `TreeSet` and `TreeMap` classes, which guarantee quick operation times. We end our discussion on trees here, but we will revisit them in a subsequent chapter on advanced object-oriented programming, where their practicality becomes more apparent.

3.7 Exercises

3.1 Design the `int[] operate(int[] A)` method that, when given an array of integers, returns a new array where the elements are the result of applying the following operation to each element: if the ith element is odd, multiply it by its index i plus one. Otherwise, divide it by its index i plus one.

3.2 Design the `int[] multiplesOf8(int[] A)` that, when given an array of integers, returns a new array where, upon finding a multiple of eight, each successive element becomes that multiple of eight. If another multiple of eight is found, it is not replaced, but all elements to its right change. Consider the following example. `multiplesOf8([3, 4, 8, 2, 19, 24, 20])` returns `[3, 4, 8, 8, 8, 24, 24]`.

3.3 This exercise has two parts. Rectangular coordinates are traditional x and y coordinates of a two-dimensional space. Polar coordinates, on the other hand, also operate in two dimensions, but instead have a radius and an angle.

(a) Design the `double[] toPolar(double x, double y)` method that, when given x and y coordinates, returns a two-element array containing the polar coordinates r in index 0 and θ in index 1, where the latter is in radians. We can convert from rectangular to polar coordinates using the following formula:

$$r = \sqrt{x^2 + y^2}$$
$$\theta = \arctan(y/x)$$

(b) Design the `double[] toRectangular(double r, double theta)` method that, when given a radius r and an angle θ in radians, returns a two-element array containing the rectangular coordinates x in index 0 and θ in index 1. We can convert from polar to rectangular coordinates using the following formula:

$$x = r \cos \theta$$
$$y = r \sin \theta$$

3.4 Design the `boolean containsOnlyPrime(int[] arr)` method that returns whether or not a given array of integers contains only prime integers. Hint: use the method you wrote in Chapter 2.

3.5 This question has two parts.

(a) Design the recursive `linearSearch` method that, when given a `String[]` S and a `String` to search for k, returns the index of k in S, and -1 if k is not in the array. This method is definitionally tail recursive, you should write a `private` helper method that actually performs the recursion.[25]
(b) Design the `linearSearchLoop` method that solves the problem using a loop.

---

[25] By "definitionally tail recursive," we mean that, even though a standard recursive variant exists, it is strongly recommended to only use a tail recursive algorithm, given the recursive definition requirement.

3.7 Exercises

3.6 Design the `int[] accSum(int[] A)` method, which receives an array of integers and returns a new array of integers that corresponds to the accumulated sum between each integer. We present some examples below.

```
accSum({1, 7, 2, 9})               => {1, 8, 10, 19}
accSum({1, 3, 3, 4, 5, 5, 6, 6, 2}) => {1, 4, 7, 11, 16, 21, 27, 33, 35}
accSum({5, 5, 5, 5, 5, 5, 5, 1, 5}) => {5, 10, 15, 20, 25, 30, 35, 36, 41}
```

3.7 Design the `String[] fizzBuzz(int min, int max)` method that iterates over the interval $[min, max]$ (you may assume $max \geq min$) and returns an array containing strings that meet the following criteria:

- If i is divisible by 3, insert "Fizz".
- If i is divisible by 5, insert "Buzz".
- If i is divisible by both 3 and 5, insert "FizzBuzz".
- Otherwise, insert "i", where i is the current number.

```
fizzBuzz(1, 12)  => {"1", "2", "Fizz", "4", "Buzz",
                     "Fizz", "7", "8", "Fizz", "Buzz",
                     "11", "Fizz"}
fizzBuzz(15, 18) => {"FizzBuzz", "16", "17", "Fizz"}
```

3.8 Using only arrays, design the `int[] findIntersection(int[] A, int[] B)` method that returns an array containing the *intersection* of two arrays. The intersection of two arrays is the set of elements that are common to both arrays. For example, the intersection of $\{7, 4, 8, 0, 2, 1\}$ and $\{8, 6, 4, 9, 26, 4, 0\}$ is $\{7, 8, 0\}$. Do not assume that the arrays are sorted, and you cannot sort them yourself.

3.9 Design the `int median(int[] A, int[] B)` that, when given two sorted (in increasing order) arrays of integers A and B, returns the median value of those two lists. You can use auxiliary data structures to help in solving the problem, but they are not necessary.

3.10 Design the `double sumOfAverages(int[] A)` method that, when given a list of arbitrary integers from 1 to 100 A, returns the average of the averages of the numbers when grouped by their right-most digit. That is, consider the list [91, 34, 87, 22, 67, 41, 10, 12, 13, 44]. If we group these by their right-most digit, we get [[10], [41, 91], [12, 22], [13], [34, 44], [67]]. The sum of the average of the "buckets" is 211. You cannot use any auxiliary Java Collections data structures, e.g., maps/lists, to solve this problem; only arrays are permitted. Your algorithm must also run in linear time, i.e., only dependent on the input array size, and use at most two traversals.

3.11 Design the `double sumNasty(ArrayList<Integer> vals)` method that returns the average of the numbers in the list with the following caveat: The number 9 should not be counted towards the average, nor should the following number, should one exist.

```
sumNasty({8, 7, 11, 9, 12, 10}) => 9.0
sumNasty({120, 99, 9})          => 109.5
sumNasty({9})                   => 0.0
sumNasty({})                    => 0.0
```

3.12 Design the `int[] countEvenOdds(int[] vals)` method that returns a tuple (an array of two values) where index zero stores the amount of even values and index one stores the amount of odd values.

```
countEvenOdds({11, 9, 2, 3, 7, 10, 12, 114})  => {4, 4}
countEvenOdds({11, 13, 15, 17})               => {0, 4}
```

3.13 This question has two parts.

(a) Design the `isAlmostStrictlyIncreasing` tail recursive method that, when given an array of integers, determines if it is strictly increasing. There is a catch to this: we also return true if the array can be made strictly increasing by removing exactly one element from the array. For instance, `isAlmostStrictlyIncreasing({1, 3, 2, 4})` returns true because, by removing 3, we get a list that is strictly increasing. Compare this with 2, 3, 2, 4, which cannot be made strictly increasing.

(b) Design the `isAlmostStrictlyIncreasingLoop` method that solves the problem using a loop.

If you write tests for one of these methods, you should be able to propagate it through the rest, so write plenty!

3.14 Design the `boolean isSubArray(int[] A, int[] B)` method, which receives two arrays of integers A and B, and determines if B is a "sub-array" of A. This means that all elements of B are elements of A.

3.15 Design the `int[] twoDimToOneDim(int[][] A)` method, which will flatten a given two-dimensional array of integers into a one-dimensional array. Hint: figure out how many elements the resulting one-dimensional array should have, and only then figure out how to position elements.

3.16 Design the `boolean canBalanceArray(int[] A)` method, which determines whether or not an array of integers A can be split into a partition that balances each side. Use the following examples as motivation.

```
canBalanceArray(new int[]{1, 1, 1, 1, 5})      => false
canBalanceArray(new int[]{2, 3, 5})            => true
canBalanceArray(new int[]{-10, 2, -58, 50})    => true
canBalanceArray(new int[]{3, -1, -1, -1, 0})   => true
canBalanceArray(new int[]{3, 2, 1, 0})         => true
canBalanceArray(new int[]{10})                 => false
```

3.17 A *span* is the distance between a value and another, distinct occurrence of the same value. Design the `int largestSpan(int[] A)` method that, when given a non-empty array of integers A, returns the largest span. It may be beneficial to write the `firstIndexOf` and `lastIndexOf` methods to help in your design process. Use the following examples as motivation.

```
largestSpan(new int[]{4, 2, 3, 2, 5})             => 3
largestSpan(new int[]{1, 2, 3, 4, 5})             => 1
largestSpan(new int[]{5, 4, 4, 4, 3, 4, 1, 4, 1}) => 7
```

3.18 A *fixed window* is a "window," or sub-array, of an array. Design the `List<List<Integer>>` `computeFixedWindows(int[] A, int k)` method that, when given an array of integers A and an integer k, returns a list of lists L where each list in L is a fixed window of size $\leq k$ that moves through A.

For example, if $A = [1, 2, 3, 4, 5, 6, 7]$ and $k = 2$, then `computeFixedWindows` returns $\{\{1,2\}\{3,4\}, \{5,6\}, \{7\}\}$.

3.7 Exercises

3.19 A *sliding window* is a "window," or subarray, of an array that slides "through the elements" of an array. Design the List<List<Integer>> computeSlidingWindows(int[] A, int k) method that, when given an array of integers A and an integer k, returns a list of lists L where each list in L is a sliding window of exactly size k that moves through A.

For example, if $A = [1, 2, 3, 4, 5, 6, 7]$ and $k = 2$, then computeSlidingWindows returns $\{\{1,2\}, \{2,3\}, \{3,4\}, \{4,5\}, \{5,6\}, \{6,7\}\}$. Note the difference between the sliding window and the fixed window.

3.20 Design the String[][] computeBowlingScores(String[] S, int[][][] scores) method that computes the bowling score for each player name in S. The scores are separated by rows, where the ith row corresponds to the ith name in S. Each row contains ten arrays of 3-element arrays. These triples, as we will call them, correspond to a bowling frame. The first nine frames only use the first two slots of the triple, whereas the last may use all three.

To compute the score of a player, there are a few rules. Note that, in bowling, the objective is to knock down all ten pins.

For frames 1 to 9:

- If the player scores a strike, meaning they hit all ten pins with one throw, it is worth ten points plus the sum of the next two frames, if they exist.
- If the player scores a spare, meaning they hit all ten points with exactly two throws, it is worth ten points, plus the sum of the next frame, if it exists.
- If the player does not score a strike nor a spare, they earn as many points as pins knocked down.

For frame 10:

- If the player scores a strike on the first throw, they get two more attempts.
- If the player scores a spare resulting from the first two throws, they get one more attempt.
- If the player does not score a strike nor a spare from the first two shots, they earn as many points as pins knocked down.

The resulting array contains n rows to represent n players, where the first element of a row is the player name alphabetized, and the second is their score.

3.21 We can represent matrices as two-dimensional arrays. For example, the matrix

$$\begin{bmatrix} 1 & 2 & 3 \\ 4 & 5 & 6 \\ 7 & 8 & 9 \end{bmatrix}$$

can be represented as the two-dimensional array

`int[][] matrix = {{1, 2, 3}, {4, 5, 6}, {7, 8, 9}};`

Design the int[][] transpose(int[][] matrix) method that returns the transpose of a given matrix. The transpose of a matrix is the matrix where the rows and columns are swapped. For example, the transpose of the above matrix is

$$\begin{bmatrix} 1 & 4 & 7 \\ 2 & 5 & 8 \\ 3 & 6 & 9 \end{bmatrix}$$

3.22 Design the int[][] rotate(int[][] matrix) method that returns the matrix rotated 90 degrees clockwise. For example, the matrix is rotated to

$$\begin{bmatrix} 1 & 4 & 7 \\ 2 & 5 & 8 \\ 3 & 6 & 9 \end{bmatrix}$$

$$\begin{bmatrix} 3 & 2 & 1 \\ 6 & 5 & 4 \\ 9 & 8 & 7 \end{bmatrix}$$

To rotate a matrix, take its transposition, then reverse each row. You may assume that the input matrix is $N \times N$, i.e., a square matrix.

3.23 Design the int[][] multiply(int[][] A, int[][] B) method that returns the product of two matrices, where A is $M \times N$ and B is $P \times Q$. Not all matrices can be multiplied, so you should return null if the matrices cannot be multiplied. Two matrices can be multiplied if and only if $N = P$. The product of two matrices A and B is the matrix C where $C_{i,j} = \sum_{k=1}^{N} A_{i,k} \cdot B_{k,j}$ for the indices i, k, and j.

3.24 Design the boolean canSum(int[] A, int t) method that, when given an array of integers A and a target t, determines whether or not there exists a group of numbers in A that sum to t. For example, if $A = \{2, 4, 10, 8\}$ and $t = 9$, then canSum returns false because there is no possible selection of integers from A that sum to 9. On the other hand, if $A = \{3, 7, 4, 5, 9\}$ and $t = 8$, then we return true because $3 + 5 = 8$. If $A = \{2, 4, 2, 11, 5, 4\}$ and $t = 9$, then we return true because $1 + 4 + 4 = 9$, but also $4 + 5 = 9$ and $5 + 4 = 9$.

There is a simple recursive algorithm to solve this problem: if you have searched through the entire array, return whether or not the target is zero. Otherwise, make two recursive calls: one for where you choose the current number and a second for where you do not. By "choose," we mean to say that the current number is subtracted from the target value. By "current number," we mean to suggest a method that resembles the tail recursive linear search algorithm. You'll need to design a helper method to solve this problem using this approach.

3.25 *Linear regression* is used to compute a "line of best-fit" for a collection of (x, y) points. In particular, we find the equation for a line $y = \hat{\alpha} + \hat{\beta}x$, where $\hat{\alpha}$ is the y-intercept and $\hat{\beta}$ is the slope. The formulas for $\hat{\alpha}$ and $\hat{\beta}$ are as follows (Krishnan, 2018):

$$\hat{\alpha} = \frac{\sum_{i=1}^{n} y_i \sum_{i=1}^{n} x_i^2 - \sum_{i=1}^{n} x_i \sum_{i=1}^{n} x_i y_i}{n \sum_{i=1}^{n} x_i^2 - \left(\sum_{i=1}^{n} x_i\right)^2}$$

$$\hat{\beta} = \frac{n \sum_{i=1}^{n} x_i y_i - \sum_{i=1}^{n} x_i \sum_{i=1}^{n} y_i}{n \sum_{i=1}^{n} x_i^2 - \left(\sum_{i=1}^{n} x_i\right)^2}$$

Design the double[] linearRegression(double[] xs, double[] ys) method that, when given two arrays of doubles xs and ys, returns a two-element array containing the y-intercept and the slope, respectively. If the two arrays are not of the same length, return null.

3.26 The correlation coefficient r is a measure of the strength and direction of a linear relationship between two variables x and y. The value of r is always between -1 and 1. When $r > 0$, there is a positive linear relationship between x and y. When $r < 0$, there is a negative linear relationship between x and y. When $r = 0$ or is approximately zero, there is no (or

3.7 Exercises

little) linear relationship between x and y. The formula for the correlation coefficient is as follows (King and Minium, 2008):

$$r = \frac{1}{n-1} \cdot \frac{1}{S_x \cdot S_y} \cdot \sum_{i=1}^{n}(x_i - \bar{x})(y_i - \bar{y})$$

Where n is the number of data points, x_i and y_i are the ith data points, $\bar{x}$ and $\bar{y}$ are the means of x and y respectively, and S_x and S_y are the sample standard deviations of x and y respectively. To compute the sample standard deviation of a set of values S, we use the formula (King and Minium, 2008):

$$S_x = \sqrt{\frac{\sum_{i=1}^{|S|}(x_i - \bar{x})^2}{|S| - 1}}$$

Design the double correlationCoefficient(double[] xs, double[] ys) method that, when given two arrays of doubles xs and ys, returns the correlation coefficient between the two arrays. If the two arrays are not of the same length, return null.

3.27 In the chapter, we presented an example of "exploding" a string into its constituent characters. Design the List<Integer> explode(int n) method that, when given an integer n, returns a list of integers that represent the digits of n. For example, explode(123) returns [1, 2, 3]. You **cannot** convert the integer to a string to solve this problem or use any auxiliary data structures.

3.28 This exercise has two parts.

(a) Design the tail recursive cycleOperationsTR method to circularly apply +, -, then * to the elements of the list. You will need to design an appropriate helper method. Remember to include the relevant access modifiers!

```
cycleOperationsTR({})
    => 0
cycleOperationsTR({1, -4, 9, -16, 25, -36})
    => ((((((0 + 1) - -4) * 9) + -16) - 25) * -36)
    => -144
cycleOperationsTR({10, 5, -2, 1, -2})
    => (((((0 + 10) - 5) * -2) + 1) - -2)
    => -7
```

(b) Design the cycleOperationsLoop method, which solves the problem using either a while or for loop.

If you write tests for one of these methods, you should be able to propagate it through the rest, so write plenty!

3.29 Design the List<Integer> sumEvenMultOdd(int[] A) method that, when given an array of integers A, returns a List<Integer> whose first element is the sum of all elements at even indices of A, and whose second element is the product of all elements at odd indices of A. If you encounter a zero at an odd index, do not continue to multiply values (i.e., don't keep multiplying subsequent values and return the multiplied value before you encountered the zero, since the product will forever be zero from that point onward).

3.30 Design the `Set<List<Integer>> twoSum(int[] A, int t)` method that, when given an array of integers A and a target t, returns all possible pairs of numbers in A that sum to t. For example, if $A = \{2, 2, 4, 10, 6, -2\}$ and $t = 4$, we return a set containing two two-element lists: $\{2, 2\}$ and $\{6, -2\}$. Do not add a pair that already exists in the set or a pair that, by reversing the pair, we get a pair in the existing set. E.g., $\{-2, 6\}$ should not be added to the set.

There is a simple brute-force algorithm to solve this problem via two loops, but by incorporating a second set for lookups, we can do much better: for every number n in A, add n to a set S, and if $t - n = m$ for some $m \in S$, then we know that $m + n$ must equal t, therefore we add $\{n, m\}$ to the resulting set of integer arrays. Walking through this with the example from before, we get the following sequence of actions:

- Initialize $S = \{\}$ and $L = \{\}$. We know that $t = 4$.
- We add 2 to S. $S = \{2\}$.
- Because $4 - 2 \in S$, the two-element array $\{2, 2\}$ is added to L. 2 is not re-added to S.
- Because $4 - 4 \notin S$, we only add 4 to S. $S = \{2, 4\}$.
- Because $4 - 10 \notin S$, we only add 10 to S. $S = \{2, 4, 10\}$.
- Because $4 - 6 \notin S$, we only add 6 to S. $S = \{2, 4, 10, 6\}$.
- Because $4 - (-2) \in S$, the two-element array $\{6, -2\}$ is added to L. We add -2 to S. $S = \{2, 4, 10, 6, -2\}$.

3.31 Design the `ArrayList<String> shift(ArrayList<String> ls, int i)` method that, when given a list of strings s and an index i, returns a new list where each element is shifted by i spots. Negative values correspond to left shifts, and positive values correspond to right shifts. If a shift is nonsensical, do not shift at all. A nonsensical shift is one of the following:

- If there are no elements in the list.
- If there is only one element in the list.
- If there are only two elements in the list, you only need to shift once. Do the math!

This method is harder than it may appear at first glance, so write plenty of tests! You **cannot** use any auxiliary data structures or methods (from, say, `Collections`) to solve this problem.

```
shift({11, 12, 13, 14}, -1)        => {12, 13, 14, 11}
shift({120, 120, 140, 140}, 2)     => {140, 140, 120, 120}
shift({99999999}, 1000)            => {99999999}
shift({}, -9999999)                => {}
shift({120, 80, 70, 50, 40, 20}, -3) => {50, 40, 20, 120, 80, 70}
```

3.32 The *centroid* of a two-dimensional shape S is the arithmetic mean position of its points. That is, it is the point that represents the "middle" of a shape.

Design the `double[] centroid(double[] P)` method that, given an array of coordinates, returns the centroid of the shape described by P. The input array has values such that every two elements $P[i], P[i+1]$ form one coordinate pair. For instance, $P[0] = x_1$ and $P[1] = y_1$, meaning there are $|P|/2$ coordinate pairs. The `centroid` method should return a two-element array whose first is the x coordinate and whose second is the y coordinate. The formula for the centroid (described as a set of points) $C(x, y)$ is as follows:

$$C(x, y) = \left(\frac{1}{|P|} \sum_{i=0}^{|P|-1} P[2i], \frac{1}{|P|} \sum_{i=0}^{|P|-1} P[2i+1] \right)$$

3.7 Exercises

3.33 For this problem you are not allowed to use an ArrayList or any helper methods, e.g., .contains, or methods from the Arrays class. You *may* (and should) use a Set<Integer> to keep track of previously-seen peaks.

Joe the mountain climber has come across a large mountain range. He wants to climb only the tallest mountains in the range. Design the int[] peakFinder(int[] H) method that returns an array H' of all the peaks in an int[] of mountain heights H. A peak p is defined as an element of h at index i such that $p[i-1] < p[i]$ and $p[i] > p[i+1]$. If $i = 0$ or $i = |H|-1$, Joe will not climb $p[i]$. Joe doesn't want to climb a mountain of the same height more than once, so you should not add any peaks that have already been added to H'. We present some test cases below.

```
peakFinder({9, 13, 7, 2, 8})                => {13}
peakFinder({8, 7, 8, 7, 8, 7, 8, 7})        => {8}
peakFinder({111, 27, 84, 31, 5, 9, 4, 3, 2, 1, 64}) => {84, 9}
peakFinder({})                              => {}
peakFinder({1})                             => {}
peakFinder({1, 2})                          => {}
peakFinder({1, 2, 1})                       => {2}
peakFinder({1, 2, 3, 2, 1})                 => {3}
```

3.34 A professor gives their students extra credit on an exam if they can guess the average within five percent of the actual average.

Design the boolean earnsExtraCredit(List<Double> D, double g) method that, when given a list of scores D and a guess g, returns whether a student is given extra credit.

3.35 Design the List<String> roundTimes(List<String> T) method that, when given a list of "times" T, returns a new list where each time is rounded to its nearest quarter hour. A "time" is a string in the 24-hour format "HHMM", where $0 \le$ HH ≤ 23, and $0 \le$ MM ≤ 59. Rounding to the nearest quarter hour means to either a minute of 00, 15, 30, or 45. For example, "1247" rounds to "1245", and "1330" stays the same at "1330". If a time rounds up to the next hour, update the hour. For instance, "2359" rounds up to "0000", whereas "1955" rounds up to "2000".

3.36 A village has members where each has a partner. These members are grouped in pairs inside an ArrayList<Integer> where each pair of indices represents a relationship of the village. I.e., A.get($2i$) and A.get($2i+1$) are in a relationship. A couple is considered the wisest if they have the highest combined age. Design the ArrayList<Integer> wisest(ArrayList<Integer> A) method that, when given a list of (integer) ages A, return a new ArrayList<Integer> containing the ages of the wisest pair. If there is a tie, return the pair that has the highest age overall. The order is not significant. We present a few test cases below. You can assume that there will always be an even number of village members.

```
wisest({31, 42, 43, 35, 21, 27, 24, 44})  => {43, 35} or {35, 43}
wisest({47, 51, 52, 48, 33, 67, 45, 35})  => {33, 67} or {67, 33}
```

3.37 Design the char missingChar(Set<Character> s) method that, when given a set of characters whose values range from $a..z$ with one missing, return the character that is missing.

3.38 Design the boolean canBecomePalindrome(String s) method that, when given a string that is *not* a palindrome s, return whether its characters can be rearranged in such a way to become a palindrome. Hint: what are the properties of a palindrome? For instance, racecar and abbbbba are both palindromes. What is similar between the two aside from that fact?

3.39 Design the `Map<String, Integer> updateTransactions(Map<String, Integer> inv, List<String> transactions)` method that, when given a map of product names to product quantities, as well as a list of transactions, returns a new inventory map of item counts. The given list of transactions contains product names, and when a product goes out of stock, it should be removed from the returned map.

3.40 (⋆) File permissions are denoted in octal notation. That is, consider a file that has three sets of permissions: owner o, group g, and users u (representing other users). There are three ways to work with a file: reading from it R, writing to it W, or execution X. We might represent this as a bit string of $R_o W_o X_o R_g W_g X_g R_u W_u X_u$. We use a 1 or 0 to denote the permissions of a file. For example, 111001000 denotes that the file owner can read, write, and execute the file, those who are in the same group as the owner can execute the file, and anyone else cannot interact at all with the file. Design the `Set<String> availableFiles(Map<int[], Integer> F, String u, int g, boolean r, boolean w, boolean x)` method that, when given a map of files to permissions F, a username u and the group identifier g for the given user, returns a list of files that satisfy the flags passed to the method. The key for the map of files to permissions is itself a 3-element array, where the first element is the file name, the second element is the username of the file owner, and the third element is the group identifier of the owner, as a string.

3.41 You're given a `HashMap` M of `String` keys to `Integer` values corresponding to their length. Design the `ArrayList<TreeSet<String>> categorize(HashMap<String, Integer> M)` that receives M and converts it to an `ArrayList` of `TreeSet` values. Each element of the `ArrayList`, therefore, is itself a `TreeSet`. These `TreeSet` elements should store the strings whose mapped value matches the index of the `TreeSet`. The order of the resulting sets, therefore, **does** matter! Below is an example test case.

```
[<"x" : 1>, <"hello" : 5>, <"world" : 5>, <"hi" : 2>]
  => [{}, {"x"}, {"hi"}, {}, {}, {"hello", "world"}]
```

3.42 Design the `List<String> tokenize(String s, char d)` method that, when given a string s and a `char` delimiter d, returns an `ArrayList` of tokens split at the delimiter. You must do this by hand; you **cannot** call any `String` methods (except `.length` and `.charAt`).

3.43 Design the `Map<String, Integer> wordCount(String s)` method that, when given a string s, counts the number of words in the list, then stores the resulting frequencies in a `HashMap<String, Integer>`. Assume that s is not cleaned. That is, you should first remove all punctuation (periods, commas, exclamation points, question marks, semi-colons, dashes, hashes, ampersands, asterisks, and parentheses) from s, producing a new string s'. Then, split the string based on spaces (remember `tokenize`?), and produce a map of the words to their respective counts. Do not factor case into your total; e.g., `"fAcToR"` and `"factor"` count as the same word. The ordering of the returned map is not significant.

```
String s = "Hello world, the world is healthy, is
            it not? I certainly agree that the world
            is #1 and healthy."
wordCount(s) => [<"hello" : 1>, <"world" : 3>, <"the" : 2>
                 <"is" : 3>, <"healthy" : 2>, <"it" : 1>,
                 <"i" : 1>, <"certainly" : 1> <"agree" : 1>
                 <"that" : 1>, <"1" : 1>, <"and" : 1>, <"not" : 1>]
```

3.7 Exercises

3.44 (⋆) Design the `LinkedHashSet<String> largeToSmall(Map<String, Integer> M)` method that, when given a `Map<String, Integer>` M, returns a `LinkedHashSet` of `String` values where the words are inserted into the set in order of decreasing count. Words that have the same count do not need to be inserted in any particular order. E.g., `"is"` may come before `"world"`. You cannot sort M. Hint: create an array of size c (where c is the highest word count) where each element is a `LinkedHashSet<String>`. For every element e in M, add e to the set at index $M[i]$, where i is the count of e in M. Then, append these sets in reverse order according to their index. We provide some pseudocode below.

```
largeToSmall(M):
  // |M| is M.size().
  c = Get Highest Count Word in M
  array = [0 .. c-1]
  for i in [0 .. c-1]:
    array[i] = new LinkedHashSet<String>();
  for every key k in M:
    i = M.get(k)
    array[i-1].add(k)
  // Append all linked hash sets in reverse order.
  return array[c-1] appended to array[c-2] ... appended to array[0]

largeToSmall(wordCount(s)) => {"world", "is", "the", "healthy",
                              "hello", "it", "i", "certainly",
                              "agree", "that", "1", "and", "not"}
```

3.45 Design the `Set<Integer> symmetricDifference(Set<Integer> s1, Set<Integer> s2)` method that, when given two sets of integers s_1 and s_2, returns a new set s_3 such that all elements of s_3 are in either of the sets, but not in their intersection. That is, it is the set of elements that are in either s_1 or s_2, but not both.

3.46 Design the `Map<String, Set<String>> trending(Map<String, Set<String>> regionTopics, Set<String> gTrending)` method that, when given a map of regions to topics that are trending in that region, returns a map of topics to regions such that the keys are topics and the values are regions where that topic is trending. A topic is trending in a region if it is not a globally-trending topic and it is trending in at least two regions simultaneously. We provide an example below.

```
trending([<"North America" : {"Tech", "Comedy", "Sports"}>,
          <"Europe" : {"Comedy", "Music", "Sports"}>,
          <"Asia" : {"Fashion, "Music"}>], {"Tech"})
  => [<"Comedy" : {"North America", "Europe"}>, <"Music" : {"Europe, "Asia"}>]
```

3.47 Design the `LinkedList<Integer> pushLast(LinkedList<Integer> lon, int v)` method that, when given a `LinkedList<Integer>` l and an `int` v, returns a newly-instantiated `LinkedList<Integer>` with the same elements plus v added to the end of l.

3.48 Design the `LinkedList<Integer> set(LinkedList<Integer> l, int v, int i)` method that, when given a `LinkedList<Integer>` l, an `int` v, and an index i, returns a *new* `LinkedList<Integer>` with the same elements, except that the element at index i is, instead, the value v. If i is less than zero or exceeds the length of l, return null.

3.49 Design the `int[] toArray(LinkedList<Integer> l)` method, which receives a linked list of integers l, returns an array containing the values from l.

3.50 Design the `LinkedList<Integer> reverse(LinkedList<Integer> l)` method that, when given a linked list of integers l, returns a *new* linked list containing the elements of l, but reversed.

3.51 Design the `HashSet<Integer> moreThanThree(int[] A)` method, which receives an `int[] A` and returns a new `HashSet<Integer>` of values containing those values from A that occur strictly more than three times.

3.52 Design the `List<String> collectComments(String s)` method that, when given a string representing a (valid) Java program, returns an list containing all comments from the input program string. You cannot use any `String` helper methods (e.g., `strip`, `split`) to solve this problem nor can you use regular expressions.

3.53 Design the `List<String> removeSideBySideDups(List<String> ls)` that receives a list of strings, returns a new list where all side-by-side duplicates are removed.

3.54 Design the `boolean isPalindromeList(LinkedList<Integer> ls)` method, which receives a linked list of integers, determines if it is a palindrome list. You cannot use `.get` to solve the problem, nor can you use a `for` loop. Think about how you can use a `while` loop, an `Iterator`, and a `Stack` to do this.

3.55 Design the `double postfixEvaluator(List<String> l)` method that, when given a list of binary operators and numeric operands represents as strings, returns the result of evaluating the postfix-notation expression. You will need to write a few helper methods to solve this problem, and it is best to break it down into steps. First, write a method that determines if a given string is one of the four binary operators: `"+"`, `"-"`, `"*"`, or `"/"`. You may assume that any inputs that are not binary operators are operands, i.e., numbers. Then, write a method that applies a given binary operator to a list of operands, i.e., an `ArrayList<Double>`.

```
postfixEvaluator({"5", "2", "*", "5", "+", "2", "+"}) => 17
postfixEvaluator({"1", "2", "3", "4", "+", "+", "+"}) => 10
```

3.56 Design the `double prefixEvaluator(List<String>) l` method that, when given a list of binary operators and numeric operands represented as strings, returns the result of evaluating the prefix-notation expression. This is slightly more difficult than the postfix evaluator, but not by much. As with the previous exercise, write helper methods for determining whether or not a string is an operator or an operand, and use a stack. Hint: traverse the input list from right-to-left, but be careful about non-commutative operations!

```
prefixEvaluator({"+", "3", "4"}) => 7
prefixEvaluator({"+", "+", "2", "10", "*", "-5", "/", "16", "4"}) => -8
prefixEvaluator({"*", "-", "100", "20", "5"}) => 400
```

3.57 (*) Design the `List<List<String>> displayOrders(List<List<String>> orderInfo)` method that, when given an array of orders, returns a series of order specifications by customer table.

To be more specific, an order is a `List<String>` whose first element is the customer name, whose second element is the table number, and whose third element is the food that the customer is ordering.

Return the data as a list of rows of information. The first row displays the table headers. The first table header should be `"Table"`, followed by the food in alphabetical order. Each successive row represents a table in increasing numerical order. Below is an input and output example.

```
{{"John", "2", "Chicken"}, {"Samantha", "3", "Pasta"},
 {"Tim", "2", "BBQ Chicken"}, {"Christina", "8", "Grilled Cheese"},
 {"Tymberlyn", "2", "Chicken"}, {"TJ", "3", "Water"}}
=>
{{"Table", "BBQ Chicken", "Chicken", "Grilled Cheese", "Pasta", "Water"},
 {"2", "1", "2", "0", "0", "0"},
 {"3", "0", "0", "0", "1", "1"},
 {"8", "0", "0", "1", "0", "0"}}
```

3.58 Design the substitute method that, when given an *exp* as a String and an environment *env* as a HashMap<String, Integer>, substitutes each occurrence of an "identifier" for its value counterpart from the map.

```
substitute("f(x) = 3 * a + b", {<"a" : 10>, <"b" : 13>})
          => "f(x) = 3 * 10 + 13"
substitute("g(h, f(x)) = y + x", {<"q" : 200>})
          => "g(h, f(x)) = y + x"
```

3.59 (⋆) Design the unifiesAll method, which receives a HashMap<String, Integer> M of unification assignments and a list of goals ArrayList<LinkedList<String>> $\mathcal{G}$. Each goal $G \in \mathcal{G}$ is a tuple represented as a LinkedList; goals consist of two values x, y, and if it is possible for these to be the same value, then we say we can unify x with y. Any successful unifications that occur with variables not present in M should be added to M. We present some examples below (assume all values are strings; we omit the quotes out of conciseness). Hint: you might want to write an isVar predicate, which determines if a value is a variable or not, i.e., a value that does not start with a number.

```
M1 = {<x : 5>, <y : 10>, <z : 15>, <w : 5>}
G1 = {{x, x}, {10, 10}, {z, 15}, {x, w}}
unifiesAll(M1, G1) => true
M2 = {<x : 5>, <y : 10>, <z : 15>, <w : 5>}
G2 = {{x, y}}
unifiesAll(M2, G2) => false
M3 = {<x : 5>, <y : 10>, <z : 15>, <w : 5>}
G3 = {{q, x}, {w, 5}, {q, 5}, {q, w}}
unifiesAll(M3, G3) => true
M4 = {<x : 5>, <y : 10>, <z : 15>, <w : 5>}
G4 = {{q, x}, {q, 10}}
unifiesAll(M4, G4) => false
```

3.60 (⋆) Two strings s_1 and s_2 are isomorphic if we can create a mapping from s_1 from s_2. For example, the strings "DCBA" and "ZYXW" are isomorphic because we can map D to Z, C to Y, and so forth. Another example is "ABACAB" and "XYXZXY" for similar reasons. A non-example is "PROXY" and "ALPHA", because once we map "A" to "P", we cannot create a map between "A" and "Y". Design the boolean isIsomorphic(String s1, String s2) method, which determines whether or not two strings are isomorphic.

3.61 Anagrams are strings that are formed by rearranging the letters of another string. For example, "plea" is an anagram for "leap", but we consider an alphabetized anagram to be the alphabetized arrangement of letters for an anagram. As an example, "aelrst" is the alphabetized anagram for "alerts", "alters", "slater", and "staler". Design the static Map<String, List<String>> alphaAnagramGroups(List<String> los) method, which maps all alphabetized anagrams to the strings in *ls* using the above criteria.

```
los = ["presorting", "plea", "introduces", "anger", "leap", "petals",
       "donate", "plates", "range", "reductions", "rediscount",
       "tapers", "pale", "atoned", "staple", "repast", "reportings"]
alphaAnagramGroups(los)
  => {{"aegnr", ["anger", "range"]},
      {"aelp", ["plea", "leap", "pale"]},
      {"aelpst", ["petals", "plates", "staple"]},
      {"aeprst", ["tapers", "repast"]}
      {"cdeinorstu", ["introduces", "reductions", "rediscount"]},
      {"adenot", ["donate", "atoned"]},
      {"eginoprrst", ["presorting", "reportings"]}}
```

3.62 A *common letter sequence* is a sequence of characters such that each character is one-letter greater than another. For example, the list ['c', 'f', 'h', 'p', 'c', 'm', 'g'] contains the common letter sequence ['f', 'g', 'h'].

Design the List<Character> findLongestCommonLetterSequence(List<Character> l) method, which receives a list of characters *l* and returns the longest common letter sequence. That is, if there are multiple disjoint common letter sequences, return the one that is the longest. For example, ['n', 'o', 'f', 'h', 'm', 'g'] contains two disjoint common letter sequences: ['f', 'g', 'h'] and ['m', 'n', 'o'] If there are multiple disjoint longest common letter sequences, return the one whose first letter is the earliest in the alphabet. You may assume that every character in *l* is lower-cased.

3.63 A SLC (simplified lambda calculus) expression takes one of the two forms: *varList* or $\lambda var.E$, where *var* is a lower-case letter from '*u*' to '*z*', *varList* is a sequence of variables, and *E* is either a *var* or another SLC expression. We provide some examples below.

$$\lambda x.\lambda y.xyz$$
$$\lambda x.x$$
$$\lambda y.yzxw$$
$$\lambda w.\lambda x.\lambda y.\lambda z.z$$

Your job is to determine which variables are bound, which are free, and which are neither.

A *bound variable* is a variable that is bound by a λ and occurs in its expression. For example, in the expression $\lambda x.x$, '*x*' is bound.

A *free variable* is a variable that is *not* bound by a λ but does occur in an expression. For example, in the expression $\lambda y.\lambda x.zwv$, '*z*', '*w*', and '*v*' are free variables.

A variable that is neither free nor bound is a variable that is bound by a λ but does not occur in its expression. For example, in the expression $\lambda x.\lambda y.yz$, '*x*' is neither free nor bound.

Design the static HashMap<String, String> classifyVars(String E) method, which returns a map of variables to their classification. We provide some examples below. You may assume that the input is a valid SLC expression and that no variables shadow one another. Use the values V, B, and N to represent free, bound, and neither, respectively.

```
classifyVars("xyz")         => <"x" : "F">, <"y" : "F">, <"z" : "F">
classifyVars("λx.λy.xyz")   => <"x" : "B">, <"y" : "B">, <"z" : "F">
classifyVars("λx.λy.x")     => <"x" : "B">, <"y" : "N">
```

3.7 Exercises

3.64 The *substitution cipher* is a text cipher that encodes an alphabet string A (also called the *plain-text alphabet*) with a key string K (also called the *cipher-text alphabet*). The A string is defined as "ABCDEFGHIJKLMNOPQRSTUVWXYZ", and K is any permutation of A. We can encode a string s using K as a mapping from A. For example, if K is the string "ZEBRASCDFGHIJKLMNOPQTUVWXY" and s is "WE MIGHT AS WELL SURRENDER!", the result of encoding s produces "VN IDBCY JZ VNHH ZXRRNFMNR!"

Design the subtitutionCipher method, which receives a plain-text alphabet string A, a cipher-text string K, and a string s to encode, substitutionCipher should return a string s' using the aforementioned substitution cipher algorithm.

3.65 (⋆) You are designing a system with querying functionality similar to a database language such as SQL. In particular, we have a 2D array of strings whose first row contains the following column headers: "ID", "Name", "BirthYear", "Occupation", and "Salary". The remaining rows should contain several contributors to not only computer science but other sciences, engineering, and mathematics as well.

Design the List<String> query(String[][] db, String cmd) method that, when given a "database" and a "Command", returns the names of all people that satisfy the criteria enforced by the command.

A Command is "SELECT <count> WHERE <predicate>"

The SELECT command receives a <count>, which is a number between 1 and n, or the asterisk to indicate everyone in the database. The WHERE clause receives a "Predicate".

A Predicate is "<header> <comparator> <value>"

Headers are one of the column headers of the database, and comparators are either =, !=, <, <=, >, or >=, or LIKE. Values are either numbers, floats, or strings.

Parsing a LIKE command is more complicated. There are four possible types of values:

'S'
'%S'
'S%'
'%S%'

The first matches an exact string, namely S. The second matches any string that ends with S. The third matches any string that begins with S. The fourth matches any string that contains S.

3.66 (⋆) Minesweeper is a simple strategy game where the objective is to uncover all spaces on a board without running into mines. If you are not familiar with the mechanics, we encourage you to find a version online and play it for a bit to understand its gameplay. In this exercise you will implement the minesweeper game as a series of methods.

(a) First, design the static boolean isValidMove(char[][] board, int mx, int my) method that receives a board and a move position, and determines whether the move is valid. A move is valid if it is located within the bounds of the board.

(b) Design the static List<int[]> getValidNeighbors(char[][] board, int mx, int my) method that receives a board and a move position, and returns a list of all the immediate neighbors to the cell (mx, my). Each element of the list is a two-element integer array containing the x and y coordinates of the neighbor. Consider the diagram below, where $(0,0)$ is the move position, and the surrounding cells are its neighbors, represents as offsets. Note that getValidNeighbors should only return neighbors that are *in bounds*. Hint: use isValidMove.

(-1, 1)	(0, 1)	(1, 1)
(-1, 0)	(0, 0)	(1, 0)
(-1, -1)	(0, -1)	(1, -1)

(c) Design the static `List<int[]> getNonMineNeighbors(char[][] board, int mx, int my)` method that receives a board and a move position, and returns a list of all the neighbors that are not mines. You *must* use `getValidNeighbors` in your definition.

(d) Design the static `List<int[]> getMineNeighbors(char[][] board, int mx, int my)` method that receives a board and a move position, and returns a list of all the neighbors that are mines. You *must* use `getValidNeighbors` in your definition.

(e) Design the static `int countAdjacentMines(char[][] board, int mx, int my)` method that receives a board and a move position, and returns the number of mines that are adjacent to the given position. This method should be one line long and contain a call to `getMineNeigbors`.

(f) With the helper methods complete, we now need a method that searches through a position and reveals all non-mine adjacent positions. In general, this is a *traversal* algorithm called *depth-first search*. The idea is to recursively extend out the path until we hit a mine, at which point we unwind the recursive calls to extend another path.

Design the static `void extPath(char[][] board, int mx, int my)` method that receives a board and a move position, and extends the path from the given position using the following rules:

   (i) If the given move position is invalid, then return.
   (ii) If the character at `board[mx][my]` is not a dash, `'-'`, then return.
   (iii) Otherwise, determine the number of adjacent mines to the move position. If the number of adjacent mines is non-zero, assign to `board[mx][my]` the number of mines at that move position.
   (iv) If the number of adjacent mines *is* zero, then we can extend out the path to all non-mine neighbors. First, assign to `board[mx][my]` the character literal `'X'`, then loop over all non-mine neighbors to the move position. In the loop body, call `extendPath` on each neighbor.

(g) Minesweeper board generation is an algorithmic problem in and of itself, and as such our implementation will be simple. Design the static `char[][] makeBoard(int N, int M, int B)` method that receives a board size of N rows, M columns, and B mines to place. To randomly place mines, create a `List<int[]>` of all the possible cells on the board, shuffle the list, retrieve the first B cells, and assign the character literal `'B'` to them. Assign the character literal `'-'` to all other cells.

(h) Finally, design the static `char[][] play(char[][] board, int mx, int my)` method that receives a board and a move position, and attempts to play the given move position on the board. If, at that position on the board, there is a mine, return `null`. Otherwise, call `extPath` on the board and position, then return `board`. In essence, `play` receives one game state and transitions it to the next state.

3.7 Exercises

3.67 Design the `List<String> dollarAll(List<Integer> lon)` method that, when given a list of numbers, returns a list of those numbers converted to strings, prefixed by a dollar sign. You must use the Stream API.

3.68 Design the `boolean containsHigh(List<int[]> lop)` method that, when given a list of two-element arrays representing x, y coordinate pairs, returns whether or not any of the y-coordinates are greater than 450. Hint: use the `anyMatch` stream method.

3.69 Design the `List<int[]> removeCollisions(List<int[]> lop, int[] p)` method that, when given a list of two-element arrays representing x, y coordinate pairs, returns a list of those arrays that are not equal to p. You must use the Stream API.

3.70 Design the `List<Integer> sqAddFiveOmit(List<Integer> lon)` that receives a list of numbers, returns a list of those numbers squared and adds five to the result, omitting any of the resulting numbers that end in 5 or 6. You must use the Stream API.

3.71 Design the `List<Integer> remvDups(List<Integer> lon)` method, which receives a list of integers, removes all duplicate integers. Return this result as a new list. You must use the Stream API.

3.72 Design the `List<String> removeLonger(List<String> los, int n)` method that receives a list of strings, and removes all strings that contain more characters than a given integer n. Return this result as a new list. You must use the Stream API.

3.73 Design the `List<Double> filterThenSquare(List<Double> lon)` method, which receives a list of doubles, removes all numbers that are multiples of seven, and squares the remaining values. Return this result as a new list. You must use the Stream API.

3.74 Design the `double filterDoubleAvg(List<Integer> lon)` method that, when given a list of integers, removes all non-prime numbers, doubles each remaining value, and computes the average of said values. Return this result as a `double` value. You must use the Stream API. You may invoke a helper method that determines primality.

3.75 Design the `Optional<Integer> maximum(List<Integer> lon)` method that, when given a list of integers, returns the maximum value in the list as an `Optional<Integer>`. If there are no values in the given list, return `Optional.empty()`. You must use the Stream API.

3.76 Design the `int sumCharacters(String s)` method that, when given a string s, returns the sum of the ASCII values of its characters. You must use the Stream API.

3.77 Design the `String conjoin(List<String> los)` method that, when given a list of strings, concatenates all the strings together into a single string, separated by a comma. You must use the Stream API.

3.78 Design the `int sumEvens(List<Integer> l)` that, when given a list of integers, filters out odd numbers and then calculates the sum of the remaining even numbers. You must use the Stream API.

3.79 Design the `List<String> addYRemoveYY(List<String> los)` that, when given a list of strings, returns a list where each string has "y" added at its end, omitting any resulting strings that contain "yy" as a substring anywhere. You must use the Stream API.

3.80 Design the `int filterSumChars(String s)` method that, when given a string s, removes all non-alphanumeric characters, converts all letters to uppercase, and computes the sum of the ASCII values of the letters. Digits should also be added, but use the digit itself and not its ASCII value. You must use the Stream API.

3.81 Design the generic `<K, V> V lookup(Map<K, V> m)` method that, when given an `Map<K, V>` M and a value k of type K, returns the corresponding value (of type V) associated with the key k in M. If the key does not exist, return `null`. You will need to use the `equals` method.

3.82 Design the generic `<T> String stringifyList(List<T> l)` method that, when given an list of values l, returns a `String` of comma-separated values where each value is an element of l, but converted into a `String`. You'll need to use the `toString` method implementation of the generic type T.

3.83 Design the generic `<T extends Comparable<T>> Optional<T> minimum(List<T> ls)` method, which receives a list of comparable elements and returns the minimum element in the list. It should return an `Optional` value of type T, where T is the type of the list. If the list is empty, return an empty `Optional`. Remember that T must be a type that implements the `Comparable` interface.

3.84 Design the `<T extends List<Integer>> boolean areParallelLists(T t, T u)` method that, when given two types of lists t and u that store integer values, determines whether or not they are "parallel." In this context, Two integer lists are parallel if they differ by a single constant factor. For example, where $t = \{5, 10, 15, 20\}$ and $u = \{20, 40, 60, 80\}$, t and u are parallel because every element in t multiplied by four gets us a parallel element in u. This factorization is bidirectional, meaning that t could be $\{100, 200, 300, 200\}$ and u could be $\{10, 20, 30, 20\}$. Note that a list of all zeroes is parallel to every other list.

3.85 Design the `<T extends Set<U>, U extends Comparable<U>> boolean equalSets(T t, T u)` method that, when given two types of sets t and u that store comparable elements, returns whether they are equal to one another. Two sets are equivalent if they are subsets of each other. You must traverse over the sets; you **cannot** use the built-in `equals` method provided by the `Set` implementations.

Part II
Objects, Classes, Exceptions, and I/O

4 Object-Oriented Programming

Abstract This chapter is divided into two halves. In the first half, we begin to introduce the basics of object-oriented programming. We start off simple with small classes that contain only immutable fields. The complexity gradually increases as we mix in mutability and aliasing. This chapter also describes the implementation of several data structures that mimic those from the Collections framework, including `ArrayList`, `LinkedList`, `HashSet`, and maps.
In the second half, we expand on the details of object-oriented programming by describing interfaces and inheritance. Interfaces ascribe behaviors and characteristics to classes, whereas inheritance denotes "IS-A" relationships across classes. We conclude the chapter by demoing a practical application of object-oriented programming and class design by writing a small programming language.

4.1 Classes

From the first page, we have made prolific use of classes, but in this chapter, we finally venture into the inner workings of a class, and how to create our own.

Classes are blueprints for *objects*. When we create a class, we declare a new type of object. Classes encapsulate data and method definitions for later use.

As we stated, we have repeatedly used classes *and* objects, e.g., strings, arrays, `Scanner`, `Random`, as well as classes from the Collections framework. Until now, however, we viewed these as forms of abstraction, whose details were not important.

To create a class, we use the `class` keyword, followed by the name of the class. The name of the class should be capitalized and, in general, describe a noun. All Java files describe a class and must be named accordingly. We previously omitted the details of class creation and merely used them as a means to design methods.

Classes can *inherit* methods from other classes, a relationship called the superclass/subclass hierarchy. For now, we will only mention that the `Object` class is the "ultimate" superclass, in which all classes are implicit subclasses. The `Object` class, in particular, has three methods that we will override in almost every class that we design: `equals`, for comparing two classes for equality, `toString`, a means of "stringifying" an object, and a third: `hashCode`, the significance of which we will return to soon. In subsequent sections, we dive more into inheritance and hierarchies.

Example 4.1. Let's design the `Point` class, which stores two `int` values representing two Cartesian coordinates x and y. By "store," we mean to say that x and y are *instance variables* of the `Point` class, also sometimes called *attributes*, *fields*, or *members* (in Java, we conventionally use the "instance variables" term). Instance variables denote the values associated with an arbitrary *instance* of that object (an instance may also be defined as an entity). For example, if we declare a Point object p, then p has two instance variables, x and y, which are the x and y coordinates of p. If we declare another Point object p2, then p2 has its own instance variables x and y, which are independent of p's instance variables. In almost all circumstances, instance variables of a class should be marked as private. Instance variables that are private are accessible only to those methods within the class definition. For the time being, instance variables are immutable. Thus, every instance variable will use the final keyword in its declaration, alongside the UPPER_CASE naming convention.

Speaking of *access modifiers*, we should mention the four that Java provides, even though we make prolific use of only three:

- A class, variable, or method declared with the public modifier is accessible to/by any other class. Variables that are public should be used sparingly.
- A class, variable, or method declared with the private modifier is accessible only to/by the class in which it is declared.
- A class, variable, or method declared without an access modifier, also called the *default access modifier*, behaves similarly to public, only that it is accessible only to/by classes in the same package. Packages are a means of organizing classes into groups, similar to directories.

The fourth and final access modifier is protected, which is similar to the default access modifier, but allows subclasses to access the variable or method.[1] We will not use protected in this text, but it is worth mentioning. As a corollary of sorts, any time that protected *can* be used, there is almost certainly a better design alternative, whether that means marking the variable/method as private or public, we are of the opinion that protected has few benefits. Moreover, because we will not use protected, the use of public will be infrequent and only when necessary.[2]

```
class Point {

  private final int X;
  private final int Y;
}
```

We now want a way to create an instance of a Point. Instances of objects are made using the new keyword, followed by the class constructor. *Constructors* are special methods that instantiate an instance of a class. Our Point class constructor receive parameters that we will use to initialize the relevant x and y instance variables. So, let's design the constructor for our Point class. Constructors, in general, should be non-private, as we need to call them from outside the class definition. On a case-by-case basis, this changes accordingly, as some classes are local to another class definition, and are thereby private.[3]

Constructors are also special in that they do not have an explicit return type, but they are non-void in that they return an object of the class type.

All classes in Java that can be instantiated have a *default constructor* only when no constructor is specified by the class implementer.[4] The default constructor of a class receives no arguments and serves only to be able to create an instance of the class.

---

[1] If you have not heard of inheritance/subclasses yet, do not worry, as we will cover this in the next chapter; we explain it here to describe the relevant difference between the access modifiers.

[2] Some methods, as we will soon see and have seen previously, are required to be public. For example, the main method must be marked as public.

[3] There are also design patterns, as exemplified in Chapter 8, that rely on a class constructor being private to prohibit unnecessary object instantiation.

[4] Later in this chapter, we will see that some classes and types cannot be instantiated.

4.1 Classes

```
class Point {

  private final int X;
  private final int Y;

  Point(int x, int y) {
    this.X = x;
    this.Y = y;
  }
}
```

Remember that the purpose of the `Point` constructor is to initialize the class instance variables. So, unless we want to use distinct identifiers for referencing the parameters and instance variables, we need to use the `this` keyword.[5] The `this` keyword refers to the current object, and aids in distinguishing between instance variables and parameters. The "current object" references the object that a method is called on.

Inside the constructor, we assign the value of the parameter x to the instance variable x. Should we not use `this` on the left-hand variable identifier, then the parameter x would *shadow* the instance variable x, meaning that writing x = x assigns the parameter to itself. At last, we can create a `Point` object by calling the constructor, but wait, we have no way of accessing/referring to the instance variables of the `Point` object! We need to create *accessor methods* to retrieve the values of the instance variables. Accessor methods are non-private and have strictly one purpose: to return the respective instance variable value.

```
class Point {

  private final int X;
  private final int Y;

  Point(int x, int y) {
    this.X = x;
    this.Y = y;
  }

  int getX() { return this.X; }

  int getY() { return this.Y; }
}
```

The principle of hiding the implementation details of a class and its properties is called *encapsulation*. Encapsulation is a fundamental idea of object-oriented programming, and is one of the primary reasons why object-oriented programming is so powerful. It can be dangerous to directly modify or access the fields of an object.[6]

Creating an instance of the `Point` class is identical to creating an instance of any other arbitrary class. Though, we should first explain a slight terminology distinction.

Declaring, or *initializing*, an object refers to typing the class name followed by the variable name. For instance, the following code declares/initializes a `Point` object p.

```
Point p;
```

By default, *p* points to `null`, since we have not yet created an instance of the `Point` class. We can create an instance of the `Point` class by invoking its constructor, an action otherwise

---

[5] Some software engineers and projects use identifier prefixes to refer to instance variables.

[6] By "dangerous," we mean to suggest that it is prone to logic errors.

called *object instantiation*. We use the `new` keyword and pass the desired x and y integer coordinates.

```
Point p = new Point(3, 4);
```

We should write some tests to ensure that our `Point` class is working as expected. We note that this may seem redundant for such a simple class, and the fact that the accessor methods do nothing more than retrieve instance variable values, but it is a good habit for beginning object-oriented programmers.

```
import static Assertions.assertEquals;

class PointTester {

  @Test
  void testPoint() {
    Point p = new Point(3, 4);
    assertEquals(3, p.getX());
    assertEquals(4, p.getY());
  }
}
```

Of course, testing the accessor methods is a little boring, so let's override the `toString` method to print a stringified representation of the `Point` class. Every object in Java has a `toString` method, which returns a string representation of the object. By default, the `toString` method returns the class name followed by the object's hash code. We can override the `toString` method by declaring a method with the signature `public String toString()` (note that this is one instance where `public` cannot be avoided.) We can then return a string representation of the object. In this case, we will return a string of the form `"(x=x, y=y)"`, where x and y refer to the respecitve instance variables.

```
class Point {
  // ... previous code not shown.

  @Override
  public String toString() {
    return String.format("(x=%d, y=%d)", this.X, this.Y);
  }
}
```

Testing the `toString` method provides more interesting results, since it requires us to not only override the default implementation of `toString`, but it also ensures that our constructor correctly initializes the instance variables.

```
import static Assertions.assertEquals;

class PointTester {

  private final Point P = new Point(3, 4);

  @Test
  void testPointAccessors() {
    assertEquals(3, P.getX());
    assertEquals(4, P.getY());
  }
```

4.1 Classes

```
@Test
void testPointToString() {
  assertEquals("(x=3, y=4)", P.toString());
}
}
```

In addition to the `toString` method, we might also design other methods associated with a `Point` object. For example, we might want to calculate the distance between two points. We can design a method that takes a `Point` object as a parameter and returns the distance between the two points, the first being the *implicit parameter*, and the second being the *explicit parameter*. We say the first is *implicit* because, under the hood, all class methods receive an implicit parameter, which is the object on which the method is called, which is accessible through the `this` pointer. We say the second is *explicit* because we explicitly pass the object as a parameter. So, in the following example, p1 is the implicit parameter, and p2 is the explicit parameter.

```
final Point P1 = new Point(3, 4);
final Point P2 = new Point(6, 42);
double dist = p1.distance(p2);
```

This is also a good time to bring up another terminology distinction. Some programming languages use *functions*, others use *procedures*, *subroutines*, or *methods*. Going from simplest to most complex, subroutines are simply a sequence of instructions that are executed in order. Procedures are subroutines that return a value. Functions are procedures that receive parameters. Methods are functions that are associated with a class. In Java, we use the term *method* to refer to all functions, procedures, and subroutines, since all methods must be associated with a class. A language like C++, on the other hand, distinguishes between the two: *functions* refer to subroutines, procedures, or parameter-receiving procedures that are not associated with a class; *methods* are subroutines, procedures, or functions embedded inside a class definition.

Returning to the `Point` class, we will now design `distance`, which receives a `Point` as a parameter and returns the Euclidean distance from `this` point to the parameter. Before doing so, however, we should write a few tests. Conveniently, the three points that we test all have a distance of five between each other.

```
import static Assertions.assertAll;
import static Assertions.assertEquals;

class PointTester {

  private final double DELTA = 0.01;
  private final Point P1 = new Point(3, 4);
  private final Point P2 = new Point(6, 8);
  private final Point P3 = new Point(0, 0);

  @Test
  void testPointDistance() {
    assertAll(
      () -> assertEquals(5, P1.distance(P2), DELTA),
      () -> assertEquals(5, P1.distance(P3), DELTA),
      () -> assertEquals(5, P2.distance(P3), DELTA));
  }
}
```

```
class Point {
  // ... previous code not shown.

  /**
   * Determines the Euclidean distance between two points.
   * @param p the other point.
   * @return the distance between this point and p.
   */
  double distance(Point p) {
    int dx = this.X - p.X;
    int dy = this.Y - p.Y;
    return Math.sqrt(dx * dx + dy * dy);
  }
}
```

The `distance` method is called an *instance method* because it is associated with an instance of the class. We can also write *static methods*, which are not associated with an object, but rather the class holistically. Static methods are useful as utility methods that are not associated with a particular instance of the class. All methods that we designed up until this chapter were static methods, which were not associated with the class in which they resided, because the classes we designed were used only to hold the methods themselves.

Method Overloading

A method is identified by two attributes: its name and its signature. Java allows us to *overload* a method or constructor by using the same identifier, but different parameters.

Example 4.2. Let's overload the `distance` method by designing a version that does not receive a parameter at all, and instead returns the magnitude/distance from the point to the origin. Fortunately, this is extremely easy, because we can make use of the existing `distance` method that *does* receive a `Point`. Namely, we pass it the origin point, i.e., `new Point(0, 0)`, and everything works wonderfully. Because this version of `distance` merely refers to the existing definition, which we have thoroughly tested, we will omit a separate set of tests.

```
class Point {
  // Previous code not shown.

  /**
   * Computes the distance from this point to the origin,
   * i.e., (0, 0).
   * @return returns the magnitude of this distance.
   */
  double distance() {
    return this.distance(new Point(0, 0));
  }
}
```

4.1 Classes

We could, if desired, overload the Point constructor as well. Though, it makes little sense to do so in this specific context, because a point is defined by its two coordinate members. In subsequent sections, however, we will overload other class constructors to demonstrate its utility/practicality.

Example 4.3. Let's design the static avgDist method, which receives a List<Point> and computes the average distance away each Point is from the origin. We already have a method to compute the distance of a point to the origin, so let's take advantage of the stream API to map distance to every point, then find the average of those resulting double values. The avgDist method returns an OptionalDouble in the event that the provided list is empty, which serves as a wrapper around the Optional<Double> type.

```
import static Assertions.assertAll;
import static Assertions.assertEquals;

import java.util.List;
import java.util.OptionalDouble;

class PointTester {

  @Test
  void testAvgDist() {
    List<Point> lop1 = List.of();
    List<Point> lop2 = List.of(new Point(4, 0), new Point(0, 4),
                               new Point(-4, 0), new Point(0, -4),
                               new Point(2, 2), new Point(-2, 2),
                               new Point(-2, -2), new Point(2, -2));
    assertAll(
      () -> assertEquals(OptionalDouble.empty(), Point.avgDist(lop1)),
      () -> assertEquals(3.414, Point.avgDist(lop2).get(), 0.01));
  }
}
```

```
import java.util.List;
import java.util.OptionalDouble;

class Point {
  // ... previous code not shown.

  /**
   * Computes the average distance to the origin of a list of points.
   * @param lop list of points.
   * @return empty Optional if the list is empty,
   * or OptionalDouble otherwise.
   */
  static OptionalDouble avgDist(List<Point> lop) {
    return lop.stream()
              .map(p -> p.distance())
              .mapToDouble(d -> d)
              .average();
  }
}
```

Example 4.4. Let's design the static random method, which returns a Point object with random x and y coordinates. We will use the Random class to generate a random radius and angle as a polar coordinate. Then, we will convert the polar coordinate to Cartesian coordinates. Let's also add a parameter that specifies a maximum radius.

Because the random method generates a random point, we cannot reasonably write a test that asserts the exact location of the point without prior knowledge of the random seed. Instead, we can write a test that asserts whether the point is within a certain radius of the origin.

```
import static Assertions.assertAll;
import static Assertions.assertTrue;

class PointTester {

  @Test
  void testPointRandom() {
    assertAll(
      () -> assertTrue(Point.random(10).distance() <= 10),
      () -> assertTrue(Point.random(1).distance() <= 1),
      () -> assertTrue(Point.random(5).distance() <= 5),
      () -> assertTrue(Point.random(5000000).distance() <= 5000000));
  }
}
```

```
import java.util.Random;

class Point {

  /**
   * Generates a random point with a maximum radius.
   * @param maxRadius the maximum radius.
   * @return a random point.
   */
  static Point random(double maxRadius) {
    Random r = new Random();
    double radius = r.nextDouble(maxRadius);
    double angle = r.nextDouble() * Math.PI * 2;
    int x = (int) (radius * Math.cos(angle));
    int y = (int) (radius * Math.sin(angle));
    return new Point(x, y);
  }
}
```

We have seen static methods, but what about static variables? A *static variable* is a variable that is associated with the class and not a specific instance thereof. Static variables are shared among all instances of a class.

Example 4.5. Suppose that we want to count how many instances of Point have been instantiated in a running program. Since counting instances is a property of the Point class, rather than an instance *of* the class, we can declare a static variable count to keep track of the number of instances, which we increment inside the constructor. To remain consistent with our recurring theme of encapsulation, count will be declared as private, and we will design a static method getCount to retrieve the number of instances, which is invoked on the class.[7] When testing, we need to be careful to only instantiate instances of Point when we

---

[7] It is also possible to invoke a static method on an instance of the class, but it is considered bad practice and unnecessary.

4.1 Classes

are ready to check the status of count, since the static count variable is updated inside the constructor.

```
import static Assertions.assertEquals;

class PointTester {

  @Test
  void testPointCount() {
    assertEquals(0, Point.getCount());
    Point p1 = new Point(3, 4);
    assertEquals(1, Point.getCount());
    Point p2 = new Point(6, 8);
    assertEquals(2, Point.getCount());
    Point p3 = new Point(0, 0);
    assertEquals(3, Point.getCount());

    // Even though we lose reference to p, the static variable still increments!
    for (int i = 0; i < 10; i++) {
      Point p = new Point();
    }
    assertEquals(13, Point.getCount());
  }
}
```

```
class Point {

  private static int count = 0;

  private final int X;
  private final int Y;

  Point(int x, int y) {
    this.X = x;
    this.Y = y;
    count++;
  }

  static int getCount() {
    return count;
  }
}
```

Notice that, inside the getCount method, we do not refer to count with this, because count is a static variable and not an instance variable. Prefixing the count variable with this results in a compiler error. Further note that the variable is not marked as final; it is not immutable and changes with every newly-instantiated Point object.

Example 4.6. Imagine we want to store a collection of Point objects in a data structure such as a HashSet. The question that arises from this decision is apparent: how do we determine if a Point is already inside the set?

We need to override two important methods from the Object class: public boolean equals and public int hashCode. The equals method of an object determines whether two instances of the class are "equal." In the circumstance of points, let's say that two points are equal according to equals only if they have the same x and y coordinates. Overriding the equals method from the Object class requires correctly copying the signature, the sole parameter being an Object that we need to check for type equality. In other words, we first need to verify that the passed object to the `equals` method is, in fact, a `Point`, otherwise they cannot possibly be equal. To "type check" a parameter, we use the `instanceof` keyword. If the input parameter is, indeed, a `Point`, we cast it to a `Point` instance, then check whether the coordinates match. Moreover, like `toString`, the `equals` and `hashCode` methods are definitionally `public`, so do not omit the access modifier.

The `assertEquals` and `assertNotEquals` methods invoke an object's `.equals` method when determining equality, which by default compares object references. Because we are finally overriding its implementation in `Point`, we can test two arbitrary `Point` instances for definitional equality.

```java
import static Assertions.assertAll;
import static Assertions.assertEquals;
import static Assertions.assertNotEquals;

class PointTester {

  @Test
  void testEquals() {
    assertAll(
      () -> assertEquals(new Point(3, 3), new Point(3, 3)),
      () -> assertNotEquals(new Point(3, 4), new Point(3, 7)),
      () -> assertNotEquals(new Point(7, 4), new Point(10, 4)),
      () -> assertNotEquals(new Point(10, 30), new Point(3, 7)));
  }
}
```

```java
class Point {
  // ... previous code not shown.

  @Override
  public boolean equals(Object obj) {
    if (!(obj instanceof Point)) { return false; }
    else {
      Point othPt = (Point) obj;
      return this.x == othPt.x && this.y == othPt.y;
    }
  }
}
```

Let's create a `HashSet<Point>`, then iterate over the elements thereof after adding two of the same `Point` instances, i.e., points that share coordinates. Doing so demonstrates a glaring flaw: the set appears to have added both `Point` instances to the set, despite having identical coordinates. The reason is incredibly subtle and easy to miss: the `Object` class invariant states that, if two objects are equal according to `equals`, then their hash codes must also be equal. The *hash code* of an object is an integer used for quick access/lookup in hashable data structures such as `HashSet` and `HashMap`. Indeed, the problem is that we forgot to override `hashCode` after overriding the `equals` method in the `Point` class. Bloch (2018) states, as a principle, that whenever we override `equals`, we should accompanyingly override the `hashCode` implementation.

Now, you might wonder: "How can I hash (compute the hash code of) an object?" Fortunately Java has a method in the `Objects` class called `hash`, which receives any number of arguments and runs them through a hashing algorithm, thereby returning the hash of the arguments. When overriding `hashCode`, we should include all instance variables of the object

4.1 Classes

to designate that all of the properties affect the object's hash code. After fixing the issue, we see that our `HashSet` now correctly contains only one of the `Point` objects that we add.

```java
import static Assertions.assertTrue;

import java.util.Set;
import java.util.HashSet;

class PointTester {

  @Test
  void testHashSetPoint() {
    Set<Point> p = new HashSet<>();
    p.add(new Point(3, 3));
    p.add(new Point(3, 3));
    assertTrue(p.size() == 1);
  }
}
```

```java
import java.util.Objects;

class Point {
  // ... previous code not shown.

  @Override
  public int hashCode() {
    return Objects.hash(this.x, this.y);
  }
}
```

Example 4.7. Let's design the static `removeLinearPoints` method that, when given a `List<Point>`, filters out all points that are "linear," meaning that their x and y coordinates are the same. As with the previous example, streams make this exercise a walk in the park. When comparing lists, the `equals` method invokes `equals` on every element of the list, meaning that we call `Point`'s implementation of `equals`.

```java
import static Assertions.assertAll;
import static Assertions.assertEquals;

import java.util.List;

class PointTester {
  // ... previous code not shown.
  @Test
  void testRemoveLinearPoints() {
    List<Point> lop = List.of(new Point(5, 10), new Point(7, 7),
                              new Point(2, 3), new Point(4, 3),
                              new Point(1, 1), new Point(-6, -10),
                              new Point(-23, -23), new Point(1, 0));
    List<Point> lopRes = List.of(new Point(5, 10), new Point(2, 3), new Point(4, 3),
                                 new Point(-6, -10), new Point(1, 0));
    assertAll(
      () -> assertEquals(List.of(), Point.removeLinearPoints(List.of())),
      () -> assertEquals(lopRes, Point.removeLinearPoints(lop)));
  }
```

```java
}
```

```java
import java.util.List;

class Point {
  // ... previous code not shown.
  /**
   * Returns a list of all points that are not "linear."
   * @param lop list of Point objects.
   * @return list where linear points are removed.
   */
  static List<Point> removeLinearPoints(List<Point> lop) {
    return lop.stream()
            .filter(p -> p.getX() != p.getY())
            .toList();
  }
}
```

Example 4.8. Suppose that we're writing a program that keeps track of orders for a local pizzeria. Let's design the `PizzaOrder` class, which stores a `Map<String, Integer>` as an instance variable. The map associates toppings (as strings) to their respective quantities on the pizza order. Toppings can be "Pepperoni", "Onion", "Pineapple", or "Anchovie". The `PizzaOrder` constructor instantiates the map to be a `LinkedHashMap` to ensure that the order of the toppings is respected. As parameters to the constructor, it receives two arrays: `String[] toppings` and `int[] toppingCount`, where each entry is added to the map. To make the constructor simpler, we will assume that `toppings` and `toppingCount` share the same length. We'll also design the `Set<String> getToppings()` method to return the toppings in the order that they were added. Finally, we'll design a method, `Optional<Integer> getToppingCount(String s)` to retrieve the number/quantity of a given topping.[8]

```java
import static Assertions.assertAll;
import static Assertions.assertEquals;

import java.util.Optional;

class PizzaOrderTester {

  @Test
  void testPizzaOrder() {
    PizzaOrder p1 = new PizzaOrder();
    PizzaOrder p2 = new PizzaOrder(new String[]{"Pepperoni","Anchovie"}, new int[]{3,2});
    assertAll(
      () -> assertEquals(Set.of(), p1.getToppings()),
      () -> assertEquals(Set.of("Pepperoni", "Anchovie"), p2.getToppings()),
      () -> assertEquals(Optional.of(3), p2.getToppingCount("Pepperoni")),
      () -> assertEquals(Optional.empty(), p2.getToppingCount("Pineapple")));
  }
}
```

---

[8] The `getToppingCount` method uses `Optional.ofNullable` that, when given a null argument, returns the empty `Optional` and otherwise wraps the value in a non-empty `Optional`.

4.1 Classes

```java
import java.util.LinkedHashMap;
import java.util.LinkedHashSet;
import java.util.Map;
import java.util.Optional;
import java.util.Set;

class PizzaOrder {

  private final Map<String, Integer> TOPPINGS;

  PizzaOrder(String[] toppings, int[] count) {
    this.TOPPINGS = new LinkedHashMap<>();
    for (int i = 0; i < toppings.length; i++) {
      TOPPINGS.put(toppings[i], count[i]);
    }
  }

  /**
   * Returns the toppings as a set.
   * @return new LinkedHashSet containing toppings.
   */
  Set<String> getToppings() {
    Set<String> set = new LinkedHashSet<>();
    this.TOPPINGS.keySet().forEach(k -> set.add(k));
    return set;
  }

  /**
   * Returns the number of a certain topping there are in this pizza order.
   * @param topping one of the four toppings.
   * @return Optional<Integer> containing value, or empty optional.
   */
  Optional<Integer> getToppingCount(String topping) {
    return Optional.ofNullable(this.TOPPINGS.get(topping));
  }
}
```

Example 4.9. Let's amplify the complexity a bit by designing a "21" card game, which is a card game where the players try to get a card value total of 21 without going over. We should think about the design process of this game, i.e., what classes we need to design. It makes sense to start with a Card class, which stores its suit and its numeric value. A suit is one of four possibilities, each of which use a different symbol, meaning that we should create another class called Suit. In Suit, we instantiate four static instances of Suit, each of which represents one of the four valid suits. Its constructor is privatized because we, as the programmers, define the four possible suits.[9] Consequently, it should not be possible for the user to define their own custom suit, at least for this particular game. The notion of Suit being an instance variable of Card, and only existing as a means to support the Card class is called *object composition*. Lastly, we will provide a method that returns an Iterator<Suit>

---

[9] Instantiating objects in this manner bears resemblance to a *design pattern* called *singleton*.

over the four suit possibilities to make our lives easier when designing the Deck class. The method should be static, so it is accessible through the class and not an instance.

```
class Suit {

  static final Suit CLUBS = new Suit("♣");
  static final Suit DIAMONDS = new Suit("♢");
  static final Suit HEARTS = new Suit("♡");
  static final Suit SPADES = new Suit("♠");
  static final int NUM_SUITS = 4;

  private final String S_VAL;

  private Suit(String s) { this.S_VAL = s; }

  static Iterator<Suit> iterator() {
    return new ArrayList<Suit>(List.of(CLUBS, DIAMONDS, HEARTS, SPADES))
                              .iterator();
  }

  @Override
  public String toString() {
    return this.S_VAL;
  }
}
```

Testing the Card class is straightforward; we only need to test one method, the toString method, since testing getValue, at this point, is superfluous. We could also test the Suit class, but we will not do so here, given that the only useful methods are accessors and the iterator retriever.

```
import static Assertions.assertAll;
import static Assertions.assertEquals;

class CardTester {

  @Test
  void testCardToString() {
    assertAll(
      () -> assertEquals("2 of ♣", new Card(Suit.CLUBS, 2).toString()),
      () -> assertEquals("3 of ♢", new Card(Suit.DIAMONDS, 3).toString()),
      () -> assertEquals("4 of ♡", new Card(Suit.HEARTS, 4).toString()),
      () -> assertEquals("5 of ♠", new Card(Suit.SPADES, 5).toString()));
  }
}
```

```
class Card {

  private final Suit SUIT;
  private final int VAL;

  Card(Suit suit, int value) { this.SUIT = suit; this.VAL = value; }

  @Override
  public String toString() {
    return String.format("%d of %s", this.VAL, this.SUIT);
  }
```

```
  int getValue() {
    return this.VAL;
  }
}
```

In a standard fifty-two deck of cards, some are "special," e.g., the Jacks, Queens, Kings, and Ace cards, otherwise called the "face" cards. To simplify the design of our game, the face cards will be treated the same as a "ten" card, showing neither a syntactic nor semantic difference. Now that we have a class to represents cards, let's design the Deck class, which stores an ArrayList<Card> representing the current state of the deck. It also contains a static variable representing the maximum number of allowed cards. For our purposes, as we alluded to, the maximum is fifty-two. In the Deck constructor, we call the populateDeck method, which adds four cards of the same value, but of each suit. So, to exemplify, there are four cards whose value is three, where each is one of the four suits. We make use of the iterator from the Suit class to simplify our deck population. Only the Deck class needs to know how to populate an initial (empty) deck, so we privatize its access.

To test a Deck, we can design the drawCard method, which retrieves the "top-most" card on the deck. According to our implementation of the iterator, the top-most cards should have values of ten and be of the same suit. From there, we can draw three more cards to ensure they have the values nine, eight, and seven, all of the same suit. The iterator places DIAMOND as the final suit, so this is what we will assume in our tester. It might also be beneficial to test the isEmpty method, which returns true if the deck is empty, and false otherwise. We can test isEmpty by drawing all fifty-two cards from the deck and ensuring that the deck is empty afterwards. Note that we draw four tens because there are no "Kings," "Queens," or "Jacks" in the deck.

```
import static Assertions.assertAll;
import static Assertions.assertEquals;
import static Assertions.assertTrue;
import static Assertions.assertFalse;

class DeckTester {

  @Test
  void testDeckDrawCard() {
    Deck d = new Deck();
    assertAll(
      () -> assertEquals("10 of ♦", d.drawCard().toString()),
      () -> assertEquals("10 of ♦", d.drawCard().toString()),
      () -> assertEquals("10 of ♦", d.drawCard().toString()),
      () -> assertEquals("10 of ♦", d.drawCard().toString()),
      () -> assertEquals("9 of ♦", d.drawCard().toString()));
  }

  @Test
  void testDeckIsEmpty() {
    Deck d = new Deck();
    for (int i = 0; i < 52; i++) {
      assertFalse(d.isEmpty());
      d.drawCard();
    }
    assertTrue(d.isEmpty());
  }
}
```

```java
import java.util.ArrayList;
import java.util.Iterator;

class Deck {

  private static final int MAX_NUM_CARDS = 52;
  private final ArrayList<Card> CARDS;

  Deck() {
    this.CARDS = new ArrayList<Card>();
    this.populateDeck();
  }

  /**
   * Retrieves a card from the "top" of the deck. If the
   * deck is empty, we return null.
   * @return the top-most card in the deck, or null if the deck is empty.
   */
  Card drawCard() {
    if (this.CARDS.isEmpty()) {
      return null;
    } else {
      return this.CARDS.remove(this.CARDS.size() - 1);
    }
  }

  /**
   * Determines if the deck is empty.
   * @return true if the deck contains no cards, and false otherwise.
   */
  boolean isEmpty() {
    return this.CARDS.isEmpty();
  }

  /**
   * Instantiates the deck to contain all 52 cards.
   * Note that the deck contains cards in-order by suit. There are
   * no face cards in the deck, i.e., no Jack, Queen, King, nor Ace.
   * All cards have a value between 1 and 10.
   */
  private void populateDeck() {
    // For every suit, create 13 cards, the last four of which all have
    // a value of ten.
    Iterator<Suit> it = Suit.iterator();
    while (it.hasNext()) {
      Suit s = it.next();
      for (int i = 1; i <= MAX_NUM_CARDS / Suit.NUM_SUITS; i++) {
        Card c = new Card(s, Math.min(10, i));
        this.CARDS.add(c);
      }
    }
  }
}
```

4.1 Classes

Hopefully, the `populateDeck` method is intuitive and not intimidating. We create fifty-two card instances, split into four equal-sized groups of suits, and add them to the deck. We use the `Math.min` method to ensure that the value of the card is at most ten, since we do not have "King," "Queen," or "Jack" cards. We also use the ternary operator to check if the deck is empty before drawing a card. If the deck is empty, we return `null`.

Finally, we come to the `Player` class, which stores a "hand" containing the cards in their possession. Fortunately, this is a very straightforward class, containing four one-line methods: `addCard`, `clearHand`, `getScore`, and `toString`. The former two are trivial to explain, as is `toString`, whereas `getScore` is the only slightly convoluted method. The idea is to return an integer that represents the total value of the cards in the player's hand. Since streams were introduced in the previous chapter, we will once again use them to our advantage.

```java
import java.util.ArrayList;

class Player {

  private final ArrayList<Card> HAND;

  Player() { this.HAND = new ArrayList<Card>(); }

  @Override
  public String toString() {
    return String.format("Score: %d\nHand: %s\n",
                         this.getScore(), this.HAND.toString());
  }

  /**
   * Adds a card to the player's hand.
   * @param c card to add to the player's hand.
   */
  void addCard(Card c) { this.HAND.add(c); }

  /**
   * Removes all cards from the player's hand.
   */
  void clearHand() { this.HAND.clear(); }

  /**
   * Determines the player's score.
   * @return the player's score.
   */
  int getScore() {
    return this.HAND.stream()
                    .map(c -> c.getValue())
                    .reduce(0, Integer::sum);
  }
}
```

Using the capabilities of `Player`, `Deck`, and `Card`, we will design `TwentyOne`: the class that runs a game of "twenty-one." The game logic is as follows: if the game is still running, clear the player's hand, create a new deck of cards, shuffle them, and give the player two. Then, ask the player if they want to draw another card. If they do, draw a card (from the deck) and add it to their hand. If they do not, then the game is over. If the player's score is greater than twenty-one, then the player loses. Otherwise, the player wins. We will also write a `main` method that runs the game. We will not write any tests for this class, since it interacts with the user through the `Scanner` class.

It should be noted that this version of "twenty-one" only has the objective of getting as close as possible to a hand containing cards with a value that sums to twenty one, compared to a more traditional card game where multiple players exist, with a dealer to distribute cards. As exercises, there are many ways to enhance the game, including adding a "high score" board to keep track of previous game outcomes, introducing CPU players to automatically poll cards from the deck to beat the main player, or even adding more human players through standard input/output interactions.

```java
import java.util.Scanner;

class TwentyOne {

  private static final int MAX_SCORE = 21;
  private final Player PLAYER;

  TwentyOne() { this.PLAYER = new Player(); }

  /**
   * Plays a game of "21", where the player has to draw cards until they
   * get as close to 21 as possible without going over.
   */
  void playGame() {
    Scanner in = new Scanner(System.in);
    boolean continuePlaying = true;
    while (continuePlaying) {
      // Clear the player's hand, and shuffle a new deck.
      this.player.clearHand();
      Deck d = new Deck();
      d.shuffleDeck();

      // First, deal two cards.
      this.PLAYER.addCard(d.drawCard());
      this.PLAYER.addCard(d.drawCard());

      // While the player has not "busted",
      // ask them to draw a card or stand.
      while (this.PLAYER.getScore() <= MAX_SCORE) {
        System.out.println(this.PLAYER);
        System.out.println("Do you want to draw? (Y/n)");
        String resp = in.nextLine();
        if (resp.equals("Y")) { this.PLAYER.addCard(d.drawCard()); }
        else { break; }
      }

      // Print the final results of the player.
      System.out.println(this.PLAYER);
      if (this.PLAYER.getScore() > MAX_SCORE) {
        System.out.println("You lose!");
      } else {
        System.out.printf("You did not go over %d!", MAX_SCORE);
      }
      System.out.println("Do you want to continue playing?");
      String resp = in.nextLine();
      continuePlaying = resp.equals("Y");
    }
  }
}
```

4.1 Classes

Designing interactive games is a great exercise in object-oriented programming, as well as the culmination of other discussed topics.

Example 4.10. Suppose that we are asked to design a simple library management system for a local library. That is, the system wants to be able to check out books, determine if they are in the system, and how much stock remains. Let's think about the components of such a system. At a minimum, we need an Author and a Book class. Authors contain only a name out of conciseness. Books contain a title, author, release date, edition number, and page count. Because books contain authors, we again use object composition. Both classes, namely Author and Book are straightforward to design. Both classes also override the equals, hashCode, and toString methods for use in a hashable data structure and equality comparison.

```java
class LibraryTester {

  private static final Author A1 = new Author("Michael Spivak");
  private static final Author A2 = new Author("Joshua Crotts");
  private static final Author A3 = new Author("Douglas Hofstader");
  private static final Author A4 = new Author("William Van Orman Quine");

  private static final Book B1
    = new Book("Calculus", A1, 4, 680);
  private static final Book B2
    = new Book("Principles of Computer Science", A2, 1, 754);
  private static final Book B3
    = new Book("Godel, Escher, Bach", A3, 2, 824);
  private static final Book B4
    = new Book("Methods of Logic", A4, 4, 344);

  @Test
  void testBook() {
    assertAll(
       () -> assertEquals("Calculus", b1.getTitle()),
       () -> assertEquals(new Author("Joshua Crotts"), b2.getAuthor()),
       () -> assertEquals(2, b3.getEditionNumber()),
       () -> assertEquals(344, b4.getPageCount()));
  }
}
```

```java
class Author {

  private final String NAME;

  Author(String name) { this.NAME = name; }

  @Override
  public boolean equals(Object o) {
    if (!(o instanceof Author)) {
      return false;
    } else {
      Author othAuthor = (Author) o;
      return this.NAME.equals(othAuthor.getName());
    }
  }

  @Override
  public int hashCode() {
    return this.NAME.hashCode();
  }
```

```java
    @Override
    public String toString() {
      return this.NAME;
    }

    String getName() {
      return this.NAME;
    }
}
```

```java
import java.util.Objects;

class Book {

    private final String TITLE;
    private final Author AUTHOR;
    private final int EDITION;
    private final int NUM_PAGES;

    Book(String title, Author author, int edition, int numPages) {
      this.TITLE = title;
      this.AUTHOR = author;
      this.EDITION = edition;
      this.NUM_PAGES = numPages;
    }

    @Override
    public boolean equals(Object o) {
      if (!(o instanceof Book)) {
        return false;
      } else {
        Book othBook = (Book) o;
        return this.NAME.equals(othBook.NAME)
            && this.AUTHOR.equals(othBook.AUTHOR)
            && this.EDITION == (othBook.EDITION)
            && this.NUM_PAGES == (othBook.NUM_PAGES);
      }
    }

    @Override
    public int hashCode() {
      return Objects.hashCode(this.NAME, this.AUTHOR,
                              this.EDITION, this.NUM_PAGES);
    }

    @Override
    public String toString() {
      return String.format("%s [%s]. Edition: %d. Page Count: %d",
                           this.NAME, this.AUTHOR,
                           this.EDITION, this.NUM_PAGES);
    }

    // Getters omitted.
}
```

4.1 Classes

With these two classes complete, let's begin to think about the Library class. Let's say that it stores an alphabetized Map<Book, Integer> of book instances to the number of copies that are not checked out. We want to be able to add books, check books out, and determine if the book is in the library. So, let's design the void addBook(Book b, int qty), Book checkout(String title), int getQuantity(String title), and boolean containsBook(String title) methods. The tests will reuse the Author and Book declarations from the previous test suite.

```java
import static Assertions.assertAll;
import static Assertions.assertEquals;

class LibraryTester {
  // ... previous test and declarations omitted.

  @Test
  void testLibrary() {
    Library l1 = new Library();
    l1.addBook(B1, 10);
    l1.addBook(B2, 1);
    l1.addBook(B3, 3);
    l1.addBook(B4, 5);
    assertAll (
      () -> assertEquals(1, l1.getQuantity("Principles of Computer Science")),
      () -> assertTrue(l1.containsBook("Methods of Logic")),
      () -> assertFalse(l1.containsBook("Frankenstein")),
      () -> assertEquals(B2, l1.checkout("Principles of Computer Science")),
      () -> assertNull(l1.checkout("Principles of Computer Science")),
      () -> assertEquals(0, l1.getQuantity("Principles of Computer Science")));
  }
}
```

```java
import static Assertions.assertAll;
import static Assertions.assertEquals;

import java.util.Map;
import java.util.TreeMap;

class Library {

  private final Map<Book, Integer> BOOKS;

  Library() {
    this.BOOKS = new TreeMap<>();
  }

  /**
   * Inserts a Book/quantity association to the map. If the book already
   * exists, we add qty to its frequency.
   * @param b Book to add to map.
   * @param qty quantity of provided book.
   */
  void addBook(Book b, int qty) {
    this.BOOKS.put(b, this.BOOKS.getOrDefault(b, 0) + qty);
  }
```

```java
/**
 * "Checks out" a book to someone. By checking out, we mean
 * that it searches for the book with the given title, and
 * returns its instance while decrementing its book counter.
 * If the associated counter is zero, we return null.
 * @param t title to search.
 * @return Book instance if it exists, or null otherwise.
 */
Book checkout(String t) {
  for (Book b : this.BOOKS.keySet()) {
    if (b.getTitle().equals(t) && this.BOOKS.get(b) > 0) {
      this.BOOKS.put(b, this.BOOKS.get(b) - 1);
      return b;
    }
  }
  return null;
}

/**
 * Searches through the books to determine if a book
 * with the given title exists.
 * @param t title of book to search for.
 * @return true if a book with title t exists, false otherwise.
 */
boolean containsBook(String title) {
  for (Book b : this.BOOKS.keySet()) {
    if (b.getTitle().equals(t)) {
      return true;
    }
  }
  return false;
}
}
```

Example 4.11. Along the lines of the previous example, let's design the `VideoGame` class, which represents a video game. A `VideoGame` contains a title and a rating. A rating is one of "C", "E", "E10+", "T", "MA", and "A", corresponding to parental and content warnings. Our `VideoGame` class also overrides the `equals` and `hashCode` methods, since we will store instances thereof in hashable data structures later on. Though, we have overridden `equals` and `hashCode` several times at this point, so our code listings will not include them, but it is extremely important to not forget about them when writing the code yourself.

```java
class VideoGame {

  private final String TITLE;
  private final String RATING;

  VideoGame(String title, String rating) {
    this.TITLE = title;
    this.RATING = rating;
  }

  // Getters omitted.
}
```

To coexist with `VideoGame` instances, let's design the `VideoGameStore` class, which rents out video games to customers. It also keeps records about its users, namely what video games are rented to them at any point. Each user is uniquely identified via an integer, which is

4.1 Classes

associated to a set of `VideoGame` instances. The constructor instantiates the stock and rental maps.

We will design two methods, the first being `boolean rent(int id, String t)`, which rents out the video game with the given title t to the user with the identifier *id*. If the user is not in the "system," they are newly-instantiated and added to the rentals map. If the video game is out of stock, not at all available, or already rented out to the passed user, then the method returns `false`. Finally, if we are able to rent the video game to the user, its stock count is decremented by one, and a *new* instance of the `VideoGame` is added to the user's video game set.

The second method, `int mostFrequentRating()`, returns the most common rating, as a number, of all video games that are rented out to users. For example, if there are 2 `"E"` games, 18 `"E10+"` games, 6 `"T"` games, 3 `"MA"` games, and 1 `"A"` game rented across all users in the system, then `mostFrequentRating` returns 2 because `"E10+"` is the most common rating and is associated with 2.

As an auxiliary method for populating the store stock, we will also create the `addGame` method to receive a title, rating, and number of copies to add to the store.

```java
import static Assertions.assertAll;
import static Assertions.assertEquals;

class VideoGameStoreTester {

  static VideoGameStore populateStore() {
    VideoGameStore vgs = new VideoGameStore();
    vgs.addGame("CuddleTime Bears Adventure", "C", 2);
    vgs.addGame("Fast Racers 2", "E", 7);
    vgs.addGame("Knight of the Republic", "E10+", 4);
    vgs.addGame("Desolation IV", "T", 1);
    vgs.addGame("Fury Combat", "M", 0);
    vgs.addGame("Alien Dating Simulator", "A", 5);
    return vgs;
  }

  @Test
  void testVideoGameStoreRent() {
    VideoGameStore vgs = populateStore();
    assertAll(
      () -> assertTrue(vgs.rent(1, "Fast Racers 2")); // Case 4
      () -> assertTrue(vgs.rent(1, "Desolation IV")); // Case 4
      () -> assertFalse(vgs.rent(1, "Fury Combat")); // Case 1
      () -> assertFalse(vgs.rent(1, "Fast Racers 2")); // Case 3
      () -> assertFalse(vgs.rent(2, "Desolation IV"))); // Case 2
  }

  @Test
  void testVideoGameStoreMostFrequentRating() {
    VideoGameStore vgs = populateStore();
    vgs.rent(1, "Fast Racers 2");
    vgs.rent(1, "Desolation IV");
    vgs.rent(2, "Fast Racers 2");
    vgs.rent(2, "Alien Dating Simulator");
    vgs.rent(3, "Fast Racers 2");
    vgs.rent(4, "Fast Racers 2");
    vgs.rent(5, "Fast Racers 2");
    assertEquals("E", vgs.mostFrequentRating());
  }
}
```

```java
import java.util.HashMap;
import java.util.Map;
import java.util.Set;
import java.util.TreeSet;

class VideoGameStore {

  private final Map<VideoGame, Integer> STOCK;
  private final Map<Integer, Set<VideoGame>> RENTALS;

  VideoGameStore() {
    this.STOCK = new HashMap<>();
    this.RENTALS = new HashMap<>();
  }

  /**
   * Attempts to rent a video game with title t to a user with the given id.
   * If the store does not have the video game in stock (whether due to it not
   * being available or a count of zero) or if the user already has a game
   * with the given title, the rental fails. Otherwise, the stock is updated and
   * the rental is added to the user's video game set.
   * If the user is not in the system, they are added.
   * @param id identifier of user.
   * @param t title of video game.
   * @return true if the rental succeeded, and false otherwise.
   */
  boolean rent(int id, String t) {
    Set<VideoGame> userSet = this.RENTALS.computeIfAbsent(id, k -> new TreeSet<>());
    // Find the VideoGame instance, if it exists, or null otherwise.
    VideoGame g = this.STOCK.keySet().stream()
                                     .filter(vg -> vg.getTitle().equals(t))
                                     .findFirst()
                                     .orElse(null);

    // Condition 1: if the store does not contain the VideoGame.
    if (g == null) {
      return false;
    }
    // Condition 2: if the store contains no copies.
    else if (this.STOCK.get(g) == 0) {
      return false;
    }
    // Condition 3: if the user already has the VideoGame.
    else if (userSet.stream().anyMatch(g -> g.getTitle().equals(t))) {
      return false;
    }
    // Otherwise, we are good to rent.
    else {
      this.STOCK.put(g, this.STOCK.get(g) - 1);
      userSet.add(new VideoGame(g.getTitle(), g.getRating()));
      return true;
    }
  }
}
```

4.1 Classes

```
/**
 * Returns the rating that occurs most frequently among the video games that
 * have been rented out to users.
 * @return the most frequent rating as an integer. If there is a tie, the
 * method returns the highest rating.
 */
String mostFrequentRating() {
  Map<String, Integer> M = new LinkedHashMap<>();
  M.put("C", 0); M.put("E", 0); M.put("E10+", 0);
  M.put("T", 0); M.put("MA", 0); M.put("A", 0);
  for (Integer i : this.RENTALS.keySet()) {
    for (VideoGame g : this.RENTALS.get(i)) {
      M.put(g.getRating(), M.getOrDefault(g.getRating(), 0) + 1);
    }
  }
  return M.entrySet().stream()
                     .max((e1, e2) -> e1.getValue() - e2.getValue())
                     .get()
                     .getKey();
}
}
```

Example 4.12. Suppose we have the following class that represents a position on a two-dimensional board of characters:

```
class BoardPosition {

  private final char CH;

  BoardPosition(char ch;) { this.CH = ch; }

  // Getter omitted.
}
```

Let's now design the Board class to represent a two-dimensional board of BoardPosition instances. Each instance thereof contains a BoardPosition that stores a single arbitrary character literal. The Board constructor receives integers representing the number of rows and columns of the board. It also receives a one-dimensional array of characters, which it uses to populate the board. This example helps to demonstrate how to convert a one-dimensional array into a two-dimensional array. To convert between the two, we use the formula rows * cols + cols.

Let's also design the Map<Integer, List<Character>> getPredecessors() method, which returns a map of the logical indices that precede each character in the board. That is, each key in the map is an index/position into the board, and its value is the list of characters that precede the character at that index on the board. For example, if the board contains the characters 'a', 'e', 'f', 'b', 'd', 'g', 'c', then the map should contain the following key-value pairs:

- 0 → []
- 1 → ['a']
- 2 → ['a']
- 3 → ['a', 'e']
- 4 → ['a', 'e']
- 5 → ['a', 'e', 'f']
- 6 → ['a', 'e', 'f']

We note that, while this example is not particularly useful in practice, it is a good exercise in traversing a two-dimensional array and converting between one-dimensional and two-dimensional arrays.

```java
import static Assertions.assertAll;
import static Assertions.assertEquals;

import java.util.List;
import java.util.Map;

class BoardTester {

  private static final char[] BOARD = {'a', 'b', 'c', 'd', 'e', 'f'};

  @Test
  void testBoard() {
    assertAll(
      () -> assertEquals(2, new Board(2, 3, BOARD).getRows()),
      () -> assertEquals(3, new Board(2, 3, BOARD).getCols()),
      () -> assertEquals('a', new Board(2, 3, BOARD).getBoard()[0][0].getChar()),
      () -> assertEquals('f', new Board(2, 3, BOARD).getBoard()[1][2].getChar()));
  }

  @Test
  void testBoardPredecessors() {
    Map<Integer, List<Character>> map
      = new Board(2, 3, BOARD).getPredecessors();
    assertAll(
      () -> assertEquals(List.of(), map.get(0)),
      () -> assertEquals(List.of('a'), map.get(1)),
      () -> assertEquals(List.of('a'), map.get(2)),
      () -> assertEquals(List.of('a', 'd'), map.get(3)),
      () -> assertEquals(List.of('a', 'd'), map.get(4)),
      () -> assertEquals(List.of('a', 'd', 'e'), map.get(5)));
  }
}
```

```java
import java.util.ArrayList;
import java.util.HashMap;
import java.util.List;
import java.util.Map;

class Board {

  private final BoardPosition[][] BOARD;

  Board(int rows, int cols, char[] chars) {
    this.BOARD = new BoardPosition[rows][cols];
    for (int i = 0; i < rows; i++) {
      for (int j = 0; j < cols; j++) {
        this.BOARD[i][j] = new BoardPosition(chars[i * cols + j]);
      }
    }
  }
```

4.1 Classes

```java
/**
 * Returns the predecessors of each character on the board.
 * A predecessor is a character that comes before the character.
 * @return map of predecessors.
 */
Map<Integer, List<Character>> getPredecessors() {
  Map<Integer, List<Character>> map = new HashMap<>();
  for (int i = 0; i < this.BOARD.length; i++) {
    for (int j = 0; j < this.BOARD[0].length; j++) {
      int index = i * this.BOARD[0].length + j;
      List<Character> list = new ArrayList<>();
      for (int k = 0; k < index; k++) {
        int row = k / this.BOARD[0].length;
        int col = k % this.BOARD[0].length;
        list.add(this.BOARD[row][col].getChar());
      }
      map.put(index, list);
    }
  }
  return map;
}
}
```

Example 4.13. Let's design the `Rational` class, which stores a rational number as a numerator and denominator. We will create methods for adding, subtracting, multiplying, and dividing rational numbers. Testing is paramount to designing a correct implementation, as is the case with all projects, but is of particular significance here. Recall the definition of a rational number: a number that can be expressed as the ratio of two integers p and q, namely p/q. We are acutely familiar with how to perform basic operations on fractions from grade school, so we will gloss over the actual mathematics and prioritize the Java implementation and class design.

The `Rational` constructor receives two integers p and q, and assigns them as instance variables. The `toString` method only involves placing a slash between our numerator and denominator. Though, let's back up for a second and think about the constructor. Do we really want to be able to store fractions that are not in their simplest form? For example, do we want to allow the user to create a `Rational` object with a numerator of 2 and a denominator of 4? The answer is probably not, meaning that we should add a method that simplifies/reduces the fraction into its lowest terms. Fractions can be reduced by finding the greatest common divisor of the numerator and denominator, and dividing both by that value. Euclid's algorithm for finding the greatest common divisor of two integers works wonderfully here. Due to its trivial implementation and the fact that it is a tail recursive algorithm exercise from the previous chapters, we will omit its implementation.

```java
import static Assertions.assertAll;
import static Assertions.assertEquals;

class RationalTester {

  @Test
  void testRationalToString() {
    assertAll(
      () -> assertEquals("1/2", new Rational(1, 2).toString()),
      () -> assertEquals("3/400", new Rational(3, 400).toString()),
      () -> assertEquals("1/1305", new Rational(5, 6525).toString()),
```

```java
      () -> assertEquals("3591/46562", new Rational(7182, 93124).toString()),
      () -> assertEquals("7/32", new Rational(7, 32).toString()),
      () -> assertEquals("9388/48122", new Rational("4694/24061").toString()),
      () -> assertEquals("1/1", new Rational(1, 1).toString()));
  }
}
```

```java
class Rational {

  private final long NUMERATOR;
  private final long DENOMINATOR;

  Rational(long numerator, long denominator) {
    long gcd = gcd(numerator, denominator);
    this.NUMERATOR = numerator / gcd;
    this.DENOMINATOR = denominator / gcd;
  }

  @Override
  public String toString() {
    return String.format("%ld/%ld", this.NUMERATOR, this.DENOMINATOR);
  }
}
```

To add two rational numbers r_1 and r_2, they must share a denominator. If they do not, then we need to find a common denominator by multiplying the denominators together, then multiplying the relevant numerators by the reciprocals of the denominator. For instance, if we want to add 2/3 and 7/9, the (not-necessarily lowest) common denominator is $3 \cdot 9 = 27$. We multiply 2 by 9 and 7 by 3 to get 18/27 and 24/27. Adding across the numerators produces 42/27, which then reduces to 14/9. Since we wish to preserve the original rational number, we will write a method that returns a new `Rational` rather than modifying the one we have in-place (this also allows us to omit a step in which we simplify the resulting fraction, since the constructor takes care of this task).

```java
import static Assertions.assertAll;
import static Assertions.assertEquals;

class RationalTester {

  @Test
  void testRationalAdd() {
    assertAll (
      () -> assertEquals("14/9",
                         new Rational(2, 3).add(new Rational(7, 9)).toString()),
      () -> assertEquals("5/6",
                         new Rational(1, 2).add(new Rational(1, 3)).toString()),
      () -> assertEquals("1/3",
                         new Rational(1, 4).add(new Rational(1, 12)).toString()),
      () -> assertEquals("1/4",
                         new Rational(1, 8).add(new Rational(1, 8)).toString()),
      () -> assertEquals("1/8",
                         new Rational(1, 16).add(new Rational(1, 16)).toString()),
      () -> assertEquals("1/16",
                         new Rational(1, 32).add(new Rational(1, 32)).toString()),
      () -> assertEquals("2/1",
                         new Rational(32, 32).add(new Rational(32, 32)).toString()));
  }
}
```

4.1 Classes

```
class Rational {

  /**
   * Adds two rational numbers.
   * @param r the other rational number.
   * @return the (simplified) sum of this and r.
   */
  Rational add(Rational r) {
    long commonDenominator = this.DENOMINATOR * r.DENOMINATOR;
    long newNumerator = this.NUMERATOR * r.DENOMINATOR + r.NUMERATOR * this.DENOMINATOR;
    return new Rational(newNumerator, commonDenominator);
  }
}
```

Due to its correspondence to addition, we leave subtraction as an exercise to the reader. We can now implement multiplication, which is even simpler than addition; all that is needed is to multiply the numerators and denominators together. We also leave division as an exercise to the reader. We encourage the reader to write methods for comparing rationals for equality, as well as greater than/less than.

Plus, we could extend this system to support BigInteger values for the numerator and denominator (rather than long types), which would allow us to represent arbitrarily large rational numbers. This, in turn, would require updating all methods to use BigInteger arithmetic, which is a good exercise in and of itself.

```
import static Assertions.assertAll;
import static Assertions.assertEquals;

class RationalTester {

  @Test
  void testRationalMultiply() {
    assertAll (
      () -> assertEquals("14/27",
              new Rational(2, 3).multiply(new Rational(7, 9)).toString()),
      () -> assertEquals("1/25",
              new Rational(1, 5).multiply(new Rational(1, 5)).toString()),
      () -> assertEquals("1/1",
              new Rational(1, 1).multiply(new Rational(1, 1)).toString()));
  }
}
```

```
class Rational {

  /**
   * Multiplies two rational numbers.
   * @param r the other rational number.
   * @return the (simplified) product of this and r.
   */
  Rational multiply(Rational r) {
    return new Rational(this.NUMERATOR * r.NUMERATOR, this.DENOMINATOR * r.DENOMINATOR);
  }
}
```

Example 4.14. Let's now use classes to demonstrate a theoretically powerful idea: translating standard recursive methods into ones that use iteration. We have seen how to mechanically translate a tail recursive method, but standard recursion was left out of the discussion. In general, any recursive method can be rewritten to use iteration. The problem we encounter with standard recursive algorithms is that they often blow up the procedure call stack, which is limited in size for most programming languages. What if we did not push anything to the call stack at all, and instead implement our own stack? In doing so, we delegate the space requirements of the recursive calls from the (call) stack to the heap, where there is orders of magnitude more memory space. This solution is neither fast nor space-efficient, but serves to show that naturally standard recursive algorithms, e.g., factorial, can still use a standard recursion algorithm, in a sense.

To create our own stack, we first need to decide what to place onto the stack. We know that each method call pushes an activation record, or a stack frame, to the procedure call stack containing the existing local variables and parameters. For the sake of simplicity, let's assume that our methods never declare local variables. We need a class that stores variable identifiers to values, which can be any type. A simple solution to the "any type" problem is to use the Object class, because all classes *are* a "kind of" Object. So, the StackFrame class stores a Map<String, Object> as an instance variable. Its constructor receives no arguments because we do not know a priori how many parameters any arbitrary user of StackFrame will require. To compensate, let's design the addParam method that receives a String and an Object, enters those into the existing map, and returns the existing instance.[10] We design the method in this fashion to prevent the need to separately instantiate the frame, then add its parameters on separate lines, which would be required if addParam were of type void.

```
import java.util.HashMap;
import java.util.Map;

class StackFrame {

  private Map<String, Object> PARAMS;

  StackFrame() {
    this.PARAMS = new HashMap<>();
  }

  Object getParam(String s) {
    return this.PARAMS.get(s);
  }

  StackFrame addParam(String s, Object o) {
    this.PARAMS.put(s, o);
    return this;
  }
}
```

Now, let's translate the standard recursive fact method, which will receive a BigInteger, and return its factorial. Below we show the recursive version. From the recursive definition, we design the factLoop method that instantiates a Stack<StackFrame> to replicate the call stack. We begin the process by pushing the initial frame comprised of the initial input argument. This is followed by a variable to keep track of the "return value," which should match the type of the standard recursive method (for our purposes of factorial, this is a

---

[10] This idea resembles the *builder* design pattern, which we will discuss in Chapter 8.

4.1 Classes

BigInteger). Our loop continues as long as there is a stack frame to pop, and the core logic of the algorithm, namely $n!$, is identical to our standard recursive counterpart.

```java
import static Assertions.assertAll;
import static Assertions.assertEquals;

import java.util.BigInteger;

class StackFrameTester {

  @Test
  void testFact() {
    assertAll (
      () -> assertEquals(new BigInteger("1"), fact(new BigInteger("0"))),
      () -> assertEquals(new BigInteger("3628800"), fact(new BigInteger("10"))));
  }

  @Test
  void testFactLoop() {
      assertAll (
        () -> assertEquals(new BigInteger("1"), factLoop(new BigInteger("0"))),
        () -> assertEquals(new BigInteger("3628800"), factLoop(new BigInteger("10"))));
  }
}
```

```java
import java.util.Stack;
import java.util.BigInteger;

class StackFrameDriver {

  /**
   * Computes the factorial of a BigInteger using natural recursion.
   * @param n instance of BigInteger to compute factorial of.
   * @return n!
   */
  static BigInteger fact(BigInteger n) {
    if (n.compareTo(BigInteger.ONE) <= 0) {
      return n.add(BigInteger.ONE);
    } else {
      return n.multiply(fact(n.subtract(BigInteger.ONE)));
    }
  }

  /**
   * Computes the factorial of a BigInteger n using the StackFrame approach.
   * @param n instance of BigInteger to compute factorial of.
   * @return n!
   */
  static BigInteger factLoop(BigInteger n) {
    Stack<StackFrame> sf = new Stack<>();
    BigInteger res = n;
    sf.push(new StackFrame().addParam("n", n));
    while (!sf.isEmpty()) { /* TODO. */ }
    return res;
  }
}
```

Turning our attention to the innards of the loop, we must accurately replicate the procedure call stack actions. Thus, we first pop the existing frame, extract the desired parameters to work with from its map, then perform the algorithm's logic.

```java
class StackFrameDriver {

  /**
   * Computes the factorial of a BigInteger n using the StackFrame approach.
   * @param n instance of BigInteger to compute factorial of.
   * @return n!
   */
  static BigInteger factLoop(BigInteger n) {
    Stack<StackFrame> sf = new Stack<>();
    BigInteger res = BigInteger.ONE;
    sf.push(new StackFrame().addParam("n", n));

    while (!sf.isEmpty()) {
      StackFrame f = sf.pop();
      BigInteger pn = (BigInteger) f.get("n");
      if (pn.compareTo(BigInteger.ONE) <= 0) {
        continue;
      } else {
        sf.push(new StackFrame().addParam("n", pn.subtract(BigInteger.ONE)));
        res = res.multiply(pn);
      }
    }

    return res;
  }
}
```

Notice two things: first, we manually mimic the behavior of the call stack. Second, by managing the stack ourselves, we drastically increase the limit to the number of possible "recursive calls," since we push instances of our StackFrame onto the heap. Theoretically, we could continuously push new "frames" to our stack so long as we have active and available heap memory. Of course, that is impossible with current hardware limitations, so in due time, with a large-enough call to factLoop, the JVM terminates the program with an OutOfMemory error.

In the relevant test suite, we do not include tests for extraordinarily large numbers to preserve space, but we encourage the readers to try out such test cases, e.g., 100000000!. We should state that these tests will not complete in a reasonable amount of time.[11]

4.2 Object Mutation and Aliasing

A limitation that we have purposefully imposed on our object/class design is the inability to modify the values of instance variables. Value mutation is a foreign concept in some programming languages, but we have made extensive use of it throughout our time in the land of Java. In this section, we discuss the implications of instance variable mutation, and how it can lead to unintended problems, but also how it can be used to our advantage.

To access a private instance variable, we design a non-private accessor method, which returns the instance variable. To *modify* a private instance variable, we design a non-private

---

[11] On an AMD Ryzen 5 3600 with 16GB of DDR4 RAM, this test did not complete within a three hour time frame.

4.2 Object Mutation and Aliasing

mutator method, which receives a parameter and assigns its value to the corresponding instance variable. Let's return to the `Point` class to demonstrate. Suppose that we instantiate a `Point` object p to the position $(7, 4)$, but we then wish to change or modify either coordinate. We can do so by calling the `setX` or `setY` methods, respectively. Testing setter methods is important to verify that a change occurred when invoking the setter/mutator method, which is confirmed through the accessor method.

Another way of phrasing such an approach is that, when testing a mutator, we care about the *side-effect* of the method rather than what it returns, namely nothing. Setter methods, or methods that modify outside values or data are definitionally *impure*. Because we want to alter an instance variable, these can no longer be marked as `final`, so we remove the keyword.[12]

```
import static Assertions.assertEquals;

class PointTester {

  @Test
  void testSetX() {
    Point p = new Point(7, 4);
    p.setX(3);
    assertEquals(3, p.getX());
  }

  @Test
  void testSetY() {
    Point p = new Point(7, 4);
    p.setY(2);
    assertEquals(2, p.getY());
    p.setY(p.getY() - 4);
    assertEquals(-2, p.getY());
  }
}
```

```
class Point {

  private int x;
  private int y;

  Point(int x, int y) {
    this.x = x;
    this.y = y;
  }

  int getX() { return this.x; }

  int getY() { return this.y; }

  void setX(int x) { this.x = x; }

  void setY(int y) { this.y = y; }
}
```

---

[12] This is not to suggest that we should never use `final` instance variables. In fact, we *should* use `final` instance variables whenever possible, since object mutation introduces the possibility of easy-to-overlook bugs.

What are some consequences to mutating an object? One such consequence comes through the notion of *object aliasing*. Recall that objects point to references in memory. Therefore, if we instantiate a Point p_1, then initialize another Point p_2 to p_1, then both objects refer to the same Point instance in memory. If we modify p_1 through a setter method, then p_2 is also affected.

```java
import static Assertions.assertAll;
import static Assertions.assertEquals;

class PointTester {

  @Test
  void testPointAliasing() {
    Point p1 = new Point(7, 4);
    Point p2 = p1;
    p1.setX(3);
    assertAll(
      () -> assertEquals(3, p1.getX()),
      () -> assertEquals(3, p2.getX()),
      () -> assertEquals(p1, p2));
  }

  @Test
  void testSetX() {
    Point p1 = new Point(11, 13);
    Point p2 = p1;
    p2.setX(100);
    assertAll(
      () -> assertEquals(100, p1.getX()),
      () -> assertEquals(100, p2.getX())
      () -> assertEquals(p1, p2));
  }

  @Test
  void testSetY() {
    Point p1 = new Point(7, 4);
    Point p2 = p1;
    p1.setY(2);
    assertAll(
      () -> assertEquals(2, p1.getY()),
      () -> assertEquals(2, p2.getY()),
      () -> assertEquals(p1, p2));
  }
}
```

Aliasing carries over to other, more complex classes as well. For example, strings, arrays, lists, and others are all objects, and therefore, are subject to object aliasing. Modifying one ArrayList instance will modify all other ArrayList instances that reference the same object. Unintentional aliasing (or its associated actions) is a common source of bugs in Java programs, and it is important to be aware of this behavior.

In the following example, we will demonstrate aliasing through the ArrayList data structure containing Point objects. We add a series of Point instances to an ArrayList, which is then aliased by another ArrayList. We then add another Point instance to the first ArrayList, followed by a verification that the lists are the same size. We traverse over the lists and verify that the elements are the same through the == operator. Remember that == returns whether or not two objects reference the same instance in memory. Because these lists are merely aliases of each other, they will, in fact, contain references to the same Point instances.

4.2 Object Mutation and Aliasing

```java
import static Assertions.assertAll;
import static Assertions.assertEquals;
import static Assertions.assertTrue;

import java.util.ArrayList;
import java.util.List;

class PointTester {

  @Test
  void testPointArrayListAliasing() {
    Point P1 = new Point(7, 4);
    Point P2 = new Point(3, 2);
    Point P3 = new Point(1, 8);

    List<Point> list1 = new ArrayList<>(List.of(P1, P2, P3));
    List<Point> list2 = list1;
    list1.add(new Point(5, 6));

    // First we can verify that the lists are actually the same.
    assertTrue(list1 == list2);

    // Size testing.
    assertTrue(list1.size() == list2.size());

    // Make sure both lists contain the same elements.
    for (int i = 0; i < list1.size(); i++) {
      assertTrue(list1.get(i) == list2.get(i));
    }

    // If we want, we can also verify that the content, i.e.,
    // the coordinates of the points in both are equal.
    for (int i = 0; i < list1.size(); i++) {
      assertTrue(list1.get(i).getX() == list2.get(i).getX()
              && list1.get(i).getY() == list2.get(i).getY());
    }
  }
}
```

Example 4.15. Now that we have classes, accessibility, and mutation, we can implement generic data structures such as an `ArrayList`. In this example, we will design a class that matches the behavior of the `ArrayList` class. Let's design the `MiniArrayList` class, which operates over any type using generics. Like generic static methods, we must quantify the generic type, but unlike static methods, however, we quantify the type over the class declaration, meaning that all instance methods observe/respect the quantify and do not need to be separately quantified. Static methods still necessitate the generic quantifier in their signatures.[13]

In addition to the class header, what else does an `ArrayList` store? Certainly, a backing array of elements and its corresponding length. The array, as we described in Chapter 3, "dynamically resizes" as we add or insert elements. The logical size of the array, i.e., the number of presently-existing elements is its `size`, whereas the current capacity, i.e., how many elements can currently be stored without a resize, is its `capacity`.

---

[13] Static methods are not tied to any instance of the class (nor its generic type), so they must be quantified separately.

Our class will provide two constructors: one that instantiates the backing array to store ten elements, and another that allows the user to specify the initial capacity. Interestingly, this shows off a great example of one constructor calling another of the same class, an idea called *constructor chaining*. "Ten," however, is a magic number: a number whose context is the only thing that determines its meaning. So, let's refactor it into a constant class variable with a relevant identifier.

```
class MiniArrayList<T> {

  private static final int DEFAULT_CAPACITY = 10;

  private T[] elements;
  private int size;
  private int capacity;

  MiniArrayList() {
    this(DEFAULT_CAPACITY);
  }

  MiniArrayList(int capacity) {
    this.size = 0;
    this.capacity = capacity;
  }
}
```

Notice that we declare an array of type T to store the elements of our mini array list. We now must instantiate the array inside the second constructor. The problem we immediately encounter is that we cannot instantiate an array of a generic type, because Java arrays utilize runtime information about the element type. Generics, on the other hand, are a compile-time feature, meaning it is impossible to directly instantiate an array of a generic type. Instead, we must instantiate an array containing (elements of) type Object, followed by a cast to contain (elements of) type T.[14] This is called an *unchecked cast*, and it is a necessary evil in Java to support powerful classes that operate over generic arrays.

```
class MiniArrayList<T> {

  private static final int DEFAULT_CAPACITY = 10;

  private T[] vals;
  private int size;
  private int capacity;

  MiniArrayList() {
    this(DEFAULT_CAPACITY);
  }

  MiniArrayList(int capacity) {
    this.size = 0;
    this.capacity = capacity;
    this.vals = (T[]) new Object[this.capacity];
  }
}
```

We now need to implement the add method, which adds an element to the end of the array list. We first check if the array is full, and if so, resize the array. We then add the element to the

---

[14] To be pedantic, the array is of type Object[], and we cast it to type T[].

4.2 Object Mutation and Aliasing

end of the array and increment the size. Resizing the array is, fortunately, not complicated; all we need to do is instantiate a new, larger array, copy the existing elements over, then reassign the instance variable. The question now is, by what factor should the array capacity increase? This decision is implementation-dependent, but we will use a doubling factor out of common practice.[15] We make resize private because it is an implementation detail that the programmer who uses MiniArrayList should not concern themselves over.

To write coherent tests, we should also write the get method, which returns the element at a given index, as well as size, which returns the number of logical elements in the list. For now, we will not consider invalid inputs, e.g., negative array indices, and all inputs to methods are assumed to be semantically correct.

```java
import static Assertions.assertAll;
import static Assertions.assertEquals;

class MiniArrayListTester {

  @Test
  void testAdd() {
    MiniArrayList<Integer> list = new MiniArrayList<>();
    list.add(100);
    list.add(200);
    list.add(300);
    assertAll(
      () -> assertEquals(3, list.size()),
      () -> assertEquals(100, list.get(0)),
      () -> assertEquals(200, list.get(1)),
      () -> assertEquals(300, list.get(2)));
  }
}
```

```java
class MiniArrayList<T> {

  private static final int RESIZE_FACTOR = 2;

  /**
   * Adds an element to the end of the list.
   * @param element the element to add.
   */
  void add(T element) {
    if (this.size == this.capacity) {
      this.resize();
    }
    this.vals[this.size++] = element;
  }

  /**
   * Retrieves an element at a given index. The index should
   * be in-bounds. If not, an ArrayIndexOutOfBoundsException is thrown.
   * @param index list index between 0 <= i < L.size()
   * @return item at the given index.
   */
  T get(int index) { return this.vals[index]; }
```

---

[15] Another logical choice is to increase the capacity linearly based on the default capacity. This choice removes the need for an extra static variable.

```
  /**
   * Returns the logical size of the list, i.e., the number of actual elements.
   * @return number of elements.
   */
  int size() { return this.size; }

  /**
   * Resizes the backing array by a factor specified by the class.
   */
  private void resize() {
    this.capacity *= RESIZE_FACTOR;
    T[] newArray = (T[]) new Object[this.capacity];
    for (int i = 0; i < this.size; i++) {
      newArray[i] = this.vals[i];
    }
    this.vals = newArray;
  }
}
```

We will write two more methods: `insert` and `remove`, which inserts an element e at a given index i, and removes an element e respectively. These two methods are similar in that they alter the backing array by shifting its values right and left. Accordingly, our implementation will contain the private helper methods `shiftRight` and `shiftLeft`. If we attempt to insert an element into a list that must be resized, we call `resize`. Both `insert` and `remove` warrant new test cases. Like the get counterpart, neither of these new methods will perform bounds checking, so testing out-of-bounds behavior is not pertinent.

```
import static Assertions.assertAll;
import static Assertions.assertEquals;

class MiniArrayListTester {

  @Test
  void testInsert() {
    MiniArrayList<Integer> list = new MiniArrayList<>();
    list.add(100);
    list.add(300);
    list.insert(1, 150);
    assertAll(
      () -> assertEquals(3, list.size()),
      () -> assertEquals(100, list.get(0)),
      () -> assertEquals(150, list.get(1)),
      () -> assertEquals(300, list.get(2)));
  }

  @Test
  void testRemove() {
    MiniArrayList<Integer> list = new MiniArrayList<>();
    list.add(100);
    list.add(300);
    list.remove(0);
    assertAll(
      () -> assertEquals(1, list.size()),
      () -> assertEquals(300, list.get(0)));
  }
}
```

4.2 Object Mutation and Aliasing

```
class MiniArrayList<T> {
  // ... previous code not shown.

  /**
   * Inserts an element at the given index.
   * @param e the element to insert.
   * @param idx the index to insert at.
   */
  void insert(T e, int idx) {
    if (this.size == capacity) {
      this.resize();
    }
    this.shiftRight(idx);
    this.vals[idx] = e;
  }

  /**
   * Removes the element at the given index.
   * @param idx the index to remove.
   * @return the element removed.
   */
  T remove(int idx) {
    T e = this.get(idx);
    this.shiftLeft(idx);
    this.size--;
    return e;
  }
}
```

```
class MiniArrayList<T> {
  /**
   * Shifts all elements to the left of the given index one position leftwards.
   * @param idx the index to shift left of.
   */
  private void shiftLeft(int idx) {
    for (int i = idx; i < this.size - 1; i++) {
      this.vals[i] = this.vals[i + 1];
    }
  }

  /**
   * Shifts all elements to the right of the given index one position rightwards.
   * @param idx the index to shift right of.
   */
  private void shiftRight(int idx) {
    for (int i = size - 1; i > idx; i--) {
      this.vals[i] = this.vals[i - 1];
    }
  }
}
```

Example 4.16. Let's see a few more examples of object aliasing and mutation. These examples will not be meaningful in what they represent, but are great exercises in testing your understanding.

Let's consider five classes: A, B, C, D, and E. Class A contains one mutable string instance variable; its constructor assigns the instance variable to the parameter thereof. Classes B and C are identical aside from the name: they contain an immutable object of type A as an instance variable. Class D stores an integer array of ten elements. Finally, class E stores a mutable integer as an instance variable.

We present several test cases that assert different pieces of these classes. We will analyze each one and determine why it uses either assertEquals or assertNotEquals in its comparison. Our first series of tests only focuses on classes A, B, and C to keep things simple. We insert blanks in the assertion statements for you to fill in as exercise before checking your answers.

```
import static Assertions.assertEquals;
import static Assertions.assertNotEquals;

class ClassTester {

  @Test
  void testOne() {
    final A a = new A("Hello!");
    B b = new B(a);
    C c = new C(a);
    assert_____(b.getA(), c.getA());
    assert_____(b.getA().getS(), c.getA().getS());
    a.setS("Hi!");
    assert_____(b.getA().getS(), c.getA().getS());
    b.getA().setS("howdy!");
    assert_____(b.getA().getS(), c.getA().getS());
    B b2 = new B(a);
    assert_____(a, b2.getA());
    assert_____(b, b2);
    b = b2;
    assert_____(a, b.getA());
    assert_____(b, b2);
  }
}
```

To set the scene, we first declare a as an immutable instance of A with the string literal "Hello!". Then, we instantiate objects b and c of types B and C respectively, each receiving a as an argument to their constructors.

Comparing b.getA() against c.getA() is a comparison of two references to the same object. Because a is immutable, we cannot change its value, so both b and c will always refer to the same object. Therefore, we use assertEquals to compare the two references. In particular, passing a to both constructors passes a reference to the same object.

```
B b = new B(a);                    C c = new C(a);
b.getA();                          c.getA();

              a = 0xffff2345
```

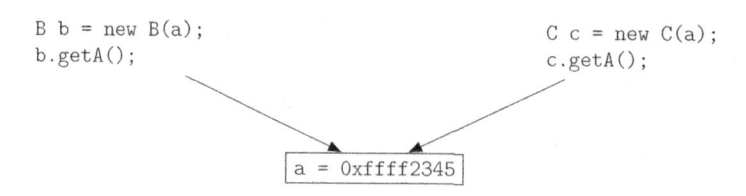

Fig. 4.1: Memory Aliasing Example

In Figure 4.1, we use memory addresses to refer to the location of a. To be a bit pedantic, objects are not stored directly in system memory per se, but rather a location accessible by the Java Virtual Machine.

4.2 Object Mutation and Aliasing

Comparing b.getA().getS() against c.getA().getS() is a comparison of two references to the same object, similar to the previous problem, right? Wrong! Recall that the String class overrides the equals method implementation to compare strings for their content rather than their reference. Should we choose to compare the two strings for referential equality, we must use the == operator. In this case, we use assertEquals since the two strings are equal in content, but using == would also work because the strings are also equal in reference.

In the third line we change the value of the string inside a to be "Hi!", which updates across all instances that point to a. Therefore, rerunning the same comparison as before still results in a true equality.

In the fifth line, we retrieve the A object instance pointed to by B and change its underlying string to be "Howdy!". Rerunning the same test as before yet again results in a true equality. Because b points to the same a that c references, this change propagates across all references to a, even if we do not directly modify a.

We then declare a new instance of B named b2, which references the same a as before. If we check the value of a against the value of a inside b2, we of course get a true equality.

We immediately follow this comparison with one in which we compare b to b2. Because these are completely distinct object instantiations, the equality does not hold true.

Up next we reassign b to point to b2. This is a reassignment of a reference, not a reassignment of an object. Therefore if we check b against b2 for equality, it is now trivially true.

Example 4.17. Let's do another aliasing test, this time to involve arrays of objects. We will operate over a class E that stores a single number, similar to how the Integer class works.

```java
class E {

  private int val;

  E(int v) { this.val = v; }

  int getNumber() { return this.val; }

  void setNumber(int v) { this.val = v; }
}
```

```java
import static Assertions.assertEquals;
import static Assertions.assertNotEquals;

class ClassTester {

  @Test
  void testTwo() {
    E e = new E(42);
    E[] arrOfE = new E[10];
    for (int i = 0; i < arrOfE.length; i++) { arrOfE[i] = new E(i); }
    assert_____(arrOfE[2], arrOfE[5]);
    assert_____(arrOfE[2].getNumber(), arrOfE[5].getNumber());

    for (int i = 0; i < arrOfE.length; i++) { arrOfE[i] = e; }
    assert_____(arrOfE[0], arrOfE[2]);
    assert_____(arrOfE[0].getNumber(), arrOfE[2].getNumber());
    arrOfE[7].setNumber(102);
    assert_____(arrOfE[0].getNumber(), arrOfE[2].getNumber());
  }
}
```

The object e is instantiated to a new instance of E, whose constructor receives 42 as an argument. Thereafter we instantiate arrOfE to be an array of ten E objects. The following loop then instantiates each index of the array to a new, distinct E object with the integer i as an argument to the constructors.

So, what happens if we compare any arbitrary element e against any other arbitrary element e' such that $e \neq e'$? Because they are all instantiated to distinct instances of E, any equality comparison is false. We can extend this to retrieving the number inside each E object and comparing them. Each E instance receives a different value of i, entailing that the equality does not hold.

The second loop assigns the e object to each index of the array. We can then compare any arbitrary element against any other arbitrary element, and they will always be equal according to both == and equals, since every element is a reference to the same memory reference. Thus, changing the stored integer value at one index propagates to every other element in the array, because again, all references point to the same object. Preceding the final assertion is an assignment of a new E instance to index four that boxes the integer 2. Changing any index aside from four modifies e, but does not modify the instance of E at index four, the converse of which also holds.

Example 4.18. Let's get even more practice with aliasing over arrays. Suppose we have the following code segment:

```
class ArrayAliasingTester {

  static int baz(int[] A) {
    A[3] = 42;
    return A[3];
  }

  static int modify(int[] A) {
    A = new int[100];
  }

  @Test
  void testBaz() {
    int[] A = new int[]{0, 0, 0, 0, 0};
    A[2] = baz(A);
    assertEquals(84, A[2] + A[3]);

    int[] B = new int[]{0, 0, 0, 0, 0, 0};
    int[] C = B;
    assert_____(84, C[3] + baz(B));

    int[] D = new int[]{0, 0, 0, 0, 0, 0, 0};
    int[] E = D;
    int res = baz(E);
    assert_____(84, D[3] + res);
    D = new int[]{1, 2, 3, 4, 5, 6, 7};
    assert_____(E, D);

    int[] F = new int[]{0, 1, 2, 3, 4};
    int h1 = F.hashCode();
    modify(F);
    assertEquals(h1, F.hashCode());
  }
}
```

4.2 Object Mutation and Aliasing

Again, we encourage the readers to stop and think about what kinds of assertions to fill in the blanks. Consider what happens when arrays are passed to methods, then continue onward to check your understanding.

We start by examining the `baz` method, which receives an array of integers A as a parameter, overwrites the value at index 3 to be 42, then returns that element.

Inside the JUnit tester method, we first instantiate an array A to contain five zeroes. Afterwards, we assign, to index 2 of A, the value of invoking `baz(A)`, meaning `A[2]` is 42, but so is `A[3]`, because passing an array to a method passes a copy of the reference to the array. Therefore, the index of the passed array is mutated. We assert whether the sum of these two elements is 84, which is true because $42 + 42 = 84$.

Second, we instantiate an array B to contain six zeroes. This is followed by an initialization of an array C to point to B, meaning C is an alias for B. We then assert whether the sum of `C[3]` and `baz(B)` is 84. The answer relies on an understanding of evaluation order. The plus operator evaluates its arguments from left-to-right. Before invoking `baz(B)`, the value of `C[3]` is zero, so the left-hand side of the addition is zero. Immediately after, we evaluate `baz(B)`, which mutates not only index 3 of B, but also index 3 of C, because again, C aliases B. The expression is now an addition of 0 and 42, which is certainly not equal to 84.

Third, we instantiate yet another array E to contain seven zeroes. We then alias the array D to E, followed by a call to `baz(E)`, whose result is stored in the `res` variable. We know for certain that `res` contains 42, and we want to know whether `D[3]` also contains 42 to sum to the expected value of 84. Because D aliases E, it must be the case that `D[3]` is also 42, meaning we assert equals.

The fourth assertion is the result of altering D's reference. Recall that D initially references the new integer array of seven zeroes. The D array becomes an alias to E, which might suggest that changing E also changes what D points to, but this is not the case. When we instantiate E to point to the new array of the integers from 1 to 7, D remains aliased to the array of seven zeroes that E was instantiated to. Therefore, the assertion should be not equals.

Finally, we instantiate an array F to contain the integers from 0 to 4 inclusive. We compute the hash code of F and store it inside h_1. Then, we pass F to the `modify` method, which appears to modify the passed reference to point to a new array. In the previous chapter we mentioned "pass by pseudo-reference," which alluded to this problem. When we pass an object to a method, we pass a copy *of* the reference rather than the reference itself. Changing what the copy points to does not change the reference outside the context of the `modify` method. So, we should assert equals on h_1 and the hash code of F after invoking `modify`, since F's reference is never altered.

Example 4.19. Some readers may question why we emphasize mutation and aliasing. When working with the Collections framework and designing data structures, proper care must be taken to avoid undesired behavior and outcomes. Consider what happens if we design a class F whose constructor receives a `List<Integer>`, which is assigned directly to an instance variable. Then, suppose we instantiate two distinct instances of F, namely f_1 and f_2, each of which receive the same (reference to a) list of numbers. If we then mutate the list somewhere inside of f_1, then the list stored as a reference inside f_2 also contains the change.

```java
import static Assertions.assertAll;
import static Assertions.assertEquals;

class ClassTester {

  @Test
  void testListAliasing() {
    List<Integer> ls = new ArrayList<>(List.of(1, 2, 3, 4, 5));
    F f1 = new F(ls);
    F f2 = new F(ls);
    f1.getList().set(2, 100);
    assertEquals(100, f1.getList().get(2));
    assertEquals(100, f2.getList().get(2));
  }
}
```

```java
import java.util.List;

class F {

  private final List<Integer> LS;

  F(List<Integer> ls) { this.LS = ls; }

  List<Integer> getList() { return this.LS; }
}
```

Example 4.20. Recall the `LinkedList` class from Chapter 3. If you have ever wondered how it works under the hood, now is the time to find out! We will design a *doubly-linked list* data structure that stores arbitrarily-typed elements.

First, remember the structure of a linked list: it is composed of nodes, which hold the data and a pointer to the next element in the chain/sequence. These types of linked lists are *singly-linked*, because nodes only refer to the successive element. In contrast, our class models a doubly-linked list, since its nodes point to their successor *and* their predecessor.

We need a generic class that stores references to the first and last elements of the list. Let's design the `DoublyLinkedList` class to receive a type parameter T, and store the first and last nodes as instance variables. It's important to realize that, whoever uses this class will not (and should not) be exposed to the innards of the class, i.e., how the links are established/constructed/altered/removed. After all, we wish to preserve the encapsulation motif.

We run into an imminent problem when declaring the types of the instance variables: what *should* they be? We need to design a class that encapsulates the value of the node, and holds references to its previous and successor nodes. Some programmers may consider designing a separate .java file for this class, but remember the encapsulation methodology: nobody outside of this class should even be aware that nodes exist in the first place. So, we can create a private and static `Node<T>` class, which is local to the definition of `DoublyLinkedList`. A privatized class can only ever be static, because it is nonsense to say that a private class definition belongs to an arbitrary instance of the class in which it resides.[16] We also override the `toString` method to output a stringified representation of underlying node data.

---

[16] Such a claim would imply that every instance of the `DoublyLinkedList` class would carry the data for instantiating nodes, which is wasteful.

4.2 Object Mutation and Aliasing

```
class DoublyLinkedList<T> {

  private static class Node<T> {

    private T value;
    private Node<T> prev;
    private Node<T> next;

    private Node(T value) { this.value = value; }

    @Override
    public String toString() { return this.value.toString(); }
  }

  private Node<T> first;
  private Node<T> last;

  DoublyLinkedList() { this.last = this.first = null; }
}
```

Notice that, in the constructor of `DoublyLinkedList`, we assign the first and last references to each other, both of which point to `null`. An empty list contains neither a first nor a last element.

To test the methods that we are about to design, we will override the `toString` method (of `DoublyLinkedList`) to print the elements inside brackets, separated by commas and a space. To traverse over the list, however, we should use a custom-defined `Iterator`, which will be its own localized class definition. We have seen iterators before, but until now we have not implemented one on our own. The idea is, fortunately, very simple: we keep track of the current node, and upon calling `hasNext`, we return whether or not the node is `null`. Similarly, invoking `next` returns the value of the stored node and moves the pointer forward via the "next" instance. Finally, we create the `.iterator` method, which returns an instance of the iterator superclass. There is no desire to expose the implementation of the iterator to the caller; they are only concerned with iterating over the doubly-linked list.

```
import java.util.Iterator;

class DoublyLinkedList<T> {
  // ... previous code not shown.

  Iterator<T> iterator() {
    return new DoublyLinkedListIterator<>(this.first);
  }

  private static class DoublyLLIterator<T> implements Iterator<T> {

    private Node<T> current;

    private DoublyLLIterator(Node<T> first) {
      this.current = first;
    }

    @Override
    boolean hasNext() {
      return this.current != null;
    }
```

```java
    @Override
    T next() {
      T value = this.current.value;
      this.current = this.current.next;
      return value;
    }
  }
}
```

Using the iterator in `toString` is straightforward: we have a while loop that continues until no more elements are present. We complete two tasks at the same time by having an iterator, which then makes subsequent traversals over the list easier.

Now we can write methods to add, retrieve, and remove elements from the list. To add an element, we need to take the links of `first` and `last`, and reassign them accordingly to remain consistent with our doubly-linked list property. If the list is empty, then we just have to assign the new node n to both the `first` and `last` references. Otherwise, we set the "next" pointer of `last` to n, and set the "previous" pointer of n to `last`.

```java
import static Assertions.assertAll;
import static Assertions.assertEquals;

class DoublyLinkedListTester {

  @Test
  void testAdd() {
    DoublyLinkedList<Integer> list = new DoublyLinkedList<>();
    assertAll(
      () -> assertEquals("[]", list.toString()),
      () -> list.add(1),
      () -> list.add(3),
      () -> assertEquals("[1, 3]", list.toString()),
      () -> list.add(4),
      () -> list.add(1),
      () -> assertEquals("[1, 3, 4, 1]", list.toString()));
  }
}
```

```java
class DoublyLinkedList<T> {
  /**
   * Adds a new node to the end of the list.
   * @param data The data to be stored in the new node.
   */
  void add(T data) {
    Node<T> newNode = new Node<>(data);
    // If the list is empty, make the new node the first and last node.
    if (this.first == null) { this.first = newNode; }
    else {
      // Otherwise, add the new node to the end of the list.
      newNode.prev = this.last;
      this.last.next = newNode;
    }
    this.last = newNode;
  }
}
```

4.2 Object Mutation and Aliasing

Retrieving an element is trivial, as it's just a matter of traversing over the list and returning the data at the index of a node. If the index is out of bounds, we return an empty `Optional`.[17]

```
import static Assertions.assertAll;
import static Assertions.assertEquals;

class DoublyLinkedListTester {

  @Test
  void testGet() {
    DoublyLinkedList<Integer> list = new DoublyLinkedList<>();
    assertAll(
      () -> assertEquals(Optional.empty(), list.get(0)),
      () -> list.add(50),
      () -> list.add(25),
      () -> assertEquals(Optional.of(50), list.get(0)),
      () -> assertEquals(Optional.of(25), list.get(1)),
      () -> assertEquals(Optional.empty(), list.get(2)),
      () -> list.add(1000),
      () -> list.add(50),
      () -> assertEquals(Optional.of(1000), list.get(2)),
      () -> assertEquals(Optional.of(50), list.get(3)),
      () -> assertEquals(Optional.empty(), list.get(4)));
  }
}
```

```
import java.util.Optional;

class DoublyLinkedList<T> {
  // ... previous code not shown.

  /**
   * Returns the element at a given index as an Optional.
   * @param idx index to retrieve.
   * @return Optional.empty() if the index is out of bounds, Optional.of(data) otherwise.
   */
  Optional<T> get(int idx) {
    Node<T> curr = this.first;
    int i = 0;
    while (curr != null && i < idx) {
      curr = curr.next;
      i++;
    }
    return idx >= 0 && curr != null ? Optional.of(curr.data) : Optional.empty();
  }
}
```

Finally we arrive at element removal, which is not as cut-and-dry. We want to pass the element-to-remove (compared via `equals`), but we need to adjust the pointers accordingly. In particular, there are four cases to consider:

(a) If the element-to-remove *e* is the first of the list, then its successor is now the first. Its previous pointer is adjusted to now point to `null`.
(b) If the element-to-remove *e* is the last of the list, then its predecessor is now the last. Its next pointer is adjusted to now point to `null`.

---

[17] It is, in general, a better idea to use *exceptions* when encountering bad inputs, but we have not covered them at this point in the text.

(c) If the element to remove e is neither the first nor the last, we retrieve its previous node p, its next node n, and assign $p_{next} = n$, and $n_{prev} = p$. This, in effect, "delinks" e from the list, and is eventually consumed/reclaimed by the garbage collector.

(d) If the element-to-remove e is not in the list, do nothing.

```java
import static Assertions.assertAll;
import static Assertions.assertEquals;

class DoublyLinkedListTester {

  @Test
  void testRemove() {
    DoublyLinkedList<Integer> list = new DoublyLinkedList<>();
    assertAll(
        () -> list.add(50),
        () -> list.add(25),
        () -> list.add(100),
        () -> list.remove(50),
        () -> assertEquals("[25, 100]", list.toString()),
        () -> list.remove(100),
        () -> assertEquals("[25]", list.toString()),
        () -> list.remove(25),
        () -> assertEquals("[]", list.toString()),
        () -> list.remove(25),
        () -> assertEquals("[]", list.toString()));
  }
}
```

```java
class DoublyLinkedList<T> {
  // ... previous code not shown.

  /**
   * Removes an element from the linked list, if it exists.
   * @param data value to be removed, compared via .equals.
   */
  void remove(T data) {
    Node<T> curr = this.first;
    while (curr != null) {
      if (curr.data.equals(data)) { // Case 1: if it's the first.
        if (curr == this.first) {
          curr.next = this.first.next;
          this.first = curr.next;
        } else if (curr == this.last) { // Case 2: if it's the last.
          curr.prev.next = null;
          this.last = curr.prev;
        } else { // Case 3: if it's anything else.
          curr.prev.next = curr.next;
          curr.next.prev = curr.prev;
        }
        break;
      } else { curr = curr.next; }
    }
  }
}
```

4.2 Object Mutation and Aliasing

Example 4.21. Some programming languages, e.g., C, do not come standard with data structures such as a map. A substitute for the common mapping data structure is called an *association list*, originating with the Lisp programming language McCarthy (1962). Its desired purpose is nearly identical to that of a map, but with worse performance implications. In this example we will design such a structure, as if Map did not exist in Java.

Associations lists, as their name implies, associate values to other values, like a map. In dynamically-typed languages, e.g., Scheme, association lists accept any type as their key and any type as their value. Therefore, we could have an association list that maps a string to an integer, or an integer to a list of strings, and so on. Should we want to use truly arbitrary types in the list, we can assign Object to both key and value types.

Our association list will support several methods that are related to their functional programming equivalents. In particular, we want a lookup method to retrieve the associated value of some element and an extend method to add a new association. Note that the extend method will, rather than modifying the current association list, return a new association list with the new association added. We want to preserve the idea of immutability, which is a common theme in functional programming. Association lists, therefore, need to have a "parent" reference to keep track of those associations in the list that we extend from.[18] We will also override the toString method to print the associations in a readable format.

```
import static Assertions.assertAll;
import static Assertions.assertEquals;

class AssociationListTester {

  @Test
  void testAssociationList() {
    AssociationList<String, Integer> list = new AssociationList<>();
    assertAll(
      () -> assertEquals("[]", list.toString()),
      () -> list = list.extend("a", 1),
      () -> assertEquals("[(a, 1)]", list.toString()),
      () -> list = list.extend("b", 2),
      () -> assertEquals("[(b, 2), (a, 1)]", list.toString()),
      () -> list = list.extend("c", 3),
      () -> assertEquals("[(c, 3), (b, 2), (a, 1)]", list.toString()),
      () -> assertEquals(Optional.of(3), list.lookup("c")),
      () -> assertEquals(Optional.of(2), list.lookup("b")),
      () -> assertEquals(Optional.of(1), list.lookup("a")),
      () -> assertEquals(Optional.empty(), list.lookup("d")));
  }
}
```

---

[18] In the next section on abstract classes and interpreters, we will revisit this idea in greater detail.

```java
import java.lang.StringBuilder;
import java.util.Optional;

class AssociationList<K, V> {

  private final K KEY;
  private final V VALUE;
  private final AssociationList<K, V> PARENT;

  AssociationList() {
    this(null, null, null);
  }

  private AssociationList(K key, V value, AssociationList<K, V> parent) {
    this.KEY = key;
    this.VALUE = value;
    this.PARENT = parent;
  }

  /**
   * Returns the value associated with a given key.
   * @param key the key to lookup.
   * @return the value associated with the key, if it exists.
   */
  Optional<V> lookup(K key) {
    AssociationList<K, V> curr = this;
    while (curr != null) {
      if (curr.KEY.equals(key)) { return Optional.of(curr.VALUE); }
      else { curr = curr.PARENT; }
    }
    return Optional.empty();
  }

  /**
   * Adds a new association to the list.
   * @param key the key to associate.
   * @param value the value to associate.
   * @return a new association list with the new association.
   */
  AssociationList<K, V> extend(K key, V value) {
    return new AssociationList<>(key, value, this);
  }

  @Override
  public String toString() {
    StringBuilder sb = new StringBuilder("[");
    AssociationList<K, V> curr = this;
    while (curr != null) {
      sb.append(String.format("(%s, %s)", curr.KEY, curr.VALUE));
      curr = curr.PARENT;
      if (curr != null) { sb.append(", "); }
    }
    sb.append("]");
    return sb.toString();
  }
}
```

4.2 Object Mutation and Aliasing

Each association list in our representation stores exactly one association. Each time we extend the association, we create a new list that points to the previous list. This is a very inefficient way to store and lookup associations, at least when compared to data structures such as a HashMap or TreeMap. But, association lists are commonly used for adding (variable) bindings in a programming language, usually when writing simple interpreted languages.

Example 4.22. In Chapter 3, we began to explore and use the Set data structure from the Collections framework. One existing implementation of sets is the HashSet, which stores non-duplicate elements according to their hash codes. In this example we will design a related data structure called a *hash table*.

Elements in a hash table are stored according to their hash code. The properties of a hash table (and the hashing function) guarantee very fast element lookup times, insertions, and removals. A straightforward hashing function is to modulo the hash code of the object by the capacity of the table. This way, every element is guaranteed a valid index into the table. The problem with this approach is that multiple objects may hash to the same "bucket." For example, if the hash code of some object o_1 is 100, and the capacity of the table is 40, then we would store o_1 at index 100 mod 40 = 2. But, consider another object o_2 with the hash code 1000, which we store at index 1000 mod 40 = 2. We cannot store multiple objects at the same index, so we need to perform *collision resolution*. A collision, as we just demonstrated, occurs when two objects hash to the same index.

As noted in our initial discussion of hashable data structures, there are several algorithms for resolving hash collisions. The simplest, albeit the least performant, is *chaining*, where each index of the hash table stores a list of elements. If two elements hash to the same index, then we walk the list at that index to query the hash table.

Let's begin by designing the constructor, fields, and method skeletons for the generic HashTable class. It stores an array of list instances, and the constructor instantiates this array to a capacity specified as a static class variable. We will include a second constructor to allow the user of the class to specify a capacity. Our hash table will not be resizable at runtime.

```
import java.util.LinkedList;
import java.util.List;

class HashTable<T> {

  private static final int DEFAULT_CAPACITY = 50;

  private final List<T>[] ELEMENTS;

  private int size;

  HashTable(int capacity) {
    this.ELEMENTS = new List<>[capacity];
    for (int i = 0; i < this.ELEMENTS.length; i++) {
      this.ELEMENTS[i] = new LinkedList<>();
    }
  }

  HashTable() {
    this(DEFAULT_CAPACITY);
  }

  /**
   * Adds a value to the hash table. We compute its hash code, then
   * insert it onto the end of the bucket at that index in the table.
```

```
 * If the value is already in the hash table, we return false and do
 * not add it into the table.
 * @param v value to add.
 * @return true if the element ∉ hash table; false otherwise.
 */
boolean add(T v) { /* TODO. */ }

/**
 * Determines whether an element exists in the hash table. We compute
 * the hash code of the input parameter, then traverse the bucket at
 * that index.
 * @param v value to search for.
 * @return true if the element ∈ hash table; false otherwise.
 */
boolean contains(T v) { /* TODO. */ }

/**
 * Returns the number of logical elements in the hash table.
 * @return # of logical elements.
 */
int size() {
  return this.size;
 }
}
```

The add method relies on contains, so we will design the latter first. We begin by computing the hash code of the given argument, then clamp that value to the bounds of the underlying array.[19] Every index in the table corresponds to a LinkedList, so we traverse the list in search of the element and return whether or not it exists.

Designing add is almost identical to contains: we compute the index-to-insert, traverse the list, and if the element is not in that list, we add it to the end and return true. Otherwise, the element is already in the table and we return false. Upon successfully adding an element to the table, we increment the size instance variable.

```
import static Assertions.assertAll;
import static Assertions.assertEquals;
import static Assertions.assertFalse;
import static Assertions.assertTrue;

class HashTableTester {

  @Test
  void testHashTable() {
    HashTable<String> t = new HashTable<>();
    assertAll(
      () -> assertTrue(t.add("Tarski")),
      () -> assertTrue(t.add("Quine")),
      () -> assertTrue(t.add("Russell")),
      () -> assertTrue(t.add("Boole")),
      () -> assertFalse(t.add("Tarski")),
      () -> assertTrue(t.contains("Quine")),
      () -> assertFalse(t.contains("Carnap")),
      () -> assertEquals(4, t.size()));
  }
}
```

---

[19] Java's modulo operator may return a negative number, so we wrap the operation in a call to Math.abs.

```
class HashTable<T> {
  // ... other methods not shown.

  /**
   * Adds a value to the hash table. We compute its hash code, then we insert it onto
   * the end of the bucket at that index in the table. If the value is already in the
   * hash table, we return false and do not add it.
   * @param v value to add.
   * @return true if the element ∉ hash table; false otherwise.
   */
  boolean add(T v) {
    if (this.contains(v)) {
      return false;
    } else {
      int idx = Math.abs(v.hashCode() % this.BUCKETS.length);
      List<T> bucket = this.BUCKETS[idx];
      bucket.add(v);
      this.size++;
      return true;
    }
  }

  /**
   * Determines whether an element exists in the hash table. We compute
   * the hash code of the input parameter, then traverse the bucket at
   * that index.
   * @param v value to search for.
   * @return true if the element ∈ hash table; false otherwise.
   */
  boolean contains(T v) {
    int idx = Math.abs(v.hashCode() % this.BUCKETS.length);
    List<T> bucket = this.BUCKETS[idx];
    return bucket.stream()
                 .anyMatch(t -> t.equals(v));
  }
}
```

4.3 Interfaces

Interfaces are a way of grouping classes together by a ubiquitous behavior. We have worked with interfaces before without acknowledging their properties as an interface. For example, the Comparable interface is implemented by classes that we want to be able to inhibit "comparable" behavior. In particular, there is a single method that must be implemented by any class that implements the Comparable interface: compareTo. The compareTo method receives a single parameter of the same type as the class that implements the Comparable interface, and returns an integer. Said integer is negative if this object instance is less than the passed argument, zero if this object instance is equal to the passed argument, and positive if this object instance is greater than the passed argument.

So, by having a class implement the Comparable interface, we group it into that subset of classes that are, indeed, comparable. Doing so implies that these classes have an ordering and are sortable in, for example, a Java collection.

In addition to the `Comparable` interface, we have worked with the `List`, `Queue`, and `Map` interfaces, which all have a set of methods that must be implemented by any class that implements the interface. Recall that `ArrayList` and `LinkedList` are "kinds of" `List` objects, and this interface describes several methods that all lists, by definition, must override.[20] To *override* a method means that we provide a new implementation of the method that is different from the default implementation provided by the interface.

Defining an Interface

Example 4.23. Imagine that we want to design an interface that describes a shape. All (two-dimensional) shapes have an area and a perimeter, so we can define an interface that, when implemented by a class, requires that the class provide an implementation of the `area` and `perimeter` methods. A common convention for user-defined interfaces is to prefix their names with `I` to distinguish them from classes. Moreover, the names of interfaces are either adjectives or, more traditionally, verbs, since they describe behaviors or characteristics of a class.[21]

```
interface IShape {

  double area();

  double perimeter();
}
```

We cannot write any tests for the `IShape` interface directly, because it is impossible to instantiate an interface. As defined, interfaces are a way of grouping classes by behavior. It, therefore, does not make sense to be able to instantiate an interface, because that would suggest that the interface in and of itself is an object. We can, however, write two different classes that implement `IShape`, and test those classes. To demonstrate this concept, we will design and test the `Pentagon` and `Octagon` classes whose constructors receive (and then store as instance variables) the side length of the shape. Fortunately, the definitions thereof are trivial because they are nothing more than regurgitations of the mathematical formulae. Notice that, when testing, we initialize the object instance to be of type `IShape` instead of `Pentagon` or `Octagon`. We want to be able to categorize these classes as types of `IShape` instances rather than solely instances of `Pentagon` or `Octagon` respectively. Instantiating a variable as an interface type, then instantiating it as a subtype is a form of *polymorphism*. Polymorphism is the ability of an object to take on many forms. In this case, the `IShape` interface is the form that the `Pentagon` and `Octagon` classes use to take on the form of a shape as we described.

When implementing the methods of an interface in a class, we must mark those methods as `public` because all interface methods are `public`, either explicitly or implicitly. In this context, the `area` and `perimeter` methods are overridden in the `Octagon` and `Pentagon` classes.

---

[20] Here we clarify that "kind of," in this context, means to implement the `List` interface.
[21] We do not add the `public` keyword to the interface definition nor any methods within because all interface methods are implicitly public.

4.3 Interfaces

```java
import static Assertions.assertAll;
import static Assertions.assertEquals;

class IShapeTester {

  private static final DELTA = 0.01;

  @Test
  void testPentagon() {
    IShape p1 = new Pentagon(1);
    IShape p2 = new Pentagon(7.25);
    assertAll(
        () -> assertEquals(1.72, p1.area(), DELTA),
        () -> assertEquals(90.43, p2.area(), DELTA),
        () -> assertEquals(5, p1.perimeter(), DELTA),
        () -> assertEquals(36.25, p2.perimeter(), DELTA));
  }

  @Test
  void testOctagon() {
    IShape o1 = new Octagon(1);
    IShape o2 = new Octagon(7.25);
    assertAll(
        () -> assertEquals(4.83, o1.area(), DELTA),
        () -> assertEquals(253.79, o2.area(), DELTA),
        () -> assertEquals(8, o1.perimeter(), DELTA),
        () -> assertEquals(58, o2.perimeter(), DELTA));
  }
}
```

```java
class Pentagon implements IShape {

  private final double SIDE_LENGTH;

  Pentagon(double sideLength) {
    this.SIDE_LENGTH = sideLength;
  }

  @Override
  public double area() {
    return 0.25 * Math.sqrt(5 * (5 + 2 * Math.sqrt(5)))
            * Math.pow(this.SIDE_LENGTH, 2);
  }

  @Override
  public double perimeter() {
    return 5 * this.SIDE_LENGTH;
  }
}
```

```
class Octagon implements IShape {

  private final double SIDE_LENGTH;

  Octagon(double sideLength) {
    this.SIDE_LENGTH = sideLength;
  }

  @Override
  public double area() {
    return 2 * (1 + Math.sqrt(2)) * Math.pow(this.SIDE_LENGTH, 2);
  }

  @Override
  public double perimeter() {
    return 8 * this.SIDE_LENGTH;
  }
}
```

Example 4.24. Recall from the previous chapter our "Twenty-one" card game example. In that small project, we designed the `Suit` class, which encapsulated four static instances of `Suit`, where each represented one of the four valid card suits. Even though this design works as intended, it fails to be elegant and demonstrate how the suits are all the same, but differ only in their string representation. Let's now design the `ISuit` interface, thereby requiring any implementing class to override the `stringify` method.

```
interface ISuit {

  /**
   * Returns the string representation of the suit.
   */
  String stringify();
}
```

From here, we define four separate classes, all of which implement `ISuit` and override the `stringify` method. These classes are incredibly simple, and as such, we show only the Diamond and Heart classes.

```
class Diamond implements ISuit {

  Diamond() {}

  @Override
  public String stringify() { return "♢"; }
}
```

```
class Heart implements ISuit {

  Heart() {}

  @Override
  public String stringify() { return "♡"; }
}
```

As shown, both `Diamond` and `Heart` implement `ISuit` and handle "stringification" differently. We can test these definitions by storing a list of `ISuit` instances and ensuring that the correct character is returned.

4.3 Interfaces

```
import static Assertions.assertAll;
import static Assertions.assertEquals;

import java.util.List;
import java.util.ArrayList;

class ISuitTester {

  @Test
  void suitTester() {
    List<ISuit> suit = new ArrayList<>();
    // Add diamonds at even indices, hearts at odd indices.
    for (int i = 0; i < 100; i++) {
      if (i % 2 == 0) { suit.add(new Diamond()); }
      else { suit.add(new Heart()); }
    }

    // Now check to verify that the stringification works.
    for (int i = 0; i < suit.size(); i++) {
      if (i % 2 == 0) { assertEquals("♢", suit.get(i).stringify()); }
      else { assertEquals("♡", suit.get(i).stringify()); }
    }
  }
}
```

One extra piece of information that we should share is that we can instantiate objects in different ways. To demonstrate why this is significant, suppose we initialize an object s_1 to be of type ISuit, but instantiate it as type Diamond. Then, we initialize another object s_2 to be of type Diamond and instantiate it as type Diamond. We would expect that s_1 and s_2 are equivalent, but this is not the case. Suppose Diamond contains a method diamondCount that does something irrelevant, but belongs solely to the Diamond class. Because s_1 is of type ISuit, we cannot invoke the diamondCount method, since ISuit knows nothing about said method. On the contrary, s_2 can certainly invoke diamondCount, but it is not polymorphic, since it is not of type ISuit. Should we want to invoke diamondCount on the s_1 object, we need to *downcast* s_1 to type Diamond.

```
ISuit s1 = new Diamond();
s1.diamondCount();          // Compile-time error!
Diamond s2 = new Diamond();
s2.diamondCount();          // Works but not polymorphic.
((Diamond) s1).diamondCount(); // Works but downcasts.
```

Example 4.25. Animals are a common example of an interface. Imagine that, in our domain of animals, every animal can speak one way or another. Speaking involves returning a string representing the sound that the animal makes. By designing the IAnimal interface, we can group all animals that have the capability of "speaking" together. We can follow this by designing classes to implement the IAnimal interface, which provide an implementation of the speak method. When testing these classes, we can instantiate a collection of IAnimal instances, and invoke speak on each of them polymorphically. In doing so, we debut a refresher of the stream API.

```java
interface IAnimal {

  /**
   * Returns the sound that the animal makes.
   */
  String speak();
}
```

```java
import static Assertions.assertAll;
import static Assertions.assertEquals;

import java.util.List;
import java.util.ArrayList;

class IAnimalTester {

  @Test
  void testCat() {
    IAnimal cat = new Cat();
    assertEquals("Meow!", cat.speak());
  }

  @Test
  void testDog() {
    IAnimal dog = new Dog();
    assertEquals("Woof!", dog.speak());
  }

  @Test
  void testListOfAnimals() {
    List<IAnimal> animals = new ArrayList<>();
    animals.add(new Cat());
    animals.add(new Dog());
    animals.add(new Cat());
    assertEquals("[Meow!, Wolf! Meow!]",
                 animals.stream()
                        .map(IAnimal::speak)
                        .collect(Collectors.toList()));
  }
}
```

```java
class Cat implements IAnimal {

  @Override
  public String speak() { return "Meow!"; }
}
```

```java
class Dog implements IAnimal {

  @Override
  public String speak() { return "Woof!"; }
}
```

4.3 Interfaces

Example 4.26. Suppose we want to design an interface that "boxes" an arbitrary value. We have seen this idea through Java's autoboxing and autounboxing mechanisms of the primitive datatypes via the wrapper classes. Our interface, however, extends the concept to any type. We can define an interface that requires any class to implement it provide an implementation of the box, get, and set methods. Boxing a value means that we can pass it around as a *reference* rather than as a raw value. Recall that, in Java, we pass primitives to methods by value and, therefore, any changes to the argument are not preserved outside the method body. If, however, we box the primitive, the box is passed by reference, and it is then possible to manipulate the contents of the box. We will first design the generic IBox interface, then we will design a class that implements the methods specified by the interface.

Interestingly, interfaces can contain static methods. Our IBox interface has the static box method, which returns a box that encapsulates the provided value. The box method can be used without having to instantiate a class that implements the IBox interface. From there, we can write the get and set methods to retrieve and change the value of the box.

```java
interface IBox<T> {

  /**
   * Boxes the value of type T.
   */
  static IBox<T> box(T t);

  /**
   * Returns the boxed value of type T.
   */
  T get();

  /**
   * Sets the boxed value of type T.
   */
  void set(T t);
}
```

```java
import static Assertions.assertAll;
import static Assertions.assertEquals;

class IBoxTester {

  private static <T> void modifyBox(IBox<T> box, T t) {
    box.set(t);
  }

  @Test
  void testIntegerBox() {
    IBox<Integer> box = IntegerBox.box(5);
    assertAll(
      () -> assertEquals(5, box.get()),
      () -> modifyBox(box, 10),
      () -> assertEquals(10, box.get()));
  }
}
```

```
class IntegerBox implements IBox<Integer> {

  private Integer value;

  private IntegerBox(Integer value) {
    this.value = value;
  }

  @Override
  public static IBox<Integer> box(Integer value) {
    return new IntegerBox(value);
  }

  @Override
  public Integer get() {
    return this.value;
  }

  @Override
  public void set(Integer value) {
    this.value = value;
  }
}
```

Example 4.27. The Java Swing API is a graphics framework for designing graphical interfaces and drawing shapes/images. In addition to these capabilities, it also supports user input through the keyboard, mouse, and other means. Compared to a class such as Scanner, which waits for the user to press "Enter" when they are finished typing input, the Swing API allows for dynamic input and whose events are processed as they occur. We call the part of the program that listens and processes events an *event listener*. A popular example in Java is the ActionListener interface, which is used to listen for a broad classification of events, ranging from button clicks to menu selections. When an event occurs, the ActionListener interface is notified and can then respond to the event however the programmer desires. The ActionListener interface has a single method, actionPerformed, that is invoked when an event occurs. The actionPerformed method receives an ActionEvent object that contains information about the event that occurred, which is then usable by the method to determine what to do in response to the event. Because graphical interface design goes beyond the scope of this textbook, we will omit a code example, but we mention action listeners to demonstrate that interfaces are not limited to the examples we have seen thus far. Moreover, the Swing API provides more specific listeners for processing keyboard and mouse events, e.g., KeyListener, MouseListener, MouseMotionListener, and so forth. We could, for instance, design a class that implements the MouseListener interface and provides an overriding implementation of the mouseClicked method. Then, inside a Java Swing graphical component, we might hook the class as a mouse listener and, when the user clicks the mouse, the mouseClicked method is invoked.

Example 4.28. An amazing insight into the power of interfaces is already present in Java, but deriving it ourselves is useful. Consider the notion of first-class methods: the concept in which methods and data are equivalent, wherein both can be passed to and returned from methods. In Java, we can pass methods around as arguments, mimicking first-class methods, by designing a *functional interface*.

Let's design the generic Function<T, V> interface, which quantifies over two types T, representing the input type, and V, representing the output type. The Function<T, V> interface

4.3 Interfaces

has a single static method, `apply`, which receives an argument of type T and returns a value of type V. We can then design a class that implements the Function<T, V> interface and provides an implementation of the `apply` method. Then, by passing the class around as an argument to other methods, we can invoke the `apply` method on the class to get the method result. An incredibly simple example is AddOne, which implements the Function<Integer, Integer> interface and adds one to its input. We mark the constructor of the implementing class as private to prevent any unnecessary instantiations; the class itself should only ever be utilized as a first-class citizen rather than an object.

```
interface Function<T, V> {

  static V apply(T t);
}
```

```
import static Assertions.assertAll;
import static Assertions.assertEquals;

class AddOneTester {

  @Test
  void addOneTester() {
    assertAll(
      () -> assertEquals(0, apply(1)),
      () -> assertEquals(3, apply(2)),
      () -> assertEquals(30001, apply(30000)));
  }
}
```

```
class AddOne implements Function<Integer, Integer> {

  private AddOne() {}

  @Override
  public static Integer apply(Integer i) {
    return i + 1;
  }
}
```

So far, we have not demonstrated the potential of first-class methods in Java with our design. Suppose that l is a list of Integer values $v_1, v_2, ..., v_n$ and f : Integer $\rightarrow$ Integer. We want to apply f to each element of the list l and produce a new list that is the result of mapping f over l. That is, we will create a new list $l' = f(v_1), f(v_2), \ldots, f(v_n)$. By passing a class that implements a functional interface as a parameter, we can design a single method that receives a list and a function f, rather than having to redundantly design several methods to work over multiple variants of f. This operation, in the functional programming domain, is called map, which we saw during our discussion on streams in Chapter 3.[22]

---

[22] Do not confuse this with the concept of a map/dictionary from our data structures/collections discussion.

```java
import static Assertions.assertAll;
import static Assertions.assertEquals;

import java.util.List;

class FunctionMapTester {

  @Test
  void testMap() {
    List<Integer> l = List.of(1, 2, 3, 4, 5);
    Function<Integer, Integer> addOne = new AddOne();
    assertAll(
      () -> assertEquals(List.of(2, 3, 4, 5, 6),
                         map(l, addOne)),
      () -> assertEquals(List.of(),
                         map(List.of(), addOne)));
  }
}
```

```java
import java.util.List;
import java.util.ArrayList;

class FunctionMap {

  /**
   * Applies the function f to each element of the list l.
   * @param l the list of elements.
   * @param f the function to apply to each element.
   * @return the list of elements after applying f to each element.
   */
  static <T, V> List<V> map(List<T> l, Function<T, V> f) {
    return l.stream()
            .map(t -> f.apply(t))
            .collect(Collectors.toList());
  }
}
```

Example 4.29. Java 8 introduced the `Function` interface, so we do not have to design our own version. When using it, we do not need to design a separate `AddOne` class to implement the interface; we can instead opt to use method referencing via the `::` operator. Let's rewrite the `addOne` example doing so. Concurrently, we will show off the fact that Java autoboxes and unboxes primitives into wrapper class counterparts in the functional interface, meaning that our `addOne` method does not need to receive and return objects, but rather primitives, which are easier to work with. Moreover, lambda expressions are passable to methods that receive `Function` arguments, since Java automatically converts them into `Function` objects, mimicking the autoboxing treatment of primitive datatypes.[23]

---

[23] In the tester code snippet below, we could omit the `FunctionMapTester::` type qualification because the method is defined inside the same class that it is used.

4.3 Interfaces

```java
import static Assertions.assertAll;
import static Assertions.assertEquals;

import java.util.List;

class FunctionMapTester {

  static int addOne(int i) { return i + 1; }

  @Test
  void testMap() {
    List<Integer> l = List.of(1, 2, 3, 4, 5);
    assertAll(
        () -> assertEquals(List.of(2, 3, 4, 5, 6), map(l, FunctionMapTester::addOne)),
        () -> assertEquals(List.of(), map(List.of(), FunctionMapTester::addOne)),
        () -> assertEquals(List.of(2, 3, 4, 5, 6), map(l, i -> i + 1)),
        () -> assertEquals(List.of(2, 3, 4, 5, 6), map(List.of(), i -> i + 1)));
  }
}
```

Example 4.30. Now that we have interfaces, we can write a very simple expression tree interpreter! What do we mean by this? Consider the arithmetic expression '5 + (3 + 4)'. According to the standard order-of-operations, we evaluate the parenthesized sub-expressions first, then reduce outer expressions. So, in our case, we add 3 and 4 to get 7, followed by an addition of 5. We can represent this idea as an evaluation tree, where we travel from bottom-up, evaluating sub-expressions as they are encountered. How does the notion of evaluation trees relate to interfaces? Suppose we create the IExpr interface, which encompasses the int value method to resolve to the value of an expression.

```java
interface IExpr {

  /**
   * Returns the value of the expression.
   */
  int value();
}
```

The simplest (atomic) values in our language are numbers, or numeric literals. A Lit stores a single integer as an instance variable, and returns this instance variable upon a value invocation, which means Lit should implement the IExpr interface. Testing this class is trivial, so we will only write two tests.

```java
import static Assertions.assertEquals;

class LitTester {

  @Test
  void testLit() {
    assertEquals(42, new Lit(42).value());
  }
}
```

```
class Lit implements IExpr {

  private final int N;

  Lit(int n) { this.N = n; }

  @Override
  public int value() { return this.N; }
}
```

How do we add two numbers? Or, rather, how do we represent the addition of two (literal) numbers? This question comes via the answer to our other question of representing literal values. Additive expressions store two IExpr objects as instance variables, and (mutually) recursively calls their value methods, followed by a summation to those results. Note the parallelism to how we do this when manually evaluating, say, parenthesized addition expressions.

```
import static Assertions.assertAll;
import static Assertions.assertEquals;

class AddTester {

  @Test
  void testAdd() {
    assertAll(
      () -> assertEquals(12, new Add(new Lit(5),
                                    new Add(new Lit(3), new Lit(4)))),
      () -> assertEquals(42, new Add(new Lit(41),
                                    new Lit(1))),
      () -> assertEquals(101, new Add(new Add(new Lit(123), new Lit(-43)),
                                    new Add(new Lit(2), new Lit(19)))));
  }
}
```

```
class Add implements IExpr {

  private final IExpr LHS;
  private final IExpr RHS;

  Add(IExpr lhs, IExpr rhs) {
    this.LHS = lhs;
    this.RHS = rhs;
  }

  @Override
  public int value() {
    return this.LHS.value() + this.RHS.value();
  }
}
```

Thus, we now have a programming language that interprets numbers and addition expressions! We could add more elements/operators to this language, and we encourage the readers to get creative.

Example 4.31. Symbolic differentiators are programs that take a mathematical expression and compute its derivative, but non-numerically. That is, symbolic differentiators examine and interpret the structure of an expression to calculate its derivative. In this example, we

4.3 Interfaces

will write a symbolic differentiator in Java using interfaces and classes. Note that you do not need any calculus knowledge to reasonably follow along and understand the high-level and pertinent object-oriented details.

The formal definition of the derivative of a function is not a necessary detail to concern ourselves of; but in short, it measures the instantaneous rate-of-change at a given point of the function, i.e., the slope of the line tangent to the point. There are several rules for computing derivatives of functions, all of which are served as common exercises in an introductory calculus course. We want to be able to construct expressions in such a way that it is trivial to differentiate their(sub-)components. As an example, the derivative of the expression $3x^2 - 16x + 100$ is $6x - 6$ due to specific rules that we will explain shortly. The idea, however, is that we have a large expression to find the derivative of, and by differentiating its sub-components, we obtain the derivative of the larger, similar to our arithmetic expression resolver. Let's see what all we need to do.

First, let's design the Expression interface, which houses one method, to compute the derivative of an Expression: Expression derivative(String v). Any class that implements Expression must override derivative. We differentiate expressions with respect to a given variable, e.g., x, so we need to pass that variable to any expression that we wish to differentiate.

Using some basic calculus derivative shortcuts/rules, we can easily think of two more types of expressions: numeric constants (e.g., 3, 0, 27) and monomials (e.g., ax^n where a, n are integers). So, let's design the ConstantExpression and MonomialExpression classes, the former of which has a constructor that receives a single integer c, whereas the latter stores the variable v, the coefficient a, and finally the exponent n. To make working with these expressions easier, as well as ensuring testability, we will override the equals, hashCode, and toString methods.

The derivative of a constant c is always zero, because the slope of a straight line, namely $f(x) = c$ is zero, i.e., non-changing. On the other hand, a monomial follows a different rule based off its coefficient and exponent: the derivative of ax^n is anx^{n-1} for any $n > 1$. If $n = 1$, then this trivially becomes a constant. There is one more edge-case to consider: if the given variable v does not match the variable of the monomial, then the derivative is zero because the monomial does not depend on the variable v.

```java
import static Assertions.assertAll;
import static Assertions.assertEquals;

class DerivativeTester {

  @Test
  void testNumberExpressionDerivative() {
      assertEquals(new NumberExpression(0),
              new NumberExpression(10).derivative("x"));
  }

  @Test
  void testMonomialExpressionDerivative() {
    assertAll(
      () -> assertEquals(new ConstantExpression(3),
              new MonomialExpression("x", 3, 1).derivative("x")),
      () -> assertEquals(new ConstantExpression(0),
              new MonomialExpression("x", 3, 10).derivative("y")),
      () -> assertEquals(new MonomialExpression("x", 6, 1),
              new MonomialExpression("x", 3, 2).derivative("x")));
  }
}
```

```java
import java.util.Objects;

class ConstantExpression implements Expression {

  private final int CONSTANT;

  ConstantExpression(int c) {
    this.CONSTANT = c;
  }

  @Override
  public Expression derivative(String v) {
    return new ConstantExpression(0);
  }

  @Override
  public boolean equals(Object obj) {
    if (!(obj instanceof ConstantExpression)) {
      return false;
    } else {
      ConstantExpression cons = (ConstantExpression) obj;
      return cons.CONSTANT == this.CONSTANT;
    }
  }

  @Override
  public int hashCode() {
    return Objects.hash(this.CONSTANT);
  }

  @Override
  public String toString() {
    return String.format("%d", this.CONSTANT);
  }
}
```

```java
import java.util.Objects;

class MonomialExpression implements Expression {

  private final int COEFFICIENT;
  private final int EXPT;
  private final String VAR;

  MonomialExpression(String v, int a, int n) {
    this.VAR = v;
    this.COEFFICIENT = a;
    this.EXPT = n;
  }

  @Override
  public Expression derivative(String v) {
    if (this.VAR.equals(v)) {
      if (this.EXPT == 1) {
        return new ConstantExpression(this.COEFFICIENT);
      } else {
        return new MonomialExpression(this.VAR, this.COEFFICIENT*this.EXPT, this.EXPT-1);
      }
    } else {
```

4.3 Interfaces

```java
      return new ConstantExpression(0);
    }
  }

  @Override
  public boolean equals(Object obj) {
    if (!(obj instanceof MonomialExpression)) { return false; }
    else {
      MonomialExpression expr = (MonomialExpression) obj;
      return this.VAR.equals(expr.VAR)
          && this.COEFFICIENT == expr.COEFFICIENT
          && this.EXPT == expr.EXPT;
    }
  }

  @Override
  public int hashCode() {
    return Objects.hash(this.VAR, this.COEFFICIENT, this.EXPT);
  }

  @Override
  public String toString() {
    return String.format("%d%s^%d", this.COEFFICIENT, this.VAR, this.EXPT);
  }
}
```

Let's move into compositional expressions, i.e., those that contain expressions as instance variables. Such an example is an additive operator: the derivative of the addition expression $(f(x) + g(x))' = f'(x) + g'(x)$, where f' is the derivative of f. In summary, the derivative of a sum is the sum of the derivatives of its operands. To represent sequential operands, e.g., $x + y + z + \cdots + w$, we will store the expressions in a list. Note that our symbolic differentiator neither simplifies expressions nor combines like terms.

```java
import static Assertions.assertAll;
import static Assertions.assertEquals;

class DerivativeTester {

  @Test
  void testAddExpressionDerivative() {
    assertAll(
        () -> assertEquals(
            new AddExpression(new MonomialExpression("x", 3, 2),
                              new MonomialExpression("x", 6, 5)),
            new AddExpression(new MonomialExpression("x", 1, 3),
                              new MonomialExpression("x", 1, 6)).derivative("x")),
        () -> assertEquals(
            new AddExpression(new MonomialExpression("x", 10, 4),
                              new MonomialExpression("x", 12, 2),
                              new MonomialExpression("x", -14, 1),
                              new NumberExpression(6),
                              new NumberExpression(0))),
            new AddExpression(new MonomialExpression("x", 2, 5),
                              new MonomialExpression("x", 4, 3),
                              new MonomialExpression("x", -7, 2),
                              new MonomialExpression("x", 6, 1),
                              new NumberExpression(9)).derivative("x")));
  }
}
```

```java
import java.util.ArrayList;
import java.util.Arrays;
import java.util.List;
import java.util.Objects;
import java.util.stream.Collectors;

class AddExpression implements Expression {

  private final List<Expression> EXPR_LIST;

  AddExpression(Expression... exprs) {
    this.EXPR_LIST = Arrays.asList(exprs);
  }

  AddExpression(List<Expression> exprs) {
    this.EXPR_LIST = exprs;
  }

  @Override
  public Expression derivative(String v) {
    List<Expression> exprs = new ArrayList<>();
    this.EXPR_LIST.forEach(e -> exprs.add(e.derivative(v)));
    return new AddExpression(exprs);
  }

  @Override
  public boolean equals(Object obj) {
    if (!(obj instanceof AddExpression)) {
      return false;
    } else {
      AddExpression expr = (AddExpression) obj;
      for (int i = 0; i < this.EXPR_LIST.size(); i++) {
        if (!this.EXPR_LIST.get(i).equals(expr.EXPR_LIST.get(i))) {
          return false;
        }
      }
      return true;
    }
  }

  @Override
  public int hashCode() {
    this.EXPR_LIST.hashCode();
  }

  @Override
  public String toString() {
    return this.EXPR_LIST.stream()
                    .map(Object::toString)
                    .collect(Collectors.joining(" + "));
  }
}
```

4.3 Interfaces

Example 4.32. Let's clarify the distinction between the Comparable and Comparator interfaces. Consider an Employee class, which stores an employee's first and last name, as well as their salary. Suppose we want to be able to compare Employee instances. One option to do so is to declare Employee to implement the Comparable<Employee> interface. Therefore, Employee must override the public int compareTo(Employee e) method. Further suppose that our method will return the result of lexicographically comparing the employee's last name.

```
class Employee implements Comparable<Employee> {

  private double salary;
  private String firstName;
  private String lastName;

  Employee(String firstName, String lastName, double salary) {
    this.firstName = firstName;
    this.lastName = lastName;
    this.salary = salary;
  }

  @Override
  public int compareTo(Employee o) {
    return this.lastName.compareTo(o.lastName);
  }

  // Getters and setters omitted.
}
```

Now, if we want to create a list of employees and sort them, we can use the static sort method from the Collections class.

```
import static Assertions.assertEquals;

import java.util.ArrayList;
import java.util.Collections;
import java.util.Collectors;
import java.util.List;

class EmployeeTester {

  @Test
  void testEmployeeComparable() {
    List<Employee> loe1 = new ArrayList<>();
    loe1.add(new Employee("John", "Doe", 100000));
    loe1.add(new Employee("Alex", "Smith", 120000));
    loe1.add(new Employee("Barbara", "Jones", 140000));
    loe1.add(new Employee("Trevor", "Wilson", 200000));
    loe1.add(new Employee("Jennifer", "Clark", 240000));
    Collections.sort(loe1);
    assertEquals("Clark, Doe, Jones, Smith, Wilson",
                 loe1.stream()
                     .map(e -> e.getLastName())
                     .collect(Collectors.join(", ")));
  }
}
```

By default, `Collections.sort` will sort the provided collection using the object's `compareTo` method. So, in this case, the employees are sorted based on their last name. Note that `Collections.sort` uses an in-place sorting algorithm, which means that the original list is modified.

Now, suppose that we want to compare employees using a *different* metric. For instance, what if we want to sort the employees based on their first name, or perhaps their salary? One approach would be to change how `compareTo` is implemented in the `Employee` class. The problem with this is that any code that relies on the last name ordering is now broken. Plus, it's possible that the source code of the `Employee` class is immutable, a commonality when working with third-party libraries or legacy codebases.

A solution to this predicament is to use a `Comparator` object. Comparators, as their name suggests, compare instances of a class. The essential difference between a `Comparator` and `Comparable` is that the class of interest, e.g., `Employee`, should *not* implement `Comparator`. Rather, we want to create a separate class that represents a comparison between `Employee` objects by an arbitrary metric. For example, in the following listing is a class `EmployeeFirstNameComparator`, which compares employees by their first name. Notice that the `Comparator` class provides the `public int compare(T o1, T o2)` method instead of `compareTo`. Another difference is that `compare` receives two arguments rather than one, because `compareTo` relies on `this` and its other argument to perform the relevant comparison. That is, `compareTo` returns a comparison result based on `this` and its argument. By contrast, `compare` receives *two* instances of the class of interest, and the returned value should be the result of however we choose to compare those two objects.

We can then pass an instance of this comparator as a second argument to the `Collections.sort` method:

```java
import java.util.Comparator;

class EmployeeFirstNameComparator implements Comparator<Employee> {

  @Override
  public int compare(Employee o1, Employee o2) {
    return o1.getFirstName().compareTo(o2.getFirstName());
  }
}
```

```java
import static Assertions.assertEquals;

import java.util.ArrayList;
import java.util.Collections;
import java.util.Collectors;
import java.util.List;

class EmployeeTester {

  @Test
  void testEmployeeComparable() {
    List<Employee> loe1 = new ArrayList<>();
    // ... assume the same list as before.
    Collections.sort(loe1, new EmployeeFirstNameComparator());
    assertEquals("Clark, Doe, Jones, Smith, Wilson",
                 loe1.stream()
                     .map(e -> e.getFirstName())
                     .collect(Collectors.joining(", ")));
  }
}
```

Let's create another comparator for comparing employees based on their salaries. A lower salary indicates a lower index in the ordering relation.

```java
import java.util.Comparator;

class EmployeeSalaryComparator implements Comparator<Employee> {

  @Override
  public int compare(Employee o1, Employee o2) {
    return (int) Math.signum(o1.getSalary() - o2.getSalary());
  }
}
```

4.4 Inheritance

When we introduced interfaces, we stated that they group classes that enact similar behaviors. *Inheritance* describes an "IS-A" relationship between two classes. That is, one class C_1 "is" another class if it extends the C_2 class. In the example, C_1 is called the *subclass*, and C_2 is called the *superclass*. A subclass inherits all the non-private methods and fields from its superclass. Classes can only extend one class at a time, unlike other programming languages such as C++ (Stroustrup, 2013).

In Java, every class has an implicit superclass: Object, which introduced the paradigm that "everything is an object in Java." The Object class serves as a barebones "template," of sorts, that provides the essentials for a class definition. These essentials include methods for comparing one object against another via equals, computing the hash code via hashCode, and stringifying the class via toString. We have seen these three methods before in a variety of contexts, but we now elaborate on their origins.

Example 4.33. When inheriting from a class, as we described, all non-private properties are inherited. So, let's consider an example that we have seen before: the Point class. As we recall, it stores x and y coordinates. Though, what if we want to store a "color" value inside the Point class? Does it make sense to modify the implementation of Point to now include a color? Absolutely not, because any existing code that makes use of Point presumes only knowledge of two coordinate values and not a color. Consequently, we should *extend* the Point class in a new subclass called ColorPoint. Importantly, do **not** copy any code from the Point class into ColorPoint, because that defeats the purpose of class extension/inheritance. Our ColorPoint class constructor will call the superclass constructor, via super, to pass the provided x and y coordinates up to the superclass definition. Remember that x and y have private access inside Point, meaning ColorPoint cannot initialize their values directly.

In designing the ColorPoint class, we will override the superclass implementation of equals, hashCode, and toString to also include the color of the point. What's convenient is that we do not need to repeat the existing comparison, hash code calculation, concatenation code respectively. Instead, we call the superclass variant of the method via 'super.equals' or 'super.toString'. Two ColorPoint instances are equal according to equals if their colors are the same and their coordinate values are equal. What we mean by "we do not need to repeat the existing comparison," is that the equals method inside ColorPoint should not (and will not) compare its x and y coordinates to those of the parameter.

Identical to interfaces, we should initialize an instance as its superclass, but instantiate it as a subclass type.

```java
class ColorPointTester {

  @Test
  void testColorPoint() {
    Point p1 = new ColorPoint(3, 4, "RED");
    Point p2 = new ColorPoint(4, 3, "GREEN");
    Point p3 = new ColorPoint(3, 4, "RED");
    assertAll(
        () -> assertEquals("Color=RED, [x=3, y=4]", p1.toString()),
        () -> assertEquals("Color=GREEN, [x=4, y=3]", p2.toString()),
        () -> assertEquals(p1, p3),
        () -> assertNotEquals(p1, p2));
  }
}
```

```java
import java.util.Objects;

class ColorPoint {

  private final String COLOR;

  ColorPoint(int x, int y, String color) {
    super(x, y);
    this.COLOR = color;
  }

  @Override
  public boolean equals(Object o) {
    ColorPoint pt = (ColorPoint) o;
    return this.COLOR.equals(pt.COLOR) && super.equals(pt);
  }

  @Override
  public int hashCode() {
    return Objects.hash(this.COLOR) + super.hashCode();
  }

  @Override
  public String toString() {
    return String.format("Color=%s, %s", this.COLOR, super.toString());
  }

  public Color getColor() {
    return this.COLOR;
  }
}
```

Some readers may question the need for inheritance; after all, could Point not be an interface and have ColorPoint implement said interface? The answer is no, because Point contains fields and private methods, neither of which are possible with an interface.

4.4 Inheritance

Example 4.34. Suppose we have the `Alien` class defined as follows, which can move forward by one unit and turn left by 90 degrees in some world that it resides within.[24]

```
import static Assertions.assertAll;
import static Assertions.assertEquals;

class AlienTester {

  @Test
  void testAlien() {
    Alien r1 = new Alien();
    assertAll(
      () -> r1.turnLeft(),
      () -> assertEquals(Alien.Direction.NORTH, r1.getDir()),
      () -> r1.moveForward(),
      () -> assertEquals(1, r1.getY()),
      () -> r1.turnLeft(),
      () -> assertEquals(Alien.Direction.WEST, r1.getDir()),
      () -> r1.moveForward(),
      () -> assertEquals(-1, r1.getX()),
      () -> r1.turnLeft(),
      () -> assertEquals(Alien.Direction.SOUTH, r1.getDir()),
      () -> r1.moveForward(),
      () -> assertEquals(0, r1.getY()),
      () -> r1.turnLeft(),
      () -> assertEquals(Alien.Direction.EAST, r1.getDir()),
      () -> r1.moveForward(),
      () -> assertEquals(0, r1.getX()));
  }
}
```

```
class Alien {
  enum Direction { NORTH, SOUTH, EAST, WEST };

  private int x;
  private int y;
  private Direction dir;

  Alien() {
    this.x = 0;
    this.y = 0;
    this.dir = Direction.EAST;
  }

  /**
   * Moves the alien forward by one unit in the direction it is facing.
   */
  void moveForward() {
    switch (this.dir) {
      NORTH -> this.y++;
      SOUTH -> this.y--;
      EAST -> this.x++;
      WEST -> this.x--;
    }
  }
```

---

[24] We base this example off of Karel J. Robot from Bergin et al. (2013) and Pattis (1995).

```
/**
 * Turns the alien left by 90 degrees.
 */
void turnLeft() {
  switch (this.dir) {
    NORTH -> this.dir = Direction.WEST;
    SOUTH -> this.dir = Direction.EAST;
    EAST  -> this.dir = Direction.NORTH;
    WEST  -> this.dir = Direction.SOUTH;
  }
}
```

We defined an incredibly primitive alien class that stores its position and direction in a two-dimensional plane. Testing the alien, as we have done, is straightforward, but even such a simple alien must turn left three times to mimic the behavior of turning right once. One solution to this problem is to write the `turnRight` method directly inside `Alien`. Though, consider a situation where the code for `Alien`, or any arbitrary class, is hidden or immutable. In such circumstances, any extendability of functionality must come via another means.

Let's extend the `Alien` class to add a `turnRight` method. We will call this class `RightAlien`, which adds a single method: `turnRight`. The other methods remain the same, since we do not want to overwrite their behavior. One important detail is that we invoke the superclass constructor without parameters, because the superclass (namely `Alien`) has no constructor that receives parameters. We invoke the superclass constructor to ensure that the x, y, and direction fields are initialized.[25]

```
import static Assertions.assertAll;
import static Assertions.assertEquals;

class RightAlienTester {

  @Test
  void testMoverAlien() {
    Alien r1 = new RightAlien();
    assertAll(
      () -> r1.turnRight(),
      () -> assertEquals(RightAlien.Direction.SOUTH, r1.getDir()),
      () -> r1.turnLeft(),
      () -> assertEquals(RightAlien.Direction.SOUTH, r1.getDir()));
  }
}
```

```
class RightAlien extends Alien {

  RightAlien() { super(); }

  /**
   * Turns the Alien right by 90 degrees.
   */
  void turnRight() {
    for (int i = 0; i < 3; i++) { this.turnLeft(); }
  }
}
```

---

[25] Not invoking the superclass constructor may result in a `NullPointerException` when trying to access the superclass fields, because those fields were never initialized nor instantiated.

4.4 Inheritance

Great, we can turn right with this flavor of the alien! Though, moving forward by one unit is absurdly slow, so let's now design the `MileMoverAlien` class, which moves ten units for every `moveForward` call. A mile, in this two-dimensional world, is equal to ten units. Because we want to override the functionality of `moveForward` from `Alien`, we must redefine the method in the subclass, and add the `@Override` annotation. Moreover, we define this particular version of `moveForward` in terms of `moveForward` from the superclass. This is a common pattern when overriding methods: we want to reuse the functionality of the superclass, but add some additional behavior. In this case, we want to move ten units forward, instead of one. In order to invoke the superclass' `moveForward`, we prefix the method call with 'super.', rather than 'this.'. Should we accidentally prefix the method call with 'this.', we would be invoking the subclass definition of `moveForward`, resulting in an infinite loop![26] One could make the argument and say that this is, in fact, a form of recursion, and while this is not incorrect, it is "nonsensical recursion" because the outcome is not only undesired, but it also never terminates.

```
import static Assertions.assertAll;
import static Assertions.assertEquals;

class MileMoverAlienTester {

  @Test
  void testMileMoverAlien() {
    Alien r1 = new MileMoverAlien();
    assertAll(
      () -> r1.moveForward(),
      () -> assertEquals(10, r1.getX()),
      () -> r1.turnLeft(),
      () -> r1.moveForward(),
      () -> assertEquals(10, r1.getY()));
  }
}
```

```
class MileMoverAlien extends Alien {

  MileMoverAlien() {
    super();
  }

  @Override
  void moveForward() {
    for (int i = 0; i < 10; i++) {
      super.moveForward();
    }
  }
}
```

Now suppose we want a alien that "bounces" throughout the world. A bouncing alien will pick a random direction to face, then move two spots in that direction, simulating a bounce. Because the alien chooses a random direction, testing its implementation is difficult without predetermined knowledge of the random number generator. Therefore we will omit a tester for this class. All we must do is override the `moveForward` method, and invoke `super.moveForward` twice after facing a random direction.

---

[26] Omitting 'this.' still causes the method to infinitely loop, since not having the qualifier will cause Java to look in the current class definition.

```java
import java.util.Random;

class BouncerAlien extends Alien {

  private final Random RNG;

  BouncerAlien() {
    super();
    this.RNG = new Random();
  }

  @Override
  void moveForward() {
    switch (this.rand.nextInt(4)) {
      case 0: { this.setDir(Direction.NORTH); break; }
      case 1: { this.setDir(Direction.SOUTH); break; }
      case 2: { this.setDir(Direction.EAST); break; }
      case 3: { this.setDir(Direction.WEST); break; }
    }
    super.moveForward();
    super.moveForward();
  }
}
```

Why not create a world for this alien to live within, and objects to interact with or collide into? Let's design the `World` class, which stores a two-dimensional array of `WorldPosition` instances. The `WorldPosition` class is a very general wrapper class to store what we will call `WorldObject` instances. Because a `WorldObject` is not very specific, we will expand upon its implementation with a single subclass, that being a `StarObject`.ABars are objects that an alien in the world can pick up and drop.

This is a lot of information to consider, so let's back up a bit and start by designing the `WorldPosition` class. A `WorldPosition` contains a list of `WorldObject` instances. Therefore, we know that `WorldPosition` encapsulates objects that exist on that particular position. We also need to write the `WorldObject` class, which does nothing but acts as a placeholder for other objects to extend; one of those being `StarObject`.

We, ideally, want aliens to be able to pick and place stars on a world position. It is nonsensical, though, for a aliens to pick stars on a `WorldPosition` that has no existing stars. Therefore, in the `WorldPosition` class, we will write a method that returns the number of instances of a given object. Doing so raises a question of, "How do we specify a class to count?," the answer to which comes via *reflection*.

Reflection is a programming language feature that allows us to inspect the structure of a class at runtime. We can use reflection to determine the class of an object, and then compare that class to the class we are using to search through the data structure. If the classes instances match (i.e., an object in the list is an instance of the desired searching class), in the case of our "counter" method, we increment the counter. To access an object's class information through reflection, we use the `getClass` method, which returns a `Class` instance. To receive any type of class as the parameter to a method, we parameterize the type of `Class` with a wildcard, `<?>`.

Why are we worrying about reflection in the first place? Would it not be easier to simply write a method that, say, returns the number of `StarObject` instances in the `WorldPosition` through perhaps an enumeration describing the type of object? The answer is a resounding yes, but forcing the programmer to write an enumeration just to describe the type of some class is cumbersome and unnecessary. Moreover, when we want to extend the functionality to

4.4 Inheritance

include a new type, we must update the enumeration, which is an additional responsibility that may be overlooked. Reflection allows us to write a single method that can count the number of instances of any class, without having to continuously/repeatedly rewrite the method.

```
class WorldObject {

  WorldObject() {}
}
```

```
class StarObject extends WorldObject {

  StarObject() { super(); }
}
```

```
import java.lang.Class;
import java.util.ArrayList;
import java.util.List;

class WorldPosition {

  private List<WorldObject> WORLD;

  WorldPosition() {
    super();
    this.WORLD = new ArrayList<>();
  }

  /**
   * Using streams, returns the number of occurrences
   * of a given class type.
   * @param cls the class to search for.
   * @return those instances of a class that exist on the position.
   */
  int count(Class<?> cls) {
    return this.WORLD.stream()
                     .filter(o -> obj.getClass().equals(cls))
                     .count();
  }
}
```

Finally we arrive at the `World` class. Perhaps we make it a design choice to disallow extension of this class. To block a class from being extended, we label it as `final`. The `World` class stores, as we stated, a two-dimensional array of `WorldPosition` instances, simulating a two-dimensional grid structure (where the plane origin lies in the top-left rather than the traditional bottom-left). Our constructor receives two integers denoting the number of rows and columns in the world. Each position in the world is directly instantiated thereof to prevent later null pointer references. Said `World` class contains two methods: `addObject`, and `countStars`, where the former adds an object to a given position in the world, and the latter counts the number of stars on a given position.

In Chapter 8, we revisit reflection and explore its potential in greater detail. Remember that reflection is a runtime mechanism and, consequently, program performance may be penalized in certain situations.

```
final class World {

  private final WorldPosition[][] WORLD;

  World(int numRows, int numCols) {
    this.WORLD = new WorldPosition[numRows][numCols];
    for (int i = 0; i < numRows; i++) {
      for (int j = 0; j < numCols; j++) {
        this.WORLD[i][j] = new WorldPosition();
      }
    }
  }

  /**
   * Assigns a WorldObject to a given position in the world by adding
   * it to the list of objects.
   * @param obj the object to assign.
   * @param x the x-coordinate of the position.
   * @param y the y-coordinate of the position.
   */
  void add(WorldObject obj, int x, int y) {
    this.WORLD[x][y].add(obj);
  }

  /**
   * Counts the number of stars on a given position in the world.
   * @param x the x-coordinate of the position.
   * @param y the y-coordinate of the position.
   * @return the number of stars.
   */
  int countStars(int x, int y) {
    return this.WORLD[x][y].count(StarObject.class);
  }
}
```

Example 4.35. Let's design a "role hierarchy" system for business users. In this system, there are employees that have different roles. For instance, we have managers and developers. An employee may be promotable if it implements the IPromotable interface. First, let's consider the hierarchy and what properties each of these roles have to offer.

An Employee contains a name and a unique identifier. Employees can be either hourly or salaried, meaning they receive an hourly pay rate or a yearly salary. Let's categorize these into HourlyEmployee and SalaryEmployee, where both extend the Employee class. Accordingly, the HourlyEmployee class stores an hourly rate, whereas the SalaryEmployee class stores an annual salary amount.

A Manager is an Employee (either salaried or hourly), and contains a list of Employee objects that they supervise.

A Developer writes code in a programming language defined as a string instance variable. They also store an integer denoting their number of years of experience. Developers are strictly salaried employees. Also, a developer can be either "junior" or "senior," and a junior developer is promotable to a senior developer after they have at least five years of experience.

Let's start by designing the Employee class. In addition to its properties, employees can String work() and must override the toString method. The work method is *polymorphic*, meaning that an Salesperson may "work" differently compared to a JuniorDeveloper, but they both "work," in essence. We will say that an Employee works by returning a string with

4.4 Inheritance

their name and `" is working."` appended. The unique identifier that an employee has is generated by a statically-incremented counter variable, similar to how we counted instances of the `Point` class in Chapter 4.

```java
import static Assertions.assertAll;
import static Assertions.assertEquals;

class EmployeeTester {

  @Test
  void testEmployee() {
    Employee e1 = new Employee("Chaitrali");
    Employee e2 = new Employee("Owen");
    assertAll(
        () -> assertEquals("Chaitrali is working.", e1.work()),
        () -> assertEquals("Owen is working.", e2.work()));
  }
}
```

```java
class Employee {

  private static int empCounter = 1;

  private String name;
  private int id;

  Employee(String name) {
    this.name = name;
    this.id = empCounter;
    Employee.empCounter++;
  }

  @Override
  public String toString() {
    return String.format("Name=%s, ID=%d", this.name, this.id);
  }

  String work() {
    return this.name + " is working.";
  }
}
```

The `HourlyEmployee` and `SalaryEmployee` classes, as aforementioned, extend the `Employee` class, the only difference being that they also receive a hourly rate and yearly salary value respectively.

To keep the conversation interesting, we refrain from overriding the `work` method, because there is no significant difference between how a generic `Employee` works and one of its direct subclasses work. By not overriding the implementation of a method, Java defaults to the existing implementation in a superclass. The `toString` method, on the other hand, is updated to contain the hourly rate or salary, depending on the subclass.

```
import static Assertions.assertAll;
import static Assertions.assertEquals;

class EmployeeTester {

  @Test
  void testHourlySalaryEmployee() {
    Employee es1 = new SalaryEmployee("Andrew", 67500);
    Employee eh1 = new HourlyEmployee("Priyanka", 42.80);
    assertAll(
      () -> assertEquals("Andrew is working.", es1.work()),
      () -> assertEquals("Priyanka is working.", eh1.work()),
      () -> assertEquals("Name=Andrew, ID=1, Salary=$67500.00", es1.toString()),
      () -> assertEquals("Name=Priyanka, ID=2, Hourly=$42.80", eh1.toString()));
  }
}
```

```
class HourlyEmployee extends Employee {

  private double hrRate;

  HourlyEmployee(String name, double hrRate) {
    super(name);
    this.hrRate = hrRate;
  }

  @Override
  public String toString() {
    return String.format("%s, Hourly=%.2f", super.toString(), this.hrRate);
  }
}
```

```
class SalaryEmployee extends Employee {

  private double annualSalary;

  HourlyEmployee(String name, double annualSalary) {
    super(name);
    this.annualSalary = annualSalary;
  }

  @Override
  public String toString() {
    return String.format("%s, Salary=%.2f", super.toString(), this.annualSalary);
  }
}
```

Up next we have the Developer class, who programs in a language, and has two supporting subclasses: JuniorDeveloper and SeniorDeveloper. The difference between these two subclasses is their years of experience and whether they are a mentee or a mentor. Junior developers have exactly one mentor, and senior developers can have many mentees, those of which are junior developers. Because a SeniorDeveloper cannot be promoted, only the JuniorDeveloper class will implement the IPromotable interface. Promotion from junior to senior developer also comes with a 25% raise in salary.

4.4 Inheritance

Upon instantiating a JuniorDeveloper, it must receive the SeniorDeveloper who is their mentor. Inside the SeniorDeveloper class, we will expose a method that adds a JuniorDeveloper to their list of mentees.[27]

Lastly we must account for how SeniorDevelopers and JuniorDevelopers "work." A senior developer works by mentoring their mentees. A junior developer works by writing in their programming language, mentored by whomever.

```java
import java.util.Set;

class EmployeeTester {

  @Test
  void testDeveloper() {
    Developer sd1 = new SeniorDeveloper("Ron", 89500, "C", 10);
    Developer d1 = new JuniorDeveloper("Calvin", 55000, "C", 1, sd1);
    Developer d2 = new JuniorDeveloper("Kushagra", 61000, "Java", 6, sd1);
    Developer d3 = new JuniorDeveloper("Tim", 57000, "C++", 2, sd1);
    assertAll(
      () -> assertEquals(Set.of(d1, d2, d3),
                         sd1.getMentees()),
      () -> assertEquals("Ron is a senior developer mentoring Calvin, 
                          Kushagra, Tim.", sd1.work()),
      () -> assertEquals("Calvin is a junior developer working in C, 
                          mentored by Ron.", d1.work()),
      () -> assertEquals("Kushagra is a junior developer working in 
                          Java, mentored by Ron.", d2.work()),
      () -> assertEquals("Tim is a junior developer working in Java, 
                          mentored by Ron.", d3.work()),
      () -> assertEquals("Name=Ron, ID=1, Salary=$89500.00, Senior 
                          Developer in C with 10yoe", sd1.toString()),
      () -> assertEquals("Name=Calvin, ID=2, Salary=$55000.00, Junior 
                          Developer in C with 1 yoe.", d1.toString()),
      () -> assertEquals("Name=Kushagra, ID=3, Salary=$61000.00, Junior 
                          Developer in Java with 6yoe.", d3.toString()),
      () -> assertEquals("Name=Calvin, ID=4, Salary=$57000.00, Junior 
                          Developer in C++ with 2yoe", d3.toString()));
  }

  @Test
  void testJuniorDeveloperPromotion() {
    Developer d1 = new JuniorDeveloper("Cole", 75000, "Python", 6);
    Developer d = new JuniorDeveloper("Adam", 45000, "Python", 0);
    assertAll(
      () -> assertTrue(d1.promote() instanceof SeniorDeveloper),
      () -> assertFalse(d1.promote() instanceof JuniorDeveloper));
  }
}

interface IPromotable {

  Employee promote();
}
```

---

[27] If this were a more robust and realistic system, we may choose to override equals and hashCode to take advantage of set lookups.

```java
class Developer extends SalaryEmployee {

  private String language;
  private int yearsOfExperience;

  Developer(String name, double salary, String language, int yoe) {
    super(name, salary);
    this.language = language;
    this.yearsOfExperience = yoe;
  }
}
```

```java
import java.util.ArrayList;
import java.util.Collectors;
import java.util.List;

class SeniorDeveloper extends Developer {

  private List<JuniorDeveloper> mentees;

  Developer(String name, double salary, String language, int yoe) {
    super(name, salary, language, yoe);
    this.mentees = new ArrayList<>();
  }

  @Override
  public String toString() {
    return String.format("%s,
                          Senior Developer in %s with %d yoe",
                         super.toString(),
                         super.getLanguage(),
                         super.getYearsOfExperience());
  }

  @Override
  String work() {
    String names = mentees.stream()
                          .map(m -> m.getName())
                          .collect(Collectors.join(", "));
    return String.format("%s is a senior developer mentoring %s.",
                         this.getName(),
                         names);
  }

  void addMentee(JuniorDeveloper jd) {
    this.mentees.add(jd);
  }
}
```

4.4 Inheritance

```
class JuniorDeveloper extends Developer implements IPromotable {

  private static final double RAISE_FACTOR = 1.25;
  private static final int PROMOTION_YEARS = 5;

  private SeniorDeveloper mentor;

  Developer(String name, double salary, String lang, int yoe, SeniorDeveloper mentor) {
    super(name, salary, lang, yoe);
    this.mentor = mentor;
    this.mentor.addMentee(this);
  }

  @Override
  public Employee promote() {
    if (super.getYearsOfExperience() >= PROMOTION_YEARS) {
      return new SeniorDeveloper(super.getName(),
                                 super.getSalary() * RAISE_FACTOR,
                                 super.getLanguage(),
                                 super.getYearsOfExperience());
    } else {
      return this;
    }
  }

  @Override
  public String toString() {
    return String.format("%s, Junior Developer in %s with %d yoe",
                         super.toString(),
                         super.getLanguage(),
                         super.getYearsOfExperience());
  }

  @Override
  String work() {
    return String.format("%s is a junior developer working in %s, mentored by %s.",
                         super.getName(),
                         super.getLanguage(),
                         this.mentor.getName());
  }
}
```

The developer series of classes were certainly a lot to write and design. The last class, namely Manager, is an hourly employee who supervises any kind of employee, including other managers. Their "work" is that they are "supervising" employee names, sorted alphabetically. The only part of this that is more complex than the others is the comparator that we provide to the TreeSet. Because the set stores employee instances, our comparator must receive two employees, but return a comparison based on their name. Let's see what this looks like:

```java
import static Assertions.assertAll;
import static Assertions.assertEquals;

class EmployeeTester {

  @Test
  void testManager() {
    HourlyEmployee m1 = new Manager("Abby", 30.00);
    m1.addDirectReport(new JuniorDeveloper("Cole", 75000, "Python", 6));
    m1.addDirectReport(new JuniorDeveloper("Adam", 45000, "Python", 0));
    m1.addDirectReport(new SalaryEmployee("Pete", 46000));
    assertAll(
      () -> assertEquals("Abby manages Adam, Cole, Pete.", m1.work()),
      () -> assertEquals("Abby, ID=1, Hourly=30.00, Manager", m1.toString()));
  }
}
```

```java
import java.util.Collectors;
import java.util.Comparator;
import java.util.Set;
import java.util.TreeSet;

class Manager extends HourlyEmployee {

  private final Set<Employee> EMPS;

  Manager(String name, double hrRate) {
    super(name, hrRate);
    this.EMPS = new TreeSet(employeeNameComparator());
  }

  @Override
  public String toString() {
    return String.format("%s, Manager", super.toString());
  }

  @Override
  String work() {
    return String.format("%s supervises %s",
                        super.getName(),
                        this.EMPS.stream()
                                .map(x -> x.getName())
                                .collect(Collectors.joining(", ")));
  }

  void addDirectReport(Employee e) {
    this.DIRECT_REPORTS.add(e);
  }

  private static Comparator<Employee> employeeNameComparator() {
    return new Comparator<Employee>() {
      @Override
      public int compare(Employee e1, Employee e2) {
        return e1.getName().compareTo(e2.getName());
      }
    };
  }
}
```

4.4 Inheritance

Example 4.36. Let's design a class hierarchy for a series of Mythicritters objects. In the exotic land of Mythicritters, there are three kinds of creatures: Mage, Warrior, and Rogue. Beneath these, each creature can transform into a more powerful form: Archmage, Berserker, and Assassin.

Mythicritters have a set number of health points, statistics about their power/strength-/speed, and two kinds of "attacks." Additionally, they have a level to indicate how strong they are. We will come back to the notion of an attack later. Finally, they also have either one or two types, which are returned via the getTypes method as a Set<IType>.[28] Let's design the Mythicritter class. Aside from the accessors and mutators, we will add one instance method for adding attacks to the Mythicritter, as long as there are less than two.

```
import java.util.HashSet;
import java.util.Set;

class Mythicritter {

  private int maxHealth;
  private int currentHealth;
  private int level;
  private int power;
  private Set<IAttack> attacks;

  Mythicritter(int maxHealth, int level, int power) {
    this.maxHealth = maxHealth;
    this.currentHealth = this.maxHealth;
    this.level = level;
    this.power = power;
    this.attacks = new HashSet<>();
  }

  void addAttack(Attack a) {
    if (this.attacks.size() < 4) {
      this.attacks.add(a);
    }
  }

  Set<IType> getTypes() {
    return Set.of();
  }
}
```

As we stated, Mythicritter have attacks, or ways to combat an opponent. Attack have a type, a base power statistic, and a number representing how many "uses" that the attack has remaining. Each time an attack is used, its usage counter is decremented. Once it reaches zero, the attack can no longer be used. Attacks also inhabit exactly one type, which cannot change.

---
[28] We will design IType in a few paragraphs.

```
class Attack {

  private final IType TYPE;
  private final int NUM_USES;
  private int remainingUses;
  private int basePower;

  Attack(String name, int numUses, int basePower, IType type) {
    this.name = name;
    this.baseDamage = baseDamage;
    this.NUM_USES = numUses;
    this.TYPE = type;
  }

  // Accessors and mutators omitted.
}
```

Finally, Mythicritters, as well as attacks, have associated types. Types in the world of Mythicritters are a property thereof, which affect the power of their attacks, as well as what types they are vulnerable to/strong against. All in all, it is akin to a game of "Rock, paper, scissors." That is, scissors beats paper, paper beats rock, and rock beats scissors. Mythicritters and attack types work similarly: if an attack is ZapType and the Mythicritter it is used against is OceanicType, the attack is "enhanced" against the Mythicritter. The defending Mythicritter thus takes more damage than it would otherwise. Conversely, if an attack is InfernoType and the Mythicritter is BoulderType, the attack is "vulnerable" against the Mythicritter. The defending Mythicritter thus takes less damage than it would otherwise.

Now, let's design a "base interface" that other classes implement. An IType contains two methods: Set<IType> vulnerableTo() and Set<IType> strongAgainst(), which returns sets to represent the types that a type is vulnerable to or strong against. These methods will call upon a data structure that we will denote as a "type registry," which defines the relationships from one type to another. Interestingly, this means that the methods inside IType should have a body to reference the type registry, but in the previous section we stated that the methods of an interface must not have bodies. *Default methods* of an interface, on the contrary, may have bodies, and serve as a "default implementation" of a method in the event that an interface does not override its definition.

```
import java.util.Set;

interface IType {

  default Set<IType> vulnerableTo() {
    return TypeRegistry.vulnerableTo(this);
  }

  default Set<IType> strongAgainst() {
    return TypeRegistry.strongAgainst(this);
  }
}
```

Out of conciseness, let's design only three types: ZapType, OceanicType, and FlameType. Repeating the rock-paper-scissors analogy, zap types are strong against oceanic type but weak to flame type. Oceanic types are strong against flame type but weak to zap. Flame types are strong against zap but weak to oceanic.

These three types, namely zap, oceanic, and flame, are designed as classes that exist solely for the purposes of instantiating exactly one instance thereof. Types do not need to be in-

4.4 Inheritance

stantiated multiple times since they are immutable and do not contain any relevant state. We are taking advantage of a *design paradigm* called *singleton*. The class constructors are private to prevent outside instantiation of the types, but the sole instance is public, static, and final for global, unrestricted, and immutable access.

```java
class FlameType implements IType {

  static final IType FLAME_TYPE = new FlameType();

  private FlameType() {}
}
```

```java
class OceanicType implements IType {

  static final IType OCEANIC_TYPE = new OceanicType();

  private OceanicType() {}
}
```

```java
class ZapType implements IType {

  static final IType ZAP_TYPE = new ZapType();

  private ZapType() {}
}
```

The aforementioned type registry is a class that stores two maps of type weaknesses and strengths. It provides two static methods: vulnerableTo and strongAgainst, identical to the IType interface, which tap into the map data structures for querying.

```java
import java.util.Map;
import java.util.Set;

class TypeRegistry {

  private static final Map<IType, Set<IType>> vulnerabilities =
    Map.of(OceanicType.OCEANIC_TYPE, Set.of(ZapType.ZAP_TYPE),
           ZapType.ZAP_TYPE, Set.of(FlameType.FLAME_TYPE),
           FlameType.FLAME_TYPE, Set.of(OceanicType.OCEANIC_TYPE));

  private static final Map<IType, Set<IType>> strengths =
    Map.of(OceanicType.OCEANIC_TYPE, Set.of(FlameType.FLAME_TYPE),
           ZapType.ZAP_TYPE, Set.of(OceanicType.OCEANIC_TYPE),
           FlameType.FLAME_TYPE, Set.of(ZapType.ZAP_TYPE));

  private TypeRegistry() {};

  static Set<IType> vulnerableTo(IType t) {
    return vulnerabilities.getOrDefault(t, Set.of());
  }

  static Set<IType> strongAgainst(IType t) {
    return strengths.getOrDefault(t, Set.of());
  }
}
```

Inside the Mythicritter class, let's design two methods: vulnerableTo and strongAgainst, both of which invoke the type registry. The problem, though, is that we potentially need to take the union of two sets, since a `Mythicritter` stores a set of types. To compensate, we can use streams to take the union of multiple sets, which collapses the problem from handling both one and two sets independently into just handling a stream. To combine the sets, we can use the `flatMap` stream method, which is a higher-order method to apply a lambda expression to a list of collections, then flatten the result into a single collection. Namely, we take the sets of types, map the `vulnerableTo` or `strongAgainst` over those types, creating a stream of sets of types. These are then converted into streams themselves and then flattened into a single stream. Finally, we collect those results into a set.

Before we write these two methods, however, let's actually create a `Mythicritter` instance to show off our hard work. Let's design the `Mage` class, which is a zap type `Mythicritter`, hence the subclass/superclass relationship. We will instantiate it to start off with 50 health, level 1, and have a base "power" statistic of 4. Because we must also pass the type information to the superclass constructor, we need to invoke `super(...)` with information provided from the subclass contructor in addition to the type(s). After creating the subclass instance, we can write tests for the type registry.

```java
import java.util.Set;

class Mage extends Mythicritter {

  Mage(int health, int level, int power) {
    super(health, level, power);
  }

  @Override
  Set<IType> getTypes() {
    return Set.of(ZapType.ZAP_TYPE);
  }
}
```

```java
import static Assertions.assertAll;
import static Assertions.assertEquals;

import java.util.Set;

class MythicritterTester {

  @Test
  void testMythicritter() {
    Mythicritter p1 = new Mage(50, 1, 4);
    assertAll(
      () -> assertEquals(Set.of(FlameType.FLAME_TYPE),
                         p1.weakTo()),
      () -> assertEquals(Set.of(OceanicType.OCEANIC_TYPE),
                         p1.strongAgainst()));
  }
}
```

Finally, let's represent an important component of Mythicritters: transformations! A Mythicritter can transform from one form to another. From this, a Mythicritter's type can change, as do its base statistics and health. For example, the transformation of Mage into Archmage adds the `MythicalType` to its type set. We can change the type that a `Mythicritter` inhabits by overriding the `getTypes` method: we retrieve the superclass type set, then add the new type earned by transforming, should it exist.

To make transformation a bit more interesting, we will design the `ITransformable` interface, which is implemented by any transformable Mythicritter. This interface contains two

4.4 Inheritance

methods: `boolean canTransform()` and `Mythicritter transform()`. The former describes the requirements before a Mythicritter can transform, e.g., whether or not it has to be at a certain level. The latter `transform` method returns a new instance of the transformation if it can transform, and itself otherwise.

Designing an interface in this way means that Mythicritters that transform once, but cannot transform thereafter must also override the methods in the `ITransformable` interface to return `false` and themselves respectively.

For contextualization, Mages transform into Archmages. A Mage can transform into an Archmage once it reaches level 30. Because `MythicalType` is almost a carbon copy of the other three types, we omit its inclusion.

```java
import static Assertions.assertAll;
import static Assertions.assertEquals;

class MythicritterTester {

  @Test
  void testTransformation() {
    Mythicritter p1 = new Mage(20, 1, 4);
    Mythicritter p2 = new Mage(1000, 40, 100);
    assertAll(
      () -> assertFalse(p1.canTransform()),
      () -> assertTrue(p1.transform() instanceof Mage),
      () -> assertTrue(p2.canTransform()),
      () -> assertTrue(p2.transform() instanceof Archmage));
  }
}
```

```java
interface ITransformable {

  boolean canTransform();

  Mythicritter transform();
}
```

```java
class Mage extends Mythicritter implements ITransformable {
  // ... previous methods not shown.

  @Override
  public boolean canTransform() {
    return this.getLevel() >= 30;
  }

  @Override
  public Mythicritter transform() {
    if (!this.canTransform()) {
      return this;
    } else {
      return new Archmage(super.getHp() * 2, super.getLevel(), super.getPower() * 3);
    }
  }
}
```

```java
import java.util.Collectors;
import java.util.Set;
import java.util.Stream;

class Archmage extends Mage implements ITransformable {

  Archmage(int health, int level, int power) {
    super(health, level, power);
  }

  @Override
  public boolean canTransform() {
    return false;
  }

  @Override
  public Mythicritter transform() {
    return this;
  }

  @Override
  Set<Type> getTypes() {
    Stream<IType> ot = super.getTypes().stream();
    Stream<IType> nt = Set.of(MythicalTypeType.MYTHICAL_TYPE).stream();
    return Stream.concat(ot, nt)
               .collect(Collectors.toSet());
  }
}
```

We went through all of this trouble to create a complex system, so what is its intended purpose? With a bit of work up front, we made it easy to extend this system to include new types, new kinds of Mythicritters, and much more.[29]

4.5 Abstract Classes

We consider a class to be abstract if it is not representable by any instance. That is, we cannot create an instance of an abstract class. Abstract classes are useful when we want to define a class that is a generalization of other classes, but we do not want to create instances of the generalization.

Example 4.37. Consider, once again, a hierarchy of animals. There is no such thing as an "animal" or something that is solely called an animal. On the other hand, everything that we would categorize as an animal *is* an animal. Therefore it makes sense to say that animals are a generalization of other types of "sub"-animals. Imagine we want to write an Animal class, where we will say that any animal can speak. The abstract class contains a superfluous constructor as well as an abstract speak method. We define speak as abstract to denote that an animal can speak, but it is nonsensical for Animal to speak. Because it is impossible to instantiate an instance of Animal, it is similarly impossible to reasonably define speak.

---

[29] We did not do anything with the attacks of a Mythicritter; this may be a good place to start expanding upon if you are interested!

4.5 Abstract Classes

```
abstract class Animal {

  Animal() {}

  abstract String speak();
}
```

Let's declare two subclasses: Dog and Cat, representing dogs and cats respectively. A cat can meow via the string "Meow!", whereas a dog woofs via the string "Woof!".

```
class Dog extends Animal {

  Dog() { super(); }

  @Override
  String speak() { return "Woof!"; }
}
```

```
class Cat extends Animal {

  Cat() { super(); }

  @Override
  String speak() { return "Meow!"; }
}
```

It might seem strange to use an abstract class, since we could write a Speakable interface to do the same logic. The differences between abstract classes and interfaces is a blurry line to beginning Java programmers (and even to some who have been programming for years), but in essence, we use abstract classes when we want to enforce a class hierarchy of "is-a" relationships, e.g., a Cat is-a Animal, and a Dog is-a Animal. Moreover, abstract classes can contain non-abstract methods, meaning that a subclass needs not to override such methods. Interfaces, on the other hand, contain only methods that the implementing class must override. In addition to the method distinction, abstract classes may contain instance variables, whereas interfaces may not.[30]

Example 4.38. Suppose we're writing a two-dimensional game that has different types of interactable objects in the world. The core game object stores the (x, y) location, with nothing more. Again, we want to design a class that specific types of game objects can extend. For instance, our game might contain circular and rectangular objects. Of course, circles and rectangles have different dimension units, namely radius versus width and height respectively. We plan for each object to be interactable with one another. Unfortunately, collision detection is a complicated set of algorithms whose discussion far exceeds the scope of this text. Conversely, there is an extremely straightforward solution that involves treating all objects as rectangles. We call this technique *axis-aligned bounding box*. Because not every object may be collidable, we will design a class AxisAlignedBoundingBoxObject that separately stores the object width and height as the dimensions of the bounding box. This class defines a method for colliding with another AxisAlignedBoundingBoxObject, which determines whether some point of o_1 is inside the bounding box of the o_2 object. This logic is not the focal point of the discussion, so we will only illustrate the example via an image and not explain the code itself. The purpose for this example is to demonstrate object hierarchy; not recreate the next best-selling two-dimensional side-scroller.

---

[30] Both abstract classes and interfaces can contain static methods and variables.

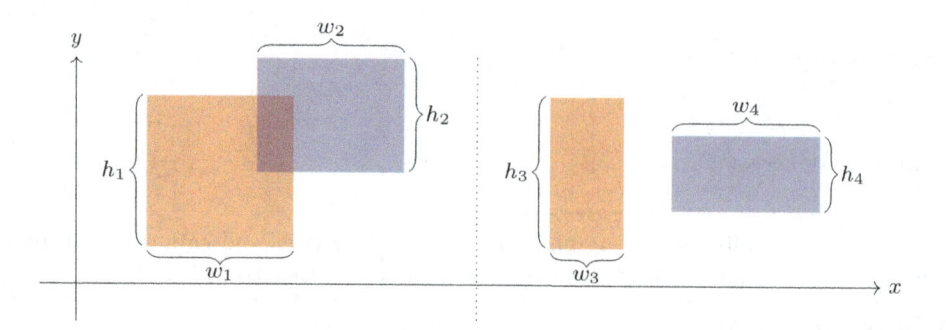

Fig. 4.2: Collision Detection Between Rectangles.

```
abstract class GameObject {

  private int x;
  private int y;

  GameObject(int x, int y) {
    this.x = x;
    this.y = y;
  }
}
```

```
abstract class AxisAlignedBoundingBoxObject extends GameObject {

  private int width;
  private int height;

  AxisAlignedBoundingBoxObject(int x, int y, int width, int height) {
    super(x, y);
    this.width = width;
    this.height = height;
  }

  /**
   * Determines whether this object collides with
   * another AxisAlignedBoundingBoxObject.
   * @param obj instance of AxisAlignedBoundingBoxObject.
   * @return true if the objects overlap and false otherwise.
   */
  boolean collidesWith(AxisAlignedBoundingBoxObject obj) {
    return (this.getX() < obj.getX() + obj.width) &&
           (this.getX() + this.width >= obj.getX()) &&
           (this.getY() < obj.getY() + obj.height) &&
           (this.getY() + this.height >= obj.height);
  }
}
```

We declared an abstract class to extend another abstract class; which is perfectly acceptable. Because it makes no sense to instantiate an entity, in and of itself, called AxisAlignedBoundingBoxObject, we declare it as abstract, but we need it to contain the functionality of GameObject, which calls for the inheritance. Normally, we would immediately write an extensive test suite for collidesWith, but because we cannot instantiate an AxisAligned-

4.5 Abstract Classes

BoundingBox directly, we cannot test collidesWith at the moment. In a couple of paragraphs, however, this will be possible, with the additions of CircleObject and RectangleObject.

```
import static Assertions.assertAll;
import static Assertions.assertEquals;

class AxisAlignedBoundingBoxObjectTester {

  @Test
  void testCollidesWith() {
    AxisAlignedBoundingBoxObject o1
      = new RectangleObject(30, 30, 1000, 2000);
    AxisAlignedBoundingBoxObject o2
      = new RectangleObject(0, 0, 5, 5);
    AxisAlignedBoundingBoxObject o3
      = new RectangleObject(400, 200, 750, 250);
    AxisAlignedBoundingBoxObject o4
      = new RectangleObject(300, 100, 300, 200);
    AxisAlignedBoundingBoxObject o5
      = new CircleObject(20, 30, 1000);
    AxisAlignedBoundingBoxObject o6
      = new CircleObject(200, 250, 500);
    AxisAlignedBoundingBoxObject o7
      = new CircleObject(30, 300, 1500);
    AxisAlignedBoundingBoxObject o8
      = new CircleObject(90, 85, 200);
    assertAll(
      () -> assertTrue(o1.collidesWith(o2)),
      () -> assertTrue(o1.collidesWith(o4)),
      () -> assertTrue(o2.collidesWith(o3)),
      () -> assertTrue(o2.collidesWith(o8)),
      () -> assertTrue(o3.collidesWith(o5)),
      () -> assertTrue(o5.collidesWith(o4)),
      () -> assertTrue(o6.collidesWith(o7)),
      () -> assertTrue(o7.collidesWith(o3)));
  }
}
```

We need to translate our circles into axis-aligned bounding box, but what does that mean? In short, we convert the given radius into the corresponding diameter, and designate this diameter as the width and height of the bounding box. Rectangular objects, on other hand, need no such fancy translation, since a bounding box is a rectangle. Neither subclasses store their dimensions as instance variables, due to the fact that the superclass takes care of this for us.

The question that we anticipate many readers are thinking of is, why do we even distinguish objects of differing "types" if they both implement collision detection in the same fashion? Since we are working in the context of a game, the way we draw these objects is certainly different! Let's, for the sake of emphasizing the distinctions, design a IDrawable interface, which provides one method: void draw(Graphics2D g2d), which gives us a Graphics2D object. We will not discuss, nor do we really care about the innards of a graphics library aside from the fact that it contains two primitive methods: drawOval(int x, int y, int w, int

h) and drawRect(int x, int y, int w, int h). Therefore our two object subclasses will implement IDrawable and override the method differently.

```
interface IDrawable {

  /**
   * Provides a means of drawing primitive graphics.
   * The inner details of "Graphics2D" are not important to us;
   * we care about the fact that we can use the following methods:
   *
   * - drawOval(int x, int y, int w, int h);
   * - drawRect(int x, int y, int w, int h);
   */
  void draw(Graphics2D g2d);
}
```

```
class CircleObject extends AxisAlignedBoundingBoxObject implements IDrawable {

  CircleObject(int x, int y, int r) { super(x, y, r * 2, r * 2); }

  @Override
  public void draw(Graphics2D g2d) {
    g2d.drawOval(this.getX(), this.getY(),
                 this.getWidth(), this.getHeight());
  }
}
```

```
class RectangleObject extends AxisAlignedBoundingBoxObject implements IDrawable {

  RectangleObject(int x, int y, int w, int h) { super(x, y, w, h); }

  @Override
  public void draw(Graphics2D g2d) {
    g2d.drawRect(this.getX(), this.getY(),
                 this.getWidth(), this.getHeight());
  }
}
```

Example 4.39. A terminal argument parser is a program/function that interprets a series of arguments passed to another program and makes it easier for programmers to determine if a flag is enabled. Without one, many programmers often resort to using a complex series of conditional statements to check for the existence of a flag. Not only is this cumbersome, but it is prone to errors, and neither extendable nor flexible to different arrangements of arguments. In this example we will develop a small terminal argument parser.

First, we need to design a class that represents an "argument" to a program. Arguments, as we described in Chapter 3, are space-separated string values that we pass to a program executable, which populate the String[] args array in the main method. In particular, however, we want to specify that an argument is not necessarily the values themselves, but are instead the flags, or instructions, passed to the executable. The simplest version of a flag is one that receives exactly one argument, which we will represent via an abstract Argument class. Later on, we want to be able to validate a flag with its given arguments, so the Argument class

4.5 Abstract Classes

includes an abstract `boolean validate` method, that shall be overridden in all subclasses of Argument.

```java
import java.util.List;
import java.util.Map;

abstract class Argument {

  private String key;

  Argument(String key) { this.key = key; }

  String getKey() { return this.key; }

  abstract boolean validate(Map<String, List<String>> args);
}
```

From here, let's design two types of arguments: one that is optional and one that receives n arguments. Namely, an optional argument is one that is always valid, according to `validate`, because it does not necessarily need to exist. The n-valued argument, on the other hand, requires that the associated passed flag contains exactly n values. For example, if we say that the `--input` flag requires exactly 3 arguments, then if we do not pass exactly three space-separated non-flag values, it fails to validate.

```java
import java.util.List;
import java.util.Map;

class OptionalArgument extends Argument {

  OptionalArgument(String key) { super(key); }

  @Override
  boolean validate(Map<String, List<String>> args) { return true; }
}
```

```java
import java.util.List;
import java.util.Map;

class NumberedArgument extends Argument {

  private final int NUM_REQUIRED_ARGS;

  NumberedArgument(String key, int n) {
    super(key);
    this.NUM_REQUIRED_ARGS = n;
  }

  @Override
  boolean validate(Map<String, List<String>> args) {
    if (!args.containsKey(this.getKey())) { return false; }
    else { return args.get(this.getKey()).size() == this.NUM_REQUIRED_ARGS; }
  }
}
```

Now comes the argument parser itself, which receives a string array of argument values, much like `main`, and extracts out the flags and arguments into a `Map<String, List<String>>` where the key represents the flag and the value is a list of the arguments to said flag. We also store a `Set<Argument>` to allow the programmer to designate arguments to the parser. The idea is straightforward: while traversing over args, if we encounter a string that begins with a double dash '--', it is qualified as a flag and the following arguments, up to another flag, are marked as arguments to the flag. We add these to the respective map as described before, and continue until we run out of elements in the array.

```java
import java.util.HashMap;
import java.util.HashSet;
import java.util.Map;
import java.util.Set;

class ArgumentParser {

  private final Map<String, List<String>> PARSED_ARGS;
  private final Set<Argument> ARGS;

  ArgumentParser(String[] args) {
    this.ARGS = new HashSet<>();
    this.PARSED_ARGS = new HashMap<>();
    String currKey = null;
    for (String arg : this.ARGS) {
      if (arg.startsWith("--")) {
        currKey = arg.split("--")[1];
        this.PARSED_ARGS.putIfAbsent(currKey, new ArrayList<>());
      } else if (currKey != null) {
        this.PARSED_ARGS.get(currKey).add(arg);
      }
    }
  }

  void addArgument(Argument arg) { this.ARGS.add(arg); }

  List<String> getArguments(String key) {
    return this.PARSED_ARGS.containsKey(key) ? this.PARSED_ARGS.get(key) : null;
  }
}
```

The parseArguments method returns whether or not the supplied arguments are valid according to the arguments populated via addArgument. Using streams, we verify that, after invoking validate on every argument, each separate call returns true, meaning that all arguments are valid and correct. Because it might be useful to return the associated arguments to a flag from a programmer's perspective who uses this parser, we include a getArguments method to return the list of arguments passed to a flag.

```java
import java.util.HashMap;
import java.util.HashSet;
import java.util.Map;
import java.util.Set;

class ArgumentParser {

  /**
   * Determines whether or not all of the arguments in the stored field are "valid."
   * @return true if all arguments are valid, false otherwise.
   */
  boolean parseArguments() {
    return this.arguments.stream()
                    .allMatch(e -> e.validate(this.parsedArguments));
  }
}
```

The ASPL Interpreter

Example 4.40. Inheritance is a truly powerful programming language construct, and we will now attempt to describe its beauty through the design of a mini-project. Said mini-project will encompass writing a small programming language called ASPL, or "A Simple Programming Language."[31] Programming language syntax and semantics, collectively, require a lot of knowledge outside the domain and scope of this text, but we will see that, even with our somewhat limited arsenal of tools, we can construct a fairly powerful programming language. Our language will start off as a recreation of the interpreter from our section on interfaces, but contains modifications to make it more flexible.

As a means of motivation, let's write a few programs in this language to show its capabilities. The first listing is a simple program to add two numbers together. The second listing binds two variables, and if their sum is equal to 42, then the result is 100, otherwise it is zero. The third listing declares a variable, followed by a conditional, both cases of which contain another binding of a variable, closing off with a product operation.

(+ 25 17)	(let ([x 10])
	  (let ([y 32])
	    (if (eq? (+ x y) 42)
	      100
	      0)))
		(let ([z 95])
		  (if (eq? (- 100 5) z)
		    (let ([w -10])
		      (* w z 2))
		    (let ([w -5])
		      (* z w -2))))

Programming language syntax is often broken up into the nodes of an *abstract syntax tree*, which at a quick glance is nothing more than a description of the operations of a language. To begin, we need to describe our programming language capabilities. To keep things simple, our language will contain integers, variables, a few arithmetic operators, and conditionals. It's important to note that, because we are glossing over the innards of lexing and parsing, all of our tests will exist in the form of abstract syntax trees. We want an abstract AST node class from which every other AST node inherits. Then, we can design purpose-specific nodes that do what we wish. Every abstract syntax tree has a list of children node. We will also define a toString method that will print out the abstract syntax tree in a readable format. Our abstract syntax tree class uses two constructors: one that receives a list of abstract syntax tree nodes, and another that is variadic over the AstNode type. We implement two different constructors for convenience purposes during testing.

Each abstract syntax tree should be evaluable as a means of reducing the expression to its simplest form. For example, numbers and booleans, the literals of our language, resolve to themselves. Primitive operations apply the operation to its arguments, then ultimately reduce to a value. Conditionals resolve to either of its branches, and "let" bindings resolve to its body. We will cover each case one-by-one as we cover the material. For now, though, the abstract syntax tree node class contains the eval method, which denotes how a node is to be evaluated.

---

[31] Originally, we called the interpreter APL, or "A Programming Language." We changed its name to include the extra 'S' so as to not cause confusion between our implementation and the actual language called APL (Iverson, 1962). If you want to have some "fun," take a slight detour and go explore *that* language!

```java
import java.util.List;

abstract class AstNode {

  private final List<AstNode> CHILDREN;

  AstNode(List<AstNode> children) {
    this.CHILDREN = children;
  }

  AstNode(AstNode... children) {
    this(List.of(children));
  }

  abstract AstNode eval();

  List<AstNode> getChildren() {
    return this.CHILDREN;
  }

  public abstract String toString();
}
```

From here, the simplest two abstract syntax tree nodes are NumNode and BoolNode, corresponding to numbers and booleans literals respectively. Nodes that encapsulate sole values, e.g., numbers and booleans, are examples of literals, and all literals are evaluated/treated the same way. As such, let's design the generic and abstract LiteralNode<T> class, which all literal types extend, those for our purposes being NumNode and BoolNode.[32]

A LiteralNode<T> stores an immutable object of type T. Literal values resolve to themselves and only themselves, which means that they return this as the object in LiteralNode's eval method. The LiteralNode class overrides equals, hashCode, and toString to compare literals, return the hash code of the stored instance variable, and "stringify" the instance variable respectively. Designing the LiteralNode class in this fashion makes designing the subclasses easier and significantly less redundant, because NumNode and BoolNode need to only provide constructors that invoke the superclass.

```java
import static Assertions.assertAll;
import static Assertions.assertEquals;

class AstTest {

  @Test
  void testNumNode() {
    assertEquals("42", new NumNode("42").toString());
  }

  @Test
  void testBoolNode() {
    assertEquals("true", new BoolNode("true").toString());
    assertEquals("false", new BoolNode("false").toString());
  }
}
```

---

[32] We say, "for our purposes," because the language could also support string or character literals.

4.5 Abstract Classes

```java
import java.util.Objects;

abstract class LiteralNode<T> extends AstNode {

  private final T VALUE;

  LiteralNode(T value) { this.VALUE = value; }

  @Override
  AstNode eval(Environment env) { return this; }

  @Override
  public boolean equals(Object o) {
    if (!(o instanceof LiteralNode)) { return false; }
    else { return this.VALUE.equals(((LiteralNode<?>) o).VALUE); }
  }

  @Override
  public int hashCode() { return Objects.hashCode(this.VALUE); }

  @Override
  public String toString() { return this.VALUE.toString(); }

  T getValue() { return this.VALUE; }
}
```

```java
final class NumNode extends LiteralNode<Double> {

  NumNode(double value) { super(value); }

  NumNode(String value) { super(Double.parseDouble(value)); }
}
```

```java
final class BoolNode extends LiteralNode<Boolean> {

  BoolNode(boolean value) { super(value); }

  BoolNode(String value) { this(Boolean.parseBoolean(value)); }
}
```

The next logical step is to add primitive operations via `PrimNode`. A primitive operator is an operation akin to addition, subtraction, value equality, and so forth. Primitive operators receive any number of arguments, and the behavior of which is handled as a case analysis of the `eval` method.

Though, evaluating a primitive operation is not as simple as applying the operator to its arguments. Consider the following code segment, where we have the primitive operation + applied to two more primitive operations '*' and '−.' We see that it is impossible to directly apply the plus operation to the two primitives, because addition only works over `NumNode` values and not `AstNode` instances. So, when applying a primitive operation, we must first recursively evaluate its children nodes, i.e., the arguments. The list of arguments is converted into a stream, where we map the `eval` method over each element. Afterwards, we write the aforementioned case analysis on the operation. For the addition operator, we sum all the values of the children nodes. Even though each node is definitionally an `AstNode`, we can safely cast them to `NumNode` because we know that the operation is semantically valid only over numbers (the same logic applies to other such primitive operators).

```java
import static Assertions.assertAll;
import static Assertions.assertEquals;

class AstTest {

  @Test
  void testPrimNode() {
    assertAll(
      () -> assertEquals(new NumNode(42),
                         new PrimNode("+",
                           new NumNode(25),
                           new NumNode(17)).eval());
      () -> assertEquals(new NumNode(42),
                         new PrimNode("-",
                           new NumNode(97),
                           new NumNode(55)).eval());
      () -> assertEquals(new NumNode(42),
                         new PrimNode("*",
                           new NumNode(6),
                           new NumNode(1),
                           new NumNode(7)).eval());
      () -> assertEquals(new BoolNode(true),
                         new PrimNode("eq?",
                           new PrimNode("+",
                             new NumNode(5),
                             new NumNode(37)),
                           new NumNode(42)).eval()):
      () -> assertEquals(new NumNode(42),
                         new PrimNode("+",
                           new PrimNode("*",
                             new NumNode(2),
                             new PrimNode("-",
                               new NumNode(57),
                               new NumNode(23))),
                           new PrimNode("-",
                             new NumNode(4),
                             new NumNode(30))));
  }
}
```

```java
import java.util.List;

final class PrimNode extends AstNode {

  private final String OP;

  PrimNode(String op, AstNode... children) {
    super(children);
    this.OP = op;
  }

  @Override
  public String toString() {
    return String.format("(%s %s)",this.OP, this.getChildren().toString());
  }
```

4.5 Abstract Classes

```java
/**
 * Interpret a primitive operation.
 * @param env the environment in which to interpret the operation.
 * @return The result of the primitive operation.
 */
@Override
AstNode eval(Environment env) {
  List<AstNode> operands = this.getChildren().stream()
                                  .map(n -> n.eval(env))
                                  .toList();
  switch (this.OP) {
    case "+": return this.primPlus(operands, env);
    case "-": return this.primMinus(operands, env);
    case "*": return this.primProduct(operands, env);
    case "eq?": return this.primEq(operands, env);
    default: return null;
  }
}

private AstNode primPlus(List<AstNode> args, Environment env) {
  return new NumNode(args.stream()
                         .map(t -> ((NumNode) t).getValue())
                         .sum());
}

private AstNode primMinus(List<AstNode> args, Environment env) {
  double res = ((NumNode) args.get(0)).getValue();
  for (int i = 1; i < args.size(); i++) {
    res -= ((NumNode) args.get(i)).getValue();
  }
  return new NumNode(res);
}

private AstNode primProduct(List<AstNode> args, Environment env) {
  return new NumNode(args.stream()
                         .map(t -> ((NumNode) t).getValue())
                         .reduce(1.0, (a, c) -> c * a));
}

private AstNode primEq(List<AstNode> args, Environment env) {
  return new BoolNode(args.get(0).equals(args.get(1)));
}
}
```

Adding the equality comparison operator provides a pathway to designing the conditional expression, namely IfNode. An IfNode contains three children nodes: a predicate, a consequent, and an alternative. The eval method of an IfNode evaluates the predicate, and if it is true, evaluates the consequent, otherwise it evaluates the alternative. The predicate *must* resolve to a boolean, assuming the program is well-formed. Because we only care about well-formed programs, we do not need to check if the predicate is a boolean, and can safely cast it to a BoolNode when evaluating the respective abstract syntax tree node.

```
import static Assertions.assertAll;
import static Assertions.assertEquals;

class AstTest {

  @Test
  void testIfNode() {
    assertAll(
      () -> assertEquals(new NumNode(100),
                         new IfNode(new BoolNode(true),
                                    new NumNode(100),
                                    new NumNode(0)).eval()),
      () -> assertEquals(new BoolNode(false),
                         new IfNode(new PrimNode("eq?",
                                                 new NumNode(5),
                                                 new NumNode(5)),
                                    new BoolNode(true),
                                    new BoolNode(false)).eval()));
  }
}
```

With numbers, booleans, primitive operations, and conditionals taken care of, we now come to the challenging part: variable bindings. We need a way of introducing variable bindings to their values, so we shall take a hint from functional programming languages via the LetNode class. The LetNode class has three children: a variable name, a value, and a body. The variable name is a string, with the value and body both being abstract syntax tree nodes. The LetNode class will have a toString method that will return a string in the form of (let ([<var> <exp>]) <body>). In tandem, we will also write the VarNode class, which represents variable placeholders. In order to do anything meaningful with both classes, we need to discuss the scope of a variable and how to handle the encompassing issues.

The *scope of a variable* refers to its lifetime. Consider the following program in our language. Initially, the program has no variable bindings. After encountering the let, we enter a scope that binds the variable identifier x to 5. The body of this let is, therefore, the *scope* of x. Inside this body, we encounter yet another variable, namely y, which binds y to 10. The body of this let is the scope of y. Outside the scope of the body, y is non-existent.

```
(let ([x 5])
  (let ([y 10])
    (* x y)))
```

When executing this program in our heads, we know intuitively that x refers to 5 and y refers to 10. To write a programming language, though, we need to formalize the notion of "variable lookup." That is, we must define how to associate variable identifiers to values. Of course, the best data structure for value association is a map, and indeed, this is the structure we will use.

Programming languages use *environments* to associate identifiers to values. Upon encountering a variable declaration, we extend the current environment to contain the new binding. This begs the question, "Why not just modify the environment?" The answer is that we want to respect the scope of variables. Modifying the environment changes the environment for all scopes, an undesired trait. In other words, if we mutate a variable binding in the existing environment, the variable's lifetime is extended to the entire program rather than to the scope in which it was declared. Instead, we *extend* the environment, which establishes a link between the current environment and the newly-declared environment. This way, we can look up variables in the current environment, and if they do not exist, we can look them up in

4.5 Abstract Classes

the parent environment. If the variable does not exist in the parent environment, we return a null value.

Environments, accordingly, contain two instance variables: a Map<String, AstNode> and a Environment parent pointer. Our environment class comprises two methods: lookup and extend.

The lookup method attempts to find a binding for the given variable identifier using the aforementioned approach. The extend method instantiates a new environment, whose parent is the current existing environment. This newly-instantiated environment, importantly, contains a new variable binding. Remember that the environment is a functional data structure, meaning that it is immutable.

```java
import static Assertions.assertAll;
import static Assertions.assertEquals;

class EnvironmentTester {

  @Test
  void testEnvironment() {
    Environment root = new Environment();
    Environment e1 = root.extend("x", new NumNode(5));
    Environment e2 = e1.extend("y", new NumNode(6));
    assertAll(
      () -> assertEquals(new NumNode(5), e2.lookup("x")),
      () -> assertEquals(new NumNode(6), e2.lookup("y")),
      () -> assertEquals(null, e2.lookup("z")));
  }
}
```

```java
import java.util.HashMap;
import java.util.Map;

final class Environment {

  private final Map<String, AstNode> ENV;
  private final Environment PARENT;

  Environment(Environment parent) {
    this.ENV = new HashMap<>();
    this.PARENT = parent;
  }

  Environment() { this(null); }

  AstNode lookup(String id) {
    if (this.ENV.containsKey(id)) { return this.ENV.get(id); }
    else if (this.PARENT != null) { return this.PARENT.lookup(id); }
    else { return null; }
  }

  Environment extend(String id, AstNode value) {
    Environment env = new Environment(this);
    env.ENV.put(id, value);
    return env;
  }
}
```

Now we can design the VarNode class. The apparent question is, "How do we evaluate a variable?" Using environments, we look up the variable identifier and return its associated abstract syntax tree. But, where does the environment come from? Environments are passed as an argument to the `eval` method, which means that all previously-existing `eval` methods must be updated to accept an environment as an argument.

Variable nodes, on their own, are simple yet relatively useless, and simply cannot exist without a means of introducing them into the environment context. This is where the LetNode class comes into play. The `LetNode` class introduces a new variable binding into the environment. A `LetNode` has two abstract syntax tree children: an expression and a body. The expression is evaluated and its value is bound to the provided variable identifier in an *extended environment* e_2, whose parent is the current environment e_1. The body of the LetNode is evaluated with respect to the extended environment, i.e., e_2.

```
import static Assertions.assertAll;
import static Assertions.assertEquals;

class AstTest {

  @Test
  void testLetNode() {
    Environment env = new Environment();
    assertAll(
      () -> assertEquals(new NumNode(42),
                         new LetNode("x",
                           new NumNode(42),
                           new VarNode("x")).eval(env)),
      () -> assertEquals(new NumNode(42),
                         new LetNode("x",
                           new NumNode(1),
                           new LetNode("y",
                             new NumNode(41),
                             new PrimNode("+",
                               new VarNode("x"),
                               new VarNode("y")))).eval(env)));
  }
}
```

```
final class VarNode extends AstNode {

  private final String NAME;

  VarNode(String name) {
    super();
    this.NAME = name;
  }

  @Override
  public String toString() {
    return this.NAME;
  }

  /**
   * Interpret a variable. We look up the variable in the environment and
   * return the value associated with it.
   * @param env the environment in which to interpret the variable.
   * @return The result of the variable lookup after interpretation.
   */
```

4.5 Abstract Classes

```
  @Override
  AstNode eval(Environment env) {
    String id = this.NAME;
    AstNode res = env.lookup(id);
    return res.eval(env);
  }

  String getName() {
    return this.NAME;
  }
}
```

```
final class LetNode extends AstNode {

  private final String ID;

  LetNode(String id, AstNode exp, AstNode body) {
    super(exp, body);
    this.ID = id;
  }

  @Override
  public String toString() {
    AstNode e = this.getChildren().get(0);
    AstNode b = this.getChildren().get(1);
    return String.format("(let ([%s %s]) %s)", this.ID, e, b);
  }

  /**
   * Interprets a let statement. The body is evaluated in the extended env.
   * The extended environment contains the binding introduced by the ID.
   * The identifier's binding expression "exp" is evaluated in "env".
   * @param env The environment to use for the let.
   * @return The result of the let statement.
   */
  @Override
  AstNode eval(Environment env) {
    String id = this.ID;
    AstNode exp = this.getChildren().get(0);
    AstNode body = this.getChildren().get(1);

    // Interpret the expression and convert it into its AST.
    AstNode newExp = exp.eval(env);
    Environment e1 = env.extend(id, newExp);
    return body.eval(e1);
  }
}
```

Finally, at long last, we can write some comprehensive tests! We will store each test in the InterpTester class, which polymorphically executes eval on the abstract syntax tree instances. All examples are initialized with an empty environment, because there are no (locally-declared) variable bindings at the start of a program. Unfortunately, we still have to write the programs as a series of compositional abstract syntax trees, but the problems of lexing and parsing raw string input into an abstract syntax tree are reserved for another time (or perhaps a separate course altogether).

```java
import static Assertions.assertAll;
import static Assertions.assertEquals;

class InterpTester {

  @Test
  void testEval() {
    assertAll(
      () -> assertEquals(new NumNode("42"),
                         new NumNode("42").eval(new Environment())),
      () -> assertEquals(new BoolNode(true),
                         new PrimNode("eq?",
                           new NumNode(42),
                           new PrimNode("-",
                            new NumNode(100),
                            new NumNode(58))).eval(new Environment())),
      () -> assertEquals(new NumNode("42"),
                         new LetNode("x",
                           new NumNode("42"),
                           new VarNode("x")).eval(new Environment())),
      () -> assertEquals(new NumNode("42"),
                         new LetNode("x", new NumNode("1"),
                         new LetNode("y", new NumNode("41"),
                           new PrimNode("+",
                            new VarNode("x"),
                            new VarNode("y")))).eval(new Environment())));
  }
}
```

Object-oriented programs with inheritance should be structured as a sequence of specific subclasses that extend an abstract class, as we have demonstrated with the different abstract syntax tree node types, and the root `AstNode` abstract class.

4.6 Exercises

4.1 Design the Car class, which stores a String representing the car's make, a String representing the car's model, and an int representing the car's year. Its constructor should receive these three values and store them in the instance variables. Be sure to write instance accessor and mutator methods for modifying all three fields. That is, you should write getMake(), setMake(String s), and so forth, to access and modify the fields directly.

4.2 Design the Dog class, which stores a String representing the breed, a String representing its name, and an int representing its age in years. You should also store a boolean to keep track of whether or not the dog is a puppy. A dog is a puppy if it is less than two years old. Its constructor should receive these three values and store them in the instance variables. Be sure to write instance accessor and mutator methods for modifying all three fields. That is, you should write getBreed(), setBreed(String s), and so forth, to access and modify the fields directly.

4.3 Design the Person class, which stores a String representing the person's first name, a String representing the person's last name, and an int representing the person's age in years. Its constructor should receive these three values and store them in the instance variables. Be sure to write instance accessor and mutator methods for modifying all three fields. That is, you should write getFirstName(), setFirstName(String s), and so forth, to access and modify the fields directly.

4.4 In this exercise you will design a class for storing employees. This relies on having the Employee class and its subclasses from the chapter available.

(a) Design the Job class, which stores a list of employees List<Employee> as an instance variable. Whether you choose to instantiate it as an ArrayList or a LinkedList is up to you and makes little difference for this particular question. Its constructor should receive no arguments. The instance variable, along with its accessor and mutator, should be named employees, getEmployees, and setEmployees respectively.
(b) Design the void addEmployee(Employee e) method, which adds an employee to the Job.
(c) Design the void removeEmployee(Employee e) method, which removes an employee from the Job.
(d) Design the Optional<Double> computeAverageSalary() method, which returns the average salary of all employees in the Job. If there are no employees, return an empty Optional.
(e) Design the Optional<Employee> highestPaid() method, which returns the employee whose salary is the highest of all employees in the Job. If there are no employees, return an empty Optional.
(f) Override the public String toString() method to print out the list of employees in the Job. To make this easy, you can simply invoke the toString method from the List implementation.

4.5 In this exercise you will design a simple music system, similar to Spotify.

(a) Design the Song class, which stores its title, artist, genre, and length. The first three fields are strings and the last is an integer. Create the accessor methods, then override equals, hashCode, and toString. You may choose how to override toString.

(b) Design the Playlist class, which stores the title of the playlist and a set of the songs in the list. In this class, create the accessor methods, then override equals, hashCode, and toString. Finally, design the boolean addSong(Song s) that attempts to add s to the set of songs. If it already exists, return false. Otherwise, add the song to the set and return true.

(c) Design the User class, which stores their name and a list of playlists. Its constructor should receive the name and assign it to the respective instance variable. Instantiate the list to a new ArrayList. Create the accessor methods, then override equals, hashCode, and toString.

   (i) Design the boolean createPlaylist(String t, Song... S) method, which receives a playlist title t and a variadic number of songs S, attempts to create a playlist with the title t. If it already exists, return false and do nothing else. Otherwise, declare a new Playlist to their list and add to it the given songs.

(d) Design the MusicSystem class, which stores a list of users and a set of all the songs in the system. In the constructor, instantiate these to an ArrayList and HashSet respectively.

   (i) Design the void addUser(User u) method that receives a user u and adds them to the list of users.
   (ii) Design the boolean addSong(User u, String t, Song s) method that, when given a user u, a playlist title t, and a song s, adds s to u's playlist with the title t. If u does not exist or t is not a title in a playlist authored by u, return false.
   (iii) Design the Map<User, Song> getLongestSong() method that returns the longest (length) song out of all the songs that a user has in their playlists. If the user has no playlists nor any songs in the playlists, do not add that user to the map.

4.6 In this exercise you will create two classes: Chocolate and ChocolateBox to store a two-dimensional array of chocolate pieces.

(a) Design the Chocolate class, which stores a string denoting its kind, and an integer representing its weight in ounces.

(b) Design the ChocolateBox class, which stores a Chocolate[][] array as an instance variable. Its constructor should receive the number of rows and columns of the box.

   (i) Design the int numberOfChocolates() method that returns the number of non-null instances of Chocolate that are in the ChocolateBox.
   (ii) Design the void shuffleChocolate() method, which randomizes the elements in the box. How you shuffle them is up to you, as long as it is a sufficient shuffle (and not just, for example, a linear shift of all chocolates).
   (iii) Design the int removeFirst(String kind) method, which removes the first occurrence, from the top, of the kind of chocolate. Removing a Chocolate means to assign the index to be null. Return what position was removed, assuming positions are numbered from 1 to n, ordered from left to right, then top to bottom (similar to a standard Gregorian calendar). If there are no kind of chocolates in the box, return -1.
   (iv) Design the ChocolateBox allergyBox(String kind) method, which returns a new ChocolateBox where all kind of chocolates are removed. If there are null spots in

between the chocolates of the old box, shift the chocolates over accordingly. Consider the following ChocolateBox:

Dark	White	Milk	Nut	Sweet
null	Nut	Dark	null	null
White	Sweet	Nut	null	Nut

Invoking allergyBox("Nut") on this box would return the following ChocolateBox:

Dark	White	Milk	Sweet	Dark
White	Sweet	null	null	null
null	null	null	null	null

4.7 In this exercise you will design a *linear congruential generator*: a pseudorandom number generation algorithm. In particular, the C programming language standard library defines two functions: rand and srand. The latter sets the *seed* for the generator, and rand returns a random integer between $[0, 2^{15})$. The formula for this generator is a recurrence relation:

$$next = |r_n \cdot 1103515245 + 12345|$$
$$r_{n+1} = \left(\frac{next}{2^{16}}\right) \% \ 2^{15};$$

(a) Design the LcgRandom class, which implements this behavior. In particular, it should have two constructors: one that receives a seed value s, and another that sets the seed to one. The seed initializes the value of r_0.
(b) Design the int genInt() method, which returns a random integer between 0 and 2^{15} using this algorithm.
(c) Design the IntStream stream() method, which returns a stream of random numbers that uses genInt to generate numbers. Hint: use generate!
(d) Design the genInt(int b) method that returns an integer between $[0, b]$. Note that $0 \le b < 2^{15}$; you do not need to account for values outside of this range. Do **not** simply loop until you find a value between that range; instead, use modulus to your advantage.

4.8 (⋆) This question has six parts.

(a) Design the `Matrix` class, which stores a two-dimensional array of integers. Its constructor should receive two integers m and n representing the number of rows and columns respectively, as well as a two-dimensional array of integers (you may assume that the number of rows and columns of the passed array are equal to m and n). Copy the integers from the passed array into an instance variable array. Do *not* simply assign the provided array to the instance variable!

(b) Design the `void set(int i, int j, int val)` method, which sets the value at row i and column j to val. If the row or column is out of bounds, do nothing.

(c) Design the `boolean add(Matrix m)` method, which adds the values of the passed matrix to the current matrix. If the dimensions of the passed matrix do not match the dimensions of the current matrix, return false and do not add the matrix.

(d) Design the `boolean multiply(Matrix m)` method, which multiplies the values of the passed matrix to the current matrix. If we cannot multiply m with this matrix, return false and do not multiply the matrix.

(e) Design the `void transpose()` method, which transposes the matrix. That is, the rows become the columns and the columns become the rows. You may need to alter the dimensions of the matrix.

(f) Design the `void rotate()` method, rotates the matrix 90 degrees clockwise. To rotate a matrix, compute the transposition and then reverse the rows. You may need to alter the dimensions of the matrix.

(g) Override the `public String toString()` method to return a stringified version of the matrix. As an example, `"[[1, 2, 3], [4, 5, 6]]"` represents the following matrix:

$$\begin{bmatrix} 1 & 2 & 3 \\ 4 & 5 & 6 \end{bmatrix}$$

4.9 This exercise has five parts.

(a) Design the `GameObject` class, which stores a `Pair<Double, Double>` denoting its center (x, y) position and a `Pair<Double, Double>` denoting its width and height respectively. Its constructor should receive four double values representing x, y, *width*, and *height*. Be sure to write instance accessor and mutator methods for modifying both fields. That is, you should write `double getLocationX()`, `void setLocationX(double d)`, and so forth, to access and modify the `Pair` values directly.

(b) Design the `boolean collidesWith(GameObject obj)` method that returns whether this `GameObject` collides with the parameter `obj`. You should design this solution as if the game objects are shaped like rectangles (which they are!).

(c) Design the `double distance(GameObject obj)` method that returns the Euclidean distance from the center of this `GameObject` to the center of the parameter `obj`.

(d) Design the `double move(double dx, double dy)` method that moves the object about the Cartesian (two-dimensional) plane. The distance should be a delta represented as two double numbers dx and dy that directly manipulate the object position. For instance, if dx is 3.0 and dy is −2.0 and the object is currently at <2.0, -9.0>, invoking `move(3.0, -2.0)` updates the object to be at <5.0, -11.0>.

(e) Override the `public String toString()` method to call the `toString` methods of the two instance variables, conjoined by a semicolon.

4.6 Exercises

4.10 This exercise has three parts.

(a) Design the `GameRunner` class, which stores a list of objects `List<GameObject>` as an instance variable. Its constructor should receive an integer representing a random number generator seed. It should first instantiate `rand` to a new `Random` object with this seed, and then populate the list with twenty random `GameObject` instances at random **integer** positions with random **integer** sizes. These random positions should be between $[-10, 10]$ for both coordinates and the random sizes should be between $[1, 10]$ for both dimensions.
(b) Design the `void moveObjects()` method, which moves each object by three positive x units and four negative y units.
(c) Design the `String stringifyObjects()` method, which converts each object in the list into its string representation, with brackets around the elements, and separated by commas. Hint: you can use one method from the `Stream` class to do this quickly!

4.11 This exercise involves the "Twenty-One" game implementation from the chapter.

(a) Change each card to use the Unicode symbol counterpart rather than the "X of Y" `toString` model, where X is the value and Y is the suit. The Unicode symbols are available on the second page of this PDF: https://www.unicode.org/charts/PDF/U1F0A0.pdf. This will be a little tedious, but it makes the game look cooler!
(b) Add the Ace, Jack, Queen, and King cards, instead of the previous implementation of using four cards whose values were all ten. A simple solution is to use a `String` that keeps track of the "name" of a card alongside the other instance variables.
(c) Add an AI to the game (you do not need to test this class). This involves writing the `AI` class and designing the `boolean play(Deck deck)` method. An AI has a `ArrayList<Card>`, similar to `Player`, but makes decisions autonomously using the following algorithm (written in a pseudocode-like language):

```
boolean play(Deck d) {
  score = getScore()
  if score < 16 then:
    cards.add(d.drawCard())
    return true;
  else if (score > 16 && score < 21) {
    k = Generate a random integer between [0, 3).
    if k is zero then:
      cards.add(d.drawCard())
      return true;
  }
  return false;
}
```

The method returns whether or not the AI drew a card. If they did not draw a card, then their turn is over. When playing the game, the player can see the first two cards dealt to an AI, but nothing more. You might want to add a static variable to the `Card` class representing the "covered card." Note that the AI knows only the context of its deck of cards; it is not aware of any other `Player` or `AI`.
(d) After designing the `AI` class and adding one to your game, create an `ArrayList<AI>` simulating multiple computer players in the game.

4.12 Design the `void set(T e, int idx)` method within the `MiniArrayList` class, which sets the element at *idx* to the given *e* element.

4.13 Design the `void isEmpty()` method within the `MiniArrayList` class, which returns whether or not the list is empty.

4.14 Design the `void clear()` method within the `MiniArrayList` class, which "removes" all elements from the list. This should not change the capacity of the list. Note that there's a reason why "removes" is in quotes. We rank this exercise as a two-star not because of its length, but because it is a little tricky.

4.15 Override the `public boolean equals(Object o)` method in the `MiniArrayList` class to compare two lists by their elements. Return `true` if all elements in the two lists are `equals` to one another, and `false` otherwise.

4.16 Using the `StackFrame` class, design an implementation of the tail recursive factorial method. Recall how to do this from Chapter 2: instead of pushing an activation record to the call stack, we can simply update the bindings in the existing frame.

4.17 This exercise has seven parts.

In this question you will design the `Time` class for working with units of time. Programming languages often support operations for handling dates and times to varying degrees of success. Java provides a few classes and methods of its own, and you cannot use these in your implementation, as that would defeat the point of the exercise.

(a) Design the `Time` class. It should contain three constructors that receive the following parameters:

- `Time(int h, int m, int s)` receives three integers h, m, and s represents times in hours, minutes, and seconds respectively.
- `Time(int s)` receives a single integer s representing the number of seconds.
- `Time(String t)` receives a string of the form `"hh:mm:ss"` with three components: hours, minutes, and seconds. The bounds on the time string are `00:00:00` and `23:59:59`.

However you choose to store the units of time is fine, as long as your class supports the remaining operations.

(b) Design the `int getNumberOfSeconds()` method, which returns the number of seconds that this `Time` object represents.

(c) Design the `int getNumberOfMinutes()` method, which returns the number of minutes that this `Time` object represents. If there are an inexact number of minutes, simply return the minutes. As an example, `new Time("02:30:45").getNumberOfMinutes()` returns 150 and not 151.

(d) Override the `public String toString()` method to return a stringified version of the time where the hours, minutes, and seconds are separated by colons. Single-digit units of time must contain a leading zero.

(e) Override the `public boolean equals(Object o)` method that returns whether a given `Time` object represents the same time as `this` instance.

(f) Design the `void addTime(Time t)` method that adds a given `Time` object to `this` instance. Take the following invocations as an example.

```
Time t1 = new Time("02:30:45");
Time t2 = new Time("11:45:18");
Time t3 = new Time("00:53:57");
t1.add(t2);
t1.toString(); => 14:16:03
```

```
t1.add(t3);
t1.toString(); => 15:00:00
```

(g) Design the `void increment(String u)` method, which receives a string u denoting the unit of time to increment. If u is not one of "HOUR", "MINUTE", or "SECOND", return `false`, and otherwise return `true`. Take the following invocations as examples. Remember to account for fringe cases, e.g., incrementing a unit that is about to roll-over to the next.

```
Time t1 = new Time("02:30:45");
t1.increment("HOUR");
t1.toString(); => "03:30:45"
t1.increment("MINUTE");
t1.toString(); => "03:31:45"
t1.increment("SECOND");
t1.toString(); => "03:31:46"
```

4.18 This exercise has six parts.

In this question you will implement the `MiniStack` data structure. This is similar to the `MiniArrayList` class from the chapter, but, of course, is a stack and not an array list.

Unlike many stack implementations, however, we will use an array-backed stack. This means that, instead of using a collection of `private` and `static` `Node` classes, the stack will use an array to store its elements. When the array runs out of space, a new one is allocated and the elements are copied over.

(a) First, design the generic `MiniStack` class. Its constructor should receive no arguments, and instantiate two instance variables: `T[] elements` and `size` to a new array and zero respectively. Remember that you cannot instantiate a generic array, so how do we do that? The initial capacity of the array should be set to `INITIAL_CAPACITY`, which is a `private static final` variable declared in the class as ten.

(b) Second, design the `void add(T t)` method, which adds an element onto the top of the stack. The "top of the stack," when using an array, is the right-most element, i.e., the element with the highest index. It might be a good idea to design a `private` helper method that resizes the underlying array when necessary. Your resize factor, i.e., how you resize the stack, is up to you.

(c) Third, design the `T peek()` method, which returns (but does not remove) the top-most element of the stack.

(d) Fourth, design the `T pop()` method, which returns *and* removes the top-most element. Be sure that your add method still works after designing pop.

(e) Fifth, design the `int size()` method, which returns the number of logical elements in the stack.

(f) Finally, override the `public String toString()` method to return a string containing the elements of the stack from top-to-bottom, separated by commas and a space. For example, if the stack contains, from bottom-to-top, 10, 20, 30, 40, and 50, the `toString` method returns "50, 40, 30, 20, 10".

4.19 (⋆) This exercise has seven parts.

A *chunked array list* data structure avoids the overhead of copying the underlying array upon running out of free spots. The idea is to break the collection into chunks, namely, as an ArrayList of arrays. Assuming that the underlying collection of chunks is adequately populated, this collection will seldom require a resizing operation. This data structure will not support arbitrary insertions or removals.

(a) Design the generic ChunkedArrayList class. It should store, as an instance variable, an ArrayList<T[]> of chunks, where T is the parameterized type. Design two constructors: one that receives a chunk size s and a number of preallocated chunks n, and another constructor that receives no parameters, defaulting n to 10 and s to 50.

(b) Design the void add(T t) method that, when given an item t, adds it to the end of the current chunk. If we run out of space in the current chunk, add it to the next chunk in succession. If there are no available chunks, add a new T[] of size s to the list. Hint: use modulus.

(c) Design the T get(int i) method that, when given an index i, returns the item at that index. The user of this data structure should not need to know about the chunks or their implementation. Therefore, if $s = 10$, and we access index 27, it should receive the element in chunk 3, index 7. Assume that i is in bounds.

(d) Design the void resizeChunks(int n) method that resizes each chunk to the input argument n. Depending on this value, you will need to either reallocate each underlying array or shift values around. For example, if we have a chunk array list with 150 elements whose chunks hold up to 50 elements each, and we resize the chunks to be 25 in maximum capacity, we will double the number of necessary chunks. On the other hand, if we resize the chunks to hold 100 elements, then the values in chunk two are shifted into chunk one, and those in chunk three are shifted into chunk two.

(e) Design the int getChunkCapacity() method that returns the maximum capacity of each chunk.

(f) Design the int size() method that returns the total number of elements in the chunk array list.

(g) Design the int getChunkSize() method that returns the number of chunks currently in-use.

4.20 (⋆) This exercise has seven parts.

A *persistent data structure* is one that saves intermittent data structures after applying operations that would otherwise alter the contents of the data structure. Take, for instance, a standard FIFO queue. When we invoke its 'enqueue' method, we modify the underlying data structure to now contain the new element. If this were a persistent queue, then enqueueing a new element would, instead, return a new queue that contains all elements and the newly-enqueued value, thereby leaving the original queue unchanged.

(a) First, design the generic, private, and static class Node inside a generic PQueue class skeleton. It should store, as instance variables, a pointer to its next element as well as its associated value.

(b) Then, design the PQueue class, which represents a persistent queue data structure. As instance variables, store "first" and "last" pointers as Node objects, as well as an integer to represent the number of existing elements. In the constructor, instantiate the pointers to null and the number of elements to zero.

(c) Design the private PQueue<T> copy() method that returns a new queue with the same elements as the current queue. You should divide this method into a case analysis: one where this queue is empty and another where it is not. In the former case, return a new queue with no elements. In the latter case, iterate over the elements of the queue, enqueuing each element into a new queue. You will need instantiate a new Node (reference) for each element.

(d) Design the PQueue<T> enqueue(T t) method that enqueues a value onto the end of a new queue containing all the old elements, in addition to the new value. You should use the copy method to your advantage.

(e) Design the PQueue<T> dequeue() method that removes the first element of the queue, returning a new queue without this first value. You should use the copy method to your advantage.

(f) Design the T peek() method that returns the first element of the queue.

(g) Design the static <T> PQueue<T> of(T... vals) method that creates a queue with the values passed as vals. Note that this must be a variadic method. Do not create a series of PQueue objects by enqueueing each element into a distinct queue; this is incredibly inefficient. Instead, allocate each Node one-by-one, thereby never calling enqueue.

(h) Design the int size() method that returns the number of elements in the queue. You should not traverse the queue to compute this value.

4.21 (⋆) This exercise has three parts.

A *deterministic finite state automaton* is an extremely primitive machine that represents transitions between the different states of a system. Think, as an example, of a light switch; there is an "OFF" state and an "ON" state, where flipping the switch flops between the two. The switch flip represents the input that causes a transition from one state to another. Programming languages most often use finite automata for character recognition, i.e., what characters are valid in the language grammar. The following is an example of a DFA diagram that accepts input strings that contain an odd number of 'a' characters from an input alphabet $\Sigma = \{a, b\}$.

(a) First, begin by designing the skeleton for the DFA class, which contains the following private and static class definitions:

- State, which stores a string identifier, an "isStart" boolean flag and an "isFinal" flag. The class should contain appropriate accessors but no mutators.
- Transition, which stores two State objects a and b representing the "from" and "to", as well as the required input to transition from a to b.

(b) The DFA constructor should be empty, and the class definition should store a Set<Transition> as well as a Set<State>.

(c) Design the void addState(State s) method, which adds a new State to the finite automaton.

(d) Design the State transition(State s, String i) method, which returns the state arrived after making the transition from s via input i.

(e) Finally, design the boolean accepts(String v) method, which receives an input string v and traverses over the automaton to determine if it accepts or rejects the input. We accept v if the last state we end on is marked as a final state.

4.22 ($\star$) A binary relation $\mathcal{R}$ is a subset of the cartesian product of two sets A and B. That is, $\mathcal{R} \subseteq A \times B$ such that $A \times B = \{\langle x, y \rangle \mid x \in A \text{ and } y \in B\}$. There are several ways that we can describe binary relations, including reflexive, symmetric, transitive, antisymmetric, asymmetric, irreflexive, and serial.

Design the generic `BinaryRelation<T, U>` class to represent a mathematical binary relation. It should store a `Set<Pair<String, String>>`, where the inner pair is the associated tuples of the set. Its constructor should instantiate the set instance variable.

Then, design the following methods:

(a) `void addTuple(T x, U y)` receives two values x and y of types T and U respectively, and adds them as a tuple to the underlying set.
(b) `boolean isReflexive()` returns true if the relation is reflexive. A relation $\mathcal{R}$ is reflexive if, for all $x \in S$, $\langle x, x \rangle \in \mathcal{R}$.
(c) `boolean isSymmetric()` returns true if the relation is symmetric. A relation $\mathcal{R}$ is symmetric if, for all $x, y \in S$, $\langle x, y \rangle \in \mathcal{R}$ and $\langle y, x \rangle \in \mathcal{R}$.
(d) `boolean isTransitive()` returns true if the relation is reflexive. A relation $\mathcal{R}$ is transitive if, for all $x, y, z \in S$, if $\langle x, y \rangle \in \mathcal{R}$ and $\langle y, z \rangle \in \mathcal{R}$, then $\langle x, z \rangle \in \mathcal{R}$.
(e) `boolean isEquivalence()` returns true if the relation is an equivalence relation. A relation $\mathcal{R}$ is an equivalence relation if it is reflexive, symmetric, and transitive.
(f) `boolean isIrreflexive()` returns true if the relation is irreflexive. A relation $\mathcal{R}$ is irreflexive if, for all $x \in S$, $\langle x, x \rangle \notin \mathcal{R}$.
(g) `boolean isAntisymmetric()` returns true if the relation is antisymmetric. A relation $\mathcal{R}$ is antisymmetric if, for all $x, y \in S$, if $\langle x, y \rangle \in \mathcal{R}$ and $\langle y, x \rangle \in \mathcal{R}$, then $x \neq y$.
(h) `boolean isAsymmetric()` returns true if the relation is asymmetric. A relation is asymmetric if it is both antisymmetric and irreflexive.
(i) `boolean isSerial()` returns true if the relation is serial. A relation $\mathcal{R}$ is serial if, for all $x \in S$, there exists a $y \in S$ such that $\langle x, y \rangle \in \mathcal{R}$.
(j) `Set<Pair<String, String>> reflexiveClosure()` returns a set representing the reflexive closure of a binary relation, which is $\mathcal{R} \cup r(\mathcal{R})$, where r returns a reflexive set over S.
(k) `Set<Pair<String, String>> isSymmetricClosure()` returns a set representing the symmetric closure of a binary relation, which is $\mathcal{R} \cup s(\mathcal{R})$, where r returns a symmetric set over S.
(l) `Set<Pair<String, String>> transitiveClosure()` returns a set representing the transitive closure of a binary relation, which is $\mathcal{R} \cup t(\mathcal{R})$, where t returns a transitive set over S.

As an added optimization, we should cache whether the current relation is one of these properties when prompted. If we do not add a pair to the relation, then it makes little sense to recompute whether or not is, say, reflexive. Implement this as an optimization, however you wish, into the class.

4.23 This exercise has five parts. Repeated string concatenation is a common performance issue in Java. As we know, Java String objects are immutable, which means that concatenation creates a new String objects. This is fine for small strings, but for larger strings (or concatenation operations performed in a loop), this can be a performance bottleneck. Each concatenation requires copying the entire string. Java provides the StringBuilder class to alleviate the issue. In this exercise, you will design a MiniStringBuilder class that mimics the behavior of StringBuilder. You cannot use StringBuilder or the older StringBuilder classes in your implementation.

(a) Design the MiniStringBuilder class, which stores a char[] as an instance variable. The class should also store a variable to keep track of the number of "logical characters" that are in-use by the buffer.
(b) Design two constructors for the MiniStringBuilder class: one that receives no arguments and initializes the default capacity of the underlying char[] array to 20, and another that receives a String s and initializes the char[] array to the characters of s.
(c) Design the void append(String s) method, which appends the given string s onto the end of the current string stored in the buffer. The given string should not simply be appended onto the end of the buffer, but rather added to the end of the previous string in the buffer. If the buffer runs out of space, reallocate the array to be twice its current size, similar to how we reallocate the array in the MiniArrayList example class.
(d) Design the void clear() method, which resets the char[] array to the default size of 20 and clears the character buffer.
(e) Override the public String toString() method, which returns the char[] array as a String object. The resulting string should contain only the logical characters in the buffer, and not the entire array. Output the characters without any additional characters, such as brackets or commas.

4.24 This exercise has twelve parts. A complex number $c \in \mathbb{C}$ has two components: a real number a and an imaginary number b. Together, these components compose into $a + bi$. In this exercise you will design a class that operates over complex numbers.

(a) Design the ComplexNumber class, whose constructor receives two double values: a and b. Store these as instance variables.
(b) Design the empty constructor that initializes a and b to 0 and 0 respectively.
(c) Implement the respective accessor and mutator methods for the real and imaginary components.
(d) Override the public String toString() method to return a string representation of the complex number of the form "a + bi" or "a - bi" when b is either positive or negative.
(e) Override the public boolean equals(Object o) method to compare two complex numbers. Of course, this entails comparing the real component and the imaginary component.
(f) Override the public int hashCode() method to return a hash code that hashes the a and b components respectively.
(g) Design the double magnitude() method, which returns the magnitude of this complex number. The magnitude of a complex number is the square root of the sum of its components.
(h) Design the double argument() method, which returns the argument, or angle, of this complex number in radians. The argument of a complex number is computed as $\tan^{-1} b/a$.
(i) Design the ComplexNumber conjugate() method, which returns the conjugate of this complex number. The conjugate of a complex number flips the parity of the imaginary component. That is, if we have a complex number $a + bi$, its conjugate is $a - bi$.

(j) Design the `ComplexNumber add(ComplexNumber c2)` method, which receives a ComplexNumber as an argument and returns a new `ComplexNumber` representing the sum of this complex number and the given number. The sum of two complex numbers is the sum of the real components and the imaginary components.
(k) Design the `ComplexNumber sub(ComplexNumber c2)` method, which receives a ComplexNumber as an argument and returns a new `ComplexNumber` representing the difference of this complex number and the given number. The difference of two complex numbers is the difference of the real components and the imaginary components.
(l) Design the `ComplexNumber mul(ComplexNumber c2)` method, which receives a ComplexNumber as an argument and returns a new `ComplexNumber` representing the product of this complex number and the given number. The product of two complex numbers is as follows:
$$(a + bi)(c + di) = (ac - bd) + (ad + bc)i$$
Hint: use `add` and `mul` to your advantage.

4.25 This exercise has 2 parts.

(a) Design the `Accumulator` class, which stores an instance variable of type `Number`. The Accumulator constructor receives a value of type `T` and stores it as an instance variable.
(b) Design the `apply` method, which receives a `Number` and adds it to the instance variable, then returns the instance variable. If `apply` has only received integers as arguments, then the result should be interpreted as an integer and not a floating-point value. We're recreating a challenge invented by Paul Graham called the "Accumulator Factory."
As an example, consider the following sequence.

```
Accumulator acc1 = new Accumulator(1);
acc1.apply(5);
acc1.apply(7);
assertEquals(13, acc1.apply(0));
assertEquals(15.3, acc1.apply(2.3));
```

4.26 This exercise has 3 parts.

The *Kotlin* programming language supports customized *ranges*. That is, we can define an interval using dot notation, e.g., `1..10`, then query a value over that interval. For instance, `x in 1..10` returns whether or not `x` is between 1 and 10, inclusive. This comparison, however, extends beyond primitive datatypes; ranges may operate over classes. For example, we can create a range `"hi".."howdy"`, which defines the range of strings in between `"hi"` and `"howdy"`.

(a) Design the generic `Range` class. It should store, as instance variables, a minimum and a maximum value, both of which are of type `<T extends Comparable<T>>`, meaning T must be a comparable type.
(b) The `Range` constructor should receive these two values as parameters and assign them to the instance variables accordingly.
(c) Design the `boolean contains(T v)` method that returns whether or not v is between the interval that this range operates over.

4.27 Design the generic static method `T validateInput(String prompt, String errResp, U extends Predicate<T> p)` that receives a prompt, an error response, and an object that implements the `Predicate` interface to test whether or not the received value,

4.6 Exercises

received through standard input, is valid. If the value is invalid according to the predicate, print the error response and re-prompt the user. Otherwise, return the entered value.

4.28 This exercise has three parts. In this exercise, you'll be developing a `Document` interface along with its implementing classes:

- `TextDocument`
- `SpreadsheetDocument`
- `PresentationDocument`

The `Document` interface is defined as follows:

```
interface Document {

  /**
   * Returns the number of pages in this document.
   */
  int numberOfPages();

  /**
   * Returns a string representing that the Document
   * is being printed.
   */
  default String print() {
    return "Printing the document!";
  }
}
```

Notice that we have a `default` method, which is one that an implementing class does **not** have to implement. It provides "default" functionality, should the "implementee" not want to implement the method (hence the name!).

(a) Implement the other three classes with the following specifications:

- A `TextDocument` consists of 100 pages. When it is printed, it should return a message `"Printing text document!"`.
- A `SpreadsheetDocument` has 50 pages. When it is printed, it should return a message `"Printing spreadsheet document!"`.
- A `PresentationDocument` contains 20 pages. It utilizes the default implementation of the `print` method.

(b) Design the `PrintingOffice` class, which includes the following static method: `static OptionalDouble avgPages(List<Document> lodocs)`. This method calculates and returns the average number of pages across the provided list of `Document` objects. Remember why we use `Optional`: if there are no `Document` objects in the list, we would be dividing by zero if we took the average!

(c) Inside the `PrintingOffice` class, modify it to include the `static void printDocuments(List<Document> documents)` method, responsible for invoking the `print` method on each object in the list of `Document` instances.

4.29 This exercise has three parts.

(a) Design the `INumberFormat` interface, which contains the `String format(int n)` method.
(b) Design the `DollarFormat` method, which implements `INumberFormat`, and returns a string where the number is prepended with a dollar sign `"$"`.
(c) Design the `CommaFormat` method, which implements `INumberFormat`, and returns a string where the number contains commas where appropriate. For example, `format(4412)` should return `"4,412"`.

4.30 (⋆) In the chapter, we described the `PizzaOrder` class. This exercise introduces readers to the visitor design pattern, which we explore in greater detail in Chapter 8.

(a) First, design the `GroupOrder` class, which keeps track of multiple pizzas in an order. Store a `Queue<PizzaOrder>` as an instance variable and instantiate it to a `PriorityQueue`. The `GroupObject` constructor should receive a `Comparator<PizzaOrder>`. Pass this to the `PriorityQueue` instantiation.
(b) Design the `ITopping` interface, which represents a topping. For now, it contains no methods. Then, design four classes: `Pepperoni`, `Onion`, `Pineapple`, and `Anchovie`, all of which implement `ITopping`.
(c) Now, let's design a class that allows us to do multiple actions with toppings. Design the generic `IToppingVisitor` class, which has four methods: `T visit(Pepperoni p)`, `T visit(Onion o)`, `T visit(Pineapple p)`, and `T visit(Anchovie a)`.
(d) Design the `ToppingPriceVisitor` class, which implements the interface `IToppingVisitor`, whose type parameter is a `Double`. The idea is that the `ToppingPriceVisitor` class serves as a way of associating a property with toppings without having to modify/amend the class definitions. Override the four methods to return 3.50, 2.50, 5.75, and 4.00 respectively.
(e) Modify the `PizzaOrder` class to have its map instance variable associate `ITopping` objects to `Integer`, rather than `String` to `Integer`.
(f) Amend the `ITopping` interface to now supply the `<T> T visit(IToppingVisitor<T> v)` method. Its subtypes should override `visit` by defining it as a call to `v.visit(this)`, where `v` is the visitor object parameter.
(g) Finally, design the `PizzaOrderPriceComparator` class, which implements `Comparator<PizzaOrder>`, and compares pizzas based on the price of its toppings. Pizzas with a higher cost are prioritized over pizzas with a lower cost.

4.31 (⋆) A *lazy list* is one that, in theory, produces infinite results! Consider the `ILazyList` interface below:

```
interface ILazyList<T> {
  T next();
}
```

When calling `next` on a lazy list, we update the contents of the lazy list and return the next result. We mark this as a generic interface to allow for any desired return type. For instance, below is a lazy list that produces factorial values:[33]

---

[33] We will ignore the intricacies that come with Java's implementation of the `int` datatype. To make this truly infinite (up to the system's memory limit), we could use `BigInteger`.

4.6 Exercises

```
class FactorialLazyList implements ILazyList<Integer> {

  private int n;
  private int fact;

  FactorialLazyList() {
    this.n = 1;
    this.fact = 1;
  }

  @Override
  public Integer next() {
    this.fact *= this.n;
    this.n++;
    return this.fact;
  }
}
```

Testing it with ten calls to next yields predictable results.

```
import static Assertions.assertAll;
import static Assertions.assertEquals;

class FactorialLazyListTester {

  @Test
  void testFactorialLazyList() {
    ILazyList<Integer> FS = new FactorialLazyList();
    assertAll(
      () -> assertEquals(1, FS.next()),
      () -> assertEquals(2, FS.next()),
      () -> assertEquals(6, FS.next()),
      () -> assertEquals(24, FS.next()),
      () -> assertEquals(120, FS.next()));
  }
}
```

Design the FibonacciLazyList class, which implements ILazyList<Integer> and correctly overrides next to produce Fibonacci sequence values. You code should *not* use any loops or recursion. Recall that the Fibonacci sequence is defined as $f(n) = f(n-1) + f(n-2)$ for all $n \geq 2$. The base cases are $f(0) = 0$ and $f(1) = 1$.

```
import static Assertions.assertAll;
import static Assertions.assertEquals;

class FibonacciLazyListTester {

  @Test
  void testFibonacciLazyList() {
    ILazyList<Integer> FS = new FibonacciLazyList();
    assertAll(
      () -> assertEquals(0, FS.next()),
      () -> assertEquals(1, FS.next()),
      () -> assertEquals(1, FS.next()),
      () -> assertEquals(2, FS.next()),
      () -> assertEquals(3, FS.next()),
      () -> assertEquals(5, FS.next()));
  }
}
```

4.32 Design the `LazyListTake` class. Its constructor should receive an `ILazyList` and an integer n denoting how many elements to take, as parameters. Then, write a `List<T> getList()` method, which returns a `List<T>` of n elements from the given lazy list.

```
import static Assertions.assertAll;
import static Assertions.assertEquals;

class LazyListTakeTester {

  @Test
  void testLazyListTake() {
    LazyListTake llt1 = new LazyListTake(new FactorialLazyList(), 8);
    LazyListTake llt2 = new LazyListTake(new FibonacciLazyList(), 10);

    assertAll(
      () -> assertEquals("[1, 2, 6, 24, 120, 720, 5040, 40320]",
                         llt1.getList().toString()),
      () -> assertEquals("[0, 1, 1, 2, 3, 5, 8, 13, 21, 34]",
                         llt2.getList().toString()));
  }
}
```

4.33 Java's functional API allows us to pass lambda expressions as arguments to other methods, as well as method references (as we saw in Chapter 3). Design the generic `FunctionalLazyList` class to implement `ILazyList`, whose constructor receives a unary function `Function<T, T> f` and an initial value `T t`. Then, override the next method to invoke f on the current element of the lazy list and return the previous. For example, the following test case shows the expected results when creating a lazy list of infinite positive multiples of three.

```
import static Assertions.assertEquals;
import static Assertions.assertAll;

class FunctionalLazyListTester {

  @Test
  void testMultiplesOfThreeLazyList() {
    ILazyList<Integer> mtll = new FunctionalLazyList<>(x -> x + 3, 0);
    assertAll(
      () -> assertEquals(0, mtll.next()),
      () -> assertEquals(3, mtll.next()),
      () -> assertEquals(6, mtll.next()),
      () -> assertEquals(9, mtll.next()),
      () -> assertEquals(12, mtll.next()));
  }
}
```

What's awesome about this exercise is that it allows us to define the elements of the lazy list as any arbitrary lambda expression, meaning that we could redefine `FactorialLazyList` and `FibonacciLazyList` in terms of `FunctionLazyList`. We can generate infinitely many ones, squares, triples, or whatever else we desire.

4.34 Design the generic `CyclicLazyList` class, which implements `ILazyList`, whose constructor is variadic and receives any number of values. Upon calling next, the cyclic lazy list should return the first item received from the constructor, then the second, and so forth until reaching the end. After returning all the values, cycle back to the front and continue. For

4.6 Exercises

instance, if we invoke new `CyclicLazyList<Integer>(1, 2, 3)`, invoking .next five times will produce 1, 2, 3, 1, 2.

4.35 (⋆) In this exercise you will design a simple particle system manager. A *particle system* is a data structure that manages particles, or small effects, in a graphical engine. Think of a video game that has smoke, fire, water, explosion, or other kinds of effects. In general, these all use particle engines for managing hundreds of thousands of particle objects. Therefore, such an engine should be efficient.

(a) In the first part of this exercise, you will design the `Particle` class.

  (i) A `Particle` contains a `double x` and `double y` representing its position, a `double width` and `double height` representing its dimensions, and a `double dx` and `double dy` representing its velocity. Finally, it contains a `double life` representing its life. The constructor should receive these as parameters and assign them to the instance variables.

  (ii) Inside the `Particle` class, design the `update` method, which adds the particle's velocity to its position. It should also decrement the `life` instance variable by one. If `life` ever becomes zero or negative, the particle is no longer alive. If the particle *isn't* alive, do not update its position (nor decrement its life).

  (iii) Design the `isAlive` method that returns whether or not the particle is alive.

(b) Now, you will design the `ParticleSystem` class for efficiently managing multiple particle instances. The idea behind this particle system is that we create a *memory pool*, and poll already-allocated particles from it when available. That is, when a particle dies, it moves to the "dead" sector, but that memory still exists. Then, when we want to create a new `Particle`, we first check to see if there are any dead particles that we can reuse. If so, we reuse that particle's allocated memory and simply reassign variables.

  (i) In the `ParticleSystem` class, store the following instance variables and instantiate them as `LinkedList` instances in the constructor. The constructor should also receive a value `maxAlive`, which is assigned to a `final int MAX_ALIVE` instance variable.
      - `List<Particle> alive`, which stores the alive particles in the system. All particles in this list should be non-null.
      - `List<Particle> dead`, which stores the dead particles in the system. All particles in this list should be non-null.

  (ii) Design the `boolean addParticle(double x, double y, double w, double h, double dx, double dy, double life)` method that adds a particle to the system with the given parameters. If there are no dead particles available, then simply allocate a new `Particle` onto the rear of the `alive` list. If there is a dead particle, use that allocated space instead and assign the parameters to the object using the respective setters. Then, move the particle out of the `dead` list and onto the rear of the `alive` list. If it is impossible to add a new particle (because there is no space for more alive particles), return `false`. Otherwise, return `true`.

  (iii) Design the `void updateSystem()` method that traverses over the alive particles, and invokes their `update` methods. After invoking a particle's `update` method, check to see if it is alive or not. If it is not alive, move it out of the `alive` list and into the dead list.

(c) In the final part of this exercise, you will design two subclass particles.

   (i) Design the SparkParticle class, which inherits from Particle. "Spark particles" move in a straight line, but their velocity decreases over time due to air resistance until they stop moving.
   - The SparkParticle constructor receives the same values as its superclass counterpart.
   - Override the update method to decrease the vertical and horizontal velocities by 10% with each call to update. Do *not* call super.update(). Instead, update the position of the particle directly inside this class. Remember that those variables are private in the Particle class.
   - Override the isAlive method to return false when its horizontal and vertical velocity values are both less than 0.01 away from zero. Otherwise, it should return true.

   (ii) Design the SmokeParticle class, which inherits from Particle. "Smoke particles" move in a straight line, but their velocity decreases over time due to air resistance until they stop moving.
   - The SmokeParticle constructor receives the same values as its superclass counterpart.
   - Override the update method to increase the width and height dimensions by 2% with each call to update. Do *not* call super.update(). Instead, update the position of the particle directly inside this class (the behavior is the same as the Particle superclass). Remember that those variables are private in the Particle class. Finally, decrement the life by 0.2 rather than 1.

4.36 Design the static <T> Predicate<T> orEq(Predicate<T> p, T x) method that, when given a predicate p and an object x, returns a *new* predicate that returns true if its argument x' is equal (using equals) to x or satisfies $p(x)$.

4.37 Design the static <T> List<T> predOrEq(List<T> ls, Predicate<T> p, BiFunction<T, T, Boolean>, T x) method that, when given a list of values ls, a predicate p, a function f, and a value x that returns the list of values in ls that either satisfy p or are equal according to f. For the purposes of this question, f is a method of two arguments of type T that determines whether or not they are "equal" according to some criteria.

4.38 Design the static <T> boolean andMap(List<T> l, Predicate<T> p) method that returns whether or not all elements of the input list satisfy the given predicate. Use the stream API to solve this problem, but do *not* use the allMatch method, as that method solves the problem we want *you* to solve!

4.39 Design the static <T, U> U foldr(List<T> ls, BiFunction<T, U, U> f, U u) method that receives a list of values ls, a function f, and an initial value u. The method should return the result of folding the list from the right with the given function and initial value. By "folding," we mean that we apply f to the last element of the list and the initial value, then apply f to the second-to-last element and the result of the previous application, and so forth. To think of this in terms of infix notation over some list, consider the list $[a, b, c, d]$. Folding it over the function $\circ$ and initial value u is $a \circ (b \circ (c \circ (d \circ u)))$. Do *not* use the reduce method, as that method solves the problem we want *you* to solve!

4.40 Design the static <T, U> List<U> buildList(int n, Function<T, U> func) method that receives an integer n and a function f and returns a list of n elements, where the ith

element is $f(i)$. For example, if we invoke buildList(6, x -> x * x), we should receive the list $[0, 1, 4, 9, 16, 25]$.

4.41 This exercise involves the doubly-linked list we wrote in the chapter. Design the int size() method, which returns the number of elements in the list. You can do this either recursively or with a loop. For better practice, try (and thoroughly test) both implementations.

4.42 This exercise involves the doubly-linked list we wrote in the chapter. Design the void set(int i, T v) method, which overwrites/assigns, at index i, the value v. If the provided index is out-of-bounds, do nothing.

4.43 This exercise involves the doubly-linked list we wrote in the chapter. Design the void insert(int i, T v) method, which inserts the value v at index i. As an example, if we insert 4 into the list $[20, 5, 100, 25]$ at index 2, the list then becomes $[20, 5, 4, 100, 25]$. If the provided index is out-of-bounds, do nothing.

4.44 This exercise involves the interpreter we wrote in the chapter. Our interpreter, so far, is very memory inefficient. The reason is not apparent at first glance, but consider every time that we create a NumberNode or, especially, a BooleanNode. There are only two possibilities for a BooleanNode: true and false, which are immutable by design. So, the interpreter should never waste time allocating an instance thereof when it can simply reference an existing one. Such an optimization follows the "factory" design pattern, which we will explore in Chapter 8.

Privatize the BooleanNode constructor, then design the static BooleanNode of(boolean b) method. It receives a boolean value v and returns a reference to a pre-allocated static true or false node. Similarly, also privatize the NumberNode constructor and design the static NumberNode of(double v) method. This method returns a new NumberNode if the given value v is not an integer between $[0, 1000)$. Otherwise, pre-cache those integer values and store them in a private lookup table.

4.45 This exercise involves the interpreter we wrote in the chapter. Add the "read-number" and "print" primitive operations to the language. The latter is polymorphic, meaning it can print both numbers and booleans.

4.46 This exercise involves the interpreter we wrote in the chapter. Functional programming languages, in general, are a composition of expressions, wherein statements are more of an afterthought. To this end, design the BeginNode abstract syntax tree node, which receives a list of abstract syntax trees. At the interpreter level, the BeginNode should evaluate each of the abstract syntax trees in the list, and return the result of the last one.

4.47 This exercise involves the interpreter we wrote in the chapter. Variables, in our language, are defined and bound exactly once, namely when they are defined within a let node. Though, in imperative programming, it is often crucial to allow variable reassignments. Design the SetNode class, which receives a variable and an abstract syntax tree, and reassigns the variable to the result of the abstract syntax tree. At the interpreter level, the SetNode should evaluate the abstract syntax tree, and reassign the variable to the result in the current environment (and only the current environment). This means that you'll need to modify the Environment class to allow for variable reassignments. Hint: create a set method in the Environment class.

4.48 This exercise involves the interpreter we wrote in the chapter. Recursion is nice and intuitive, for the most part. Unfortunately, it is not always the most efficient way to solve a problem. For example, the Fibonacci sequence, as we saw in Chapter 2, is often defined recursively, but it is much more efficient to define it iteratively (or even with tail recursion). Design the WhileNode class, which receives a condition and an abstract syntax tree, and evaluates the abstract syntax tree until the condition is false. At the interpreter level, the WhileNode should evaluate the condition, and if it is true, evaluate the abstract syntax tree, and repeat until the condition is false. To test your implementation, you will need to combine the WhileNode with both the SetNode and BeginNode classes.

4.49 (⋆) This exercise involves the interpreter we wrote in the chapter. Having to manually update our case analysis on the primitive operator type is cumbersome and prone to mistakes. A better solution would be to store the operator and its corresponding "handler" method, i.e., the method that receives the operands and does the logic of the operator. We can do this via a map where the keys are the string operators and the values are functional references to the handlers. Unfortunately, Java does not directly support passing methods as parameters, meaning they are not first-class. Conversely, we can make use of Java's functional interfaces to achieve our goal. Namely, the interface will contain one method: AstNode apply(List<AstNode> args, Environment env), where args is the list of evaluated arguments. We will call the interface IFunction and make it generic, with the first type quantified to a list of AstNode instances, and the second type quantified to AstNode. Hopefully, the connection between these quantified types and the signature of apply is apparent. Using the below definition of IFunction, update PrimNode to no longer perform a case analysis in favor of the map. We provide an example of populating the map with the initial operators in a static block.

```
@FunctionalInterface
interface IFunction<T, R> {

  R apply(T t);
}
```

```
import java.util.List;
import java.util.Map;
import java.util.HashMap;

class PrimNode extends AstNode {

  private static final Map<String, IFunction<List<AstNode>, AstNode>> OPS;

  static {
    OPS = new HashMap<>();
    OPS.put("+", this.primPlus);
  }

  @Override
  AstNode eval(Environment env) { /* TODO. */ }

  private AstNode primPlus(List<AstNode> args, Environment env) { /* ... */ }
}
```

4.6 Exercises

4.50 (⋆) This exercise is multi-part and involves the interpreter we wrote in the chapter.

(a) First, design the `ProgramNode` class, which allows the user to define a program as a sequence of statements rather than a single expression.

(b) Design the `DefNode` class, which allows the user to create a global definition. Because we're now working with definitions that do not extend the environment, we should use the set method in environment. When creating a global definition via `DefNode`, we're expressing the idea that, from that point forward, the (root) environment should contain a binding from the identifier to whatever value it binds.

(c) Design the `FuncNode` node. We will consider a function definition as an abstract tree node that begins with `FuncNode`. This node has two parameters to its constructor: a list of parameter (string) identifiers, and a single abstract syntax tree node representing the body of the function. We will only consider functions that return values; void functions do not exist in this language.

(d) Design the `ApplyNode` class, which applies a function to its arguments. You do not need to consider applications in which the first argument is a non-function.

Calling/Invoking a function is perhaps the hardest part of this exercise. Here's the idea, which is synonymous and shared with almost all programming languages:

   (i) First, evaluate each argument of the function call. This will result in several evaluated abstract syntax trees, which should be stored in a list.

   (ii) We then want to create an environment in which the formal parameters are bound to their arguments. Overload the extend method in `Environment` to now receive a list of string identifiers and a list of (evaluated) AST arguments. Bind each formal to its corresponding AST, and return the extended environment.

   (iii) Evaluate the function abstract syntax tree to get its function definition as an abstract syntax tree.

   (iv) Call eval on the function body and pass the new (extended) environment.

This seems like a lot of work (because it is), but it means you can write really cool programs, including those that use recursion!

```
new ProgramNode(
    new DefNode("!",
      new FuncNode(
        List.of("n"),
        new IfNode(
          new PrimNode("eq?",
            new VarNode("n"),
            new NumNode(0)),
          new NumNode(1),
          new PrimNode("*",
            new VarNode("n"),
            new ApplyNode("!",
              new PrimNode("-",
                new VarNode("n"),
                new NumNode(1))))))),
    new ApplyNode("!", new NumNode(5)))
```

4.51 This exercise involves the interpreter we wrote in the chapter, and relies on the addition of `FuncNode` and `ApplyNode`. Our current version of the interpreter uses *dynamic scoping*. A dynamically-scoped interpreter is one that uses the value of the closest declaration of a variable. This seems like nonsense without an example, so consider the following code listing.

```
(define f
  (let ([x 10])
    (λ ()
      x)))

(let ([x 3])
  (f))
```

Under dynamic scoping, this program outputs 3, because the binding of x takes on the value 3. On the other hand, if we were using a *lexically-scoped* interpreter, the program would output 10, which seems to make more sense due to the binding that exists immediately above the function declaration. The question is: how do we implement lexical scoping into our interpreter? The answer is via *closures*, which are data structures that couple a function definition with an environment. Then, when we apply a closure to an argument (if it exists), we restore the environment that was captured by the closure.

To this end, design the `ClosureNode` class, whose constructor receives a `FuncNode` and an `Environment`. The respective `eval` method returns `this`, but `FuncNode` changes slightly. Rather than returning `this`, we return a `ClosureNode`, which wraps the current `FuncNode` and the environment passed to `eval`. Finally, inside `ApplyNode`, evaluating the function definition should resolve to a closure. Evaluate the arguments to the closure inside the passed environment, but *extend* the captured environment, and bind the formals to the arguments in this extended environment. The body of the closure's function definition is then evaluated inside this new environment.

Making this alteration not only causes our programs to output the "common sense" result, but also means we can implement recursive functions using *only* a `LetNode`. See if you can figure out how to do this!

4.52 (⋆) This exercise involves the interpreter we wrote in the chapter. Data structures are a core and fundamental feature of programming languages. A language without them, or at least one to build others on top of, suffers severely in terms of usability. We will implement a *cons*-like data structure for our interpreter. In functional programming, we often use three operations to act on data structures akin to linked lists: *cons*, *first*, and *rest*, to construct a new list, retrieve the first element, and retrieve the rest of the list respectively. We can inductively define a cons list as follows:

```
A ConsList is one of:
- new ConsList()
- new ConsList(x, ConsList)
```

Implement the cons data structure into your interpreter. This should involve designing the `ConsNode` class that conforms to the aforementioned data definition. Moreover, you will need to update `PrimNode` to account for the `first` and `rest` primitive operations, as well as an `empty?` predicate, which returns whether or not the cons list is empty. Finally, override `toString` inside `ConsNode`, which amounts to printing each element, separated by spaces, inside of brackets, e.g., $[l_0, l_1, \ldots, l_{n-1}]$.

4.6 Exercises

4.53 This exercise involves the interpreter we wrote in the chapter. Having to manually type out the abstract syntax tree constructors when writing tests is extremely tedious. Design a *lexer* for the language described by the interpreter. That is, the text is broken up into tokens that are then categorized. For example, '(' might become OPEN_PAREN, "lambda" might become SYMBOL, "variable-name" might become SYMBOL, and 123.45 might become NUMBER. The output of the lexer is a list of tokens. Part of the trick is to ensure that after reading an open parenthesis, the next token is not grabbed as part of the open parenthesis.

4.54 (⋆) This exercise involves the interpreter we wrote in the chapter. Design a parser for the language described by the interpreter. The idea is to tokenize a raw string, then parse the tokens to create an abstract syntax tree that represents the program. A good starting point would be to parse *all* parenthesized expressions into what we will call SExprNode, then traverse over the tree to "correct" them into their true nodes, e.g., whether they are IfNode, LetNode, and so forth. Realistically, all programs in our language are, at their core, either primitive values or s-expressions.

4.55 This exercise involves the interpreter we wrote in the chapter. The Scheme programming language and its derivatives support *code quotation*, i.e., the ability to convert an evaluable expression into data. As an example, if we evaluate new QuoteNode(new VarNode("x")), we receive a symbol as the output, rather than the evaluated symbol via environment lookup. Add the QuoteNode class to your interpreter.

4.56 (⋆) In Chapter 2, we discussed tail recursion and an action performed by some programming languages known as tail-call optimization. We know that we can convert any (tail) recursive algorithm into one that uses a loop, and we described said process in the chapter. There is yet another approach that we can mimic in Java with a bit of trickery and interfaces.

The problem with tail recursion (and recursion in general) in Java is the fact that it does not convert tail calls into iteration, which means the stack quickly overflows with activation records. We can make use of a *trampoline* to force the recursion into iteration through *thunks*. In essence, we have a tail recursive method that returns either a value or makes a tail recursive call, such as the factorial example below. Inside our base case, we invoke the done method with the accumulator value. Otherwise, we invoke the call method containing a lambda expression of no arguments, whose right-hand side is a recursive call to factTR. Functions, or lambda expressions, that receive no arguments are called thunks.

```
import static Assertions.assertEquals;
import static Assertions.assertDoesNotThrow;
import java.lang.BigInteger;
import java.lang.StackOverflowError;

class FactorialTailRecursiveTester {

  @Test
  void testFactTailRecursiveTrampoline() {
    assertEquals(BigInteger.valueOf(120),
                 factTailCall(BigInteger.valueOf(5), BigInteger.ONE));
    assertDoesNotThrow(StackOverflowError.class,
                       factTailCall(BigInteger.valueOf(50000),
                                    BigInteger.ONE));
  }
}
```

```java
import java.lang.BigInteger;

class FactorialTailRecursive {

  /**
   * Tail-recursive factorial function. Uses BigInteger to
   * avoid number overflow and thunks to avoid stack overflow.
   * @param n the number to compute the factorial of.
   * @param ac the accumulator.
   * @return a tail call that is either done or not done.
   */
  static ITailCall<BigInteger> factTailCall(BigInteger n, BigInteger ac) {
    if (n.equals(BigInteger.ZERO)) {
      return TailCallUtils.done(ac);
    } else {
      return TailCallUtils.call(() ->
              factTailCall(n.subtract(BigInteger.ONE), ac.multiply(n)));
    }
  }
}
```

The idea is that we have a helper class and method, namely `invoke`, that continuously applies the thunks, **inside a while loop**, until the computation is done. The trampoline analogy is used because we bounce on the trampoline while invoking thunks and jump off when we are "done."

First, design the generic `ITailCall<T>` interface. It should contain only one (non-default) method: `ITailCall<T> apply()`, which is necessary for the `invoke` method. The remaining methods are all default, meaning they must have a body. Design the `boolean isDone()` method to always return false. Design the `T getValue()` method to simply return `null`. Finally, design the `T invoke()` method that stores a local variable and constantly calls `apply` on itself until it is "done."

Second, design the `TailCallUtils` final class to contain a private constructor (this class will only utilize and define two static methods). The two methods are as follows:

- `static <T> ITailCall<T> call(ITailCall next)`, which receives and returns the next tail call to apply. This definition should be exactly one line long and as simple as it seems.
- `static <T> ITailCall<T> done(T val)`, which receives the value to return from the trampoline. We need to create an instance of an interface, which sounds bizarre, but is possible only when we provide an implementation of its methods. So, return a new `ITailCall<>()`, and inside its body, override the `isDone` and `getValue` methods with the correct bodies.

Finally, run the factorial test that we provided earlier in its JUnit suite. It should pass and not stack overflow, hence the inclusion of an `assertDoesNotThrow` call.

4.6 Exercises

4.57 (⋆) In this series of problems, you will design several methods that act on very large/small *integers* resembling the BigInteger class. You **cannot** use any methods from BigInteger, or the BigInteger class itself.

(a) Design the BigInt class, which has a constructor that receives a string. The BigInt class stores a List<Integer> as an instance variable, as well as a boolean for keeping track of whether it is negative. You will need to convert the given string into said list of digits. Store the digits in reverse order, i.e., the least-significant digit (the ones digit) of the number is the first element of the list. Leading zeroes should be omitted from the representation.

The possible values for the parameter are an optional sign (either positive **or** negative), followed by one or more digits.

Below are some example inputs.

```
new BigInt("42")         => [2, 4], isNegative = false
new BigInt("0420")       => [0, 2, 4], isNegative = false
new BigInt("-42")        => [2, 4], isNegative = true
new BigInt(0000420000)   => [0, 0, 0, 0, 2, 4], isNegative = false
new BigInt("+42")        => [2, 4], isNegative = false;
```

(b) Override the public boolean equals(Object o) method to return whether this instance represents the same integer as the parameter. If o is not an instance of BigInt, return false.

```
new BigInt("42").equals(new BigInt("42"))       => true
new BigInt("00042").equals(new BigInt("0042"))  => true
new BigInt("+42").equals(new BigInt("42"))      => true
new BigInt("42").equals(new BigInt("-42"))      => false
new BigInt("-42").equals(new BigInt("-42"))     => false
new BigInt("422").equals(new BigInt("420"))     => false
```

(c) Override the public String toString() method to return a stringified version of the number. Remember to include the negative sign where appropriate. If the number is positive, you do not need to include it.

(d) Implement the Comparable<BigInt> interface and override the method it provides, namely public int compareTo(BigInt b2). Return the result of comparing this instance with the parameter. That is, if $a < b$, return -1, if $a > b$, return 1, and otherwise return 0, where a is this and b is b2.

(e) Design the BigInt copy() method, which returns a (deep)-copy of instance representing the same integer as this instance of BigInt. Do *not* simply copy the reference to the list of digits over to the new BigInt (this violates the aliasing principle that we have repeatedly discussed and can be the cause of relentless debugging).

(f) Design the BigInt negate() method, which returns a copy of this instance of BigInt, but negated. Do *not* modify this instance.

(g) Design the private boolean areDifferentSigns(BigInt b) method, which returns whether this instance and b have different signs. That is, if one is positive and one is negative, areDifferentSigns returns true, and false otherwise.

(h) Design the private BigInt addPositive(BigInt b) method, which returns a BigInt instance that is the sum of this and b under the assumption that this and b are non-negative. *Be sure you thoroughly test this method!*

(i) Design the private BigInt subPositive(BigInt b) method, which returns a BigInt instance that is the difference of this and b under the assumption that this and b are non-negative, and the minuend (the left-hand operand) is greater than or equal to the subtrahend (the right-hand operand). *Be sure you thoroughly test this method!*

(j) Design the `private BigInt mulPositive()` method, which returns a `BigInt` instance that is the product of `this` and `b` under the assumption that `this` and `b` are non-negative. *Be sure you thoroughly test this method!*

(k) Design the `BigInt add(BigInt b)` and `BigInt sub(BigInt b)` method that returns the sum/difference of `this` and `b` respectively. Note that these methods should be a case analysis of the signs of the operands. Use the following equivalences to guide your design. Do *not* over-complicate these methods.

$$A + (-B) = A - B \text{ if } A \geq B. \text{ Otherwise, } - (B - A).$$
$$(-A) + (-B) = -(A + B).$$
$$A - (-B) = A + B.$$
$$(-A) - B = -(A + B).$$
$$(-A) - (-B) = (-A + B) \text{ if } A \geq B. \text{ Otherwise, } (B - A).$$

(l) Design the `BigInt mul(BigInt b)` method that returns the product of `this` and `b`. The product of two negative integers is a positive integer, and the product of exactly one positive and exactly one negative is a negative integer.

4.58 (⋆) Recall the unification exercise from Chapter 3. We can take the idea of unification a step further, which is the basis for almost all logic programming languages such as Prolog. For instance, take the expression `p(X, f(Y))`; attempting to unify this with `p(q(r(x)), f(b(x)))` returns a unification assignment of `X : q(r(x)), Y : b(x)`. It is possible for a unification to not return any possible assignment. As an example, unifying `p(a, b)` with `p(Y, Y)` returns an empty assignment because it is not possible to unify `a` with `Y`, then unify `b` with `Y`.

Design three classes: `Variable`, `Constant`, and `Predicate`. Each of these should implement the `IUnifiable` interface, which supplies one method: `Assignment unify(IUnifiable u, Assignment as)`. An `Assignment` is simply a mapping of `IUnifiable` objects to `IUnifiable` objects, resembling a map data structure. Variables in this small language will be represented as upper0cased letters, whereas constants are lowercase. If two `IUnifiable` objects cannot be unified, then `unify` should return `null`.

Constants are straightforward: constants can only be unified with other constants if they are equivalent. Constants can only be unified with variables if that variable does not have an existing assignment and, if it does, it must be equal to `this` constant. Constants cannot be unified with predicates.

Variables can only be unified with constants if the variable does not have an existing assignment and, if it does, it must be equal to the constant passed as an argument. Variables can only be unified with other variables if at least one is bound to a constant; if they are both bound, then they must be equivalent constants.

Predicates can only be unified with variables if the variable does not have an existing assignment and, if it does, it must be equal to `this` predicate. Predicates can only be unified with predicates if it is possible to successfully unify all of its arguments. E.g., `p(a, z(b), c)` unifies with `p(X, z(Y), Z)` because we return the assignment `X : a, Y : b, Z : c`.

4.59 (⋆) Quine's method of truth resolution van Orman Quine (1950) is a method of automatically reasoning about the truth of a propositional logic statement (recall the exercise from Chapter 2). The method is as follows:

1. Choose an atom P from the statement. Consider two cases: when P is true and when P is false. Derive the consequences of each case. The rules follow those of the propositional logic connectives.
2. Repeat this process for each sub-statement until there are no more sub-statements, and you have only true or false results. If you have *both* true and false results, the statement is a contingency. If all branches lead to true, the statement is a tautology. If all branches lead to false, the statement is a contradiction.

Design several classes to represent a series of well-formed schemata in propositional logic, namely `CondNode`, `BicondNode`, `NegNode`, `AndNode`, `OrNode`, and `AtomNode`, all of which extend a root `Node` class, similar to our representation of the abstract syntax trees within the ASPL interpreter. Then, design the `boolean isTautology(Node t)`, `boolean isContingency(Node t)`, and the `boolean isContradiction(Node t)` methods, which return whether or not the given statement is a tautology, contingency, or contradiction, respectively. You may assume that the input is a well-formed schema. Note that only one of these methods needs a full-fledged recursive traversal over the data; the other two can be implemented in terms of the first.

5 Exceptions and I/O

Abstract With the foundations of Java, data structures, and classes/objects covered, we now move into more advanced topics, such as exception handling and I/O. This chapter will discuss unchecked and checked exceptions, as well as how to handle them. We will also discuss several means of working with file I/O, including more advanced topics such as serialization. Finally, the chapter ends with an explanation of more modern Java I/O techniques.

5.1 Exceptions

Exceptions, at their core, are effect handlers. We use exceptions to identify and respond to events that occur at runtime. Java uses objects to implement an exception type hierarchy, with Throwable being the highest class in the chain. Any subclass or instance of Throwable can be thrown by Java. We will discuss several different exception types by categorizing them into one of two categories: unchecked versus checked checked exceptions.

5.1.1 Unchecked Exceptions

We handle exceptions at either compile time or runtime. The exceptions themselves are thrown at runtime, but some exceptions must be explicitly handled and referenced by the program. An *unchecked exception* is a form of exception whose behavior is dictated by the runtime system, or is caught by the programmer manually. A convenience factor of unchecked exceptions is that we do not *have* to explicitly state what happens when one is thrown. We should also note that the RuntimeException class serves as the superclass of all unchecked exceptions.

Example 5.1. Consider what happens when a program contains code that may or may not divide a numeric value by zero. If the bad division operation occurs, Java automatically throws an ArithmeticException with a relevant explanation of the problem, that being a divide-by-zero. The exception halts program execution at the point thereof, but what's interesting is that we can control the behavior of an unchecked exception through a try/catch block. Within a try block, we include the code that potentially raises the exception. In the associated catch block, we declare a variable for the exception we aim to catch, such as ArithmeticException, and then manage it within that block. Let's write a method that does nothing more than divides the sum of two numbers by the third.

```
import java.lang.ArithmeticException;

class ArithmeticExceptionExample {

  double div(int a, int b, int c) {
    return (a + b) / c;
  }

  double div2(int a, int b, int c) {
    try {
      return (a + b) / c;
    } catch (ArithmeticException ex) {
      System.err.println("div2: / by zero!");
      return 0;
    }
  }
}
```

We define two versions of div, where the first does not perform an explicit check for the exception, and the second does. In the latter, we print a message to the standard error stream and return zero. The preferable resolution is certainly up to the programmer, but it makes more sense in this scenario to throw the exception and halt program execution, rather than propagating a zero up to the caller. Another solution might be to return an Optional from the method, but the Optional class is more about compositionality of stream methods rather than exceptions.

Example 5.2. In the preceding example, we catch the ArithmeticException that Java throws. Though, suppose we have a situation in which *we* want to throw the exception. Because the div problem arises from a bad parameter, we might wish to throw an IllegalArgumentException, which designates exactly what its name suggests. We insert a conditional check to test if the divisor, namely c, is zero and, if so, we throw a new IllegalArgumentException. Because IllegalArgumentException is an unchecked exception, the caller needs not to handle nor necessarily know that it may raise the exception. Should we want to signal that as a hint, the method signature may specify that the method potentially throws an IllegalArgumentException. As the callee that defines the location of an exception invocation, we *only* throw the exception; it is not our responsibility to control the outcome.

We can unit test a new version of div by determining whether it throws an exception through the assertThrows and assertDoesNotThrow assertion methods. The thing is, though, neither assertThrows nor assertDoesNotThrow are not as simple as they appear on the surface; we need to specify *what* exception the code might throw as a reference to the class definition.[1] Additionally, the argument must be passed as an executable argument. Remember though have worked with executable constructs before via lambda/anonymous functions! Simply wrap the code that might raise an exception inside a lambda, and everything works as expected.

---

[1] To reference a class definition as an object, we access .class on the class as if it were a static method.

5.1 Exceptions

```java
import static Assertions.assertDoesNotThrow;
import static Assertions.assertThrows;

import java.lang.IllegalArgumentException;

class IllegalArgumentExceptionExampleTester {

  @Test
  void testIllegalArgumentException() {
    assertAll(
      () -> assertDoesNotThrow(div(5, 3, 1))),
      () -> assertThrows(IllegalArgumentException.class, () -> div(5, 3, 0)),
  }
}
```

```java
import java.lang.IllegalArgumentException;

class IllegalArgumentExceptionExample {

  int div(int a, int b, int c) throws IllegalArgumentException {
    if (c == 0) {
      throw new IllegalArgumentException("div: / by zero");
    } else {
      return (a + b) / c;
    }
  }
}
```

What if we wanted to call `div` from a separate method and process the exception ourselves? Indeed, this is doable. Should we wish to retrieve the exception message (i.e., the message passed to the exception constructor), we can via calling the `.getMessage` method on the exception object, which is helpful for producing custom error messages/responses or redirecting the message to a different destination.

```java
import java.lang.IllegalArgumentException;

class IllegalArgumentExceptionExample {

  int div(int a, int b, int c) throws IllegalArgumentException {
    if (c == 0) {
      throw new IllegalArgumentException("div: / by zero");
    } else {
      return (a + b) / c;
    }
  }

  public static void main(String[] args) {
    try {
      double res = div(2, 3, 0);
    } catch (IllegalArgumentException ex) {
      System.err.printf("main: %s\n" ex.getMessage());
    }
  }
}
```

Example 5.3. Arrays and strings both produce unchecked exceptions when incorrectly indexed via `ArrayIndexOutOfBoundsException` and `StringIndexOutOfBoundsException` respectively, both of which inherit from the `IndexOutOfBoundsException` class. We imagine that these have both been received, in great frustration, from the readers a indeterminate number of times. An index out of bounds exception stems from accessing data beyond the permissible bounds of some collection or structure.

```java
import static Assertions.assertAll;
import static Assertions.assertDoesNotThrow;
import static Assertions.assertThrows;

import java.lang.StringIndexOutOfBoundsException;

class IndexOutOfBoundsExceptionExampleTester {

  @Test
  void testOobException() {
    String ex1 = "String";
    int[] ex2 = new int[]{5, 3, 1, 2, 4, 6};
    assertAll(
      () -> assertDoesNotThrow(() -> ex1.charAt(0)),
      () -> assertDoesNotThrow(() -> ex1.charAt(ex1.length() - 1)),
      () -> assertDoesNotThrow(() -> ex2[0]),
      () -> assertDoesNotThrow(() -> ex2[ex2.length - 1])
      () -> assertThrows(StringIndexOutOfBoundsException.class, () -> ex1.charAt(17)),
      () -> assertThrows(StringIndexOutOfBoundsException.class, () -> ex1.charAt(-1)),
      () -> assertThrows(ArrayIndexOutOfBoundsException.class, () -> ex2[17]),
      () -> assertThrows(ArrayIndexOutOfBoundsException.class, () -> ex2[-1]));
  }
}
```

Another uncomfortably common unchecked exception that many Java programmers encounter is the `NullPointerException`. The `NullPointerException` most often discovered when referencing an object that has yet to be instantiated, or was accidentally never instantiated at all.

Example 5.4. Casting an object of type τ_1 to an incompatible type τ_2 results in an unchecked `ClassCastException`. By "an incompatible type," we mean to say that the object is either not an instance of the τ_2 type, or τ_1 and τ_2 are not in a *discernible* superclass/subclass relationship.[2] Primitive datatypes are not subject to this exception, as they are not objects.[3] All primitive datatypes, minus booleans, can be casted into one another. For example, the statement `int x = (int) 'A';` is valid, as is `char c = (char) 65;`. On the other hand,

```
String x = (String) new Integer(5);
```

is an invalid cast. Importantly, the cast operation (or this kind) results in a compile-time error instead of a runtime exception, because `Integer` and `String` share no discernible inheritance relationship, i.e., `Integer` is not a superclass/subclass of `String`, nor vice-versa.

We can, however, treat `List<T>` as an `AbstractList<T>` by performing a cast, such as

```
AbstractList<T> x = (AbstractList<T>) ls;
```

---

[2] We elaborate on discernibility below.

[3] No pun intended.

where `ls` is defined as being of type `List<T>`, because the `AbstractList` class implements the `List` interface.

Example 5.5. Sometimes, a program can reach a state where continuing is impossible or illogical. In these circumstances, we can throw an `IllegalStateException`, designating that the program has reached a point that it should not under normal pretenses. An example is attempting to access a closed `Scanner` instance.

```
Scanner in = new Scanner(System.in);
in.close();
String s = in.nextLine(); // Throws IllegalStateException!
```

5.1.2 Checked Exceptions

A *checked exception* is one that the programmer must explicitly handle. Java will fail to compile a program that does not enclose a checked exception type within a `try/catch` block, or when the method signature does not specify that it throws the exception. Almost all checked exceptions arise from I/O operations, such as reading from or to a data source, so further elaboration at this point the discussion at this point is not particularly helpful. We will discuss checked exceptions in the context of I/O operations in the following (non-sub)section.

5.1.3 User-Defined Exceptions

We can define our own exceptions in terms of other exceptions. Exceptions are nothing more than class definitions, which may be extended/inherited.

Example 5.6. Consider defining the `BadStringInputException` class, which inherits from `RuntimeException`. We might define `BadStringInputException` as an exception that Java throws when, after reading the user's input, we find that the input is not a "alpha string," i.e., a string that contains only letters. Let's define a constructor that takes a string as an parameter, serving as the exception message.[4]

```
class BadStringInputException extends RuntimeException {
  BadStringInputException(String msg) {
    super(String.format("BadStringInputException: %s", msg));
  }
}
```

Then, if we write code that reads a string from the user (through standard input), we can throw a `BadStringInputException` if said input is a non-alphabetic string. The following code segment uses the `matches` method, which receives a regular expression and returns whether the string satisfies the expression. More specifically, `[a-zA-Z]+` states that there must be at least one lowercase or uppercase character in the provided string. A method that calls `readAlphaString` does not need to handle the exception, as it unchecked and will be caught by the runtime system.

---

[4] We note that, broadly speaking, creating new types of exceptions is rarely beneficial, because Java provides a plethora of exception definitions that cover most use cases.

```java
import java.util.Scanner;

class BadStringInputExceptionExample {

  static void readAlphaString() {
    Scanner in = new Scanner(System.in);
    String s = in.nextLine();
    if (!s.matches("[a-zA-Z]+")) {
      throw new BadStringInputException(s);
    }
  }
}
```

5.2 File I/O

Presumably this section discusses the syntax and semantics of file input and output. Although this is correct, we will explain reading data from "non-plain-text" sources such as websites and network connections through sockets.

5.2.1 Primitive I/O Classes

Example 5.7. Let's write a program that reads data from a file and echos it to standard output.

```java
import java.io.IOException;
import java.io.FileNotFoundException;
import java.io.FileInputStream;

class FileInputStreamExample {

  public static void main(String[] args) {
    FileInputStream fis = null;
    String inFile = "file1.in";
    try {
      fis = new FileInputStream(inFile);
      // Read in data byte-by-byte.
      int val = -1;
      while ((val = fis.read()) != -1) {
        System.out.print(val);
      }
    } catch (FileNotFoundException ex) {
      System.err.printf("main: could not find %s\n", inFile);
    } catch (IOException ex) {
      System.err.printf("main: I/O err: %s\n", ex.getMessage());
    } finally {
      fis.close();
    }
  }
}
```

5.2 File I/O

Recall that in the previous section we mentioned checked exceptions, and deferred the discussion until generalized input and output. Now that we are here, we can refresh our memory and actually put them to use. A checked exception is an exception enforced at compile-time. We emphasize the word "enforced" because the exception is not handled until runtime, but we must place the line(s) that possibly throws the checked exception within a try/catch block. Namely, in the preceding code, the FileInputStream constructor is defined to potentially throw a FileNotFoundException, whereas its read method throws a generalized IOException if an input malfunction occurs. Since FileNotFoundException is a subclass/-subexception type of IOException, we could omit the distinct catch clause for this exception.

When reading from an input source that is not System.in, it is imperative to always close the stream resource. So, after we read the data from our file input stream object fis, inside the finally block, we invoke .close on the instance to release the allocated system resources and deem the file no longer available.[5] Expanding upon the finally block a bit more, it is a segment of code that *always* executes, no matter if the preceding code threw an exception. The finally block is useful for releasing resources, e.g., opened input streams, locks, that otherwise may not be released in the event of an exception or program redirection.[6] Many programmers often forget to close a resource, and then are left to wonder why a file is either corrupted, overwritten, or some other alternative. To remediate this problem, Java provides the *try-with-resources* construct, which auto-closes the resource.[7]

Example 5.8. Let's use the try-with-resources block to copy the contents of one file into another. In essence, we will design a program that opens a file input stream and a file output stream, each to separate files. Upon reading one byte from the first, we write that byte to the second.

```java
import java.io.*;

class FileCopyExample {

  public static void main(String[] args) {
    try (FileInputStream fis = new FileInputStream("file1.in");
         FileOutputStream fos = new FileOutputStream("file1.out")) {
      int val = -1;
      while ((val = fis.read()) != -1) { fos.write(val); }
    } catch (FileNotFoundException ex) {
      System.err.printf("main: could not find file1.in\n");
    } catch (IOException ex) {
      System.err.printf("main: I/O err: %s\n", ex.getMessage());
    }
  }
}
```

The file input/output stream classes receive/send data as raw bytes from their source/destination streams. In most instances, we probably want to read *characters* from a data source or to a data destination rather than the raw bytes themselves. To do so, we can instead opt to use the FileReader class, which extends Reader rather than the InputStream class. Namely, FileReader is for reading textual data, whereas FileInputStream is for reading raw byte

---

[5] We can check whether an input stream is available via the .available method.

[6] A lock is a construct used in concurrent programs, which we will exemplify in Chapter 8.

[7] Not every resource can be auto-closed; the class of interest must explicitly implement the AutoCloseable interface to be wrapped inside a try-with-resources block.

content of a file. Therefore a `FileReader` can read only textual files, i.e., files without an encoding, examples include .pdf, .docx, and so forth.

Example 5.9. Using `FileReader`, we will once again write an "echo" program to read data from its file source and writes its contents to standard output. Of course, we may want to output data to a file, in which case we use the dual to `FileReader`, that being `FileWriter`. In summary, `FileWriter` provides several methods for writing strings and characters to a data destination. In the following example we will also write some data to a test file, then examine its output based on our choice of method invocations.

```java
import java.io.*;

class FileReaderWriterExamples {

  public static void main(String[] args) {
    try (FileReader fr = new FileReader("file1.in")) {
      int c = -1;
      while ((c = fr.read()) != -1) { System.out.print((char) c); }
    } catch (IOException ex) {
      throw new RuntimeException(ex);
    }

    try (FileWriter fw = new FileWriter("file2.out")) {
      fw.write("Here is a string");
      fw.write("\nHere is another string\n");
      fw.write(9);
      fw.write(71);
      fw.write(33);
    } catch (IOException ex) {
      throw new RuntimeException(ex);
    }
  }
}
```

If we open `file2.out`, we see that it contains "Here is a string" on one line, followed by "Here is another string" on the next line. Then, we might expect it to output the numeric strings "9", "71", and "33" all on the same line. The `write` method coerces (valid) integers into their ASCII character counterparts, meaning that the file contains the tab character, an uppercase 'G', and the exclamation point '!'. As we will soon demonstrate, working directly with `FileReader` and `FileWriter` is rarely advantageous.

The problem with the file input and output stream classes, as well as the file reader and writer classes, is that they interact directly with the operating system using low-level operations. Constantly calling these low-level operations is expensive on the CPU because they read individual bytes, sequentially, which is horribly inefficient. The `BufferedReader` and `BufferedWriter` classes aim to alleviate this problem by utilizing data buffers. A better approach is to read data in chunks, rather than byte-by-byte, to reduce the number of operating system-level calls. When the allocated buffer is full, the data within is flushed to either the source or destination. By chunking the data in this manner, we reduce the number of times that the program interacts with the operating system, which consequently reduces the CPU overhead. To read from a stream using buffers, we use the `BufferedReader` class. Its constructor receives a `Reader` instance, which may be one of several classes. For example, to read from a file, we provide a `FileReader` to the `BufferedReader` constructor. Wrapping a `FileReader` inside a `BufferedReader` allows the buffered reader to interplay (using its optimization techniques) with the file reader, which in turn interacts with the operating system.

5.2 File I/O

> **BufferedReader Methods**
>
> The BufferedReader class provides methods for reading from a data source using a buffered mechanism.
>
> R = new BufferedReader(new FileReader(f)) creates a new buffered reader instance that reads from the file f, where f is either a String or a File object.
> int R.read() reads a single character from the input stream R. Calling read advances the location of the file pointer by one byte. If the stream is empty or reads an EOF character, returns -1.
> String R.readLine() reads a line of text from the input stream R. Calling readLine advances the location of the file pointer to the next line. If the stream is empty or has no further lines to consume, returns null.
> void R.close() closes the input stream R.

Fig. 5.1: Useful BufferedReader Methods.

> **BufferedWriter Methods**
>
> The BufferedWriter class provides methods for writing to a data source using a buffered mechanism.
>
> W = new BufferedWriter(new FileWriter(f)) creates a new buffered writer instance that writes to the file f, where f is either a String or a File object.
> void W.write(s) writes a string s to the output stream W.
> void W.close() closes the output stream W.

Fig. 5.2: Useful BufferedWriter Methods.

To output data using buffers, we use the analogous BufferedWriter class, which receives a Writer instance.

Example 5.10. Using BufferedReader and BufferedWriter, we will write a program that reads data from a file and outputs it to another file.

```java
import java.io.*;

class BufferedReaderWriterExample {

  public static void main(String[] args) {
    try (BufferedReader br = new BufferedReader(
                        new FileReader("file1.in"));
         BufferedWriter bw = new BufferedWriter(
                        new FileWriter("file1.out"))) {
      String line = null;
      while ((line = br.readLine()) != null) { bw.write(line + "\n"); }
    } catch (IOException ex) {
      throw new RuntimeException(ex);
    }
  }
}
```

The benefits of buffered I/O are not obvious to us as the programmers who use these classes. We can, however, directly compare the execution time of buffered I/O to non-buffered

> **PrintWriter Methods**
>
> The `PrintWriter` class provides utility methods for writing different types of data to a data destination.
>
> P = new PrintWriter(new FileWriter(f)) creates a new print writer instance that writes to a file f, where f is either a `String` or a `File` object.
> void P.print(x) writes the string representation of x to the output stream P.
> void P.println(x) writes the string representation of x to the output stream P, followed by a newline character.
> void P.printf(f, x) writes a formatted string to the output stream P, where f is a format string and x is the value to be formatted.
> void P.close() closes the output stream P.

Fig. 5.3: Useful `BufferedReader` and `BufferedWriter` Methods.

I/O operations. The following code shows two implementations of reading the contents of a very large file and echoing them to another. We have defined two methods: buffered and nonbuffered, which utilize the `BufferedReader/Writer` and `FileInput/OutputStream` classes respectively. Upon testing, we see that the buffered variant takes around three seconds to finish, whereas the non-buffered version took over four minutes!

```java
import java.io.*;

class PerformanceExamples {

  private static void buffered() {
    try (BufferedReader br = new BufferedReader(
                             new FileReader("huge-2m-file.txt"));
         BufferedWriter bw = new BufferedWriter(
                             new FileWriter("bigfile.out"))) {
      int c = -1;
      while ((c = br.read()) != -1) { bw.write(c); }
    } catch (IOException ex) { throw new RuntimeException(ex); }
  }

  private static void nonbuffered() {
    try (FileInputStream br = (new FileInputStream("huge-2m-file.txt"));
         FileOutputStream bw = (new FileOutputStream("bigfile.out"))) {
      int c = -1;
      while ((c = br.read()) != -1) { bw.write(c); }
    } catch (IOException ex) { throw new RuntimeException(ex); }
  }
}
```

The classes that we have explored thus far are primarily for reading/writing either binary or text data. Perhaps we want to output values that are not strictly strings or raw bytes, e.g., integers, doubles, floats, and other primitives datatypes. To do so, we can instantiate a `PrintWriter` instance, which itself receives an instance of the `Writer` class. A concern for some programmers may be that we lose the performance benefits of buffered I/O, but this is not the case; the constructor for `PrintWriter` wraps the writer object that it receives in an instantiation of a `BufferedWriter` object. Therefore, we do not forgo any performance gains from buffered writing, while gaining the ability to write non-strictly-text data.

5.2 File I/O

Example 5.11. Using `PrintWriter`, let's output some arbitrary constants and formatted strings to a file.

```java
import java.io.*;

class PrintWriterExample {

  public static void main(String[] args) {
    try (PrintWriter pw = new PrintWriter(new FileWriter("file4.out"))) {
      pw.println(Math.PI);
      pw.println(false);
      pw.printf("This is a %s string with %c and %d and %f and %b\n",
                "formatted", '&', 42, Math.E, true);
    } catch (IOException ex) {
      throw new RuntimeException(ex);
    }
  }
}
```

And thus the contents of `file4.out` are, as we might expect:

```
3.141592653589793
false
This is a formatted string with & and 42 and 2.718282 and true
```

We now have methods for reading strings and raw bytes, as well as methods for outputting all primitives and formatted strings to data destinations. We still have one problem: how can we output the representation of an object? For example, take the `BigInteger` class; it has associated instance variables and fields that we also need to store. For this particular class, it might be tempting to store a stringified representation, but this is not an optimal solution because, what if a class has a field that itself is an object? We would need to recursively stringify the object, which is prone to mistakes and requires updating the "stringification" any time a field is added, removed, or altered. Instead, we can use the `ObjectOutputStream` and `ObjectInputStream` classes, which *serialize* and *deserialize* objects respectively. Serialization is the process of converting an object into a stream of (transmittable) bytes, whereas deserialization is the opposite process. In summary, when we serialize objects, we save the object itself, alongside any relevant information about the object, e.g., its fields, instance variables, and so forth. Upon deserializing said object, we can restore the object to its original state, initializing its fields.

Example 5.12. Let's use `ObjectInput/OutputStream` classes to serialize an object of type `Player`, which has a name, score, health, and array of top scores. To designate that an object can be serialized, it must implement the `Serializable` interface. `Serializable` is a *marker interface*, meaning that it has no methods to implement. Instead, it is a "flag," of sorts, that informs the compiler that the class can be serialized. The `ObjectStreamExample` class defines the private and static `Player` class as described above. Should we open the `player.out` file, we see that it contains incomprehensible data; the data within is intended to be read only by a program.

> **Scanner Constructor Methods**
>
> The Scanner class has several constructors for reading from different data sources.
>
> S = new Scanner(System.in) instantiates a scanner that reads from the standard input stream.
> S = new Scanner(f) instantiates a scanner that reads from the file f, where f is a File object.
> void S.close() closes the input scanner S.

Fig. 5.4: Useful Scanner Constructors.

```java
import java.io.Serializable;

class ObjectStreamExample {
  // ... previous code not shown.

  private static class Player implements Serializable {
    private String name;
    private int score;
    private int health;
    private double[] topScores;

    Player(String name, int score, int health, double[] topScores) {
      this.name = name;
      this.score = score;
      this.health = health;
      this.topScores = topScores;
    }

    @Override
    public String toString() {
      return String.format("Player[name=%s, score=%d, health=%d, topScores=%s]", name, score, health,
                           Arrays.toString(topScores));
    }
  }
}
```

Suppose, on the contrary, that we want to store objects as strings in a file. This has two problems: first, as we said before, we would need to recursively serialize all compositional objects of the object that we are serializing. Second, we would need to write a parser to read the stringified object and reinitialize its fields. In essence, we have to reinvent worse versions of pre-existing classes.

Example 5.13. In Chapter 1, we saw how to use the Scanner class to read from standard input. Indeed, standard input is a source of data input, but we can wrap any instance of InputStream or File inside a Scanner to take advantage of its helpful data-parsing methods. Let's design a method that reads a series of values representing Employee data for a company. We just saw that we can take advantage of Serializable to do this for us, but it is helpful to see how we can also use a Scanner to solve a similar problem.

5.2 File I/O

We will say that an Employee contains an employee identification number, a first name, a last name, a salary, and whether or not they are full-time staff. Each row in the file contains an Employee record.

```java
class Employee {

  private long employeeId;
  private String firstName;
  private String lastName;
  private double salary;
  private boolean fullTime;

  Employee(long eid, String f, String l, double s, boolean ft) {
    this.employeeId = eid;
    this.firstName = f;
    this.lastName = l;
    this.salary = s;
    this.fullTime = ft;
  }

  @Override
  public String toString() {
    return String.format("[%d] %s, %s | %.2f | FT?=%b",
                         this.employeeId, this.lastName, this.firstName,
                         this.salary, this.fullTime);
  }
}
```

Our method returns a List<Employee> that has been populated after reading the data from the file. In particular, the nextLong, nextDouble, nextBoolean, and next methods will be helpful. The next method, whose behavior is not obvious from the name, returns the next sequence of characters prior to a whitespace.

To test, we will create a file containing the following contents:

```
123 John Smith 100000.00 false
456 Jane Doe 75000.00 true
789 Bob Jones 50000.00 false
```

```java
import static Assertions.assertAll;
import static Assertions.assertEquals;

import java.util.List;

class EmployeeScannerTester {

  @Test
  void testReadRecords() {
    List<Employee> emps = readRecords("employees.txt");
    assertAll(
      () -> assertEquals(emps.get(0).toString(),
                         "[123] Smith, John | 100000.00 | FT?=false"),
      () -> assertEquals(emps.get(1).toString(),
                         "[456] Doe, Jane | 75000.00 | FT?=true"),
      () -> assertEquals(emps.get(2).toString(),
                         "[789] Jones, Bob | 50000.00 | FT?=false"));
  }
}
```

> **Scanner Querying Methods**
>
> The Scanner class has several methods for determining the type of data that is next in the input stream.
>
> boolean S.hasNext() returns true if the scanner has another token in its input.
> boolean S.hasNextInt() returns true if the scanner has another integer in its input.
> boolean S.hasNextDouble() returns true if the scanner has another double in its input.
> boolean S.hasNextBoolean() returns true if the scanner has another boolean in its input.
> boolean S.hasNextLine() returns true if the scanner has another line in its input.

Fig. 5.5: Useful Scanner Querying Methods.

```java
import java.util.Scanner;
import java.util.List;
import java.util.ArrayList;
import java.io.File;
import java.io.IOException;

class EmployeeScanner {

  /**
   * Reads in a list of employee records from a given filename.
   * @param fileName name of file.
   * @return list of Employee instances.
   */
  static List<Employee> readRecords(String fileName) {
    List<Employee> records = new ArrayList<>();

    try (Scanner f = new Scanner(new File(fileName))) {
      while (f.hasNextLine()) {
        long eid = f.nextLong();
        String fname = f.next();
        String lname = f.next();
        double s = f.nextDouble();
        boolean ft = f.nextBoolean();
        records.add(new Employee(eid, fname, lname, s, ft));
      }
    } catch (IOException ex) { throw new RuntimeException(ex); }

    return records;
  }
}
```

At this point, we have seen several methods and classes for reading data from different data sources. Let's now write a few more meaningful programs.

Example 5.14. Let's write a program that reads a file containing integers, then outputs (to another file) the even integers. Because our input file has only integers, we can use the Scanner class for reading the data and PrintWriter to output those even integers. To make the program a bit more interesting, we will read the input file from the terminal arguments, and output the even integers to a file whose name is the same as the input file, but instead with the .out extension.

5.2 File I/O

> **Scanner Methods**
>
> The Scanner class has several methods for reading different types of data from its input stream.
>
> String S.next() returns the next token from the scanner. Any leading whitespace is skipped. Generally, this method should not be used, instead opting for one of the four methods below.
> int S.nextInt() returns the next integer from the scanner. If there is a newline character following the integer, it is left in the buffer. If there is no integer to be read, throws an InputMismatchException.
> double S.nextDouble() returns the next double from the scanner. If there is a newline character following the double, it is left in the buffer. If there is no double to be read, throws an InputMismatchException.
> boolean S.nextBoolean() returns the next boolean from the scanner. The same rules apply as for nextInt and nextDouble.
> String S.nextLine() returns the next line from the scanner. The newline character is removed from the input buffer, but *not* included in the returned string.

Fig. 5.6: Useful Scanner Methods.

```
import java.io.*;
import java.util.Scanner;

class EvenIntegers {

  public static void main(String[] args) {
    if (args.length != 1) {
      System.err.println("usage: java EvenIntegers <input-file>");
      System.exit(1);
    }

    String inFile = args[0];
    String outFile = inFile.substring(0, inFile.lastIndexOf('.')) + ".out";

    try (Scanner f = new Scanner(new File(inFile));
         PrintWriter pw = new PrintWriter(new FileWriter(outFile))) {
      while (f.hasNextInt()) {
        int val = f.nextInt();
        if (val % 2 == 0) {
          pw.println(val);
        }
      }
    } catch (IOException ex) {
      throw new RuntimeException(ex);
    }
  }
}
```

Example 5.15. Let's write a program that returns an array containing the number of lines, words, and characters (including whitespaces but excluding newlines) in a given file. The array indices correspond to those quantities respectively. To simplify the program, words will be considered strings as separated by spaces. For example, if the file contains the following contents:

```
This is a test file.
It contains three lines.
Here is the last line.
```

The returned array should be [3, 14, 46]. We can write JUnit tests to verify that our program works as intended.

```java
import static Assertions.assertAll;
import static Assertions.assertEquals;

class LineWordCharCounterTester {

  @Test
  void count() {
    int[] counts = LineWordCharCounter.count("file1.in");
    assertAll(
      () -> assertEquals(counts[0], 3),
      () -> assertEquals(counts[1], 14),
      () -> assertEquals(counts[2], 46));
  }
}
```

```java
import java.util.Scanner;
import java.util.File;
import java.io.IOException;

class LineWordCharCounter {

  /**
   * Counts the number of lines, words, and characters in a given file.
   * @param fileName name of file.
   * @return array of counts.
   */
  static int[] count(String fileName) {
    int[] counts = new int[]{0, 0, 0};
    try (Scanner f = new Scanner(new File(fileName))) {
      while (f.hasNextLine()) {
        String line = f.nextLine();
        counts[0]++;
        counts[1] += line.split(" ").length;
        counts[2] += line.length();
      }
    } catch (IOException ex) {
      throw new RuntimeException(ex);
    }
    return counts;
  }
}
```

Example 5.16. Going further with terminal arguments, let's write a program that receives multiple file names from the terminal, and outputs a file with all of the data concatenated into one. We will throw an exception if the user passes in files that do not all share the same extension. As an example, should the user input the following:

```
java ConcatenateFiles file1.txt file2.txt file3.txt output-file.txt
```

Then the program should output a file `output-file.txt` that contains the contents of `file1.txt`, `file2.txt`, and `file3.txt`, in that order.

5.2 File I/O

```java
import java.io.*;
import java.util.Arrays;

class ConcatenateFiles {

  /**
   * Determines whether all files have the same extension.
   * @param files array of file names.
   * @return true if all files have same extension, false otherwise.
   */
  private static boolean sameExtension(String[] files) {
    if (files[0].lastIndexOf('.') == -1) { return false; }
    else {
      String extension = files[0].substring(files[0].lastIndexOf('.'));
      for (String file : files) {
        if (file.lastIndexOf(".") == -1
           || !file.substring(file.lastIndexOf('.')).equals(extension)) {
          return false;
        }
      }
      return true;
    }
  }

  /**
   * Concatenates the contents of a list of files into a single file.
   * @param files array of file names.
   * @param outFile name of output file.
   */
  private static void concatenate(String[] files, String outFile) {
    try (BufferedWriter bw = new BufferedWriter(new FileWriter(outFile))) {
      for (String file : files) {
        try (BufferedReader br = new BufferedReader(new FileReader(file))) {
          String line = null;
          while ((line = br.readLine()) != null) {
            bw.write(line + "\n");
          }
        }
      }
    } catch (IOException ex) { throw new RuntimeException(ex); }
  }

  public static void main(String[] args) {
    if (args.length < 3) {
      System.err.println("usage: java ConcatenateFiles <i-files> <o-file>");
      System.exit(1);
    } else {
      String[] inFiles = Arrays.copyOfRange(args, 0, args.length - 1);
      String outFile = args[args.length - 1];
      if (!sameExtension(inFiles)) {
        System.err.println("ConcatenateFiles: bad extensions");
        System.exit(1);
      } else {
        concatenate(inFiles, outFile);
      }
    }
  }
}
```

5.3 Modern I/O Classes & Methods

Aside from the aforementioned classes for working with files and I/O, Java's later versions provide methods and classes that achieve the same task as those that we might otherwise need to write several lines of code.

Example 5.17. To read the lines from a given file, we might open the file using a BufferedReader and FileReader object, read the values into some collection, e.g., a list, then process those lines accordingly. Repeatedly writing these almost identical lines of code is repetitive, so it might be a good idea to write a method that does this for us, and is an exercise that we provide to the reader. Java 8 introduced two classes: Files and Path that work with files and paths respectively. Let's use a handy method from Files, namely readAllLines to, as its name implies, read the lines from an input file and store them in a List<String>.

```java
import java.nio.file.Files;
import java.util.List;

class ReadAllLines {
  public static void main(String[] args) {
    try {
      List<String> lines = Files.readAllLines(Path.of("test.txt")));
      // Some processing with lines...
    } catch (IOException ex) {
      throw new RuntimeException(ex);
    }
  }
}
```

We still need to catch an IOException because readAllFiles might throw one in the event of some I/O error. What may be slightly disappointing is the fact that we cannot wrap this in a try-with-resources block, because readAllLines opens and closes the file it receives, resulting in what might appear to be less succinct code. Moreover, the method receives a Path, rather than a String, which we believe to be an attempt made by Java to prevent the programmer from needing to mess with strings and other input resources directly.

Example 5.18. Unfortunately, readAllLines is extremely memory-inefficient, requiring us to store a list of every line in the file. Consider an extremely large dataset, where the input contains one billion rows. Storing this data directly into running memory is not a particularly viable option, at least at the time of writing this text. A solution is to process each line one at a time, similar to how we work with a BufferedReader instance. As the section title suggests, though, there is a better way that incorporates streams into the mix. The Files class provides the lines method, which returns a stream of the lines in the file. Therefore, appealing to the lazy nature of streams, if we never actually use the data from the stream, nothing happens at all. This is a meaningless exercise, so let's write a method that solves the 1BR challenge: given a file of data points representing measurements of temperatures in differing locations, return an alphabetized string containing the location and, separated by an equals sign, the minimum, maximum, and average temperatures across all data points for that location (Morling, 2023).

To start the exercise, let's consider our options: we have one billion rows of text in the following format: "LOCATION;TEMP", so storing this in direct memory is a challenge that we will not overcome. Instead, let's create a Map that maps location identifiers to Measurement objects. A Measurement stores a number of occurrences, its minimum, maximum, and total-

5.3 Modern I/O Classes & Methods

accrued temperature. Each line we read either updates an existing Measurement in the map or inserts a new key/value pair.

To start, let's design the skeleton for our method, which we will name computeTemperatures, as well as the Measurement private class. Moreover, when instantiating a new Measurement instance, its current minimum, maximum, and total are all equal to the value on the current line.

```
import java.io.IOException;
import java.nio.file.*;
import java.util.*;

class TemperatureComputer {

  /**
   * Returns a string with the locations and their
   * minimum, maximum, and average temperatures.
   * @param filename input file with locations and
   * temperature separated by ';'.
   * @return String formatted as aforementioned.
   */
  static String computeMeasurement(String filename) {
    // TODO.
    return null;
  }

  private static class Measurement {

    private double min, max, total;
    private int noOccurrences;

    Measurement(double t) {
      this.numOccurrences = 1;
      this.min = t;
      this.max = t;
      this.total = t;
    }

    /**
     * Adds a temperature to this measurement's total.
     * We update the minimum, maximum, total, and
     * number of occurrences respectively.
     */
    void add(double t) {
      this.noOccurrences++;
      this.total += t;
      this.min = Math.min(this.min, t);
      this.max = Math.max(this.max, t);
    }
  }
}
```

As stated, using a map is the appropriate data structure, so let's instantiate a HashMap due to its quick lookup times. Then, we declare, inside a try-with-resources, a Stream<String>, returned by the lines method. Once either the stream is fully consumed, the stream is closed, or the program execution finishes the try block, then the file is also closed. From the stream, we could use a traditional for-each loop, but let's use stream operations instead. For every line, we want to split it on the semicolon, retrieve the location and temperature, then update the map as necessary. Because we need to update the state of an object if it exists in the map, we will utilize the `putIfAbsent` method, which returns the associating `Measurement` if the key-to-put already exists.

Lastly, we must conjoin the sorted pairs in the map with commas, which we can do via the `sorted()` and `Collectors.joining()` methods. In addition to this, we added a `toString` method to `Measurement` that returns a formatted string containing the minimum, average, and maximum temperatures floated to one decimal.

```java
import java.io.IOException;
import java.util.stream.Stream;
import java.nio.file.*;
import java.util.*;

class TemperatureComputer {

  /**
   * Returns a string with the locations and their
   * minimum, maximum, and average temperatures.
   * @param filename input file with locations and
   * temperature separated by ';'.
   * @return String formatted as aforementioned.
   */
  static String computeMeasurement(String filename) {
    Map<String, Measurement> mMap = new HashMap<>();
    try (Stream<String> lines = Files.lines(Path.of(filename))) {
      lines.forEach(x -> {
        String[] arr = x.split(";");
        String location = arr[0];
        double temp = Double.parseDouble(arr[1]);
        Measurement ms = mMap.putIfAbsent(location, new Measurement(temp));
        if (ms != null) {
          ms.add(temp);
        }
      });
    } catch (IOException e) {
      throw new RuntimeException(e);
    }
    return mMap.keySet()
            .stream()
            .sorted()
            .map(s -> String.format("%s=%s", s, mMap.get(s)))
            .collect(Collectors.joining(", "));
  }

  // ... other class not shown.
}
```

With inputs as large as what we assume them to be, we must make reasonable considerations with our choice of data structure. We could, theoretically, use a `TreeMap` and have the program autosort the measurement map pairs, but this is a performance penalty that is greater than using the `sorted` method as provided by the stream API over the map keys. In our tests, using a `TreeMap` amounted to a forty second performance penalty.

Example 5.19. Our last example of working with File I/O is a simple Sudoku solver. *Sudoku* is a game where the objective is to fill each row, column, and sub-grid with exactly one of possible entries, generally from 1 to 9. There are nine 3 × 3 sub-grids that form a square, which results in a 9 × 9 grid.

5.3 Modern I/O Classes & Methods

The most straightforward way to mechanically solve a Sudoku puzzle is via a backtracking algorithm. That is, we try to place a number in a cell and, if it leads to success, we continue with the solution. Otherwise, we undo the placement and try again. We will use I/O to read in a partial Sudoku puzzle and to write the solution out to another file.

Let's write the `SudokuSolver` class, whose constructor receives a file that represents a partial Sudoku puzzle. The input specification contains nine rows and nine columns, with dots to denote a missing number. From here, we will design the `boolean solve()` method, which returns whether or not a solution exists. If there is one, it is stored in an instance variable of the class. We will also design the `void output(String fileName)` method to output the solution to a file. If there is no possible solution, the program will throw an `IllegalStateException` to indicate a failure.

```java
import java.io.IOException;
import java.nio.file.*;
import java.util.*;

class SudokuSolver {

  private static final int N = 9;
  private int[][] board;
  private int[][] solution;

  SudokuSolver(String filename) {
    this.board = new int[N][N];
    this.solution = new int[N][N];
    try (Stream<String> lines = Files.lines(Path.of(filename))) {
      int row = 0;
      lines.forEach(x -> {
        for (int i = 0; i < x.length(); i++) {
          this.board[row][i] = x.charAt(i) == '.' ? 0 : x.charAt(i) - '0';
          this.solution[row][i] = this.board[row][i];
        }
        row++;
      });
    } catch (IOException e) {
      throw new RuntimeException(e);
    }
  }

  boolean solve() {
    /* TODO. */
    return false;
  }

  void output(String filename) {
    /* TODO. */
  }
}
```

Our `solve` method jump-starts a backtracking algorithm that attempts to solve the puzzle using recursion. Let's design a private helper method to receive the row r and column c of the cell to fill. If r and c are both equal to N, then we have reached the end of the board and therefore have a solution. Otherwise, we need to find the next empty cell to fill. This is a three-step process:

(i) First, if the y coordinate is equal to N, then we have reached the end of the row and need to move onto the next.

(ii) If the cell is not empty, we move onto the next cell.
(iii) If the cell is empty, we try to place a number in the cell. If the number is valid, we continue with the solution. Otherwise, we undo the placement and try again.

What does it mean for a number to be valid? A number is valid in its placement if it does not already exist in the row, column, or sub-grid. Let's write another private helper method that, when given a cell at row r and column c, and a number n, determines whether or not the number is valid.

```java
import java.io.IOException;
import java.nio.file.*;
import java.util.*;

class SudokuSolver {
  // ... previous code not shown.

  SudokuSolver(String filename) { /* Implementation omitted. */ }

  /**
   * Returns whether or not a number is valid in a given cell.
   * @param r row of cell.
   * @param c column of cell.
   * @param n number to place in cell.
   * @return true if number is valid, false otherwise.
   */
  private boolean isValid(int r, int c, int n) {
    // Check the row and column simultaneously.
    for (int i = 0; i < N; i++) {
      if (this.board[r][i] == n || this.board[i][c] == n) {
        return false;
      }
    }

    // Check the sub-grid.
    int sr = (r / 3) * 3;
    int sc = (c / 3) * 3;
    for (int i = sr; i < sr + 3; i++) {
      for (int j = sc; j < sc + 3; j++) {
        if (this.board[i][j] == n) {
          return false;
        }
      }
    }
    return true;
  }
}
```

From this we can begin to work on the recursive backtracking algorithm, using the outline we provided earlier.

5.3 Modern I/O Classes & Methods

```java
import java.io.IOException;
import java.nio.file.*;
import java.util.*;

class SudokuSolver {
  // ... previous code not shown.

  SudokuSolver(String filename) { /* Implementation omitted. */ }

  /**
   * Returns whether or not a solution exists. If a solution does not
   * exist, the variable that stores the solution is set to null.
   * @return true if a solution exists, false otherwise.
   */
  private boolean solve() {
    if (solve(0, 0, this.solution)) {
      return true;
    } else {
      this.solution = null;
      return false;
    }
  }

  /**
   * Recursive backtracking algorithm to solve the puzzle.
   * @param r row of cell.
   * @param c column of cell.
   * @param sol solution array.
   * @return true if we have a solution, and false if the current
   * placement is invalid or leads to a "dead end".
   */
  private boolean solve(int r, int c, int[][] sol) {
    if (r == N) {
      return true;
    } else if (c == N) {
      return solve(r + 1, 0, sol);
    } else if (this.board[r][c] != 0) {
      return solve(r, c + 1, sol);
    } else {
      for (int i = 1; i <= N; i++) {
        if (isValid(r, c, i)) {
          this.sol[r][c] = i;
          if (solve(r, c + 1, sol)) {
            return true;
          } else {
            this.sol[r][c] = 0;
          }
        }
      }
    }
    return false;
  }
}
```

Finally, the output method is straightforward. We use a `PrintWriter` to write the solution to a file. If there is no solution (meaning the solution instance variable is set to null), then we throw an `IllegalStateException`.

```java
import java.io.IOException;
import java.nio.file.*;
import java.util.*;

class SudokuSolver {
  // ... previous code not shown.

  SudokuSolver(String filename) { /* Implementation omitted. */ }

  /**
   * Outputs the solution to a file. The solution is just a 9x9 grid of
   * numbers, and does not attempt to format the output in any way.
   * @param filename name of output file.
   */
  void output(String filename) {
    try (PrintWriter pw = new PrintWriter(new FileWriter(filename))) {
      if (this.solution == null) {
        throw new IllegalStateException("No solution exists.");
      } else {
        for (int i = 0; i < N; i++) {
          for (int j = 0; j < N; j++) {
            pw.print(this.solution[i][j]);
          }
          pw.println();
        }
      }
    } catch (IOException e) {
      throw new RuntimeException(e);
    }
  }
}
```

5.4 Exercises

5.1 Design the `EchoOdds` class, which reads a file of line-separated integers specified by the user (using standard input), and writes only the odd numbers out to a file of the same name, just with the `.out` extension. If there is a non-number in the file, throw an `InputMismatchException`.

Example Run. If the user types `"file1a.in"` into the running program, and `file1a.in` contains the following:

```
5
100
25
17
2
4
0
-3848
13
```

then `file1a.out` is generated containing the following:

```
5
25
17
13
```

Example Run. If the user types `"file1b.in"` into the running program, and `file1b.in` contains the following:

```
5
100
25
17
THIS_IS_NOT_AN_INTEGER!
4
0
-3848
13
```

then the program does not output a file because it throws an exception.

5.2 Design the `String[] readStrings()` method, which reads an indeterminate number of line-separated strings from standard input. You *cannot* store the strings in a collection—that is, you can only use Java arrays. Remember how to dynamically "resize" an array? Return the array of strings that are read from standard input. Your array should not contain "null slots" at the end. You may assume that a blank line indicates no further input.

5.3 Design the `Capitalize` class, which contains one `static` method: `void capitalize(String in)`. The `capitalize` method reads a file of sentences (that are not necessarily line-separated), and outputs the capitalized versions of the sentences to a file of the same name, just with the `.out` extension (you must remove whatever extension existed previously).

You may assume that a sentence is a string that is terminated by a period and only a period, which is followed by a single space. If you use a splitting method, e.g., `.split`, you must remember to reinsert the period in the resulting string. There are many ways to solve this problem!

Example Run. If we invoke `capitalize("file2a.in")` into the running program, and `file2a.in` contains the following *(note that if you copy and paste this input data, you will need to remove the newline before the "hopefully" token)*:

```
hi, it's a wonderful day. i am doing great, how are you doing. it's
hopefully fairly obvious as to what you need to do to solve this problem.
this is a sentence on another line.
this sentence should also be capitalized.
```

then `file2a.out` is generated containing the following *(again, remember to remove the newline before "hopefully".)*:

```
Hi, it's a wonderful day. I am doing great, how are you doing. It's
hopefully fairly obvious as to what you need to do to solve this problem.
This is a sentence on another line.
This sentence should also be capitalized.
```

5.4 Design the `SpellChecker` class, containing the `static void spellCheck(String dict, String in)`. The `spellCheck` method reads two files: a "dictionary" and a content file. The content file contains a single sentence that may or may not have misspelled words. Your job is to check each word in the file and determine whether or not they are spelled correctly, according to the dictionary of (line-separated) words. If a word is not spelled correctly, wrap it inside brackets [].

Output the modified sentences to a file of the same name, just with the .out extension (you must remove whatever extension existed previously). You may assume that words are space-separated and that no punctuation exist. Hint: use a Set! Another hint: words that are different cases are not misspelled; e.g., `"Hello"` is spelled the same as `"hello"`; how can your program check this?

Example Run. Assuming `dictionary.txt` contains a list of words, if we invoke the method with `spellChecker("dictionary.txt", "file3a.in")`, and `file3a.in` contains the following:

```
Hi hwo are you donig I am dioing jsut fine if I say so mysefl but I
will aslo sya that I am throughlyy misssing puncutiation
```

then `file3a.out` is generated containing the following:

```
Hi [hwo] are you [donig] I am [dioing] [jsut] fine if I say so
[mysefl] but I will [aslo] [sya] that I am [throughlyy] [misssing]
[puncutiation]
```

5.5 Design the `OrderWebUrls` class, which contains one `static` method: `void orderWebUrls(String in)`. The `orderWebUrls` method reads in a file of line-separated web URLs. A web URL contains a protocol separated by a colon and two forward slashes, and a host name. For example, in the URL https://www.joshuacrotts.us, the protocol is https and the host name is www.joshuacrotts.us. The method should read in web URLs in this specific format and sort them, lexicographically, based on the hostname. If two hostnames are identical and only differ by the protocol, then the order becomes based on the protocol.

5.4 Exercises

5.6 Recall the `Optional` class and its purpose. In this exercise you will reimplement its behavior with the `IMaybe` interface with two subtypes `Just` and `Nothing`, representing the existence and absence of a value, respectively. Design the generic `IMaybe` interface, which contains the following three methods: `T get()`, `boolean isJust()`, and `boolean isNothing()`. The constructors of these subtypes receive either an object of type `T` or no parameter, depending on whether it is a `Just` or a `Nothing`. Throw an `UnsupportedOperationException` when trying to get the value from an instance of `Nothing`.

5.7 Redo the "Maybe" exercise, only this time implement it as an abstract class/subclass hierarchy. That is, `Maybe` should be an abstract class containing three abstract methods: `T get()`, `boolean isJust()`, and `boolean isNothing()`. The `Just` and `Nothing` classes should be subclasses of `Maybe` and override these methods accordingly. Do not create constructors for these classes. Instead, create static factory methods `Just.of(T t)` and `Nothing.of()` that return an instance of the appropriate class.

5.8 A sum type is a type T that stores differing types. For example, `Either<L, R>` is a sum type that encapsulates one value that is either of type L or is of type R, called the "left" and "right" respectively. Haskell programmers (or other functional programmers) frequently use `Either` to indicate failure and success outcomes, where the "left" is populated upon failure and "right" is populated upon success. The common example is designing a function to safely divide integers. Namely, if the divisor is zero, it returns an `Either` whose "left" is a `String` with the value `"ERR / by zero"`, or something related. Oppositely, if the divisor is not zero, then the division is declared "safe," and the quotient is stored in the "right" value of the returned `Either`. In this exercise you will implement the `Either` class to simulate Haskell's `Either` sum type.

(a) Design the generic `Either<L, R>` class. Its constructor should be private and receive values of types L and R, and assign them to instance variables.
(b) Design the `static <L, R> Either<L, R> left(L v)` and `static <L, R> Either<L, R> right(R v)` methods, which receive parameters of types L and R respectively. These two methods should invoke the `private` constructor and pass `null` for the object of the other type.
(c) Design the `isLeft()` and `isRight()` methods, which returns whether the `Either` represents a "left" or a "right."
(d) Override the `public String toString()` method to print out `"Left "` or `"Right "` followed by the stored value, depending on what value is stored.
(e) Now, design the `static <L, R> Either<L, R> safeDiv(int a, int b)` method, which returns an instance of `Either` based on the criteria in the preceding definition of `safeDiv`.

5.9 A common use for file input and output is data analysis. Design a class `StatisticsDescriptor` that has the following methods:

(a) `void read(String fileName)`, which reads in a list of numbers from a file into a collection. These numbers can be integers or floating-point values.
(b) `double mean()`, which returns the mean of the dataset.
(c) `double stddev()`, which returns the standard deviation of the dataset.
(d) `double quantile(double q)`, which receives a quantile value $q \in [0, 1]$ and returns the value such that there are q, as a percentage, values below said value. As an example, if our dataset contains 3, 2, 1, 4, 5, 10, 20, and we call `quantile(0.30)`, then we return 2.8 to indicate that 30% of the values in the dataset are below 2.8.
(e) `double median()`, which returns the median, or the middle value, of the dataset.

(f) `double mode()`, which returns the mode, or the most-frequent value, of the dataset.
(g) `double range()`, which returns the range, or the difference between the maximum and minimum values of the dataset.
(h) `List<Double> outliers()`, which returns the numbers that are outliers of the dataset. We consider a value an outlier if it is greater than three standard deviations away from the mean. Refer to the formula for z-score calculation in the exercises from Chapter 1.
(i) `void output(String fileName)`, which outputs all of the above statistics to the file specified by the parameter (the order is irrelevant). You should output these as a series of "key-value" pairs separated by an equals sign, e.g., mean=X. Put each pair on a separate line.

For all methods (except read), if the data has yet to be read, throw an `IllegalStateException`.

5.10 You are teaching an introductory programming course and you want to keep a seating chart for your students. A seating chart is an arrangement of numbers 1..n, the location in the classroom of which is defined by the instructor. Numbers that are lower in the range are closer to the front of the room. Design the `SeatingChart` class, which has the following methods:

(a) `SeatingChart()` is the constructor, which initializes the seating chart to be empty. The seating chart is represented as a `List<Student>`, where `Student` is a private and static class, inside `SeatingChart`, that you design. Students should have a name, a seat number, and an accommodation parameter. The seat number is an integer, and the accommodation parameter is a boolean.

(b) `void read(String fileName)` reads in a list of students from a file into the seating chart. The file contains a list of students, one per line, with their name. A student also has an optional accommodation parameter, which means they should sit in a seat closer to the front of the room. The file is comma-separated, and if the student has an accommodation, it is represented by true after the student's name.

```
Alice
Bob,true
Charlie
```

(c) `void scramble()` scrambles the seating chart. That is, it randomly shuffles the students in the seating chart. This also accounts for the accommodations, so that students with accommodations are closer to the front of the room.

(d) `void alphabetize()` sorts the seating chart alphabetically by the students' names. This "mode" does not account for accommodations, and is thus strictly alphabetical.

(e) `List<Student> getStudents()` returns the seating chart as a list of students.

(f) `List<Student> getAccommodationStudents()` returns the students with accommodations as a list.

(g) `void output(String fileName)` outputs the seating chart to a file specified by the parameter. The file should contain the students' names and their seat numbers, one per line, separated by a comma. The output list should be in the order of the seating chart.

5.4 Exercises

5.11 (★) You are designing a system for looking up car information, similar to that of, say, Kelly Blue Book or Carvana.

(a) First, design the Car class, which stores the make, model, color, trim, and VIN (vehicle identification number) of the car as strings, the year and number of prior owners as an integer, an enumeration that contains its title status (e.g., Clean, Salvaged, or Rebuilt), and its MSRP (in USD) as a floating-point value.[8]

(b) Make the Car class serializable, like we did in the chapter. That is, implement the Serializable interface and override the writeObject and readObject methods respectively.

(c) Override the public boolean equals(Object o) and public int hashCode() methods. Two Car objects are the same if they share the same VIN. When overriding hashCode, return a hash code that hashes all instance variables.

(d) Finally, override the public String toString() method, which returns a string similar to the following (with a tab character before each line):

```
Make: Honda
Model: Accord
Color: Silver
Trim: LX
Year: 2007
VIN: 1G4HDSLVRLX
Number of Previous Owners: 2
Title Status: Salvaged
MSRP: $20,475.00
```

(e) Now, design the CarDatabase class, whose (no parameter) constructor instantiates a List<Car> instance variable to store the list of cars. Then, design the following methods:

(i) void addCar(Car car), which adds a car with the given values to the database.

(ii) boolean removeCar(String vin), which removes a car with the given VIN. If the car was in the database, the method returns true, and false otherwise.

(iii) boolean contains(String vin), which returns true if a Car with the given VIN exists in the database, and false otherwise.

(iv) boolean contains(Car car), which returns true if the given car exists in the database, and false otherwise. Note that this method should be one line long and call the other variant of contains.

(v) void readFile(String in), which populates the database with the Car objects from the given file. The file should contain only serialized Car objects and not plain-text.

(vi) void writeFile(String out), which writes all cars in the database out to a file with the given file name. The file should contain only serialized Car objects and not plain-text.

(vii) void sort(Comparator<Car> cmp), which sorts the database of Car objects according to the provided Comparator implementation.

(viii) void sort(), which sorts the database of Car objects according to their VIN.

---

[8] As a tip: if you are ever writing real-world software that works with currency values, you should *never* store currency as floating-point numbers, e.g., double or float. This is because of the inaccuracies that come with such representations in a computer. The preferred solution is to use an object type that separately stores cents and dollars such as BigDecimal.

5.12 You're interested in determining the letter statistics of a file containing text. In particular, you want to design a program that reports the frequency of each alphabetic character. Design the LetterFrequency class, which has the following methods:

(a) LetterFrequency(String fileName) is the constructor, which reads a file containing text into a long[] instance variable with 26 elements. Convert all upper-case letters into lower-case. Index 0 of the (frequency) array corresponds to 'a', and index 25 corresponds to 'z'. Before reading the contents of the file, initialize the array to contain all zeroes.
(b) void add(char c) adds a character c to the frequency map. If c is not alphabetic, throw an IllegalArgumentException.
(c) void add(String s) calls the other add method on each character in the given string s.
(d) long get(char c) returns the frequency of a given character, which should be converted to lowercase. If c is not a letter, throw an IllegalArgumentException.
(e) char get(int i) returns the ith most frequent character. If $i \notin [0, 25)$, throw an IllegalArgumentException.
(f) List<Character> getMostFrequentChars(int n) returns the n most frequent characters. If $n \notin [0, 25)$, throw an IllegalArgumentException. Hint: invoke the get method n times for values 1 to n inclusive.

5.13 This exercise has two parts. A *stack-based* programming language is one that uses a stack to keep track of variables, values, and the results of expressions. These types of languages have existed for several decades, and in this exercise you will implement such a language.

Design the StackLanguage class, whose constructor receives no parameters. The class contains two instance methods: void readFile(String f) and double interpret().

- The readFile method reads a series of "stack commands" from the file. These can be stored however you feel necessary in the class, but you should not interpret anything in this method, nor should you throw any exceptions. You may want to create a private static class for storing commands.
- The interpret method interprets the stored list of instructions. If no instructions have been received by a readFile command, throw an IllegalStateException. Here are the following possible instructions:

  (a) DECL v X declares that v is a variable with value X.
  (b) PUSH X pushes a number X to the stack.
  (c) POP v pops the top-most number off the stack and stores it in a variable v. If v has not been declared, an IllegalArgumentException is thrown.
  (d) PEEK v stores the value at the top of the stack in the variable v. If v has not been declared, an IllegalArgumentException is thrown.
  (e) ADD X adds X to the top-most number on the stack.
  (f) SUB X subtracts X from the top-most number on the stack.
  (g) XCHG v swaps the value on the top of the stack with the value stored in variable v. If v has not been declared as a variable, an IllegalArgumentException is thrown.
  (h) DUP duplicates the value at the top of the stack.

If the command is none of these, then throw an UnsupportedOperationException. You may assume that all commands, otherwise, are well-formed (i.e., they contain the correct number of arguments and the types thereof are correct). After interpreting all instructions, the value that is returned is the top-most value on the stack. If there is no such value, throw a NoSuchElementException.

Hint: use a Map to store variable identifiers to values.

5.4 Exercises

5.14 (⋆) Java provides many forms of input and output stream classes, e.g., BufferedReader/BufferedWriter. Unfortunately, it does not have classes, say BitInputStream and BitOutputStream, for outputting raw bits to a file. In this exercise you will implement these classes. [9]

(a) Design the BitOutputStream class, which extends OutputStream. It should store two instance variables: an instance of OutputStream and an array of eight integers. Each integer index corresponds to a bit to send to the output.

   (i) Design three BitOutputStream constructors: one that sets the stored output stream instance to null, a second that receives an OutputStream object and assigns it to the instance variable, and a third that receives a file name, and instantiates the stored output stream as a FileOutputStream. All three constructors should instantiate the array of "bits."

   (ii) Override the public void flush() throws IOException method from OutputStream to output the bits, as a single byte, to the file. This does *not* mean that you should output the raw '1' and '0' characters that are stored in the buffer. Instead, convert those bits into a single int, and write that value to the output stream. Hint: the bitwise operations << and | may come in handy.

   (iii) Override the public void write(int b) throws IOException method from OutputStream to assign bit b to the next-free index in the array. If you run out of bits to store in the array, call this.flush().

   (iv) Design the void writeBit(int b) method, which adds a bit to the ith index of the array. If the input b is not a 0 or 1, throw an IllegalArgumentException, otherwise call this.write with b.

(b) Design the BitInputStream class, which extends InputStream. This class should also store an instance of an InputStream as a field, as well as an array of bit values.

   (i) Design three BitInputStream constructors that mimic the behavior of the BitOutputStream class constructors.

   (ii) Design the private int readBit() method, which reads a bit from the buffer. Your code should call read on the input stream once every eight bits, i.e., every byte.

   (iii) Override the public int read() method, which returns the next bit from the buffer. If you run out of bits to return, read a byte from the input stream. If there are no more bytes to read, return −1. Hint: read() itself returns −1 when there are no bytes remaining.

---

[9] This exercise is common in Java textbooks, and in our opinion, is worth repeating.

5.15 (⋆) A maze is a grid of cells, each of which is either open or blocked. We can move from one free cell to another if they are adjacent. Design the `MazeSolver` class, which has the following methods:

(a) `MazeSolver(String fileName)` is the constructor, which reads a description of a maze from a file. The file contains a grid of characters, where '.' represents an open cell and '#' represents a blocked cell. The file is formatted such that each line is the same length. Read the data into a `char[][]` instance variable. You may assume that the maze dimensions are on the first line of the file, separated by a space.

(b) `char[][] solve()` returns a `char[][]` that represents the solution to the maze. The solution should be the same as the input maze, but with the path from the start to the end marked with '*' characters. The start is the top-left cell, and the end is the bottom-right cell. If there is no solution, return `null`.

We can use a backtracking algorithm to solve this problem: start at a cell and mark it as visited. Then, recursively try to move to each of its neighbors, marking the path with a '*' character. If you reach the maze exit, then return `true`. Otherwise, backtrack and try another path. By "backtrack," we mean that you should remove the '*' character from the path. If you have tried all possible paths from a cell and none of them lead to the exit, then return `false`. We provide a skeleton of the class below.

(c) `void output(String fileName, char[][] soln)` outputs the given solution to the maze to a file specified by the parameter. Refer to the above description for the format of the output file and the input `char[][]` solution.

```
class MazeSolver {

  private final char[][] MAZE;

  MazeSolver(String fileName) { /* TODO read maze from file. */ }

  /**
   * Recursively solves the maze, returning a solution if it exists,
   * and null otherwise. We use a simple backtracking algorithm
   * in the helper.
   * @return a solution to the maze, or null if it does not exist.
   */
  char[][] solve() {
    char[][] soln = new char[MAZE.length][MAZE[0].length];
    return this.solveHelper(0, 0, soln) ? soln : null;
  }

  /**
   * Recursively solves the maze, returning true if we ever reach
   * the exit. We try all possible paths from the current cell, if
   * they are reachable. If a path ends up being a dead end, we
   * backtrack and try another path.
   * @param r the row of the current cell.
   * @param c the column of the current cell.
   * @param sol the current solution to the maze.
   * @return true if we are at the exit, false otherwise.
   */
  private boolean solveHelper(int r, int c, char[][] sol) {
    /* TODO. */
  }
}
```

5.4 Exercises

5.16 (⋆) The cut program is a command-line tool for extracting pieces of text from data. For this exercise, you will implement a very basic version of the program that reads data from the terminal.

(a) First, add support for the -c $X, Y, \ldots, Z$ flag, which outputs the characters at positions $X, Y, \ldots, Z$ in each line. If any number is less than 1, throw an IllegalArgumentException.
(b) Second, add support for the -c X-Y flag, which outputs the characters between and including positions X and Y. This option should also work with comma separators.
(c) Third, add support for the -c X- and -c -Y flags, which print the characters from X to the end of the line, and all characters up to Y.
(d) Fourth, Add support for the -dD and -fX flags. The former serves as a single character delimiter, and the latter indicates that X is either an interval or a range of fields to print. The fields are delimited by D. Note that these two flags cannot be used without the other. The format of X mirrors that of the input to the $-c$ flag. If D does not exist on a line, then the entire line is printed.

5.17 (⋆) The sort program is a command-line tool for sorting input from a data source. For this exercise, you will implement a very basic version of the program that reads data from the terminal.

(a) First, allow the sort command to receive either a file or a list of data. If the -dD flag is passed, use D as the delimiter. The default for a file is a newline, and the default for a non-file is the space.
(b) Second, add support for the -r flag for reversed sorting.
(c) Third, add support for the -i flag for case-insensitive sorting.
(d) Fourth, add support for the -c flag for checking to see if a file is sorted. Reports the first occurrence of out-of-order sort.
(e) Fifth, add support the the -n flag for sorting the values as if they are numbers. Notice the difference between sorting 9, 10, 8 with and without this flag.
(f) Sixth, add support for the -u flag for removing duplicate values.
(g) Seventh, add support for the -o flag for outputting to the file specified immediately after.

Any of these flags should be composable with another, with the exception of -o whose output file is the next argument, and -c, which outputs any disorders to standard out.

5.18 (⋆) The awk program is a command-line tool for text parsing and processing. For this exercise, you will implement a very basic version of the program that reads data from the terminal. Be aware that this exercise is more in line with a mini-project.

(a) Add support for the -F flag that, when immediately followed by a delimiter, uses that delimiter as a "field separator" when parsing input lines. For example, -F, uses a comma as the delimiter.
(b) Add the -h flag that ignores the first row in all subsequent commands. This is particularly useful when working with files that have headers, e.g., comma-separated value files.
(c) Next, add the 'print ...' command. That is, the user should be able to type an open brace, followed by print, then some data, then a closing brace, all enclosed by single quotes. The print command receives multiple possible values, including 'column labels', i.e., N, where N is a column number. For example, awk -F, 'print $1' input.csv should print the first column of each row in the input file.

(d) After getting the previous command to work, add support for inlined prefix operations in the print command. That is, suppose we want to print the sum of the second and fourth column of each row. To do this, we might write awk -h -F, 'print (+ $2 $4)' input.csv. For simplicity, you may assume that there are only four operations: '+', '-', '*', and '/'.

(e) After getting the previous command to work, add multiple-argument support for print. That is, if we want to compute the product of the first three columns, output a string saying " multiplied is " , followed by the product, we could write awk -h -F, 'print $1,$2,$3 " multiplied is " (* $1 $2 $3) '. Note that the delimiter between the column labels must match that passed by -F, otherwise there is no separator.

(f) After getting the previous command to work, add support for conditional expressions. That is, suppose we want to print the second column of a row only if it has a value greater than 200. We can achieve this via awk -h -F, 'print $2(> $2 200)'. If you *really* want a challenge, you can add support for inlining other arithmetic expressions into a conditional. For example, if we want to print the third column only if the sum of the first two columns exceeds 1000, we might write awk -h -F, 'print $3(> (+ $1 $2) 1000)'.

(g) Finally, add the -v=N:V flag that acts as a variable map that can be used in a print command. That is, suppose we want to create a variable called val and assign to it 30. We can do this via -v=val:30, then reference it in a print via $, e.g., awk -F, 'print $val'.

5.19 (⋆) A thesaurus is, in effect, a dataset of words/phrases and information about those words/phrases. For example, a thesaurus may contain a word's definition, synonyms, antonyms, part-of-speech, and more. There are hundreds of collections online that researchers use for sentiment analysis, natural language processing, and more. In this exercise you will create a mini-thesaurus parser that allows the user to lookup information about a word/phrase.

(a) First, design the skeleton for the Thesaurus class. It should store a Set<Word> S as an instance variable.

(b) Design the private and static Word class inside the Thesaurus class body. A Word stores a String s and a Map<String, List<String>> M as instance variables. The string is the word itself, and the map is an association of information "categories" to a list of content. For example, we can create a Word that represents "happy", with an association of "synonym" to List.of("content", "cheery", "jolly"). Design the respective getters and setters for these two instance variables.

(c) In the Word class, design the boolean updateCategory(String c, String v) method, which receives a category c and a value v, and updates the list mapped by c to now include v. If c did not previously exist for that Word, add it to the map and return false. On the other hand, if c did previously exist for that Word, update its association and return true.

(d) In the Word class, override the equals and hashCode methods to compare two Word objects for equality and generate the hash code respectively. Two Word objects are equal if they represent the same word.

(e) In the Thesaurus class, design the List<String> getInfo(String c) and List<String> getInfo(String w, String c, int n) methods, where the former calls the latter with Integer.MAX_VALUE as n. The latter, on the other hand, looks up w in S, and

- If $w \notin S$, return null.
- Otherwise, return n items from the category c of w. If n is Integer.MAX_VALUE, return the entire list.

Part III
Searching, Sorting, and Algorithms

6 Searching and Sorting

Abstract This section is divided into two parts. In the first part, we discuss the two popular searching algorithms: linear and binary search. In the second part, we describe the five most popular sorting algorithms: bubble, selection, insertion, merge, and quick sort. All algorithms are implemented using generics with a functional and in-place approach.

6.1 Searching

In this section we describe two fundamental searching algorithms: linear and binary. To conserve space, we will show the test inputs below, and assume they are appropriately defined in all subsequent code.

```
AbstractList<Integer> LS1 = new ArrayList<>(List.of(78, 43, 22, 101, 29, 34, 23, 12, 33));
AbstractList<Integer> LS2 = new ArrayList<>(List.of(1,2,3,4,5,6,7,8,9,10,11,12));
```

6.1.1 Linear Search

The *linear search* algorithm is a sequential searching algorithm. That is, we check element-by-element to determine if the element we are looking for is in the list. If the element is in the list, we return the index of the element. If the element is not in the list, we (generally) return -1, because -1 is not a valid (list) index in Java. Linear search is nonsensical for non-constant-time access data structures, such as linked lists, because the whole point of linear search is to retrieve an element at its index quickly, then determine if it is the element we are searching.

Standard Recursive Linear Search

We might think that a standard recursive linear search works, and indeed it is possible to write such an algorithm, but in Java it is almost nonsensical to do so. Consider the possible base cases: if the list is empty, what do we return? As described earlier, we might choose to return -1, but think about what happens when the recursive calls unwind. If we add one to the result of the recursive calls when searching, then if the element is not in the list, the returned value will always be the length of the list minus one. Should we find the desired element, we might return zero, which works as expected. It's only in the cases when we do not find the element that we run into trouble. There are two possible solutions: throw an exception if the element is not present, which diverts program control to the exception handler, or simply do not use a standard recursive linear search.[1] We might also think to use `Optional`, but this is also not a good idea, since we would need to check the result of each recursive call, which detracts from the simplicity of the algorithm.

Another reason why the standard-recursive version is suboptimal is because we have no way of passing the index-to-check; we instead have to create sub-lists of the original list, which induces a non-insignificant performance penalty.

First, let's create an interface for designing linear search algorithms. Recall when we stated that the data structure of choice should guarantee constant-access times. The `List` interface does not provide this promise, so we will instead opt for a generic `AbstractList<V>` (where V is any comparable type) which guarantees that any list type that extends `AbstractList` guarantees constant-access time for elements. The method provided by the interface should receive the list and the element to search.

```java
import static Assertions.assertAll;
import static Assertions.assertEquals;

import java.util.AbstractList;
import java.util.NoSuchElementException;

class ILinearSearchTest {

  @Test
  void testSrls() {
    ILinearSearch<Integer> ls = new StandardRecursiveLinearSearch<>();
    assertAll(
      () -> assertEquals(2, ls.linearSearch(LS1, 22)),
      () -> assertThrows(NoSuchElementException.class, () -> ls.linearSearch(LS1, 102)),
      () -> assertEquals(2, ls.linearSearch(LS2, 3)),
      () -> assertThrows(NoSuchElementException.class, () -> ls.linearSearch(LS2, 13)));
  }

  @Test
  void testTrls() {
    ILinearSearch<Integer> ls = new TailRecursiveLinearSearch<>();
    assertAll(
      () -> assertEquals(2, ls.linearSearch(LS1, 22)),
      () -> assertThrows(-1, ls.linearSearch(LS1, 102)),
      () -> assertEquals(2, ls.linearSearch(LS2, 3)),
      () -> assertThrows(-1, ls.linearSearch(LS2, 13)));
  }

  @Test
  void testLLs() {
    ILinearSearch<Integer> ls = new LoopLinearSearch<>();
    assertAll(
      () -> assertEquals(2, ls.linearSearch(LS1, 22)),
      () -> assertThrows(-1, ls.linearSearch(LS1, 102)),
      () -> assertEquals(2, ls.linearSearch(LS2, 3)),
      () -> assertThrows(-1, ls.linearSearch(LS2, 13)));
  }
}
```

---

[1] Some languages, e.g., Scheme, use *continuations* to represent "jump-out" states; allowing the program to forgo unwinding the call stack when returning -1. Since Java does not support continuations by default, we cannot take this approach.

6.1 Searching

```java
import java.lang.Comparable;
import java.util.AbstractList;

interface ILinearSearch<V extends Comparable<V>> {

  int linearSearch(AbstractList<V> ls, V v);
}
```

```java
import java.lang.Comparable;
import java.util.AbstractList;
import java.util.NoSuchElementException;

class StandardRecursiveLinearSearch<V extends Comparable<V>> implements ILinearSearch<V> {

  @Override
  public int linearSearch(AbstractList<V> ls, V v) {
    if (ls.isEmpty()) {
      throw new NoSuchElementException();
    } else if (ls.get(0).equals(v)) {
      return 0;
    } else {
      return 1 + linearSearch((AbstractList<V>) ls.subList(1, ls.size()), v);
    }
  }
}
```

As demonstrated, we must handle the no-element case as an exception, which would otherwise be left as a decision to the programmer that calls this version of the `linearSearch` algorithm.

Tail Recursive Linear Search

The tail recursive linear search is much more intuitive to understand compared to its standard recursive counterpart. We use an accumulator to keep track of the current index, and if we reach the end of the list, then -1 is returned. If we find the element v, we return its index, which does not unwind the stack, since there is no work remaining after each tail call, making this extremely efficient (again, at least in comparison to the standard recursive version).

```java
import java.lang.Comparable;
import java.util.AbstractList;

class TailRecursiveLinearSearch<V extends Comparable<V>> implements ILinearSearch<V> {

  @Override
  public int linearSearch(AbstractList<V> ls, V v) {
    return this.linearSearchHelper(ls, v, 0);
  }

  private int linearSearchHelper(AbstractList<V> ls, V v, int idx) {
    if (idx == ls.size()) { return -1; }
    else if (ls.get(idx).equals(v)) { return idx; }
    else { return linearSearchHelper(ls, v, idx + 1); }
  }
}
```

Loop Linear Search

Even though the tail recursive linear search is relatively straightforward to understand, almost all linear search implementations prefer the iterative version because the call stack becomes irrelevant. With the standard or tail recursive versions, a semi-large input list overflows the stack.

We presented the linear search briefly in Chapter 3, and also ask readers to write the tail recursive and loop variants as an exercise. So, our description of the loop linear search algorithm is kept to a minimum.

```java
import java.lang.Comparable;
import java.util.AbstractList;

class LoopLinearSearch<V extends Comparable<V>> implements ILinearSearch<V> {
  @Override
  public int linearSearch(AbstractList<V> ls, V v) {
    int idx = 0;
    for (int i = 0; i < ls.size(); i++) {
      if (ls.get(i).equals(v)) {
        return i;
      }
    }
    return -1;
  }
}
```

6.1.2 Binary Search

Binary search is the alternative to linear search, and fortunately proves to be significantly faster, but with a catch: the data must be sorted in order to correctly use a binary searching algorithm. Here's how it works: we compare the middle element e of the list against our target value k and if they are equal, we return the middle element index. If $e < k$, we know that k is greater than all elements to the left of e because the data is in sorted order. Therefore, we can search exclusively on the right-half. Without loss of generality, this idea applies to the left-half as well; if $e > k$, then k must be less than all elements to the right of the middle.

Binary search makes even less sense to design as a standard-recursive algorithm because of the fact that we have to search separate partitions of the list. So, we will only design tail-recursive and loop versions. The tail-recursive variant is extremely simple and directly follows from the English description of the algorithm: we keep track of the indices to search between l and h, assuming $l \leq h$. Given this assumption we compute the middle element index as $(l+h)/2$, and recursively update l/h as necessary to change the bounds of the search "zone." If $l > h$, the bounds have crossed, meaning the search element does not exist in the list.

When we state that binary search is faster than linear search, this is of course relative to the problem context; if we want to search an unsorted list exactly once, then taking the time to sort the data, then run binary search, it is not optimal. Repeatedly searching for elements in a list containing many values should be done by first sorting the list, then repeatedly binary searching. As an example, if we were to use linear search on a sorted list containing half a billion elements for an element that is not present, we must check all half a billion values.

6.1 Searching

Binary search, on the other hand, is logarithmic in the number of elements. So, taking the base two logarithm of our input size places an upper-bound of 30 comparisons (after rounding). To say that binary search is a substantial performance increase over linear search is underselling its potential to the extreme.

```java
import static Assertions.assertAll;
import static Assertions.assertEquals;

import java.util.AbstractList;

class IBinarySearchTest {

  @Test
  void testTrbs() {
    IBinarySearch<Integer> ls = new TailRecursiveBinarySearch<>();
    assertAll(
      () -> assertEquals(1, ls.binarySearch(LS1, 22)),
      () -> assertEquals(-1, ls.binarySearch(LS1, 102)),
      () -> assertEquals(4, ls.binarySearch(LS1, 33)),
      () -> assertEquals(7, ls.binarySearch(LS1, 78)),

      () -> assertEquals(2, ls.binarySearch(LS2, 3)),
      () -> assertEquals(-1, ls.binarySearch(LS2, 13)),
      () -> assertEquals(8, ls.binarySearch(LS2, 9)),
      () -> assertEquals(0, ls.binarySearch(LS2, 1)));
  }

  @Test
  void testLbs() {
    IBinarySearch<Integer> ls = new LoopBinarySearch<>();
    assertAll(
      () -> assertEquals(1, ls.binarySearch(LS1, 22)),
      () -> assertEquals(-1, ls.binarySearch(LS1, 102)),
      () -> assertEquals(4, ls.binarySearch(LS1, 33)),
      () -> assertEquals(7, ls.binarySearch(LS1, 78)),

      () -> assertEquals(2, ls.binarySearch(LS2, 3)),
      () -> assertEquals(-1, ls.binarySearch(LS2, 13)),
      () -> assertEquals(8, ls.binarySearch(LS2, 9)),
      () -> assertEquals(0, ls.binarySearch(LS2, 1)));
  }
}
```

```java
import java.lang.Comparable;
import java.util.AbstractList;

interface IBinarySearch<V extends Comparable<V>> {

  int binarySearch(AbstractList<V> ls, V v);
}
```

Tail Recursive Binary Search

```java
import java.lang.Comparable;
import java.util.AbstractList;

class TailRecursiveBinarySearch<V extends Comparable<V>> implements IBinarySearch<V> {

  @Override
  public int binarySearch(AbstractList<V> ls, V v) {
    return binarySearchTRHelper(ls, v, 0, ls.size() - 1);
  }

  private int binarySearchTRHelper(AbstractList<V> ls, V v, int low, int high) {
    if (low > high) { return -1; }
    else {
      int mid = (low + high) / 2;
      if (ls.get(mid).compareTo(v) > 0) {
        return binarySearchTRHelper(ls, v, low, mid - 1);
      } else if (ls.get(mid).compareTo(v) < 0) {
        return binarySearchTRHelper(ls, v, mid + 1, high);
      } else {
        return mid;
      }
    }
  }
}
```

Loop Binary Search

```java
import java.lang.Comparable;
import java.util.AbstractList;

class LoopBinarySearch<V extends Comparable<V>>
                    implements IBinarySearch<V> {

  @Override
  public int binarySearch(AbstractList<V> ls, V v) {
    int low = 0;
    int high = ls.size() - 1;
    while (low <= high) {
      int mid = low + (high - low) / 2;
      if (ls.get(mid).compareTo(v) > 0) { high = mid - 1; }
      else if (ls.get(mid).compareTo(v) < 0) { low = mid + 1; }
      else { return mid; }
    }
    return -1;
  }
}
```

6.1.3 Using Comparators for Searching

Recall the use of comparators from 3 when discussing priority queues. Our implementations of linear and binary search, at the moment, require the generic class that we parameterize over to be Comparable, which can be slightly limiting on the types of classes we can search over because it is not feasible to modify a class that already exists in the Java library. Plus, having to go back and write a definition of compareTo in a Java source file is cumbersome, and is outright irresponsible to amend if the class already contains a definition of compareTo. The solution to this problem is to define a custom Comparator object and pass that to the search methods.

Example 6.1. Let's amend our definition of IBinarySearch to also include a method that receives the Comparator object. Note that we need to specify in the definition of the comparator that the type it receives should be a superclass of the list element type. Therefore, we will use the dual to extends: namely super, in the parameterized type. We do not necessarily care about the type variable of this element, so we can use a wildcard '?' instead of another random letter from the alphabet. With this modification, however, it no longer makes as much sense to quantify that V extends Comparable<V>, because the latter method does not require its type to implement that interface. So, let's remove it from the interface signature and move it down to the type quantification.

```java
import java.lang.Comparable;
import java.util.Comparator;
import java.util.AbstractList;

interface IBinarySearch {
  <V extends Comparable<V>> int binarySearch(AbstractList<V> ls, V v);
  <V> int binarySearch(AbstractList<V> ls, V v, Comparator<? super V> c);
}
```

Now, we do not want to have to rewrite the entire definition of binarySearch just to make use of a different comparator, and indeed, we do not have to do so. All we must do is move the logic of the search into the version that receives a comparator and update the other one that operates over comparable elements. This means that we need to instantiate a Comparator that uses the compareTo method from the elements, which is trivial to do via a lambda expression. We also must change the definition from using compareTo, which comes from Comparable to use compare from the c object.

```java
import static Assertions.assertAll;
import static Assertions.assertEquals;
import java.util.AbstractList;

class IBinarySearchTester {

  @Test
  void testBinarySearchComparator() {
    IBinarySearch<Integer> search = new TailRecursiveBinarySearch<>();
    assertAll(
      () -> assertEquals(0, search.binarySearch(ls, 1, (o1, o2) -> o1.compareTo(o2))),
      () -> assertEquals(4, search.binarySearch(ls, 5, (o1, o2) -> o1.compareTo(o2))),
      () -> assertEquals(-1, search.binarySearch(ls, 11, (o1, o2) -> o1.compareTo(o2))));
  }
}
```

```java
import java.lang.Comparable;
import java.util.AbstractList;
import java.util.Comparator;

class TailRecursiveBinarySearch implements IBinarySearch {

  @Override
  public <V extends Comparable<V>> int binarySearch(AbstractList<V> ls, V v) {
    return binarySearchTRHelper(ls, v, 0, ls.size() - 1, (o1, o2) -> o1.compareTo(o2));
  }

  @Override
  public <V> int binarySearch(AbstractList<V> ls, V v, Comparator<? super V> c) {
    return binarySearchTRHelper(ls, v, 0, ls.size() - 1, c);
  }

  private <V> int binarySearchTRHelper(AbstractList<V> ls, V v, int low, int high,
                                       Comparator<? super V> c) {
    if (low > high) {
      return -1;
    } else {
      int mid = low + (high - low) / 2;
      if (c.compare(ls.get(mid), v) > 0) {
        return binarySearchTRHelper(ls, v, low, mid - 1, c);
      } else if (c.compare(ls.get(mid), v) < 0) {
        return binarySearchTRHelper(ls, v, mid + 1, high, c);
      } else {
        return mid;
      }
    }
  }
}
```

We leave changing the loop variant to use comparators as an exercise. It does not make sense to update `ILinearSearch` because linear search uses `equals` for comparing objects, rather than `.compareTo` or `.compare`, since directionality of the comparison is not necessary for linear search.

6.2 Sorting

In this section we will begin our discussion on the implementation of sorting algorithms. Each algorithm contains two variants: a functional and in-place variant. The functional variant will return a new list that is sorted, while the in-place variant sorts the list passed as a parameter. The functional variant is, in principle, easier to implement, but the in-place variant is more efficient in terms of memory usage. Moreover, all lists that are parameters to the sorting algorithms are assumed to be constant-access lists. Accordingly, we specify that the input list extends `AbstractList` class, which guarantees the constant-access property.

For each algorithm, we will assume the same three lists are declared and properly instantiated within the respective unit testing files. To conserve space, we enumerate their values below only once.

```java
AbstractList<Integer> LS1 = new ArrayList<>(List.of(5, 4, 2, 1, 3));
AbstractList<Integer> LS2 = new ArrayList<>(List.of());
AbstractList<Integer> LS3 = new ArrayList<>(List.of(10, 8, 6, 7, 2, 10, 3, 3, 3, 10));
```

6.2.1 Bubble Sort

Our sorting journey begins with the worst-performing sort out of the five that we will discuss: *bubble sort*. With bubble sort, we repeatedly swap adjacent elements if they are in the wrong order. We repeat the process until the list is sorted, which is guaranteed after at most n^2 iterations, where n is the size of the input list. Figure 6.1 illustrates the in-place bubble sort algorithm. Note the use of two iteration variables i and j, where i represents the outer loop and j represents the inner loop. The inner loop is responsible for the actual swapping of elements, whereas the outer controls the number of traversals over the list. The idea is to "bubble" the elements to the top/end of the list via repeated comparisons and swapping, hence the name. There are optimizations that can be made to the bubble sort algorithm. For example, if we traverse through the entire list without swapping at all, then the list must be in sorted order and we can terminate early. We will not implement the optimization, but it is worth considering.

```
import static Assertions.assertAll;
import static Assertions.assertEquals;

class BubbleSortTester {

  @Test
  void fbs() {
    IBubbleSort<Integer> fbs = new FunctionalBubbleSort<>();
    assertAll(
      () -> assertEquals(List.of(1, 2, 3, 4, 5),
                         fbs.bubbleSort(LS1)),
      () -> assertEquals(List.of(),
                         fbs.bubbleSort(LS2)),
      () -> assertEquals(List.of(2, 3, 3, 3, 6, 7, 8, 10, 10, 10),
                         fbs.bubbleSort(LS3)));
  }

  @Test
  void ipbs() {
    IBubbleSort<Integer> ipbs = new InPlaceBubbleSort<>();
    assertAll(
      () -> ipbs.bubbleSort(LS1),
      () -> assertEquals(List.of(1, 2, 3, 4, 5), LS1),
      () -> ipbs.bubbleSort(LS2),
      () -> assertEquals(List.of(), LS2),
      () -> ipbs.bubbleSort(LS3),
      () -> assertEquals(List.of(2, 3, 3, 3, 6, 7, 8, 10, 10, 10), LS3));
  }
}
```

```
import java.lang.Comparable;
import java.util.AbstractList;

interface IBubbleSort<V extends Comparable<V>> {
  AbstractList<V> bubbleSort(AbstractList<V> ls);
}
```

Functional Bubble Sort

The functional bubble sort removes exactly one instance of the largest element in the list, then recursively sorts the remaining list. Once we know that list is sorted (by the recursive invariant property), we insert the largest element back into the list.

```java
import java.lang.Comparable;
import java.util.AbstractList;
import java.util.ArrayList;

class FunctionalBubbleSort<V extends Comparable<V>> implements IBubbleSort<V> {

  @Override
  public AbstractList<V> bubbleSort(AbstractList<V> ls) {
    if (ls.size() <= 1) {
      return ls;
    } else {
      // Find the largest element.
      V largest = getLargest(ls);
      boolean removed = false;

      // Get all elements but the largest. Removes only
      // one occurrence of the largest element.
      AbstractList<V> rest = new ArrayList<>();
      for (V v : ls) {
        if (v.equals(largest) && !removed) {
          removed = true;
        } else {
          rest.add(v);
        }
      }

      // Bubble sort the rest, then add the largest as the last element.
      AbstractList<V> newLs = bubbleSort(rest);
      newLs.add(largest);
      return newLs;
    }
  }

  /**
   * Retrieves the largest element in the list. If the list is
   * empty, null is returned.
   * @param ls the list to search.
   * @return the largest element in the list.
   */
  private V getLargest(AbstractList<V> ls) {
    return ls.stream()
            .max(Comparable::compareTo)
            .orElse(null);
  }
}
```

6.2 Sorting

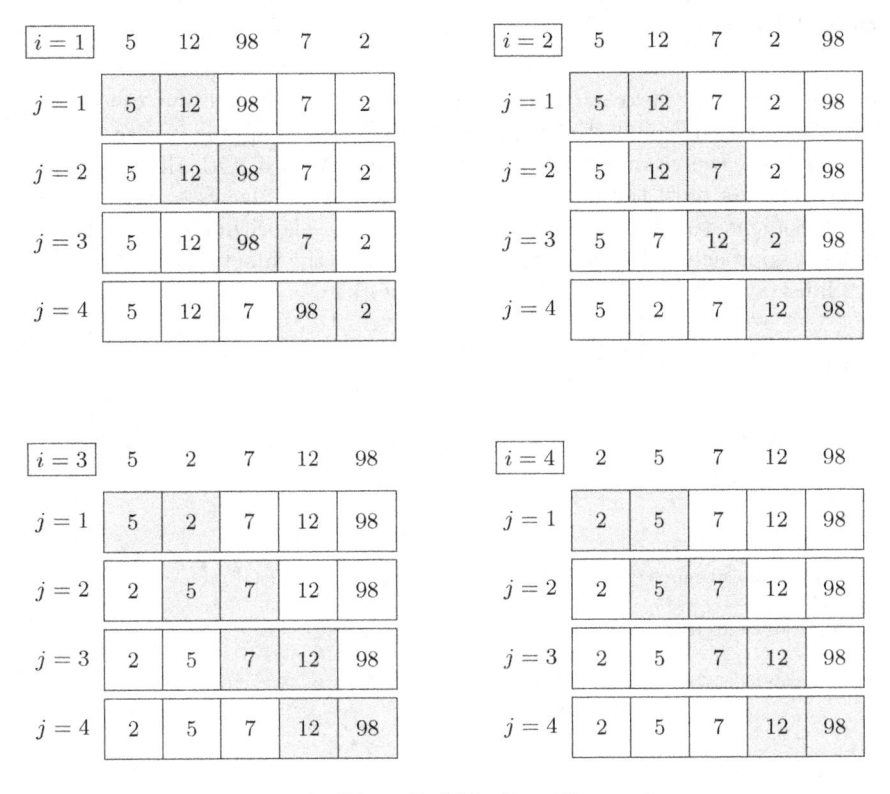

Fig. 6.1: In-Place Bubble Sort Illustration

In-place Bubble Sort

```java
import java.lang.Comparable;
import java.util.AbstractList;
import java.util.Collections;

class InPlaceBubbleSort<V extends Comparable<V>> implements IBubbleSort<V> {

  @Override
  public AbstractList<V> bubbleSort(AbstractList<V> ls) {
    for (int i = 0; i < ls.size(); i++) {
      for (int j = 0; j < ls.size() - i - 1; j++) {
        if (ls.get(j).compareTo(ls.get(j + 1)) > 0) {
          Collections.swap(ls, j, j + 1);
        }
      }
    }
    return ls;
  }
}
```

6.2.2 Selection Sort

The *selection sort* is the next sorting algorithm that we will describe. Selection sort works by first searching for the smallest element in the list, then swapping it with the first element. Then we search for the second smallest element, and swap it with the second element. We continue this process until the list is sorted. Being that we always search the entire list for the smallest element, this is a horrendously slow sorting algorithm and should be avoided in favor of faster approaches. Nevertheless, we show both the functional and in-place versions. Figure 6.2 illustrates the in-place selection sort algorithm.

```java
import static Assertions.assertAll;
import static Assertions.assertEquals;

import java.util.List;

class SelectionSortTester {

  @Test
  void fSelSort() {
    ISelectionSort<Integer> ss = new FunctionalSelectionSort<>();
    assertAll(
      () -> assertEquals(List.of(),
                         ss.selectionSort(LS2)),
      () -> assertEquals(List.of(2, 3, 3, 3, 6, 7, 8, 10, 10, 10),
                         ss.selectionSort(LS3)));
  }

  @Test
  void ipqsTester() {
    ISelectionSort<Integer> ss = new InPlaceSelectionSort<>();
    assertAll(
      () -> ss.selectionSort(LS2),
      () -> assertEquals(List.of(), LS2),
      () -> ss.selectionSort(LS3),
      () -> assertEquals(List.of(2, 3, 3, 3, 6, 7, 8, 10, 10, 10), LS3));
  }
}
```

```java
import java.lang.Comparable;
import java.util.AbstractList;

interface ISelectionSort<V extends Comparable<V>> {
  AbstractList<V> selectionSort(AbstractList<V> ls);
}
```

6.2 Sorting

Functional Selection Sort

```java
import java.util.*;

class FunctionalSelectionSort<V extends Comparable<V>> implements ISelectionSort<V> {

  @Override
  public AbstractList<V> selectionSort(AbstractList<V> ls) {
    if (ls.isEmpty() || ls.size() == 1) { return ls; }
    else {
      // Recall that min returns an Optional, but we know it is nonempty.
      int minIdx = IntStream.range(0, ls.size())
                            .boxed()
                            .min((i1,i2) -> ls.get(i1).compareTo(ls.get(i2)))
                            .get();

      // Swap the minimum element with the first element.
      Collections.swap(ls, 0, minIdx);
      // Sort the rest of the list (excluding the first element).
      List<V> rest = new ArrayList<>(ls.subList(1, ls.size()));
      AbstractList<V> sortedRest = selectionSort(rest);
      // Construct the final sorted list.
      AbstractList<V> sortedList = new ArrayList<>();
      sortedList.add(ls.get(0));
      sortedList.addAll(sortedRest);
      return sortedList;
    }
  }
}
```

In-place Selection Sort

```java
import java.util.*;

class InPlaceSelectionSort<V extends Comparable<V>> implements ISelectionSort<V> {

  @Override
  public AbstractList<V> selectionSort(AbstractList<V> ls) {
    for (int i = 0; i < ls.size(); i++) {
      V min = ls.get(i);
      int minIdx = 0;
      boolean needToSwap = false;
      // Find the minimum value. If we get a value < curr min, swap at end.
      for (int j = i + 1; j < ls.size(); j++) {
        if (ls.get(j).compareTo(min) < 0) {
          min = ls.get(j);
          minIdx = j;
          needToSwap = true;
        }
      }
      if(needToSwap) { Collections.swap(ls, minIdx, i); }
    }
    return ls;
  }
}
```

| $i=0$ | 5 | 2 | 1 | 13 | 98 | 12 | 7 | 6 | 97 |

| $i=1$ | 1 | 2 | 5 | 13 | 98 | 12 | 7 | 6 | 97 |

| $i=2$ | 1 | 2 | 5 | 13 | 98 | 12 | 7 | 6 | 97 |

| $i=3$ | 1 | 2 | 5 | 13 | 98 | 12 | 7 | 6 | 97 |

| $i=4$ | 1 | 2 | 5 | 6 | 98 | 12 | 7 | 13 | 97 |

| $i=5$ | 1 | 2 | 5 | 6 | 7 | 12 | 98 | 13 | 97 |

| $i=6$ | 1 | 2 | 5 | 6 | 7 | 12 | 98 | 13 | 97 |

| $i=7$ | 1 | 2 | 5 | 6 | 7 | 12 | 13 | 98 | 97 |

| $i=8$ | 1 | 2 | 5 | 6 | 7 | 12 | 13 | 97 | 98 |

| $i=9$ | 1 | 2 | 5 | 6 | 7 | 12 | 13 | 97 | 98 |

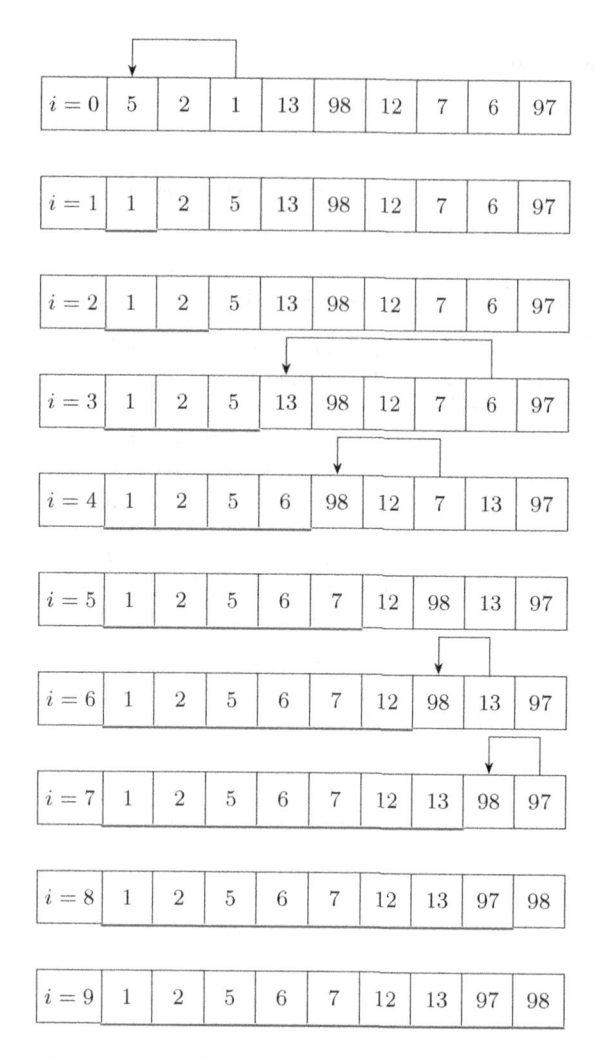

Fig. 6.2: In-Place Selection Sort Illustration

6.2.3 Insertion Sort

The insertion sort is the last of the three poorly-performing sorting algorithms that w will discuss. Insertion sort, in general, works by taking an element from the unsorted list and inserting it into the correct position in a sorted list. Figure 6.3 illustrates the in-place insertion sort algorithm; each iteration of the outer loop is represented by a row in the figure, with the red under-bars representing the now-sorted sub-list.

6.2 Sorting

```java
import static Assertions.assertAll;
import static Assertions.assertEquals;

class InsertionSortTester {

  @Test
  void fInsSort() {
    IInsertionSort<Integer> ss = new FunctionalInsertionSort<>();
    assertAll(
      () -> assertEquals(List.of(1, 2, 3, 4, 5),
                         ss.insertionSort(LS1)),
      () -> assertEquals(List.of(),
                         ss.insertionSort(LS2)),
      () -> assertEquals(List.of(2, 3, 3, 3, 6, 7, 8, 10, 10, 10),
                         ss.insertionSort(LS3)));
  }

  @Test
  void ipInsSort() {
    IInsertionSort<Integer> is = new InPlaceInsertionSort<>();
    assertAll(
      () -> is.insertionSort(LS1),
      () -> assertEquals(List.of(1, 2, 3, 4, 5), LS1),
      () -> is.insertionSort(LS2),
      () -> assertEquals(List.of(), LS2),
      () -> is.insertionSort(LS3),
      () -> assertEquals(List.of(2, 3, 3, 3, 6, 7, 8, 10, 10, 10), LS3));
  }
}
```

```java
import java.util.AbstractList;

interface IInsertionSort<V extends Comparable<V>> {

  AbstractList<V> insertionSort(AbstractList<V> ls);
}
```

Functional Insertion Sort

The functional insertion sort is a recursive sorting algorithm; it sorts the list by recursively sorting its tail (i.e., the list without the first element). Once the tail is sorted, the algorithm inserts the first element into the sorted tail. We know how to insert an element into a sorted list: we compare the element to insert with the first element of the sorted list. If the list is empty, then we return a list containing only the provided element. If the element to insert is less than the first element of the sorted list, we insert the element at the beginning of the list, which is provably correct because the list is sorted. Otherwise, we (recursively) insert the element into the sorted tail of the list.

```java
import java.lang.Comparable;
import java.util.AbstractList;
import java.util.ArrayList;

class FunctionalInsertionSort<V extends Comparable<V>> implements IInsertionSort<V> {

  @Override
  public AbstractList<V> insertionSort(AbstractList<V> ls) {
    if (ls.isEmpty()) {
      return new ArrayList<>();
    } else {
      AbstractList<V> rest = (AbstractList<V>) ls.subList(1, ls.size());
      return insert(ls.get(0), insertionSort(rest));
    }
  }

  /**
   * Inserts an element into a sorted list of values.
   * @param val value to insert.
   * @param sortedRest a sorted sub-list.
   * @return the sorted sub-list with the new value inserted.
   */
  private AbstractList<V> insert(V val, AbstractList<V> sortedRest) {
    if (sortedRest.isEmpty()) {
      ArrayList<V> ls = new ArrayList<>();
      ls.add(val);
      return ls;
    } else if (val.compareTo(sortedRest.get(0)) < 0) {
      ArrayList<V> ls = new ArrayList<>();
      ls.add(val);
      ls.addAll(sortedRest);
      return ls;
    } else {
      ArrayList<V> ls = new ArrayList<>();
      ls.add(sortedRest.get(0));
      ls.addAll(insert(val, (AbstractList<V>)
                          sortedRest.subList(1, sortedRest.size())));
      return ls;
    }
  }
}
```

In-place Insertion Sort

```java
import java.lang.Comparable;
import java.util.AbstractList;
import java.util.Collections;

class InPlaceInsertionSort<V extends Comparable<V>> implements IInsertionSort<V> {

  @Override
  public AbstractList<V> insertionSort(AbstractList<V> ls) {
    for (int i = 1; i < ls.size(); i++) {
      V curr = ls.get(i);
      int j = i - 1;
      while (j >= 0 && ls.get(j).compareTo(curr) > 0) {
        Collections.swap(ls, j+1, j);
        j--;
      }
    }
    return ls;
  }
}
```

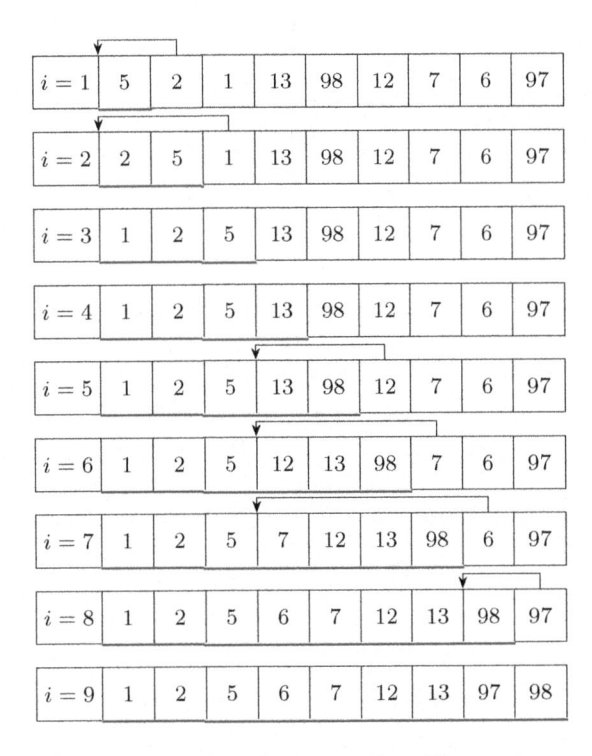

$i=1$	5	2	1	13	98	12	7	6	97
$i=2$	2	5	1	13	98	12	7	6	97
$i=3$	1	2	5	13	98	12	7	6	97
$i=4$	1	2	5	13	98	12	7	6	97
$i=5$	1	2	5	13	98	12	7	6	97
$i=6$	1	2	5	12	13	98	7	6	97
$i=7$	1	2	5	7	12	13	98	6	97
$i=8$	1	2	5	6	7	12	13	98	97
$i=9$	1	2	5	6	7	12	13	97	98

Fig. 6.3: In-Place Insertion Sort Illustration

6.2.4 Merge Sort

The *merge sort* is one of the first explicitly divide-and-conquer algorithms that programmers encounter. We "divide" the sorted list into halves, and recursively sort those halves. The base case is when the list is either empty or a singleton, since we certainly know how to sort these kinds of lists. After dividing comes the "conquering," which consists of taking two now-sorted lists and combining their elements to create yet another sorted list. Recall that, at the base case, we know the singletons are sorted by definition. Because of this *invariant*, we know that merging the contents of two sorted lists is not an issue: we compare each element one-by-one, putting the smaller of the two before the subsequent value.

In Figure 6.4, we sort the list $[5, 2, 1, 13, 98, 12, 7, 6, 97]$ by decomposing the list into two smaller lists: $[5, 2, 1, 13, 98]$, and $[12, 7, 6, 97]$. We recursively decompose these two further until we end with the base case, at which we proceed to merge the now-sorted sub-lists back into one overall sorted list.

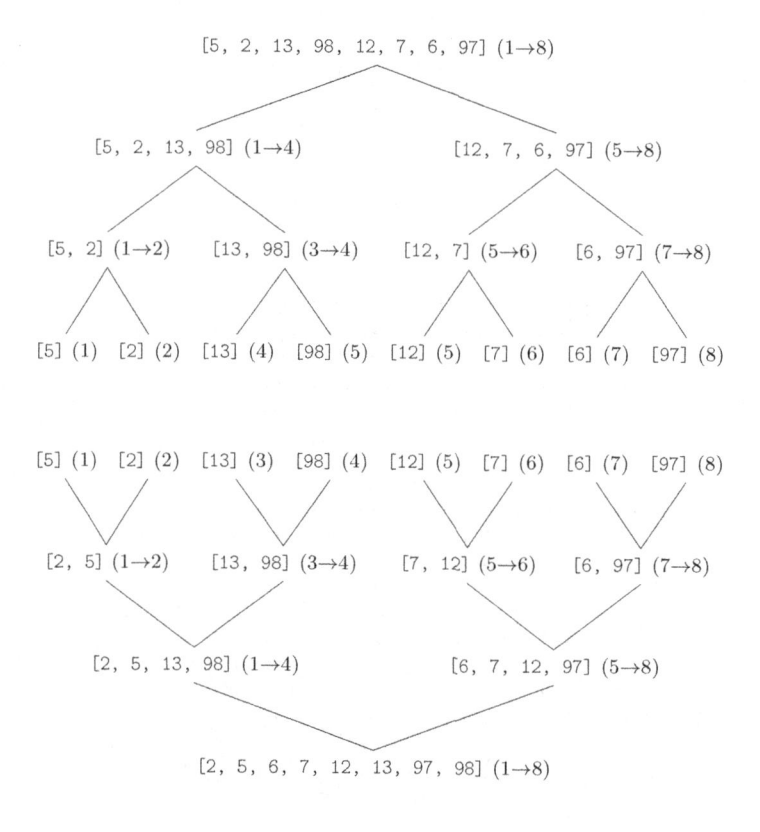

Fig. 6.4: Merge Sort Illustration

6.2 Sorting

Example 6.2. Consider merging the lists $l_1 = [9, 11, 14]$, and $l_2 = [2, 20]$. We create a new list l_3 whose size is the sum of the sizes of l_1 and l_2. Then, we compare 9 against 2, of which the latter is smaller, meaning it goes first in l_3. Then, we compare 20 against 9, of which the latter is smaller, meaning it is second. Then, we compare 20 against 11, of which the latter is smaller, meaning it is third. Then, we compare 20 against 14, of which the latter is, once again, smaller, meaning it is fourth. Since we have exhausted all elements of l_1, and we know for certain that l_2 is sorted, we can just copy the remaining elements of l_2 into l_3.

```
import static Assertions.assertAll;
import static Assertions.assertEquals;

class MergeSortTester {

  @Test
  void fmsTester() {
    IMergeSort<Integer> ms = new FunctionalMergeSort<>();
    assertAll(
      () -> assertEquals(List.of(1, 2, 3, 4, 5),
                         ms.mergeSort(LS1)),
      () -> assertEquals(List.of(),
                         ms.mergeSort(LS2)),
      () -> assertEquals(List.of(2, 3, 3, 3, 6, 7, 8, 10, 10, 10),
                         ms.mergeSort(LS3)));
  }

  @Test
  void ipmsTester() {
    IMergeSort<Integer> ms = new FunctionalMergeSort<>();
    assertAll(
      () -> ms.mergeSort(LS1),
      () -> assertEquals(List.of(1, 2, 3, 4, 5), LS1),
      () -> ms.mergeSort(LS2),
      () -> assertEquals(List.of(), LS2),
      () -> ms.mergeSort(LS3),
      () -> assertEquals(List.of(2, 3, 3, 3, 6, 7, 8, 10, 10, 10), LS3));
  }
}
```

```
import java.util.AbstractList;

interface IMergeSort<V extends Comparable<V>> {

  AbstractList<V> mergeSort(AbstractList<V> ls);
}
```

Functional Merge Sort

```java
import java.lang.Comparable;
import java.util.AbstractList;
import java.util.ArrayList;
import java.util.List;

class FunctionalMergeSort<V extends Comparable<V>> implements IMergeSort<V> {

  @Override
  public AbstractList<V> mergeSort(AbstractList<V> ls) { return this.msHelper(ls); }

  /**
   * Recursive helper method for merge sort. Splits the list
   * in half and merges the two halves after recursively sorting them.
   * @param ls the list to sort.
   * @return the sorted list.
   */
  private AbstractList<V> msHelper(AbstractList<V> ls) {
    if (ls.isEmpty()) { return new ArrayList<>(); }
    else if (ls.size() == 1) {
      AbstractList<V> newLs = new ArrayList<>();
      newLs.add(ls.get(0));
      return newLs;
    } else {
      int mid = (ls.size() - 1) / 2;
      List<V> left = ls.subList(0, mid + 1);
      List<V> right = ls.subList(mid + 1, ls.size());
      AbstractList<V> leftSort = this.msHelper((AbstractList<V>) left);
      AbstractList<V> rightSort = this.msHelper((AbstractList<V>) right);
      return this.merge(leftSort, rightSort);
    }
  }

  /**
   * Merges two sorted lists into one sorted list. Compares each
   * element one-by-one and adds the smaller element to the new list.
   * If one list is exhausted, the elements of the other list are
   * added to the new list.
   * @param ls1 the first sorted list.
   * @param ls2 the second sorted list.
   * @return the merged sorted list.
   */
  private AbstractList<V> merge(AbstractList<V> ls1, AbstractList<V> ls2) {
    int i, j = 0;
    AbstractList<V> newLs = new ArrayList<>();
    // Merge the lists, comparing the elements.
    while (i < ls1.size() && j < ls2.size()) {
      if (ls1.get(i).compareTo(ls2.get(j)) < 0) { newLs.add(ls1.get(i++)); }
      else { newLs.add(ls2.get(j++)); }
    }
    // Finish copying ls1.
    while (i < ls1.size()) { newLs.add(ls1.get(i++)); }
    // Finish copying ls2.
    while (j < ls2.size()) { newLs.add(ls2.get(j++)); }
    return newLs;
  }
}
```

6.2 Sorting

In-place Merge Sort

```java
import java.lang.Comparable;
import java.util.AbstractList;
import java.util.ArrayList;

class InPlaceMergeSort<V extends Comparable<V>> implements IMergeSort<V> {

  @Override
  public AbstractList<V> mergeSort(AbstractList<V> ls) {
    this.msHelper(ls, 0, ls.size() - 1);
    return ls;
  }

  /**
   * Recursively sorts the list by splitting it in half and merging the halves.
   * @param ls the list to sort.
   * @param low the lower bound of the sub-list.
   * @param high the upper bound of the sub-list.
   */
  private void msHelper(AbstractList<V> ls, int low, int high) {
    if (low < high) {
      int mid = low + (high - low) / 2;
      this.msHelper(ls, low, mid);
      this.msHelper(ls, mid + 1, high);
      this.merge(ls, low, mid, high);
    }
  }

  /**
   * Merges two sorted sub-lists into one sorted list.
   * @param ls the list to sort.
   * @param low the lower bound of the sub-list.
   * @param mid the middle index of the sub-list.
   * @param high the upper bound of the sub-list.
   */
  private void merge(AbstractList<V> ls, int low, int mid, int high) {
    AbstractList<V> ls1 = new ArrayList<>();
    AbstractList<V> ls2 = new ArrayList<>();
    for (int i = low; i <= mid; i++) { ls1.add(ls.get(i)); }
    for (int j = mid + 1; j <= high; j++) { ls2.add(ls.get(j)); }
    int mergeIdx = low;
    int i, j = 0;
    // Merge the elements into the existing list.
    while (i < ls1.size() && j < ls2.size()) {
      if (ls1.get(i).compareTo(ls2.get(j)) < 0) {
        ls.set(mergeIdx++, ls1.get(i++));
      } else {
        ls.set(mergeIdx++, ls2.get(j++));
      }
    }
    // Copy the rest of the elements over.
    while (i < ls1.size()) { ls.set(mergeIdx++, ls1.get(i++)); }
    while (j < ls2.size()) { ls.set(mergeIdx++, ls2.get(j++)); }
  }
}
```

6.2.5 Quick Sort

At last, we arrive at the *quick sort* algorithm. Quick sort works by choosing a *pivot*, which is some value in the list. We then recursively sort all elements that are less than the pivot and all those that are greater than the pivot. Our implementation of the in-place quicksort works slightly differently, which is why we favor the functional version over the in-place counterpart.

Quick sort performs optimally when the median is selected as the pivot because roughly half of the elements are less than the pivot and roughly half are greater than the pivot, allowing for a performance similar to that of merge sort. Unfortunately, finding the median a priori to sorting ultimately defeats the point. In the subsequent chapter, we will analyze the sorting algorithms in more detail.

```java
import static Assertions.assertAll;
import static Assertions.assertEquals;

class QuickSortTester {

  @Test
  void fqsTester() {
    IQuickSort<Integer> fqs = new FunctionalQuickSort<>();
    assertAll(
      () -> assertEquals(List.of(1, 2, 3, 4, 5), fqs.quicksort(LS1)),
      () -> assertEquals(List.of(), fqs.quicksort(LS2)),
      () -> assertEquals(List.of(2, 3, 3, 3, 6, 7, 8, 10, 10, 10),
                         fqs.quicksort(LS3)));
  }

  @Test
  void ipqsTester() {
    IQuickSort<Integer> ipqs = new InPlaceQuickSort<>();
    assertAll(
      () -> ipqs.quicksort(LS1),
      () -> assertEquals(List.of(1, 2, 3, 4, 5), LS1),
      () -> ipqs.quicksort(LS2),
      () -> assertEquals(List.of(), LS2),
      () -> ipqs.quicksort(LS3),
      () -> assertEquals(List.of(2, 3, 3, 3, 6, 7, 8, 10, 10, 10), LS3));
  }
}
```

```java
import java.lang.Comparable;
import java.util.AbstractList;

interface IQuickSort<V extends Comparable<V>> {
  AbstractList<V> quicksort(AbstractList<V> ls);
}
```

Functional Quick Sort

The functional implementation of quick sort is beautiful and elegant. We choose a pivot $p \in L$ at random, then create three sub-lists $l_<$, $l_>$, $l_=$, where $l_<$ stores all elements less than p, where $l_>$ stores all elements greater than p, and $l_=$ stores all elements equal to p. Each sub-list, excluding $l_=$, is recursively sorted, followed by concatenating the three sub-lists in order.

```
import java.lang.Comparable;
import java.util.AbstractList;
import java.util.stream.Collectors;

class FunctionalQuickSort<V extends Comparable<V>>
                    implements IQuickSort<V> {

  @Override
  public AbstractList<V> quicksort(AbstractList<V> ls) {
    if (ls.isEmpty()) { return ls; }
    else {
      // Choose a random pivot.
      V pivot = ls.get((int) (Math.random() * ls.size()));

      // Sort the left-half.
      AbstractList<V> leftHalf = (AbstractList<V>)
                              ls.stream()
                                .filter(x -> x.compareTo(pivot) < 0)
                                .collect(Collectors.toList());
      AbstractList<V> leftSorted = quicksort(leftHalf);

      // Sort the right-half.
      AbstractList<V> rightHalf = (AbstractList<V>)
                              ls.stream()
                                .filter(x -> x.compareTo(pivot) > 0)
                                .collect(Collectors.toList());
      AbstractList<V> rightSorted = quicksort(rightHalf);

      // Get all elements equal to the pivot.
      AbstractList<V> equal = (AbstractList<V>)
                          ls.stream()
                            .filter(x -> x.compareTo(pivot) == 0)
                            .collect(Collectors.toList());

      // Merge the three.
      leftSorted.addAll(equal);
      leftSorted.addAll(rightSorted);
      return leftSorted;
    }
  }
}
```

In-place Quick Sort

```java
import java.lang.Comparable;
import java.util.*;

class InPlaceQuickSort<V extends Comparable<V>> implements IQuickSort<V> {

  @Override
  public AbstractList<V> quicksort(AbstractList<V> ls) {
    this.quicksortHelper(ls, 0, ls.size() - 1);
    return ls;
  }

  /**
   * Recursive helper method for quicksort.
   * @param ls the List to sort.
   * @param low the lower bound of the partition.
   * @param high the upper bound of the partition.
   */
  private void quicksortHelper(AbstractList<V> ls, int low, int high) {
    if (low < high) {
      int pivot = quicksortPartition(ls, low, high);
      quicksortHelper(ls, low, pivot - 1);
      quicksortHelper(ls, pivot + 1, high);
    }
  }

  /**
   * Creates a quicksort partition, where all elements less than
   * the pivot are to the left of the pivot, and all elements
   * greater than the pivot are to its right.
   * @param ls the list to partition.
   * @param low the lower bound of the partition.
   * @param high the upper bound of the partition.
   * @return the index of the pivot.
   */
  private int quicksortPartition(AbstractList<V> ls, int low, int high) {
    int rand = new Random().nextInt(high - low + 1) + low;
    Collections.swap(ls, rand, high);
    V pivot = ls.get(high);
    int prevLowest = low;
    for (int i = low; i <= high; i++) {
      if (ls.get(i).compareTo(pivot) < 0) {
        Collections.swap(ls, i, prevLowest++);
      }
    }
    Collections.swap(ls, prevLowest, high);
    return prevLowest;
  }
}
```

6.2.6 Priority Queue Sort

As a bonus, let's briefly discuss the priority queue sort, which leverages the power of, you guessed it: a priority queue. Recall from Chapter 3 that priority queues sort elements based on their priority, which itself is defined as either the natural ordering of the elements or a custom comparator. The priority queue sort algorithm works by first adding all elements from the given list into the queue, then repeatedly removing the maximum element from the heap, and placing it at the end of a list. Each time an element is polled from the priority queue, its underlying structure is adjusted to reassign the maximum element to the top of the queue.

We create a priority queue from the list, repeatedly poll the queue until it is empty, and add the polled elements to the rear of a new list. Remember that inserting elements onto the front of an `ArrayList` list is slow, so we return a `LinkedList` instead.[2]

```java
import java.lang.Comparable;
import java.util.AbstractSequentialList;
import java.util.List;

interface IPriorityQueueSort<V extends Comparable<V>> {

  AbstractSequentialList<V> pqSort(List<V> ls);
}
```

```java
import java.lang.Comparable;
import java.util.AbstractSequentialList;
import java.util.LinkedList;
import java.util.List;
import java.util.PriorityQueue;
import java.util.Queue;

class FunctionalPriorityQueueSort<V extends Comparable<V>>
                              implements IPriorityQueueSort<V> {

  @Override
  public AbstractSequentialList<V> pqSort(List<V> ls) {
    Queue<V> pq = new PriorityQueue<>(ls);
    AbstractSequentialList<V> sorted = new LinkedList<>();
    while (!pq.isEmpty()) {
      sorted.add(pq.poll());
    }
    return sorted;
  }
}
```

---

[2] The other sorting algorithms return instances of `AbstractList` to guarantee (constant-time) random access to elements. The heap sort, on the contrary, will instead return an `AbstractSequentialList` to ensure that adding elements to the front of the list is constant-time. The `LinkedList` class is a subclass of `AbstractSequentialList`.

7 Algorithm Analysis

Abstract This chapter introduces readers to how we analyze algorithm performance through asymptotic analysis. We will discuss Big-Oh, Big-Omega, and Theta notation, as well as the best, average, and worst-case analysis of algorithms. We then use these tools to analyze the performance of the searching and sorting algorithms discussed in Chapter 6.

7.1 Analyzing Algorithms

Asymptotic analysis, or in general, the analysis of function growth, relates heavily to the performance of an algorithm. We can represent algorithms as mathematical functions and describe their relative performance in terms of the input size.

Example 7.1. Consider the linear search algorithm. We know that, in the best case, the item that we are searching for is the first element in the list. In the average case, it is found in the middle of the list. In the worst case, the element does not exist in the list. Because we have to traverse through n elements, namely the n elements of our input list, we say that the linear search grows linearly in proportion to its input size. *Best-case, average-case,* and *worst-case* describe the potential inputs to a function. We can ascribe similar attributes to binary search, the sorting algorithms from the previous chapter and beyond. Though, we need a notation to denote the growth rate of a function. In computer science, we most often make use of *Big-Oh notation*, which denotes the upper bound on the growth of a function. That is, a function $f(n) = \mathcal{O}(g(n))$ if, at some point, $f(n)$ begins to forever grow slower than or equal to $g(n)$. We can roughly replace the equals '=' sign with a less-than-or-equal-to '$\leq$' sign. One detail to note is that the end-behavior of a polynomial is determined by its highest-order term. For example, $f(n) = 0.5x^2 + 0.5\cos(\deg(5x))$ is upper-bounded by $g(n) = 0.5x^2$, because the cosine function is upper-bounded by 1. When describing a function in terms of asymptotic bounds, we can drop/ignore all coefficients and lower-order terms.

Example 7.2. Consider the following functions $f(n) = 0.5x^2 + 0.5\cos(\deg(5x))$ and $g(n) = 0.2x^3 + 0.3\sin(\deg(4x))$. As we stated, we can drop all lower-order terms and coefficients, meaning $f(n) = n^2$ and $g(n) = n^3$. From here, it is trivial to see that for any $n \geq 1$, $g(n)$ grows faster (or at least as fast) than $f(n)$. Thus, we say that $f(n) = \mathcal{O}(g(n))$.[1]

---

[1] There is a bit more to the formalism of Big-Oh, but we will explain those details in due time.

© The Author(s), under exclusive license to Springer Nature Switzerland AG 2024
J. Crotts, *Learning Java*, https://doi.org/10.1007/978-3-031-66638-4_7

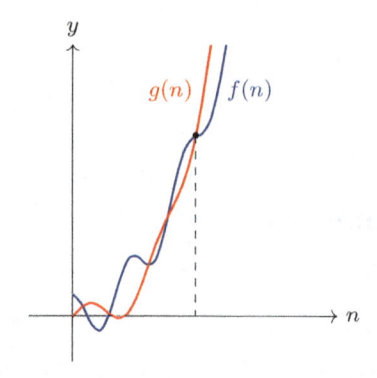

Fig. 7.1: $f(n) = \mathcal{O}(g(n))$

There are two other common notations for asymptotic analysis: Big-Omega and Theta. *Big-Omega* describes the lower-bound of the growth of a function, and Theta describes the tight bound of a function. That is, $f(n) = \Omega(g(n))$ if there is a point at which $f(n)$ begins to grow faster than or equal to $g(n)$. We can roughly replace the equals '=' sign with a greater-than-or-equal-to '$\geq$' relation. Similarly, $f(n) = \Theta(g(n))$ if $f(n) = \mathcal{O}(g(n))$ and $f(n) = \Omega(g(n))$. We can roughly replace the equals '=' sign with an equivalence '$\equiv$' sign. Examples for Omega and Theta are harder to come by without a formalized definition, so we will defer them until later.

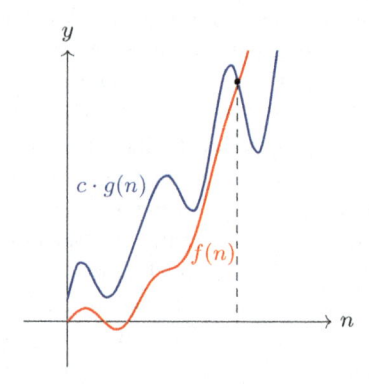

Fig. 7.2: $f(n) = \Omega(g(n))$

7.1 Analyzing Algorithms

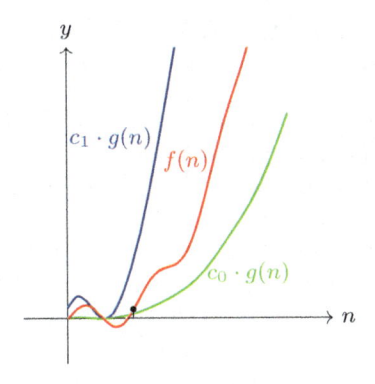

Fig. 7.3: $f(n) = \Theta(g(n))$

The term "asymptotic analysis" stems from the fact that "asymptotic" behavior describes the behavior of a function as its input approaches infinity.

Programmers often conflate Big-Oh as meaning the "worst-case" of an algorithm, Big-Omega as the "best case," and Theta as the "average case." In actuality, these have no precise and deterministic relation to one another, and this misconception will be further addressed in a subsequent section. Remember that Big-Oh is the upper-bound, Big-Omega is the lower-bound, and Theta exists if the function is Big-Oh and Big-Omega of the same function.

Example 7.3. Consider the following function.

```
// foo receives an array of integers.
foo(ls) {
  // v is a random integer between 0 and 100, with equal probability.
  v := RNG()
  n := len(ls)
  if v == 100
    return 42
  else if v == 0
    for i := 0 to n do
      for j := 0 to n do
        n := n + i * j;
  else
    for i := 0 to n do
      n := n + i;
  return n;
}
```

The best-case for this algorithm is for v to be 100, meaning we immediately return 42. Therefore, we are upper-bounded by $\mathcal{O}(1)$, since this is a constant-time operation. We are similarly lower-bounded by this operation, meaning it is $\Omega(1)$. Therefore, it is also $\Theta(1)$ in the best case.

In the worst case, v is zero, meaning we have a nested for-loop over the length of the input list, meaning we are (strictly) upper-bounded by $\mathcal{O}(n^2)$. The for-loops must always execute, meaning that we are lower-bounded by $\Omega(n^2)$ as well. We can conclude similar reasoning for $\Theta(n^2)$.

In the average case, i.e., when n is neither 0 nor 100, we loop once over the length of the input list, meaning we are both upper and lower-bounded by $\mathcal{O}(n)$ and $\Omega(n)$ respectively.

Example 7.4. Recall the binary search algorithm. In the best case, we find the element immediately. Therefore, we can conclude that we are lower-bounded by $\Omega(1)$, but we can also reasonably conclude that we are upper-bounded by $\mathcal{O}(n^3)$. This reasoning seems odd, but it's certainly true; finding the element immediately will never exceed $\mathcal{O}(n^3)$. It's logically correct to conclude that we are upper-bounded by $\mathcal{O}(n^n)$ as well; we will never grow faster than $\mathcal{O}(n^n)$. These are what we call *loose (upper)-bounds*, and are a bit sloppy to state for binary search. In the best case, we find the element immediately, so proclaiming anything other than that the upper-bound is $\mathcal{O}(1)$ is, while technically correct, loose. Moreover, in these instances, should we say that the upper-bound is not $\mathcal{O}(1)$ in the best case, we lose the ability to conclude that the algorithm, in the best case, is $\Theta(1)$.

In the worst case, the element is not in the list. Therefore, we are upper-bounded by $\mathcal{O}(\lg n)$, but lower-bounded, yet again, by $\Omega(\lg \lg n)$. This is similarly a sloppy argument to make, because while it is true that we will never find the element faster that $\Omega(\lg \lg n)$ in the worst case, it's not a tight lower bound, meaning we lose the ability to use Theta notation, should we opt for this lower bound.

In the average case, we land somewhere in the middle of finding the element immediately and it not existing at all, meaning that we are upper-bounded by $\mathcal{O}(\lg n)$, and lower-bounded bounded by $\Omega(1)$. Therefore, concluding $\Theta(\lg n)$ is incorrect for binary search.

Example 7.5. Recall the insertion sort algorithm. We can analyze that, in the best case, the structure is already sorted, meaning nothing needs to be (recursively) sorted and inserted. Therefore, we require exactly one traversal over the data, meaning it is upper-bounded by $\mathcal{O}(n)$. Additionally, because we do require exactly one traversal over the input data, we are also lower-bounded by $\Omega(n)$. Hence, we can also conclude that, in the best-case, insertion sort is $\Theta(n)$.

In the worst-case, the list is in reversed order. So, we must insert each element in the correct position, with respect to every other element. Therefore we are upper and lower-bounded by $\mathcal{O}(n^2)$ and $\Omega(n^2)$ respectively.

7.1.1 Formalizing Big-Oh, Big-Omega, and Theta

We have informally introduced Big-Oh, Big-Omega, and Theta notations. For proving a mathematical function's asymptotic bounds, a formal demonstration is essential. In the following subsections, we will outline these important demonstrations.

Big-Oh

A function $f(n) = \mathcal{O}(g(n))$ if there exists a constant $c > 0$ and a number n_0 such that $f(n) \leq cg(n)$ for every $n \geq n_0$ (Cormen et al., 2009). Interestingly, we can describe all three notations in terms of limits. We say that $f(n) = \mathcal{O}(g(n))$ if $\lim_{n \to \infty} f(n)/g(n) < \infty$. Unfortunately there is no hard-and-fast rule to apply when finding the c and n_0 constants. What is convenient

7.1 Analyzing Algorithms

about it, however, is that multiple solutions may work, hence the existential quantifiers in the definition.

Example 7.6. Prove that $3n^2 + 6n = \mathcal{O}(n^2)$. We need to find a constant $c > 0$ and a number n_0 such that $3n^2 + 6n \leq cn^2$ for every $n \geq n_0$. Let's move $3n^2$ to the right-hand side of the inequality and divide both sides by n^2.

$$3n^2 + 6n \leq cn^2$$
$$6n \leq cn^2 - 3n^2$$
$$6n \leq n^2(c - 3)$$
$$\frac{6n}{n^2} \leq c - 3$$
$$\frac{6}{n} \leq c - 3$$
$$\frac{6}{n} + 3 \leq c$$
$$c \geq \frac{6}{n} + 3$$

If we assign n to be 1, then $c \geq 9$, and the inequality holds for all $n \geq 1$. Therefore we can conclude that $3n^2 + 6n = \mathcal{O}(n^2)$. We can also evaluate this as a limit:

$$\lim_{n \to \infty} \frac{3n^2 + 6n}{n^2} = \lim_{n \to \infty} \frac{3n^2}{n^2} + \frac{6n}{n^2}$$
$$= \lim_{n \to \infty} 3 + \frac{6}{n}$$
$$= 3 + 0$$
$$= 3 < \infty$$

Example 7.7. Prove that $0.25n^4 - 6000n^3 + 25 \neq \mathcal{O}(n^3)$. To show that this relationship does not hold, we can do either a proof-by-contradiction or use the limit definition. Let's write a proof-by-contradiction. Assume the opposite, that $0.25n^4 - 6000n^3 + 25 = \mathcal{O}(n^3)$. Then there exists a constant $c > 0$ and a number n_0 such that $0.25n^4 - 6000n^3 + 25 \leq cn^3$ for every $n \geq n_0$.

$$0.25n^4 - 6000n^3 + 25 \leq cn^3$$
$$25 \leq cn^3 - 0.25n^4 + 6000n^3$$
$$25 \leq n^3(c + 0.25n + 6000)$$
$$\frac{25}{n^3} \leq c + 0.25n + 6000$$
$$c \geq \frac{25}{n^3} - 0.25n - 6000$$

The problem here is that, no matter what constant we choose for c, there is always an $n \in \mathbb{N}$ that falsifies the inequality. Therefore we can conclude that $0.25n^4 - 6000n^3 + 25 \neq \mathcal{O}(n^3)$. We can also evaluate this as a limit:

$$\lim_{n \to \infty} \frac{0.25n^4 - 6000n^3 + 25}{n^3} = \lim_{n \to \infty} \frac{0.25n^4}{n^3} - \frac{6000n^3}{n^3} + \frac{25}{n^3}$$
$$= \lim_{n \to \infty} 0.25n - 6000 + \frac{25}{n^3}$$
$$= \infty - 6000 + 0$$
$$= \infty$$

Example 7.8. Prove that $(2n^2 + n)(4n) = \mathcal{O}(n^3)$. Expanding the expression, we get $8n^3 + 4n^2$, meaning we need to find constants c and n_0 such that $8n^3 + 4n^2 \leq cn^3$ for all $n \geq n_0$.

$$8n^3 + 4n^2 \leq cn^3$$
$$4n^2 \leq cn^3 - 8n^3$$
$$4n^2 \leq n^3(c - 8)$$
$$\frac{4n^2}{n^3} \leq c - 8$$
$$\frac{4}{n} \leq c - 8$$
$$\frac{4}{n} + 8 \leq c$$
$$c \geq \frac{4}{n} + 8$$

For $n_0 = 1$, we have $c \geq 12$. Therefore we can conclude that $(2n^2 + n)(4n) = \mathcal{O}(n^3)$. We can also evaluate this as a limit:

$$\lim_{n \to \infty} \frac{(2n^2 + n)(4n)}{n^3} = \lim_{n \to \infty} \frac{8n^3 + 4n^2}{n^3}$$
$$= \lim_{n \to \infty} 8 + \frac{4}{n}$$
$$= 8 + 0$$
$$= 8 < \infty$$

Example 7.9. Prove that $(4n)^n \neq \mathcal{O}(n^n)$. Assume the opposite, $(4n)^n = \mathcal{O}(n^n)$. Then, there exists a constant $c > 0$ and a number n_0 such that $(4n)^n \leq cn^n$ for every $n \geq n_0$. Expanding the left-hand side, then dividing both sides by n^n gets us:

$$4^n \cdot n^n \leq cn^n$$
$$4^n \leq c$$

7.1 Analyzing Algorithms

The problem is that we cannot pick a constant c without finding an n that falsifies the inequality. Therefore, by contradiction, $(4n)^n \neq \mathcal{O}(n^n)$.

Example 7.10. Prove that $3n + n\lg n = \mathcal{O}(n^2)$. Dividing both sides of the equation by n gets us:

$$3n + n\lg n \leq cn^2$$
$$3 + \lg n \leq cn$$
$$\lg n \leq cn - 3$$

Suppose $c = 3$. Then, $\lg n \leq n$ for any $n > 2$, so we can let $n_0 = 3$. Thus, $3n + n\lg n = \mathcal{O}(n^2)$.

Big-Omega

A function $f(n) = \Omega(g(n))$ if there exists a constant $c > 0$ and a number n_0 such that $f(n) \geq cg(n)$ for every $n \geq n_0$. We can describe this in terms of limits as well. We say that $f(n) = \Omega(g(n))$ if $\lim_{n \to \infty} f(n)/g(n) > 0$.

Example 7.11. Prove that $(2n^3 - 6n^2) = \Omega(n^2)$. We need to find a constant $c > 0$ and a number n_0 such that $(2n^3 - 6n^2) \geq cn^2$ for every $n \geq n_0$. First, let's factor out the n^2 on the left-hand side of the inequality.

$$2n^3 - 6n^2 \geq cn^2$$
$$n^2(2n - 6) \geq cn^2$$
$$2n - 6 \geq c$$
$$c \leq 2n - 6$$

We know that $2n - 6$ is always greater than 0 for $n > 3$, so we will let $n_0 = 4$ and $c_0 = 1$. Therefore, we can conclude that $(2n^3 - 6n^2) = \Omega(n^2)$.

Example 7.12. Prove that $3n^2 + 4n - 8 = \Omega(n^2)$. We need to find a constant $c > 0$ and a number n_0 such that $3n^2 + 4n - 8 \geq cn^2$ for every $n \geq n_0$. We can divide both sides by n^2:

$$3n^2 + 4n - 8 \geq cn^2$$
$$3 + \frac{4}{n} - \frac{8}{n^2} \geq c$$
$$c \leq 3 + \frac{4}{n} - \frac{8}{n^2}$$

Choosing $n_0 = 8$, we need a value of c to satisfy the inequality $c \leq 3 + 1/2 - 1/64$, which reduces to $c \leq 3.484375$. So, picking $c = 3$ works, and we have proved that $3n^2 + 4n - 8 = \Omega(n^2)$.

Theta

A function $f(n) = \Theta(g(n))$ if there exists constants $c_0, c_1 > 0$ and a point n_0 such that $c_0 g(n) \leq f(n) \leq c_1 g(n)$ for every $n \geq n_0$. We can also say that $f(n) = \Theta(g(n))$ if $f(n) = \mathcal{O}(g(n))$ and $f(n) = \Omega(g(n))$.

7.1.2 Misconceptions About Asymptotic Analyses

As we mentioned before, many programmers conflate best, average, and worst-cases with Big-Omega, Theta, and Big-Oh respectively. *There is no discernible relationship between these concepts.*

Example 7.13. Consider the absolutely egregious statement, "linear search is n." The big problem here is that we are using n without any qualification; n what? A slightly better, but still poor, way to phrase it is, "linear search is $\mathcal{O}(n)$," which introduces the upper-bound. The problem now is that we have yet to state under what conditions is linear search $\mathcal{O}(n)$, i.e., best-case, average-case, or worst-case. So, we can state, "linear search, in the worst-case, is $\mathcal{O}(n)$." Even though this is an accurate statement, using a loose upper-bound when the lower-bound is known and is equal to the upper-bound is sloppy. We *should* assert that, "linear search, in the worst-case, is $\Theta(n)$," which is a tight bound. Being specific about the conditions under which an algorithm is $\mathcal{O}(n)$, $\Omega(n)$, or $\Theta(n)$ is important, as is using tightened bounds when possible.

Example 7.14. Consider the statement, "Insertion sort is faster than merge sort since it is $\mathcal{O}(n)$ while merge sort is $\Theta(n \lg n)$."[2] There are two problems with such a claim: first, it omits the qualification of what case analysis we wish to reference. To fix it, we need to add "in the best case" immediately after "is faster than merge sort." Second, we could tighten the bound of insertion sort because it is $\mathcal{O}(n)$ and $\Omega(n)$ in the best case.

Example 7.15. Consider the statement, "The worst-case running time of selection sort is $\mathcal{O}(n^2)$ and the worst-case running time of merge sort is $\mathcal{O}(n \lg n)$; therefore, merge sort is asymptotically faster in the worst-case." Is this statement correct? Unfortunately, it is not, and we can fix the statement by changing only the asymptotic functions. It is incorrect because Big-Oh only describes the upper-bound of a function. We cannot conclude that merge sort is asymptotically faster in the worst-case because we do not know the lower-bound of either algorithm. To correct the statement, we ascribe a tight-bound on the growth of the functions via $\Theta(n^2)$ and $\Theta(n \lg n)$ respectively. We could also just place the tight-bound on only $\Theta(n^2)$, which then provides the lower-bound of selection sort, but as we have continuously stated, using tight-bounds is always the preferred option.

7.1.3 Analysis of the Sorting Algorithms

We can analyze the five sorting algorithms described in Chapter 6 in terms of their asymptotic behavior in the best, average, and worst cases.

---

[2] Thanks, Steve Tate, for this (practice) exam problem.

Bubble Sort

Starting off with bubble sort, in the best case, the array is already sorted, meaning we only need to traverse the array once. Therefore, we are upper and lower-bounded by $\mathcal{O}(n)$ and $\Omega(n)$ respectively. Hence, we can conclude that bubble sort is $\Theta(n)$ in the best case.

In the average case, each element is roughly "half way" to its sorted position. We can compute the expected number of swaps/inversions as follows: an array of length n has an inversion $I_{i,j} = 1$ if we must swap the values (i,j). Therefore, the expected value of there being an inversion for any arbitrary pair is $1/2$ because either a pair must or must not be inverted. Our loop traverses from $i = 1$ to n, with an inner loop of $j > i$ to n. In the average case, each element is roughly "half way" to its sorted position. We can compute the expected number of swaps/inversions as follows: an array of length n has an inversion $I_{i,j} = 1$ if we must swap the values (i,j). Therefore, the expected value of there being an inversion for any arbitrary pair is $1/2$ because either a pair must or must not be inverted. Our loop traverses from $i = 1$ to n, with an inner loop of $j > i$ to n, both of which correspond to summations. Because the inner term depends on neither i nor j, we need to determine how many pairs are such that $1 \leq i < j \leq n$. We are, in effect, choosing two values out of a possible n, which collapses to $\binom{n}{2}$, which resolves to $\dfrac{n(n-1)}{2}$.

$$\mathbf{E}\left(\sum_{i=1}^{n}\sum_{j>i}^{n} I_{i,j}\right) = \sum_{i=1}^{n}\sum_{j>i}^{n} \frac{1}{2}$$
$$= \binom{n}{2} \cdot \frac{1}{2}$$
$$= \frac{n(n-1)}{2} \cdot \frac{1}{2}$$
$$= \frac{n(n-1)}{4}$$
$$= \frac{n^2}{4} - \frac{n}{4}$$

Dropping lower-order terms and coefficients shows that, in the average case, we are upper and lower-bounded by $\mathcal{O}(n^2)$ and $\Omega(n^2)$ respectively. Hence, we can conclude that bubble sort is $\Theta(n^2)$ in the average case.

In the worst case, the array is sorted in reverse order, meaning we must traverse the array n times, and each traversal requires n swaps. Therefore, we are upper and lower-bounded by $\mathcal{O}(n^2)$ and $\Omega(n^2)$ respectively, so we also conclude that bubble sort is $\Theta(n^2)$ in the worst case.

Selection Sort

Up next we come to selection sort, which as we know from the previous chapter, always finds the minimum element and places it at the beginning of the array. Finding the minimum element requires n comparisons, and we must do this for every element in the list, meaning in all cases, finding the minimum element takes $\Theta(n)$ time. Therefore, in all cases, no matter the input, selection sort is upper and lower-bounded by $\mathcal{O}(n^2)$ and $\Omega(n^2)$ respectively. Hence, we can conclude that selection sort is $\Theta(n^2)$ in the best, average, and worst cases. Moreover, we now understand why selection sort is considerably worse than the other four sorting algorithms, because even in the best case, its asymptotic time complexity is still $\Theta(n^2)$.

Insertion Sort

Insertion sort, similar to bubble sort, has a good start with its best case. The in-place insertion sort algorithm traverses through the list, and swaps the out-of-order elements. Therefore, in the best case, the list is already sorted, meaning it traverses over the data exactly once, meaning it is upper and lower-bounded by $\mathcal{O}(n)$ and $\Omega(n)$ respectively. Hence, we can conclude that insertion sort is $\Theta(n)$ in the best case.

In the average case, we perform a similar analysis to bubble sort, in which we determine that every element is "roughly halfway" sorted. This brings about the conclusion that we are upper and lower-bounded by $\mathcal{O}(n^2)$ and $\Omega(n^2)$ respectively. Hence, we can conclude that insertion sort is $\Theta(n^2)$ in the average case.

In the worst case, the list is sorted in reverse order, and every element must be swapped down to the ith index, starting from 1 up to n. So, the element at the last index is swapped n times, the element at the second-to-last index is swapped $n - 1$ times, and so on.

$$\sum_{i=1}^{n} i = 1 + 2 + \cdots + (n-1) + n$$
$$= \frac{n(n+1)}{2}$$
$$= \frac{n^2}{2} + \frac{n}{2}$$

Therefore, we are upper and lower-bounded by $\mathcal{O}(n^2)$ and $\Omega(n^2)$ respectively, both of which correspond to summations. Hence, we can conclude that insertion sort is $\Theta(n^2)$ in the worst case.

Merge Sort

Merge sort is a bit more complicated to analyze, but we can do so by using a recurrence relation. We know that merge sort splits the input list into two halves, and recursively sorts each half. We also know that the base case is when the input list is of length 1, in which case we return the list. Accordingly, we can write the recurrence relation, as a function $T(n)$, as follows:

$$T(n) = \begin{cases} \Theta(1), & \text{if } n \leq 1 \\ 2T(n/2) + \Theta(n), & \text{if } n > 1 \end{cases}$$

Using this definition, we continuously expand the recurrence relation to determine its asymptotic behavior.

7.1 Analyzing Algorithms

$$\begin{aligned}T(n) &= 2T(n/2) + \Theta(n) \\ &= 2(2T(n/4) + \Theta(n)) + \Theta(n) \\ &= 2(2(2T(n/8) + \Theta(n)) + \Theta(n)) + \Theta(n) \\ &= 2^k T(n/2^k) + k \cdot \Theta(n)\end{aligned}$$

At this point, we have a relationship that is dependent on k, representing the depth of the recurrence. Suppose $n = 2^k$. This implies that $\lg n = k$, because of the base two logarithm properties. Therefore, after substituting we get

$$\begin{aligned}T(n) &= 2^k T(2^k/2^k) + k \cdot \Theta(n) \\ &= 2^k T(1) + k \cdot \Theta(n) \\ &= \lg(n) \cdot \Theta(1) + \lg(n) \cdot \Theta(n) \\ &= \Theta(\lg(n)) + \Theta(n \lg n) \\ &= \Theta(n \lg n)\end{aligned}$$

So, we conclude that merge sort is $\Theta(n \lg n)$ in the best, average, and worst cases. We make this conclusion because, no matter the input, we always subdivide the input into two halves, and merge the two halves together.

Quick Sort

Finally, we will analyze the quick sort algorithm. In the best case, the pivot is always the median, indicating that half of the data is to either of its sides. This relationship resolves to the recurrence relation of the merge sort, whose analysis was in the previous section. Therefore, in the best case, the quick sort time complexity is $\Theta(n \lg n)$.

Jumping down to the worst case, the pivot is always either the minimum or the maximum, meaning that all of the data is to one side of the pivot. As a piecewise equation, we know that the base case of quicksort is $T(n) = 1$ if $n \leq 1$. So, we get

$$T(n) = \begin{cases} \Theta(1), & \text{if } n \leq 1 \\ T(n-1) + \Theta(n), & \text{if } n > 1 \end{cases}$$

The added $\Theta(n)$ accounts for the time partitioning the list, which is linear in terms of the input size. Solving the recurrence relation gets us

$$\begin{aligned}T(n) &= T(n-1) + \Theta(n) \\ &= (T(n-2) + \Theta(n-1)) + \Theta(n) \\ &= ((T(n-3) + \Theta(n-2)) + \Theta(n-1)) + \Theta(n) \\ &\vdots \\ &= T(1) + \Theta(2) + \Theta(3) + \cdots + \Theta(n-1) + \Theta(n) \\ &= 1 + 2 + 3 + \cdots + (n-1) + n\end{aligned}$$

The result is an arithmetic series $\sum_{i=1}^{n} i = n(n+1)/2$, which resolves to $\Theta(n^2)$ after dropping constants and lower-order terms. Therefore, in the worst case, the quicksort time complexity is $\Theta(n^2)$.

The average case is significantly harder to analyze and the full proof goes beyond the scope of this book. It is known that, in the average case, quicksort is $\Theta(n \lg n)$ (Cormen et al., 2009).

7.1.4 Lower Bound for Comparison-Based Sorting Algorithms

The performance and time complexity of sorting algorithms largely depend on the underlying implementation. We will now prove that, for any comparison-based sorting algorithm, i.e., a sorting algorithm that answers "YES" or "NO" to the question, "Is $a_i < a_j$?" for any list a and arbitrary indices i and j, it must perform $\Omega(n \lg n)$ comparisons to sort n randomly-accessible elements (Cormen et al., 2009).[3]

Proof. We need two auxiliary lemmas, or true statements, to prove our theorem.

(a) There are $n!$ ways to permute a list of distinct elements $\langle x_1, x_2, \ldots, x_n \rangle$.
(b) Exactly one of these permutations is the correct ordering such that each element $x_{i+1} > x_i$ for all i such that $0 \leq i \leq n-1$.

Assume that we have a set S containing answers to every question (i.e., the "YES"/"NO" question we described above) found so far when attempting to sort using comparisons. By definition, this set must be such that $|S| = n!$ to start. If we answer the first question, we create two groups S_1 and S_2 describing those inputs for which the answer is "YES" and those inputs for which the answer is "NO." Each time we make a decision, we half the problem size, meaning it becomes a (base-two) logarithmic relationship. In the end, we reach the base case of $|S| = 1$, which means the algorithm knows which output is correct. Thus,

$$\lg n + \lg(n-1) + \cdots + \lg 2 + \lg 1 = \lg n! \tag{7.1}$$
$$= \Omega(n \lg n) \tag{7.2}$$

Recall the definition of additive logarithms: $\lg a + \lg b = \lg ab$. Thus, $\lg a + \lg b + \lg c = \lg abc$, and so forth ad infinitum. Therefore we get the equivalence shown in line (7.1). Using Stirling's approximation, we get the equivalence in line (7.2) (Knuth, 1998). □

---

[3] Randomly-accessible means that we can access any element in the list in $\Theta(1)$ time.

Part IV
Modern Java

8 Modern Java and Advanced Topics

Abstract In this final chapter, we begin to discuss modern features of Java, such as pattern matching, reflection, and its attempts to remove the notion that Java is an extremely verbose programming language. We also discuss advanced programming topics, e.g., concurrency, networking, and design patterns.

8.1 Verbosity

8.1.1 Main Method and Anonymous Classes

All the way back in Chapter 1, we introduced the `main` method, and stated that all methods must belong inside a class. Prior to Java version 21, this was indeed true. Java 21, however, has a much cleaner and succinct syntax for writing the `main` method that does not need `public`, nor `static`, nor the input array of strings. These changes make Java much more beginner-friendly. Let's see what a "Hello, world!" program looks like with the improvements.

```java
class MainMethod {

  void main() {
    System.out.println("Hello, world!");
  }
}
```

Additionally, these changes mean that any methods that we want to reference/invoke within `main` (that are defined inside the respective class) do not need to be marked as static. For instance, let's once again write the `double fToC(double f)` method, only this time, we will call it from inside the `main` method.

```java
class MainMethod {

  double fToC(double f) {
    return (f - 32) * (5.0 / 9.0);
  }

  void main() {
    System.out.printf("%d deg F = %d deg C.\n", 32, fToC(32));
  }
}
```

Whether we label `fToC` as static is irrelevant in this circumstance. Unfortunately, if we want to create unit tests for this method, it needs to be static, as we cannot reference it outside the class definition without the static qualifier. Though, what if we could write unit tests within the `MainMethod` class, rather than writing an entirely separate file? Making such an alteration couples the logic of the method with the tests, which, in a large project is not an advisable choice.

To write the unit test, all we need is the `void testFToC()` method and prepend the `@Test` annotation.[1] Then, our IDE will automatically detect that we have a test method in the file and is executable.[2] Since we wish to emphasize writing tests *before* the (method) implementation, we place the testing method above the method that it tests.

```java
import static Assertions.assertAll;
import static Assertions.assertEquals;

class MainMethod {

  @Test
  void testFToC() {
    assertAll(
      () -> assertEquals(0, fToC(32)),
      () -> assertEquals(-40, fToC(-40)),
      () -> assertEquals(100, fToC(212)));
  }

  /**
   * Converts a temperature in Fahrenheit to Celsius.
   * @param f degrees Fahrenheit.
   * @return degrees Celsius.
   */
  double fToC(double f) {
    return (f - 32) * (5.0 / 9.0);
  }
}
```

In addition to a less-verbose `main` method, Java 21 also introduces *nameless/anonymous classes*, which reduces the required keystrokes even further by removing the need for a class definition. So, if all we want to do is write the `main` method (and perhaps other methods callable from `main`), we might write the following:

```java
/**
 * Converts a temperature in Fahrenheit to Celsius.
 * @param f degrees Fahrenheit.
 * @return degrees Celsius.
 */
double fToC(double f) {
  return (f - 32) * (5.0 / 9.0);
}

void main() {
  System.out.printf("%d deg F = %d deg C\n", 32, fToC(32));
}
```

Note that nameless classes (or the methods contained within) cannot be referenced from outside the definition of the class, nor can we write and execute JUnit tests. So, the utility of nameless classes is little, in our opinion.

---

[1] The respective import statements are also necessary.
[2] We will note that we could have done this back in Chapter 1, but we favor separating the tests and the method definition, even if this means we must use the `static` keyword.

8.2 Pattern Matching

Pattern matching is a powerful tool for working with data. It allows the programmer to declare temporary bindings for identifiers that match a given pattern. Pattern matching helps when extracting data out of a data structure, or when testing whether a data structure inhibits a certain pattern. Java added support for pattern matching inside `switch` expressions in Java 21. Prior to Java 21, the best that could be done was to use `instanceof` to test whether an object was an instance of a given class or interface, and then cast the object to that type. Pattern matching is significantly more concise.

Example 8.1. Suppose we want to write a method that uses pattern matching to compute the perimeter of an `IShape`. We can do this by matching on the shape and then computing the perimeter for each type of shape.

```java
import static Assertions.assertAll;
import static Assertions.assertEquals;

class PatternMatchingTester {

  @Test
  void testPatternMatching() {
    assertAll(
      () -> assertEquals(31.41592653589793, perimeter(new Circle(5))),
      () -> assertEquals(30, perimeter(new Rectangle(5, 10))),
      () -> assertEquals(15, perimeter(new Triangle(5))));
  }
}
```

The definitions of `Rectangle`, `Circle`, `Triangle`, and `IShape` are trivial and have been shown in previous chapters. The `perimeter` method, which is static inside `PatternMatching`, is shown below. We return the result of a `switch` expression, which matches against the possible subtypes of `IShape`. We create a temporary binding for the identifier `shape` that is bound to the `IShape` object passed into the method. This, in effect, casts the `IShape` to the subtype that is pattern matched, and we can then access the respective non-private methods and fields of the specific subtype rather than being restricted to only members of the `IShape` interface.

```java
import java.lang.IllegalArgumentException;

class PatternMatching {

  /**
   * Computes the perimeter of a given shape.
   * @param shape the IShape whose perimeter to compute.
   * @return the perimeter of the shape.
   */
  static double perimeter(IShape s) {
    return switch (s) {
      case Rectangle r -> 2 * r.getWidth() + 2 * r.getHeight();
      case Circle c -> 2 * Math.PI * c.getRadius();
      case Triangle t -> 3 * t.getSideLength();
      default -> throw new IllegalArgumentException("perimeter: bad shape " + s);
    };
  }
}
```

We can also use "guard expressions" when constructing patterns to only match a pattern if a condition holds for that pattern.

Example 8.2. Suppose that we want to design a factorial method that uses pattern matching. We can do so by matching on the argument to the factorial method. If the argument is zero, we return one. Otherwise, we return the argument multiplied by the factorial of the argument minus one. We can use a guard expression to ensure that the argument is non-negative.

```java
import static Assertions.assertAll;
import static Assertions.assertEquals;

class FactorialTester {

  @Test
  void testFactorial() {
    assertAll(
      () -> assertEquals(1, factorial(0)),
      () -> assertEquals(1, factorial(1)),
      () -> assertEquals(2, factorial(2)),
      () -> assertEquals(6, factorial(3)),
      () -> assertEquals(24, factorial(4)),
      () -> assertEquals(120, factorial(5)));
  }
}
```

```java
import java.lang.IllegalStateException;

class Factorial {

  /**
   * Computes the factorial of an integer using pattern matching.
   * @param n integer.
   * @return n!.
   * @throws IllegalStateException if n is not an integer or is <0.
   */
  static Integer fact(Integer n) {
    return switch (n) {
      case Integer v when v == 0 -> 1;
      case Integer v when v > 0 -> v * fact(v - 1);
      default -> throw new IllegalStateException("fact: bad value " + n);
    };
  }
}
```

Notice that we have to use the wrapper class, since Java permits only special types of pattern matching over the primitive data types, and otherwise works with objects. We could replace the first case with a match against the literal zero, since Java autounboxes the `Integer` object to a primitive `int`, e.g., `case 0 -> 1;`. Unfortunately, we cannot use guard expressions over primitives.

Pattern matching is not restricted to switch-case expressions. We can also use pattern matching in cases where we check the instance of an object, namely in the `equals` method. As an example, the traditional `equals` methods look like the following:

8.2 Pattern Matching

```
@Override
public boolean equals(Object o) {
  if (o instanceof MyClass) {
    MyClass other = (MyClass) o;
    return this.field1.equals(other.field1) &&
           this.field2.equals(other.field2) &&
           ...
           this.fieldN.equals(other.fieldN);
  } else { return false; }
}
```

The need to cast the object to the type of the class on its own separate line is tedious. Pattern matching allows us to write the `equals` method in a more concise manner by providing an identifier to the pattern that is bound to the object being tested. We can wrap the check in either an `if` statement or as a logical AND, because the pattern matching expression returns a boolean and fails to match if the object is not an instance of the stated class.

```
@Override
public boolean equals(Object o) {
  return (o instanceof MyClass other)    &&
         this.field1.equals(other.field1) &&
         this.field2.equals(other.field2) &&
         ...
         this.fieldN.equals(other.fieldN);
}
```

Example 8.3. Suppose that we want to override the `equals` method inside `Rectangle` using pattern matching. It's possible to use an `if` statement rather than resolving the `instanceof` check in an expression, but the latter is much more concise and solves the same problem.

```
import static Assertions.assertAll;
import static Assertions.assertEquals;

class RectangleTester {

  @Test
  void testEquals() {
    Rectangle r1 = new Rectangle(5, 10);
    Rectangle r2 = new Rectangle(5, 10);
    Rectangle r3 = new Rectangle(10, 5);
    assertAll(
      () -> assertEquals(r1, r2),
      () -> assertNotEquals(r1, r3),
      () -> assertNotEquals(r1, "Hello!"));
  }
}
```

```
class Rectangle implements IShape {

  private final double WIDTH;
  private final double HEIGHT;

  Rectangle(double width, double height) {
    this.WIDTH = width;
    this.HEIGHT = height;
  }

  @Override
  public boolean equals(Object o) {
    return o instanceof Rectangle r && this.WIDTH == r.WIDTH && this.HEIGHT == r.HEIGHT;
  }

  double getWidth() { return this.WIDTH; }

  double getHeight() { return this.HEIGHT; }
}
```

8.2.1 Record Types

Our perimeter pattern matcher is helpful and convenient, but what is not-so-convenient is that we have to write a lot of boilerplate code just to design, for example, a class that represents a rectangle. Each subtype of IShape needs instance variables, a constructor, and accessors at a minimum. Moreover, we have to manually extract the fields from the object that is bound by the variable binding. In modern (versions of) Java, we can utilize *record types*, which are immutable classes whose boilerplate code (as described previously) is compiler-generated. We can also add methods to the record type, but other static or instance variable are disallowed.

Example 8.4. Using record types, let's design a small interpreter for a simple language that supports arithmetic expressions and boolean expressions, similar to the one presented in Chapter 4. Instead of the interface approach that we took before, we will use records and pattern matching to evaluate the expressions. With this, our interpreter makes use of var: a new keyword for a variable whose type is inferred from the type of the expression on the right-hand side of the assignment operator. Type inference allows us to omit the specification of verbose and complex types such as BigDecimal.

```
import static Assertions.assertAll;
import static Assertions.assertEquals;
import java.lang.BigDecimal;

class EvaluatorTest {

  @Test
  void evalTest() {
    assertAll(
      () -> assertEquals(new BigDecimal("42"), Evaluator.eval(new Number(42))),
      () -> assertEquals(new BigDecimal("42"), Evaluator.eval(new Add(new Number(41),
                                                                     new Number(1)))));
  }
}
```

8.2 Pattern Matching

```java
interface IExpr {}
```

```java
import java.lang.BigDecimal;

record Number(BigDecimal value) implements IExpr {

  Number(int value) { this(new BigDecimal(value)); }
}
```

```java
record Add(IExpr left, IExpr right) implements IExpr {}
```

```java
import java.lang.IllegalArgumentException;
import java.lang.BigDecimal;

class Evaluator {

  /**
   * Evaluates a given expression using records and pattern matching.
   * @param exp the expression to evaluate as a subtype IExpr.
   * @return result of evaluating the expression: a BigDecimal.
   */
  static BigDecimal eval(IExpr e) {
    return switch (e) {
      case Number(var n) -> n;
      case Add (var left, var right) -> eval(left).add(eval(right));
      default -> throw new IllegalArgumentException("eval: bad expr "+e);
    }
  }
}
```

In the interpreter, we pattern match on the constructors of our record types. For example, inside the `eval` method, when pattern matching on the `Add` constructor, we create temporary bindings for the identifiers `left` and `right` that are bound to the respective `Expr` objects passed into the constructor. We then recursively call `eval` on these objects and add the results together. We do the same for the other constructors of `Expr`. To make testing the program easier, we designed a secondary constructor for `Number` that receives an integer and converts it to a `BigDecimal`. Note that self-defined constructors of a record can only reference other constructors via `this(...)`.

Example 8.5. Let's use some of Java's modern features to write a lexer and parser for the interpreter that we designed in Chapter 4. We presented this as an exercise to the readers, but we imagine it was quite a hassle if they restricted themselves to older versions of Java. In particular, we can use records and pattern matching to greatly reduce the amount of necessary boilerplate code. Our language capabilities will be greatly reduced for the time being, however, since our focus is the lexing and parsing of the raw language rather than its evaluation. Therefore, let's restrict the language to supporting numbers, symbols, and s-expressions, i.e., expressions enclosed by parentheses. Below we present some examples of expressible programs this language.

```
7
(+ 2 40)
(+ 10 (* 4 5) 30)
```

For the uninformed, a *lexer* is a program that converts input into *tokens*, also called a tokenizer. Tokens are components of an input string. For example, we can create five tokens from the input string "(+ 2 3)":

```
L_PAREN "("
SYMBOL  "+"
NUMBER  "2"
NUMBER  "40"
R_PAREN ")"
```

It's the job of the lexer to categorize the input into patterns ascribed by the programmer, e.g., NUMBER or SYMBOL. Our lexer assumes that tokens are separated by whitespace, and for the most part, this holds true. Consider the simplest case of applying an operator to a list of operands: "(+ 2 40)". Should we delimit the string on the space character, we accidentally group an opening parenthesis and the plus into "(+", an undesired token. The solution is to add a whitespace after each opening parenthesis and a whitespace before each closing parenthesis.

Before we write the lexer and test cases, we need to determine what comprises a token. Tokens have token types, e.g., L_PAREN and so forth, as well as an associated string. In the case of, say, a NUMBER, the associated string *is* that number represented by the token, e.g,. 40. Let's use a Java record to represent a Token, and an enumeration for the types of tokens. We will integrate tokens into the lexer tests, so it makes little sense to write separate tests for tokens and token types.

```
enum TokenType {
  L_PAREN, R_PAREN, NUMBER, SYMBOL
}
```

```
record Token(TokenType type, String data) { }
```

The implementation of the lexer is not complicated—the static `lex` method receive a `String` and returns a `Queue<Token>` containing all identified tokens. As we stated earlier, we first add the required spacing, then split on the whitespace character, producing a `String[]` of raw tokens. Then, we iterate over these strings and enqueue an instance of `Token` with the respective token type and data. For identifying numbers, we determine if an attempt to parse the string as a number results in an exception and, if not, it resolves to a NUMBER token. Otherwise, the only option (assuming we identify parentheses before this case) is some kind of symbol token.

8.2 Pattern Matching

```java
import static Assertions.assertAll;
import static Assertions.assertEquals;
import java.util.LinkedList;
import java.util.List;

class LexerTester {

  @Test
  void testLex() {
    String in1 = "42";
    String in2 = "(+ 2 40)";
    String in3 = "(+ 27 (* 5 3) 10)";
    assertAll(
      () -> assertEquals(new LinkedList<>(
                         List.of(new Token(TokenType.NUMBER, "42"))),
                       Lexer.lex(in1)),
      () -> assertEquals(new LinkedList<>(
                         List.of(new Token(TokenType.L_PAREN, "("),
                                 new Token(TokenType.SYMBOL, "+"),
                                 new Token(TokenType.NUMBER, "2"),
                                 new Token(TokenType.NUMBER, "40"),
                                 new Token(TokenType.R_PAREN, ")"))),
                       Lexer.lex(in2)),
      () -> assertEquals(new LinkedList<>(
                         List.of(new Token(TokenType.L_PAREN, "("),
                                 new Token(TokenType.SYMBOL, "+"),
                                 new Token(TokenType.NUMBER, "27"),
                                 new Token(TokenType.L_PAREN, "("),
                                 new Token(TokenType.SYMBOL, "*"),
                                 new Token(TokenType.NUMBER, "5"),
                                 new Token(TokenType.NUMBER, "3"),
                                 new Token(TokenType.R_PAREN, ")"),
                                 new Token(TokenType.NUMBER, "10"),
                                 new Token(TokenType.R_PAREN, ")"))),
                       Lexer.lex(in3)));
  }
}
```

```java
import java.util.Collectors;
import java.util.LinkedList;
import java.util.Queue;

class Lexer {

  /**
   * Splits the input of our language into tokens.
   * @param s raw string input.
   * @return queue of tokens.
   */
  static Queue<Token> lex(String s) {
    // First, we need to add a space after each left parenthesis
    // and before each right parenthesis. Then split on the space.
    String newS = s.replaceAll("\\(", "( ").replaceAll("\\)", " )");
    String[] rawTokens = newS.split(" ");
    return Arrays.stream(rawTokens)
                 .map(Lexer::createToken)
                 .collect(Collectors.toCollection(LinkedList::new));
  }
```

```java
/**
 * Creates a token from a string.
 * @param t the string to create a token from.
 * @return the token.
 */
private static Token createToken(String t) {
  return switch (t) {
    case "(" -> new Token(TokenType.L_PAREN, t);
    case ")" -> new Token(TokenType.R_PAREN, t);
    default -> {
      try {
        Double.parseDouble(t);
        yield new Token(TokenType.NUMBER, t);
      } catch (NumberFormatException ex) {
        yield new Token(TokenType.SYMBOL, t);
      }
    }
  };
}
```

As shown, we can make use of streams and collectors to populate the queue of tokens. The `createToken` method is responsible for creating the respective token type from the input. Subsequent updates to the grammar of the language would result in only needing to update `createToken` rather than requiring a change to the internals of the lexer algorithm itself. Suppose that we want to add boolean literals into the language. Thus, we need two modifications: 1) add a boolean `TokenType` and 2) add a clause in the switch expression to return a `Token` that represents a `TokenType.BOOLEAN` or something similar.

Example 8.6. We will break the mini-project into two separate examples since both the lexer and parser are complicated pieces of the puzzle. The parser receives tokens and, in general, creates an abstract syntax tree to represent the input data.[3]

Our parser implementation contains a single static method: `parse`, which receives a queue of tokens and returns the root of an abstract syntax tree. We need to create three kinds of abstract syntax trees: `NumNode`, `SymbolNode`, and `SExprNode`, all of which extend the abstract `AstNode` class. An `AstNode`, like the one presented from chapter 4, contains a list of children, as well as a way to add children to that list. The former two subclasses, namely `NumNode` and `SymbolNode`, store their data, i.e., the number and symbol respectively, as instance variables inside their class definitions. Because we have seen these two class definitions previously, we will omit their implementation. What we have not seen before, however, is the `SExprNode` class. Because our language is so small, an `SExprNode` is identical to an `AstNode` aside from the fact that it is not abstract.

To parse the list of tokens, we peek at the head of the queue and match on its type. If it is either a number or a symbol, we instantiate an instance of the appropriate subclass type. If we encounter a left parenthesis, then we must do more work, that work being to parse the contents inside the parentheses. Namely, we traverse over the tokens until we encounter a right parenthesis, recursively parsing and adding each abstract syntax tree node to a running `SExprNode` instance. Because the process is recursive, we handle the cases in which an s-expression is nested inside another, which was the case in the third test case from the lexer tester.

---

[3] We say "in general" because a parser might also forego an AST and go straight to an interpreter or program instructions.

8.2 Pattern Matching

```
import static Assertions.assertAll;
import static Assertions.assertEquals;

class ParserTester {

  @Test
  void testParse() {
    String in1 = "42";
    String in2 = "(+ 2 40)";
    String in3 = "(+ 27 (* 5 3) 10)";

    assertAll(
      () -> assertEquals(new NumNode(42),
                         Parser.parse(Lexer.lex(in1))),
      () -> assertEquals(new SExprNode(
                         new SymbolNode("+"),
                         new NumNode(2),
                         new NumNode),
                         Parser.parse(Lexer.lex(in2))),
      () -> assertEquals(new SExprNode(
                         new SymbolNode("+"),
                         new NumNode(27),
                         new SExprNode(
                           new SymbolNode("*"),
                           new NumNode(5),
                           new NumNode(3)),
                         new NumNode(10)),
                         Parser.parse(Lexer.lex(in3))));
  }
}
```

```
import java.util.Objects;
import java.util.Queue;

class Parser {

  /**
   * Parses a list of tokens into an AST.
   * @param tokenList queue of tokens to parse.
   * @return constructed AST from the tokens.
   */
  static AstNode parse(Queue<Token> tokenList) {
    if (!tokenList.isEmpty()) {
      return switch (tokenList.peek().type()) {
        case NUMBER -> new NumNode(tokenList.remove().data());
        case SYMBOL -> new SymbolNode(tokenList.remove().data());
        case BOOLEAN -> new BooleanNode(tokenList.remove().data());
        case L_PAREN -> parseSExpression(tokenList);
        default ->
          throw new IllegalArgumentException("parse: unexpected token "
                                    + tokenList.peek().type());
      };
    } else {
      return null;
    }
  }
```

```java
/**
 * Constructs an s-expression from a list of tokens. The precondition
 * for entering this method is that the first token in the queue is
 * the opening parenthesis of the s-expression, i.e., an L_PAREN.
 * @param tokenList queue of tokens to parse as the sexpr.
 * @return constructed SExpressionNode from the tokens.
 */
private static AstNode parseSExpression(Queue<Token> tokenList) {
  if (tokenList.isEmpty()) { return null; }
  else {
    // Remove the left parenthesis.
    tokenList.remove();
    SExpressionNode sexpr = null;

    // Parse the tokens until we reach the right parenthesis.
    while (!tokenList.isEmpty()
        && tokenList.peek().type() != TokenType.R_PAREN) {
      // Get the first token.
      sexpr = sexpr == null ? parseFirstToken(tokenList) : sexpr;
      sexpr.addChild(parse(tokenList));
    }

    // Remove the right parenthesis.
    tokenList.remove();
    return sexpr;
  }
}

/**
 * Instantiates a subclass of SExpressionNode to the type
 * defined by the first token in the queue. This can be
 * anything represented as an s-expression.
 * @param tokenList list of tokens.
 * @return new SExpression of the parsed values.
 */
private static SExpressionNode parseFirstToken(Queue<Token> tokenList) {
  switch (Objects.requireNonNull(tokenList.peek()).type()) {
    default: { return new SExpressionNode(); }
  }
}
```

Fortunately, the parser is also not too terribly difficult to understand. We perform a case analysis on the token and either return an abstract syntax tree node or create one from an s-expression.

We decided to write a helper method, `parseFirstToken`, as a precursor to more advanced features in the language. Many special forms are represented as s-expressions and should be converted into appropriate abstract syntax tree nodes. As an example, we can write a conditional expression, i.e., `(cond pred cons alt)` via an s-expression. Therefore, it makes logical sense to have a separate method that reads the first token and instantiates the correct node for that token, whether it be a `CondNode` or something else. Our implementation has only one case, `default`, since we do not have conditional expressions, but we encourage the readers to add them as additional language features!

8.3 Reflection

Reflection, while not a necessarily new computer science concept, is a powerful way for programming languages to interpret and potentially modify its own structure (Forman and Forman, 2004). We made an example of reflection in Chapter 4 to pass around a class type as a parameter.

Example 8.7. Suppose that we want to be able to search, then invoke, a method based on its name. Reconsider the primitive calculator example from many chapters ago, where we utilize a case dispatch on the operator received as a terminal argument. As we add functions to the system, we must proportionally add code in the main method to account for the new case, which is tiresome at best. Java allows us to lookup a method and pass parameters, at runtime, using its reflection API. As a substitute for terminal arguments (and the main method in general), we will pass an "argument array" to a static calculate method, so we can easily run unit tests.

```java
import static Assertions.assertAll;
import static Assertions.assertEquals;

class ReflectiveCalculatorTester {

  private static final double DELTA = 0.0001;

  @Test
  void testCalculator() {
    assertAll(
      () -> assertEquals(5,
                         calculate(new String[] {"add", "2", "3"}),
                         DELTA),
      () -> assertEquals(5,
                         calculate(new String[] {"subtract", "10", "5"}),
                         DELTA),
      () -> assertEquals(10,
                         calculate(new String[] {"multiply", "2", "5"}),
                         DELTA),
      () -> assertEquals(2,
                         calculate(new String[] {"divide", "10", "5"}),
                         DELTA));
  }
}
```

To retrieve a method at runtime, we first need to retrieve the class in which it lives through the Class.forName method. In this case, we pass ReflectiveCalculator, as that is the name of our class. Note that the return value is of type Class<?>, denoting that it is a reflective class type.

With the class type object in hand, we must now get the method object to call. To do so, we need two values: its identifier, and its parameter types. We will assume that the arguments to the calculator functions are strings, which can be converted inside the respective methods. This approach makes it significantly easier to inform the reflection API of our parameter type(s). Therefore, we use the getDeclaredMethod method, which takes the name of the method as a string, and a variadic number of Class<?> objects that represent the parameter types. In our case, the parameter type is a String[], so we pass String[].class. Because we might attempt to reference a non-existent method, we must wrap this in a try-catch block to catch the NoSuchMethodException checked exception.

Finally, we invoke the method encapsulated by the `Method` using the conveniently named `invoke` method, which receives the object on which to invoke the method (in this case, `null` because the method is static), and the necessary arguments. The return value is an `Object`, so we must cast it to the appropriate type. There are several issues that may arise when calling a method, such as the method being inaccessible due to its access modifier, the method throwing a checked exception, or passing the wrong number of arguments. We must handle these issues accordingly via `try-catch` blocks.[4] The four calculator methods are trivial and have been omitted; all they do is convert the string arguments to numbers and perform, then return, the corresponding operation.

There is one small intricacy with how Java handles variadic arguments and passing arrays to reflective methods. Passing an array to a variadic argument method unwraps the arguments and passes them individually. For example, if we have a method `foo(String... args)`, and we pass `foo(new String[] {"Hello", "World"})`, the method receives two arguments: `"Hello"` and `"World"`. In our case, this is problematic, since we want our computation methods to receive the entire array of arguments. To accomplish this, we can cast the array to an `Object` and pass it to `invoke` as a single argument.

```java
import java.lang.reflect.Method;
import java.lang.reflect.InvocationTargetException;
import java.lang.IllegalAccessException;
import java.lang.NoSuchMethodException;

class ReflectiveCalculator {

  /**
   * Calculates the result of a given operation on two numbers.
   * @param args the operation to perform, and the two numbers.
   * @return the result of the operation.
   */
  static double calculate(String[] args) {
    Class<?> cls = ReflectiveCalculator.class;
    try {
      Method mtd = cls.getMethod(args[0], String[].class);
      return (double) mtd.invoke(null, args);
    } catch (NoSuchMethodException
          | InvocationTargetException
          | IllegalAccessException ex) {
      throw new RuntimeException(ex);
    }
  }
}
```

Example 8.8. The Python programming language, including many others, offer a REPL, or a read-evaluate-print-loop, that users can run at the terminal to evaluate expressions and programs. This is done to alleviate the need to open a source file in a text editor, type the code, then run the file with the respective command. Java is not one of these languages out-of-the-box, unfortunately. There is an application, namely JShell, which introduces this functionality. In this example, we will write our own version of JShell, where the programmer can type and evaluate expressions and statements at the terminal.[5]

---

[4] Our code uses the Java 7 feature of the vertical pipe '|' to catch/handle multiple exceptions at once, removing duplicate code.

[5] Credit goes to Terence Parr for this example and "assignment" from his graduate course on programming languages at the University of San Francisco. That's right–this is a graduate-level programming example!

8.3 Reflection

First, we need to establish a few details. Our program will read, from standard input, a subset of Java code. After reading, we spin up an instance of the Java compiler and compile the source code into a .class file. Finally, using reflection, we search for and execute that code. This is the goal at a high level, but we certainly need to break this down into sub-components. Let's see some examples of what we will be able to do in due time:

```
> int i = 5;
> System.out.println(i)
5
> class Animal { String speak() { return ""; }}
> class Dog extends Animal { String speak() { return "Woof!"; }}
> Animal a = new Dog();
> System.out.println(a.speak());
"Woof!"
> System.out.println(List.of(i, i + 2));
[5, 7]
> System.out.println(IntStream.iterate(0, i -> i + 5).limit(10));
[0, 5, 10, 15, 20, 25, 30, 35, 40, 45]
```

As we can see, powerful programs are a possibility only by using the REPL. The question now is, how do we get to that point?

The idea with this project is to output our lines of source code into a temporary Java class. In essence, we create a temporary directory on the system that that stores a separate class (file), enumerated from zero, containing whatever we enter at the REPL. Each time we enter code, we wrap it inside a class called "InterpX" where X is the current class identifier, so to speak. These classes are extended with each new segment of code received to allow access to prior declarations/definitions. As an example, consider the following class definitions generated after inputting the first two lines that we showed earlier:

```
class Interp0 {
  static int i = 5;
  static void execute() {}
}
class Interp1 extends Interp0 {
  static void execute() {
    System.out.println(i);
  }
}
```

The execute method is always generated, but we only care about its contents (i.e., we only populate its body) when we write something that is not a declaration. For example, if we write a class definition or a variable, it is nonsensical to place it inside the execute method body, since in the former case it would not compile, and in the latter case it would be local to only that version of execute. So, we need a way of determining whether or not a piece of code *is* a declaration/definition. All declarations in our subset of Java will be restricted to the following grammar:

```
<expr> ::= <varDecl> | <methodDecl> | <classDecl>

<varDecl> ::= (<type> ' ' <id> ';') | (<type> '[]' ' ' <id> ';')

<methodDecl> ::= <type> ' ' <id> '(' <params> ')' '{' <body> '}'

<classDecl> ::= ('class ' <id> (' extends ' <id>)? '{' <body> '}')
```

Fig. 8.1: Extended-BNF Grammar for Declarations

Let's assume that the type rule is any arbitrary sequence of characters representing a type in Java (e.g., void, int, Dog), as is an identifier. Under these assumptions, it is simple to parse a string to determine if it's a declaration. We will further assume that the user is acting in good faith and typing only valid Java code that compiles under said assumptions; responses to inputs such as intttt x = 5; will not be considered.[6]

```java
class JavaRepl {

  private boolean isDeclaration(String s) {
    return this.isVariableDeclaration(s)
        || this.isMethodDeclaration(s)
        || this.isClassDeclaration(s);
  }

  /**
   * Determines if a given string is a type of Java variable declaration.
   * Types of var declarations:
   * - int x;
   * - int x = 5;
   * - int[] a = new int[5];
   * - String x = "Hi!";
   * - ArrayList<Integer> foo;
   */
  private boolean isVariableDeclaration(String s) {
    return s.matches("[a-zA-Z_\\[\\]<>]+\\s*[a-zA-Z0-9_]+"
            + "(\\s*=\\s*.+?)?;");
  }

  /**
   * Determines if a given string is a type of Java method declaration.
   * Types of method declarations:
   * - int foo() {}
   * - int bar(int x, int y) {}
   * - String baz(ArrayList<Integer> foo) {}
   */
  private boolean isMethodDeclaration(String s) {
    return s.matches("[a-zA-Z_\\[\\]<>]+\\s+[a-zA-Z0-9_]+
            + "\\(.*?\\)\\s*\\{.*?\\}");
  }

  /**
   * Determines if a given string is a type of Java class declaration.
   * Types of class declarations:
   * - class Animal {}
   * - class Dog extends Animal {}
   */
  private boolean isClassDeclaration(String s) {
    return s.matches("class\\s+[a-zA-Z_<>]+\\s+\\{.*?\\}")
        || s.matches("class\\s+[a-zA-Z_<>]+\\s+extends\\s+[a-zA-Z_<>]+\\s
                    *\\{.*?\\}");
  }
}
```

Anything that is not a declaration is something else that belongs inside the body of execute, and is executed accordingly. For instance, if we declare i to be zero, then use a post-

---

[6] We make prolific use of regular expressions in this next section. You are free to gloss over these details or use "raw string parsing" with substring and equals.

8.3 Reflection

increment operator on i, the i++ statement is stored inside Interp1's execute body, and is invoked prior to the next standard input reading.

Now, onto the main event. We know how to read lines/data from standard input, so that's nothing more than a rehashing of what we've seen before. We create an infinite loop, read in a single string (line), and create a File object out of that string by storing it in a temporary class file. Where do we create that temporary class file? In a temporary directory, which is created by a static method in theFiles class. Let's set this up in the constructor of JavaRepl, since the temporary directory (path) won't change for the lifetime of the program. Let's also instantiate the standard input reading mechanism, i.e., a BufferedReader that operates over an InputStreamReader.

```java
import java.io.*;
import java.nio.file.Files;
import java.nio.file.Path;

class JavaRepl {

  private final Path TMP_DIR;
  private final BufferedReader IN;
  private int classNo;

  JavaRepl() {
    try {
      this.TMP_DIR = Files.createTempDirectory();
    } catch (IOException ex) {
      throw new RuntimeException(ex);
    }

    this.IN = new BufferedReader(new InputStreamReader(System.in));
    this.classNo = 0;
  }
}
```

With this, we know that we want to store the class and what its name should be, thanks to a counter that starts at zero. In the createJavaFile method, we create a File at the correct location, with its contents populated by a writer of some kind. Here is where we make use of the isDeclaration method—if the source code that we pass is, in fact, a declaration, we precede it with the static keyword. Otherwise, it resides inside the static void execute() method. Creating and returning this file is straightforward. We need to account for the fact that if the class number is zero, we do not extend any class. As a corollary point, to be able to use certain classes, e.g., List, at the REPL, we include two wildcard imports from the I/O and utilities Java packages.

```java
import java.io.*;
import java.nio.file.Files;
import java.nio.file.Path;

class JavaRepl {
  // ... other methods not shown.

  private File createJavaFile(String src) {
    File f = new File(String.format("%s/Interp%d.java",
                                    this.TMP_DIR,
                                    this.classNo));
    try (PrintWriter pw = new PrintWriter(new FileWriter(f))) {
      pw.println("import java.io.*;");
      pw.println("import java.util.*;");
```

```java
      // If it is the starting class we do not have it extend anything.
      pw.println(String.format("class Interp%d %s", this.classNo,
                               this.classNo == 0
                                 ? "{"
                                 : "extends Interp"
                                    + (this.classNo - 1)
                                    + " {"));

      // If it's a declaration, it cannot be inside a method.
      if (this.isDeclaration(src)) {
        pw.printf("static %s\n", src);
        pw.println("static void execute() {}");
      } else {
        pw.printf("static void execute() { %s }\n", src);
      }
      pw.println("}");
    } catch (IOException ex) {
      throw new RuntimeException(ex);
    }
    return f;
  }
}
```

Here, we run into our first of two roadblocks: how to compile the file at runtime. Fortunately, there exists the Java compiler API, which contains methods and classes to compile a file definition. Most of this code is boilerplate "setup," so understanding it completely is unnecessary. At the core, we instantiate a compiler object, as well as a list of diagnostics that may result from compiling the program (e.g., error messages). These values are passed into a compilation unit that executes the compiler. Upon its success, it produces a .class file in the temporary directory, as we would if we were compiling our Java code by hand. We will instantiate the JavaCompiler, StandardJavaFileManager, and DiagnosticCollector objects in the constructor. More importantly we have the executeRepl method, which starts the REPL and listens for data on standard input. This is where we use the API to compile and produce the .class file.

```java
import javax.tools.*;
import java.lang.StringBuilder;

class JavaRepl {
  // ... other instance variables not shown.
  private final JavaCompiler JAVAC;
  private final StandardJavaFileManager FILE_MANAGER;
  private final DiagnosticCollector<? super JavaFileObject> DS;

  JavaRepl() {
    // ... other instantiations not shown.
    this.JAVAC = ToolProvider.getSystemJavaCompiler();
    this.DS = new DiagnosticCollector<>();
    this.FILE_MANAGER = this.JAVAC.getStandardFileManager(this.DS, null, null);
  }

  /**
   * Continuously loops, reading in lines of input representing valid Java
   * programs. These are converted into statements/expressions that are
   * fed into a skeleton Java class file. We use Java's runtime compiler
   * to execute these, and the reflection API to dynamically load the
   * class at runtime.
   */
```

8.3 Reflection

```java
  private void executeRepl() throws Exception {
    List<File> programs = new ArrayList<>();
    while (true) {
      // For now assume that one line is the entire program.
      StringBuilder sb = new StringBuilder();
      System.out.print("> ");
      sb.append(this.IN.readLine());
      programs.add(this.createJavaFile(sb.toString()));

      // Create the compiler from these files.
      var units = this.FILE_MANAGER.getJavaFileObjectsFromFiles(programs);
      this.task = (JavacTask) this.JAVAC.getTask(null, this.FILE_MANAGER,
                                                 this.DS, null, null,
                                                 units);

      // Compile the list of programs.
      boolean ok = this.task.call();
      if (!ok) {
        for (var diag : this.DS.getDiagnostics()) {
          System.err.println(diag);
        }
      } else {
        // TODO.
      }
    }
  }
}
```

If the compilation was unsuccessful, thereby meaning `ok` is false, we iterate over the diagnostics received from the compile and print them to the standard error stream. Otherwise, we know it successfully compiled and we now have a class file.

Now comes the second roadblock: we want to load this file into memory via the reflection API and preserve changes to static fields. For example, if we increment/reassign a variable, its state should be updated across the REPL. To do so, we must use a common class loader, which persists changes to static fields and means we can load a new class at runtime. Indeed, we want to load the new class that we just compiled, namely $InterpX$, and invoke its `execute` method. This is nothing new, but what we have not seen is the common class loader approach; we store an instance of `URLClassLoader` that gets instantiated to refer to the temporary directory path, in our constructor. Therefore, when loading a class via `loadClass`, any changes we made to previous variables remain loaded into memory.

```java
class JavaRepl {

  // ... other instance variables not shown.

  private final URLClassLoader CLASS_LOADER;

  JavaRepl() {
    // ... other instantiations not shown.
    try {
      this.CLASS_LOADER = URLClassLoader.newInstance(
                          new URL[]{this.TMP_DIR.toUri().toURL()});
    } catch (MalformedURLException e) {
      throw new RuntimeException(e);
    }
  }
```

```java
/**
 * Continuously loops, reading in lines of input representing valid Java
 * programs. These are converted into statements/expressions that are
 * fed into a skeleton Java class file. We use Java's runtime compiler
 * to execute these, and the reflection API to dynamically load the
 * class at runtime.
 */
private void executeRepl() throws Exception {
  List<File> programs = new ArrayList<>();
  while (true) {
    // ... compilation omitted.
    if (!ok) {
    // ... omitted.
    } else {
      Class<?> cls = CLASS_LOADER.loadClass("Interpret" + this.classNo);
      Method method = cls.getMethod("execute");
      method.invoke(null);
      this.classNo++;
    }
  }
}
```

In summary, we load the current class, reflectively grab its `execute` method, then execute it with `null` as an argument, designating that it is a static method in the class. Finally we increment the class number for the next line.

8.4 Concurrent Programming

There is sometimes a conflation between concurrency and parallelism, two related but different methodologies. *Concurrency* describes actions/computations that occur at the same time, whereas *parallelism* refers to simultaneous actions/computations (Silberschatz et al., 2012). A non-concurrent program sequentially completes tasks $t_1, t_2, \ldots, t_n$ one after the next. Concurrent programs will start t_1, then start t_2, and so forth, without necessarily finishing t_1 before starting subsequent tasks. The order of execution and completion depends on the operating system's scheduler, but what is important is that no tasks t_i and t_j operate at the exact same moment. Contrast this idea with parallelism, which executes tasks t_i and t_j to be worked on at the exact same moment.

We can simulate the concurrency/parallelism distinction with two queues of people A and B in line for a ride at an amusement park. A concurrent system might poll a person from A, then from B, then back to A, but never from A and B at the same time. On the other hand, consider a kiosk that has multiple cashiers serving several people simultaneously, polling from both A and B. The kiosk system is, therefore, operating in parallel.

8.4 Concurrent Programming

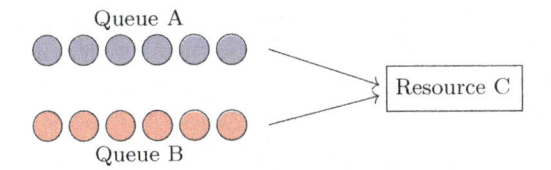

Fig. 8.2: Diagram of Concurrency

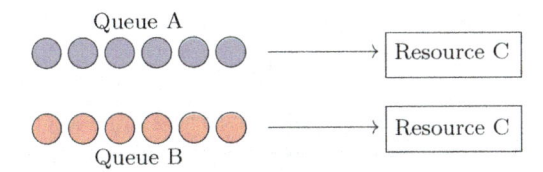

Fig. 8.3: Diagram of Parallelism

8.4.1 Threads

Java supports concurrent programming through its Thread API, but what is a thread? In essence, a *thread* is a single lightweight process that executes a task, or a sequential set of tasks.

Example 8.9. Multiple threads may access shared data at the same time, which is convenient. The problem is the fact that threads can *context switch* at arbitrary points, which may include during an *atomic operation*. Atomic operations are operations that must be executed in their entirety, without interruption. For example, suppose that we have a variable counter that we want to increment. We might write the following code:

```
import java.lang.*;

class RaceConditionExample {
  private static int counter = 0;

  public static void main(String[] args) {
    Thread t1 = new Thread(new Incrementer());
    Thread t2 = new Thread(new Incrementer());
    t1.start();
    t2.start();
    try {
      t1.join();
      t2.join();
    } catch (InterruptedException ex) { throw new RuntimeException(ex); }
    System.out.println(counter);
  }

  private static class Incrementer implements Runnable {
    @Override
    public void run() {
      for (int i = 0; i < 1_000_000; i++) { counter += 1; }
    }
  }
}
```

Upon running the program, we might expect the output to be 2_000_000, but this is not the case. The output is, in fact, nondeterministic, meaning that it is not guaranteed to be the same every time we run the program. This is because the `counter += 1` operation is not atomic. That is, the following sequence of events can occur:

1. Thread t_1 reads the value of `counter` as 0.
2. Thread t_2 reads the value of `counter` as 0.
3. Thread t_1 increments the value of `counter` to 1.
4. Thread t_2 increments the value of `counter` to 1.
5. Thread t_1 writes the value of `counter` as 1.
6. Thread t_2 writes the value of `counter` as 1.

Thus, we need a way of synchronizing access to the `counter` variable. We will discuss synchronization, alongside a more-detailed example, in the next section.

Synchronization

Example 8.10. Let's suppose that we're writing a Java class to represent a bank account, which allows users to withdraw and deposit money. Further suppose that we have multiple threads that access the same bank account at once, each depositing, then immediately withdrawing, five hundred dollars.

```
class BankAccount {

  private int amt;

  BankAccount(int amt) {
    this.amt = amt;
  }

  void deposit(int more) {
    this.amt += more;
  }

  void withdraw(int less) {
    if (amt >= less) {
      this.amt -= less;
    } else {
      System.err.printf("withdraw: insufficient funds %d\n", less);
    }
  }

  int getAmount() {
    return this.amt;
  }
}
```

Let's design a `TransactionThread` class that implements `Runnable`, which executes one thousand "transactions," i.e., a deposit of $500, then a withdrawal of $500.[7] At the end, assuming everything works as we expect, we should net zero dollars in the account.

---

[7] It is an implementer's choice to either extend the `Thread` class or implement the `Runnable` interface. We choose the latter because Java allows us to implement multiple interfaces, but we can only extend one parent class. This does, however, mean that any time we want to instantiate a thread, we must also instantiate a separate instance of the `Runnable` subtype.

8.4 Concurrent Programming

```java
import java.lang.Runnable;

class TransactionThread implements Runnable {

  private BankAccount acc;

  TransactionThread(BankAccount acc) {
    this.acc = acc;
  }

  @Override
  public void run() {
    for (int i = 0; i < 1000; i++) {
      this.acc.deposit(500);
      this.acc.withdraw(500);
    }
  }
}
```

```java
import java.lang.Thread;

class BankAccountRunner {

  static void runTransactionThreads() {
    BankAccount acc = new BankAccount(0);
    Thread t1 = new Thread(new TransactionThread(acc));
    Thread t2 = new Thread(new TransactionThread(acc));
    Thread t3 = new Thread(new TransactionThread(acc));

    t1.start();
    t2.start();
    t3.start();

    // Wait on the threads to finish, then print the result.
    try {
      t1.join();
      t2.join();
      t3.join();
    } catch (InterruptedException ex) {
      throw new RuntimeException(ex);
    }

    System.out.printf("%d\n", acc.getAmount());
  }

  public static void main(String[] args) {
    runTransactionThreads();
  }
}
```

Running the program may produce the following output:

```
withdraw: insufficient funds
withdraw: insufficient funds
0
```

It seems that we have an unpredictable problem: rerunning the program produces different results each time, but the error stems from the fact that our accesses to the bank account are not *synchronized*. To understand why, let's expand out the code that performs a withdraw operation.

```
void withdraw(int less) {
  int currAmt = this.amt;
  if (currAmt >= less) {
    int newAmt = currAmt - less;
    this.amt = newAmt;
  } else {
    // ... print not shown.
  }
}
```

Recall how threads work: a thread t_1 might reach the third line of this method, and store some value in newAmt. At this point, suppose another thread t_2 makes a deposit of $500. Finally, t_1 updates newAmt to zero, because currAmt - less must be zero, so we effectively nullify the deposit action by our second thread! As we showed with the previous example, this is a *data race* for the amt instance variable. To fix the problem, we want to ensure that our withdraw and deposit methods are synchronized, which we can do via marking the methods as synchronized. Synchronization of a method solves the problem of atomicity, i.e., a synchronized method can only be accessed by a single thread at any time. Let's mark our methods then rerun the code to check the result, which should never display an error. Even though the calls to deposit and withdraw might not be inside a synchronized environment, we end up netting zero dollars in the account, because three successive calls to deposit must be followed, at some point, by three calls to withdraw, which our synchronization action guarantees.

Example 8.11. Let's design a transfer method as part of the BankAccount class, which receives another BankAccount b_2 and an amount n as parameters. We will transfer n dollars from this bank into b_2, which resolves to a call to withdraw on this and a call to deposit on b_2.

```
import static Assertions.assertAll;
import static Assertions.assertEquals;

class BankAccountTester {

  @Test
  void testTransfer() {
    BankAccount b1 = new BankAccount(0);
    BankAccount b2 = new BankAccount(100);
    assertAll(
      () -> b2.transfer(b1, 30),
      () -> assertEquals(30, b1.getAmount()),
      () -> assertEquals(70, b2.getAmount()));
  }
}
```

```
class BankAccount {

  private int amt;

  BankAccount(int amt) {
    this.amt = amt;
  }
```

8.4 Concurrent Programming

```java
/**
 * Transfers money from one account to another.
 * @param b2 other bank account to deposit money into.
 * @param amt the amount to withdraw from this account.
 */
void transfer(BankAccount b2, int amt) {
  this.withdraw(amt);
  b2.deposit(amt);
}

// deposit and withdraw not shown.
}
```

The code has the problem of not being synchronized; if multiple threads call `transfer` on the same bank account, we run into the same problem as before. To fix it, we may think that we need to synchronize `transfer`, but this is not the case, because a method that is synchronized means that only one thread can enter the method, but we need to synchronize the bank objects themselves from access and mutation. We can do so by synchronizing on the bank objects themselves, which we can do by using the `synchronized` keyword on a block of code. First, we synchronize on `this` (the bank account that we are withdrawing from), followed by a synchronization on `b2` (the bank account that we are depositing into). This ensures that only one thread can access both bank accounts concurrently.

Let's now create another class that implements `Runnable` to manage multiple transfers between bank accounts. Each thread will deposit $500 into its first bank b_1, then transfer $500 from b_1 to b_2, followed by a withdrawal of $500 from b_2 to ensure that both accounts net zero dollars. Our tester creates two threads: one that initiates a transfer from b_1 to b_2, and another that transfers from b_2 to b_1.

```java
import java.lang.Runnable;

class TransferThread implements Runnable {

  private final BankAccount B1;
  private final BankAccount B2;

  TransferThread(BankAccount b1, BankAccount b2) {
    this.B1 = b1;
    this.B2 = b2;
  }

  @Override
  public void run() {
    for (int i = 0; i < 1000; i++) {
      this.B1.transfer(this.B2, 500);
    }
  }
}
```

```java
import java.lang.Thread;

class BankAccountRunner {

  static void runTransferThreads() {
    BankAccount b1 = new BankAccount(0);
    BankAccount b2 = new BankAccount(0);
    Thread t1 = new Thread(new TransferThread(b1, b2));
    Thread t2 = new Thread(new TransferThread(b2, b1));

    t1.start();
    t2.start();

    try {
      t1.join();
      t2.join();
    } catch (InterruptedException ex) {
      throw new RuntimeException(ex);
    }
  }

  public static void main(String[] args) {
    runTransferThreads();
  }
}
```

```java
class BankAccount {

  private int amt;

  BankAccount(int amt) {
    this.amt = amt;
  }

  /**
   * Transfers money from one account to another.
   * @param b2 other bank account to deposit money into.
   * @param amt the amount to withdraw from this account.
   */
  void transfer(BankAccount b2, int amt) {
    synchronized (this) {
      synchronized (b2) {
        this.withdraw(amt);
        b2.deposit(amt);
      }
    }
  }

  // deposit and withdraw not shown.
}
```

Upon running the program, it is very likely to encounter an unexpected problem: an infinite "loop," so to speak. The "loop" occurs because we have a *deadlock*, which happens when two or more threads are waiting on each other to release a lock. In our case, thread t_1 synchronizes on itself and acquires the lock. Then, suppose we context switch into t_2 and it synchronizes on itself. At this point, t_1 is waiting for the lock held by t_2, and t_2 is waiting on t_1's lock. There are several possible solutions to this problem, where one is to use a Java-defined Lock object.

8.4 Concurrent Programming

As we will discuss in the subsequent example, a *reentrant lock* allows a thread to acquire the lock multiple times, which is useful in the event that a thread needs to call a synchronized method from within a synchronized block. In particular, we will lock transfer, deposit, and withdraw using the same static lock. We will also use a try/finally block to ensure that the lock is released, even if an exception is thrown.

```java
import java.util.concurrent.locks.Lock;
import java.util.concurrent.locks.ReentrantLock;

class BankAccount {

  private int amt;

  private static Lock lock = new ReentrantLock();

  BankAccount(int amt) {
    this.amt = amt;
  }

  /**
   * Transfers money from one account to another.
   * @param b2 other bank account to deposit money into.
   * @param amt the amount to withdraw from this account.
   */
  void transfer(BankAccount b2, int amt) {
    BankAccount.lock.lock();
    try {
      this.withdraw(amt);
      b2.deposit(amt);
    } finally {
      BankAccount.lock.unlock();
    }
  }

  void deposit(int more) {
    BankAccount.lock.lock();
    try { this.amt += more; }
    finally { BankAccount.lock.unlock(); }
  }

  void withdraw(int less) {
    BankAccount.lock.lock();
    try {
      if (amt >= less) {
        this.amt -= less;
      } else {
        System.err.printf("withdraw: insufficient funds\n");
      }
    } finally {
      BankAccount.lock.unlock();
    }
  }
}
```

Example 8.12. A *thread-safe data structure* is one that supports reentrancy, i.e., multiple threads working over it at the same time. Java's ArrayList class is not thread-safe, so we will implement our own thread-safe array list using locks.

The idea is to wrap all pieces of the code that multiple threads may access with a lock. Recalling our `MiniArrayList` class from Chapter 4, we see that `add`, `remove`, `insert`, `get`, and `size` all either access or modify the state of the list, which could conflict with another thread and cause a dangerous race condition. Thus, we will surround the code with a lock. Note that some methods do not, themselves, need to be synchronized, e.g., `shiftLeft`/`shiftRight`/`resize`, because they are only ever called from within a synchronized context. Should we wrap those methods in the same lock, then the thread who owns the lock would be unable to call those methods, causing a deadlock.[8] Moreover, because the `remove` method calls `get`, acquiring the lock immediately in `remove` is a bad idea. So, we acquire the lock in `get`, then release it, then acquire it again in `remove`. Certain methods, e.g., `size` and `get`, need to be updated to account for releasing the lock before the return statement; in these cases we store the result in a (local) temporary variable, release the lock, then return.

In the code segment, we omit the comments for the sake of brevity. In all cases, we use `try/finally` blocks to ensure that, even in the case of exceptions, the lock is released, which is especially important with data structural methods.

```java
import java.util.concurrent.locks.Lock;
import java.util.concurrent.locks.ReentrantLock;

class ThreadSafeArrayList<T> {
  // ... other instance variables not shown.
  private Lock lock;

  ThreadSafeArrayList(int capacity) {
    this.size = 0;
    this.capacity = capacity;
    this.elements = (T[]) new Object[capacity];
    this.lock = new ReentrantLock();
  }

  void add(T element) {
    this.lock.lock();
    if (this.size == this.capacity) {
      this.resize();
    }
    this.elements[this.size] = element;
    this.size++;
    this.lock.unlock();
  }

  void insert(T e, int idx) {
    this.lock.lock();
    try {
      if (this.size == capacity) {
        this.resize();
      }
      this.shiftRight(idx);
      this.elements[idx] = e;
      this.size++;
    } finally { this.lock.unlock(); }
  }
```

---

[8] As we showed with the bank account example, Java's `ReentrantLock` class is reentrant, meaning that a thread can safely acquire the lock multiple times. So, this problem is not necessarily an issue, but we will still avoid it for the sake of clarity and adaptability to other languages that may not have reentrant locks.

8.4 Concurrent Programming

```
  T remove(int idx) {
    this.lock.lock();
    try {
      T e = this.get(idx);
      this.shiftLeft(idx);
      this.size--;
    } finally { this.lock.unlock(); }
    return e;
  }

  T get(int index) {
    this.lock.lock();
    try { T e = this.elements[index]; }
    finally { this.lock.unlock(); }
    return e;
  }

  int size() {
    this.lock.lock();
    try { int sz = this.size; }
    finally { this.lock.unlock(); }
    return sz;
  }
}
```

Java, in fact, does have a data structure in the Collections framework that supports multithreading and is therefore thread-safe: the Vector class serves this purpose. Though, should we not want to use Vector, since some Java programmers consider it "deprecated," we can invoke the static synchronizedList method on Collections to return a synchronized/thread-safe version of the input list. There are also other data structures in the Collections framework that are thread-safe, such as ConcurrentHashMap and ConcurrentLinkedQueue, as well as methods to convert a non-thread-safe data structure into one that is thread-safe, e.g., synchronizedMap and synchronizedSet.

Example 8.13. If the event that we want to block concurrent access to a variable, we need to enforce a few more precautions than simply marking methods that access the variable as synchronized. Moreover, should we want to not deal with locks but still require atomic operations over access to an integer, we can use, for example, AtomicInteger. Let's revisit the counter example from earlier, but this time we will use an AtomicInteger to ensure that the increment operation is atomic.

```
import java.util.concurrent.atomic.AtomicInteger;
import java.lang.Thread;
import java.lang.Runnable;

class AtomicIntegerExample {

  private static AtomicInteger counter = new AtomicInteger(0);

  public static void main(String[] args) {
    Thread t1 = new Thread(new Incrementer());
    Thread t2 = new Thread(new Incrementer());

    t1.start();
    t2.start();
```

```java
    try {
      t1.join();
      t2.join();
    } catch (InterruptedException ex) {
      throw new RuntimeException(ex);
    }

    System.out.println(counter);
  }

  private static class Incrementer implements Runnable {

    @Override
    public void run() {
      for (int i = 0; i < 1_000_000; i++) {
        inc();
      }
    }

    static synchronized void inc() {
      counter.incrementAndGet();
    }
  }
}
```

Condition Variables

Example 8.14. Imagine that we are writing a multithreaded program, where thread t_1 is a "consumer," and there are multiple "producer" threads $t_2, \ldots, t_n$. The producer threads add data to a list, and the consumer polls them when available. We want to ensure that the consumer only polls the list when it is non-empty. So, one might think to write the following code for the consumer:

```java
import java.lang.Runnable;
import java.util.Vector;

class Consumer<T> implements Runnable {

  private final Vector<T> LIST;

  Consumer(Vector<T> ls) { this.LIST = ls; }

  @Override
  public void run() {
    while (true) {
      while (this.LIST.isEmpty()) { /* Do nothing. */ }
      T e = this.LIST.remove(0);
      System.out.printf("Consumed: %s\n", e.toString());
    }
  }
}
```

The consumer thread "busy-waits" until the list is non-empty. A busy-wait loop is not recommended because the thread has to continuously check the list to determine if an element exists, which wastes CPU time. Plus, there's the added problem that this code is not thread-

8.4 Concurrent Programming

safe; by not acquiring a lock, we run into the potential of a race condition where one thread polls the queue and another is about to poll the queue. Even though our queue definition *is* thread-safe, this does not solve the problem of a thread trying to remove an element that does not exist. The solution is to use a *condition variable*, which serves as a signal between threads. While the list is empty, our consumer thread awaits on the condition variable, thereby putting it to sleep. Then, the producer thread(s) issues a signal to the condition variable when inserting data into the list. Condition variables are always associated with a lock, so we need to define one in our main program and pass it around to both the producer(s) and consumer.

When the consumer acquires the lock, it checks if the list is empty. If so, it awaits on the condition variable, which releases the held lock and puts the thread to sleep. When the producer acquires the lock, it adds an element to the list, then issues a signal to the condition variable, which wakes up the consumer thread. The signal causes the consumer to reacquire the lock, check if the list is empty, and, if not, remove (and process) the head element from the list, followed by releasing the lock.

For the sake of our example, suppose that a producer adds data to the list using a random number generator.[9] That is, we generate a random number, determine if it is within a specific range and, if so, add data to the list. This then means that the producer thread signals on the condition variable, awaking the consumer.

```java
import java.util.concurrent.locks.Condition;
import java.util.concurrent.locks.Lock;
import java.util.Random;
import java.util.Vector;

class Producer implements Runnable {

  private static final Random RAND = new Random();

  private final Vector<Integer> LIST;
  private final Lock LOCK;
  private final Condition COND_VAR;

  Producer(Vector<Integer> ls, Lock lock, Condition condVar) {
    this.LIST = ls;
    this.LOCK = lock;
    this.COND_VAR = condVar;
  }

  @Override
  public void run() {
    while (true) {
      this.LOCK.lock();
      int n = this.RAND.nextInt(100);
      if (n < 10) {
        this.LIST.add(n);
        this.COND_VAR.signal();
      }
      this.LOCK.unlock();
    }
  }
}
```

---

[9] The Random class is thread-safe (Gosling et al., 2023).

Further note that awaiting on a condition variable may throw an InterruptedException, meaning we must surround the call with a try/catch block.[10] An important fact to also consider is that, if a thread that issues a signal on a condition variable does not own the respective lock, Java will throw an IllegalMonitorStateException.

```java
import java.util.concurrent.locks.Condition;
import java.util.concurrent.locks.Lock;
import java.util.Random;
import java.util.Vector;
import java.lang.Thread;

class ConditionVariableExample {

  private static final Lock LOCK = new ReentrantLock();
  private static final Condition COND_VAR = LOCK.newCondition();
  private static final Vector<Integer> LIST = new Vector<>();

  public static void main(String[] args) {
    Thread t1 = new Thread(new Consumer<>(LIST, LOCK, COND_VAR));
    Thread t2 = new Thread(new Producer<>(LIST, LOCK, COND_VAR));
    Thread t3 = new Thread(new Producer<>(LIST, LOCK, COND_VAR));

    t1.start();
    t2.start();
    t3.start();
  }
}
```

If we fix our input seed to 212, the output is deterministically as follows:

```
Consumed: 1
Consumed: 6
Consumed: 1
Consumed: 7
Consumed: 7
Consumed: 8
Consumed: 1
Consumed: 4
Consumed: 5
```

Example 8.15. Suppose that we have a very large collection of files, and we want to count the number of occurrences of a specific word in all of them. The standard approach would be to read in each file, then count the number of occurrences of the word. Let's design the countWordInFiles method that, when given a word to search for and a directory, returns a Map<String, Integer> of file names to the number of occurrences of the word in each file.

Java provides the Files.walk method, which returns a stream of all paths in a directory, including subdirectories. We can leverage walk to read in the .txt files in a directory, then process each file sequentially to count the number of occurrences of the given word. We will also design the process method that reads in a file and counts the number of occurrences of a word.[11] These occurrences are added to a map that is passed as a parameter.

So, to recap, we read in all .txt files in a directory, then process each file to count the number of occurrences of a word, storing the results in a map.

---

[10] Should we not want to do this, we can instead invoke the awaitUninterruptibly method.
[11] In the code listing, the process method reads in the file as a stream of lines, then splits each line into space-separated tokens using the flatMap method. The flatMap method is used to flatten the stream of streams into a single stream of words.

8.4 Concurrent Programming

```java
import java.util.Map;

interface IFileSearcher {

  /**
   * Count the number of occurrences of the word in all .txt files in the given
   * directory. The word is case-insensitive. Different implementations of the method
   * may use different strategies to count the occurrences.
   * @param word the word to count.
   * @param dir the directory to search.
   * @return a map from file names to the number of occurrences.
   */
  Map<String, Integer> countWordInFiles(String word, String dir);
}
```

```java
import java.io.IOException;
import java.nio.*;
import java.util.*;

class StandardFileSearcher implements IFileSearcher {

  @Override
  public Map<String, Integer> countWordInFiles(String word, String dir) {
    // Find all .txt files in the given directory.
    try (Stream<Path> paths = Files.walk(Path.of(dir))) {
      List<String> files = paths.filter(Files::isRegularFile)
                                .map(Path::toString)
                                .filter(f -> f.endsWith(".txt"))
                                .toList();

      // Count the number of occurrences of the word in each file.
      Map<String, Integer> M = new TreeMap<>();
      files.forEach(f -> process(f, word, M));
      return M;
    } catch (IOException e) {
      throw new RuntimeException(e);
    }
  }

  /**
   * Count the number of occurrences of the word in the given file.
   * @param file the file to process.
   * @param word the word to count.
   * @param M the map to store the count.
   */
  static void process(String file, String word, Map<String, Integer> M) {
    try (Stream<String> lines = Files.lines(Path.of(file))) {
      Stream<String> words = lines.flatMap(l -> Stream.of(l.split(" ")));
      M.put(file, (int) words.filter(w -> w.equalsIgnoreCase(word))
                             .count());
    } catch (IOException e) {
      throw new RuntimeException(e);
    }
  }
}
```

Testing the program with the word "the" and a directory of over 3,000 .txt files, we find that the program runs in about 12 seconds.[12] Depending on how many files there are, and how large they are, the "standard" algorithm could take even longer to finish. We can speed up the process by using multiple threads to read in the files concurrently. The idea is to have a *pool* of threads, each of which reads in a file and counts the number of occurrences of the word. When a thread finishes with a "task,", it moves on to the next file in the queue, if any remain. We can use Java's `ExecutorService` to manage the pool of threads, and a sychronized `LinkedBlockingQueue` to store the files that need to be processed. We want to utilize as many threads as the runtime allows, so we can call `Runtime.getRuntime().availableProcessors()` to determine the number of threads that we should pass to the `Executors.newFixedThreadPool` method. The `process` method does not change between the implementations, so we omit it from the code listing.

```java
import java.io.IOException;
import java.nio.file.*;
import java.util.*;

class MultithreadedFileSearcher implements IFileSearcher {
  // ... other methods not shown.

  @Override
  public Map<String, Integer> countWordInFiles(String word,
                                               String dir) {
    // Find all .txt files in the given directory.
    try (Stream<Path> paths = Files.walk(Path.of(dir))) {
      Queue<String> files = paths.filter(Files::isRegularFile)
                        .map(Path::toString)
                        .filter(f -> f.endsWith(".txt"))
                        .collect(Collectors.toCollection(LinkedBlockingQueue::new));

      // Count the number of occurrences of the word in each file.
      int cores = Runtime.getRuntime().availableProcessors();
      ExecutorService es = Executors.newFixedThreadPool(cores);
      Map<String, Integer> M = new ConcurrentSkipListMap<>();
      files.forEach(f -> es.execute(() -> process(f, word, M)));

      // Block until all tasks are complete.
      es.shutdown();
      try {
        boolean term = es.awaitTermination(1, TimeUnit.MINUTES);
      } catch (InterruptedException e) {
        throw new RuntimeException(e);
      }
      return M;
    } catch (IOException e) {
      throw new RuntimeException(e);
    }
  }
}
```

Rerunning the program with the same input, we find that the program finishes in less than 3 seconds, which is a significant improvement over the single-threaded version.

---

[12] This statistic was measured on a ThinkPad X1 Carbon Gen 11.

8.4.2 Network Programming

Computers communicating with one another is not a revolutionary concept, but being able to write programs that act as *clients* and *servers* is certainly cool. A server is a program that listens for incoming connections over a network and processes them accordingly. Clients connect to servers to do different things, e.g., receive information from a server, talk to other connected clients, and so on. In this section, we will demonstrate Java's networking/socket API and how to write a few programs that incorporate a server.

Example 8.16. The simplest kind of server is one that receives an incoming connection and outputs/relays some data to the client, then closes said connection. Our first example using a server will accept a client, then send it the current server clock date and time, and close the connection. Servers operate on *ports* over a connection, which, simply put, are virtual places where connections occur. Our server will be hosted on port 8080: a common default port. So, we instantiate an object of type `ServerSocket` to listen on port 8080, and set up an infinite loop to forever listen for connections. Upon receiving one, we accept the client as a `Socket` and instantiate a data stream to print information out to the client. One important detail to note is that we need to designate the `PrintWriter` output stream to "autoflush" its data. In essence, this means that as soon as the client reads data from the server, it gets emitted to their standard output stream. Note that we do not need to declare a reader stream from the client, since our server does not receive data.

The server *blocks* until it receives a connection, similar to how many of the input reader classes, e.g., `Scanner`, `BufferedReader`, wait until data is sent to the input stream to continue execution. A blocking server that is implemented in this fashion, as we have done, can only serve one client at a time, since it has to accept the client, set up the output stream, print the data, then close the connection before being able to accept another.

```java
import java.io.*;
import java.net.*;

class TimeEchoServer {

  private static final int PORT = 8080;

  public static void main(String[] args) {
    try (ServerSocket ss = new ServerSocket(PORT)) {
      System.out.printf("Server listening on port %d...\n", PORT);
      // Continuously listen for clients.
      while (true) {
        // Accept the incoming client, block until we receive one.
        Socket client = ss.accept();
        System.out.printf("Client connected: %s\n", client.getInetAddress().toString());
        PrintWriter pw = new PrintWriter(new OutputStreamWriter(
                                    client.getOutputStream()),
                                    true);
        pw.println("The server time is " + java.time.LocalDateTime.now());
        System.out.printf("Client disconnected: %s\n",
                      client.getInetAddress().toString());
        client.close();
      }
    } catch (IOException ex) {
      throw new RuntimeException(ex);
    }
  }
}
```

To connect to this server, we can use the Unix nc "netcat" command to connect to localhost, e.g., `nc localhost 8080`, while the server is running.

Example 8.17. Let's write a server that, upon receiving a connection, allows the client to type a number. This number is then translated by the server into an index, grabbing them the nth most populous country. So, our server first reads in a list of countries from most populous to least. From there, we establish the same server connection, only this time we use both the input and output streams of the client, so we can read the number that they enter, as well as output to them the corresponding country.

```java
import java.io.*;
import java.net.*;
import java.nio.file.*;
import java.util.*;

class CountryPopulationRankServer {

  private final int PORT;
  private final List<String> COUNTRIES;

  CountryPopulationRankServer(int port) {
    this.PORT = port;
    this.COUNTRIES = Files.readAllLines(Paths.get("clist.txt"));
  }

  void start() {
    try (ServerSocket ss = new ServerSocket(this.PORT)) {
      while (true) {
        Socket s = ss.accept();
        BufferedReader br = new BufferedReader(
                      new InputStreamReader(s.getInputStream()));

        // Read in the country from the user.
        String line = br.readLine();
        int country = Integer.parseInt(line) - 1;
        PrintWriter pw = new PrintWriter(socket.getOutputStream(), true);

        // Output the nth most populous country.
        pw.printf("%d country: %s\n", country + 1, this.COUNTRIES.get(country));
        socket.close();
      }
    } catch (IOException ex) {
      throw new RuntimeException(ex);
    }
  }

  public static void main(String[] args) {
    new CountryPopulationRankServer(8080).start();
  }
}
```

Example 8.18. Let's use what we have learned to write a *multithreaded* chat server. That is, we will write a program that acts as server for a chat room.

Clients can connect to the server and send messages to each other. The server will be multithreaded so that it can simultaneously serve clients.

8.4 Concurrent Programming

First, we need to decide on a protocol for communication between the server and the clients. For this example, to minimize the number of features necessary to convey the important ideas, we will only allow the user to log into the "room," type messages to all users in the room, or to disconnect via the \quit command. The server houses a thread pool that spins up a thread to communicate with a connected client. Fortunately for us, because we are in Java, we have access to synchronized data structures such as Vector. Therefore, we do not need to manually insert locks into a data structure for storing those connected clients. After a server receives a client, as we stated, we dedicate a thread to that user, then resume listening for more clients. We will also have a server thread that actively listens for messages that are then relayed to every other user.

The notion of the server having a thread to listen for messages is known as a *task-handler*, whose tasks are queued away in a synchronized LinkedBlockingQueue data structure. When reading a command from the user, we enqueue it into the server's queue of tasks, which blocks until a task is available. The task-handler then dequeues the task and broadcasts it to all users. It will be up to the client to determine whether or not they are the intended recipient.[13]

```
import java.lang.Runnable;

class Server {
  // ... other data not shown.

  private static class TaskHandler implements Runnable {

    private final Server SERVER;

    TaskHandler(Server server) {
      this.SERVER = server;
    }

    @Override
    public void run() {
      while (this.SERVER.running) {
        try {
          Task task = this.SERVER.TASKS.take();
          this.SERVER.CLIENTS.forEach(c -> c.send(task));
        } catch (InterruptedException e) {
          throw new RuntimeException(ex);
        }
      }
    }
  }
}
```

---

[13] From a security standpoint, broadcasting a message in this fashion is incredibly insecure, since a client can simply decide if it is the intended recipient no matter if the message is not intended for them.

```java
import java.io.IOException;
import java.net.ServerSocket;
import java.net.Socket;
import java.util.concurrent.BlockingQueue;
import java.util.concurrent.LinkedBlockingQueue;
import java.util.concurrent.ExecutorService;
import java.util.Vector;

class Server {

  private final ExecutorService THREAD_POOL;
  private final Vector<Client> CLIENTS;
  private final BlockingQueue<Task> TASKS;
  private final int PORT;
  private boolean running;

  Server(int port) {
    int cores = Runtime.getRuntime().availableProcessors();
    this.running = true;
    this.PORT = port;
    this.THREAD_POOL = Executors.newFixedThreadPool(cores);
    this.CLIENTS = new Vector<>();
    this.TASKS = new LinkedBlockingQueue<>();
    this.THREAD_POOL.execute(new TaskHandler(this));
  }

  void start() {
    try {
      ServerSocket server = new ServerSocket(this.PORT);
      System.out.printf("Server connected on port %d...\n", this.PORT);
      while (this.running) {
        Socket client = server.accept();
        System.out.printf("Client %s connected!\n",
                          client.getInetAddress());
        Client c = new Client(client, this);
        this.CLIENTS.add(c);
        this.THREAD_POOL.execute(c);
      }
    } catch (IOException e) { throw new RuntimeException(e); }
  }

  void addTask(Task t) {
    if (t != null) { this.TASKS.add(t); }
  }

  public static void main(String[] args) { new Server(8080).start(); }
}
```

Clients contain an output and input stream, which are used to send and receive messages to and from the server, as we saw with the country population ranking server. The client thread is responsible for reading messages from the server and printing them to the user's console, as well as receiving messages from the clients' standard input stream, and feeding those lines to the server. We will also designate that a client has a user identifier and stores a flag indicating whether the client is "logged in", which represents if they can receive broadcast messages. By default, the user identifier will be the IP address of the connected socket, which is replaceable/alterable via the `"login"` command. In case a client disconnects from the server,

8.4 Concurrent Programming

we utilize the `connected` flag to prevent the thread from reusing the now-closed input stream. We will disable this flag once we implement the functionality for handling "quit" commands.

```
import java.io.BufferedReader;
import java.io.IOException;
import java.io.PrintWriter;
import java.lang.Runnable;
import java.net.ServerSocket;
import java.net.Socket;

class Client implements Runnable {

  private final Socket SOCKET;
  private final Server SERVER;
  private final BufferedReader IN;
  private final PrintWriter OUT;

  private boolean loggedIn;
  private boolean connected;
  private String userId;

  Client(Socket socket) {
    this.SOCKET = socket;
    this.SERVER = server;
    this.IN = new BufferedReader(new InputStreamReader(socket.getInputStream()));
    this.OUT = new PrintWriter(socket.getOutputStream(), true);
    this.loggedIn = false;
    this.connected = true;
    this.userId = socket.getInetAddress().toString();
  }

  @Override
  public void run() {
    try {
      String line;
      while (this.connected && (line = this.IN.readLine()) != null) {
        this.SERVER.addTask(parseCmd(line));
      }
    } catch (IOException e) {
      throw new RuntimeException(e);
    }
  }
}
```

We now need to write the `parseCmd` message, which receives an unparsed string from the client and returns a `Task` object, which we will design momentarily. Commands, in our system, will be prefixed via a forward slash /, followed by the arguments thereof. As an example, /login joshua will set the user's identifier to joshua. We will also allow the user to send messages to all other users via the /send command, which is followed by the message to broadcast. Finally, the /quit command disconnects the user from the server.

```java
class Client {
  // ... other information not shown.

  Task parseCmd(String line) {
    String cmd = line.substring(0, line.indexOf(' '));
    String msg = line.substring(line.indexOf(' ') + 1);
    switch (cmd) {
      case "/login" -> { return this.handleLoginCmd(msg); }
      case "/send"  -> { return this.handleSendCmd(msg); }
      case "/quit"  -> { return this.handleQuitCmd(); }
      default -> throw new IllegalArgumentException("bad cmd " + cmd);
    }
  }
}
```

Our tasks consist of a hierarchy of objects. Namely, a Task contains an enumeration of its type, as well as the raw data. A SenderTask is a task that contains a sender information, which stores an instance variable denoting the Client who the message originated from. Finally, a BroadcastTask is a task that contains a message to be broadcast to all users, which is itself a subclass of SenderTask. Tasks are operations that must be sent to the server and handled by one of its threads. Certain commands may remain local to the server due to their simplicity, e.g., "/login" and "/quit" do not need to be relayed to other users (and therefore are not wrapped as Task instances).

```java
enum TaskType { BROADCAST }
```

```java
abstract class Task {

  private final TaskType TYPE;
  private final String RESPONSE;

  Task(TaskType type, String response) {
    this.TYPE = type;
    this.RESPONSE = response;
  }

  TaskType getType() { return this.TYPE; }

  String getResponse() { return this.RESPONSE; }
}
```

```java
abstract class SenderTask extends Task {

  private final Client SENDER;

  SenderTask(TaskType type, String response, Client sender) {
    super(type, response);
    this.SENDER = sender;
  }

  Client getSender() { return this.SENDER; }
}
```

8.4 Concurrent Programming

```java
class BroadcastTask extends SenderTask {

  BroadcastTask(Client sender, String response) {
    super(TaskType.BROADCAST, response, sender);
  }
}
```

We now must write the Client's send method, which receives a Task from the server and interprets it accordingly. The only task that our server can send is BROADCAST, so we simply need to check whether the client is logged in and, if so, deliver the message to their output stream. At the same time, we can also take care of privatized parsing command methods. Only one of these three should return a non-null object. It is also a design decision to make handleQuitCmd and handleLoginCmd return null, because they do not need to be broadcast to other users. We do so to ensure consistency among the methods.

```java
class Client {
  // ... other information not shown.

  void send(Task t) {
    switch (t) {
      case BroadcastTask tb -> {
        if (this.loggedIn) {
          this.OUT.printf("%s: %s\n", tb.getSender(), tb.getResponse());
        }
      }
      default -> {
        throw new IllegalArgumentException("bad task "+t.getType());
      }
    }
  }

  private Task handleLoginCmd(String msg) {
    this.userId = msg;
    this.loggedIn = true;
    return null;
  }

  private Task handleSendCmd(String msg) {
    return new BroadcastTask(this, msg);
  }

  private Task handleQuitCmd() {
    this.loggedIn = false;
    try {
      this.SOCKET.close();
      this.IN.close();
      this.OUT.close();
    }
    catch (IOException e) { throw new RuntimeException(e); }
    finally { return null; }
  }
}
```

Now we can run the server! Clients connect via the "netcat" command nc, which is a Unix utility for reading and writing to network connections. We can connect to the server, using multiple terminals, via nc localhost 8080.

8.5 Design Patterns

Part of the reason that we have spent so much time discussing object-oriented design is because it is a fundamental aspect of software engineering. In particular, we have talked about the importance of designing classes that are cohesive, loosely coupled, and adhere to the single responsibility principle. We have also discussed the importance of designing classes that are extensible, and how to do so through the use of inheritance and polymorphism. As software engineers, we are responsible for designing and implementing software that is scalable and maintainable. Scalable software does not explode in complexity when adding new features/functionality, or as the user-base grows. Maintainable software, on the other hand, is simple to understand and make incremental changes and fixes as time passes.

In this section, we will discuss several *design patterns*, which are common solutions to specific problems that arise largely in the context of object-oriented design. Design patterns are, of course, not specific to Java and can be implemented in any reasonable object-oriented language.

8.5.1 Command

The *command* pattern is a simple pattern that encapsulates a request, of sorts, to some type of handler. The handler knows nothing about the request itself, only that the handler acts as a dispatch for invoking the request.

Example 8.19. Suppose that we're writing a game that involves moving a player around an environment. We want to design a class that handles moving the player, but remains independent of the player implementation. First, we will say that the player executes some type of ICommand, which is an interface containing a sole execute method. Then, we will design the Player class containing move and jump methods, where the former increments their x coordinate and jump increments their y coordinate, starting from the origin.

```java
interface ICommand {

  void execute();
}
```

```java
class Player {

  private int x;
  private int y;

  Player() { this.x = 0; this.y = 0; }

  // Getters and setters omitted.
}
```

Now, we will design two subtypes of ICommand, namely MoveCommand and JumpCommand, that each implement execute, where the only difference is the intended behavior. The Move-Forward command receives the Player instance and a direction, whereas JumpCommand only needs to receives a Player instance.

8.5 Design Patterns

```java
class MoveCommand implements ICommand {

  private Player player;

  MoveCommand(Player p) {
    this.player = p;
  }

  @Override
  public void execute() {
    this.player.setX(this.player.getX() + 1);
  }
}
```

```java
class JumpCommand implements ICommand {

  private Player player;

  JumpCommand(Player p) {
    this.player = p;
  }

  @Override
  public void execute() {
    this.player.setY(this.player.getY() + 1);
  }
}
```

Lastly, we must implement a "command dispatch handler," of sorts, which we might envision to be a controller. In particular, we will design the `InputHandler` class to store two commands that respond to presses to an 'X button' and presses to a 'Y button'. The methods to 'press' each button correspond to invoking `execute` on the respective commands. The general idea behind the command pattern is that we can pass an arbitrary implementation of a command to the handler to change/update the behavior of a button press or action.

```java
class InputHandler {

  private ICommand xButton;
  private ICommand yButton;

  InputHandler(ICommand xButton, ICommand yButton) {
    this.xButton = xButton;
    this.yButton = yButton;
  }

  void pressXButton() {
    this.xButton.execute();
  }

  void pressYButton() {
    this.yButton.execute();
  }
}
```

Now, we can test the system. Under other circumstances we would write JUnit tests before writing the separate commands, but we needed to create the handler before writing coherent tests.

```
import static Assertions.assertAll;
import static Assertions.assertEquals;

class CommandTester {

  @Test
  void testCommand() {
    Player p = new Player();
    InputHandler handler = new InputHandler(new MoveCommand(p), new JumpCommand(p));
    assertAll(
        () -> assertEquals(0, p.getX()),
        () -> assertEquals(0, p.getY()),
        () -> handler.pressXButton(),
        () -> assertEquals(1, p.getX()),
        () -> handler.pressYButton(),
        () -> assertEquals(1, p.getY()));
  }
}
```

As shown, we have decoupled the player from the handler, and the handler from the implementation of the commands. This, consequently, allows us to alter or modify the behavior of commands without redesigning the handler or player classes.

8.5.2 Factory

Example 8.20. To showcase our next pattern, we will design the Fraction class to represent mathematical fractions containing integer numerators and denominators. This example greatly resembles the rational number class presented in Chapter 4, but we introduce a twist to exemplify the benefits of the *factory* pattern.

```
import static Assertions.assertAll;
import static Assertions.assertEquals;

class FractionTester {

  @Test
  void testFraction() {
    assertAll(
        () -> assertEquals("1/1", new Fraction(1, 1).toString()),
        () -> assertEquals("1/2", new Fraction(1, 2).toString()),
        () -> assertEquals("17/312", new Fraction(17, 312).toString()),
        () -> assertEquals("321/199", new Fraction(321, 199).toString()));

    // Test random allocations of 1/2.
    for (int i = 0; i < 500_000; i++) {
      assertEquals("1/2", new Fraction(1, i).toString());
    }
  }
}
```

8.5 Design Patterns

```
class Fraction {

  private int num;
  private int den;

  Fraction(int num, int den) {
    this.num = num;
    this.den = den;
  }

  @Override
  public String toString() {
    return String.format("%d/%d", this.num, this.den);
  }
}
```

Notice that one of our test cases loops five hundred thousand times, repeatedly allocating the same fraction, namely 1/2. It is almost certainly true that, whatever application uses the Fraction class, will not need separate/distinct instances of a fraction. Accordingly, we are unnecessarily allocating Fraction instances, using a lot of CPU time and memory. The solution is to design a form of object caching, wherein we create a lookup table of the most "common" fractions and, whenever someone wants to construct a Fraction, we first determine if it can be polled from the table. If not, we have no choice but to allocate the fraction. We call this the *factory* pattern, because we have a class that represents and processes the creation of Fraction objects, rather than allowing the user to directly instantiate one themselves.

In designing the FractionFactory class, we declare a five-hundred element array to store the fractions $1/n$, where n is an integer such that $1 \leq n \leq 500$. Its constructor allocates the fraction "cache." We now need a method to take the role of building fractions; namely a Fraction create(int num, int den) method, which either looks up and returns the shared instance of a common fraction or allocates a new instance.

```
import static Assertions.assertAll;
import static Assertions.assertEquals;

class FractionFactoryTester {

  @Test
  void testFractionFactory() {
    FractionFactory ff = new FractionFactory();
    assertAll(
      () -> assertEquals("1/1", ff.create(1, 1).toString()),
      () -> assertEquals("1/2", ff.create(1, 2).toString()),
      () -> assertEquals("17/312", ff.create(17, 312).toString()),
      () -> assertEquals("321/199", ff.create(321, 199).toString()));

    // Check to see that all of the allocations are the same.
    Fraction f1 = ff.create(1, 2);
    for (int i = 0; i < 500_000; i++) {
      assertEquals("1/2", ff.create(1, 2).toString());
      assertEquals(true, f1 == ff.create(1, 2));
    }
  }
}
```

```
class FractionFactory {

  private static final int LIMIT = 500;

  private static final Fraction[] CACHE;

  FractionFactory() {
    this.CACHE = new Fraction[LIMIT];
  }

  /**
   * Creates a new Fraction instance, or looks it up in the cache.
   * @param num numerator of fraction.
   * @param den denominator of fraction.
   * @return a new instance of Fraction, or a shared instance if cached.
   */
  Fraction create(int num, int den) {
    if (den >= 1 && den <= LIMIT) {
      return this.CACHE[den - 1];
    } else {
      return new Fraction(num, den);
    }
  }
}
```

Example 8.21. Imagine that we have a file of data containing information about a "Person," which entails their university records. A person can be either a student, faculty, or staff member, and each type of person contains a name. For the purposes of this example, this is the only information that we care about, but we could easily extend the classes to include other datapoints. The idea is that we want to read in these records and create a Person object for each record. We could store 'type' of person as, say, an enum, or a string, but this is not ideal, because the type of the person is already available as a property of the class itself. Instead, let's use the *factory* pattern to create a Person object for each record, and the factory will instantiate the subclass type of person based on the record.

Let's design the abstract Person class, which contains a name field, a getName method, and an abstract String getRole() method to-be overridden in each subclass. We will also design the Student, Faculty, and Staff classes, which extend Person and contain the overridden getRole method that returns the type of person. Instead of directly instantiating Person objects, we take advantage of the factory pattern by writing the PersonFactory class, which contains a create method that receives a name and role as parameters, and returns the relevant subclass of Person.

To read the input file, we will design the PersonDatabase class, which stores a Map of Person objects, where the key is the name of the person and the value is the Person object. The PersonDatabase class contains a readFile method that takes a String argument rep-

8.5 Design Patterns

resenting the path to the file, and reads the file line-by-line, creating a `Person` object for each record and storing it in the `Map`.

```java
import java.nio.file.Files;
import java.nio.file.Paths;
import java.util.HashMap;
import java.util.List;
import java.util.Map;

class PersonDatabase {

  private final Map<String, Person> DATABASE;

  PersonDatabase() { this.DATABASE = new HashMap<>(); }

  void readFile(String path) {
    List<String> lines = Files.readAllLines(Paths.get(path));
    lines.forEach(l -> {
      String[] tokens = l.split(",");
      this.DATABASE.put(tokens[0],
                        PersonFactory.create(tokens[0], tokens[1]));
    });
  }

  Person lookup(String name) { return this.DATABASE.get(name); }
}
```

```java
class PersonFactory {

  /**
   * Creates a new Person object based on the role.
   * @param name name of person.
   * @param role role of person.
   * @return a new subclass of Person.
   */
  static Person create(String name, String role) {
    return switch(role) {
      case "student" -> new Student(name);
      case "faculty" -> new Faculty(name);
      case "staff" -> new Staff(name);
      default -> throw new IllegalArgumentException("invalid role "+role);
    };
  }
}
```

```java
abstract class Person {

  private final String NAME;

  Person(String name) { this.NAME = name; }

  String getName() { return this.NAME; }

  abstract String getRole();
}
```

```
class Student extends Person {

  Student(String name) { super(name); }

  @Override
  String getRole() { return "student"; }
}
```

```
class Faculty extends Person {

  Faculty(String name) { super(name); }

  @Override
  String getRole() { return "faculty"; }
}
```

```
class Staff extends Person {

  Staff(String name) { super(name); }

  @Override
  String getRole() { return "staff"; }
}
```

If we assume that our input records are line-separated and comma-delimited, then we can write a simple test case to verify that the `PersonDatabase` class correctly reads the file and creates the appropriate `Person` objects. The following file (titled `"records1.dat"`) will be used for testing purposes. As expected, all tests pass.

```
Willard Van Orman Quine,faculty
Alan Mathison Turing,student
John von Neumann,staff
Stephen Cole Kleene,faculty
```

```
import static Assertions.assertAll;
import static Assertions.assertTrue;

class PersonDatabaseTester {

  @Test
  void testPersonDatabase() {
    PersonDatabase db = new PersonDatabase();
    db.readFile("records1.dat");
    String n1 = "William Van Orman Quine";
    String n2 = "Alan Mathison Turing";
    String n3 = "John von Neumann";
    String n4 = "Stephen Cole Kleene";
    assertAll(
      () -> assertTrue(db.lookup(n1) instanceof Faculty),
      () -> assertTrue(db.lookup(n2) instanceof Student),
      () -> assertTrue(db.lookup(n3) instanceof Staff),
      () -> assertTrue(db.lookup(n4) instanceof Faculty));
  }
}
```

8.5.3 Builder

When creating instances of classes, it is not always feasible or possible to pass all of the necessary arguments to a constructor. The *builder* pattern allows us to write "partial constructors," i.e., methods that take a subset of the arguments and return an object with partially-populated fields.

Example 8.22. Suppose that we are designing a `Url` class to represent a URL, which contains a schema, host, port, and path. We will design the `Url` class that allows us to construct a `Url` object by passing arguments one-at-a-time to a series of methods. In particular, each instance variable, namely `_schema`, `_host`, `_port`, and `_path` have corresponding methods of the same name, sans the underscore. Each method returns `this`, which allows us to chain method calls together. Moreover, returning `this` and forgoing the constructor means we do not need to unnecessarily allocate a new `Url` object for every method call.

We will designate that a "complete" URL is one that, at the very least, contains a schema and a host. To complement this, we now design the `build` method that returns a `Url` object if the schema and host are non-`null`, otherwise, it throws an `IllegalStateException`. When the optional fields are not specified, they are set to default values, namely 0 for the port and "" for the path.

To test the implementation, we chain together a series of method calls on a `Url` instance and verify that the resulting `Url` object is correct through its `toString` representation.

```java
import static Assertions.assertAll;
import static Assertions.assertEquals;

class UrlTester {

  @Test
  void testUrlBuilder() {
    Url url = new Url().schema("http")
                       .host("www.google.com")
                       .port(80)
                       .path("search");
    assertAll(
      () -> assertEquals("http://www.google.com:80/search",
                         url.toString()));
  }
}
```

```java
class Url {

  private String _schema;
  private String _host;
  private int _port;
  private String _path;

  private Url() {}

  @Override
  public String toString() {
    return String.format("%s://%s:%d/%s", this._schema,
                         this._host, this._port, this._path);
  }
}
```

```
  Url schema(String schema) {
    this._schema = schema;
    return this;
  }

  Url host(String host) {
    this._host = host;
    return this;
  }

  Url port(int port) {
    this._port = port;
    return this;
  }

  Url path(String path) {
    this._path = path;
    return this;
  }

  Url build() {
    if (this._schema == null || this._host == null) {
      throw new IllegalStateException("build: incomplete URL");
    }
    this._port = this._port == 0 ? 80 : this._port;
    this._path = this._path == null ? "" : this._path;
    this.complete = true;
    return this;
  }
}
```

Partially-constructed objects may seem odd at first, but they are useful in situations where we want to instantiate an object piecemeal, i.e., one instance variable at a time. Plus, we can reuse the same builder with multiple objects. As an example, suppose that we want to create a Url for a particular host and schema, but without a specific port or path. We can then reuse this object repeatedly to populate an partially-constructed instance with differing ports and paths, rather than having to unnecessarily repeat the known schema and host.

8.5.4 Visitor

The *visitor* pattern is the most complex pattern that we will work with, but it offers a host of benefits. Consider a situation in which we do not have access to class definitions, but want to modify their implementation to add some functionality.[14] In particular, if those classes support the use of visitors, then we can design almost any type of functionality without needing to modify those classes at all.

Example 8.23. Let's design a visitor that prints out a programming language expression in a human-readable format. We will use a simplified version of the programming language that we wrote an interpreter for in Chapter 4. First, we need to design the visitor interface, which contains a visit method for each type of expression, namely NumNode, PrimNode, VarNode,

---

[14] Further assume that we cannot use reflection or similar runtime techniques.

8.5 Design Patterns

and `LetNode`. Each variant of the `visit` method receives an expression of the corresponding type as a parameter and returns a string.

```
interface IExpressionVisitor {

  String visit(NumNode node);
  String visit(PrimNode node);
  String visit(VarNode node);
  String visit(LetNode node);
}
```

Next, we need to modify the `AstNode` class to include the abstract `visit` method, which receives a `Visitor` object, and calls the appropriate `visit` method using polymorphic dispatch. By labeling `visit` as abstract, we require all (non-abstract) subclasses of `AstNode` to provide an overridden implementation of `visit`.

```
class AstNode {
  // ... other methods and variables not shown.

  abstract String visit(IExpressionVisitor visitor);
}
```

Now, we update each subclass to override the `visit` method and call the appropriate `visit` method. Fortunately, this is trivial, since all we must do is add the method signature and call `visit` with `this` as the argument to represent that the visitor is visiting the current node. Because making this alteration is consistently redundant, we will only show the implementation of the `NumNode` class, but the remaining classes are identical with respect to this method.[15]

```
class NumNode extends AstNode {
  // ... other methods and variables not shown.

  @Override
  String visit(IExpressionVisitor visitor) {
    return visitor.visit(this);
  }
}
```

From here, we need to design a variant of the interface that implements the expression printing behavior. Thus, we will write the `ExpressionPrinterVisitor` class, which implements the `IExpressionVisitor` interface. The new class, namely `ExpressionPrinterVisitor`, overrides the respective methods from the `IExpressionVisitor` interface to print the expression, to standard output, in a "stringified" format.

The corresponding tester is nothing different from previous tests; we instantiate an instance of `IExpressionVisitor` to `ExpressionPrinterVisitor`, followed by a call to `visit` on the root node of the expression tree. The result is a string representation of the expression, which we then verify.

---

[15] Remember that we said that we could not alter/update these classes (or rather that the visitor pattern guarantees this invariant), but we rely on the assumption that they support the visitor pattern, which serves as the only internal modification.

```java
import static Assertions.assertAll;
import static Assertions.assertEquals;

class ExpressionPrinterVisitorTester {

  @Test
  void testPrimExprPrint() {
    AstNode expr = new PrimNode("+",
                        new NumNode(1),
                        new PrimNode("*",
                          new NumNode(2),
                          new NumNode(3)));
    String result = expr.visit(new ExpressionPrinterVisitor());
    assertAll(
      () -> assertEquals("(+ 1 (* 2 3))", result));
  }

  @Test
  void testLetExprPrint() {
    AstNode expr = new LetNode("x",
                        new NumNode(1),
                        new PrimNode("+",
                          new VarNode("x"),
                          new NumNode(2)));
    String result = expr.visit(new ExpressionPrinterVisitor());
    assertAll(
      () -> assertEquals("(let ([x 1])\n (+ x 2))", result));
  }
}
```

```java
import java.lang.StringBuilder;

class ExpressionPrinterVisitor implements IExpressionVisitor {

  @Override
  public String visit(NumNode node) {
    return String.valueOf(node.getValue());
  }

  @Override
  public String visit(PrimNode node) {
    StringBuilder sb = new StringBuilder();
    sb.append("(");
    sb.append(node.getOperator() + " ");
    sb.append(node.getChildren().stream()
                            .map(c -> c.visit(this))
                            .collect(Collectors.joining(" ")));
    sb.append(")");
    return sb.toString();
  }

  @Override
  public String visit(VarNode node) {
    return node.getValue();
  }
```

8.5 Design Patterns

```java
@Override
public String visit(LetNode node) {
  StringBuilder sb = new StringBuilder();
  sb.append("(let ([" + node.getVar() + " ");
  sb.append(node.value.visit(this));
  sb.append(")]\n ");
  sb.append(node.body.visit(this));
  sb.append(")");
  return sb.toString();
}

@Override
public String visit(IfNode node) {
  StringBuilder sb = new StringBuilder();
  sb.append("(if ");
  sb.append(node.condition.visit(this));
  sb.append(" ");
  sb.append(node.thenExpr.visit(this));
  sb.append(" ");
  sb.append(node.elseExpr.visit(this));
  sb.append(")");
  return sb.toString();
}
}
```

Example 8.24. As another example, suppose that we have classes to represent items at a grocery store. Namely, we have a IGroceryItem interface, and subtypes Fruit, Milk, and Cereal. Additionally, we can extend the IGroceryItemVisitor interface, which itself contains corresponding "visit" methods for each subtype to describe how to visit an IGroceryItem object. Let's take advantage of Java's generics to allow a specification of the return type for visit methods. A visitor that always returns nothing severely limits the capabilities of the visitor pattern.

```java
interface IGroceryItemVisitor<R> {

  R visit(Fruit fruit);
  R visit(Milk milk);
  R visit(Cereal cereal);
}
```

```java
interface IGroceryItem {

  <R> R visit(IGroceryItemVisitor<R> visitor);
}
```

The subtypes of IGroceryItem, as we stated, are Fruit, Milk, and Cereal. Fruits have a name and a weight in ounces, milk is either skim milk or regular (designated by a boolean) and a weight in fluid ounces, and cereal has a mascot and a weight in ounces. While we are in the realm of modern Java, let's once again use records to our advantage to remove redundant code. Conveniently, this means that we only have to override the visit method in each record type.

```java
record Fruit(String name, int oz) implements IGroceryItem {

  @Override
  public <R> R visit(IGroceryItemVisitor<R> visitor) {
    return visitor.visit(this);
  }
}
```

```java
record Milk(boolean skim, int fluidOz) implements IGroceryItem {

  @Override
  public <R> R visit(IGroceryItemVisitor<R> visitor) {
    return visitor.visit(this);
  }
}
```

```java
record Cereal(String mascot, int oz) implements IGroceryItem {

  @Override
  public <R> R visit(IGroceryItemVisitor<R> visitor) {
    return visitor.visit(this);
  }
}
```

Now, let's extend the capabilities of our classes by designing a visitor that calculates the total price of a grocery list. Let's design the `GroceryListTotalVisitor` class, which implements the `IGroceryItemVisitor` interface. The new visitor, `GroceryListTotalVisitor`, overrides the respective methods from the `IGroceryItemVisitor` interface to calculate the total price of the grocery list. For the sake of the example, fruits are priced at $0.25 per ounce, milk is priced at $2.00 by the gallon, and cereal is priced at $0.10 per ounce. If the milk is skim, we add $0.50 to its price.

The corresponding tester is nothing different from previous tests; we instantiate an instance of `IGroceryItemVisitor` to `GroceryListTotalVisitor`, followed by a call to `visit` on each item in the grocery list.

```java
import static Assertions.assertAll;
import static Assertions.assertEquals;

class GroceryListTotalVisitorTester {

  @Test
  void testGroceryListTotalVisitor() {
    IGroceryItemVisitor<Double> vs = new GroceryListTotalVisitor();
    List<IGroceryItem> groceryList = List.of(new Fruit("apple", 4),
                                             new Fruit("banana", 2),
                                             new Milk(true, 128),
                                             new Cereal("Tony the Tiger", 16));
    assertAll(
      () -> assertEquals(0, List.of().stream()
                                     .mapToDouble(item -> item.visit(vs))
                                     .sum()),
      () -> assertEquals(5.60, groceryList.stream()
                                          .mapToDouble(item -> item.visit(vs))
                                          .sum()));
  }
}
```

```java
class GroceryItemPriceVisitor implements IGroceryItemVisitor<Double> {
  private static final double FRUIT_PRICE_PER_OZ = 0.25;
  private static final double MILK_PRICE_PER_GALLON = 2.0;
  private static final double CEREAL_PRICE_PER_OZ = 0.1;

  @Override
  public Double visit(Fruit f) {
    return f.oz() * FRUIT_PRICE_PER_OZ;
  }

  @Override
  public Double visit(Milk m) {
    double gallonsPrice = m.fluidOz() / 128.0 * MILK_PRICE_PER_GALLON;
    return m.skim() ? gallonsPrice + 0.5 : gallonsPrice;
  }

  @Override
  public Double visit(Cereal c) {
    return c.oz() * CEREAL_PRICE_PER_OZ;
  }
}
```

There are dozens of other design patterns that have been covered in much greater detail. Gamma et al. (1995) serves as a gold standard text for design patterns, albeit in C++ and Smalltalk.

8.6 API Connectivity

Writing programs that interact with the outside world is outrageously common in modern programming. We have explored working with data from standard input, files, and other data streams. There are many ways to connect a program to the outside world, one of which is via an API, or Application Programming Interface. In this context, an API refers to the functions that a server provides to allow external programs to connect and retrieve data. Understanding how an API connection works is a valuable skill to have, and we will show some examples of how to 1) connect to an API, 2) parse the data, and 3) use the data in a meaningful way.

Example 8.25. Consider a program that needs to retrieve the current weather conditions for a given latitude and longitude. Let's design a program that connects to the "OpenMeteo" Weather API, sends a request for weather data, and parses the received response (Zippenfenig, 2023).

First, we need to understand how to connect to an server-based API in Java. In general, when querying a server, we are sending what's called a GET request over HTTP (Hypertext Transfer Protocol). A GET request comprises an address, as well as parameters to tell the API what data the request asks for. In our case, we want to send a GET request to the OpenMeteo API, that asks for the current weather conditions at a given latitude and longitude. The address for the OpenMeteo API is https://api.open-meteo.com/v1/forecast. Because we want to retrieve the weather for a given latitude and longitude case, we need to add these parameters latitude and longitude onto the end of the address. Parameters to a GET request are separated by ampersands, and preceded by a question mark. For instance, the full address to fetch the weather for Bloomington, Indiana is `https://api.open-meteo.com/v1/forecast?latitude=39.1653&longitude=86.5264&hourly=temperature_2m&timezone=EST&temperature_unit=fahrenheit`. If we paste the URL into a web browser, we see that the browser executes the request and receives a response in the form of a JSON (JavaScript Object Notation) object, which is a common format for data transfer. To make adding additional parameters down the road easier, we will store them as strings that map to strings in a map, then concatenate them onto the resulting URL string.

In Java, we can create a URL instance with our desired destination address, and open a connection to the server by casting the URL to a `HttpURLConnection`. We also must tell the connection what type of request we are making, which in this case is a GET request. After establishing the connection, we check the response code to ensure that the request was successful. Success is indicated by a response code of 200. Should the connection return a response code other than 200, we can throw some form of exception. Possible sources of error include a malformed URL, a server that is down, or a server that is not responding. On the other hand, if the connection succeeded, we read the response back from the server via some input stream reader. The simplest way is to use a `BufferedReader` to read the response line-by-line.

```java
import java.io.*;
import java.lang.StringBuilder;
import java.net.HttpURLConnection;
import java.net.URL;

class ApiConnection {

  public static void main(String[] args) {
    try {
      // Bind the parameters to their values.
      String webUrl = "https://api.open-meteo.com/v1/forecast?";
      Map<String, String> parameters = new HashMap<>();
      parameters.put("latitude", "39.1653");
      parameters.put("longitude", "-86.5264");

      // Create a URL with the link, then concatenate each parameter.
      StringBuilder baseUrl = new StringBuilder(webUrl);
      for (String s : parameters.keySet()) {
        baseUrl.append(String.format("%s=%s&", s, parameters.get(s)));
      }

      // Open the connection and set the request to GET.
      baseUrl = baseUrl.delete(baseUrl.length()-1); // Remove the last &.
      URL url = new URL(baseUrl.toString());
      HttpURLConnection conn = (HttpURLConnection) url.openConnection();
      conn.setRequestMethod("GET");
      if (conn.getResponseCode() != 200) { throw new RuntimeException("bad resp code"); }
      else {
        // Read the response from the connection line-by-line.
        try (BufferedReader br = new BufferedReader(
                         new InputStreamReader(conn.getInputStream()))) {
          StringBuilder response = new StringBuilder();
          String inputLine = null;
          while ((inputLine = input.readLine()) != null) { response.append(inputLine); }
        }
      }
    } catch (IOException e) { throw new RuntimeException(e); }
  }
}
```

8.6 API Connectivity

Again, the response that we receive from the API is in the JSON format, but at the moment, all we have is a large string returned from the API that takes the form of a JSON object. We, therefore, need to parse this string into a JSON object that we then query in our program to retrieve fields and values. The question is, how do we do that? We need to take advantage of a library that can parse JSON data.[16] There are dozens of such libraries choose from, but thankfully, JSON is a simple format to understand, meaning many of the APIs are largely the same, so we shall use *JSON-java* by "stleary".[17] We wrap our received data inside the constructor of a `JSONObject` instance. Doing so converts our raw string data into an object that we can traverse and access element keys inside.

JSON stores its data in terms of keys and recursive values. By "recursive values," we mean that the values may, themselves, be keys to other objects. Therefore, it is sensible to conclude that JSON is somewhat akin to a "multi-level" map.

Looking at the raw JSON is a good idea, since it helps us to distinguish between the important keys and values returned from the API. Passing only the latitude and longitude as HTTP parameters is not sufficient; we also need to tell the API what data we want associated with that particular location. According to the Open-Meteo API, to view the current temperature, we append the `current` key with the `temperature_2m` value into the request parameters. Rerunning this request now shows the data split into two distinct JSON Objects: `current_units` and `current`. The former, as its name might suggest, acts as a one-to-one mapping to the keys in `current`, where each entry associates the data with a specific unit. By default, the temperature is reported in degrees Celsius, which the API informs us. We also see the interval at which the API polls its temperature sensors/collectors: every 900 seconds, or every fifteen minutes. Now, how do we access the data in our program? We have a `JSONObject` instance, namely *e*, that encapsulates the parsed JSON data, and we need to retrieve the temperature. From looking at the response, as we said, the temperature is a key inside the "current" object, which resides within *e*. We access this object by calling .`getJSONObject` on the JSONObject, which, itself, is a JSONObject that we can manipulate. Finally, we retrieve the value associated with the "temperature" key, that of which we know to be a `double`, i.e., a numeric temperature.

---

[16] We could, and is indeed a great exercise in working with real-world data and parsing techniques, write our own JSON parser.

[17] The GitHub repository for JSON-java can be found at https://github.com/stleary/JSON-java.

```java
import java.io.BufferedReader;
import java.io.IOException;
import java.io.InputStreamReader;
import java.net.HttpURLConnection;
import java.net.URL;
import org.json.JSONObject;

class ApiConnection {

  public static void main(String[] args) {
    try {
      // Bind the parameters to their values.
      String webUrl = "https://api.open-meteo.com/v1/forecast?";
      Map<String, String> parameters = new HashMap<>();
      parameters.put("latitude", "39.1653");
      parameters.put("longitude", "-86.5264");
      parameters.put("current", "temperature_2m");

      // Create a URL with the link, then concatenate each parameter.
      StringBuilder baseUrl = new StringBuilder(webUrl);
      for (String s : parameters.keySet()) {
        baseUrl.append(String.format("%s&%s", s, parameters.get(s)));
      }

      // Open the connection and set the request to GET.
      URL url = new URL(baseUrl.toString());
      HttpURLConnection conn = (HttpURLConnection) url.openConnection();
      conn.setRequestMethod("GET");
      if (conn.getResponseCode() != 200) {
        throw new RuntimeException("response code was not 200.");
      } else {
        // Read the response from the connection line-by-line.
        try (BufferedReader br = new BufferedReader(
                                  new InputStreamReader(
                                    conn.getInputStream()))) {
          StringBuffer response = new StringBuffer();
          String inputLine = null;
          while ((inputLine = input.readLine()) != null) {
            response.append(inputLine);
          }

          // Now that we have the data, we can parse it.
          JsonElement jsonElement = JsonParser.parseString(resp.toString());
          JsonObject jsonObject = jsonElement.getAsJsonObject();
          JsonArray times = jsonObject.get("hourly")
                                      .getAsJsonObject()
                                      .get("time")
                                      .getAsJsonArray();
          JsonArray temps = jsonObject.get("hourly")
                                      .getAsJsonObject()
                                      .get("temperature_2m")
                                      .getAsJsonArray();
        }
      }
    } catch (IOException e) {
      throw new RuntimeException(e);
    }
  }
}
```

8.6 API Connectivity

And that (which, admittedly, is a lot) is all there is to reading data from an API. The weather API project introduces many new concepts, but it simultaneously opened up a new world of possibilities for programs; we can now connect to any (public) API, retrieve data, and make decisions based on that data.

A JUnit Testing

Welcome to the back of the book; we hope this is not after you have finished the book but rather before you have even started the main content! In this Appendix, we will discuss how to use and setup the JUnit testing framework.

A.1 JUnit

There are many testing frameworks that we could use during our Java adventure, but we will stick to the industry-standard JUnit library. JUnit allows us to write test cases for methods as a means of determining whether they function correctly. Most beginning programmers debug or test their methods by calling them in, for example, the `main` method with inputs, then verifying that their output matches what they expect, usually through the console. This is neither robust nor elegant, and is prone to mistakes. Moreover, it introduces an unnecessary step: having to check to see whether the terminal contains the correct output. JUnit bypasses this inconvenience and we will demonstrate with some examples.

A.1.1 Installing & Using JUnit

Firstly, we need to install JUnit. We will assume that the users are working with the IntelliJ IDE and have it installed on their computer. Each project has to have JUnit separately configured, but doing so is trivial. There are two primary ways of integrating JUnit into a project: with or without Maven, which is a complex dependency manager. Our examples do not use Maven.

We need to create a class definition that has our method to test. Let's redo the example from Chapter 1, where we convert a temperature from degrees Fahrenheit to degrees Celsius.

```java
class TempConverter {

  /**
   * Converts a temperature from Fahrenheit to Celsius.
   * @param f degrees Fahrenheit.
   * @return f in degrees Celsius.
   */
  static double fToC(double f) {
    return 0.0;
  }
}
```

(1) In IntelliJ, right-click the class name, i.e., `TempConverter`, then click "Show Context Actions" (you can also press a shortcut combination such as Alt+Enter). This pops up a menu with a few options, one of which is "Create test."
(2) Click this option and a dialog box will appear labeled "No Test Roots Found," which asks if you want to create the tests in the same directory as the source files. In large projects, it is a good idea to separate the source files from tester files, but for our purposes, they will remain together.
(3) Click "OK," and another dialog box should appear, containing various options, the first of which is a piece of text saying that "JUnit5 library not found in the module." Beside of this text is a button labeled "Fix".
(4) Click "Fix", then hit "OK" in the following dialog box.
(5) Now, at the bottom, there is a box with all the visible methods for which we can write tests. In our case, the only option is `fToC`, which is to be expected. Click the checkbox to its left, the hit "OK" to generate the test file.
(6) From here, IntelliJ generates a new and separate class/source called `TempConverterTest`. Assuming everything is working up to this point, there are two pieces of red text, one of which is "Assertions" on line one and the other is "Test" on line five.
(7) Hover your cursor over the "Assertions" word and wait for about two seconds. A tooltip should appear saying that it "Cannot resolve symbol 'Assertions'." Below this is a button that says "Add library JUnit 5.X.Y to classpath," where X and Y are arbitrary versions of JUnit (as long as it is not JUnit 4).
(8) Click "Add library JUnit 5.X.Y to classpath" bring JUnit 5 into the project and the other error should disappear.
(9) Inside the tester file is the `fToC` method with a preceding *annotation*. This `@Test` annotation tells JUnit that this method contains JUnit tests and should be interpreted as such.[1]

Let's write a few tests! To do so, we can use the `assertEquals` method, which receives two arguments: the expected value and the actual value. The expected value, as its name might imply, is the expected output of a method that we test. The actual value, on the other hand, is where we call the method we are testing. So, we might write a test case saying that 212°F is equal to 100°C and another test to assert that 32°F is equal to 0°C. To emphasize that we are working inside a test method, we will prefix `fToC` with test, which also helps to eliminate accidentally referencing the `fToC` method defined in this file versus the one inside the TempConverter class.

```
import static org.junit.jupiter.api.Assertions.*;

class TempConverterTest {

  @org.junit.jupiter.api.Test
  void testfToC() {
    assertEquals(0, TempConverter.fToC(32));
    assertEquals(100, TempConverter.fToC(212));
  }
}
```

To execute this test (and only this test) method, click the green arrow immediately to the left of the method declaration. This will run the tests inside the method. At the bottom of

---

[1] Initially, your annotation will contain more than just `@Test`; IntelliJ qualifies the annotation with its full location in the Java library.

A.1 JUnit

the IDE, any failed assertions will be displayed. Of course, the second one fails because we have no meaningful implementation of fToC yet.

Should we want to write multiple test methods for different methods in the source file, we can do so easily.

(1) Head back to the TempConverter.java file and write the c2f method, which converts a temperature in degrees Celsius to degrees Fahrenheit.
(2) Then, click on the class name, "Show Context Actions", and "Create Test."
(3) The same dialog box with the selectable methods appears, so be sure to check c2f.
(4) Hitting "OK" at this point displays an error dialog box saying that the test file already exists. This is correct and IntelliJ is making sure that we are okay with updating the contents of that file by introducing a new method stub for testing c2f.
(5) Hit "OK" and you will see that the c2f method now has a corresponding tester method.

Writing assertions in this method is similarly straightforward, and if we do not want to rerun the tests for fToC just yet, we do not have to; clicking on the arrows beside a tester method's signature runs only the assertions inside that particular testing method. Should we want to run all the tests, we do not need to click each arrow, as that would be cumbersome. Instead, at the class declaration, i.e., class TempConverterTest, there is another green arrow; clicking this button runs all declared test methods inside our class definition.

One issue that arises when running tests with assertEquals and other variants is that, if an assertion fails, JUnit stops execution at the point of failure and refuses to run subsequent tests. This is not very convenient, so to circumvent the issue, we wrap all assertion statements inside a call to assertAll, which acts as a "dispatch" of sorts. We provide, to assertAll, a list of assertions to execute, and it executes them one after another, regardless of if one fails. A syntax warning to be aware of is that each assertion must be prefaced with '() -> ', without the quotes, and all but the last assertion must have commas.[2] Below is an example.

```
import static org.junit.jupiter.api.Assertions.*;

import org.junit.jupiter.api.Test;

class TempConverterTest {
  @Test
  void fToC() {
    assertAll(
      () -> assertEquals(0, TempConverter.fToC(32)),
      () -> assertEquals(100, TempConverter.fToC(212)),
      () -> assertEquals(-40, TempConverter.fToC(-40)));
  }
}
```

Rerunning this test demonstrates that, even though the second assertion fails, the last is still executed because all of the assertions reside within a call to assertAll.

Figure A.1 provides a table of helpful JUnit assertion methods.

---

[2] The significance of '() ->' is unimportant for now.

JUnit 5 Testing Methods

assertEquals(e, a) asserts that the actual value, namely a, should be equal to the expected value e. When these are primitive datatypes, e.g., int, their values are compared. If they are objects, it uses their equals method implementation.

assertNotEquals(e, a) is the dual to assertEquals in that, if assertEquals(e, a) returns true, then assertNotEquals(e, a) returns false.

assertTrue(p) asserts that p is an expression that resolves to true.

assertFalse(p) asserts that p is an expression that resolves to false.

assertArrayEquals(A_2, A_1) asserts that the contents of an expression generating the array A_1 are equal to the expected array of values A_2.

assertThrows(E, e) asserts that the executable code e throws the exception E.

assertNull(e) asserts that e is null.

Fig. A.1: Useful JUnit Methods.

B Binary Search Tree Library

In this Appendix, we provide the implementation to the binary search tree data structure described in Chapter 3. To use the class, copy the provided code into your development environment, and import all necessary packages.

Binary Search Tree Code

```java
import java.util.Comparable;

/**
 * This interface represents any possible tree data structure that
 * supports insertion and search.
 * @param <T> the type of elements stored in the tree.
 * Whatever type is used must implement Comparable.
 */
interface Tree<T extends Comparable<T>> {

  void insert(T data);

  Tree<T> contains(T data);
}
```

```java
import java.util.Comparable;
import java.util.Comparator;

/**
 * This class represents a binary search tree.
 * The tree is ordered according to the natural order of
 * the elements or a custom comparator.
 * The tree does not allow duplicate elements.
 * @param <T> the type of elements stored in the tree.
 * Whatever type is used must implement Comparable.
 */
class BinarySearchTree<T extends Comparable<T>> implements Tree<T> {

  /**
   * Data associated with this node.
   */
  private final T DATA;

  /**
   * Comparator instance used to order the elements.
   * If no comparator is passed, the natural order of the elements is used.
   */
  private final Comparator<T> COMPARATOR;

  /**
   * Left child of this node, or null if it doesn't exist.
   */
  private BinarySearchTree<T> left;

  /**
   * Right child of this node, or null if it doesn't exist.
   */
  private BinarySearchTree<T> right;

  /**
   * Parent of this node.
   */
  private BinarySearchTree<T> parent;

  BinarySearchTree(T data) {
    this(data, Comparator.naturalOrder());
  }

  BinarySearchTree(T data, Comparator<T> comparator) {
    this.DATA = data;
    this.COMPARATOR = comparator;
    this.left = this.right = this.parent = null;
  }

  /**
   * Inserts a new (non-null, non-duplicate) element into this binary search tree.
   * - If the element is less than this node, it is inserted into the left subtree.
   * - If the element is greater than this node, it is inserted into the right subtree.
   * @param data the element to insert.
   */
  @Override
```

B Binary Search Tree Library

```java
  public void insert(T data) {
    if (this.COMPARATOR.compare(data, this.DATA) < 0) {
      if (this.left == null) {
        this.left = new BinarySearchTree<>(data, this.COMPARATOR);
        this.left.parent = this;
      } else {
        this.left.insert(data);
      }
    } else {
      if (this.right == null) {
        this.right = new BinarySearchTree<>(data, this.COMPARATOR);
        this.right.parent = this;
      } else {
        this.right.insert(data);
      }
    }
  }

  @Override
  public Tree<T> contains(T data) {
    if (this.COMPARATOR.compare(data, this.DATA) == 0) {
      return this;
    } else if (this.COMPARATOR.compare(data, this.DATA) < 0) {
      return this.left == null ? null : this.left.contains(data);
    } else {
      return this.right == null ? null : this.right.contains(data);
    }
  }

  @Override
  public String toString() {
    return (this.left == null ? "" : this.left + ", ") + this.DATA
        + (this.right == null ? "" : ", " + this.right);
  }

  T getData() {
    return this.DATA;
  }

  BinarySearchTree<T> getLeft() {
    return this.left;
  }

  BinarySearchTree<T> getRight() {
    return this.right;
  }

  BinarySearchTree<T> getParent() {
    return this.parent;
  }

  boolean isLeaf() {
    return this.left == null && this.right == null;
  }

  boolean isRoot() {
    return this.parent == null;
  }
}
```

References

[1] Bergin, J., Stehlik, M., Roberts, J., and Pattis, R. (2013). *Karel J Robot: A Gentle Introduction to the Art of Object-Oriented Programming in Java*. John Wiley & Sons.

[2] Bloch, J. (2018). *Effective Java*. Addison-Wesley, Boston, MA, 3 edition.

[3] Code, R. (2024). Disarium numbers — rosetta code,. [Online; accessed 27-April-2024].

[4] Cormen, T. H., Leiserson, C. E., Rivest, R. L., and Stein, C. (2009). *Introduction to Algorithms*. The MIT Press, 3rd edition.

[5] Crotts, L. J. (2023). *Principles of Computer Science: An Invigorating, Hands-on Approach*. J. Ross Publishing.

[6] Felleisen, M., Findler, R. B., Flatt, M., and Krishnamurthi, S. (2018). *How to Design Programs: An Introduction to Programming and Computing*. The MIT Press.

[7] Forman, I. R. and Forman, N. (2004). *Java Reflection in Action (In Action series)*. Manning Publications Co., USA.

[8] Friedman, D. P. and Felleisen, M. (1996). *The Little Schemer (4th ed.)*. MIT Press, Cambridge, MA, USA.

[9] Friedman, D. P. and Wand, M. (2008). *Essentials of Programming Languages, 3rd Edition*. The MIT Press, 3 edition.

[10] Gamma, E., Helm, R., Johnson, R., and Vlissides, J. (1995). *Design patterns: elements of reusable object-oriented software*. Addison-Wesley Longman Publishing Co., Inc., USA.

[11] Gardner, M. (1990). *Mathematical magic show: More puzzles, games, diversions, illusions and other mathematical sleight-of-mind from scientific American*. The Mathematical Association of America.

[12] Gosling, J., Joy, B., Steele, G., Bracha, G., Buckley, A., Smith, D., and Bierman, G. (2023). *The Java Language Specification, Java SE 22 Edition*. Oracle, 1st edition.

[13] Iverson, K. E. (1962). *A programming language*. John Wiley & Sons, Inc., USA.

[14] Katherine Ritchey, Sarah Patterson, B. P. and Ritchey, N. (2023). Wordle as a teaching tool. *PRIMUS*, 33(8):901–915.

[15] King, B. M. and Minium, E. W. (2008). *Statistical reasoning in the behavioral science*. John Wiley, 5th ed. edition.

[16] Knuth, D. E. (1998). *The art of computer programming, volume 3: (2nd ed.) sorting and searching*. Addison Wesley Longman Publishing Co., Inc., USA.

[17] Krishnan, M. (2018). Maths behind polynomial regression.

[18] McCarthy, J. (1962). *LISP 1.5 Programmer's Manual*. The MIT Press.

[19] Morling, G. (2023).

[20] Pattis, R. E. (1995). *Karel The Robot: A Gentle Introduction to the Art of Programming*. John Wiley & Sons.

[21] Polignac, D. (2013).

[22] Riesel, H. (1994). *Prime numbers and computer methods for factorization (2nd ed.)*. Birkhauser Verlag, CHE.

[23] Sebesta, R. W. (2012). *Concepts of Programming Languages*. Pearson, 10th edition.

[24] Silberschatz, A., Galvin, P. B., and Gagne, G. (2012). *Operating System Concepts.* Wiley Publishing, 9th edition.

[25] Stroustrup, B. (2013). *The C++ Programming Language.* Addison-Wesley Professional, 4th edition.

[26] Sussman, G. J. and Steele, G. L. (1975). Scheme: An interpreter for extended lambda calculus. Technical Report AI Memo No. 349, Massachusetts Institute of Technology, Cambridge, UK.

[27] van Orman Quine, W. (1950). *Methods of Logic.* Harvard University Press.

[28] Weiss, M. A. (1998). Data structures and problem solving using java. *SIGACT News*, 29(2):42–49.

[29] Willans, C. P. (1964). On formulae for the nth prime number. *The Mathematical Gazette*, 48(366):413–415.

[30] Zippenfenig, P. (2023). Open-meteo.com weather api.

Index

`Comparator`, 133
`StringBuffer`, 68
`AbstractList`, 368
`ArrayList`, 114
`Comparator`, 133
`HashMap`, 140
`HashSet`, 136
`LinkedHashMap`, 141
`LinkedHashSet`, 137
`LinkedList`, 132
`Map`, 140
`Math.random()`, 18
`PriorityQueue`, 133
`Queue`, 132
`Random`, 18
`Scanner`, 16
`Set`, 135, 136
`StringBuilder`, 68
`TreeMap`, 140
`TreeSet`, 137
`finally`, 331
`nextLine`, 16
`printf`, 15

access modifier, 192
accessor method, 193
accumulator-passing style, 35
activation record, 34
aliasing, 116
amortized analysis, 115
argument, 4
array, 88
ArrayList, 114
association, 140
average case, 387

best case, 387
Big-Oh, 387
Big-Oh notation, 387

Big-Omega, 388
Big-Omega notation, 388
binary search tree, 166
block, 435
body, 4
bounded type parameters, 161
bubble sort, 369

cast, 20
casting, 20
checked exception, 329, 331
class, 3, 191
classes, 191
coerce, 57
collision resolution, 241
column-major, 99
command pattern, 442
common class loader, 419
comparator, 133
comparator object, 132
concatenate, 11
concatenation, 11
concurrency, 68
conditional expression, 28
constant access, 92
constant cost, 115
constructor, 12, 192
continuation-passing style, 50

deadlock, 426
default method, 276
delta argument, 5
dequeue, 131
design pattern, 203
design patterns, 442
downcast, 247
driver method, 36
dynamic programming, 103, 104, 108, 109, 127

edge case, 4
encapsulation, 37, 193
enhanced `for` loop, 89
enqueue, 131
entry, 140
Euclid's algorithm, 217
exception, 14
exponential time, 63

factory pattern, 444
final class, 267
first-in-first-out, 131
format characters, 15
format specifiers, 15
format string, 15
function, 3

generic, 114
generics, 160

hash code, 200
hash collisions, 136
hash function, 136
hash map, 140
hash set, 136
hash table, 241
head, 128

impure, 223
in-place sorting, 260
initialize, 193
initializer lists, 87
instance variables, 191
instantiation, 12, 194
interface, 131
invariant, 378

JUnit, 4

key set, 141

last-in-first-out, 130
lexer, 408
line buffered, 16
linked hash map, 141
linked hash set, 137
linked list, 128
logical index, 112

map, 140
marker interface, 335

merge sort, 378
method, 3
method access modifiers, 36
method application, 4
method body, 4
method call, 4
method call stack, 34
method invocation, 4
method overloading, 12, 110, 196
method signature, 3
mutator method, 223

natural ordering, 132
node, 128

object, 191
object composition, 203
object initialization, 193
object instantiation, 194

parameter, 3
parameteric polymorphism, 160
parameterized types, 114
peek, 130
persistency, 113
persistent, 113
persistent data structure, 304
polymorphic, 268
polymorphism, 268
pop, 130
predicate, 25
primitive datatypes, 5
priority, 132
priority queue, 132
priority queues, 132
pseudorandom, 18
pseudorandomness, 18
push, 130

queue, 131, 132

reflection, 413
return type, 3
return value, 4
row-major, 99

selection sort, 372
sentinel, 114
sentinel indicator, 114
serialization, 335
server, 435

INDEX

set, 135, 136
setter method, 223
shadow, 193
side-effect, 10, 121, 223
signature, 3, 4
singleton, 203
stack, 130
stack frame, 34
standard data streams, 15
standard error stream, 15
standard input, 16
standard input stream, 16
standard output stream, 15
standard recursion, 34
static variable, 198
string, 11
string literal, 12
string pool cache, 12

tail call optimization, 44
tail position, 35
tail recursion, 35
tail recursive, 35
terminal arguments, 96
ternary expression, 28
ternary operator, 28
test cases, 4
Theta, 388
Theta notation, 388
thread pool, 434, 437
tree map, 140
tree set, 137
try-with-resources, 331
type cast, 20
type coercion, 57
type parameterization, 114, 160
type parameters, 161

unchecked exception, 325

variable shadowing, 193
variadic-argument method, 118
visitor, 450

worst case, 387

Made in United States
North Haven, CT
19 June 2025